THE FATHER'S ALMANAC

THE FATHER'S ALMANAC

S. Adams Sullivan

with illustrations by the author

DOUBLEDAY
NEW YORK LONDON TORONTO SYDNEY AUCKLAND

Excerpts from *Theodore Roosevelt's Letters to His Children*, edited by
Joseph Bucklin Bishop. Copyright © 1919 Charles Scribner's Sons; renewal
copyright © 1947 Edith K. Caron Roosevelt. Reprinted by permission of
Charles Scribner's Sons.

We wish to thank the following organizations for permission to use photographs of works from their collections:

p. 23   Kobberstiksamling
         Statens Museum for Kunst
         Copenhagen, Denmark

p. 39   The Art Institute of Chicago

p. 328   Graphische Sammlung Albertina
         Vienna, Austria

p. 330   Staatliche Graphische Sammlung
         Munich, Germany

p. 333   The Art Institute of Chicago

Photo Credits:

Rita Baragona, p. 168, p. 198.

Gay Courter, p. xviii, p. 52, p. 296.

Phil Courter, p. 22.

Judith Palfrey, p. 142, p. 214.

Sean Palfrey, p. ii, p. 78, p. 337.

United Press International, p. 55.

DESIGNED BY MARILYN SCHULMAN

Library of Congress Cataloging in Publication Data

Sullivan, St. Clair Adams, 1938–
    The father's almanac.

    (A Dolphin book)
    Bibliography: p.
    Includes Index
    1. Children — Management.   2. Father and child.
3. Fathers — Handbooks, manuals, etc.   I. Title.
HQ772.S794   649'.1

ISBN: 0-385-13626-9

Library of Congress Catalog Card Number 78-22650

To Rita
and Gregory and Timothy

CONTENTS

ACKNOWLEDGMENTS

CONTRIBUTING FATHERS

Julio Acevedo
John Achenbach
Rick Allen
Louis Baragona
Antony J. Barry
Leland Bell
James Bohary
Edward Brewer
James Carey, Jr.
David Cole
Joel Corcos Levy
Phil Courter

Thomas J. De Coster
David Dewey
Robert L. Elmore
Erich Grau
David Gumpper
William Hall
Eugene Heath
Benjamin Huberman
Robert L. Hurvitz
Norman Paul Hyett
Brian Jones
James Robert Jones III

Steven N. Kaplan
Ingimundur S. Karval
Richard A. Lake
Charles V. Lord
Robert W. Lubrano
Leslie Lumley
Benjamin Mendelsund
Lewis P. Miller
Michael Murphy
Charles O'Connor
William K. Olson
Sean Palfrey

A. MacDonough Plant
Philip Puzzo
Gordon A. Raupp
Bill Salter
Arthur L. Seugling
Terry I. Seymour
Denny Shaw
Lawrence Stryker
Scott Sullivan
Yuval Waldman
Dick Wenner
Gerald M. Whelan

The men whose names are listed here all made contributions to this book. They come from many walks of life; some of their jobs and professions are: lawyer, physician, investment banker, roofer, harpsichordist, building contractor, school principal, landscape architect, accounting manager for a communications corporation, journalist, a trader in international commodities markets, analytical chemist, film maker, social work administrator, partner in a public accounting firm, toolmaker, psychologist, personnel manager, engraver, bongo drummer, utility company line splicer. They live in seven different states, one in D.C., and one abroad. Some live in rural areas, but the majority are pretty evenly divided between suburbs and big cities. About the only thing they all have in common is kids — two are wise grandfathers who have many years of experience with children, some have big families, a few are just starting out as fathers with first babies. Divorced fathers and single dads are represented in the group as well, and the great majority have two or three kids, most of them still preschoolers.

A few of these contributing fathers are old friends whose adventures as fathers I've watched over the years, but the majority are men I contacted specifically to get a wide variety of viewpoints. When I undertook writing THE FATHER'S ALMANAC at the suggestion of my publisher, I was confident that I was close to the subject and the material since I was — and still am — in the midst of raising two boys. But my experience, like every father's, was clearly limited. So for months I asked everyone I talked with to introduce me to men they thought of as good fathers, men who were interested in and closely involved with their kids as babies and preschoolers. Many of these men were good enough to sit down with me for long sessions with a tape recorder and talk in detail about the activities they share with their kids, their pleasures as fathers, and their difficulties. The first half dozen or so interviews were informal, but then I found that some subjects and concerns came up repeatedly in these conversations, and on the basis of them I worked up fifty questions that I used to pry "expert testimony" out of the rest of the men I interviewed. A few of the interviews were brief, though useful and revealing, but many of the fathers became so involved that the conversations went on for four, five, and six hours at a stretch. Many said they enjoyed the experience because it gave them a chance to recap their years as fathers and to think about fatherhood in a systematic way.

Mothers are forever getting together to discuss their kids and how they deal with them — it's their form of shop talk. But fathers seldom share much conversation about their children or swap experiences and advice in the same way mothers do. "How are the kids?" "Fine." And then the conversation turns to sports or cars or business. These interviews gave me a surplus of ideas — the kind that ordinarily don't come up in talk between fathers — because every father has something special he does with his kids and every father knows a few tricks of the trade. I've tried to compile the best of all this material and let the contributing fathers speak for themselves through direct quotes wherever possible. Naturally I don't hold the contributing fathers responsible in any way for ideas or opinions I have expressed in this book.

While I was conducting these interviews, I tried at the same time to educate myself on current scholarly thinking about fatherhood. My wife's mother, Rosalie Baragona, a sensitive and successful child psychologist, was a great help in steering me toward the best books available in her field and related ones, as were my sister, Judy Palfrey, and her husband, Sean, both of them hospital-based pediatricians on teaching faculties. Judy even lured me up to Boston for two weeks to take a summer course at Harvard on "Educating the Infant and Toddler," in which she was lecturing. And in Boston Judy introduced me to colleagues of hers who were conducting detailed scientific investigations into early father-child interaction. My close friends Gay and Phil Courter, who run an educational films outfit called Parenting Pictures, and who have produced several widely distributed movies about childbirth, were a big help in filling me in on aspects of the chapter on fathers and childbirth.

Additionally, I forced myself to read through a mountain of popular books about child care — most of them, unfortunately, aimed at mothers. And I plowed through most of the available social-scientific literature on fatherhood — which isn't a lot of reading since the psychologists and sociologists have only started seriously to study fatherhood in very recent years. The majority of social-scientific research into fatherhood is concerned with "father absence" and its possibly detrimental effects on kids, which wasn't a great help, because this book is very much about father presence and its certain benefits both to kids and fathers.

In the long run, of all the work I did trying to prepare myself to write THE FATHER'S ALMANAC, far and away the most useful and thought-provoking material came directly from my interviews with the contributing fathers named above. They helped me fill out my limited experience with a broad view of how men are actually going about being fathers today. A short note of thanks to the following people for putting me in touch with some of the contributing fathers: Jacqui De Coster of the Surprise House Child Care Center, Belvidere, New Jersey; Donald Pierson and Pamela MacLean of the Brookline (Massachusetts) Early Education Project; Lois Roberts of the Morris Plains (New Jersey) Cooperative Playschool.

Another important group of helpers who couldn't conceivably be left out here are the kids at the

Surprise House Child Care Center in Belvidere, New Jersey. Because my son Gregory started his education there, and because my wife, Rita, has been involved with the center from its founding as an adviser and part-time teacher, I served with her on the center's board of trustees. But much more interesting, and an awful lot more fun, is the time I spend playing with the kids there for several hours each week — a luxury that free-lance work allows me to fit into my schedule. We do acrobatics together, play ball, hammer nails, saw off pieces of cardboard, drill holes, build crazy-looking constructions out of scrap wood, holler and chase each other in the play yard, and have long quiet discussions indoors about Australia and rocket ships and alliga-

tors and other subjects of mutual interest. It's certain that I've learned a lot more from these kids about what preschool girls and boys think and do than they've learned from me. Many of their ideas and all of our good experiences together have gone into making this book.

For me, the greatest bonus of working on THE FATHER'S ALMANAC was to be able to spend long hours with my own kids, Gregory and Timothy, sharing projects and pleasures that we would never have had the time for under other circumstances. Whenever we do something together that's fun, Gregory says: "Put *that* in your father book, Dad. Tell those fathers to do *that* with their kids." His choices and Timothy's were usually the deciding factor in whether or not an activity or a project was included.

MOTHER'S ALMANAC – FATHER'S ALMANAC

This book is roughly patterned after THE MOTHER'S ALMANAC by Marguerite Kelly and Elia Parsons. I'm especially grateful to them for pioneering the notion that a helpful book for parents can be written by practicing parents — they are both experienced mothers with big families, not so-called child care "experts." Since it was published in 1975, the tremendous popularity of their book with mothers has proved their point, and made it possible for this companion volume to appear — a book specifically about fatherhood and young kids written from the viewpoint of a father with the help of other fathers.

Of all the complimentary things I might say about the wise and useful MOTHER'S ALMANAC, I think the most telling is simply that it's a tough act to follow.

PREFACE

If you had had to fill out a job application for the position of father before your first child arrived, would you have had anything to put in under Prior Experience? Related Training? I've asked dozens of fathers this question, and most of the answers were like this one from a CPA with a brand-new first-born boy: "I'd have to put down Unqualified. It's going to be a learning experience for both my wife and myself, and I'm sure we'll adapt."

Most of us come on fatherhood cold: no background, no education. There probably wasn't a course at your school to teach you about male parenthood. If your father said seven words to you while you were growing up about what you could expect as a father, they were: "Wait till you have kids. You'll see." Chances are, the first diaper you ever changed was on your own child, not somebody else's. And if you ever did baby-sitting as a teenager, it was probably your girl friend who did the child care part of the job.

One man suggested that his Ph.D. in psychology might have given him some useful training for fatherhood — but no, he thought better of it, that was "eminently impractical." I asked a pediatrician if he thought his schooling and professional experience with children had set him up for fatherhood. "In fact, I think it works just the other way around," he said. "Having children of your own teaches you a lot about kids that can help you in your practice as a pediatrician. As a doctor you're never really close enough to the kids to learn very much about them as people. We know all about their medicine, but we don't get to handle them and fondle them and talk to them."

Some men have learned a lot about child care firsthand, from having grown up as the eldest in big families and having been obliged to help out with the younger kids. Not surprisingly, many of the fathers I talked to who seemed particularly confident and easygoing in their dealings with their kids had come from big families. It's clearly the best — and nearly the only — school you can have, real practical on-the-job training. Of course there's plenty more to learn as a father — child care is only one small part of the job. But a man from a big family

has at least known young children intimately and has some idea of what they're about.

A landscape architect I talked with had grown up in a family with five kids and changed plenty of diapers, fed plenty of bottles to the two youngest. When his first baby arrived, he felt stronger than his wife in his knowledge and experience of infants — he was sure of himself and raring to go. But he discovered a "striking difference between what I anticipated before I was a father and the reality of being a father. . . . In your own children, you see a strong, thriving individual character that you don't necessarily perceive in your own brother or someone else's child — a strong, demanding being with its own wants and needs who at a very early age begins to develop its own preferential course through life."

Exactly what all parents discover — a new personality in the group, a new relationship to be formed. Not just a typical child whom you can deal with as a typical father with a typical set of father responses, but a very particular child, who deals with you as one person with another.

Here's another man who was an "experienced" beginner, again from a family of five kids: "I knew all about it. There was nothing you could tell me. . . . There were so many things about my childhood and growing up that wanted to do *my way* this time. I knew how I was brought up and this time it was going to be all mine. So I think the first time around I was maybe a little bit overconfident." There were plenty of surprises in store for him and there still are — every day. "Fatherhood — as ready as I was for it and as much as I thought I knew about it — I think is more a state of mind than anything. For me it's something that's still going on, so it's taken at least seven years that I know of. And every day I look at something I've done and say to myself: 'Well, jeez, that's not something you should do as a father, or something you could do better, or a situation you could handle better.' It's an ongoing thing."

One man pointed out that he had had the useful experience of being a child himself. We can all draw a little on the same source, but how much do we remember? Several men looked back to their own fathers as examples, and one man felt that his thirteen years of psychoanalysis might have sorted things out enough to make him ready for fatherhood. One noted that before his kids arrived he and his wife had often visited with friends who already had families. They would observe and discuss how their friends were bringing up their kids: "We picked out the good points and threw away the bad and said: 'I'll never do *that* with *my* kids.'" And of course when their kids came, they found themselves doing *that*, too.

Of all the men I talked to, only one had what seemed like a rock-solid foundation for being a father. He had been a father — a Roman Catholic priest — for ten years, until he changed his life and started from scratch as a biological father. "Very definitely I was a father. . . . I was a father to sixty-five-year-old women dying of cancer, or thirty-five-year-old men with alcoholic problems." He had been a confidential member of hundreds of families, helping young kids, teen-agers, and parents sort out their family problems. He had learned things about being a father that take most of us a lifetime to arrive at finally — not simple child care, but how to help people: your own kids when they are the people who need help. "It all boils back to the same thing: you have to have a love for the person; you have to have a respect for the person; and you treat them that way and try to get them to have love for themselves, a respect for themselves. . . . I never *solved* a problem for anybody; they solved their own. I pointed out ways; I reinstilled love of themselves, respect for themselves, but never, never once did I give the solution. *They* gave the solution." A very special kind of background and understanding to be able to bring to family life. The rest of us, however, have to learn that lesson and a thousand others from our own kids.

So it looks as if we're all pretty much in the same boat as fathers: Unqualified. It's going to be a learning experience, but I'm sure we'll adapt.

A CHILD'S-EYE VIEW

In every child's eyes, Daddy is BIG. I've asked dozens of preschoolers to tell me about their fathers: what Dad looks like, what they do together. I've even done tape-recorded interviews with nursery school kids where we discussed their ideas about their fathers and how they were different from their mothers. The really striking thing about all these discussions was that Daddy was invariably described as tall and strong. "He goes right up to the ceiling." "He's so strong he could punch out a whale." "He could knock down a tree, even." "And I can squeeze his muscles." How big is your dad? "THAT BIG!!!"

Many of those fathers who go right on up to the ceiling are just little guys — I've seen or know a lot of the men who were being described as giants. What a terrific deal. Without lifting a finger, without even being big, and whether or not we deserve it, we are automatically looked up to, respected, possibly worshiped. Because our kids have to look up to us in the simplest physical sense, they look up to us in other ways as well.

One father I talked with, a psychology professor who has two kids, put it this way: "From the viewpoint of kids, all adults just have a real natural authority, and especially the parents. And you really don't have to exert that. Simply by being big and being competent and being able to do things

that they want to do, we just have an incredible amount of authority. And you can just let it flow naturally."

Kids respect a father's towering strength just as they respect all other big things: giants, dragons, dinosaurs, and whales. But with a difference. Dad is so close that they needn't be intimidated by his strength; they can use it as a refuge; they can use him for protection. A child enlists superheroes as allies against the monsters and bad guys in his world. But probably even more useful to a four-year-old than Batman and Super Woman is a father who is right there when he's needed to punch out a whale or banish brontosaurs from the hall closet. Whether or not you may feel like it at the end of a hard day, your return each evening, in your child's eyes, is a little like the return of Superman, ready to do battle with the foes of law and order.

I thought it would be interesting to include in this book drawings by preschoolers of their fathers, naturally assuming that kids would draw their dads as gigantic figures, and probably put themselves in the pictures as tiny specks by way of comparison; so I carried a black crayon in my pocket for a couple of months and collected quite a pile of drawings of fathers by kids. None of them fits my little theory. Dad drawn by a three- or a four-year-old is just another face with arms and legs sticking out from it. And Dad drawn by a five- or a six-year-old is sometimes the smallest guy in the picture. If the rest of the family is in the picture, Mom is bigger, and the artist may be bigger still. What seems to be happening is that the drawings show the relative importance of the people in the child's life, rather than how the child sees them physically. Just as ancient Egyptian tomb decorations show the Pharaoh and his wife as huge, while court officers are medium-sized and slaves are quite small. A child draws herself big because she is the center of her world. Mom is big because she is there all the time. And Dad is small in the picture because he's not around as much.

Whenever you *are* there, though, your child is watching your every move. Dad is every child's first idea of what a man is like — a son's first image of what he may become, a daughter's first view of what she'll have to cope with.

"Things that I'm not even conscious that I do he picks right up," says one father about his oldest son, three. "I'm putting shakes on the outside of the house — you know how many nails are in those shakes? At least five hundred million. So I'll pick up a handful and put like eight in my mouth and pretty soon he's walking around with nails in *his* mouth. . . . That's the way kids learn. I never catch Luke reading any books, so he must be doing it just by looking."

They also do it by listening — to Dad. Kids are all ears for whatever you have to tell them, whether you're explaining to a baby how her spoon works for eating or showing a toddler how to catch a ball, whether you've opened up the tank top on the toilet to demonstrate to a preschooler how the fascinating flush mechanism functions or you're reading your child a book about space exploration. Whatever the subject, no matter how fundamental or complex, kids rely on a father's — and a mother's — superior knowledge of the world to give them clues to what goes on in it. Never again will you have so attentive an audience as you do when your kids are still so young that they don't question your judgment.

Gregory, at four, showed me a twisted little piece

of plastic one day, a nondescript thing that could have come from a broken toy or a broken appliance. "What is this?" he wanted to know.

"I can't tell," I said.

"How come you don't know what this is? Grownups know everything that kids don't know."

It's too bad he's wrong. But for a while it feels pretty good to know that someone thinks of you as infallible.

WORKING AT FATHERHOOD

It's one of the clichés of child care advice books to admonish fathers to make fatherhood as important in their lives as their jobs or careers. This is a nice thought, but it is quite literally impossible — at least in terms of hours of family time compared to hours of work — for anyone who is working overtime or who is goaded by the demands of a career, or who travels in his work.

The week has only 168 hours. Say work takes up 40 hours; commuting, 5; sleep, 56; and there are about 21 hours a week when Dad is home awake, but young children are in bed — the hours from eight to eleven in the evening. Simple arithmetic leaves 46 hours in the week, on this uncomplicated schedule, during which a man could be spending time with his kids. Add a little overtime, a long commute, or one short business trip a month, and you're already under 40 hours possible family time. Add a moonlighting second job, or devotion to a

career, and the scales are tipped all the way. And add some frills — say tennis twice a week or some community service responsibility, heavy handyman work around the house, or an evening course . . .

It's a rare man who is putting in a regular 40-hour week on straight fatherhood. But it's also a rare father who *feels* his job or career is qualitatively more important than his family — the two things can't be compared one to one. You can certainly be devoted to a career, or be tied down by financial burdens and two jobs, and be devoted at the same time to your kids. I know dozens of men in this position, and there's no contradiction there, even though there may be stiff competition for their time between the two sides of their lives.

There's one point, though, where a one-on-one comparison between a man's working life and his family life makes sense and can be valuable. I think every father can try to devote the same *kind* of energy to his family life that he devotes to his job. Though there's no simple way to find time parity, your dealings with your kids can receive the same high level of attention you give to matters at work, and your family life can benefit from the same kind of imaginative, creative thinking you use when tackling job-related problems.

We all know that bringing up kids is a task as important to us and to the rest of the world as any we ordinarily take on at work. But we relax at home, tune out. We put in our strenuous efforts on the job, and when we get home we want to prop up our feet and breathe easy for a minute — which is only natural. It's just that the relaxed atmosphere can dictate a slack attitude toward the whole at-home enterprise. We tend to slog along through family activities and crises, where we are always on our toes at work. We tend to take the easiest way out in family situations, while at work we zero in on the problem and search diligently for inventive solutions. We find ourselves losing touch with our kids from time to time in the press of events — yet we would never dream of losing touch with developments, changes, advances in our fields of work.

I think a lot of this difference lies in the simple fact that we're being paid for what we do at work and there's no immediate reimbursement for fatherhood. When I signed a contract with my publisher to work on this book, I became perhaps the only man in the country who was actually being paid for fatherhood. I could spend a couple of hours playing with my own kids and have no lurking feeling that I was squandering the time. Fatherhood itself was bringing home the bacon. And I found myself regarding fatherhood in a new light — as a significant, useful, and dignified undertaking. Not that I had regarded it as trivial before — it's just that I discovered a whole new sense of respect for the enterprise.

It's so easy for fatherhood to become a side issue

in our lives, something we can spend some time on if and when we get a spare hour. If a paycheck came in each week for fatherhood, though, we'd all feel obligated to stay current with the family scene, to be on top of things at home. I'm certainly not advocating tax-supported pay for fatherhood. On the contrary, I'd suggest that we all recognize that we *are* being paid for fatherhood. It's not a dollars-and-cents proposition, and it doesn't come in regular installments with periodic increases. It comes whenever our kids laugh, whenever they jump on us with unsolicited hugs.

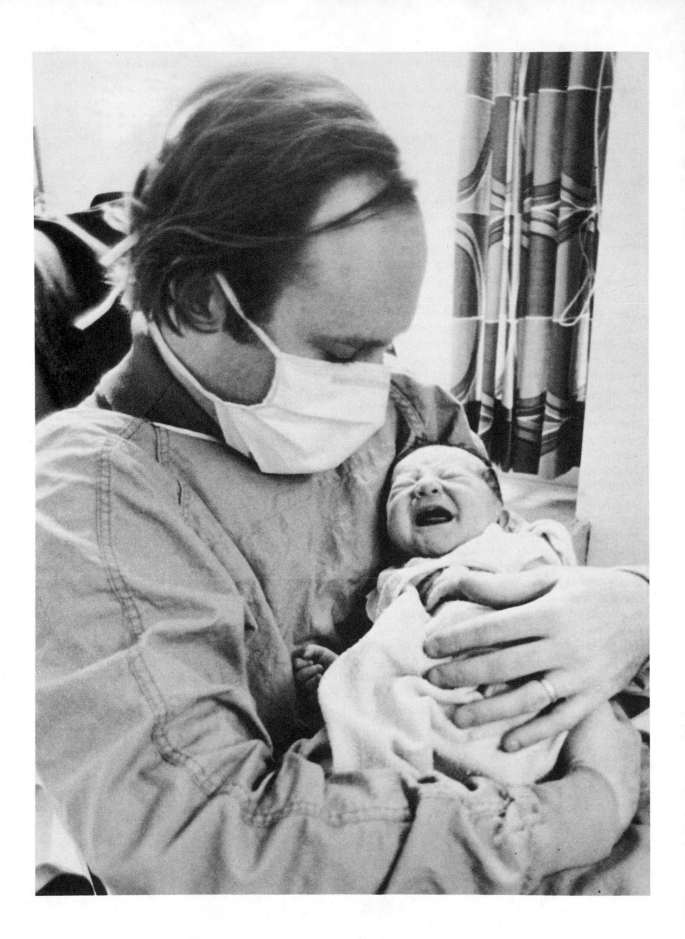

Chapter 1

THE GRAND ARRIVAL

Not too long ago it was only the avant-garde father who was in the delivery room for his child's birth. But the childbirth scene has changed remarkably and today most hospitals and doctors welcome fathers, and most fathers are right in there helping and cheering as the baby comes out into the world bloody and screaming and absolutely beautiful.

The director of a childbirth education program in a suburban hospital told me that fathers participated in 90 per cent of births in the hospital — and this was in an institution with a reputation for being a little behind the times in terms of father involvement. Fathers in childbirth classes and in the delivery room could think of themselves as pioneers in the sixties and early seventies, but today they are very much in the mainstream. When your wife is pregnant, your next-door neighbor or another man at work will corner you and talk rapturously about how he shared childbirth with his wife, and badger you until you promise to get involved and take a childbirth class.

A father interested in shared childbirth will talk your ear off — I have a file full of glowing testimonials from involved dads. One striking thing about these is that the most ardent enthusiasts are almost always men who have experienced the other side of childbirth, who with other births have spent long, dismal, alienating hours in the fathers' waiting room. "It wasn't a matter of just adding another one on this time," says an investment banker who finally got into the act with his fourth child. "It was a real process, and I was part of that process." He held Victoria five minutes after she was born and he's certain that he feels somehow closer to her than he does to his other kids — directly because of this experience.

When fathers rhapsodize about their experiences in the delivery room, the emphasis is nearly always on the fact that they were *part* of things, that they actually participated. "It's what it did for me — not 'You owe it to your wife,'" says a regional sales manager for a large publishing firm, the father of twin girls. "I think a father owes it to himself." Ask any mother, though, who has had her husband with

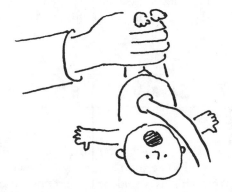

her during a birth and she'll tell you the other side of the story: many say, "I couldn't have done it without him." That's perhaps an exaggeration, but they couldn't have done it the same way — or with the same sense of pleasure and accomplishment — without him.

Fathers have earned widespread acceptance of their place in the labor and delivery rooms because of the tremendous support a man gives his wife through the pain and effort of childbirth. During the climactic minutes of the birth the father gives physical support as well as the moral kind, propping the mother's back up off the delivery table so she'll be in the right position to "push" the baby out. And through the whole process, the father is busy and involved — timing the relentless progress of the

contractions as they build in intensity; coaching the distracted mother through the breathing exercises they have learned and practiced together; constantly soothing and reassuring her; and often for hours on end grinding the heel of his hand into the base of her back to relieve some of the intense "back labor" pain she feels there.

And a father shares completely the excitement of the actual arrival. "There's nothing missing" is the way several men I talked to put it. Their job didn't end when the baby was conceived; they went on being part of things; and for a lot of men, this involvement seems to make a huge difference — the difference between indifference to their kids and true fatherly caring. "Being able to go through that process really saved me," one man said, "because I didn't want to be a parent; I didn't want anything to do with it. It was an accidental pregnancy and I didn't feel at all ready for that responsibility. I just totally was not prepared for it. And getting involved in that basic level of the whole process, the biological level of it, really saved me. It made me able to be a conscious participant."

For men who are looking forward to having kids, being on hand when they arrive is one of the ultimate good things in life. Childbirth, one man said, "pretty much was like what the marriage ceremony is supposed to be — representing the act of making two into one."

GETTING INVOLVED

Don't count yourself in on the birth unless you're willing to spend some time preparing for what will happen. You can't just decide at the last minute and come panting in from work saying, "Doc, I think I'd like to watch" — because it's a participation event, not a spectator sport.

Early in your wife's pregnancy, you should go with her on a regular prenatal checkup visit and meet her obstetrician. You'll probably want to talk with the doctor about costs and charges to get straight exactly what you're in for. And if you want to be involved in the childbirth process, you'll definitely want to talk to the doctor about your role. If the obstetrician isn't receptive to the idea of your being in the delivery room, find another doctor who is. The obstetrician who resists father participation is happily becoming a rarity, but there are still holdouts, so don't assume your wife's doctor will welcome you — ask.

A doctor who encourages father participation will almost certainly be associated with a hospital that does, too. Again, there are still some holdouts — hospitals where fathers are excluded from the deliv-

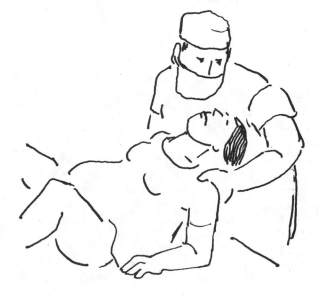

ery room — but they are fewer every year. If you run into trouble trying to find a hospital in your area where fathers are welcome, contact the International Childbirth Education Association, P. O. Box 5852, Milwaukee, Wisconsin 53220.

The obstetrician should be able to put you in touch with a "prepared childbirth" course — which is the right way to get ready for the grand arrival.

LEFT OUT

Why were fathers excluded from childbirth for so long? Probably for reasons similar to the ones that for centuries forced Moslem women to hide behind veils. And then over a hundred years ago, Queen Victoria set the fashion for heavily sedated childbirth by being one of the first women chloroformed for a delivery — since which time, fathers have been extraneous during childbirth. You can't comfort or help a drugged zombie who doesn't even know you're there. In this dreary process, even the baby is knocked out by the general anesthetic, which passes through the placenta from mother to child. The doctor slaps the baby to get him to breathe and cry mainly because the baby is drugged and groggy. Normally delivered, a newborn person may not need this slap at all, but will usually breathe naturally and scream readily when he discovers where he's arrived.

Mothers are now rejecting general anesthesia in favor of being mentally present when their children are born and in favor of having their husbands with them. When Queen Victoria's great-great-great-granddaughter Princess Anne had her first baby in November 1977, the proud papa, Mark Phillips, was on hand in the delivery room.

So-called "natural" childbirth — without drugs of any sort — is only one of the options open to a modern mother. Sophisticated techniques of anesthesia allow pain killers to be administered during labor and local anesthetics to be given for delivery. Whatever route is chosen — and these are choices to be made in consultation with your doctor — there is nothing to stop Dad from being on hand. Doctors were at first hesitant to allow fathers access to the birth process, particularly to the delivery room — after all, a father is just an ordinary klutz with no medical training. But fathers quickly proved to be so helpful and supportive that now many doctors actively encourage them to get into the act. After thousands of father-present deliveries, Dr. Robert

A. Bradley* wrote: "No husband has fainted in the delivery room or otherwise made a nuisance of himself. On the contrary, he has added an element of humor and joy and has become very much a member of the team."

In point of fact, fathers haven't always been excluded from childbirth in the past; when they could be useful, they were right in there helping. A grandfather told me how his father — a worker in a cement factory — had always helped the midwife with the births of his six kids; and he wasn't just boiling the water and stepping aside for the midwife to do the whole job; he was in the thick of things. The older kids would all be gathered in the other room of their tiny Jersey City apartment, and the proud papa would bring the new baby in to show to them, wrapped carefully in a laundered cement bag — the finest, softest linen in the household.

And I'm sure there have always been fathers who have insisted on being in on the birth of their kids. One famous such father was the great Russian novelist Leo Tolstoy, who was nearly always on hand when his wife, Sonia, gave birth to one of their thirteen babies. His biographer H. Troyat calls him "a habitué of the delivery room." On the birth of his ninth child — a son, Andrey — Tolstoy wrote to a friend: "Even though it has come to be a sort of routine for me, I am stirred and moved and filled with happiness every time."

SQUEAMISHNESS

Don't let squeamishness cheat you out of involvement in your child's birth. Many men "brave it through" and discover that they are so caught up in the event that they simply don't have time to be squeamish.

Here is a father who resisted going into the delivery room, among other reasons because he got sick watching a birth movie in the childbirth preparation class: "At first I didn't want to because I have a personal sensitivity to — well . . . blood [he even seemed to be having a little trouble saying the word]. When they take my blood, my knees start to knock. So I said I just can't see any usefulness in being a participant when I'm sick, and it would just make me feel dizzy. But still I thought, 'Maybe you can get by by not looking in any particular direc-

*Author of *Husband-Coached Childbirth* (New York: Harper and Row, 1965).

tion.'" He gave it a try and, "I guess when I got all dressed I felt like I was part of the team. My wife said I looked more like a doctor than a doctor." He helped out in the delivery room and took photos — the works — and, "I didn't feel squeamish at all; I don't exactly know why."

I suffer with a similar kind of squeamishness — faintness at the sight of a hypodermic needle, dizziness on seeing blood — but when Gregory was born, those feelings simply suspended themselves. I suspect that I was just too busy and interested in what was going on for the squeamish feelings to get a foothold. I was much more edgy and uncomfortable three years later stuck in the fathers' waiting room while Timothy was delivered by Cesarean than I had been right in the bloody midst of things.

CHILDBIRTH CLASSES

There are plenty of how-to-do-it books on the subject of childbirth, but the best training a husband and wife can get is through the "prepared childbirth" courses now widely offered by hospitals. These mini-courses are generally inexpensive and take only six or eight evening sessions; your wife's obstetrician or your hospital can tell you how to sign up. The courses offer a wealth of information about the birth process, including, for instance, fascinating films on the development of the baby in the uterus. Films, plaster models, and diagrams are used to explain just how the great rhythmic contractions of the uterine muscle push the baby down and out through a birth canal that has miraculously widened itself, dilating a spectacular ten centimeters to let the baby's head pass through.

For many fathers, learning the mechanics of birth is a revelation; it takes the mystery out of the process — not the extraordinary, essential mystery of reproduction but the annoying mystery caused by ignorance that makes you feel like an absolute sap

when confronted with knowledgeable doctors and nurses. No father is right on top of things as his child is being born; the tension and excitement tear you apart. But armed with some knowledge of the situation, you're in a far stronger position than if you go in cold and everything that happens is new, strange, and possibly a cause for extra worry. Most childbirth courses include a tour of the labor and delivery rooms in the hospital. Seeing the setup in advance and knowing what the surroundings will be like really makes a difference when you arrive at the hospital for the big event; you march in as an old hand and get right down to work, rather than having to poke foolishly — or desperately — around hospital corridors getting lost and asking directions.

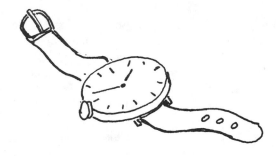

Breathing Techniques

The real substance of the childbirth classes is the relaxation exercises and breathing techniques that you and your wife learn and practice together. Proper techniques of controlled breathing are the key to relaxation during labor; if a woman is breathing correctly, she can "ride out" much of the pain of the contractions. In this process, mother and father truly become a team. The father uses a watch to time the contractions, which come at quite regular intervals; you can tell your wife when to start the rhythmic breathing so that it will be co-ordinated with the onset of the next contraction. This stopwatch timing isn't just a gimmick to make fathers feel involved; during actual labor it's an important job. Practicing before the event, your wife can easily keep time by herself and remember the breathing techniques, but when labor starts and the powerful waves of the contractions are surging through your wife's body, she's in no condition to keep her thoughts on timing or on how she should be breathing. Your calm coaching sees her through. So you practice together and though you may feel a little superfluous in rehearsal, when you go on for the real performance you'll recognize how important your participation actually is.

There's a different breathing technique for each of several progressive stages of labor, none of them difficult to master, but all best taught by a trained person in a class situation.

Watching the class group practice one of the exercises — the pelvic rock, which is just for the women, to strengthen muscles used in childbirth — is worth the price of admission. A spectacle of this sort is available nowhere else that I know of: a dozen heavily pregnant women on their hands and knees bumping and grinding.

Fringe Benefits

Besides teaching the ins and outs of the childbirth process, childbirth classes put you in touch with other people who live near you, who are going through the identical experience you are, and whose child will be almost exactly your child's age. Many people — especially the women, but fathers, too — form attachments with others in the group and stay in touch for years. Class groups often have yearly picnic get-togethers where everyone can compare notes on how the kids have grown. There's a spirit of camaraderie among the people in these groups, and the kids — who are childbirth twins — sometimes grow up good friends.

ALTERNATIVES

Here are thoughts on a few alternate systems of childbirth. You may be interested in trying home birth or father delivery; and you should definitely be aware of how commonplace Cesareans have become — your baby could easily be a candidate for a C-section delivery.

Father Deliveries

Today's avant-garde father is not only in the delivery room, he "delivers" his own baby. In this new-style obstetrics, the doctor stands discreetly in the background and literally coaches the father through all the steps of the procedure: "Now, Mr. Smith, with your left hand please grasp the clamp being passed to you by the nurse . . ." This looks like a good way to get to know your child at the earliest conceivable moment, and the experience must be thrilling. But I hope father delivery doesn't

become the childbirth style of the future, because I'm convinced a father does the most good at the other end of the delivery table, holding his wife's hand and encouraging her as she pushes out the baby.

Home Birth

Clearly your own bedroom is the most comfortable place for a family event like childbirth. But a hospital is the safest place — in case there are complications. When your wife's and your baby's life and health are at stake, you don't want to be miles away from help. Interesting compromises are being worked out between hospital and home so parents who want to can have their children safely in the intimacy of their bedrooms.

One couple I talked with had an ambulance waiting outside their Boston apartment building during the birth of their first baby in case the doctor decided that complications necessitated getting to the hospital fast. In rural areas in some states, home births are attended by well-equipped hospital vans.

Another couple told me they had gone for the birth of their second child to a family-centered birth clinic — a situation halfway between home and hospital. The clinic was next door to a hospital and had two comfortable birth rooms. Their daughter, six, was with them through the whole labor — though she apparently got a little bored. And a couple of hours after the baby arrived, they bundled him up; the whole family got in the car, and drove home. It's also possible in a birth clinic situation like this one to check into the hospital after the baby arrives, and of course to be rushed next door to the hospital if there are complications.

Talk with your wife's obstetrician about home birth if the idea appeals to you.

Cesareans

Be prepared for the possibility of your baby's being delivered by Cesarean section, because it has recently become a very common route for births. It used to be a relatively rare operation, but at this writing some hospitals have as many as 30 per cent Cesarean deliveries, and the trend still seems to be on the upswing. Sophisticated devices like the fetal heart monitor have given doctors the means for spotting problems and possible complications before the baby descends from the uterus into the birth canal; and if they detect that the baby is suffer-

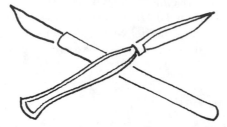

ing some distress, the next step is often a C-section.

The operation saves the baby a narrow, difficult, painful passage, and it often saves the baby's life or her normal brain function. From the baby's point of view, Cesarean delivery is wonderful — toil and trouble free.

From the mother's point of view, however, it's not such a terrific deal. A C-section is a major operation and it can take a woman a *long* time to recover. Instead of bouncing back physically in a couple of weeks or a month, as from a conventional birth, it sometimes takes a Cesarean mother months to feel like herself again, and there are plenty of sharp pains along the way. Cesarean mothers, because they feel so depleted, can also experience difficulty nursing.

From a father's viewpoint, too, a Cesarean operation has big drawbacks. In most hospitals fathers aren't welcome during Cesarean deliveries, no matter how well prepared they may be to share in the childbirth process. When the doctor decided at the last minute to deliver our second son, Timothy, by Cesarean, I was banished to the fathers' waiting room and an hour of bleak anxiety that started me smoking cigarettes for the first time in seven years. And I accepted this fate, thinking that an operating theater was no place for me. But months later I learned that because Cesareans are so common some hospitals are beginning to change the rules and are allowing father to stay with their wives during the delivery.

A screen can be placed across the mother's chest so that the father, sitting at the head of the operating table, won't be a spectator at a major operation, but will be able to hold his wife's hand throughout, soothe and comfort her, share the experience, and see the baby when it arrives. Local anesthetics are commonly used for Cesareans, so the mother is awake and fully able to appreciate the moral support. Rita was irate when she learned that in another hospital I might have been allowed to stay with her; she had expected me to be with her through the whole birth and had felt desperately lonely when at the ninth hour she was carted off alone to the operating room.

Ask your wife's obstetrician about the hospital's policy on fathers and Cesarean delivery, and insist on your right to be there. This, probably even more than during a conventional delivery, is a time when your wife can really use your support. Many C-sections are decided on and scheduled months ahead of time — and here you'll have plenty of time to try to arrange to accompany your wife.

After the baby is born by Cesarean, your support is going to be needed for months to come — far more help than you might ordinarily have contributed. Your wife's hospital stay will last a week or more, and when she comes home, she will probably be sore and dismal and not up to much. Hire help if you can afford to, and make peace with your mother-in-law — gratefully accept any assistance from any quarter.

Women who are prepared for childbirth and excited about it can experience an emotional letdown if the baby has to be delivered by C-section; they feel thwarted, disappointed, cheated. So besides simple physical help, you should be ready to provide lots of understanding and sympathy.

Cesarean deliveries cost far more than conventional ones, and some of the extra cost may not be absorbed by your insurance. A lot of parents who have paid the financial, physical, and emotional costs of a Cesarean operation grumble that doctors are cutting babies out more often not so much for the babies' good but because they're afraid of malpractice suits if every precaution is not taken. Maybe there's a grain of truth in this, but a baby's chances actually are improved by Cesarean delivery, and that, in the long run, is what really counts.

A Cesarean probably won't leave an ugly scar running up and down your wife's abdomen. Most doctors currently use horizontal "bikini" incisions that fall well below the top line of a bikini bottom and which you will hardly notice several months after the operation. And one little plus in Cesarean births is that Cesarean babies are better-looking than babies who have had to struggle down through the birth canal. The head of a C-section baby isn't all mashed out of shape from the effort.

Emergency Delivery

There's only the very slimmest chance that you'll have to "deliver" the baby or that it will arrive

during the drive to the hospital; the vast majority of babies wait until it's convenient. If the baby does arrive unexpectedly, just remember: Don't try to play doctor with your Swiss Army knife. If you're in the car on the way to the hospital, keep driving and try to keep calm. These are usually the easy births — the babies that come shooting out with no trouble. Don't stop the car; don't try to cut the cord or deliver the placenta. Just drive on to the emergency entrance of the hospital. Meanwhile your wife can hold the baby, with the umbilical cord intact, and put it to her breast if she wants to.

If events overtake you and your wife at home, call the doctor for instructions. When your wife is pushing to expel the baby, remind her to pant as she was taught in the childbirth class; this will help to slow down the birth and minimize the possibility of damage to the surrounding tissue. Handle the baby with care, because he'll be slippery. Hold the baby upside down by the feet so water and mucus can drain from his mouth and nose, and if he doesn't start to cry right away, give him a gentle slap on the bottom.

Don't cut the umbilical cord or pull on it. With the cord intact, put the baby on the mother's breast — whether or not she intends to breast-feed. This can help prevent hemorrhaging and ease delivery of the placenta. The cord is usually long enough so the baby will reach the breast; if it's not long enough, wait until the placenta slips out, and then put the baby to the breast. Wrap baby and placenta in a clean blanket and keep mother and baby warm. The next step is getting mother and baby to the hospital — following your doctor's instructions as you have throughout.

DURING PREGNANCY

The first three months and the last three are the hard ones for your wife. In the middle, there's usually a welcome change of pace. The queasy feelings of "morning sickness" that devil mothers-to-be for the first three months are rare after the fourth, because a woman's body has grown accustomed to its new boarder by this point. It's then that most women take on that wonderful healthy, radiant glow of pregnancy.

And it's around that time — in the fourth or fifth month — that the baby starts to kick. Powerful kicks, too; the baby's really making contact. You'll feel them just by touching where your wife tells you to.

In the seventh month you can start listening for the baby's heartbeat. Doctors use a gadget called a fetoscope to listen to the heartbeat, but it doesn't have any advantage over the simple method you will use — pressing your ear to your wife's abdomen. In fact, the fetoscope — unless it's a fancy model connected to an amplifier — muffles the sound a little; the doctor uses it primarily for the sake of dignity.

Babies commonly lie upside down on their backs and usually a little to the mother's left side; so start

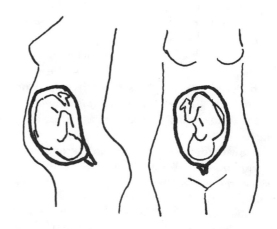

your search by pressing your ear slightly lower than and to the left of the navel, and then work over the whole field till you locate it. The heartbeat will sound a little like a ticking watch — it's much faster than you'd expect, varying from 100 to 160 beats per minute, but usually around 140. One tricky part in locating the heartbeat is sorting it out from other internal noises you'll be hearing — gurgles and swishes produced by the intestines and the flow of blood through the uterus. But keep at it for a while — it's like detective work and it's very exciting when you finally hear the little ticker.

"My wife and I each month would read a chapter together on what's going on internally with her and with the baby," one new father told me, "and so we kind of stayed current like that. I was aware with her what was happening in each month of the development." An excellent book to use for following the baby's development this way is Ashley Montagu's *Life Before Birth* (New York: Signet, 1964).

In the last three months — or final trimester — things get progressively rougher for your wife. The baby takes up so much space by this point that he starts interfering with various normal functions of her body. Pressure upward can cut off her breath from time to time and even give her suffocation sensations. In the last month or so the baby and uterus take up most of the room the bladder used to occupy, so your wife will be running to the john every few minutes. The baby's feet can block the mother's stomach, not allowing it to empty at the right time, which causes heartburn and burping.

In the last three months many women suffer from "hot flashes," caused by the intermittent exchange of rather large amounts of blood between the uterus and the mother's regular circulatory system. "Hot flashes" can give a woman terrible nightmares — she dreams that the baby will be born dead, or dozens of babies will be born alive — and even when she's awake the alternation of circulation can make her feel panicky and terrified that she won't be a good mother. And in the last months many women are generally high-strung and jumpy, and so are candidates for a little extra understanding and patience.

Some women work right up to the end with no interruptions, but most bog down in the last month, because the baby is a very heavy burden to carry around. This is the time for an interested father to be around with lots of reassurance and some help with the household.

HELPING OUT

You can give your wife wonderful relief during the later months of pregnancy by rubbing at the base of her back with the heel of your hand. The whole weight of the uterus with the growing baby inside pulls directly on the small of the back, because this is the single point in the mother's body to which the uterus is attached — by a set of muscles called the uterosacrals. And with all that weight tugging against them, these muscles get really tired and sore.

To do a professional job of relieving the weary uterosacrals, sprinkle on some talcum powder or use a little cold cream so the heel of your hand will slide freely as you rub firmly and slowly.

Another big help — if you're attending childbirth classes — will be to practice together at bedtime the relaxing exercises you've learned. Besides being good training for both of you for childbirth, the relaxation exercises are also an excellent first step toward a sound, refreshing night's sleep — just what an exhausted pregnant woman needs.

From the first signs of pregnancy people fetch chairs for women and try to help them down the stairs as if they were invalids, and most of these solicitous gestures are pure nonsense. Pregnant women can lead energetic lives that include vigorous sports like tennis and skiing — and without endangering their babies in the least. Babies are remarkably well protected by the surrounding sac of fluid, and — contrary to popular belief — a woman won't miscarry simply because she falls down stairs.

But in the last months, the vigor flags and the belly sags and though the baby is still safe and snug inside, you can readily see that Mom can now use some solicitous gestures. Why not sit down with her during the seventh or eighth month and make a list of the jobs she routinely does, and see if there aren't a few that you could take over to save her some bending and stooping and standing for long periods? Washing out the bathtub, for instance, is a brutal task for a pregnant woman, and one you can easily assume.

If you have a cat, one small job you should take over at the very beginning of pregnancy is tending to the litter box. An infection called toxoplasmosis, which is caused by organisms that may be found in cat feces, if contracted by a pregnant woman can be passed on to the baby in her womb, with serious consequences including blindness. The effect of the infection on the mother is mild, so she may not even know she has it at the time.

Sex

There's no reason to let pregnancy interrupt your sex life; you can usually keep making love right into the last month. When your wife's belly has filled out, she'll be uncomfortable on her back with you on top — but there are plenty of other positions. Also remember that your wife's vaginal flesh may be puffy and sensitive, which will call for gentleness.

Some women are turned on by pregnancy, while others become less responsive. And men react in both ways, too. Among other things, there's the fear of hurting the baby — which doesn't happen. And a lot of people feel a loss of privacy with the baby right there in the midst of things. It makes a lot of sense to talk about these feelings if you have them — get everybody's cards out on the table so there won't be any misunderstandings.

Misunderstandings crop up easily. Say you're a little reluctant to make love during pregnancy and your amorous advances slow down or stop altogether. If you don't talk it out and tell your wife what's going on, she can easily conclude that you're turned off by her lumpy figure, that *she's* doing something wrong, even that there's another woman.†

†Elisabeth Bing, the great popularizer of the Lamaze childbirth techniques, and Libby Colman have written an interesting in-depth study of sex for expectant parents: *Making Love During Pregnancy* (New York: Bantam, 1977).

PREGNANT WORRIES

The nine months of pregnancy are a man's worry time: worries about the new responsibilities ahead, about how tied down he'll be, about the loss of income if his wife has a job. Worries that for some of us are as burdensome as the extra weight our wives are lugging around.

I don't think I've ever known an expectant father who wasn't tied up in knots over some aspect of pregnancy. Lurking at the back of everyone's mind is the question of how the baby is doing; she's hidden from view and anything could be going on in there. Even if you're well read on fetal development, you may still be worried by the nagging possibility that something's not right — and you're simply not going to know until the baby arrives.

Many men worry about their wives. If your wife is knocked out with morning sickness in the first months or bogs down toward the end or is always irritable, your next-door neighbor will surely say: "My wife loves being pregnant. She's never happier; it's like all her fulfillment comes from being pregnant." And you start thinking there must be something wrong with your wife — maybe she's ill and needs more medical attention, maybe she's just not as capable as the next woman. There's probably nothing wrong with her at all. Pregnancy affects every woman differently — both physically and emotionally. A *normal* course for pregnancies doesn't exist; even the nine-month time period varies.

And there's another one that really gets you worrying — lateness. One day over that magic "due date" and you start to be concerned; a week, two weeks, and you're jumping out of your skin. Even though you know there's nothing magic about due dates, that you could have guessed at a due date as easily as the obstetrician did, simply by adding nine months to the date your wife suspected she got pregnant.

By arriving too early or too late your baby is telling you something important — a lesson we learn over and over as parents. Kids are never convenient; they resist being scheduled and organized — and try as we will to fit our kids into the orderly structures we've set up, they'll always figure out a way to get *us* to change to take care of *their* needs. Late babies, no matter how much we worry, do arrive — when they're ready.

Money accounts for a lot of worry time. No man,

rich or poor, is certain he'll be able to provide correctly for a bigger family. And now without your wife's income, it's all on your shoulders for the time being. Writing this, I'm getting a little panicky just thinking back through all the things that used to torture me while Rita was pregnant. Each of us has his own special set of problems that nag him during a pregnancy: some men are sure they won't be good fathers; some don't want to be fathers at all; some are sure the baby will interfere with the way they enjoy living. And whatever it is that gets you down, you've got those nine long months to dwell on it, nine months of anticipating a huge change in your way of life, and building up the problems you see — blowing them up out of all proportion. Small wonder then that fathers start to get frantic when the baby holds out past the due date. You just want to get it over with, make the change and let come what may . . .

Strangely enough a lot of these pregnant worries seem to be "delivered" along with the baby. When the baby comes, some of them disappear because they were in our imaginations, and the concrete ones find whatever half-baked solutions they can, and our lives go on — in a rather different course.

ARRANGEMENTS

Your wife's bag will be packed weeks before the first pangs of labor. Here are a few items that *you* should make sure are taken care of well in advance:

Paying

Visit or call the hospital several weeks before your wife's due date and talk with the admissions office or business office about finances, the cost of a private room vs. a semiprivate one, etc. At this point you may be able to fill out a preadmission form so you won't have to mess around with insurance plan identification cards and hospital forms when you

arrive with your wife in labor. If the hospital doesn't have preadmission forms, ask for a standard admission form that you can fill out and present when you arrive.

Childbirth costs plenty, especially if there are complications like premature birth or Cesarean delivery. Check your insurance coverage carefully in advance to see if you have maternity coverage and how much. I wrote to the national Blue Cross Association and the National Association of Blue Shield Plans asking whether their plans were consistent throughout the country on maternity coverage. Not at all. "Most policies," they wrote back, "cover full cost of hospitalization. However, some certificates pay an indemnity, i.e., a certain dollar amount, which may not cover the total cost. Especially persons who are not members of a group should check their certificates for this feature. . . . Maternity coverage is usually included as part of family coverage. However, it could be an option which the employer may choose not to purchase. . . . In all cases, the fathers should be advised to check their health care coverage ahead of time. The rationale behind insurance and prepayment is that such coverage is for unforeseen health care needs. Since pregnancy can be foreseen and planned for, some schools of thought put it in a different category than other medical conditions. Therefore, coverage may not be as comprehensive."

If you don't have health insurance when your wife gets pregnant, you probably won't be able to buy insurance with maternity benefits, since there's commonly a nine-month waiting period for new subscribers before these benefits go into effect.

Family health insurance premiums are not increased when a baby is born — he's included in the family coverage at the same rate, and *ill* babies are covered from birth. If you have maternity benefits, they will probably pay the nursery charges for a well baby in the hospital. But once the baby is discharged from the hospital, you'll be picking up the whole tab for well-baby care (i.e., regular checkup visits to the pediatrician and immunizations) as well as for the usual run of childhood infections and diseases.

Paternity Leave

You'll need to take some time off from work when the baby arrives — certainly the day after, just to rest up and catch your breath. If you can't afford a lot of time off the job, go back to work for the days your

wife is in the hospital — especially if this is going to be a week or more of recovery from a Cesarean operation or because the baby is premature or under observation. You can visit and get to know the baby in the evenings — and at lunch time if it's convenient — and save your days off from work for the time when your wife and baby are home from the hospital and you can truly provide some help and get to see a lot of the baby. After the birth of a second baby, you should try to take half days off from work — or even full days — while your wife is in the hospital, so you can spend some time alone with your first child — for more thoughts on second babies see p. 19.

Some companies offer a special employee benefit called paternity leave — several days or a week off with pay when a baby arrives. And several of the fathers I talked with had taken some form of paternity leave. One man, who worked for a large pharmaceutical manufacturer, told me he'd had a week's paternity leave available but hadn't taken it because he'd been busy at the time. When his wife, who was with us, heard this, she was furious, because he'd never mentioned it at the time and she would of course have loved to have had him home for the first week.

Check with your employer or personnel department to see if some form of paternity leave is available. The odds are against it, but it's worth a try. Otherwise you'll probably have to take your own paternity days off — possibly as compensatory time for overtime worked or as some type of personal time off with pay — usually vacation time or accumulated sick days. Some school systems and other organizations have instituted another type of "paternity leave" — an unpaid leave of absence that allows a man months off the job to stay home and take care of an infant. Early reports on these programs, however, indicate that very few men have chosen to take this type of paternity leave.

Also consider taking another week of vacation time — or more if you have it coming — about three weeks or a month after the baby arrives. Around this time your wife is liable to be down in the dumps from the demands of full-time baby care and she probably could use your company and help. For more along this line, see p. 16 on postpartum blues and the possibility of escaping them by taking a newborn along on a vacation trip.

Help

You'll be doing a lot of baby care and housework in the first weeks after mother and baby come home. Mothers don't bounce right back from childbirth; they need all the help they can get. If you've never been much help before, there's no point in playing hero and pretending you'll be able to take everything over capably.

Hiring help for the first two weeks or more is a great idea if you can afford it and your quarters aren't too cramped. Be careful, though, to try to find someone who won't take over your household and baby and treat you like a hopeless male oaf who can't be trusted to hold his own child — helpers with this attitude are pretty common.

Grandmothers often behave this way. But with a grandmother, a lot of this can be shrugged off and laughed at, because the help is free and it's given with love. Of course avoid having a relative move in to "help" if it's going to cause too much friction and make everybody miserable. On the other hand, this is as good a time as any to learn the important lesson that most parents learn about grandparents: they are a wonderful help and you'll lean on them and like it. Even where there's a little strain between the generations, the birth of a grandchild will fre-

quently pull the extended family together with a shared interest in the baby.

One thing to avoid is having a relative arrive on the baby's due date to help out. The baby may be weeks late and you'll be stuck with a house guest who'll just be an extra worrier. Help isn't needed till the baby is home from the hospital.

Trial Run

Make a practice run to the hospital several weeks before the due date. It doesn't have to be a big deal, waking up in the middle of the night and timing everything with a stopwatch to get the drill down perfectly. But do drive the route that you intend to use — say for an evening outing. If you already have kids, they'll think it's an adventure.

Find out what door of the hospital you should be arriving at; usually it will be the main entrance during the day, but at night that door will probably be locked after a certain hour and you'll have to go to the emergency room entrance, perhaps on the other side of the hospital. Besides knowing which door to go to at which hour, you'll want to check out the parking lots so you'll know the fastest way to ditch the car once your wife has gotten out.

Also think with some care about the route you'll be driving to get there: is any part of it usually clogged with traffic during rush hours and if so, is there an alternate, back route that will get you there almost as quickly? When your wife is in labor, you won't want to be sitting in a traffic jam or find yourself blundering up a one-way street in the wrong direction.

CHILDBIRTH

LABOR

In most hospitals, fathers are welcome to stay with their wives in the labor room — whether or not they've attended "prepared childbirth" classes. Labor can be a long-drawn-out wait, and your wife will need you just for company. During the first phase of labor, when the contractions are mild and widely spaced, couples often walk around the halls chatting, trying finally to settle on a name.

But then the work — that labor is named for — starts in earnest. The contractions come more and more regularly and the force increases. "What's it like to give birth to a baby?" says one father. "I mean, my wife struggled. You know, you hear all about labor pains and all that stuff — I *heard* it but I didn't realize it until you could see the sweat breaking out . . ."

Fathers who are trained and know the ropes can help their wives ride through the pain; they are ready to whisper sweet nothings at the appropriate time to distract their wives. Here's a father who wasn't trained: "I really felt that my feet were enormous and that I was going to fall all over them. And that might have been my own fault, because we didn't go to the course. I didn't know what things to say and what things would be helpful and I felt that if

I were just saying certain things I would be foolish because I wasn't experiencing the pain — I might sound absurd."

Many fathers are surprised to find out how very helpful they are in the labor room. "I wasn't expecting to be as much of a *participant* in it as I actually turned out to be," says a social work administrator about the birth of his daughter. "I'd gotten the idea that I was just going to be there and hold Sloane's hand and time the contractions and feed her ice water — and it turned out to be a whole other thing. Her labor was very protracted and it really made a big difference to her that I was there to support her in what she was doing."

SNAGS

Every couple is prepared for a perfectly smooth, by-the-book experience of childbirth, but unfortunately there's no such thing. There's always some hitch in your plans. The contractions may stop and you may have to go home again with your tails between your legs, or the baby may decide to turn around backward and present her bottom for a difficult "breech" delivery, or any one of dozens of other possible complications.

In two births, Rita and I batted a thousand for complicating factors. With the first, her labor had to be "induced" to get the process going; a drug is administered intravenously that stimulates uterine contractions. And does it ever stimulate them! Instead of starting out slow and easy and gradually building up in intensity, they come on hard and violent and irregular from the start. The orderly breathing techniques we had learned in class were no match for this onslaught. But Rita was trained and confident and managed to improvise through the contractions to go on to a splendid finale.

The next time around we ended up spending eight hours watching a jumping mechanical pen scratch out on graph paper the evidence that Timothy's heartbeat wasn't quite as strong as it should have been. That was truly tense, sitting there staring at the fetal heart monitor — which uses a receiver strapped to the mother's belly to measure the infant's vital signs — hoping the signs would change. But the heartbeat stayed low and other tests convinced the doctors to deliver Timothy by Cesarean section, so all our plans and training for this birth were shot.

Childbirth classes try conscientiously to cover most of the common types of problems that you may run into in labor and delivery, but you always expect *your* baby to be born without a hitch. If it is, you're in the lucky minority. Most of us end up muddling through complications that we only half understand.

DELIVERY

Fathers are always steady, calm, and sure of themselves as they suit up in hospital uniform gowns to accompany their wives to the delivery room. "I didn't know how to put on the gown," said one father, "so it was like a Jerry Lewis act. I'd untie it and tie it and it would fall off, and meanwhile the doctors were all preparing. And I said: 'I'm going to miss this whole thing getting these booties on,' and I put the head thing on backwards — I was tying it up front and saw that they all had it in the back . . . I had no idea how to put that stuff on."

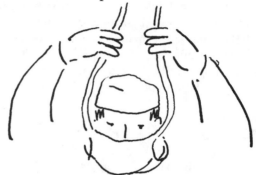

But once in the delivery room, most fathers do themselves proud supporting their wives.

When the baby finally arrives, it is a magnificent thing to see. Books about childbirth always point out that newborns are ugly — presumably to prepare parents for the shock of seeing that their long-awaited darling is blue and covered with a cheesy substance called vernix caseosa. And looked at in a moment of calm and impartiality, a newborn isn't too cute; the genitals and breasts of both sexes are likely to be enlarged; the head is huge in proportion to the body; the belly may stick out; the eyes may wander and cross; the baby may feel cool to the touch. But when you see your baby for the first time, ugly and pretty are totally irrelevant. Spectacular is more like it. I'll never forget the huge black circle of Gregory's mouth as he blasted out his greeting to the world. Ugly? Not at all — he was heroic.

All parents count the fingers and toes. I've asked dozens of men what they noticed first about their new babies. Almost inevitably it's that the baby's healthy, alive, intact. For nine months we've managed pretty well to hold in check the fear that something will go wrong, that the baby won't be all right, but in the hospital and especially in the delivery room, that fear is riding high; it's getting control.

What a wonderful relief there is in seeing that the baby is *all* there. This of course is one big reason why men like to be in on the delivery — the men down the hall in the fathers' waiting room get the news late and second hand.

And then we take a second look at this remarkable arrival. "Up until then it's just like something under a sheet you just can't see for nine months," said one father the day after his second child was born, ". . . something that keeps poking around and you don't know it's really a human being and all of a sudden it assumes a human shape, and it's a person . . ." Another brand-new father, who owns a sporting goods store, says: "What was the first thing that came into my mind? I thought that he was awful small for being a fisherman and a football player and all kinds of stuff — but I had to put up with it." And another father: "She looked exactly like the Star Child from the end of the movie *2001.*"

AFTER THE BIRTH

Just because the baby is born, activity in the delivery room doesn't stop. Your wife's contractions resume, but painlessly, and the placenta, or afterbirth, is delivered. The doctor then sets to work stitching up an episiotomy if he has performed one — an episiotomy is a cut in the flesh of the perineum (the area directly behind the vaginal birth opening) that is made during the final moments of most deliveries so that the baby's head won't tear the flesh as it passes through. The incision is painless when it is made, but the healing hurts.

The baby gets drops in his eyes; he's footprinted; he's examined and receives various other ministrations. In between all these activities, your wife will get to hold the baby and probably to nurse him if she chooses to — and you may get in a little baby holding, too.

BONDING

Take the first opportunity anyone offers you to hold the baby. There is a good deal of talk these days about the phenomenon of mother-infant bonding, or imprinting — the notion that a special kind of attachment is formed between mother and infant that is at its strongest when the two have met and the baby has nursed only moments after he's born. Many people believe this bond was often weakened in the past by the practice of using general anesthesia for childbirth, so that mother and child didn't get together intimately until hours after the birth, when Mom had come to and could make sense, and that the bond was further weakened by officious nursery practices that continued to separate mother and baby throughout their stay in the hospital except for special feeding times. Hospitals and doctors are much more sensitive now to the need for letting mother and baby be together to form their close attachment.

There is father-infant bonding, too. It starts the first moment you hold your baby, and for fathers it's a compelling experience. So when your wife says, "You hold the baby now," don't back off in deference to her; get in there and get to know your baby. Or even better, find some way to get your arms around mother and child to start forming the bond that hopefully will be stronger than a mother-infant or a father-infant bond — the whole family bond.

Handle the baby often when you visit the hospital in the following days. The nurses are usually delighted to show you how to hold the baby, give her a bath, etc. All of which can only tighten the bond.

BIRTH PHOTOS

Delivery-room photos taken by enthusiastic dads have become so common a part of the childbirth scene that one father told me the hospital had provided a mimeographed sheet of hints for camera-wielding fathers. It suggested, for instance, using a blue filter to correct for the light in the delivery room, and it had similar tips for movie making and tape recording.

Another father told me that the obstetrician, a camera buff, had advised him to use black-and-white film in the delivery room — nobody wants to see all that blood in living color.

If you plan to take photos, check first with the

recorder than a participant in the event, so I'd encourage you to save the camera for the end — you can do much more good by simply holding your wife's hand. And the picture you really want anyway is the one that comes at the finale, when the agony is over and your wife is holding the baby — a person only smiles like that a few times in a lifetime, and you want to capture it on film. You'll be smiling the same way, so ask the nurse to snap a couple of shots of the whole family — obstetric nurses are very good at this because they get a lot of practice. The photo will be an excellent piece of evidence to show your child a few years later that you've been a family group from the very start.

hospital or the person who runs the childbirth class to see if there are any restrictions on camera use, and tell the doctor that you want to take photos. Flash photography is usually banned in the delivery room to avoid any chance of igniting the often oxygen-rich atmosphere. But the strong lighting used in delivery rooms should be sufficient to give you good clear photos, especially if you use high-speed film. Some men like to get a kind of photo-journalistic sequence of shots showing the whole progress of the birth. But that takes you away from your wife's side and makes you more a spectator or

If you bring along a cassette tape recorder, you can get your baby's first utterance on tape. Don't wait till the baby arrives to push the Record button(s) or you may miss the first cry by getting caught up in the excitement of the moment. Turn the machine on when you arrive in the delivery room; you may enjoy having a recording of the whole thing — your wife's moaning and the doctor's wry comments *and* that powerful first scream. The half-hour side of a sixty-minute tape should be plenty, since events usually progress swiftly once you make it to the delivery stage; but you may want to use a longer tape to be sure.

CELEBRATING

Fathers who pass out cigars are running into rejection these days; one new father told me that one out of two Tiparillos he'd offered had been turned down flat. Another new dad said he'd seen so many cigars refused at work that he hadn't even bothered with them; he got a box of fancy cookies to pass out instead — women will take cookies, he explained, but they turn down candy because they're all on diets.

What a great event for a celebration — your child's initial birthday. It's a time for giving presents all around — better than Christmas. Many new fathers bring a football for the baby, but forget to bring something for Mom — who deserves most of the credit and who will be very touched when you remember her. One man told me he'd picked out a bracelet for his wife weeks before the birth and

arranged with the jeweler for a rush engraving job; after the baby arrived, his third phone call — following calls to the grandparents — had been to the

jeweler, and the bracelet had been ready the same day, engraved with the baby's name and birth date.

Frilly, sexy nightclothes make an excellent present for a new mom. Every new mother wants very much to be reminded that she is a *woman* and that you think of her that way. Pull out all the stops; bring a bottle of champagne to the hospital to celebrate; it's a time for extravagance and sentiment.

TIME CAPSULE

Many fathers make up a "time capsule" when their kids are born. Usually this is as simple a matter as putting aside a newspaper from the day the baby arrived, or a weekly news magazine, so that when your child is old enough to be interested, she can read what else happened all over the world on that momentous day. One meticulous father, though, showed me a clear plastic sweater box crammed with dated memorabilia that he had assembled to mark the occasion of his son's birth. There were political campaign buttons and stickers, first-issue stamps, mint-fresh coins from that year, the usual birthday newspaper, but also articles he'd clipped from a variety of specialized magazines and papers to show the fads and attitudes of the moment, and a postcard picture of the hospital and a large map and guidebook to the city.

Another father, a wine fancier, showed me two cases in his cellar that held bottles from a variety of the great wines of 1970 and 1974, the years his two daughters had been born. He planned to turn the cases over to the girls on their twenty-first birthdays. And of course each case came with a bottle of champagne to be opened on that occasion.

A dated bottle of champagne for the twenty-first birthday can be bought years after the event. But the news of the day has to be bought fresh. In the midst of the excitement of the baby's arrival, you probably won't have the time or the presence of mind to put aside a daily paper, and the next day, when you do think of it, the newsstand will be sold out of birth-dated papers. No problem — because what you want anyway is the paper from the day after, since it reports the news from the day of the birth. You may want to get two newspapers — a big-city paper like the New York *Times* or Washington *Post* for the international news, and a local paper for the weather news and events close to home.

TREE TWINS

A tree planted the year your child is born grows up with her. She will get to know the tree well and think of it as a kind of companion. Almost any tree you choose to plant will have special advantages — an oak, for instance, will still be there, grown huge, permanent, and shady when your child returns as an old woman to the place where she grew up. But fruit trees and evergreens have real bonuses for young kids. Most fruit trees will begin to bear during a child's preschool years, and she'll love picking the fruit from her own tree. And evergreens can be decorated at Christmas.

Even if you live in a city apartment you may find it's possible to plant a tree when your child is born. Check with your local block organization, the municipal government, or the parks department. Some city governments sponsor matching-fund programs through which local residents and block organizations can pay part of the price of having trees planted in tree-poor city neighborhoods. And failing that, why not start an avocado pit growing? By the time your child is five or six you may have an indoor tree taller than he is that can grow in a bucket of dirt on the floor.

Remember to get your wife to take a photo of you and the baby with the newly planted tree to put in the baby book.

POSTPARTUM BLUES

A couple of days after the baby is born you discover your wife in tears. "I should be the happiest woman on earth, with the baby and all," she sobs. "I don't know why I'm crying like this . . ." And the tears flow freely. She probably even knew that these "postpartum blues" were on the way — most new mothers are prepared for this natural emotional letdown by childbirth classes or have heard about the "blues" from other women. But knowing about it in advance doesn't head it off or make it much easier for a woman to accept what's happening while she's going through it.

Just like the monthly "downs" your wife may go through before or during her periods, only much more severe, the postpartum blues are the result of sweeping changes in her body. A woman crying with the postpartum blues is an irrational spectacle — Rita would half smile and say, "I knew it was coming . . ." and cry some more. If your wife is one of those women who become irritable before they get their period and you have been able to be understanding, you may be some comfort and help to her during the blues. But if you've never come to terms with her monthly female traumas, you'll find that this one is a real humdinger.

SECOND-PHASE BLUES

A week or so after the birth, another phase of the postpartum blues can set in — though much less spectacular this time. New mothers often feel slightly depressed — for weeks at a time, and for dozens of reasons. This time it's not all hormones and body changes and total irrationality, but the kind of dull feeling that comes after the excitement of the main event.

Drudgery and loneliness close in on a woman when the visits from friends and relatives have slowed down and she finds herself alone all day with the baby. She'll feel tied down, and other common feelings she may have include: a sense of inadequacy as a mother; helplessness in this new way of life; resentment at the baby for having stuck her with it; anger that her job or career has been interrupted. And she'll feel guilty, guilty, guilty for feeling these things. On top of this, she may be physically low, overtired from round-the-clock baby care, and if the baby was delivered by Cesarean, she may be weak and painfully sore for some time to come. On top of that, when she thinks of you, she may feel inadequate as a wife, and her dismal thoughts will dwell on how frumpy she looks with her body still all stretched out of shape and no clothes that fit that aren't homely. . . . It's enough to bring down the spirits of even the most resolutely cheerful woman.

During this phase of the postpartum blues, you

have a little better chance of providing succor and comfort than you did during the crying jag of the first phase. I've asked a number of women what they need from their husbands during this trying period and the consensus is: Help and Sympathy. Ask your wife what she thinks she needs and try to supply it.

None of the women I asked said they needed Romance during the postpartums, but it's my pet theory on this that Romance is precisely what *is* needed. It's certainly what has disappeared from a woman's life — not just the hugs-and-kisses variety of romance, but the whole wide spectrum of romantic possibility. A woman who spends the whole day and night changing diapers and meeting an infant's demands *knows* that she isn't a likely candidate for adventure and excitement. So why not try to put a little romance into her life? Candlelight dinner, flowers, chewing on the back of her neck, jewelry . . . You know what turns your wife on and makes her feel like a woman — use it. If you're certain she won't feel guilty about leaving the baby with a sitter, go out somewhere where you'll both feel a little excitement and romance — whether it's disco dancing or an evening at the symphony. If she can't leave the baby without feeling uncomfortable, go out anyway and take the baby along.

One of a newborn's nicest traits is portability; a newborn will sleep through dinner at a restaurant, sleep through an afternoon at a museum, sleep through a ball game. With your first newborn baby, you really aren't tied down — you can move around almost as much as you like. And the moving may even cheer *you* up somewhat if you happen to be going through a little postpartum blues of your own.

DAD'S POSTPARTUMS

Though it's not as well advertised a phenomenon as a woman's postpartums, lots of men take a bit of an emotional dive after the birth of a baby. The elation and exhilaration of the first hours after the big event, the feeling of importance and the thrill of creating a new life, aren't going to last until your kid is through high school. And they may disappear pretty quickly when you start thinking about what you have set in motion here.

"When the baby is just born or just about to be born," said one new father, "people ask you about it; you're sort of a *person* and they'll pay attention. But once the baby is born, forget it — cause everybody's got little kids." The hearty congratulations at work last a few days, but then your status as a celebrity wears off and you begin to notice that you're coming home every night to a demanding baby and a distraught wife, and the bills are piling up, and the changes and excitement of the birth have set you back a couple of weeks on every front. . . . Sure, it's depressing.

You look at your wife and she *does* look dowdy, just as she complains she does; the healthy, radiant glow that made her beautiful while she was pregnant has disappeared, and you're tempted to agree with her when she gripes about her looks. The baby may be crying all night and you're getting maybe four and a half hours of sleep, total, and that's broken up into hour-and-a-half naps, so that you're nodding off every day at work and falling behind.

Yes, men get postpartum blues, just as women do. But they go away after a while, just as your wife's will. Your baby settles down and sleeps through the night; you start to be able to function at work again. Your wife's body miraculously stretches itself back into a semblance of its former glory. The world looks a lot better; you may even get a chance to relax for a minute.

There are also some lucky people — men and women, too — who claim they sail right through the whole experience with hardly a melancholy moment; I hope you're one of these.

GETTING OUT

It may be possible just to flee the whole depressing postpartum scene — literally run away from it. A newborn baby is such a good traveler that this could be the moment to take the big vacation you've been putting off for years — a kind of second honeymoon. Wait six months or a year and you've nearly missed your chance; your child will never be so portable again. Naturally, check with your pediatrician before undertaking a long trip.

I know an Episcopal minister and his wife who packed up their first baby just a little over two weeks after he arrived and flew to Acapulco for a conference/vacation and a marvelous time.

Air fare for babies is only 10 per cent of the regular fare on most flights — for the first two years. On charter flights babies go free. Traveling with a newborn, there's less paraphernalia to lug along than there will be for years to come. A newborn can sleep in a dresser drawer and if he's being breast-fed, there's no food or food preparation equipment to carry.

If you're leaving the country, ask a travel agent whether disposable diapers will be available where you're going; sometimes they can be found at places like Hilton hotels at such outrageous prices that you could buy local cloth diapers for less and throw them away. But the best policy is to stuff suitcases and bags with disposable diapers before you leave — your burden will grow lighter as you go. And if you buy presents for the folks back home, there will be lots of extra luggage space to pack them in.

For a trip out of the country you may need a passport with the baby's photo taken with you or your wife. And check with your pediatrician about inoculations.

Make sure to take along a good front-position

baby carrier (p. 29); your baby will go everywhere in it. One of the real pleasures of traveling with a newborn is that people are helpful and considerate wherever you go. Everyone smiles at a newborn baby, which is good medicine for a couple of slightly dispirited new parents.

SECOND BABY

For the arrival of a second baby, you'll want to arrange to have extra time off from work to spend with your first child — who will need you. This will be one of the few times, and maybe even the only time, he's been separated from his mother for a period of days. Preschool kids usually have a surprisingly clear picture of what goes on in hospitals: birth, sickness, and death. And it's easy for a child to conclude that Mommy is in for all three. Having Daddy around a lot will be some reassurance that the whole world hasn't collapsed.

The arrival of a new baby is so obviously a time when a father can help with the kids that even some monkey fathers — who otherwise show little interest in infants — step in and lend a hand. Male leaders in groups of Japanese macaques take over the care of one- and two-year-olds when their mothers are delivering.

ARRANGEMENTS

Well in advance of the birth, make plans for your first child to stay with someone very close while you're at the hospital — preferably grandparents who will spoil her. You'll have prepared her for the arrival of the baby (see p. 90), but she can also use some special preparation for the rush and bustle of the big night. Some practice in sleeping away from home will help if it's included in the plans and she's never done it. A month or so before the birth, give her a trial run at sleeping over with grandmother or whoever will be taking her — so everything won't be new and possibly scary when the baby arrives.

Delivering a child or children to a close neighbor or to grandmother's and your wife to the hospital all at the same time can become a major logistical hassle. So consider alternative setups. Ideally, your child can stay put at home — sound asleep through the whole business if the baby arrives conveniently in the middle of the night — and a neighbor or relative can come to your house. The shift to grandmother's house can be made later.

REVIEW COURSE

"We panicked in there," a financial analyst told me shortly after the birth of his second child. For the first birth he and his wife had taken the childbirth course and practiced the breathing exercises at home, and sailed through labor and delivery with flying colors. But for the second, they hadn't taken the time to brush up: "We knew everything. . . . Our babies are only eighteen months apart, so we didn't have that long a period to forget it, but we still forgot — enough to make us panic."

A number of fathers and mothers who neglected to brush up the second time around have told me the same story. "It was as though we were in training right along for the big game," said another man, "and the second time we'd sort of skipped practice a little bit." He had a feeling of hesitancy during the second labor and delivery and felt it had been a less satisfying experience than the first.

"It's like anything else — the only reason a person is good at his work is from repetition," says a father who has taken two refresher courses.

FIRST CHILD

Many fathers bear gifts when returning from the hospital to tell the first child about the new baby. The theory behind this — which I think makes a lot of sense — is that the child will equate getting a new baby with getting a gift — a nice positive start. The most usual gift, both for girls and boys, is a baby doll that your child can use to visualize the new baby. For Gregory at three, having a rubber doll to handle seemed to make the invisible event of Timothy's arrival something of a reality. Another good way to help an older child comprehend the event is to stage a little birthday party for the new baby.

Polaroid photos of Mom and the new baby will also help your child understand what's going on. Of course there should be frequent phone calls from Mom. And you can carry home little written messages and small presents from her — tangible things like this are often more help to a preschooler than a disembodied voice on the phone. I carried tape-recorded messages back and forth between Rita and Gregory for ten days following her Cesarean, which seemed to help both of them — Rita even a bit more than Greg.

While Mom is in the hospital spend as much time as you can manage with your first child. If he has regular daily activities — nursery school or the like — there's no point in interrupting them; in fact, it's probably best if his life goes on in as routine a way as possible for these few days. But between visits to the hospital, try to take him on special outings and spend time alone with him playing and talking. One good excursion will be a trip to a store where he can pick out a present to give the new baby.

When third and fourth kids come, the first two or three have each other for company and reassurance, and the first is a case-hardened veteran who can show a younger child the ropes. But your kids will still miss Mom, and you should still be right there to make them feel wanted and loved.

HOSPITAL VISITS

An older child will want desperately to visit the hospital — not so much to see the new baby as to see Mommy and satisfy herself, among other things, that Mommy is still alive.

But of course most hospitals have strict rules against visits by children. Rules, however, are made to be bent, so if there are complications of any kind that mean Mom will be in for more than a few short days, start putting pressure on the doctor to okay a brief visit. Beg a little; say your child is hopelessly attached to Mom — a visit can often be arranged.

A pediatrician told me this story: A father whose second child had been born a couple of days before smuggled his firstborn — a two-year-old — into the hospital in a brown paper bag. He was just taking the little boy out of the bag when the obstetrician came in to do a routine checkup, so the man hastily stuffed the kid back into the brown paper bag. The doctor of course saw what was going on; he made his visit brief and left without saying anything about the subterfuge. Two years later, when the family's next baby was nearly due, the obstetrician was examining the mother on her eighth-month visit. As he felt her belly, he said, "There's just one thing I want to know. Does your husband plan to bring both of your children in brown paper bags this time?"

CHANGES

The big surprise of childbirth for many men is that it doesn't bring about the cataclysmic changes they expected.

A night-owl father I talked to had been tied up in knots while his wife was pregnant, worrying that they would never again be able to pick up at ten-thirty or eleven and go out on the town. "I *really* anticipated a change and it just never came. We

kind of slid into it rather than being thrown into it. Like you figure as soon as the child's here — that's it. . . . There's a lot more planning and a lot more moving — we had to get a bigger car cause we have to cart more stuff around. And a lot of little changes like that. But I honestly don't believe that it changed our life as much as we thought it was going to. We managed to work around it and work it into our life-style." They found out they could take the baby along pretty much anywhere they'd gone before, and by the time he was a toddler and too old to come along, they were settled into new family patterns.

Another man, the father of twin girls, put it this way: "It changes your sense of values. Where before it was nice to go out to dinner, now, all of a sudden, the babies are more important. So they're small, and they're eating every hour on the hour through the night and things like that, and you're too tired to go out. And by the time you get used to all that and your kids are sleeping, your values have switched and now for some strange reason, you've become a family man."

I watched a friend suffer real pangs of anxiety about the responsibilities he was sure would come with fathering. But after his daughter was born, those burdens never seemed to materialize. "As a matter of fact," he says, "I'm even less conservative in my financial dealings and other things that one would tend to see in terms of anxiety, than I was before she arrived. I'm doing many more things and spreading myself thinner and I've committed myself much more to expenses. . . . It didn't affect me as I thought it might — that it might make me very tight and scared. . . . It didn't do that at all. It's given me a new strength, and an enormous sense of satisfaction. And taking care of her and all that stuff, I look forward to."

And the advent of a baby can have a variety of downright positive effects on our lives. One man told me: "It realigned our whole married life. We were having some problems and instead of driving us further apart, the baby brought us much closer together. So really, I could say that she saved our marriage."

But then it's not *all* roses; one father said: "Today and for as long as we have kids I'm sure there'll be times when we'll grumble about it. As long as you can still remember what it was like when you were married but had no children, as long as you can remember those times, you can't help but notice the differences — and some you lament and some you just don't care about."

Chapter 2

BABIES

A group of five-year-olds were discussing what their fathers did all day. "My daddy takes care of babies," said a pediatrician's son. "Oh no, he doesn't," said a little girl imperiously. *"Daddies don't take care of babies."*

Fathers don't have a long history of close involvement with infants. Check through all the old familiar nursery rhymes, and you discover that Daddy only makes it into one of them:

> Bye, baby bunting,
> Daddy's gone a-hunting,
> Gone to catch a rabbit skin
> To wrap the baby bunting in.

Off Daddy goes to work — hunting for rabbit skins. All he has to say to the baby is "Bye."

Take a look, though, by way of contrast, at the drawing by Rembrandt reproduced here of a father spoon-feeding his baby in 1643. It shows a side of father-infant relations that has always existed — a private, rich, fulfilling side. And it's a side that more men are enjoying today, I think, than ever before.

You still hear men who say, as my brother does: "They don't interest me as babies; children are savages until they are at least three — that's about the time they can start to contribute something new to the conversation." There are plenty of men who avoid babies and baby care like the plague, who try to dodge all the hollering and hold out until the child is old enough to be a "pal."

But there's another group of men who want to get to know their kids as newborns. "After all," one of these fathers observed, "when you buy a new car,

Drawing by Rembrandt, 1643.

you don't wait six months or a year to start driving it." And these men discover that a baby, even a newborn one, can add quite a lot to the conversation — if it happens to be the right conversation. At first it's just bumping foreheads and finger grabbing, but it progresses rapidly to swapping smiles and tickling and then to passing blocks back and forth, and rolling balls, and it's really not that long before you're using words. And all along you've been good pals.

Again and again, men who had two kids or more told me they'd ignored the first one as a baby or had been preoccupied with work or studies and hadn't gotten to know the first for months or even years. But when the second came and they were used to having a child around, they'd gotten to know the baby right away and had loved it. These men all regretted the good times they'd missed with the first.

Some men get so excited when they are involved in the birth of their kids that the day-to-day business of child rearing seems an anticlimax by comparison. I asked many men if they could identify their proudest moment as a father, and the majority of them said it was the moment the child was born — all the things they had done with the kids and all the children's new accomplishments paled beside this great event.

One new father, though, whose baby girl was one, had an interesting approach to this question: "If you've ever seen a colt or a calf born, you know

that the birth part is interesting enough — seeing the legs come out and the head and so forth. But the real fascination when you watch an animal be born is watching him get to his feet. Nobody leaves right after the calf is delivered; you stay around and watch him struggle to get his legs under him and stand up. And I think it's like that with babies, too. I loved being in the delivery room — it was really exciting. But for me, watching the baby grow up and try to get her feet under her like the calf — that's the good

part. And it's funny; with a baby you have a whole year of this instead of just the short time it takes an animal, so it's stretched out for you to kind of savor."

Attachment

The bond between you and your baby will change from week to week and month and month. He'll go through periods of passionate attachment to Mom, when he'll be afraid to let her leave the room — eight months is one time when this regularly happens. And you're likely to be pretty well forgotten in the midst of this kind of mother dependence. When you try to comfort the baby, he'll cry for Mom, and you'll feel superfluous.

The pendulum will eventually swing back, and the baby will come to you again. There are even times when you become an important celebrity in the baby's life, and when you're home, most of her attention will be directed toward you. Both of my boys at one and a half, for instance, reached a kind of high-water mark of father attachment. "Da-dy, Da-dy," they'd shout over and over fervently, and throw themselves on me. It feels great to be wanted like this, and it makes up for most of the times you got nothing for your efforts but screams and maybe a stray poke in the eye.

Rival

People talk glibly about sibling rivalry, but there's not much said about father-infant rivalry. We'd just as soon not admit that it exists. After all, fathers think, how petty can you get — being jealous of a little baby? But it's not all that petty; the baby *is* taking up an enormous amount of your wife's time and attention, at least some of which probably came your way in the past.

In some places, the baby is easily recognized as a rival. In traditional Japanese families, for instance, the new baby sleeps on the mat between mother and father — no wonder Japanese fathers are known for finding their pleasure outside the family, out on the town. The American setup minimizes father-infant rivalry by including fathers in many ways; one father said the close bond between mother and child never made him feel left out: "I was too busy taking pictures." American fathers are involved, which makes the baby less of a rival, more of a pleasure. But aside from the involvement, there's still a sense in which the baby is sleeping between you and your wife. You make love and both have an ear cocked toward the baby's room; or you don't make love because the baby is crying or because you're so tired from being awake for weeks to comfort her during colicky spells.

We don't blame a first child for being jealous when a second comes along to assume the place of honor on Mom's breast; we recognize that it's only a natural reaction and we try to help the first child cope. But we don't allow ourselves to benefit from the same understanding attitude. We pretend that we couldn't possibly be the least bit jealous of our own loved new baby; and even if we do feel put out or excluded because of the remarkable new closeness between mother and baby, it's a subject we studiously avoid mentioning.

COMPETENT BABIES

Fathers and mothers have always thought their newborn babies were remarkable, but the scientific community used not to give the human infant much credit. Until quite recently the newborn was regarded as virtually blind and not much good at hearing — an unformed lump of clay in almost every respect. In the past ten years or so, however, medical and psychological researchers have reversed that verdict as they continue to discover through sophisticated testing procedures that the baby is a competent, capable little fellow.

A newborn baby can't see as well as an older child, but he can make crude visual distinctions, responding, for instance, to black-and-white patterns and black-and-white drawings of faces. He will reach out to touch objects he sees presented to him — though since he apparently doesn't know how long his arms are, he'll often miss them. A baby in the first weeks will defend himself against an object approaching his face by putting up his arms and hands and pulling back his head — to do this he must be comfortably supported, not lying in the usual baby position on his back.

In the hearing department a newborn is pretty sophisticated; within seconds of birth an infant can turn her head toward the source of a sound — which seems to show a whole complex of abilities, since turning the head toward a sound suggests that the newborn expects there to be something at the source and also expects to see it. Newborns will also turn away from unpleasant odors.

Many of a baby's early abilities disappear after a few weeks. Try your baby out on two of the more dramatic newborn special skills while he still has them: neonate walking and mimicry. Hold the baby upright and press his foot down on a level surface,

and he will proceed to "march" along impressively; you have only about eight weeks to play this game with your baby before "walking" will disappear from his repertoire.

You have only three or four weeks to check out your baby's early talent for imitating before it likewise fades. The optimum time for this is between two and three weeks of age. Seat yourself in front of the baby — comfortably held in an infant seat or by Mom — and make faces and finger movements. Stick out your tongue and the baby is

likely to come right back at you. Try opening and closing your mouth repeatedly, and making a big yawning O. The baby's imitations won't always be exact and right on cue, but you should be able to see strong indications that she's trying to copy what you're doing. The remarkable thing about this behavior, of course, is that this newly arrived person figures out how to match her tongue and its action to your tongue's action without, presumably, knowing much of anything about tongues, that she acts as a mirror without knowing anything at all about mirrors.

In the first three or four weeks, you will also be able to observe your baby's early reaching ability; again the baby should be supported comfortably rather than flat on his back. Present him with various objects and watch him reach for them. Timothy reached most readily for black objects — a tape recorder and a bottle of ink.

Newborns have a fairly wide repertoire of automatic "reflexes"; most pediatricians will be delighted to demonstrate some of these for you, or you can try to set a few of them off for yourself. Stroke the baby's hand or foot and the whole arm or leg will withdraw. Try a sudden noise or a bright flash of light and she will startle. Stroke the palm of the hand and your baby will grasp your finger; try this on the sole of her foot as well. Stroking the cheek or around the mouth sets off a "rooting" reflex: the baby will turn toward the source of the stroking to find a breast and nipple.

Babies are quite as remarkable as parents have always thought they were. And they go on being that way. To watch a baby acquiring physical skills later in the first year and then starting in on spoken language in the beginning of the second is to watch a really superior learner.

TELLING THE DIFFERENCE

In their very earliest weeks, babies can tell the difference between Mom and Dad, and they show this by acting differently toward their two parents. I talked with pediatricians Michael Yogman and T. Berry Brazelton, who have made a detailed study of father-infant interaction at Boston Children's Hospital Medical Center.

By videotaping scenes of infants playing first with their fathers, then with their mothers, and then with a total stranger, they were able to analyze with precision and compare how the babies responded to each; and they found that there were rather striking differences. By the time they were two months old, and in some cases even earlier, the babies tended to

frown more at the strangers than at Mom and Dad, and their dealings with the strangers were "more tentative and cautious." With Mom, their movements "appeared smoothly modulated and contained," while with Dad, their interactions "could be characterized as heightened and playful."

Whether babies learn fast, picking up their cues from the ways we act toward them, or whether they make these distinctions instinctively, there's of course no way of knowing. But clearly they have us pegged at a very early moment — Mom is comfortable and Dad is there for some lively play.

INDIVIDUALS

"He's much bouncier, much more throw-aroundy than Leah ever was," said one father. "And you work those things out with feedback from the kids. The first couple of times I took Leah when she was little and bounced her and started to throw her up, she cried and hated it. And he just loved it. He's a lot more cuddly, too; he likes to be snuggled more."

With your first baby it's still possible to believe that all infants are pretty much alike, that they are all like your baby — and also like the standard, average baby you may read about in child care books. As soon as your second baby arrives on the scene, though, you know that every child is an individual from the very beginning. This one looks different, smiles differently, acts in ways you hadn't expected. If the first one cried all the time, this one is placid; if the first one settled easily into a convenient feeding schedule, this one will want to eat every twenty minutes; if the first one had trouble sleeping, this one will sleep through thunderstorms. Babies are out to prove that they can't be stereotyped, that each one arrives with a distinct personality and a unique personal approach to the rest of the world.

DROPPING BABIES

"My mother-in-law didn't think I knew anything and my wife's aunt didn't think I was a suitable watcher for the child," says one father. "They couldn't leave the child in the same room with me for five minutes or I'd do something terribly bad — hold the baby by an arm. . . . I didn't feel that comfortable with other people's babies. But when it's yours, it's easy to learn. I'd get a little holding time in there when my mother-in-law wasn't around. You can figure it out pretty easily, you know. . . . But then I'd put the baby in the bassinet and my mother-in-law would take her out; she'd fold everything differently; she put the baby in a different position. She'd make you feel like you were really screwing up. She was thinking: You see, that's the way a baby's put in; I don't know what this guy's doing, but he's messing it up."

And it isn't always from mothers-in-law that we get this treatment; sometimes our wives aren't too sure we won't drop the baby on his head. Modern mothers know that Dad is to be included in taking care of the baby from the word Go. But sometimes there's a little hesitancy. Maternal instinct maybe.

On the other side of this question, fathers for centuries have lent their willing support to the little myth that a big man is going to be clumsy with such a tiny, frail thing as a baby. It's almost a social convention to admit you were shaky the first time you held the baby — just one of a whole complex of social conventions that until only recently have spared men from almost all the day-to-day care of infants and children.

And I'm sure most of us *are* a little shaky when we pick up our firstborn that first time. This is the youngest baby we've ever held, and for many of us it's the *only* baby we've ever held. We haven't had any practice and we've just been through an extraordinary event — the baby's birth. But time and again, what happens is what happened to this father: "She was two days old the first time I held her and I was scared to death I was going to drop her. But she sat there and she wiggled and kind of punched at me a little bit — I knew then that she was pretty sturdy."

And from there on out you're doing fine. You will also notice that your wife is just the least bit awkward at first in handling the baby; it's not all instinct.

Football Hold

When you first hold a baby it's usually in a careful "cradle" hold, with one hand supporting the head and the other hand and arm under the body. You've got a firm grip on the baby, but your hands are both tied up.

Take a cue from the pediatricians and try a truly professional baby hold that firmly supports the baby but leaves you a free hand. It's even appropriately named for fathers — the football hold.

The baby's head goes in your hand and her body lies along your horizontally held forearm, with the legs hanging down on either side of your elbow. It

may look a little precarious, so convince yourself how securely your baby is held in this position by practicing the football carry within inches of your lap or the top of the bed.

Your other hand is free so the baby can tug at your fingers, or so you can give him a bottle or pat his head or drink a glass of beer. And his face is in a position where you can see and enjoy it. The football hold is also an excellent way to handle a newborn as you bathe him; just dip your forearm and the baby together into the baby tub. In fact, this hold has so many advantages you're sure to miss it when your baby grows too long for your arm.

Hip Carry

We borrow the football carry from one professional infant handler — the pediatrician. For older babies we can borrow another excellent hold from another pro — Mom. When your baby is big enough to hold up her head and cling a little, you can start to take her on your hip — as smart mothers have done since time began. Hip carrying leaves one hand more or less free, and as your baby grows heavier, you'll be thankful for the support that your hip provides — it takes maybe a third of the weight off your arm.

In the hip-carry position, your baby is securely supported with his legs straddling your body, your arm around his back, and your other hand under his bottom. The common alternative to hip carrying is the comparatively insecure cradle hold. Cradling is fine while you're sitting down. But carrying a baby around in your arms in front of you puts the baby in a chancy position. Should you trip or fall, the baby is likely to go flying. While in the hip-carry position, if you take a dive, your embracing arm acts as a safety strap and you can roll with the fall, protecting the baby with your elbow and shoulders.

Hip Baby Seat

Because a man's hip doesn't provide a natural ledge for a baby to perch on, I devised a simple hip extender for fathers. You can put this baby seat together in less than an hour; the materials you will need are:

> one scrap piece ½" x 6" pine
> one 13" length 1" x 3" pine
> one 6" x 5" shelf bracket
> six ½" No. 8 wood screws
> one 28" length ½" flat sewing elastic
> staples OR tacks

Cut the triangular seat from the ½" pine; round the corners and sand the edges thoroughly. Drill pilot holes for the screws and assemble. Staple the sewing elastic about an inch above the bottom end of the 1" x 3" strut. A few coats of shellac, varnish, or

polyurethane, or a piece of contact paper on the seat, will help keep diaper dampness from soaking into the wood.

The hip baby seat is worn as shown in the illustration. To put it on, wind the elastic around the bottom of the strut and push the strut down between your belt and pants, one belt loop back, and on the left side for right-handers; right side for southpaws. Pull the elastic around your thigh and tie in a bow knot just as you would tie on a six-gun holster.

With the baby perched on this seat, your hips take almost all the weight; your arm is around the child just to steady her, and your other hand is free. I used this seat less as a carrying device than as a

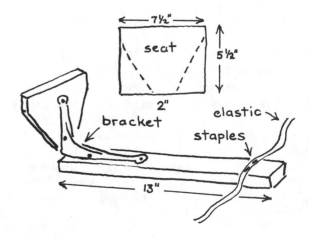

"gentling" seat. Timothy liked to sit on it when he was tired, and snuggle close, and I'd just stand there and rock back and forth from foot to foot until he was sound asleep. For a number of months at the end of his first year it was a sure source of comfort whenever he was cranky and overtired, which with Timothy was the rule rather than the exception — he was a chronic screamer. But when he'd see me put on the hip seat, he'd motion toward it and make an "Ah — ah — ah" sound, and once rocking away on it, he'd quiet right down.

I can't promise the same kind of success with your baby, but this is such a simple little project that it may be worth the time to try. Make it while your baby is still quite young; by about twelve months, Timothy's weight was more than my hip felt like lugging around — though we kept using the seat for a year more from time to time because he insisted.

Front Carriers

The most useful carrying device you can have is the "snuggly" type, worn is front — many fathers I talked with were great advocates of these. A front-worn carrier supports a newborn's head, so the baby becomes portable in her first weeks. You carry your baby snuggled next to your heart, where she's warm and comforted by your heartbeat, where you can see her easily, and you still have both hands free. When the baby's crying and you have some light work to do around the house, just wrap her onto your chest in the carrier and go on with what you're doing; your movement will quiet her as well as anything else would.

Check the fit before you buy a front carrier; one man told me the one he had was cut skimpily and pulled his shoulders forward uncomfortably — but several six-footers I talked with had used front carriers with no discomfort.

The Cadillac of these front-position carriers can be ordered from Snugli, Route 1, Box 685, Evergreen, Colorado 80439.

Papoose Carriers

Aluminum-frame backpack carriers are also a great boon to parents. A baby can be taken around in one of these from the time he can hold his head firmly erect, and the papoose carrier continues to be useful long after the baby has outgrown the front-carry type. The back carrier has one problem, though: you can't see what's going on behind your head. So you walk past a bush and you sense that your baby has snatched off a handful of leaves or some poisonous berries and is cramming them into her mouth . . . Obviously, the woods isn't a good place to walk alone with a baby in a backpack. The best time to use it is on family excursions — so one parent can carry and the other can keep an eye on what's happening.

Timothy and I had a lot of fun with a small "rear-view" mirror I carried to check on what he was doing back there. The mirror would entertain him wherever we were, because he likes nothing better than to admire himself.

Lap Holding

When you're sitting down with your baby and want to play a little, put your knees together and lay the baby on her back with her head on your knees and her back and bottom supported by your thighs. Babies are usually very happy in this position — because they can see your face. This is the perfect situation for early father-baby conversations and games of finger grabbing and nose tweaking. It's also the recommended position for leg-pump burping, described on p. 37 below.

BABY CARE

WORLD CHAMPION DIAPER CHANGER

"I'm not changing no diapers. That's a woman's job," said the Champ, Muhammud Ali. *But his wife, Veronica, said he did it all the time.*

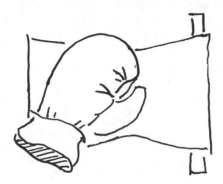

A few men I talked to claimed they had managed to shirk all diaper changing and most of the other routine baby care duties, but only a very few. The majority were pitching in when they were home. In families where both parents have jobs, baby care is almost as a matter of course a shared responsibility. And fathers intent on being involved with their kids' upbringing — often hooked on the idea because they got so much satisfaction from being in on the birth — are taking on baby care duties because they recognize that this is the direct route toward "involvement." There is another large group of fathers, too, who are never mentioned in trendy magazine articles about "The Changing Role of Men" — men who pitch in simply because they want to, because it's part of family life.

Every father plays with his baby when he comes home at night and on the weekends. It's how we get acquainted; it's a kind of courtship. But playing with the baby is only the icing on the cake. You really get acquainted with your baby and share her life if you are meeting her needs. And child care is the name of the game. It's not particularly ennobling work, but it's also not particularly hard. And if it's shared by two people, neither is likely to feel entirely martyred by it.

Some men feel they're going to end up being auxiliary mothers if they get into child care — that somehow they'll compromise their position as fathers by performing tasks that a mother traditionally performs. This line of reasoning sounds good — especially as it seems to offer a respectable way out of changing diapers — but it just doesn't hold up. Because a man's position as a father can only be strengthened through closer involvement with his kids — at every point in their lives and no matter what kind of involvement it is. Wiping a few bottoms isn't going to change you. To your child you will always be Daddy — who keeps different hours than Mom does, who smiles, smells, looks, plays, and acts in every respect differently than Mom does. You are indelibly and unequivocally Dad, and whatever you do for or with your kids will be in their eyes something that fathers do.

In practical terms, the sharing of child care is hardly ever a fifty-fifty proposition, especially where Dad goes to work each day and Mom is home with the baby. I'm always amused when a man with a full-time job tells me, as a number of men have, "Sure, we split the routine care right down the middle." Fathers like this are so proud to have a piece of the action, they exaggerate their share. There's just not enough time in the day for this statement to be literally true. And it looks like a lot of mothers wink at this kind of exaggeration — who would bother to set her husband straight when he actually is being a tremendous help?

The situation that irks mothers is one where Dad comes home from work and plays with the baby — and that's it. A woman who sees this day in and day out starts to feel jealous: "I do all the dirty work — and *he* gets all the fun." But the father here is apt to feel, often sincerely, that he *is* helping out by taking the baby off his wife's hands, that playing is what a father does with his child, that it's his form of child care. This rationale is a kind of Fifth Amendment for fathers — if you can't find any other way out of baby care, plead Playing. It's a sound enough argument: playing with babies and kids obviously does contribute to child care; and it's one of a father's traditional strong points. But it's an argument that will never convince a woman who is doing 100 per cent of the dirty work, and who has friends whose husbands actually lend a hand.

So why not eat the icing and the cake together by combining some play and some hard-core baby care? You can have a great time with a baby feeding her, and diaper-changing time, with the baby on her back and refreshed, you'll discover, is the perfect time for tickling and other games and also for giving the baby's arms and legs a good exercise workout. As a new father put it: "I thought I was going to hate the caretaker part, but you find out pretty quick that it's not all divided up neatly that way, with baby care over here and fun and good times over here — they're all sort of mixed in together. And I can have fun with him — it doesn't matter what we happen to be doing. Like last week I gave him a bath for the first time, because I'd been pretty hesitant to do that, and he had such a fantastic time in the water . . ."

Another man made this observation: "You know, when you get right down to it, diapering is the only shitty deal in the lot. The rest of the things you do for a baby are pretty ordinary. You spoon in some mashed peas, or you warm a bottle, or you walk her till she falls asleep — that part I like, and the rest isn't hard."

In this section I'm including pointers on basic baby care operations and tips from other fathers that may help you execute some of them in a professional manner. You'll need a copy of Dr. Spock, too, for ready reference. Dr. Spock is a little long, though, for sitting down and boning up on child care to learn the essentials. If you'd like a short, succinct primer on infant care that will give you an excellent background briefing — just the right length for a father — send one dollar to the Superintendent of Documents, U. S. Government Printing Office, Washington, D.C. 20402, and ask for the best-selling booklet *Infant Care*, Stock Number 1791-0178.

You'll naturally want to co-ordinate all your baby care activities with your wife so you'll know all about schedules and special needs, and so that you can work together as a team to ease the burden both ways. This kind of teamwork is simple enough with the first baby, mostly just a matter of passing the ball from time to time, but when a second baby arrives, there are needs to be met on every hand, and you'll wish there were more players on your team.

Animal Fathers   If you're unconvinced that fathers have a place in the business of baby care, take a look at the animal kingdom. The male sea horse actually "gives birth" to his young. The mother deposits the eggs in a pouch on the father's belly, where they hatch and where the minuscule sea horses develop for six weeks. The father then coils his tail around a

strand of seaweed and begins to flex his body back and forth, tightening his muscles until all the little sea horses — as many as 150 of them — are shot out into the water.

Bird fathers are wonderfully attentive to the needs of their young. There are some eight thousand species of birds who live in monogamous pairs — sometimes for a single breeding season and sometimes for life — and among most of these the male helps build the nest and feed the young and in some cases sits on the eggs. Male birds also defend the female, protect and instruct the young. The huge greater rhea of South America is famous as a concerned father. For five weeks he sits on the two-pound eggs that several of his female friends have left in the nesting hole he has prepared. When the rhea chicks hatch, he alone tends and protects them for three or four months until they can make it on their own. Male emperor penguins stand shoulder to shoulder in huge groups to protect the eggs and the new chicks from winds up to a hundred miles an hour and temperatures to forty below. A feathered flap of skin hanging from the father penguin's sagging belly keeps the egg warm. The chick huddles between its father's feet and is nourished by sticking its head into its father's mouth and drinking a milky liquid from his throat.

Bird fathers have a much greater opportunity to help out with infant care than mammal fathers do. Among mammals, of course, the mother has the biological equipment for hatching the babies and for feeding the young, but among the birds, the female's only unique contribution to the process is laying the eggs. A male bird can take it from there, or, more to the point, share in all the tasks as the couple take it from there.

Mammal fathers, with less of an opportunity for involvement in baby care, don't hang around to help out with raising their progeny; in the majority of mammal species, the parents don't even stay together after copulation. But there are also striking instances among mammals of close paternal involvement in infant caretaking. Some concerned mammal fathers are the coyotes, wolves, jackals, hunting dogs, and foxes. These animals live, as birds and people do, in pairs; male coyotes and others will bring food to pregnant females, will prechew and regurgitate food to nourish their young, will play with and carry around the young, and will protect them by distracting predators away from them. And the father fox takes the litter out for hunting lessons.

A little closer to us, there is a very wide variety of fathering styles among the nonhuman primates. Chimpanzee males, for example, show no interest in infants, and are sometimes aggressive toward them — which makes sense considering the completely promiscuous sex lives of chimps; there's no way a male chimp can identify his own kids. Baboons, however, live in orderly social groupings, and the males often are very involved with the young.

In South and Central America live the superfathers among the nonhuman primates: marmosets and tamarins. Male marmosets will assist during the

birth of infants; they prechew food for their infants during the first week; they carry the babies around on their backs for at least the first six weeks and sometimes for three months, transferring them to the mother only for nursing, every two or three hours; and the males continue to carry the young even after weaning. A couple of factors set the tiny marmosets apart from other nonhuman primates; they are among the only species who live — as birds and people do — in monogamous family units. And unlike most primates, they commonly give birth to twins. It's possible that the marmoset father pitches

in so helpfully for the same reason a human father of twins finds himself pitching in — the sheer necessity of having two caretakers for two babies.

Other New World monkey fathers who show exceptional involvement with their young — tamarins, night monkeys, and titi monkeys — likewise live in monogamous families. And among other monogamous primates in other parts of the world — the gibbons, siamangs, and humans — fathers also show a considerable interest in the care of infants.

COMFORTING CRIERS

"I'm a stander and carrier and singer of lullabies, nursery rhymes, nonsense songs — whatever seems to be appetizing at the moment," said a man who felt he had inherited from his dad a knack for comforting babies. "I tend to stand, and my father tends to rock. I think it's a propensity for being very comfortable feeling or being very boring, but in any case the kid seems to go to sleep agreeably. And that's about the most significant block of time that I've been able to spend with Karina and Sasha on a regular basis since we've had them."

There are almost as many methods for calming a crying baby as there are parents — rocking and patting and back rubbing and walking and singing and holding next to the heart, and an infinite number of variations on these. It's remarkable that during the aeons that people have been engaged in this activity, human ingenuity and technology have failed to come up with a universal foolproof method for quieting a bawling infant.

Each baby responds to a slightly different approach and the trick is to find it — by trial and error. The closest thing to a universal foolproof method that exists is the rocking chair.

Womb Returns

Babies like to be held close and next to the heart so they can feel and hear your heartbeat. Theoretically, hearing the beat of the heart up so close reminds a baby of that happy, fluid, stress-free environment where she spent her first blissful nine months listening to the loud thump of her mother's heart. Amplified recordings of heartbeats are available commercially and some parents play these in the baby's room and find that the baby is comforted by the regular sound. A noisily ticking windup clock can have pretty much the same soothing effect. But for actually calming down an upset or fretful baby, holding close and a real heartbeat are more to the point. A front-position baby carrier (p. 29) holds the baby snugly next to your heart and allows you the freedom to move around and do some light work; meanwhile your motion adds another soothing dimension. The hip baby seat (p. 28) soothes in a similar way.

Two mechanical devices that sometimes work wonders for quieting a screamer are the automobile and the dishwashing machine. Many parents, when the crying has gone on longer than they can endure, put the baby in the infant car seat and take a spin — and with most babies this works like magic, the motion of the car putting them out within a mile or two. If you have a dishwasher, definitely try it as a calmer-downer; its churning may be very much like what your baby remembers in the womb — loud churning sounds of mother's intestines and circulation. Just strap the baby in an infant seat and put it on top of the dishwasher; but stay close as babies shouldn't be left alone in infant seats, especially not up high.

"We got a water bed when Amber was about three months old," one father told me, "and we had a party the day we put it in and filled it up — kind of the latter-day equivalent of a barn raising. And so she was the first person we put on it. There were about six adults in the room and all of us agreed that she thought she was back in the womb." Water beds are heated from beneath to maintain a temperature close to body temperature, so the sensation for a baby could be very much like being back inside, where she came from. Amber, at seven, continues to love the water bed — but now it's for roughhouse play.

Some parents use the small-time equivalent of the water bed — the water bottle — for calming a

baby. Not too hot, and lay the baby on it on his stomach, with a towel between, and rub his back.

Back Rubs

Back rubbing gets results, but it's been my experience that each baby needs a different stroke. Gregory liked a circular motion around his whole back with the flat of the hand; but Timothy goes for fingertips working up the middle. Try a variety of rubs and if you have an electric massage device that straps onto the hand, test it out on the baby, too. It's very awkward and tiring to lean over the side of a crib to rub a baby's back; you'll do better sitting down with the baby across your knees for the back rub, and then praying that he doesn't wake up when you transfer him to the crib.

Lullabies

Crooning to the baby is an integral part of any effective calming-down system; whether you walk or rock or rub, sing at the same time. The all-time expert in the lullaby department was Johann Sebastian Bach; he had twenty kids altogether, so there was always a baby squalling in the Bach household. The master would leave his keyboard to comfort the babies, and he is said to have crooned to them this lovely chorale, "Beside Thy Cradle, Here I Stand."

The song you sing needn't be an actual lullaby — just any song that seems gentle and soothing; I find, for instance, that "Ol' Man River" works better for me than "Rock-a-bye, Baby." Maybe it's because I prefer to sing it, so I put a little bit of soul into it, or maybe it's the combination of voice and tune and the lucky chance that I found a song both babies liked. You may have to try a variety of songs before you discover one that hits home.

One inventive father told me he'd found two lullaby records in the local library, and played them in the evening for his baby son, noting which tunes seemed to appeal. He'd tried records of folk music, too, and Indian ragas and classical guitar recordings. "Now, the classical guitar always did the trick, except for a couple of pieces, but I could have saved myself the trouble with the songs and lullabies, because, you know, there were five or six that kind of worked, but the only one with real knockout effectiveness was 'Rock-a-bye, Baby.'"

"Rock-a-bye, Baby," incidentally, is said to have been written by a young Pilgrim who came over on the *Mayflower* and was impressed by the way the Indians hung their birchbark cradles from the branches of trees so the wind and the flexing of the branch would lull the baby to sleep.

BREASTS AND BOTTLES

The father of a breast-fed baby may get a stiff dose of rejection; the baby knows who's doing the feeding

and it isn't you. Bottle feeding puts a father where the action is; for months the central issue in a baby's life is food (for some of us it's the central issue from cradle to grave), and if you're feeding the baby, you'll be a Very Important Person in her life.

Breast feeding has big advantages for fathers, too. "The milk's prewarmed; you don't have to do anything else. Our first child was adopted, so I was up in the middle of the night making bottles. I appreciate how easy it is: the child cries, you go get him and put him in bed with you — that's all there is to it." Did this man feel left out because mother and baby were so close through breast feeding? "No, my wife allowed me to change all the diapers I wanted."

There's plenty of room for a father to help out with breast feeding, too, because many nursing mothers run into stumbling blocks and need support. "Dora's mother implied that it was unsanitary, that it wasn't ladylike; she laid it on heavy and it really gave my wife fits," said one father. "She was sure she wanted to do it, but it was like she had to buck the system. It made her really nervous about it

and if the milk didn't come just right one time, she'd be in tears, because she felt she had to prove herself."

Opposition can come from other quarters, too. Rita and I went through two pediatricians before we found one who didn't discourage breast feeding. Most young pediatricians, and older ones who have stayed current, encourage mothers to nurse, but there are still many who love the advantages of bottles. Bottles make the doctor's job easier — if the baby isn't thriving, the formula can be adjusted, but you can't adjust mother's milk.

With family and professional advice and pressure running counter to a mother's simple desire to feed her baby the way Nature intended, a father's positive interest and backing can make a huge difference. But we're not always right there with that strong support and sense of conviction. A pediatrician told me: "I've advised women for years that they should choose breast feeding. But when my wife was breast-feeding our second child, I never stopped asking her: 'Do you think you *really* have enough milk?' 'Are you sure you can do it?' All the wrong questions."

Some husbands actively oppose breast feeding because they fear they'll be embarrassed by seeing their wives' breasts exposed in public for nursing. As a practical matter, this is generally a needless fear, since a woman who wants to nurse discreetly can almost always manage to do so by retiring to a private room. If you are concerned about this aspect of breast feeding, though, it's best to discuss it openly and frankly with your wife well before the baby arrives.

Pros and Cons

Most of us were raised on bottled formula, and many a new father has never even seen a baby nursed until he sees his own wife nursing their first-born. This most natural of processes just isn't that natural to us, so if your wife and you choose breast feeding, it's important that you understand something of its advantages — and its drawbacks.

Advocates of breast feeding point out that human milk is designed specifically for human needs — just as the milk of other mammal species has special properties according to the needs of the species. Seals' milk, for example, is extremely rich in fats to help the newborn seal stay warm in his icy home. In human milk, an element called taurine is thought to

contribute to brain development. Mother's milk is also believed to provide babies with important immunities to childhood illnesses. Mother's milk is generally easier for a baby to digest than formula, so there's less spitting up. A breast-fed baby smells better than a bottle-fed one, as do her bowel movements, and her skin is said to be much softer to the touch than the skin of a bottle-fed baby. You won't save a fortune on breast feeding, but it is cheaper than buying formula. Clearly nursing is the more portable of the two possibilities, so you may be a little less tied down to home base, or, at any rate, there will be less paraphernalia to lug along.

There are disadvantages to breast feeding, too. Some women have trouble nursing; some simply can't. For some it's purely physical. Mothers who have had Cesarean sections are sometimes so knocked out by the surgery they may have difficulty nursing. For others, attitudes get in the way — some women aren't sure they can nurse successfully, and well-meaning friends and grandmothers may be quick to assure them that they can't.

To help cope with these problems, nursing mothers founded the La Leche League, a national organization that supplies women with information about breast feeding and sponsors group discussions where new nursing mothers can get together to air their problems and feelings. A local chapter of the La Leche League will probably be listed in your phone book. A nursing mother can always pick up the phone and call an experienced member of the group for advice if she's having difficulty — nursing mothers find this a terrific boost. But for all the comfort another woman in the La Leche League can offer, an understanding and supportive husband can offer more — day in and day out.

How about bottles? For a woman who plans to go back to work shortly after the baby is born, they're the answer — though many women like to nurse for a month or so before making the switch. Bottles are safe, dependable, convenient — perfect for a woman who honestly isn't interested in nursing or who can't. Here again, though, attitudes may get in the way. "My wife didn't want to nurse our son," one father told me, "but every time she turned around, here was one of these breast-feeding fanatics. We have a neighbor who thinks breast feeding is more exciting than orgasm, and my wife has a friend who told her that she wouldn't be a woman unless she nursed — in so many words." So whichever brand of milk your wife and you choose, you'll probably be called on to support the decision.

Nursing

With a breast-fed baby you won't be running for bottles in the middle of the night, but you should be running for the baby. A nursing mother is drained from feedings around the clock whenever the baby demands milk, and she can use your help. It's tempting just to pull the covers up around your head when the baby hollers, and hope your wife will get up and take care of the whole job. But your wife will have a much easier time with nursing if you let her conserve some of her strength by staying in bed while you go get the baby and bring him to her. Your sleep is interrupted in any case, and this simple act of stumbling through the dark to bring the baby will make you part of the process. Your wife will know that you're supporting her — and not just morally — and your baby may learn to recognize you as part of the food chain.

Another way you can get into the food chain is by giving the occasional supplementary bottles of water that breast-fed babies sometimes get. And

you'll want to start spooning in the mush as soon as your baby is ready for solid foods.

Any other help you can give with the baby or the household chores will help your wife maintain the strength she needs to feed the baby — if she's overtired, excited, or overanxious, the milk may not flow easily.

Moral support you can give aplenty. A nursing mother wants to know that you're certain she'll do a good job, that you're confident of her ability, that you *approve*. "When I took photographs of my wife with the baby nursing," one father said, "she said it made her feel really good that I enjoyed watching them together and that I was proud of it." If friends or relatives have discouraged your wife, your encouragement can help her stand firm. You can try to educate a grandmother from the old school and convince her that nursing is the right way, but your actions and attitudes are more likely to sway her, especially if you stay by your wife when she nurses — whether she nurses in company or leaves and goes into another room for privacy. This kind of family solidarity is very impressive to older women, many of whom never experienced anything like it. And your wife will appreciate it, too.

You and your wife will want to find a pediatrician who is solidly in favor of mother's milk; shop around before the baby arrives and don't settle for less than a breast-feeding enthusiast. Too often a nursing mother is confounded when she has difficulties and the doctor, instead of trying to help her through them, insists that she switch to bottles. This is no time to discover that the doctor is lukewarm on breast feeding, because at this point a nursing mother will suspect the doctor's motives and not know where to turn. The confusion of looking for a new pediatrician will only add to her problems. If you're confident of your doctor's interest in breast feeding, at least your wife can be certain that a decision to switch to bottles is based on real concern for her condition.

A nursing mother who has to stop for medical reasons will be crushed. Every woman seems to wonder whether she'll be up to it, and finding out she isn't is a big emotional blow — this time she'll really need your sympathy and strength.

For most women, there are traumas at the beginning of breast feeding — panic when the baby cries and the breasts seem empty. But with a husband who understands and wants to help, and hours on the phone talking to other women in the La Leche League, most nursing mothers manage to perform beautifully. And proud fathers enjoy the performance. "Personally, it's as satisfying to watch my wife nurse the baby as it is to hold the baby myself," said a father of two girls. "That sort of clear, comfortable situation is easy enough to appreciate without actually taking a part in it. To see it and know that it's happening is really, I think, sufficient."

Sex and Breast Milk   Couples are sometimes surprised to discover that when the woman reaches a climax, she also has a let-down of milk that may drench her husband — this happens with some, not all, women.

Some men are turned on by tasting breast milk; others are embarrassed by this possibility; and many wonder just what is "right." As far as I can make out, there are no rules in this area; it's a question to be decided privately — whatever you and your wife like is "right."

FEEDING

The path to your baby's heart is through her stomach. Especially if you feel a little left out of things because the baby is nursing, take every opportunity to feed her. If she's taking supplementary bottles of water, be the one to give them. And when solid foods start — usually somewhere between two and four months, depending on your pediatrician's way of doing things — you can do the shoveling.

Heating Bottles

When you're up three times in the middle of the night heating bottles, you start to experiment with ways to speed up the process so you can quickly plug the bottle into the screaming baby and get back to bed. Bottles can be heated most quickly in a relatively tall, narrow container with a couple of inches of water in the bottom so that there is very little water to bring to a boil. Some fathers use a large beer can on the stove.

Glass bottles will usually stand up under quick heating, but there's always a chance they'll break, and I'll never use another glass bottle again after the day we found Timothy at five months cheerfully playing in his crib with the jagged shards from a

smashed bottle. Plastic bottles are harder to clean than glass, but they have distinct advantages.

Some parents dispense with heating the bottles altogether, because babies don't seem to mind drinking formula cold and because some pediatricians say heating makes no difference. We've always heated, though, because it seemed it would be a little more like the real thing.

Whether you heat or serve it up cold, always shake or squirt a few drops on the back of your hand first. For warmed formula, this tells you whether you've made it too hot and need to cool the bottle under cold running tap water. And for both warm and cold formula you learn whether the nipple is functioning; blocked nipple holes are common and give a baby fits of frustration. Blockage can usually be cleared up instantly with the point of a sharp knife.

Try always to hold your baby close while you give him a bottle. The bottle is already a mechanical replacement for the warm mother's breast, so propping the baby in a seat with the bottle is a pretty cold act of rejection. Hold the baby close and you give a passable imitation of the real thing.

Burping

By mastering a couple of good burping techniques early in your child's life, you may add many hours of sleep and peace to your life. Everyone knows how to hold a baby up on his shoulder and thump away on her back, but all babies don't respond to this treatment. Try these two systems:

Leg-pump Burping Lay the baby on his back on your lap, head on your knees. Take him by the ankles and gently bend his legs back and forth, "pumping" out the burp.

Massage Burping Instead of thumping the baby's back, massage along the lower part of her sides, trying to feel the bubble and gently squeeze and push it up on its way to relief. You can do this in the traditional over-the-shoulder position, or with the baby lying face down across your lap; you'll want to support the head of a newborn in this position.

Spoon Feeding

Spoon feeding is simple enough. In the beginning, when the baby drools the food back out, just scrape it off her chin and pop it back in. After a while you both get very skilled at spooning and eating and you've got a neat, orderly rhythm worked out. And then the baby starts to grab for the spoon all the time — at around twelve months or possibly earlier. She's not trying to foul up feeding time; she's just indicating that she wants to do it herself. Let her.

She'll have a hard time with the spoon for weeks — at first getting hardly anything on it and later getting lots of food on herself. And meanwhile you'll use another spoon to get some food to its destination. This is usually called "co-operative feeding," though it's hard to tell — from the mess that results and the trouble both parent and baby have for a while — just who is co-operating with whom. The end result, however, is that the baby learns to use a spoon, just as she set out to do, and you're out of a job that had become a little boring anyway.

DIAPER TECHNIQUES

Before you change it, you check to see if it's full or wet. There are the smell test and the finger inspection for a full diaper, both self-explanatory. On a girl, the side of the diaper that is down as she is lying in her crib is the one to check; the rest of the diaper may be bone dry while that part is soaked. On boys check the top front of the diaper first; they pee up. In fact, one step in the correct diapering of a boy baby is to aim him downward before fastening the diaper, so he won't just squirt out the top of it.

Changing tables are fine, but unless you go to a lot of trouble and strap a baby down, he can always find some way to wriggle free and fall off, especially as he gets older. A baby can't fall off the floor and it's an excellent surface for changing a diaper. The exercise of kneeling down is good for you, too. If you think the floor's not clean enough for the job, throw down a towel or a rubberized baby mat. Also assemble all the equipment you'll need on the floor: tissues, wet washcloth, new diaper, ointment, if it's needed for a rash, and powder, if it's used in your household.

In cleaning a baby, you use the tissues first and then the wet cloth and you always work from front to back, regardless of sex, for hygienic reasons. In using baby powder, the temptation is to shake a lot of it on to do a bang-up job. Don't. Talcum is an abrasive, which is no good for a baby's lungs, so if you use powder, sprinkle a little first into your hand, holding the dispenser well away from the baby, and then pat it onto her bottom.

If the tape on a disposable diaper gets torn off or won't stick, don't throw out the diaper — close it up with masking tape. This is a little refinement that most mothers don't know about, and you can get a few points by providing a roll of masking tape for the changing table.

The thirty-six men questioned in a small poll I made were unanimous in preferring disposable diapers to the cloth variety.

Diaper Pleasures

When you get the easy routine of diapering down pat, you can concentrate on the pleasurable part. Many babies love diaper changing; it's obviously a time of relief for the baby — and if the person who's doing the changing is relaxed and ready for fun, it can be a fine time to play. As you're doing the changing, there's room for conversation and singing and once business is out of the way there's time for some little exercises where you work the baby's arms and legs back and forth. And it's a time for all the silly little endearments — tickling and tummy kissing and toe tweaking and "This Little Piggy Went to Market" . . .

As in all things, though, not all babies react the same way. With some, diapering is truly a pain. They squeal and resist and squirm and holler and the only thing you can do is pretend that you are very calm and self-possessed and go about the business of changing in a crisp, composed, and professional manner. This is an almost impossible pose to maintain, though, as you wrestle with this filthy little protester.

BABY CLOTHES

The fastening systems of baby clothes are designed purposely to frustrate fathers. No two work in quite the same way and you usually can't even tell where the front is. Look for a label; labels are always sewn in the back, so you'll at least know which end is up. Start snapping from bottom to top, but don't worry if there are a couple of extra snaps left over — these are put in by the manufacturers as part of their plot to make you feel inept.

Babies' heads are huge by proportion to the rest

of them, a fact that baby clothes makers choose to ignore, so often you have a small neck hole that gets stuck on top of the baby's head and sets off a screaming fit. Stretch the neck hole wide and start from the *back* of the head; once it's over, poke the arms through. In pulling it off, reverse the procedure: arms first; grab the hole at the front and pull up over the baby's face.

SLEEP

We're all prepared to get up several times every night for a new baby and we know we'll miss a month or so of sleep. That's par for the course, but it's not what always happens. Sometimes you luck out, like this man, whose daughter was one when I talked to him: "Pamela never wakes up, never has. Waking up is not as universal as I thought it was. A lot of people say, 'My baby never wakes up either.' I always thought you had to get up with a baby, especially when they're young, but that's not true."

There's another side to that coin, though, as Rita and I found out when Timothy was born. He was up every night, not just a few times, but six times, eight times, and for month after wearying month. We were daytime zombies. This didn't fit at all with our earlier experience with Gregory, who had been an average waker-upper. It wasn't colic; Timothy

Honoré Daumier, pen and ink drawing, 1857.

would go back to sleep after some rocking or walking, but then he was back awake again an hour later. We read all the advice in all the books and followed some of it, let him cry it out until we wanted to flee from the house. We called my sister, who is a pediatrician, and she said not to worry, *all* babies sleep through the night by the fourth month, no exception. We had the exception; it went on for the better part of eight months. But meanwhile, as we complained bitterly to anyone who'd listen, we discovered that we didn't have the only exception. Many other parents have kids who cry through the night and keep them awake for months on end. If you have a baby like this, I can't tell you to take heart, because I know you won't care to — you're too tired of the whole thing.

But do try to remember, if it's any comfort, that you're not alone — in this or in any of the other things your kids do that don't happen to fit conveniently into the "norms."

ALONE WITH THE BABY

Your wife goes out and you are alone with the baby for the first time. You feel pretty confident for a start; you've got a good idea of what needs to be done, plus detailed instructions from Mom about the schedule and the routine. And then the baby cries . . . and cries, and goes on crying. "And if you can't get them to stop crying, you get kind of frantic," said one new father. "I would think to myself: Either she's hungry or she needs to be changed or she has a stomach-ache, and I tried all these three and if that didn't work, I started worrying that maybe I didn't do something right."

With the first baby, and particularly the first few times alone together, there's always that doubt — you must be screwing up. New mothers feel the exact same way. But you're not screwing up. The baby is — by crying. Make sure you've followed all the simple steps on this checklist: Diaper, Bottle, Burp, Rock:

DIAPER — Check and change it if necessary. If the baby continues to cry, try a

BOTTLE — Offer food; if the baby's problem is hunger, he'll take it. If he ignores or refuses it and continues to cry, try a

BURP — If burping doesn't relieve him, it's probably not gas, so

ROCK — Or walk him or rub his back or sing a

lullaby or whatever else you usually do to calm him, because the chances are about fifty to one the problem is merely that he's tired.

With those four simple steps, you cover about 99 per cent of the possible causes of crying. I've never been much good at remembering formulas, so I wrote out these steps on a card and put it in a plastic window in my wallet, and it was a great help with both babies to have this little checklist handy. It's surprisingly easy to leave out one step when you're irritated or confused by a baby's crying, and that step may be the solution. And if you've followed the steps faithfully, you can at least feel confident you're doing the right thing.

But if the baby keeps crying after all the steps check out and after you've walked her and rocked and crooned to her for an hour or more, you start to think, as one father expressed it: "My God, how do you turn this thing off!" Meanwhile you've felt the back of her neck for a fever and found it cool as a cucumber, and now you're holding the baby in one arm and trying to thumb through Dr. Spock with the other hand and hoping your wife will come home early. Or the baby is hot, red, and sweaty, but it's obvious that he's done all this to himself by crying and carrying on.

Now you remember that you read or heard somewhere that babies pick up on the moods of their parents and that if a parent is tense it will make a baby irritable — so you blame yourself. But hold on a minute and remember that it works the other way around, too. Parents pick up on a baby's mood, and this baby is crying — which is making *you* irritable.

The problem is that you're stuck with a cranky baby who is crying for obscure reasons. Don't bother to blame yourself. Nobody else will be blaming you either, especially your wife — unless she's very undiplomatic — because she will want you to feel as good as you can about the experience so you won't try to weasel out of it the next time she wants to go out.

FAMOUS FATHER STARS AT BABY CARE

In Springfield, Illinois, a young lawyer named Abraham Lincoln took care of the baby every Sunday while his wife went to church. The neighbors said they would see the tall young lawyer pulling the baby up and down the street in front of their house in a little wagon, and as he pulled the wagon he habitually had his nose buried in a book. Legend has it that one Sunday the neighbors saw the baby fall out of the wagon, screaming, while the young lawyer proceeded on up the street, absorbed in what he was reading. And just then Mary Todd Lincoln rounded the corner on her way home . . .

Baby Furniture

Take all the hand-me-down baby furniture and equipment that's offered; there are plenty of other things to spend your money on. Even solicit hand-me-downs, because there are always forgotten cribs and baby swings, etc., cluttering up other people's storage space. But look these gift horses in the mouth, especially old cribs, which often aren't safe — the section below on cribs tells what to look out for.

Make sure all old baby furniture is solidly put together — reinforce where needed. If you paint old baby furniture to spruce it up, use lead-free paint — babies chew on everything, and lead is poisonous. Since February 1978, federal regulations have limited the lead content of all ordinary household paints to an acceptably low level — 0.06 per cent by weight of the dried film — but I always feel better if the label specifically states that the paint is safe for use on children's furniture. Older furniture may be covered with leaded paint; the safest course is always to strip it and repaint it, as the lead in the old paint doesn't disappear just because you cover it with a new coat of paint — the lead is even said to leach up into the new paint.

If you're an ardent handyman/carpenter and want to build your own baby furniture from scratch, an excellent source for plans is Mario Dal Fabbro's *How to Make Children's Furniture and Play Equipment* (New York: McGraw-Hill, 1975); the book includes plans for a bassinet, crib, portable crib, high chair, etc. In building your own baby furniture, also follow the safety guidelines given below.

Bassinet

For a baby's first bed you can fix up any box, basket, or dresser drawer — or a fine old cradle or

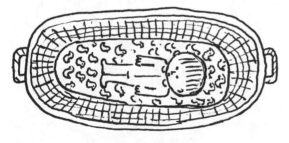

bassinet if one's available. A wicker laundry basket is cheap, good-looking, and the ideal size. Foam rubber cut to fit will make a fine mattress; just make certain the mattress fits firmly against the sides — see notes on tight-fitting mattresses below under Cribs for more on this necessary safety precaution. Standard fitted sheets for bassinets are made 16″ x 32″.

A bassinet made by converting a box or basket should be kept on the floor, where it can't fall off — the high sides will protect the baby from drafts.

Crib

In 1974 the U. S. Consumer Product Safety Commission started to regulate the manufacture of

cribs, and newly built ones are designed along fairly safe lines, but there are millions of sturdy old cribs around that don't measure up to the federal standards. The slats of a crib should be as closely spaced as possible; the government standard space is 2⅜″, but closer is better. The problem isn't babies stuffing their heads between the bars — it's that a baby can wriggle her body down between widely

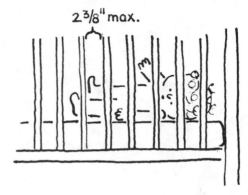

2⅜″ max.

spaced bars, catch her head, and strangle. If there's too much space between the bars of your crib, get bumper pads that go all the way around the crib; they should tie or snap securely into place at at least six points along the bars. Bumper pads should be removed when a baby is old enough to pull up to a standing position, so she won't use them to climb up on and fall out — by this point the baby will be much too big to fit between the bars.

Be sure the mattress fits the crib snugly; it is too small if you can fit two fingers between the mattress and the side of the crib. Here the problem is that an infant might wedge his head between the mattress and the side of the crib and suffocate. Don't throw out a perfectly good, though slightly small mattress; instead, make rolls from large bath towels and fit them tightly between mattress and crib side. The standard size for fitted crib sheets is 27″ x 51″.

The lock or latch on the drop side of the crib should be one that a baby can't reach through the bars and release; some older cribs have a quick-release bar directly under the middle of the drop side, designed to be operated with the parent's knee; and this is easy for a baby to trip.

When the release catches start to squeak horribly as you run the side up and down its metal rails, lubricate the catches and the rails with ordinary petroleum jelly — it's the safest lubricant for all baby things, including wheels on strollers, and it's very effective.

Once your baby is up off her back and moving

around, you'll have to check the crib every now and again with a wrench and screwdriver to be sure all the bolts and screws are tight; a child can really wiggle a crib apart. Some kids stand up in the crib and rock and bump and hump, and get the thing going across the room. If the crib has casters, remove them; if the baby still manages to move the crib around, try fastening the legs of the crib to the

baseboard with small metal angle brackets; this same technique can be used to anchor tippy pieces of furniture that your kids habitually pull over.

As soon as your child can pull up to a standing position, lower the crib mattress to its very bottom position, and set a policy of not leaving big objects like large stuffed animals in the crib; kids will climb up on anything, and a fall from the top of a crib side is a nasty one. A child is ready to leave the crib for a bed when he's grown so much that the side rail is less than three quarters his height.

Don't put a crib near furniture that a child can climb out and onto. And don't put it near draperies or venetian blinds, because a baby can grab the cords, become entangled, and strangle — it sounds bizarre and farfetched, but it happened to a friend's baby, so I'm hoping this little note of caution will save someone else's child.

Crib Gym

Quick and easy to make, a crib gym will give your baby lots to do while lying on his back, and may give him his first good handhold when he tries to lift himself up to stand. All that's needed are:

    20″ length ¾″ dowel OR broom
        handle OR ½″ PVC pipe
    sturdy cord
    baby toys
    string and round sewing elastic

The bar can be longer or shorter than 20″, depending on the width of the crib and your whim. Drill a hole about ½″ in from each end to accept the stout cord that you will use to tie it to the top rails of the crib. An even quicker way to make this hanging bar is to thread the cord through a 20″ length of ½″ PVC pipe and tie big knots at both ends so it can't slip back and forth along the cord.

From the support bar you can hang any objects that are safe and fun for a baby to bat and kick at or play with — rubber animals, plastic rings and clacking disks, a plastic cup. Tie some on with string and others with round sewing elastic so they'll pull and snap back when the baby lets go. Drill a small hole for the string in an object that can't be hung up easily another way.

The crib gym can be moved easily to hang over the playpen, or you can put the baby in an infant seat on the floor and hang the thing over her, suspended between the legs of a couple of chairs.

When the baby has mastered pulling himself up to stand, the crib gym should go. It will only be another boost up for the baby's next step, which is up and over the side of the crib.

Changing Table

A changing table can be improvised from almost any old table with a top surface of at least 2′ x 3′. To make a waterproof mattress for the changing surface, you will need:

½″ foam rubber pad to fit surface
polyethylene film
silver-color duct tape

Just wrap the foam rubber pad in the polyethylene as you would wrap a parcel for the post, and seal all seams with the wide duct tape. Polyethylene film is the widely available plastic sheeting used in building construction and sold in all building supply and hardware stores. The taped side of the mattress will be down and the mattress should be covered with a cloth sheet. An excellent size for a changing table mat is 24″ x 38″, because standard fitted sheets come in these dimensions.

Changing tables are sometimes rigged up with a strap from side to side to hold the baby down. You can use an old leather belt cut in half and held on with screws, but I prefer omitting the strap, because it encourages you to leave the baby strapped — insecurely — and turn around to attend to something else. Babies are so good at wriggling free that I think it's best to set the situation up so you'll always *have* to pick up the baby if you turn away from the table.

A low guardrail around the edge, made with 1″ x 4″ wood, will be some help when the baby is still quite small, but it tends to get in the way after eight or nine months.

The best changing table will have shelf space under and above it. The shelves underneath are for diapers and clothes, and a narrow shelf above and well out of the baby's reach will be for diaper rash ointment, petroleum jelly, etc.; it may also give you a place to hang a mobile from. Good lighting is important over a changing table; you definitely don't want the table placed so that a light behind the changer throws his or her shadow across the changee.

High Chair

A high chair has to be stable, with legs that slant outward to give it a firm base; so don't waste your time fixing up a pretty, but steep and wobbly older wooden high chair, because your baby will rock it over as soon as he's big enough to. Mothers prefer metal high chairs, because they can be cleaned easily, and your baby's chair will be cleaned thousands of times before you're through with it.

Vinyl is the best surface to have under a high chair; you have to be able to wash up easily after the baby throws food all around. Baby food throwing

will destroy a finished wood floor in a few weeks, especially if you wash the floor off liberally with water. Wood floors should be cleaned off with floor wax or a solvent like turpentine, which isn't practical each time the baby lobs some mashed beets or spills some apple juice. A large drop cloth of heavy oilcloth is an excellent solution in a room with a wooden floor or carpeting. Put rubber feet on the ends of the high chair legs to protect the oilcloth from tearing. You can also put down a big piece of vinyl under the high chair. Floor-covering stores usually keep the short end pieces from big rolls,

which they sell cheaply. Cut the mat in a circle or oval rather than a square so there won't be corners for a child to bend back and break. The edges of a vinyl mat like this will chip after a while, but you probably won't go through more than two mats per child.

If you want to win a few points with Mom, attach a towel rack to the back of the high chair seat for hanging a bib and damp washcloth ready at hand. Depending on the type of chair and its measurements, you can use either a metal towel rack from a hardware store or improvise with a dowel and a couple of pieces of scrap wood.

When your baby learns to rock the high chair, there's every chance he'll manage to turn it over — even if it has a good wide base. Try fastening the bottoms of the rear legs to a baseboard with hooks and eyes. The hooks are screwed into the baseboard to engage eyes in the back legs of the high chair.

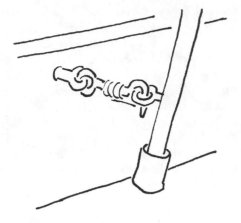

This setup can be easily undone whenever you want to move the chair. "Childproof" hooks that have a little spring closing device make this more secure.

Mobiles

After a month or two a baby does a lot of looking up, and a mobile is about the easiest way to provide your baby with something to look at. A "mobile" can be as simple a thing as a stuffed doll hung over the baby on a string. Screw a large eye bolt or screw hook into a ceiling beam directly over the crib so you will have a permanent, sturdy place to hang things from; install a mobile hook over the changing table, too, while you're at it.

You can make mobile structures from string and sticks of any sort; wire coat hangers also make good mobile frameworks to hang light objects from. If the mobile is to hang over a baby who's on her back, make sure the big interesting sides of the objects you hang are facing down so she can see them. Too often you see a bright, good-looking mobile hanging over a crib that only the parents can appreciate; say it's a bunch of colorful flat fish shapes — the baby will see only the narrow undersides of the fish. Hang any shiny or bright or interesting objects you come across. Keep them as close to the baby as you can and still have them well out of reach — a baby focuses best on objects that are close up. Very young babies seem to see black-and-white objects best, and they are attracted to pictures of faces; try hanging over your baby a large simple drawing of a face made with a black marker on white cardboard — just a big pair of eyes and a mouth on an oval shape will do.

ACCOMPLISHMENTS

We sometimes think of a baby's lot as an easy one: no job, no responsibilities, lie around all day eating. But in fact a baby has his hands full learning to cope with forces that we take totally for granted. He's expending much of his considerable energy and keen intellect in coming to terms with many aspects of a slightly hostile environment. Take gravity for example.

It's easy to assume that a child knows about gravity from birth — that this knowledge is simply part of our human equipment, as instinctively under-

stood as the fact that we have to eat to stay alive. But kids are coming to us from a relatively weightless environment. For her first nine months, a child is suspended in a sac of fluid, so that her earliest experience of the physical world is of a buoyant, cushiony environment very different from the one she'll be born into.

Astronauts and cosmonauts go through years of sophisticated training to prepare them for a new environment, for a force field unlike the one they're used to. And I think much of what a child does and goes through during his first year is a kind of on-the-job training program to develop skills similar to the ones the astronauts have to master. The astronaut is learning to cope with a situation in which a ribbon of toothpaste may float away as he squeezes it onto his brush; and the child is learning to cope with a world where that same squeeze of toothpaste will inevitably fall on the floor and get dirty if he doesn't keep the brush directly under it.

Of course kids eventually learn to deal with gravity, but you will notice that for the first months of a child's life, gravity, not the child, is pretty much in control — the baby is lying down. With muscles developed to sit up and then to stand and walk, the baby makes repeated and increasingly successful attempts to stay upright, and the toddler goes through an extraordinary course of trial-and-error learning to come to that point where he can not only stay upright but also keep moving and not fall. It's a daily struggle, a thousand pratfalls before the trick is mastered. I wonder if astronaut training is as rough.

By acquiring the rudiments of language and getting up off his back to become erect and self-propelled, in one short year a baby is transformed into a new creature — from cocoon to butterfly. It's fascinating to watch, and we try to help the process along a little, too, talking at the baby to supply him with words and holding him up so he can practice walking, all of which definitely helps. How much direct formal "learning" goes on is open to question — the baby will learn to walk and talk without your conscious effort at teaching him. But the backing you give your baby really counts as he moves on confidently from accomplishment to accomplishment. It's Dad and Mom in the cheering section who boost that confidence and give him the courage he needs for his mighty exploits.

STIMULATION

Child care books always admonish parents to provide a "stimulating, enriched environment" for their kids — from birth. And the alternative, by implication, is dull kids. Toy manufacturers create elaborate — and very expensive — "educational" machines and "toy systems" for babies; you can drop a big piece of cash stimulating a baby; his crib can be hung with more gaudy equipment than a Christmas tree. And most of this will do the baby no more good, and provide him with no more stimulus, than a half-dozen thirty-nine-cent plastic toys; in fact, it's perfectly possible that too much "stimulus" will confuse a baby.

There's a little misunderstanding going on here between parents and well-meaning child care experts on this score that's abetted by manufacturers of fancy equipment for kids. The "stimulating environment" that's meant isn't the overstimulation of gadgetry. The enrichment that kids need is the stimulation of interested, loving parents who enjoy introducing them to the things in their world — it's as simple as that.

With a new baby, your attention and warmth and play will provide far more enrichment than her "interaction" with an elaborate "educational" plastic crib toy might. Of course, interesting toys and an interesting place to live stimulate a child, too. And the first order of business in this department is to make your household available to your baby as soon as she can get around a little by crawling. Baby-proofing the house can be done in two ways. Either you strip the whole place down, put everything of any value up high or under lock and key so the baby can do no harm to your things, in which case you're protecting the place from the baby. Or you can eliminate all real hazards to the baby and set the place up so she has maximum access to everything she can't easily destroy — in which case you're actually enriching her environment. If you put everything interesting up high, observed one father, "the child's part of the environment is barren and the adult's is rich. . . . All those wonderful things up there. People wonder why their kids risk their necks by climbing up the bookcase. . . . You have to be willing to pick a lot of stuff up. We had this long low bookcase in our living room when Leah was a toddler. Several times a day she'd start at one end and go on down to the other end just pulling out all the books so they'd fall down on the floor. And we always let her do it because she was having so much fun and it wasn't that much work to put them back. But also because she'd get interested in the books and pick them up and look at the pretty covers. It's difficult to hurt a book unless you tear a page out."

In the kitchen you want to set things up safely (see p. 118 for more on the mechanics of babyproofing), but you also want to make the baby part of the concern; after all, she may be spending the better part of the day crawling around on the kitchen floor. Pots and pans and plastic kitchen containers are

always among a child's favorite toys, so give her the "run of the Tupperware," as one father put it. And let her have a low kitchen drawer or part of a cabinet to keep other toys in as well.

There are always times when we have to stick the baby in a playpen just so we can get necessary tasks accomplished. A little occasional quiet playpen time isn't going to deprive your child of his sense of freedom. But regularly penning a baby up doesn't expand his horizons at all, and babies are eager to get around and explore, see and do things for themselves so they can learn about the furniture and the stairs and the place under the table. Try to do just the opposite of penning your child up; think of ways you can expose him to new things that he can't reach or see from his vantage point on the floor. Lift a

child up to the ceiling; it's thrilling for him to be able to touch this faraway place. Hold your child up to the window from time to time so he can see what's going on outside — it's easy to forget that a baby or a toddler can only see the sky or the tops of trees or buildings from a window — the way a prisoner does in a cell with a high window.

Nearly everything a baby sees or touches is new and "stimulating." Any object that is safe for her to handle is an "educational" toy — she will learn about its shape and its taste and its feel and she'll learn how to grasp it so it doesn't get away. The house or apartment you live in is an "enriching environment" for your baby — all you need to do is help her get at it.

CRAWLING AND WALKING

A baby will learn to crawl without any special instruction, but it's fun to give crawling lessons on the theory that a baby who has never seen it done will have trouble doing it. It was especially fun when Gregory and I together "taught" Timothy how to crawl.

Walking is the big step, and again babies figure out by themselves when and how to go about doing it — some at around a year, and many much later. You'll help and cheer, of course, and take pictures — movies if you can — of the first steps.

Between crawling and walking, a wheeled walker gives a child a lot of mobility. Mothers often object to walkers; they think of them as newfangled and suspect and they have heard it rumored that babies grow dependent on them and then have difficulty learning to walk, that the walker makes the bones grow crooked, and other such like. Apparently some doctors object to a walker if it makes a baby's toes turn out or in drastically — check with your pediatrician if you're unsure. But walkers are hardly newfangled; simple wheeled wooden-frame walkers were common in the Middle Ages. If you don't give a child a walker, he'll try to invent his own from any piece of light furniture he can shove along in front of him; second children use the tricycle or wheel toy of the first.

CLIMBING

A father's body (or a mother's) is the best climbing apparatus a baby can have. You're a human jungle gym, and all you need to do is lie down and let your baby explore and crawl and climb all over you. You are steps and a hill and a steep wall — and what's more, you have hands to catch and stop a big tumble or fall.

You can vary the terrain and the baby's climbing possibilities by getting in any and every position you can. With a little rolling and rearranging, you can always be there as a new mountain when the bear climbs over the mountain to see what he can see. He saw another mountain, and whadaya think he did?

Babies readily find the best ready-made, nonhuman climbing equipment in house or apartment. What looks to you like a perfectly normal, sedate living space, looks to a baby like a challenge, a Mount Everest to be climbed because it's there. Some kids are climbers and others are not; both kinds are wonderful. If you've got a climber, keep your eyes and ears open and babyproof with a little extra care. But try not to babyproof your child out of a job. Her job is exploring the place she lives in and discovering what it's like, and she needs as much access to it as you can give her.

You can also supply a baby with a few hurdles and obstacles to crawl over. An inner tube is great for this, and large cardboard boxes are always fun to crawl into and over. A crawler loves to be put in a cardboard box and pushed or pulled by Daddy all around the floor. If you're a builder, perhaps you'll knock together a few 2″ x 4″s and some 1″ dowels to make a low obstacle or climber for your baby. No need to make this elaborate. *Your* design will be the best one, because you know how far along your child is and can gauge what his next step will be. If you haven't a table or desk with a horizontal crosspiece near the floor, I'd suggest you make something like the over-and-under baby hurdle pictured here. As with all wooden things you make for kids, no splinters, please.

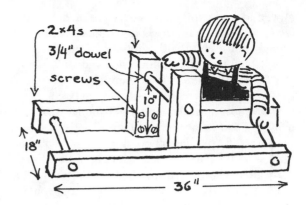

STAIRS

It's hard to imagine what a flight of stairs looks like to a baby who has never climbed them; it must be an awesome sight. I know that to many a first-time parent that flight of stairs looks even more awesome — you see your baby crawling up and you *know* he isn't ready for it, that he will reel and tumble backward. You know that the first climb is an important step toward independence for the baby, but you hover along behind, hands cupped inches away from the baby's butt, ready to catch him when he stumbles.

The surprise for most first-time parents is how little difficulty a kid actually has crawling up the stairs. As with almost every other early enterprise, a child seems to *know* when the time has come for this new conquest, and will show a clear interest in climbing the stairs when she's ready for it. Going down is more difficult for a baby than the ascent, and a little more dangerous — and babies seem to know this, too. As a matter of course, babies master the uphill climb before they even try going down; there are normally weeks between the first climb up and the first one down, during which the baby gets plenty of practice and becomes thoroughly familiar with the stairs. And when she does decide she's ready for the descent, a baby will almost always choose the safest approach, which is to crawl down backward. If your baby decides to follow the other possible course, which is bouncing from step to step on her bottom, you'll have to intervene and get her turned around.

Carpeting on the stairs makes the job easier for everyone; the baby gets more traction and the parents get some feeling of reassurance. But carpeting isn't a necessity; I've had stair carpeting on my list of household things to attend to for a good six years now, and meanwhile both kids have made out perfectly well on painted wooden stairs. Watch out, though, for a child with slippery rayon clothes or shiny-soled new shoes on uncarpeted stairs — you can hit the bottoms of the new shoes with some rough sandpaper. A barefoot baby gets good traction on most surfaces; and you'll notice that your baby is good at providing himself with this extra traction — by peeling off every sock and bootie and little shoe his parents painstakingly put on him.

By attaching the guard gate at the bottom of your stairs at the level of the third or fourth step, you give your baby a little practice stairway to work on all

alone, without Mom or Dad hovering. Usually, though, you'll find it's easier to attach the gate at the bottom of the stairs, where there's more likely to be woodwork to screw it to. For more on stairway gates, see p. 120.

Stairs are a place for purposeful climbing and not for play, and this becomes a rule in most households with small children. But rules are made to be broken and there is one little stairway game that is so much fun for a baby that we can maybe bend the rule from time to time. Carpeted stairs are best here; and the game is as simple as this: the baby sits on a stair and Dad takes him by the legs and *gently* pulls him forward, Bump, Bump, Bump, down the stairs.

Apartment Stairs

A child in a walk-up apartment will learn stair climbing before a baby in a suburban house, but what about a child in an elevator apartment? A resourceful father of a one-year-old who lives uptown in Manhattan told me his daughter has had no problem with stairs. Every time they enter or leave the building they use the stairs for one flight and the elevator for the rest of the trip. While the baby was still practicing the *up* climb only, they always went to the floor above theirs on the way out of the building, and to the floor below on their way in. Now that she has mastered the stairs in both directions, they choose the floor to go to by whim.

PROTECTIVE FATHERS

If stereotypes fit in every case, Mom would always be the one who protected the kids, while Dad would always be pushing them toward riskier feats of derring-do. In some families it works just that way, and gives the kids a nice balance of possibilities. But plenty of fathers are just as protective as mother hens, and sometimes it's Mom who ends up prodding the kiddies out of the nest.

I think *every* father has crept up on the baby in the middle of the night to reassure himself that the baby is still breathing. And most of us remember all the details of the first time we dropped the baby, and can usually remember the feelings of guilt and horror when it happened. The baby takes a lot more spills, and worse ones, after that, and we discover happily that babies do bounce — a little — and manage to survive some pretty rough treatment.

One father remembered how he was always making "saves" when Eben, his first son, was a toddler. As Eben would start to go down, he would dive across the room to grab him. He was all hands, and he felt a little like a goalie as he performed these antics. When he realized what he was doing, he backed off and let Eben take some of the falls that were coming his way, and when, three years later, Jesse was going through the same stage, his father's hand was seldom there to catch him.

NONVERBAL – VERBAL

"I remember being able to pick out the different sorts of cries," said the father of three girls, "but then those were just signals; they weren't really communications. You know, they were like a fog horn and a fire horn. I got the message but I didn't enjoy the communications."

If you tune your ear sharply, as this man did, you may learn to tell the difference between a hunger scream and a wet diaper scream, and several other demands may have their own intonations. Some people call this nonverbal communication, which certainly dignifies it. By the time most kids are one, however, they've worked out pretty efficient systems of nonverbal communication. They point to things they want and say, "Ah, ah, ah," and do charades. Some kids get so good at this that they find their needs being met without their using words, and as a consequence they are slow to begin talking.

It's often fun guessing what a baby is trying to say to you with gestures and grunts, but the sooner we can get in a little language, the quicker we can begin to communicate. Talking a lot to a baby probably helps. We always feed the baby words and phrases after he starts to use an occasional word, which is usually around his first birthday. We respond naturally to what we see as his interest in language and his growing ability to use it. Before that, though, there's less impetus to talk to a baby — no feedback. But in fact, at about six months babies can use some talking to, because they understand much of what is being said. The ability to receive and comprehend language runs way ahead of the ability to reproduce it. You'll notice that after one and a half your child will love to follow detailed directions and commands, even though his spoken language is still in the one-word-at-a-time stage.

I remember reading years back in a book on child care the advice that a parent should always talk to a baby, and thinking: "What rot. Of course talk to a baby. What else are you supposed to do, grunt at him?" But with Timothy, I noticed that even though I talked to him from the very first day, when he began to respond with a word or two, at one, the amount of language I was using at least doubled. And the way I was talking to him changed as well. Where before I had mainly been making quips and jokes that he had no way of understanding, now I was systematically feeding him words, names of the things he was using every day: banana, car, refrigerator — I was *teaching* him these words. And I realized that if I had been on the ball, I could have started feeding him words this way at least five months earlier, and that he would have been able to understand and conceivably make use of them.

The first vocal step a baby makes away from simple screaming is cooing, which starts sometime between two and four months. At about six months babbling begins, and all kids around the world, no matter what language their parents speak, make similar babbling noises. One of the sounds they make is da-da, and it's fun to pretend that your baby has identified and labeled you this early in the game. At around ten months the babbling has begun to sound a little like language, and this is the point at which deaf children — who coo and babble just as hearing children do — stop vocalizing. Single words come in around twelve months, and a year later most kids are making telegraphic two-word sentences: "Daddy cookie."

You may not be able to speed up the onset of speaking by talking to your baby, but there can be no doubt that exposure to plenty of language will make it easier for your child to learn to talk. Twins, it is well known, are commonly behind single children in early language development — theoretically because the parents of twins have so much child care to attend to that they get less of a chance to talk to their babies, and there are two babies to share the talk between. Statistically, second children run a little behind first children in early language ability, possibly for the same reason — parents too busy with child care to lavish direct attention and intimate talk on the second baby.

CLINK

Make sure to teach your baby to toast when he drinks. Some babies will lift a bottle in salute when they are still only crawling around, and a toddler who's saying a few words will rapidly add "Clink" to his small vocabulary when you show him how to touch cups or bottles in a toast.

Gregory and Timothy both loved Clinking — our dinner table sometimes sounded like a scene from *The Student Price*. For a baby or toddler, toasting is

an easy, sure-fire conversational gambit that doesn't require any real language — a wonderful social tool that small kids readily make use of. Timothy at a bluegrass music festival when he was one strutted around with his belly hanging out over the top of his diaper, lugging along his "bobble," until he found another guy with a similar belly. He marched up to this beer-bellied six-footer, squared off in front of him, and raised his bobble high. "Clink," he shouted, and he was instantly accepted as a hearty drinking companion, and many rousing toasts followed.

OBSERVING

During the first year, many fathers enjoy making observations on how their babies develop — what new things the baby does each day or each week, what breakthroughs she's made: turning over, sitting up, first responsive smiles, first understanding of words. Several men told me they had kept notebooks in which they jotted down the changes and stages they noticed their babies going through.

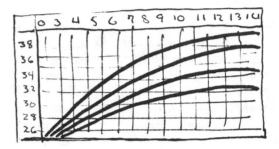

Father notekeeping has, in fact, led to the most significant work in the scientific field of child development studies. Jean Piaget, the great Swiss leader in the field, began his pioneering exploration of the developing minds of children by minutely observing the development of his own kids.

Many parents enjoy following along month by month in a good popularly written guide to child development and noticing how closely their child conforms to the established relatively predictable developmental patterns that most children seem to follow. A few good books of this sort are listed under Further Reading: Child Development (p. 340). Parents are usually eager to know if their kids fit into the developmental "norms" established by the scientific community. We are proud of a baby in the ninety-fifth percentile — even if it's in a category like weight. And real pride comes when your baby takes a step or says a few words weeks or months ahead of the date this is supposed to happen according to Gesell or some other authority.

It's a good policy to use child development information with discretion, and even with a little skepticism — especially if it is in a distinctly popularized form, which is likely to mean that it's inexact. "Norms" are very useful to determine whether a child is grossly out of line in some area of development — for spotting kids with handicaps and disabilities when they are many months behind others in their age group. And as the years go by and your kids change dramatically from year to year, some years acting like angels and other years driving you crazy, books on child development are a wonderful source of comfort, because they point out that all kids go through predictable behavioral "downs" toward the end of the first year, during the so-called Terrible Twos, the Out-of-Bounds Fours, etc. With a baby, a book on development can give you excellent clues on what new feats to watch for from your child, and may provide a fairly accurate timetable for these events — and we're always delighted when a baby performs right on cue, just as we're delighted when a horoscope seems to give an accurate reading of our personality.

Many parents, however, get their sense of competitive pride in their kids' accomplishments tangled up with notions they glean from popular books on child development, and the result can be disappointment with a child who doesn't perform exactly on cue, or even a little ahead of time — we always want Johnny to be first in the class, even if the test is whether or not he can roll over in his crib. Or we can end up with inflated pride in Johnny and unrealistic expectations for his future accomplishments if he happens to be a fast starter and has the jump in a couple of categories on the sample of kids in the "norm." Johnny will probably be as average as the next guy, and his parents' determination that he'll be a genius because he scored high in early walking will only be a hindrance to him in years ahead. So if you do read books on child development, try to use them to learn about how kids grow and perform in general, and not as infallible testing devices for measuring your own child's abilities.

FIRSTS

With or without a guide to child development, you'll be watching for the milestones in your child's career — the first time her smile is clearly directed at you or Mom, and isn't just an involuntary happy expression; the first time she understands something you've said, which will be in the middle of the first year, months before she does any real speaking; of course first walking and first talking . . . but also the first time she gives you a real kiss, the first time she turns to you for comfort, the first time she leads you somewhere, instead of the other way around. For me, this was a truly remarkable feeling with both my boys — to be prodded and pushed and then pulled by the hand across the room by a baby who could hardly walk; after a year of carrying this same child around, almost completely dependent, to be directed, even compelled by his powerful, independent will and determination to move me across the room.

I like to think of a child's new accomplishments as "firsts," and one great pleasure I've had from my kids is watching their excitement and photograph-

ing their expressions as they experience some of the really big "firsts" in their careers: first time seeing fire, first time in the ocean, first ice cream cone. And from time to time — though never on a regular basis — I've taken the trouble to jot down a few of the kids' firsts with significant details and save the

notes. Here is a list of firsts from a couple of red-letter weeks in the middle of Timothy's seventh month:

3 July   Pulled himself up to standing, on straight chair in Dedham at Sean and Judy's house.

4 July   Crawled successfully — for first time — to the strains of Arthur Fiedler and the Boston Pops playing patriotic music on the radio.

5 July   Waved by-by to Judy by opening and closing his hand, and said, "Bbbb . . ."

17 July   First ice cream cone — soft vanilla — at Twirl Top in Tuscarora, Pa. He wouldn't stop eating it.

18 July   First real interest in animals. Very turned on by Buckram and Underfoot, the cats. With much prompting, he said, "Kkkk . . ." for cat.

As with any diary, going through your entries months or years after the events can bring back to life scenes and events that you've completely forgotten. But as with any diary, it's hard to be faithful about making entries. Usually by the time a child is one this kind of father diary lapses because the "firsts" are coming so thick and fast that you hardly have time to enjoy them, let alone write them up.

IT DOESN'T LAST

When you're holding your baby and she's falling asleep in your arms slowly and the evening is slipping away and your mind is racing through the thousand things at the top of your list, and you begin to feel – as all fathers and all mothers inevitably feel from time to time – that you're wasting your time taking care of this little kid, try to remember that next year you won't be able to hold her in the same way, she won't go to sleep in your arms, and after a few more years you'll be happy to get a hug on the run. Our children are here to stay, but our babies and toddlers and preschoolers are gone as fast as they can grow up – and we have only a short moment with each. When you see a grandfather take a baby in his arms, you see that the moment hasn't always been long enough. So – urgent as the other demands in your life may be – try to remember this: A baby in the hand is worth two teen-agers behind a bush.

Chapter 3

JOB

The daughter of an undertaker in a small community where business is slow says: "My dad is around home a lot and I get to see him — only except when he has a body." Our jobs cast the deciding vote on how much time we get to spend with our kids. And in many other ways, too, our jobs and professions determine what kinds of fathers we will be.

When a man chooses a career or a permanent job, about the last thing that's likely to concern him is whether the work will fit in well with family life and fatherhood. Career decisions are usually made long before we become fathers — as often as not while we're still bachelors with no thought in the world about family and responsibilities. So we get ourselves established working at what we want to do or what we feel we have to do, and only later our families enter the picture.

There's always some friction between job and family, no matter how well the two fit together in your life. As I talked with dozens of fathers about their kids, our conversations constantly turned back to their jobs — how the pressures and extra demands of their work interfered with their family lives, how business travel or commuting cut so much time out of their schedules they hardly ever saw their kids, how temporary assignments and transfers had turned their families upside down. Most of us are acutely aware of the intimate link-up between job and home life and feel squeezed between the legitimate demands from both sides. You want to spend plenty of time with the kids, but you have to spend most of your time on the job — or the family will simply collapse. When Scott, five, says, "Daddy, we've got enough money; I don't think you have to go to work tomorrow," his dad can only laugh — much as he'd like to, he can't seriously consider staying home the next day to play ball with his son.

In some jobs the nature of the work makes it next to impossible even to have a family life. Take the merchant marine, for example. Here you don't find too many devoted dads. Months at sea on an oil tanker or down the river with the barges are no help in keeping homes together. A recently divorced executive in a merchant seamen's union, father of a two-year-old girl, told me that the nature of the work tends to rule out family men from the start. And a seaman who decides to marry and settle down has a statistically minuscule chance of staying married. Some find a berth on a tug in a harbor and here the chances are a little better, but the family man in this business is the rare exception rather than the rule.

In working on this book, I've been fascinated to discover that there is one particular job that seems ideal for fatherhood and where involved fathers abound. For months I asked friends and acquaintances to introduce me to friends of theirs whom they thought of as "good fathers" — men who were interested in their kids and in family life — so I could talk with them and gather their thoughts on fatherhood. I found no shortage of good fathers, but strangely most of the men who were being referred to me were schoolteachers. After half a dozen schoolteachers, I stopped bothering to contact teachers when people suggested them, so that I wouldn't end up with a totally lopsided sampling of opinion; and I concentrated on finding involved fathers in a broad range of jobs and professions. But I continued to keep a rough count of schoolteachers, and out of a little over a hundred men suggested, nearly every third "good father" was a schoolteacher. And this wasn't schoolteachers I knew suggesting teacher friends of theirs — I don't have a single teacher friend or acquaintance. This was people from a wide variety of jobs and positions in the community recognizing men they knew in this single job as involved fathers.

Obviously, men who teach are interested in kids, and likely to be interested in their own kids. But teaching also offers a nearly ideal schedule for an involved dad. As the teacher-fathers I talked with pointed out, the hours are regular; in many school situations there aren't heavy after-hours or evening obligations; and the summer vacation gives a man a real opportunity to spend some fulfilling time with his kids. Schoolteachers were the only men I talked with who said they had taken family life into consideration when they chose a career, that they had been conscious of the advantages a teacher's situation had for raising kids. And most of the teachers I talked to were happy to trade off the possibility of high earnings for these advantages.

The other "good fathers" people referred me to represented a surprisingly wide spectrum of types of employment, both blue and white collar — there's a partial list of their jobs on p. ix. There was a fairly good showing of free-lancers, men working out of their own homes — which I had expected because free-lance work with its flexible scheduling has given me such a great opportunity to be close to my kids. But the vast majority of the "good fathers" were nine-to-fivers. I was pleased that aside from the one special case of schoolteachers, involved fatherhood appears to be pretty equally distributed through our society. It seems that only a very few jobs actually deter or prevent a man from being an involved father. But surely every job manages to throw a few obstacles in your path. Even schoolteaching. Since the pay is relatively low, many teachers take a second, moonlighting job in order to feed those kids they are so close to, so there go all the evenings, or maybe the weekends, and then in the summer break many teachers are obliged to take a seasonal job, again to stay ahead of the bills, and that blows the wonderful vacation with the family.

Whatever the conditions of the work, there will be conflicts with family time. A highly paid corporate executive may have no financial worries, but he may have to devote so much time to his career that he becomes a stranger to his kids. Another father, who has trained for a stage career, will give up the struggle to find acting jobs when the kids arrive in his life, and take a steady job in theater management — and he ends up resenting the kids because of his lost opportunities. Still another father will increase his earnings by going on rotating swing shifts in a factory. The pay is good, but the schedule may completely disrupt his life with his family; for six days he works the midnight shift; two days off; six days now on the morning shift; two days off (but notice that these aren't the same two days as last time, and not the standard weekend); then six nights again . . . When they are still young enough to be home all day, this man will see something of his kids, but his times with them are constantly shifting, so the scheduled regularity and predictability that children thrive on are completely missing. And when the kids reach school age, rotating shifts will mean that their father seldom sees them.

On another side of the issue, kids often learn to resent "Daddy's work" because it is obviously what keeps him away from home so much, and what often preoccupies him when he is home. A striking example of this syndrome comes from a harpsichordist I talked with, who has two preschool kids. When I asked him how he went about introducing his children to music, he seemed surprised that I would ask such a question. He hadn't tried to introduce them to music at all, because they wouldn't take to it — they regarded music as a *rival*. Music was Daddy's other love, which took him away from them, and they would have none of it.

Certainly you know where the friction lies in your

own job-family situation, and you also know that there aren't a lot of easy solutions on the horizon. But the two sides of your life needn't be completely set apart, and they needn't be antagonistic. Many fathers I talked with enjoyed teaching their kids about their jobs by taking them on visits to the places where they work and also by bringing home tools, gadgets, and scrap materials to show their children what they do.

A child who is included early on in his father's working life and understands something about it on his own level gets to know what his father is all about — his dad is more than just a man who regularly comes and goes from home and loves him and is alternately kind and angry. His dad has a special working identity that is always a great source of pride to a child and that is one of his first keys for unlocking the mystery of how the world outside his home is set up.

I've talked with many men whose families have made minor adjustments in their schedules that have allowed them some time with the kids — changes as simple as keeping the baby up late so Dad could play with her when he got home from his long commute, as simple as getting everyone in the family up for an early breakfast together. In the sections that follow, I go a little more into the kinds of problems that crop up, but also into ways that fathers have found for building bridges between job and family, and some solutions they've found for balancing out the needs on both sides.

PERSONALITY SPLIT

A man's personality can be split dramatically in two by his working life and his family life. One father may face a fierce daily struggle for survival at the office, real dog-eat-dog competition; he may spend his days trying to subvert the efforts of competitors — both corporate enemies and his own personal rivals — and his business style may be tough as nails — all gruff orders and efficiency. At home he's expected to be a nice guy, genuinely interested in his wife and kids and ready to support them with his affection and his help.

Another father may go every day to a job that he's come to regard as a dead end; for him there's no incentive at work and he continues on simply because he has the job, and now with the kids there's no time to look for a new one — he's stuck and a lot of the reason seems to him to rest with the kids, with the family. At night when he gets home from a day of drudgery, he's expected to be fun-loving and enthusiastic with his kids, to perk up the dreary atmosphere of a household where Mom and the kids have spent the day wearing each other out.

Still another father will work in an absolutely fascinating job, so interesting to him, in fact, that it is his consuming passion. He eats and sleeps his job — it is never out of his mind. At home he's expected to devote himself — his precious time — willingly to helping with the upkeep of the house and the care of the kids.

I doubt that anyone ever completely reconciles these differences. Certainly no one manages to be that perfectly cheerful, helpful, decent sort of Dad most of us feel we're supposed to be. A lot of the working personality will spill over into the way we deal with our kids. We carry our troubles and aggravations back and forth from home to work and we end up taking out on the kids anger we feel over

situations at work. Of course this will spell big trouble for the whole family if it gets out of hand. But most fathers manage to keep it more or less in check, with maybe a weekly outburst where you scream at your wife: "How in hell can I be expected to keep this place going and pay for these kids and stay up with my work . . . !" And the effect on your kids isn't to make them think less of you because you aren't that perfect upright family man, but to make them know that you're a normal human being with the same kinds of strong feelings and emotions that are always sending *them* into violent fits.

One important thing to watch for, though, when you do let off a little steam at home: from about three years old on, kids insist on blaming themselves for everyone's problems. Small children are so egocentric that they often feel they are responsible for everything that happens around them. If you're angry about something that happened at work, and fume and gripe and swear, your child may decide — with no evidence at all except your bad humor — that you're angry at him for something he did. He may even figure out what it was he did that was so bad, have a whole scheme worked out, feel guilty as hell about it — but not tell a soul. A kid with ideas like this will go around glumly or act up terribly to draw down the wrath he is sure he deserves. A child can usually open up and get these feelings off his chest if you pry a little, ask leading questions, and explain that Daddy really was angry at someone else altogether, and why.

PRESSURES

There are always times when the burden at work is increased and you simply have to pitch in. A lawyer with an extra case load or a big trial to prepare for

will be backed up with paperwork that will keep him at the office every night, and on the weekend he'll arrive home with a cram-packed brief case, and even more than that, a mind full of legal quibbles. There's no space here for little kids.

And here I was writing this book about fatherhood, and very conscious that I should have been acting as a model father, always taking the time to be involved with my kids, but with the pressure on to get the text written and delivered on schedule to the publisher, I ended up chained to a desk, spending day and night on the book to the point that I began to feel estranged from Gregory and Timothy. Even though I work at home, I was spending so little time with them that we were growing distant.

A line splicer for a metropolitan power company told me how well his job fit in with his life as a father. His hours — 7 A.M. to 3 P.M. — allow him to give his wife some really substantial help taking care of their severely handicapped baby. He takes over child care for the afternoon-evening shift. But following the big New York blackout of the summer of '77, everyone in the power company worked nearly around the clock for a week or more. There were no afternoons off to take care of the baby.

Many men find their jobs cutting into their family lives not only in emergency situations, but on a regular basis. With a career at stake, or a pressing need for more income, there's often no choice but to cut down on time with the kids. The time has to come from somewhere, and that's usually the only available source.

Add to the demands of a father's career the demands of a company's career, and you really have some pressure. "It's been a young company struggling to get a foothold and they've been really overworking the people that have been there," one man told me about the computer firm he works for. "The people that are in upper management — there've been several levels of upper management purges in the last two or three years, as I guess with any struggling company there are, and they've gone through a number of vice-presidents, that kind of thing — those guys just push and push and push and expect people on down the line to do the same thing, and if you don't . . . for the most part, they weed them out pretty quickly." In the midst of this kind of push, push, push, it's not easy to find time to play with babies.

An analytical chemist who supervises a lab for a

large pharmaceutical corporation says that his company has "enlightened" personnel policies, that in theory the company strives to make the workers happy and take care of their needs as family men so they will do a better job. "But I feel that the production facility kind of chews people up. The people who implement the rules of the company don't always consider these enlightened personnel policies, because a lot of them aren't trained; they're under pressure, you know; they've got to get out twenty thousand kilos of Vitamin C in twelve hours; they just have to. And they just take people and use them as much as they possibly can. Because that's the only thing they can do. . . . And I guess I make decisions like that to a certain degree. . . . It comes to a point where you really have to make a choice whether it's for the company's good or the individual's, and usually it's quite clear what the company's good is; and it's not quite so clear what the individual's is — so you have to go in that direction: with the company."

In small businesses, relations between worker and boss are likely to be easygoing and informal and the boss may be able to understand a father's desire to take a day or more off to help out with a family crisis — say Mom is just recovering from the flu and

both kids are down with it. Some big companies are even able to cope gracefully with situations like this and make the men who work for them feel their needs as family men are understood. But the majority of men I talked with who worked for big organizations knew that the family had better not be sick and need help both Friday and Monday — "I don't think that cuts it with any employer" was the way an insurance underwriter put it. And here's another father, who works for a large, impersonal corpora-

tion: "They understand if you have to take off, but they don't like it, they don't condone it; they're always worried that somebody's going to take off Monday morning. . . . That's just big business — so tied up in rules that they lose perspective. And a lot of the guys making the decisions — their families are already grown, so it's not their problem any more. It's fine to work for them, but I have to realize that they're not going to be any help at all."

Transfers

"If they want somebody to move someplace, it's done pretty much on an arbitrary basis," said one father who works for a giant communications corporation; his small family has already made two major moves since the first child, five, arrived, besides two temporary assignments of four and six months that meant he was several hundred miles away from his kids all week, and only spent weekends with the family.

Businesses with far-flung operations shift their employees around like chessmen. Which is fine if you happen to be a chessman, but when you have small kids who obviously thrive on permanence and regularity, it's a different story. If you have any say in the matter, try to get most of your shifting and transferring out of the way before your child is four. A big move won't make as dramatic a change in the life of a baby or younger child as it will in the life of a child who is already established with friends in the neighborhood or in a nursery school or day care center.

But few men have much say in the matter; if the company feels you can do more good in Topeka than you've been doing in Bridgeport, you pull up stakes and go — family or no family. And kids adapt to new places; there's even a sense of excitement and expectation about moving. It's important to remember, though, in the rush and bustle of getting established in the new place, that your child will be pretty lonely at first, until he gets into a new neighborhood gang or starts in a new school — and an excellent companion for a lonely child is an under-

standing father. You may even feel the need of someone to pal around with yourself in a new town, and since the place is new there'll be no trouble finding things to explore and investigate with your kids.

CHANGES

A trusts and estates lawyer told me that when he went to work for his firm fifteen years ago, all lawyers as a matter of course worked after five evenings, took work home with them, and regularly went to the office on Saturdays. He still carries the pressures of work home with him every night, but he says that the climate has changed a little over the years for a family man in the law — today a lawyer doesn't feel his career will be ruined if he misses working on a Saturday.

Other small changes in the working world are giving men more opportunity to spend time with their kids. Flex-time, or flexitime as it's sometimes called, is the most widespread and dramatic change. Many large companies have adopted this system, which gives employees — usually office workers — some flexibility in their working schedules. Under the system, an employee puts in a regular forty-hour week, but he can choose his hours daily. In a typical flex-time setup, you can start at seven and work till three-thirty, or come in at nine and leave at five-thirty, so long as you are always there during "core hours" — say, nine to eleven and one to three-thirty, which will be the hours during which meetings, conferences, and the like are scheduled.

Flex-time wasn't designed to give fathers more time with their kids. Companies have adopted it because it seems to increase productivity by cutting down on absenteeism; it alleviates rush-hour traffic problems, and it was also designed to give working mothers some chance to align their job hours with child care needs. By working early on flex-time, a woman can pick up a small child at a day care center at a reasonable time in the afternoon — not have to leave him there until it's dark in the winter. And when the kids are older and coming home from school in the middle of the afternoon, Mom can make it home shortly after they do. But the same advantages that flex-time holds for a mother apply to a father as well. It gives you an option between a long breakfast with the family and spending the latter part of the afternoon with the kids; and if both parents have jobs, Dad can be the one to pick the child up from the day care center.

In some few special job situations, husbands and wives with the support of very understanding employers are developing family job-sharing setups so that both parents can contribute equally to child care. Typically, a man and wife will split up the duties of a single teaching position at a college — drawing a single salary, and meanwhile splitting child care duties down the middle. Husband-wife teams who own their own small businesses sometimes split the management duties on pretty much this same basis, and a father in a situation like this can truly be involved with his kids. But obviously the applications of family job sharing are limited.

Somewhat more widespread is the shift to part-time work by fathers seriously interested in sharing the care of their young children with their wives. The women's movement has concentrated much effort on improving possibilities for part-time work so that mothers can find convenient employment. State governments are beginning to make civil service jobs available on a part-time basis with full job security and fringe benefits. And the climate for part-time work is improving as employers adapt their policies to the needs of the ever growing female work force. So part-time work is becoming a much more available option for fathers intent on really taking part in their kids' lives.

DADDY'S WORK

Any preschooler will understand what Daddy does if he sells things in a store, or drives a truck or a combine harvester, or paints a picture, or wears a blue uniform, a badge, and a pistol. And fathers who have jobs like these that are accessible even to toddlers can have a great time showing their kids what they do, because explaining is such a straightforward task. The independent trucker

parks his cab or even the whole eighteen-wheel rig in the driveway of his house on the weekend and the kids all help him wash it down with the hose, and polish the chrome. A big-city public transit bus driver I talked with drives his bus blocks off his assigned route on special occasions to pick up his kids in front of their apartment house. An artist's kids may spend hours during the day in his studio, playing their own games, but also watching Daddy work.

But there are many more jobs that young children can't see and experience so directly and understand so easily. An insurance salesman's work isn't easily explained to a three-year-old, or a bank officer's, or the work of a clerk in a government welfare office. In fact, the majority of office jobs are difficult to explain to kids, and the more complex and sophisticated the industry involved, often the harder explaining becomes.

There are also many jobs that kids could understand pretty well if they were allowed in to see what their fathers were doing, but kids can't usually visit factories, laboratories, construction sites, hospitals, garages, and a great many other places of work.

I've heard dozens of charming anecdotes that illustrate how poorly kids understand what their fathers do at work, the kind of anecdote in which the child knows only that Daddy goes to work to make money and firmly believes that Daddy is running off five-dollar bills on a little printing press. Stories like this are cute enough in small doses, but the big dose of them I've had points to a conclusion that I don't think is at all cute: many preschool kids are literally ignorant of what their fathers do all day. Which means that these kids have a very slender idea of who their fathers are.

When people ask you at a party, "What do you do?" you don't say, "I'm the father of two preschool boys," or, "I'm a weekend handyman." You tell what you do for a living. It's what defines you — even if you don't enjoy doing it. And if you enjoy it, your job is your life. I think our kids deserve to learn even more about us than people we meet casually at parties do. I think a preschooler should know as much about his father's job as he is capable at his age of understanding. And I don't believe it's all that hard to show him or explain to him what we do.

A three-year-old may not be ready to understand exactly what you do all day, but from a visit to the place where you work or a photo of you at work if the place is off limits to kids, she can certainly have a clear notion of where you work and how you do it — let's say it's done with a phone and a dictating machine and file folders. On a visit she will be proud to see her picture on your desk and know that she has this place in your daily life when you're away from home. A four-and-a-half- or five-year-old can definitely be expected to remember the name of what you do even if he doesn't yet understand it in depth. John, five, the son of an investment banker, is in a unique position to say with accuracy, "My daddy makes money," but he says with true accuracy, "My daddy makes money for other people. And they pay him for doing it." I don't think you could pin him down on the precise mechanics of this — his father's job is a sophisticated one. But he has a firm basis for learning more over the years about Daddy's work — always at the level he can understand at the time. And this way he'll be able to learn a lot about his dad.

As fathers we're in an excellent position to explain the whole world of things and ideas to our kids — what better place to begin than by explaining ourselves?

VISITS

Taking your kids with you to the place where you work is the single most important thing you can do to let them share something of your working life. You can tell them all about it — and it's important to do that as well — but preschool kids learn about 90 per cent by direct observation, and only pick up little bits and pieces theoretically. Something a child sees and experiences first hand is real and understandable. A preschooler understands your job on his own terms only if he has seen the desk you sit behind or the machine you operate at work. The process that you're involved in, the product your company makes, the people you work with — every aspect of your job will probably be interesting to your child. But nothing is more useful to him than simply establishing what the devil you do during those nine or more hours you're away from home every day — where you sit, what toys you play with, what tools you use, what it looks like.

I emphasize this seemingly obvious point because so many men have told me that the reason they haven't taken their preschoolers to work with them is that they think the kids won't be interested in what they see there — it's just desks and files. It may indeed be just desks and files to you, or whatever your workplace looks like may well be humdrum and boring to you after five or ten years day in and day out. But remember, your preschooler has probably never seen a desk or a filing cabinet before, and kids are interested in everything they see and in everything *you* do. I've talked to fathers who have taken their kids at great expense to Disney World and Great Adventure amusement parks, but never to their own offices — because the kids would be bored at the office. But I've also talked to many other men who have taken their kids to the office and several have said things like this: "You know,

taking the kids with me to work is like a trip to Disneyland for them; they really dig it."

"Ordinary" Offices

You don't need anything glamorous or exciting in the place where you work to make your kids happy. The most important part for them is simply being there and seeing what it's like. And beyond that there will be plenty for a child to do on a short visit, no matter how "ordinary" the place. Very few kids can resist the allure of perfectly routine office supplies: pencils, pens, erasers, paper clips, staplers, tape, paper.

Make a quick inventory of the gadgets and machines in the place and let the kids have a go at these. Almost every office of any kind has a calculator that the kids can punch the buttons on without doing any harm. And don't forget the office copier — which makes wonderful prints of children's hands. Or a child can make a copier collage by arranging some small objects — bent paper clips, coins, pieces of chewing gum (still in wrappers,

please), anything that comes to hand — and copying them. Copiers do silhouettes of kids' rings, belt buckles, and braids, and whatever else they can think to put in there. It's always a good idea for a child on a visit to bring along a favorite book and a couple of small toys to fill in some time when you will be busy, and these can go in the copier, too. A drawing that a child does at your office can be copied — or favorite drawings can be brought along from home specially to be copied.

Kids can sing or recite rhymes or talk into a dictation machine and hear it played back.

The ordinary old office typewriter is a kind of spectacular toy in the eyes of most kids. You can usually leave a child of two or older alone with a manual typewriter and no harm will come to either of them beyond the keys all getting pushed at once and the works sticking temporarily, but I think you should supervise preschool kids on electric typewriters, particularly on sophisticated models with interchangeable type face balls and other fancy features — I can jam a machine like this through simple ignorance, so I'm sure a preschooler could play havoc with one.

There's always something around to delight your child, even if it's the elevator you arrive in, a water cooler to be held up to for a drink, or a new bathroom to explore.

Co-workers

The people you work with are another attraction for your kids. No matter how reserved or aloof they may act toward you, they will be curious and interested to meet your kids and will welcome them with smiles. The crabbiest and most officious office workers regularly become genial, animated, and helpful when kids come for a visit. So, among other things, you may be cheering up the lives of some of your fellow workers.

Some men hesitate to take the kids to work for fear they will embarrass them with a lot of silly behavior or a temper tantrum. But the risk of this kind of embarrassment is really very small. We always see our kids at home, where they are totally relaxed — and they do their worst at home — at every age and stage. But in a special situation like a visit to Daddy's office, most kids can be counted on

to behave (almost) like angels. Of course if your child is in the throes of the "Terrible Twos" and pulls supermarket tantrums with regularity, or if he's going through some other siege of antisocial behavior, don't take him to the office. But please don't exclude him just on the grounds of ordinary rambunctious childish behavior. It's about five to one he'll do you proud. And if he whimpers or pouts or plays shy or runs in the corridor or knocks a stack of papers over, no one will blame you. Most of the others have kids, too.

More than One

Fathers who have taken groups of their children to work with them point out that it's a lot harder situation to manage than one at a time. As always with two kids or more, the group mentality can take over — and that's a silly mentality. It's certainly safer to take your kids for solo visits. But then you and they may have more fun in the long run in a bunch, and there won't be any recriminations about who got the first turn and who got to go for the longest visit and so on. I'd prefer risking a little screeching outside the boss's office to having to listen to this kind of contentious quibbling at home.

Getting There

Getting to the place where you work can be more than half the fun, especially if you use public transportation. When I talk to preschoolers about their visits to Daddy's work, they often have much more to say about the bus or the subway or the train they rode there on than about the actual visit; they will describe the ride in detail, telling about the people on the bus or the noise of the subway. In fact, kids

who haven't the vaguest idea what Daddy does at work, because they've never been on a visit, can always tell you how he gets there, and they are usually very proud of the fact that he travels on a commuter train or drives his car.

If your preschooler isn't accustomed to riding on public transportation — and most who live outside the largest metropolitan centers aren't — taking an ordinary public bus can be a very big deal. It's new and it's an adventure. A train or subway is even more of an adventure — a little scary, too, sometimes for a child as young as three.

Even if you regularly drive to work, think about the possibility of taking your kids there by public transportation — which may make it a truly memorable occasion for them.

Timing

Finding a good time for the kids to visit Daddy's work may be tricky. Of course if you live near where you work and you have a flexible schedule in an easygoing work situation, your kids will probably be in and out of the place regularly — with you when you stop by in the evening or on the weekend to attend to some small matter, or coming by with your wife for a short visit during the day. You may even bring them along for brief periods during the working day when no one else can take care of them. But for most men at work, things aren't quite so relaxed and convenient. The place where you work may be an hour's commute or more in each direction and the atmosphere there may be orderly and formal.

A preschooler obviously can't be expected to stay contented through a day-long visit to an office, which in practical terms means that the visit will have to be on a day off — and best on a weekday off, when there will be people and activity. Since going back to work on a day off is hardly a treat for most of us, the visit to Daddy's work sometimes gets sidetracked and then put off indefinitely. But considering how much your child can learn about you through the visit, it's worth a day of vacation time. And you can look at the visit as a special vacation excursion for the kids, and even add other activities that might give you some pleasure. After all, the actual visit is only going to last an hour — tops. More than that and a preschooler will be restless and ready to leave, and may become a distraction to people who are trying to work. Probably the best time of day for a visit is around the lunch hour, when people are free to stop and talk with the kids, and there won't be anything happening that they can interrupt.

You may find yourself enjoying the visit to Daddy's work as much as your kids will. One man told me: "You know, I resisted taking Becky and Rich to the office for years; it seemed like a crazy long trip for nothing — forty-five minutes each way on the train and you have to take the tubes into the city and a subway four stops from there, and my kids have never traveled well. But when we finally got it organized and went, they had such a ball the whole way and at the office — it was like seeing the whole daily commuting grind and the office and all through their eyes, and, you know, it didn't look so bad that way."

You'll want to come prepared with a bag full of snacks, equipment to keep the kids clean, and a few books and toys to keep them occupied in odd moments; see p. 172 for more on preparations for day trips with kids. There's no reason to wait till your child is toilet trained to take her where you work, especially if it's nearby and convenient — everybody loves a baby or a toddler, and you can always carry disposable diapers and wet wash-up cloths.

Another point to remember is that the trip to Daddy's work doesn't have to be an exclusively father-child event; Mom is welcome to come along, though she may well opt to stay behind and have a moment for herself if she has the choice.

KIDS AT WORK

Sometimes you get into a situation that calls for keeping a child with you at work for more than just a casual visit — anything over an hour. And here you need careful preparation and plenty of things to keep your child entertained and occupied, especially if you won't be free to play with her. You know your child's attention span, and just because she's in the novel surroundings of a workplace, it isn't magically going to triple or quadruple itself. So if your child is going to stay at the office for a couple of hours — say between the end of nursery school and the end of your day — you'll need to make more than routine preparations.

Some small room or a space behind a screen or the like will be needed — a mini child care center. You'll have to have a sizable collection of kids' books and some basic toys like a set of blocks — your child's current favorites. And you or someone the child is familiar with will have to be in a position to look in regularly — at least every twenty minutes. Of course, this kind of setup is usually only possible for the boss or the owner of the business.

NO KIDS ALLOWED

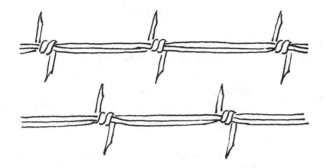

Most of this section has been directed toward men who work in offices. But there are plenty of other places where men work: construction sites, factories, workshops, garages, laboratories, hospitals. And kids would love to visit their fathers in these places, too, but they're simply not allowed in. Safety considerations and regulations exclude kids in many situations, and security rules cut them out of others. You can't childproof a factory or a lab or a hospital, so you make it off limits to kids.

A research scientist explains why his four kids can't visit his lab: "Any major pharmaceutical company will not allow children in the buildings. Everybody up here's afraid of getting sued. . . . I have benzene in my laboratory and if somebody spilled benzene and a child got a lot of it in the lungs and for some reason got liver toxicity — then you've run into a problem and the company could be sued for allowing that to happen. But I have a neat job and it would be exciting for the kids to see."

A father I talked with who works on big roofing jobs has no way to take his two preschoolers up and show them what he does: it's high and there are no guardrails. Another man's kids weren't allowed in the Research and Development department he worked for because the secrecy surrounding the operation excluded all visitors.

Job Photos

If your kids are shut out of the place where you work, take along a camera one day and shoot lots of pictures of the place. Have someone else snap shots of you actually doing your job — talking on the telephone, operating a machine, whatever you do. With good hard documentary evidence like this your preschooler can have a relatively clear idea of what you do during the time you're away from home. And making a few photos won't take any time

or strenuous effort, and won't seriously interrupt anyone's working day.

A slide presentation of photos like this will make a big impression on your kids, or they can have prints to look at whenever they like. If you work in a particularly noisy place, it might be fun to make a tape recording of the sounds of the place to play for the kids: the clatter of typewriters, the grinding of machinery.

Other Evidence

Tours of factories and labs are sometimes offered to employees' families on a yearly basis, but preschoolers and even kids up through the middle teens may be excluded. On the weekend you can take your kids by and show them the outside of the place where you work; it isn't much, but it will give them another clue to go on.

Men in construction trades can sometimes get their kids into a work site on the weekend. A building contractor I talked to takes his three kids on Saturday or Sunday to see the progress of houses his company is putting up. Around construction machinery, if you can't get the kids up in the cab for safety reasons, at least let them touch the machines. This sounds like a very little thing, but it is what a three-year-old will passionately want to do: simply touch the side of the bulldozer. Just looking at it doesn't do the whole job; running up and touching it is the thrill.

EXPLAINING

If your job is so complex that you feel your wife isn't even sure what you do every day or you have an "invisible" job where your kids are literally excluded from seeing what you do, it will probably take some ingenuity to explain to your preschoolers.

When we talk to foreigners or visit another country and have to make ourselves understood, we go to a lot of trouble to get across the simplest ideas. We resort to pantomime and sign language, draw pictures, and do charades just to get directions to the cathedral or to drive a bargain for a souvenir. We can go to the same kind of trouble to explain to our preschool kids — who are essentially still speaking "tourist" English — what we do all day.

I don't mean they need to know all the details, all the intricacies of your job or profession. A lawyer joked that he couldn't explain his work to his kids on this level: "Now, children, pay close attention to your father as he changes the Whereas clause in this document. A lesser practitioner would only have bungled this delicate operation . . ." Naturally you won't go into subtleties. But a preschooler can understand basic notions — whether you sit at a desk or stand up to use a tool. What kinds of machines or tools you use — including the dictaphone, the wrench, the paper clip, the brief case, and the sample book.

One inventive father I talked to, in an effort to explain his complex job in the computer industry, brought home from work a projector and a marketing film that describes his company and its services, and showed it to his preschoolers. Pictures in books — including union magazines, trade magazines, and other business publications — may be some help in explaining an invisible or complicated job. And you might try simple dramatic skits where you and your wife and kids — at ages five and six — act out the things you do at work.

How much kids are able to understand about what Daddy does depends very much on their ages. At three a child is doing fine if she can characterize Daddy's job by the tools he uses; a three-year-old can understand that an author is a typist, and that an executive talks to people on the phone. By four and a half, though, a child should have a ready and generally correct answer to "What does your daddy do at work?" — something much more specific than "He makes money." Even if he doesn't understand exactly what it is, he can say, "He's a chemist," or, "He makes automobiles in a factory," or, "He's a

market analyst." And little by little at the level our kids are ready for and by using some imagination, we can fill them in on the details.

BRINGING WORK HOME

Keep an eye on the things you handle every day at work, especially the ones you and the people around you are throwing out — you may find lots of things to bring home for your kids. Fathers who work in offices often have access to reams of waste computer paper, teletype paper, and other materials like the ends of reels of punch paper tape.

Children who draw a lot will love to have big supplies of paper from your office. Used computer paper, in fact, has become the standard nursery school drawing paper in places where local firms contribute it; Gregory's drawings from nursery school usually had long printed-out lists of numbers on the opposite side with headings like "Daily Inventory of Chemical Product Lots [1221–1231]." Someday industrial spies will start snooping around child care centers.

One man showed me a big collection of heavy-duty cardboard cylinders that his son, four, uses as building blocks; they're the rollers the paper for the office copier comes on, and he had salvaged them from the wastebasket. If you're in construction, there will always be blocks of wood to bring home for the kids to nail together; and there'll be short ends of pipe and pieces of many-colored telephone wire and dozens of other scraps that preschoolers can make things with.

A furniture salesman brings home the world's longest rubber bands, which are used to wrap carpeting, and sometimes he has plastic bubble packaging material from around lamps, and his kids sit there by the half hour popping the bubbles. From other jobs, fathers bring home styrofoam "peanuts" that are used for packing, and which kids string with needle and thread to hang around the Christmas tree and around themselves. Sturdy cardboard boxes often arrive home with fathers — which the

kids can convert into cars, trains, stoves, playhouses, or just climb on.

A doctor's kids get to play with some of the equipment in his bag, just as a plumber's kids are always grabbing the wrenches from his truck. But if you don't ordinarily bring home the tools of your trade, see if there isn't some gadget that's easily carried that would fascinate the kids. Several fathers told me they had brought home office calculators and lightweight computer terminals. There's bound to be something around, even if it's as commonplace as an office stapler — if you use it at work, your child will be interested in it.

So be on the lookout for tangible parts of your work that you can bring home to share with your kids. This is just one more little link between work and family life that will make your children feel they have a stake in what you do all day.

PROXY VISITS

Occasionally take some small thing of your child's to work with you. Borrow a toy for the day — not a favorite toy, because no kid wants to part with a treasure. But let's say your three-year-old has a small Big Bird figure she occasionally plays with. Big Bird can ride in your pocket or brief case or lunch box when you go to work. And in the evening, Big Bird can tell the story of his exciting visit when he gets home, describing the ride there, the people he saw and talked to, the things that were happening. Coming from Big Bird or some other puppet friend, the story will be a vivid one for your child.

COMMUTING

When a friend asked Melissa, three, where her daddy worked, she was quick to answer because she knew for certain that she and her mom drove him there every morning and picked him up there every evening: "My daddy works at the train station."

And her commuter dad is working *long* hours at that train station. If Melissa could count and keep time, she'd discover that there are over twelve hours between the time he arrives at the station ready for work and the moment they pick him up. When the family car pulls into the driveway at home each evening, she'll kiss Daddy good night and it's off to bed for her. And next morning she'll see him, but only briefly and on the way to the train station, and there won't be time for play. Another nice hug and a kiss and Daddy's gone again for the day.

It's a familiar story. The city's a lousy place to bring up kids, you reason, but it's the only place you can make a living. So you look for a place to live within commuting distance, and it quickly becomes obvious that the kind of house you'd like for your family is way out of your price range if it's anywhere near the city. The circle you've drawn on the map that puts you within a half-hour commute is replaced by a much wider circle after your first talk with a real estate agent. By the time you find a house you can almost afford, the commuting time is up to an hour and a half each way. But those are the breaks, and that's what the other guys you work with do for their families, you reason. So you join the army of family men that advances and retreats every day from the city. The only problem is that you get to see much less of that nice little family you're setting up in a comfortable establishment.

Three hours a day commuting is fifteen hours a week — which is to say, almost two full working days. You are in effect working nearly a seven-day week.

Or say you work for a corporation that has moved out of the city to spacious quarters near a small town. Again you find that the real estate close by is at a premium. Or word has it that the school system is no good, so you look further and by the time you've found a house and a school system that's up to snuff, you may be a forty-five-minute drive from where you work, a drive that you'll discover actually takes a full hour during peak times when everybody else is making it.

In many parts of the country it's unusual for a young family man to live near where he works; where I live, men commonly spend as many as four hours a day commuting. For young commuting fathers it's almost always the same circular story: you buy the house and put up with the commuting for the kids' sake, but the commuting keeps you from seeing those kids — except in the briefest encounters — five days out of the week.

There's no ready solution to this enigma; it's part of our national system. The system allows you the eventual possibility of moving closer to where you work; with success and advancement you may be able to afford a house closer in toward the city. I often take suburban trains into Manhattan, and it's interesting to notice that at the stations furthest out on the line, the commuters who get on are mostly in their twenties and thirties, while closer to Manhattan in expensive communities, the passengers who board the train are mostly successful-looking men in their late forties and fifties. These older guys can afford to spend less time commuting, and presumably could spend more time with their kids. But by another funny twist of circumstance, their kids are teen-agers who haven't any time for Dad, or they're already away at college.

LATE BEDTIMES

One way that several commuter fathers I talked to came to terms with the problem of never seeing their kids in the evening was simply by changing bedtime from the traditional seven-to-seven-thirty slot and putting the kids to bed around nine. These were men who had been leaving work late — around five-thirty or six — spending well over an hour in transit, and getting home to a hushed house and sleeping kids.

At the end of a long, hard day, sleeping kids look just great — no screeching, no begging for attention, no climbing on your tired back, no knees in the groin. Just what the doctor ordered: little angels dreaming of sugarplums while you relax, have a leisurely dinner . . .

But there's another side to this. A father of two preschool girls who commutes three and a half hours daily told me: "I hardly even saw the baby during the week. I'd sneak in at night and kiss her, but I was usually awake and gone before she woke up, so it was like I only saw her on the weekends, and I know *divorced* guys who see their kids as often." A little adjustment of the baby's schedule let him play with her for an hour every evening.

Most babies can have their timetables adjusted to fit yours. The specific hour at which a baby goes to sleep or wakes up isn't important; the important part is only that she get the right *amount* of sleep — which is never a problem, because children always take the amount of sleep they need. But let's say your baby needs twelve hours a night. It doesn't make a bit of difference if those hours run from 7 P.M. to 7 A.M. or from 11 P.M. to 11 A.M. By shifting nap time a little each day, and putting the baby to bed a little later each night, you can change her hours to fit better with yours. If you've ever been in a siesta-taking country like Spain or Mexico, you know that infants and toddlers keep hours much different from those in our country — they're up till late in the evening because it's convenient for their parents that way.

When kids reach three, though, the situation changes, and it isn't as easy to let them stay up to nine o'clock or later. A three-year-old may have started nursery school and will have to be up on time with the rest of the world, which in practice means that bedtime will be around seven-thirty or eight.

Many fathers of preschoolers find that the best time to see their kids each day is over a long breakfast, and change their kids' schedules and their own to fit in an early meal together; see p. 76 for some fathers' thoughts on kids and early rising.

There's so little leeway in a schedule that includes a full working day plus a long commute that you may find yourself having to contrive strict schedules and think of your time with the kids very formally — as a Father's Hour that shouldn't be missed — in order to keep those times from slipping away and disappearing from your life and your children's.

COMMUTER'S WELCOME

If you are met, as so many commuters are, at the station or the bus stop by your wife and kids, you might try organizing a little fanfare for your own daily return. In common practice the commuter return scene looks like this: the station wagon pulls up punctually as Dad walks out of the station; Dad gets into the front seat with a peck for Mom and maybe some playful hair-tousling over the back of the seat for the kids, who continue on with their eternal strife.

But the scene doesn't have to be played out in this humdrum way. If you can convince your wife and kids to park the car and get out each time they pick you up, you may find yourself getting a big warm welcome. Especially if the kids can get out on the station platform and see the train or the bus pull in. For kids there's magic and romance in the arrival of

a train or a bus, and you'll be the beneficiary of this magic. Of course it takes a little longer; a greeting like this will take an extra seven to ten minutes a day — possibly even longer if you dawdle on the platform playing with the kids after the train pulls out.

If you're a veteran commuter, this little vision of a warm family welcome on the station platform may sound very farfetched and contrived, because it's hardly something you see every day. But I actually know a man who gets this royal welcome each evening from his wife and two preschool boys as he steps bone-weary at seven-thirty from the BMT train at Boston's Forest Hills station. He's my brother-in-law, and whenever I visit him and my sister, I like to go along for the ride on these evening commuter pickups because they're such cheerful events — the boys are always keyed up with the excitement of the train's arrival, and they fling themselves on their dad.

Maybe you, too, can trade off a little drive-up convenience for some warm welcoming hugs.

FAMILY FIFTEEN

Even though the long hours of commuting are a kind of transition between family and work, work and family, for most train and bus commuters, these hours belong firmly in the world of work, and aren't identified in any way with family life. References to families in commuters' conversations are only passing ones: "How are the wife and kids?" "Fine." Talk centers on business or sports or other subjects men have in common. And some men spend their commuting time with an open attaché case, actually working.

A number of men who commute by train have told me that they have a hard time "shifting gears" between their working personalities and their personalities as family men when they get home. But men who drive to work say they are able to relax on the way home and change over with little difficulty. I think this is largely because a train or bus commuter is still in a kind of working environment on the way home — surrounded by others like himself who may be relaxing a little, having a drink together, but who are still behaving essentially as one business or professional man to another. Whereas the guy driving his own car is in fact in a state of transition between work and home life; he's left job and fellow workers behind and as he drives home his thoughts are just as likely to be about his family and their needs as they are to be about his job and its demands. So by the time he gets home he is a family man, whereas the train or bus commuter steps off onto the platform at home still thinking and acting pretty much as he does at work.

My modest suggestion for bus and train commuters is that you assign say fifteen minutes on the return trip to thinking of yourself as a family man, as a father, and actually doing something that relates to your family during that time. You could take out a pad and pencil and try to design that sandbox you've been meaning to build for the kids for two years now. Or you could mull over why your son at five is always pushing you away, and try to figure out what the next step is. You could make up a new bedtime story, or you might have along a book about a hobby you want to get into with the kids. These are just random suggestions; you'll certainly know best how to use your own family fifteen minutes.

MORNING FAREWELLS

If you're up and gone before the kids are awake, there's no chance for a fond farewell. But one father

— a pediatrician who is out of the house at six each morning — has found a small solution to this one. He pours glasses of fruit juice for his preschoolers and sometimes leaves notes to them under the glasses of juice. Just little tokens of his having been there and having thought about them. But tokens like these are important to kids. Those morning glasses of juice poured by Daddy on his way to work are like the empty glass of milk consumed by Santa Claus as he stops on his busy rounds. They are hard evidence, visible proof that somebody who cared very much was there.

BUSINESS TRAVEL

"Unfortunately, I think I missed what would have been my proudest moment as a father," said one man I talked to. "It was one of her great performances. I was on a business trip and I missed the first-grade play, and there were glowing reports of how she was bound for a major New York stage — and here I was in Chicago. I'd been called away on something I couldn't get out of."

Business travel can take a heavy toll on family life, too. An investment banker, father of a boy, five, and

a baby girl, told me he had been traveling an average of six days a month to points as far away as Nome, Alaska, to service bond accounts for the New York bank he was working for. Six days out of thirty — not *that* many. But he thought it had been enough to set up a bad situation for the whole family. He felt that he simply wasn't on the scene, and he knew his wife had started to feel that way too. His family is much closer now that he has a new position working for an investment banking firm, most of whose clients are within the metropolitan area — a job with more responsibility and much less travel.

Other fathers I've talked to, though, are certain that they and their families can take six days of business travel a month and more in their stride. In fact, several men who travel extensively for business felt that their kids took their regular absences pretty much as a matter of course — just as kids take any working father's daily absences from home as a matter of course. It's what they expect.

INFREQUENT TRAVEL

Regular business travel by fathers seems actually to be much less of a problem for infants and preschoolers than special one-time trips taken by fathers who are normally home every evening. Kids are apt to become upset when their routines are broken and it's a big break when one trusty, regular parent disappears for a while. Some fathers even find themselves rejected when they get home from a trip, by a child who is apparently angry that she was deserted. I have read about this happening and I've been told second hand by a number of people stories of men who came home to a silent treatment by a preschooler. But I have never actually talked to anyone who experienced it, so I'm sure it isn't an everyday phenomenon. Many of the fathers I've talked with have been on infrequent trips with no dire consequences — as I have.

Kids really miss their fathers when they're away — of that I'm certain. On a two-week stay in southern Maryland, I called home every other night, and one evening I told Gregory, four, "I'll see you in only two more days. That's not long." "But, Daddy," he groaned, "I miss you. Two days — that's an awful lot of weeks."

PREPARATIONS

It's a good idea to keep your kids abreast of travel plans — especially if you aren't a regular business traveler and your trip is going to make a major change in family routine. I don't mean that you should make a big deal of an upcoming trip for a month in advance till your toddler or preschooler expects some cataclysmic event in his life. I just mean that you can include him in family conversations about the trip, answer his questions about it, and point out that a trip means Daddy will be gone for a few days (or a week, or whatever), but that Daddy will come home, just as he comes home every night from work.

Until a baby is over a year old, when an object or a person disappears from view or leaves the room, as far as she's concerned, that's it for the object or person — poof, it vanishes, never to return. Her world is still so self-centered that she can't yet understand that things continue to exist somewhere outside her field of vision. In the language of child development specialists, she doesn't have a good working concept of "object permanence."

In the latter part of the first year, a baby is likely to cry bitterly each time Mom leaves the room — he's become strongly attached to her, completely dependent on her, but he isn't yet positive she hasn't vanished — poof. Babies love the game of peek-a-boo because it helps them to come to terms with this quandary: you're gone, but you come right back. Every baby of course eventually learns that things are still there, even though he isn't looking at them. But for the rest of our lives, I think, a bit of that doubt lingers — when someone very close to us goes away for a while, we worry, and I suspect that somewhere at the bottom of that worrying is the infantile fear that Poof — there will be no return.

Certainly some of this doubt lingers in the minds of toddlers and preschool kids — and we can reassure them before we leave for a trip that we definitely are coming back.

A day or two before you leave, make a big deal of the trip, so that your kids can feel they're in on it, and so that they understand on their level what you're about to do. By a big deal, I mean spreading out road maps or opening an atlas or spinning around a globe and pointing out where you're going.

Or tack a road map up on a wall and trace out your route with a thick-tipped marker.

A two- or three-year-old won't have much of an idea how a map works, unless you've worked with her on it, and even then her concept will be very sketchy. And though a four-year-old may understand roughly that they represent places, maps and charts for him are still peopled with monsters like the maps of Columbus' time. If you put a big X to mark your destination, he will be certain you're going into the lair of the pirates. Your road map won't give your child a clear-cut idea of where and how far you're going. But it will give him something real to look at that represents the trip, and even a two-and-a-half-year-old is up to learning to point and say: "My daddy is going *there*."

You can also explain, on your child's level, why you're going and what you plan to do while you're there. And definitely if you're flying or going by train, talk about airplanes or railroads; have the kids get out a toy plane, or read a bedtime story about a train.

Packing your suitcase can be another big deal that the kids can share. They can help by fetching shoes and deciding which necktie you should take and arranging things in the suitcase, and always by sitting on the lid to squeeze all the stuff in so the fasteners will snap closed.

Reminders

If you travel regularly, there should be a picture of Daddy permanently posted in the kids' room or on the bulletin board or the refrigerator door. Even if you travel infrequently, it's good idea to post a picture of yourself before you go. Any snapshot will do, but the best picture is one that shows you with the whole family, all smiles.

You can leave other little reminders of yourself before a trip. Most preschoolers will be honored by being entrusted with some object of yours while you're gone. One man told me that when he was a boy his father would always bring his meerschaum pipe in its rosewood stand to his room before he left on a business trip. "I am entrusting this to you, son," he would say, "because I value it highly. Guard it with your life." But you don't need high drama for this routine. Say your three-year-old is passionately attached to your reel-in tape measure; leave it with her — let her play with it as a special treat while you're away. Or a six-year-old could be allowed to keep your calculator in his room on condition that he be super careful with it.

A baby can also be given something to remember Daddy by — if there's anything he associates with you that can't be hurt by a little chewing: a set of keys like yours but not the real thing, because they're bound to get lost, or a slipper, or an old cap or hat.

Taped Bedtime Stories I think the best reminder you can leave your kids is your voice on tape. If you simply turn on a tape recorder while you're reading a bedtime story one evening shortly before your trip, your child will have something of you to listen to over and over until you get back. I make new recordings before each trip I take because it's so easy to do and because the kids have usually out-

grown or lost interest in the last stories on the tape after an interval of three months or half a year, which is as often as I travel. Even at that slow rate, we're building up quite a backlog of titles on Daddy's Tape.

One nice embellishment you can add to these bedtime story tapes is the trick used on professionally made story records for kids: whenever the page should be turned so the child can follow along and look at the right page with the appropriate illustration, there is a little bell sound or a gong. "Now, children, when you hear this sound [ting-a-ling], turn the page." When you're going to make your

story tape, find a bell or a whistle or any little noisemaker — a water glass and a wooden spoon will do the job — and get your child poised and ready to ring or tinkle or toot whenever the page is turned. There will probably be a lot of extraneous tinkling or tooting between pages or you both may miss a couple of turns if the story is going along interestingly, but after hearing the tape a couple of times your child will find her way through the illustrations perfectly, no matter how goofed up the page-turning cues are. And all the tinkling and tooting and the giggles, too, will remind her of the important part about making the tape: "That's *me*. I ranged that bell with my daddy." See p. 335 for notes on getting good clear sound on your tape.

If you're a bedtime story *teller*, by all means turn the tape on for your own story, rather than just for a store-bought one.

At the end of the story, I let the tape run on Record while we go through the rest of the current bedtime ritual, which in our house has never been very elaborate. Later I sign off with a little thought like: "I love you and I'll be back at the end of my trip."

While I'm away, the kids actually get to hear more of me each evening than they usually do, because I only read the story and do the ritual a few times a week, and they play the tape over and over before bed while I'm gone.

For a child who isn't yet old enough for a bedtime story, it's still fun to leave a tape. For Timothy at eight months, I did a tape of several phrases I thought he might pick up on, repeating them over and over, each for a couple of minutes. Rita and he enjoyed listening and he waved a little on by-by, but couldn't be jollied into playing peek-a-boo with the tape recorder. At eighteen months, though, he would say "Da-Da" excitedly while listening to an updated list of phrases, and he was able to follow some standard eighteen-month questions: "Where are Timothy's ears?" "Where is Timothy's nose?" and point, respectively, to his hair and his eyes.

Your tapes may end up being stored and treasured for years. My wife still has and occasionally plays a disc recording her father made for her at age one during World War II. It was cut in a coin-operated booth in Grand Central Station and on it he croons "Daddy's Little Girl."

STAYING IN TOUCH

Regular phone calls are the way most of us stay in touch when we're on a trip, and for kids it's great to hear your voice and know you're still around, but long-distance conversations are brief, especially for kids — who aren't allowed to hang on the line and be silly. And it's just your disembodied voice — no better, really, than a tape recording. Which is one reason I like the taped bedtime story, which can be played at a child's leisure and as often as he likes if he's up to pushing the buttons in the right sequence.

Postcards

Postcards from a trip are hugely appreciated by kids; they're visible, physical proof that you remembered. If you're going to send them and have them arrive home before you do, you have to make it the first order of business on getting to your destination. Postcards theoretically go at the same speed as all other first-class mail, but anyone who has ever sent them knows it doesn't work that way. Carry some stamps in your wallet; buy postcards in the airport or at the hotel desk when you check in;

write them quickly; and get them in a mail slot.

If you have more than one child, their postcards will never arrive on the same day. To avoid the griping and hurt feelings that will inevitably follow when one gets a card and the others don't, put all the cards together in a single envelope with all their names on it, or place each card in an individually addressed envelope with a first-class stamp.

Letters

Letter writing is disappearing fast in our world of steep postal rates and inexpensive long-distance telephoning, but in the past, it was of course the only way to stay in touch from a distance, and many kids got thoughtful, long letters from their fathers that they could squirrel away and take out and look at over and over — even if they were too young to read. And since the letters of famous men eventually find their way into print, we have some wonderful examples of how fathers corresponded with their kids in the past.

In a cheerful letter to his young daughter Chouchou, the composer Debussy dashes off a line of music that he calls a Ballet for Fleas. And here are romantic lines from a letter by the poet Samuel Taylor Coleridge to his son Derwent, seven, when Coleridge was on a visit to his friend Wordsworth in 1807: "It will be many times the number of years, you have already lived, before you can know and feel thoroughly, how very much your dear Father wishes and longs to have you on his knees, and in his arms. . . . For you are a big Thought, and take up a great deal of room in your Father's Heart: and his eyes are often full of tears thro' his Love of you, and his Forehead wrinkled from the labor of his Brain, planning to make you good, wise and happy." I won't quote the rest of this long letter, which is made up of some of the heaviest-handed moralizing in the English language; Derwent is admonished never to vex his father and mother because it is wicked, and other such — which was the parenting style of the day. I assume that Derwent ignored the good advice but treasured and read and reread the romantic thoughts of his father that I have quoted.

Teddy Roosevelt was forever writing notes and letters to his children — from his camp near Santiago, from wild animal hunts around the country, from the White House when the kids were away. These letters, complete with lively illustrations he drew when the kids were still too young to read, were published in 1919 as *Theodore Roosevelt's Letters to His Children*, and he said at the time, "I would rather have this book published than anything that has ever been written about me." It is indeed a fascinating record of the unofficial side of the Rough Rider that shows how much time, care, and thought a man with such a pressing career could devote to his kids and how much joy he derived from his family life. Here are a couple of samples, both to his youngest son, Quentin.

White House, June 12th, 1904.
The little birds in the nest in the vines on the garden fence are nearly grown up. Their mother still feeds them.

You see the mother bird with a worm in her beak, and the little birds with their beaks wide open!

I was out walking the other day and passed the Zoo; there I fed with grass some of the two-year-old elk; the bucks had their horns "in the velvet." I fed them through the bars.

White House, April 1, 1906.
Slipper and the kittens are doing finely. I think the kittens will be big enough for you to pet and have some satisfaction out of when you get home, although they will be pretty young still. I miss you all dreadfully, and the house feels big and lonely and full of echoes with nobody but me in it; and I do not hear any small scamps running up and down the hall just as hard as they can; or hear their voices while I am dressing; or suddenly look out through the windows of the office at the tennis ground and see them racing over it or playing in the sand-box. I love you very much.

PRESENTS

Should you always bring presents home from a business trip? Most traveling fathers have strong views on this point. Here is a regional sales manager who is on the road three days out of each week and who purposely doesn't bring presents to his twin girls: "There's nothing worse than a guy coming home from a trip — and say he's depressed — he comes in and stoops over to kiss the kids and they grab his suitcase to see what he brought them. I want them to kiss *me*. . . . If you're down in the dumps — nobody appreciates you and all that — and all of a sudden you're walking in the house and your little kids are grabbing your suitcase, then you *really* know nobody appreciates you."

Other men tell me they routinely pick up trinkets and don't mind a little present begging when they get home. A middle-of-the-road view on this issue was expressed by the most seasoned traveler I talked with, a partner in the consulting division of a public accounting firm who seldom sees a week go by without a flight somewhere nationally or internationally: "I don't believe I should bring Alec [five] a toy every trip, because I don't want him to be in the habit; I want it to be a fun thing, an exciting thing. . . . Now, this week I gave him something two times in a row; it just depends on my mood and his mood

and how we're going, but he really doesn't expect it. In other words, there are many times when I'll say, 'Daddy didn't bring you a toy this time,' and then there'll be times when Daddy forgot. As far as picking out something he wants, my 'hit ratio' is less than fifty per cent. Of course, the selection at airports is very limited and very expensive and Bea gets very upset with me if I spend money on him that's unnecessary. . . . This time I decided not to get something at the airport and I went to Child World on the way home — it's right down the street — and I got him a neat dollar-and-twenty-cent shiny airplane. It was a jet like the one I had been riding on." And the airplane was a smash hit.

Simple Gifts

Many traveling fathers point out that a gift you bring home doesn't have to be expensive and it doesn't have to be a toy. If your kids are used to elaborate novelties and frequent gifts, of course you won't be able to fob them off with some little throwaway goodies you picked up on the trip. But most kids are absolutely delighted to get bars of hotel soap with the name of the place where you stayed on the wrapper.

Bring home the sturdy plastic dinner plates from the airplane; preschoolers will use these to mix paints or to play a game of airline dinner in the sandbox. Pocket the miniature bottle if you have a drink on the flight home; these are made of heavy glass and with a minimum of supervision a four-year-old or older can have a great time at the kitchen sink with a miniature bottle, a big plastic bowl, and maybe some food coloring. Ask the airline stewardess for replicas of the wings pins she and the pilot wear; many airlines supply these as favors for child passengers and for kids who stayed home. The publisher of a music magazine who is on "red-eye" flights to and from the West Coast almost weekly told me that these simple airline and hotel giveaway

and throwaway items are always the biggest present hits with his two preschool boys. And on international flights, he noted, you really clean up.

There usually isn't time or opportunity on a business trip to stop in a dime store or a toy store. Try for a late-night drugstore, either in or near the hotel; it will be an excellent place to grab a little remembrance after your business appointments are over for the day and evening — even if it doesn't have a selection of Golden Books and bags of balloons. Kids of both sexes love little cosmetics presents; a can of shaving cream from Dad goes at the top of this list. Other sure-fire hits from the cosmetics counter are: a stick of flavored lip balm in winter; a small plastic bottle of hand lotion; miniature tubes of toothpaste; new toothbrush; toothbrush holder; sunglasses. A big bar of mild soap makes a good present for a baby.

The stationery section is a gold mine for small presents. Every child loves to get a small ring-bound notebook; a two-year-old will scribble in it and enjoy ripping out the pages, and a six-year-old may cover every page of it with pictures and words. Any pad, for that matter, makes a fine present. Pens, pencils, washable, nontoxic markers, crayons, glue, or paste are all good standard gifts. Preschoolers love to have their own envelopes to stuff and lick. Key chains, paper clips, gummed rings . . . in fact it's hard to go wrong with any type of stationery supplies.

And for last-ditch quickie presents, you can always grab a package of Life Savers, or hand-deliver an accordion fold-out postcard that will show where you've been.

It really isn't the present that counts — it's the thought behind it. The present is definitely the proof of the thought, though, and for a preschooler it may be easier to understand the thought by way of a small object than by way of an abstract explanation like "I really missed you, kid."

TAKING THE FAMILY ALONG

Several well-traveled fathers I talked with had managed to include their kids in business trips. Usually it was a matter of Mom and the kids taking a separate flight and joining Dad for a short vacation after the business part of his trip was over.

A concert violinist told me how he had flown to Tel Aviv for an appearance with the Israel Philharmonic, and his wife and son, one, had joined him later. The security guards who checked his luggage at the airport found it odd that a man should arrive in their country carrying nothing but a violin, a tuxedo, and two suitcases crammed full of disposable diapers.

For a child's first two years, she can be taken along cheaply — for only 10 per cent of the regular fare on most scheduled flights, and free on charters. If you're lucky enough not to have to worry about expenses and it fits everybody's schedule, the preschool years are the time to take the family with you; as soon as they start school there'll be little chance of including your kids in trips.

If you're sent on a distant temporary assignment or training stint that will keep you away from home for weeks or months, consider every possible way to take your family along. When he was a congressman in Washington, John Lindsay's family continued to live in New York. One day he walked into the house with a group of political friends, and his daughter, six, said loudly: "How come everybody else gets to see Daddy and we don't?" The next step was a family move to Washington, about which Mrs. Lindsay said: "I think it saved the children."

LONG ABSENCES

One man — an artist — told me that his in-laws and friends had warned him that Amanda, one, wouldn't remember him if he took the month-long trip he planned to the West Coast, where his paintings were being exhibited. He went anyway, of course, and when he arrived home he woke her from her nap, and she reacted as if he'd only been gone since she'd been asleep. It takes a lot more than a month for a child of any age to forget a parent.

It is well known, though, that when a father is away for a long time — say in the service during a war — he's liable on returning to run into a very chilly reception from a young child. There's nothing unnatural or ungrateful about a child who gives the cold shoulder to a father who's been gone for a year or more. Dad arrives in this case just as a stepfather would; he's in effect an intruder in his own home. The child has grown used to not sharing Mom with anyone, and suddenly here is a very big rival — Dad — so jealousy sets in. On top of which, the new rival is in a position to tell the child what to do, and that doesn't sit too well either. After a week of trying hard to please, many kids ask, "Mom, can't we send Daddy back to the war?"

So if you find yourself separated from your family for really lengthy periods — let's say six months and up — don't come home expecting glowing smiles and all hugs and kisses for Dad. If no problems crop up — fine. But there may be real adjustments to make before the household is running smoothly — lots of talk from all sides and lots of getting reacquainted. After a long absence you return to a whole new child; he will be at a stage entirely different from the one he was at when you left, and you missed the slow transformation that intervened. You've come home to a child with a new set of physical abilities, a new set of intellectual equipment, new responses to the world, and new and very different responses to you.

You may find yourself having to establish your credibility and gain respect just as a new stepfather must — a task that will take patience and diplomacy. With every child the adjustments to be made will be unique, but I think in every situation like this the thing to be on the lookout for and to try to steer clear of is an early and head-on clash of wills. There's a perfect setup for this with both father and child feeling entitled to the center of the stage — Dad because he's just arrived back and thinks he deserves some special treatment, and the child because she's held the center of the stage since Dad left months ago. Nobody comes out of this kind of clash of wills a winner, because there aren't any personal winners in families — either the family wins, or it's everybody's loss.

Communications

For many years, professional military men have used tape-recorded letters to stay in touch with their families when they're away on distant assignments. "My kid thinks his father's a tape recorder," said a GI in Vietnam. He had left for his year-long tour of duty shortly after the baby's birth, and just about the only thing the baby knew about Daddy was that every now and then a tape recorder would be held toward him and Mom would say brightly: "Say hello to Daddy."

In the early 1960s I worked at Green Beret headquarters at Fort Bragg, North Carolina, and my boss was a lieutenant colonel who sent long tape recordings to his family in Colorado several times a week. I'll always remember eavesdropping with the other young soldiers at his office door as this man listened to long tapes from his wife and kids and dictated his replies into the tape recorder. We were all bachelors and cocky, so we sniggered and joked about his wife's tiresome accounts of dripping noses and infected ears, her mushy, drawn-out ramblings as she tried to sign off, and the kids' hesitant recitations of nursery rhymes. But, you know, I think we all somewhere deep down envied that man what he had. And looking back at it now, I realize that he and his wife had found a wonderful way to keep their family tightly together over a distance of thousands of miles and through what I recall as something more than a six-month separation.

I find, however, that civilian fathers seldom take advantage of the tape recorder to stay in touch with the home front — even on long-term temporary assignments. It's said that the military is always in the forefront in putting technology to work — as they did with nuclear power — and perhaps this is just another example of that syndrome. Or maybe it's that separation is so routine a part of family life for them that military people have found ways to deal with it.

In any event, whether you're a civilian or in the service, if you're going to be away for a month or more it will be worthwhile setting things up so that you can exchange tapes with your family. You'll need an inexpensive tape recorder on each end, cassette tapes, and mailers. At stereo equipment stores you can buy little cardboard mailers specially designed for sending tape cassettes, but they make a very small package that looks as if it could be easily mislaid — even by our super-efficient postal service. So I prefer using the smallest size padded mailing envelope, which are sold in stationery stores and sometimes in post offices.

Your first few tapes may be a little stilted. It's not all that natural talking to a tape recorder. But try to imagine that you're just talking on the phone — even though there's no immediate feedback — and perhaps jot down a few notes before your first tapes so you'll have an idea of what you're going to say. You get used to it quickly.

QUALITY TIME

There's a persistent myth among busy, career-oriented fathers that a man can spend "quality time" with his kids — that even though a demanding job and other family and community responsibilities may keep him away from his kids for all but a few hours a week, it is still possible to maximize the mutual benefit that can be had from these hours, to squeeze the truly essential parts of a relationship into the little time available. Proponents of this notion point out that it is much better to spend a half hour of enjoyable, productive time with a child than to drag around together for days on end in a blue

funk. Theoretically, the idea of "quality time" is swell, and if your job makes heavy demands on you, yet you still want to be close to your kids, you are pretty well stuck with it — there aren't a lot of alternatives.

Unfortunately, though, kids aren't as easily organized as business schedules, and what often happens in practice is that a father — fresh and raring to go to squeeze in those precious weekend good times — runs headlong into a toddler in a hateful negative mood, or a strung-out, silly-acting preschooler. And in this case the only "quality" their time together will have will be the quality of annoyance — or maybe the quality of disappointment. Dad is hurt and possibly a little puzzled by this hitch in his plans; it was all worked out, they were scheduled to have FUN. And the child is likely to sense the father's disappointment — which certainly isn't going to

snap her out of a bad mood. She wants to please her dad, but can't, and knowing he's let down only makes things drearier.

An advertising executive I talked with said: "I get maybe an hour and a half tops on Sunday with Joan and Tommy, and I've hardly seen them all week; they're usually in bed by the time I get there. So I'm psyched up for a roll on the lawn or throw the ball around — you know — but half the time they could care less. They're down the street playing with their friends or they're angry at Jo-ann because she won't give them gum with sugar in it or some damn thing, or they're angry at each other because one of them got the stick of gum first. Frankly, this kind of stuff turns me off completely."

Of course this doesn't always happen; there *are* "quality times" for every parent and child, times when the sun is shining and it's all smiles and jolly-up. But it's unrealistic to expect this every time, just as it's unrealistic to expect success with every venture in your business or work — you win a few, you lose a few. Small kids are changeable and moody, as you've no doubt observed, so if you're a "quality timer" of necessity, it's better to face this and figure on a win-loss ratio of maybe one to three. If you're a top-notch organizer and your luck is running, and you beat that ratio — terrific. But try not to approach your quality time with a fantasy image of good pals getting together for instant cheer. It simply doesn't work that way.

A work-oriented father who puts high hopes in quality time and gets shot down repeatedly is a very

likely candidate to give up trying on the home front and tip the balance all the way toward his career. I hate to see a good man lost this way from the ranks of fatherhood, a man who would sincerely like to be close to his kids, but who becomes disillusioned when it turns out there's no way to schedule children's moods — or is there?

Children at every age are generally easier to deal with when they're fresh — after a nap or after a bath. During the bath, they're usually relaxed and easygoing, too. Many fathers I've talked to feel there's a definite difference in their kids in the early morning, that they are fresher, happier, and much more fun to be with than the same kids with their spirits blunted and their bodies worn at the end of the afternoon or at bedtime. (Not all men agree; some see their kids as being on the go at about the same level of animation and cheerfulness at all times, and others have kids who wake up on the wrong side of the bed and do their worst pouting and complaining first thing in the morning.) In the next section, I include the comments of several fathers on why they enjoy early-morning times with their kids.

But before we leave the notion of quality time, one parting shot. If your quality time gets whittled down to as little as an hour or so a week, even if you have the knack of pulling off a success nine times in ten, it's a good chance that the most striking "quality" of the time you spend will be that it is fleeting and all too brief — a quality that will be clearly recognized both by father and child.

MORNING CHEER

One man told me that for years he had left for work before his wife and kids were awake, and he missed having breakfast with his family. He was looking forward to seeing Jessica in the mornings when she started school. But when kindergarten started: "Fine. Maybe she got up at quarter to seven and I'd see her while I was brushing my teeth and then whizz out the door, into a car pool or whatever. What a drag, because in the morning they're bright but not too alert. It's kind of like they're docile — it's a nice time. So now I've thrown convention out the door: I've got my own business, so I get up when I feel like, more or less, and if I leave at eight-thirty, nobody's going to yell at me. So I get up and take a shower and the kids are down there and we talk a little bit — 'What are you going to do in school today?' — Russell [two] is running around and sometimes he'll shave with me. It's a good time, a real good time."

At night, on the other hand, he feels: "If you saw them for half an hour, it was maybe the worst half hour of the day." And he adds: "The morning is just so enjoyable right now. And I appreciate it so much because it's something I was always denied. . . . I spend less time with the kids since I started the business, but I seem to be happier with the time I spend with them."

Here is a father who enjoys teaching new things to his two preschool kids: "By the time I get home at night, they're really not in good shape to participate in learning. They're tired. They may want to sing some songs or have me read them a story or roughhouse with them — but they're not ready to sit down and learn anything. . . . Basically they're at an age when you still have to do things when they're ready, and I find that I get compartmentalized, that there are certain things that they want to do at certain times of the day that they *can* do; and those are the things that I have to share with them.

"But take this morning; I didn't have to go to work because of the snowstorm. Scott rounded the corner and he had a little pad and pencil and he wanted to do arithmetic. We sat down and he was fresh and it was like two different children, because I've tried working with stuff like that at night and it just doesn't work; he has no attention span; he gets frustrated at the least little thing. And those types of things weren't bothering him this morning."

And here is another morning-loving father: "I have a policy at my work that I don't go home unless I've gotten through my mail. . . . So I've got a problem with seeing Alec [five] at night. One thing I've done with him is have breakfast. Bea doesn't like to get up in the morning. So he and I have a private time in the morning. He's an early riser and

he gets up with me and we make our breakfast. He'll make mine some days. At first, all he could put on the table were the utensils, but now he can literally serve me — I can read some mail and he'll set the

table and put out the bowl and then he'll pour the Cheerios, and in the last year he's started to be able to pour the milk, which is one of the hardest things." For father and son it is a quiet, private, special time before the rest of the world is awake.

This is just a small sample of testimonials to the pleasures of eating breakfast with the kids that early-rising fathers gave me. If your time with your family is severely limited, this may be the best place to start trying to fit a little family togetherness into an overloaded schedule. Of course if your kids are grumpy in the morning you might as well forget it. And it will help a lot if your children are usually awake at an early hour. Kids vary considerably in their rising habits. Some wake up chipper and ready to go. I'll never forget Gregory at one waking every morning punctually at six and calling loudly and happily from his crib: "Hel-lo; Hel-lo." But from stage to stage and age to age, the same child takes on new rising habits, and now it takes at least ten minutes to roust Gregory.

But if your child is fresh and easy in the morning, you probably have a sure bet for some real "quality" time.

Chapter 4

FAMILY

The old song tells you to stop your ramblin', stop your gamblin', stop stayin' out late at night, stay home with your wife and family, and sit by the fireside bright. Every man fears that family life will bog him down, rob him of freedoms, possibly bore him. While your wife is pregnant with the first baby, you balk just as you did on the morning of your wedding day. You want to go through with it, you look forward to it — but, on the other hand, how in hell have you gotten yourself into this fix?

And it's a terrible fix for some men — ever mounting divorce rates attest to that. But for hundreds of thousands of others it's only a baffling fix, and they meet it squarely, as they meet any challenge, and have hard struggles and good times grappling with it. Certainly few fathers end up bored sitting by the fireside bright, the way the song describes it — we're too busy trying to pay for everything and help keep the family going at the same time.

Keeping the family "going" is a tall order and it takes hard work, because families are forever bogging down. A Chinese sage said: "It is easier to rule a kingdom than to regulate a family." Family morale sags and collapses every time you turn around. The kids are always getting tired and cranky — and so are their parents. It takes a concerted effort to rescue a family from its doldrums and get it back on its feet day after day, year after year, and most families that succeed find that the concerted effort can only be achieved through teamwork. One parent work-ing without support seldom has the buoyancy to keep the whole family afloat. It takes a mom and dad partnership.

And as the family grows and the kids get older, everyone has to be in on the partnership for the business really to work. Families that are truly blessed develop a shared interest where everyone is involved in the same venture — whether it's blue-grass music or swimming or paleontology. And other families manage to make common cause around family chores and games and celebrations. But however it works out, if it works to everyone's satisfaction, there'll be some kind of teamwork at the bottom of it.

In the past, father and mother were stuck with a coy game: who was the true head of the family? Was it father, by coming in occasionally and acting domineering? Or was it mother, by being on hand always and being *truly* in control of the scene? Families are now happily more or less free of this tedious little contest. The time and effort that used to be wasted on it can be put into the common effort of two parents working and guiding their family together. Each one brings a special point of view and a personal set of values, skills, and strengths to the partnership that complement each other and reinforce each other — and sometimes grate a little on each other. But the climate is there for a combining of strengths rather than a contest of wills.

RETURNING HERO

The nightly return to the hearth is the big Father Event of each day. The baby has heard your car pulling into the garage or your footfalls in the hall and is already shouting Da-Da and waving her

spoon over her head as you come into the kitchen. Your preschooler rushes in and throws his arms around your knees, begging to be lifted up. Your wife, delighted to have you home, wraps her arms around you. You are momentarily a celebrity. It's supposed to be like that, at any rate.

Some men come home to hugs and kisses every night, but for others it's more like this: "You've had a rough day and you get off the train and get in the car and walk in the front door and she starts yelling and the kid's crying . . ." Other fathers arrive home to the dazed expressions of young televiewers and find themselves ignored; their only greeting is the droning voice of Mr. Rogers.

The returning hero scene will be played out differently in the same home from month to month and even from day to day. It makes a big difference how old your kids are, what time you get home, and what has been going on in the household all day. It can be a heavy disappointment after months of cheery greetings from a baby to find yourself coming home every evening to an eighteen-month-old grouch, or a disheveled, demoralized household tyrannized by a Terrible Two, but kids go through big changes, and during a siege of negative behavior the whole family scene will inevitably be altered. See p. 143 for a brief rundown of the major predictable behavior changes most kids undergo during their first six years.

TUG-OF-WAR

Many fathers find themselves being pulled from opposite sides the instant they get home; they see it as a kind of tug-of-war between a full-time mom nearly desperate for adult company and kids demanding Daddy's undivided attention, wanting to start right in to play with him or show him what they've made that day. Most of the fathers I talked to who face this daily dilemma said that the kids usually won — that their demands were so urgent, Mom had to be fobbed off for later.

In homes where Mom has an outside job, this problem doesn't come up; both parents arrive home on more or less common ground or equal footing. But a mother who has been with a baby or small children all day needs someone to talk to. "I understand that when he comes home he doesn't want to hear a lot of nonsense about how many outfits she wet through today, and her fights with the dog," says one new mother. "But somehow when you don't have anything more stimulating that's been

occurring that day, you want to share it, and not that many friends are interested in that trivia either, and you think, 'Well, if there's anyone who should be interested in it, it's the baby's father.' So I start spitting out all this stuff that's pure trivia — I acknowledge that — but still it was my day and I want to share it. He sits and yesses me to death, you know. And I know that he just wants to get on and eat supper and read his paper. But I think he should understand that nothing more exciting happened to me that day and I enjoyed it, but I want to share it."

When the kids are older and literally pulling on Daddy to come and play, Mom still has that burden of "trivia" to unload, plus there's often a need for a serious consultation between parents about some problem that has come up during the day. Mom sees a glimmer of hope — maybe you'll have a fresh outlook on things, and even be able to offer a solution since you haven't been up against the problem all day.

It's hard to respond at this point; you're tired and hardly ready to start in on family problems (and "trivia"). And it's inconvenient, since the kids are insisting that you come with them and play, insisting that you pay attention to them. The simplest course is to shelve the parent discussion and go with the kids. But if you want to stay current with the family scene and be a fully active parent, this is the time to listen, to get the news of the day while it's still hot. Later — when the kids are in bed — is a great time for mother-father discussions, too, but by then the day's news *will* be trivia — stale and nearly useless. Once you know the news of the day, you have most of the clues you need for understanding the morale level of the family you've come home to. You'll know who and what needs your attention or, if everything is running smoothly, you'll know that you can relax and enjoy.

Listening to everyone at once — the kids as they pull you toward playing and your wife as she tries to fill you in — can be a hectic proposition. And it takes considerable diplomatic skill to convince all the people concerned that they have your full and undivided attention. I doubt that any father is ever entirely successful at this; but keep trying, because the alternative is picking one party and letting the other feel out-and-out rejected.

BAD DAYS

As you stumble through the door at the end of an impossible day, you don't feel like the returning hero your kids see you as. You're just drained and ready to slump. If the kids are in a good mood, that may be the medicine you need. Baby smiles have been known to relieve office-problem headaches faster than the leading brand of buffered aspirin. But there are plenty of other days when that relief isn't waiting for you; the place looks like a dump when you walk in and the kids are surly or silly and that headache you carried home from work starts to throb with redoubled energy.

"I don't bring work home," one father said, "but sometimes I bring home bad attitudes — I've had a bad day, that kind of thing. And the hardest thing for me to remember is that my children can have bad days, too, and I tend not to recognize that early enough."

Listening attentively to the family news bulletin is the only way to find out, and then you know it's not *all* your problem. One father told me he has a sure-fire solution for evenings like this when he's had it and the kids have, too. He and the kids, who are six and four, leave Mom alone for a moment's peace and take a warm shower together. In the summertime, they use the garden hose for the same effect.

SUPPORT

I asked dozens of fathers to tell me what kinds of things they thought their wives needed from them — as mothers. Support was the almost unanimous answer. And I asked most of their wives the same question, from their standpoint: what did they, as mothers, need most from their husbands? Again: Support. But when I pinned them down on what they meant by Support, it turned out that the men and the women were talking about two essentially different things.

When the men spelled out what they meant by support, in most cases it was help — physical help with the household chores and with child care. But the women were talking about Moral Support — recognition that the job they were doing as mothers was an important one, understanding and sympathy for how difficult it was, and praise for doing it well.

I got the distinct impression that the men were talking about physical help because they felt guilty that they weren't supplying enough of it. And from the women I got the sense that they really did want moral support — and that many of them weren't getting much of it. A number of women said that they were always happy to have some help with the household chores, that they were overjoyed when the bed got made or the kids bathed or the dinner cooked, but that they would gladly give up every bit of that kind of help for some real solid understanding of what they were doing and some moral support.

In families where both parents were working, there was much more unanimity of opinion on the question of what mothers needed from fathers. Here both men and women know that the support that's needed is physical help — sharing so both parents can work. One man who shares much of the child care for their toddler daughter with his working wife said, "The nonworking woman tends to get less respect because she's not producing income, and she tends to value less what she's doing. . . . Women who don't have regular, regimented jobs have a harder time justifying to their husbands that they need time."

Two parents both working outside the home have common problems and common aspirations, while a working father and a full-time mother live in two very different worlds. It's clearly not hard for a man to understand the needs of a working wife; they are very similar to his own needs. But understanding the life and the needs of a full-time mother takes some persistence and imagination. We know roughly what it's like. We know what our wives' routines and activities are. We've all had the kids for a day or so at a time, and we've all heard the complaining of mothers. But the world of full-time motherhood is so very remote and different from the world of men's work, does any of us *really* know what it's like — or understand?

SWITCHING ROLES

"You really appreciate what the wife is going through if she should get sick and for the weekend the burden is on you. You don't get away, you're shackled to the children; they're there and particularly at a young age they can't do anything for themselves. You really realize what she has to go through and, thank God, on Monday morning you go to work for a rest." Two days obviously gave this man some insight into full-time motherhood.

I talked with a couple who had switched places for three months. He had been a high school shop teacher at the time, so while he stayed home with the kids for the summer vacation, she took a nine-to-five job. He said: "It was nothing I couldn't cope with, but when the whole thing was over, I think we were both glad it was over. I mean, when she came home from work and lay down on the sofa and went to sleep, I was mad."

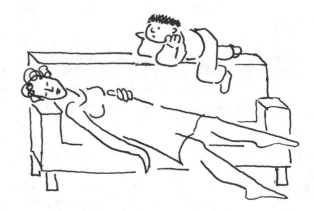

She said: "I'll tell you, we fought the whole summer. From my first day of work, we fought about everything; it was just seething and constant. We both got a lot out of it; we've talked a lot about it since. . . . But there was his whole attitude, his whole feeling about it — he said he liked being home, but . . . But the thing about dinner — when I didn't say it was a nice dinner, he was crushed, he really was. In fact he told me at the end of the first week the worst thing would be if I were to come home late for dinner — and we'd been married for years of late dinners; I don't know how many dinners he missed. At the time I didn't want to hear that. It was very hard to work out."

He said: "She wasn't accepting of my feelings. I would start preparing dinner at two o'clock in the afternoon; I would read the cookbook; I would get some fantastic recipe. . . . And to do that just can't go unnoticed. She ate it, she'd get up from the table and come out here and go to sleep until seven o'clock. . . . I don't think I was as good with the kids during the day as she is. I really don't think I was. We had a good time and I got Courtney in for her naps at the proper time and Jessica and I swam in the pool and occasionally we went out places, but I felt as though I was more compelled to do the housework than to play with them."

She said: "Oh, but you *are*. That's it — being home. You *are* more compelled to do housework."

There had been other reasons why he'd stayed in with the housework: "If you're a house father, it's very difficult to go out and coffee-klatch with the neighborhood ladies during the day, and when you go out and visit your friends, if they're not into kids, so to speak, there's nothing to say."

Had it all been worth it? "It gives you a little bit of insight when you come home and you walk in and things are all disheveled — it gives you a little bit of understanding of why. I think it gave us each a little bit of insight into the other's life. But it was really tense. I'm not ready to do it again. I think if somebody wanted to do it permanently, the adjustment might be easier, but it seemed like we had to cram so much into those three months . . ."

I talked with a couple who had "switched" permanently and their adjustment did seem easier; in fact, it looked as if the whole thing was working quite smoothly. The father was a drummer and most of his work was at night, so he spent the day with their daughter while his wife went to a nine-to-five job in an insurance office, and this arrangement had worked well for them since shortly after the baby

arrived three and a half years earlier; another baby was on the way and the father planned to take charge of this one as well.

Father and child were a well-known team in the neighborhood. They went everywhere together, doing the shopping and the other chores, playing in the park. If there was a recording session for Dad during the day, Alexis went right along with him. When she was a baby, he'd played his bongo drums in recording sessions with her strapped to his chest in a snuggly baby carrier, but now she would sit behind a glass wall in a control booth.

Coming home tired from the office in the evening, Alexis' mom would shoo her away while she tried to read the newspaper. And in this family it was Mom who was helping out with the bedtime ritual, sometimes reading a bedtime story; and it was Mom who was in charge of the big weekend outing.

Alexis' father had grown up in a fatherless family of seven kids, and as a teen-ager he'd done a good share of the child care. So he'd had no trouble stepping right in and taking charge of the baby; and he'd been having a great time with his daughter ever since, and obviously had no regrets as he looked forward to the arrival of the next child.

It's interesting to me that of the three men I've talked about in this section, the one who has had a full experience of "motherhood" liked it best, while the one who had three months of exposure had a lot of trouble adjusting, and the one who got only a weekend glimpse wanted to flee back to work. Of course they were men with three very different personalities, but isn't it just possible that full-time parenthood is a very demanding and trying job that takes a lot of getting used to, but that once a person has learned the ropes, become accustomed to the long hours and the miserable working conditions, and otherwise generally settled into the pattern, it can be an extremely fulfilling way of life? This, apparently, is what many *women* discover.

RELIEF PITCHING

Frazzled full-time mothers look forward to the moment each day when Dad returns and can lend a hand. Here's how a mother of three kids — seven, four, and two — sees it: "When he comes home I can share the burden. I don't have to keep after them. I know he's home and so I'm not so quick to yell at them. I know *he* will; or he'll take care of it. And just knowing that makes it a lot better. Because you get tired of saying for the sixty-eighth time: 'Don't do this,' or, 'You have to do that.' And now I can hear him say it instead of me, and that means a lot. 'Cause that's the day-to-day parenting; that's what you have to put up with every day. All the other stuff — what you do with them to enjoy them — that's real nice. But it's getting through that everyday draggy stuff. I'm sure the kids think that, too; they must think: 'Oh, here she goes again — put my cup in the sink, pick up my toys.' So it helps that *he* can be the drag once in a while."

HOME	1	3	3	4	5	5	5		
VISITORS	0	0	1	2	2	4	6		

Many fathers I talked to thought of themselves as relief pitchers coming in in the seventh inning of the day-long family ball game, when Mom is starting to fade. "It's just that I'm like relief," said the father of a first baby. "In other words, if Myra's had enough pulling and poking and taking things away, then I'm fresh, and I'm not used to it and I won't be frustrated for another hour until I get tired of it. I'm not faced with it all the time, so I don't mind doing it." And in big families, fathers perform the identical function. Here's a man who has four kids: "Being that I'm away all day, I'm more receptive to them when I come home. . . . I'll have a little more reserve for them than my wife. She's used it up all day; she's comforted them all day long, and you only have so much to give — and toward the end of the day she's had it."

Taking over, helping out, or even just playing with the kids for a while — it all helps a full-time mother. This is one place where a father's job is uniquely different from a full-time mother's. Most of the things they do for the kids, either parent can do equally well, but here the setup gives Dad a special daily opportunity to give everyone in the family a new and possibly brighter perspective on the world. You may not feel too fresh as you arrive home from work, but to Mom and the kids you're a fresh face.

One man put it this way: "If you don't watch TV for a week and then you turn it on, sometimes you'll be more interested in it than if you've been watching it day after day — it may have more impact on you. So sometimes my impact on the kids probably is greater just because they haven't been with me." For your kids your daily return from work is a comfortable, predictable pattern, but it also has a big element of novelty — your arrival can break up the cloud of monotony that has settled over your family.

PITCHING IN

It's said that young fathers in Russia get a good laugh when they hear that American family men do the dishes, change diapers, and otherwise help around the house. Our Soviet brothers are apparently unreconstructed male chauvinist swine who let their wives hold down jobs and bear the whole burden of the household and the kids as well. Maybe we're a little further along toward the collective society than they are.

Of course many American men duck housework and child care — but it's less and less acceptable to admit that you do. I spent a day at a nearby hospital in the maternity section talking to most of the new fathers as they came to visit their wives and babies.

When I asked them if they intended to help out at home with the baby, they were unanimous in claiming they would. "Oh yes, of course, we're going to share the child care," was the way many of them put it. We know what society expects, and there's plenty of willingness to pitch in.

When I talk to fathers months and years after the baby is born, though, I get a slightly different story: "I know I should be doing more to help out — and of course if Betty had a full-time job, I'm sure I would be . . ." With a capable wife on duty and in control of things it's easy to relax a little on that good resolve to lend a hand.

DUAL CAREERS

In families where both parents have jobs, there's almost always real sharing of the chores and responsibility for the kids. Here are the thoughts of a high school English teacher who has two girls, three and six, and who expresses what many men feel who split the effort with their working wives: "My feelings about sharing the upbringing of the children are quite strong. I believe that were only one of us working — if my wife were home all day — I would miss out on a great opportunity to get to know my children better. On a number of occasions my wife's work has taken her out of town for several days and even up to a week and this has meant that I've been responsible for carrying out all the chores which we ordinarily share. While the prospect of this does not particularly excite me, I find that once involved in a routine, everything goes along very smoothly. In almost every case, in retrospect, I've found the experience to be highly rewarding, simply because I've been forced under these circumstances to spend a great deal more time with my children than I would under ordinary circumstances. And it seems to me that the relationship I have with my children as a result is a good deal closer."

In this man's family, the chores are divided up specifically his and hers, and there are strict routines for mornings and evenings. He dresses one child and cooks breakfast for all, while his wife straightens up upstairs. In the evening he does the grocery shopping and cooks supper; his wife does the laundry. In every family the details will work out differently according to the skills and interests of the two parents — though it's interesting to me that Dad more often than not becomes the cook. One

feature that's common to nearly all families where two working parents share the housework is a strict, formalized division of labor.

Partners find out quickly that you can't just let things swing easy. "It was all nagging and recriminations," says another sharing father, "until we actually sat down and got it down on paper — task by task and day by day." If you have a business partner or know anyone who does, you know that partnerships never succeed unless both sides know exactly where they stand, with the details worked out with precision, and everything down in writing. The same holds for husband-wife partnerships. A family doesn't need a legal document to square things away and of course the arrangements are always open to revision, but two-job couples find that *all* chores have to be assigned, and that the easiest way is to write it down; they also discover that weekly lists help, too, or a family calendar, to detail who will take the kids to the doctor for shots or pick them up from the birthday party.

HELPING MOM

If you're serious about pitching in evenings and weekends to ease your wife's burden of full-time motherhood, you may want to take a cue from the two-job families discussed above — chore assignments and lists help in any sharing arrangement. Without some formal agreement on who will do what, it's the easiest thing in the world to let your wife take over in every household department. When everything's getting done, you stop noticing how it's being accomplished, follow your own goals, and don't lift a finger beyond setting out the trash on Sunday night — I'm always falling into this one. The daily schedule changes, and the kids' needs change, and before I know it, I've dropped a task here and a duty there and I'm not pulling my weight. Then Rita and I have to get together and reschedule our lives, divide up the duties again, and write down the results, and for a while longer I can make a concrete contribution.

In every family the needs of the situation will be different and to a great extent, your contributions at home depend on your working schedule. But there is one time of day when every full-time mother is desperate for help: the hour before dinner.

Father's Hour

No matter how early dinner is scheduled, the kids' appetites run at least a half hour ahead of the time it's possible to serve it, so preparing dinner is always hectic, with children underfoot demanding to be fed. And it comes at the end of the day, when tempers are short and the kids are so exhausted they revert to their lowest forms of behavior.

The educational TV people have alleviated a little of this daily madhouse by scheduling kiddie programs in the predinner slot so the children can be parked in front of the mechanical baby-sitter. This is a big help to full-time mothers, but the late-afternoon scene in most households with small kids is still a hairy one. It's a scene that calls for two parents: one to cook and one to cope. If you can get

home in time, your efforts on either front will be more than welcome.

If you choose "coping," call it a Father's Hour and find things to do with the kids that will be fun for you all — well away from the kitchen. Outdoor activities are best of all. One father I know takes out his guitar for Father's Hour every evening while his wife cooks dinner and he and his two preschool boys sing "Old MacDonald" and other favorites. Mothers who get this kind of help really love it; I've talked with several and they tell about it with pride and a twinkle in their eyes.

Fathers Don't Baby-sit

Baby-sitting is done by baby-sitters, never by fathers. It's a generally underpaid and not terribly rewarding job — not something you would be likely to take on with someone else's kids for low pay, so why take it on with your own for nothing? What fathers do is spend time alone with their children — there's a big difference and it's not just a semantic one.

If you think of yourself as a baby-sitter, you might as well be one. It makes me cringe a little when I hear a woman say: "Wasn't it nice of George to baby-sit the kids Saturday so I could get out for the afternoon?" Because if she can lightly call her husband a baby-sitter, she may very well think of him as one, and he may too. And if George's kids grow up also thinking of him as an occasional baby-sitter, believe me, he's in trouble.

When your wife goes out for the day or evening, consider it a good opportunity to spend some time with your child, to get to know her better, to learn about her and be close to her. It's also a good policy to figure you will spend the *whole* time with your child. Too often we try to get some other simple task accomplished as well, and end up feeling put out when child care consumes the whole time — and it always does consume the whole time. Ask any mother; she knows this is true. If your child goes to sleep and you manage to get something else done — great. But don't expect it to happen or you're bound for disappointment. Says one new father about being alone with his baby: "It's like being at work with the phone constantly ringing and people asking you questions, and you never get to sit down and do something."

FAMILY MORALE

Before you have kids, you can iron out mood clashes with your wife and the constant emotional ups and downs of living together by discussing the problem, talking things through. But with kids in the picture, the whole emotional climate of the family changes. It's no longer two people capable of getting on each other's nerves (and of loving each other richly), but three or four or more. The new ones are even more emotionally unstable than you are, and they don't know the first thing about talking problems through. They're equipped only with primitive, infantile emotional responses, so you've introduced into your home a Pandora's Box of mood changes.

With babies and preschool kids, too, it's all the way up or all the way down to despair and wailing, and very little even ground in the middle. It takes

masterful self-control not to let this affect you. Even the relatively quiet crying of a newborn will get to you if it goes on for a while. The screaming of a toddler can get right under your scalp; and later you have a preschooler who can pull the whole household with him into an exaggerated funk—and even when he's cheerful and riding high he'll screech so loud you'll want to flee.

There are constant emotional crosscurrents in a family with little kids, or maybe cross fire would be a better way to describe it. The baby has been crying all day; Mom is irritable because she's had to listen to it; Dad arrives home from a hard day in no mood to pamper anyone, in a foul humor and needing some comfort . . . and that's only a three-way logjam; add a preschooler who is also out of sorts be-

cause the baby has been crying and because Mom has been irritable . . . The permutations are endless — parents and children triggering off each other's irritability and taking it out on one another. I'd love to see a family that's completely free of these hassles.

Happily, small kids go up just as fast as they plunge down, so a lot of this is in short squalls and thunderstorms, and then the kids' smiles light up the place again. And of course as soon as your kids can use more language than ba-ba and car-car, you start teaching them to figure out what's wrong and to look for solutions for themselves, ways to change the scene and break the mood — and preschoolers do learn to cope with their small traumas and even with some of the biggies. You also try to stay on your toes and rise above the infantile emotional squalor that you find yourself surrounded with, while you look for solutions. Talking things through to a successful conclusion, though, is one of the least likely ways out of a volatile emotional situation with little kids, so we need other tools to work with.

I find it helps to think of the whole business in terms that are simple enough for a preschooler to understand. We talk about Family Morale in our house and we try to keep it high so that the emotional cross fire will have a little harder time taking over in the first place.

FAMILY CHEER

We've had fairly good results from the kinds of crude tactics that are used to keep morale running high during a football game. Kids love to shout something out, so we instituted a simple cheer:

Sullivan Family, Rah, Rah, Rah!!!!!

I do the cheerleading, and the kids do the yelling, and Rita joins in, too. It's not a regular everyday thing — just when someone wants to do it; or I'll suggest it if family morale is looking pretty low, but it hasn't completely collapsed yet. Some cheering can get things going again on a different footing, but for us it won't reverse a thoroughly dreary household.

FAMILY HUG

For reversing a bad scene, the best tool I know of is the Family Hug. One parent calls for a Family Hug, and Mom and Dad and kid(s) all have a big snuggle session. Everybody (usually) feels a lot better. You can't just save this for the rocky moments, however, or it would quickly become a very dreary exercise indeed. Most of our Family Hugs come at the happiest times, when this is precisely what everybody feels like doing.

I naturally thought that we'd invented this marvelous technique, but my work on this book has turned up a number of families that practice the same amiable custom — and who report uniformly good results. In our case, the proof that it was working came when Gregory at three interrupted his mom and dad in the midst of a domestic squabble with, "Aw, come on, let's have a Family Hug." Broke our hearts; and of course it ended the squabble.

BIRTHDAY PARTIES

If you don't mind a lot of birthday celebrations, you can use candle-blowing-out ceremonies on a regular basis to improve family morale when it starts to dip. All that's needed for a birthday party is a dark place, a lighted candle, and a small child. The formula can't be repeated too often, at least not for the kids. The song can be sung over a hundred times on the same evening, the candle relighted just as often — and the magic is still there.

Put the candle on a cookie or a dill pickle or whatever you have and celebrate anyone's birthday. We have a calendar that gives the birthdays of Famous American Women, so we sometimes celebrate birthdays for people like Margaret Sanger, but as often as not I cheat and look at the calendar and say: "Oh boy, today is the birthday of the world-famous Cookie Monster," or Batman or Isis or Scoobie-Doo.

CHANGE OF SCENE

A basic technique you can use to cope with a bad family scene is simply to change it. It's the same thing you do with an unruly toddler when you pick him up and move him to another place to switch off his mood by shifting his activity. Try it with the whole family. The best time for an unadvertised special dinner out at a fast-food place is when you get home to a household where family morale has collapsed. A ride out in the car will sometimes turn the tables, or even a family walk around the block. Just get everybody up and moving (if you haven't collapsed yourself).

Sometimes you spot regular patterns of family morale breakdown — say four mornings in a row everyone has been in tears as you leave for work; or getting everybody into the car for a family drive has become an ordeal. It's time to change the scene; if you can't move it physically to another place, change the timing; alter any conditions that can be adjusted. This is the time for family morale strategy sessions with Mom, to put your heads together for a little brainstorming and figure out what's going wrong — and how to change it.

There's often some practical solution, something as simple as everybody getting up fifteen minutes earlier in the morning so that everyone's needs can be met. Let's say one of the kids has started to dawdle over dressing in the morning; this results in Mom's not getting a shower, which puts her out of sorts, and with the whole family running behind

schedule, you're tense because you're getting out the door just in the nick of time — morning family morale is shot. The solution to this one really is as simple as everybody getting up fifteen minutes earlier; the new timing changes the scene. Other breakdowns of family morale are going to call for more complex adjustments, often for Mom and Dad figuring out new teamwork approaches for taking care of the kids.

As children grow, their needs change dramatically from week to week and month to month, and I've noticed that family morale is a pretty good barometer of these changes: it starts to drop off when the existing order isn't satisfying new demands. Say, for instance, the baby has been walking on her own for a week now. Predinner time has become a squalid torment: cross toddler, harassed Mom, dismayed Dad. Up until last week, when she started to walk, the baby was content to sit in her high chair and eat some finger foods while Mom cooked, but now she's on the prowl; she's learned to walk and nobody is going to keep her down. So she's bumping into Mom's legs while Mom is trying to fry the burgers in sputtering grease, and Mom, annoyed, keeps having to leave her cooking to lead her away. Meanwhile, the potato water boils over; Mom is in a fit; and Dad, coming up from the cellar, where he's been trying to adjust the water heater, wonders why the situation is so tense. The baby's made a big leap forward and the whole family scene is going to

have to be changed to accommodate her new ability. In this case the change will probably be that Dad will now spend the half hour before dinner running around with his daughter.

The solution, of course, is seldom so simple, nor is it always easy to spot the problem. Often it takes a lot of discussion between mother and father and some pretty keen detective work to pinpoint the cause. No parents are wise enough to stay one jump ahead, always aware exactly how the kids are changing and how to adjust the situation accordingly. I've asked dozens of families if they had any kind of thought-out child-rearing program, if mother and father ever got together to scope out what needed to be done. No program, they all said, nothing figured out in advance, but almost all said they got together for necessary strategy sessions. It's the way we all end up operating as parents. And it works if there are enough of those necessary strategy sessions, if we read the family morale barometer regularly and make sure we talk about and concentrate on any precipitous dips well before family morale hits bottom.

FAMILY POLICIES

Many families discover that morale runs higher if there are definite family policies to cover common situations, policies that Dad and Mom have hashed out and agreed to follow and enforce. Kids who know what to expect will only push a little beyond the limits you've set, rather than turning over the whole apple cart. Children gripe sometimes when limits are set and they throw tantrums other times, but they do learn to live fairly comfortably with them, whether the limits are on the number of hours of TV cartoons they can watch on Saturday morning or on the amount of noise they're allowed to make indoors.

SIBLINGS

All brothers and sisters fight, all are jealous of each other; they've been at it since Cain and Abel. They're also capable of being very close and loving and playing together beautifully — but that's the easy part. It's the rivalry that we have to cope with as parents.

PREPARING THE FIRST

Parents are usually careful to prepare an older child properly for the arrival of the new baby. A big event is going to take place and the preliminaries are already changing many things in the household besides Mommy's shape. Kids ask plenty of questions about what's going on and are fascinated by the process if we can find ways to describe it briefly and in words they can understand. Bedtime stories during the last months of the pregnancy are usually about bear families or groundhog families who have new babies, and the stories talk a little about the difficulties the little boy bear or the little girl hedgehog had adjusting to the new baby.

If anything, kids are often a little too well prepared for the advent of the new baby. In an effort to sell the baby to the child, we sometimes go overboard — "This is going to be your very own special baby to love and play with." "This baby is going to be an extra special playmate for you." Those are sweet ideas and they make good advertising copy, but they're simply not true. And I think many preschool kids who have been fed this line are sorely disappointed when they learn what a baby *really* is — a little one who just lies there on his back and cries and eats and monopolizes everyone's attention. A newborn baby is anything but a playmate, and a preschool child isn't able to visualize how this runt is

going to grow into the promised bosom buddy. As far as this being the child's "special baby to love and play with," the child soon learns that except in rigidly supervised situations, it's hands off the baby for him. Anybody else who walks in the door — relatives, neighbors, whoever — can pick the baby up and go goo-goo all over her, but he's hardly even allowed near the bassinet.

On the other hand, I don't think there's any need to paint a grim picture of what the baby's arrival will represent. Nor do you need to present a preschooler with a scaled-down psychology course designed to teach or warn her about the feelings of anger, jealousy, or sibling rivalry she may have when the baby comes; this isn't concrete enough to make much of an impression on a preschool child. You can save for later, when your child is grappling with her own real problems, the storybook about the little bunny who finds he hates all the bunnies in the new litter because he never gets attention any more from Mom and Dad rabbit.

Probably the most important message to get across is that a big change in coming for the family. And beyond that, in the last months of the pregnancy, a child can use clear descriptions of how that change is going to come about: where and when; the mechanics of birth; where *he* will be and what *he* will be doing while the baby is arriving; when the baby will come home — the works. And he can use clear, responsible information about what a newborn baby is — not a playmate, but a new member of the family who will be loved by everyone, lavishly, and whom he, too, can love. And sometimes he'll be able to help Mom and Dad do things for the baby and play with her.

NEW RIVAL

With kids who are very close in age, especially with the older one under three when the baby arrives, you have to watch like a hawk. If you leave them alone together, the older one can do real damage to the baby. Keep a sharp eye on a three-year-old, too.

Many parents, sensitive to the question of sibling rivalry and prepared to see the older child take a poke at the baby the first day home from the hospi-

tal, are surprised when the older child acts beautifully with the baby. And this model behavior may go on for months, with only an occasional "accidental" shove or jab at the eyes by the older one. The older child is probably trying very hard to please Mom and Dad, and she also has genuine good feelings toward the baby — and besides, the baby is just lying there, he hasn't yet truly invaded her turf. Wait till the baby can grab the older one by the hair or the nose and pull, till the baby can grab a toy that the older one wants — then the bickering begins in earnest. And from there on out your kids will compete daily for toys and attention and first turn and biggest serving of ice cream and a thousand other things, just as they will compete with others — not just brothers and sisters — at play and school and sports and job for the rest of their lives.

On top of this ordinary competitiveness, a first child is likely to believe that you and Mom love the baby more than you love him. He's never known anything but your undivided attention, and now the baby is in the center of things. Visitors come to see the baby and walk right past him, where before they made a fuss over him. The baby is always in Mommy's arms or on her breast. There is probably no question in the first child's mind that he has been supplanted. At three or four a child doesn't think in degrees or in the subtle ways that will let him understand that he is still loved fully and that his mom and dad have been able to come up with a separate but equal surplus stock of love to heap on the new baby. Even as adults, are we any more capable of understanding when we see someone new on the breast of the woman we love?

Happily, the first child has a pal to turn to — Dad. With Mom wrapped up in the baby, child and father both find themselves out in the cold, and this is a time when kids naturally turn to Dad for comfort and fun, and fathers are usually delighted by the attention. It's a good time to club together, and you can talk about the feelings you may have in common

and let your child know that you, too, feel you're getting the short end of the stick from Mom — because misery loves company. You can also give your older child some of the time alone with Mom that he desperately longs for — by taking over the baby so she can smother him with love for a while.

COPING

All parents of more than one child know that two are much more than twice the trouble of one. The added element is family friction. If you space your kids ten or twelve years apart, it's possible to have two who get along without a hitch, but kids who are close in age will squabble whatever you do.

Right from the time the new baby enters the picture, you'll want to set limits and indicate exactly what is approved behavior for the older child — and firmly.

But when the second child is old enough to defend herself, usually the best thing to do is to try to ignore the bickering, except to separate the kids when the going gets too rough. Mixing into kids' squabbles brings you right down on their petty level: "He did it to me." "No, she hit me first." It's demeaning. If the kids insist you play judge, try the case in a matter of seconds, render judgment, and clear out — you're bound to be right at least as often as if you'd listened with care to both convoluted arguments in full.

By not getting embroiled in the argument, you maintain your effectiveness as arbitrator and limits-setter — and this is where you can do the most good, by letting both or all of the kids know precisely how things stand and how far they are allowed to go. Of course they'll overstep the limits you set — constantly — to test your resolve, and to practice their independence, and because when a fight flares up rules are quickly forgotten — that's only natural. But they will have guidelines that they understand and respect, and your resolve and strength in administering the guidelines will give them an example to follow in trying to stick by them. The rules will be different for every family, and will change as the kids grow and change, but they'll provide a constant source of stability and direction.

At the same time that you work to keep the lid on the inevitable family frictions, you can also work at setting up a climate for sibling co-operation.

SIBLING CO-OPERATION

Two kids or more can play beautifully together as companions — sometimes — and I think it helps to show them how. A three- or a four-year-old will try to play with the new baby just as he plays with other kids his own age — very roughly. The baby will usually be delighted with this treatment — but only for a short while until she's overwhelmed by it or gets bumped too hard, knocked over, or smashed in the face. "Now, play nicely with the baby. You have to play gently with a baby because babies get hurt easily." This must be really frustrating for the older child; for months he listened to adults advertising the fantastic new playmate who would arrive just for his benefit, and the minute he tries to play with the baby, it turns out that babies are untouchable.

There are necessarily strict limits on the kinds of playing an older child can do with a baby. But you can give him as many openings as you think are possible, considering his age and abilities, and demonstrate, supervise, teach him how to act with the baby. You stand by a little anxiously as a three-year-old rocks the baby in a baby swing, ready to pounce when he starts to push too hard. The older one will learn to hold the baby — on the floor and on his lap so there's nowhere for the baby to fall to — and to sing a lullaby, and to help a little with diaper changing. Whatever you do with the baby, try to find some way for the older child to get in on it.

It's always easiest to play with each child on his own level, alone — and a lot of this is necessary, because neither child wants the other one always there; each wants to know he's valued for himself, and the older one needs sessions alone with you like the ones he had when he was the uncontested ruler of the household. But they both also need practice in doing things together.

A good first roughhouse game for the two of them is to get the older child down on hands and knees in the horse position; then you hold the baby and rest

her lightly on the back of the horse and hang on to her for the duration of the ride. You can do this when the baby is still only a few weeks old. The baby may not get much out of it, but the horse will love it.

For the first half year it's hard to find things for the older child to do with the baby. When in the latter half of the year, the baby is sitting up by herself and holding on to things, there's more chance for interaction, but the baby is still hardly the ideal playmate who was promised. Try a simple game of handing an object around, say a small block. You hand it to the older child, who hands it to the baby, who (theoretically) hands it to you. Gregory and Timothy and I got into a pretty good rhythm on this game by Timothy's eighth month, though we never could reverse the current and get Timothy to pass the block to his big brother. Gregory, who was four at the time, asked for this game nearly every day — because it was something we could all work at together. And we're still playing it in an improved version with a rolled ball instead of a passed block.

Toward the end of her first year, you have to start teaching the baby to be gentle with the older child, because the baby is now grabbing fistfuls of hair and going for the eyeballs. Teach her to say, "Nice," and pat and stroke the older child, and remind her to do it when she starts attacking him.

You can also provide the older child with a useful line of defense. Show him how to distract the baby, using the same technique that is so successful for parents. When the baby cries or attacks or takes a toy the older one wants, he can change her activity and her mood by offering her another toy or distracting her with another activity.

Always keep an eye open for opportunities to get the two children sharing in the same activity. If you're doing some roughhousing, try to find ways to double up instead of simply going one on one. For instance, when the baby is over a year old, you can hold her firmly around her body under the arms while the older child holds her by the ankles and the two of you swing her gently back and forth. You are firmly in control and can break up the game if the older one starts to swing too hard. As the year goes on, you can swing harder and harder till you're swinging almost at a rate the older child thinks is right. Another favorite in our house is one kid on each knee for bouncing; my knees are spread and the kids hold hands in between and I hold onto the other hands — it's kind of a seated ring-around-the-rosy. Holding hands this way, the kids can lean way back while they're being knee-bounced.

Don't neglect ring-around-the-rosy. You can start playing it almost as soon as the baby can walk. It is *the* classic in the field — no child can resist it. And it's actually a lot of fun for parents, too.

It's only for a year and a half or two years that you have to work at finding ways for kids to play cooperatively. By the time the baby hits two, she'll be standing on the back of the tricycle for a ride and will have grown not into the perfect playmate who was promised, but at least into a pretty good imitation.

FIRST CHILD/SECOND CHILD

"The first child suffers the most," says one father, "because you don't know what you're doing. Well, she gets good and bad, I should say, because she gets most of your attention, but then you make most of your mistakes with her."

Even after the family expands, the first child continues to be the beneficiary of your extra attentions and mistakes, because he continues to be in the vanguard, always the one you're learning on. And the second child never gets the same kind of attention the first one did — you've seen it before, and there are two kids or more to split the time and interest between. Several fathers told me they felt they were slighting their other children by not giving them as much time and attention as they had given the first. Simpler than worrying about establishing attention parity for your kids and more helpful to everyone concerned is to work at ignoring the first one a little — he could probably use some practice at playing alone, or even at being lonely. You won't need to work consciously at ignoring a second child or a third.

SONS AND DAUGHTERS

"The girls I'm more apt to cuddle and fondle and pat," said a father of four. "With the boy we always punch each other and roll around on the floor and have pillow fights — and he responds to that, he likes that very much. . . . Not that the boy doesn't cook and do things like that — but he's a boy. Even his whole make-up — he's constantly moving; something's always happening around him and it's very *noisy* when it happens."

Whether it's the way we treat them, or whether they're born with different "make-ups," there's no question that boys and girls are different — temperamentally. Any parent who has both will tell you so. The big general difference most parents see is that boys are boisterous and girls are "easier to live with" — though there are plenty of exceptions.

And hurrah for the differences; they keep the world interesting. But of course they also color our dealings with our kids. Many fathers told me they felt they were stricter and more demanding with their sons than with their daughters, that there were frictions and tensions with a son — even as a toddler — that just didn't come up with a daughter. One man, for instance, said: "I want to give them full equal treatment — you know, no sex discrimination, everybody's on the same ball club, the whole thing. But, God, that boy gets under my skin, and it can grate on you, and it's like I'm *up against* him. Where with her it's a different story . . ." It's an age-old story, too, this business of fathers and sons and fathers and daughters, and considering the way people are, it's not likely to change much in the near future.

But there's a new twist in the story that will make a huge difference to our kids — which is that fathers are thinking about equal opportunities for their boys and girls, and trying hard to provide them. When a man sees his newborn daughter for the first time he says: "One day she'll be President." It's an old joke by now, but it spells a major change in how we look at our kids' futures.

Some important parts of a father-daughter relationship exist specifically because daughters are members of the other sex. Fathers and daughters enjoy a wonderful innocent flirtation — it's the way girls learn about men, since Daddy is the first man in a girl's life. In many ways he's her model for all men. Dad is a model of manhood for a boy, too, but hardly in the same way.

And many things in a father-son relationship are determined by the fact that we're members of the same sex. We have been boys and know what it's like, and this is valuable knowledge that we want to pass along to our sons, just as we want to teach them how to be men.

Social change isn't going to take sex distinctions out of our lives with our kids — they're here to stay. But social change is already giving our daughters a fairer shake in the world than girls and women used to get. A father of two preschool girls who is conscientiously raising them as first-class citizens with a full and equal place in the world says: "Karina rides to nursery school with three little boys and they say that they have secrets that Karina can't share because she's a girl, and that girls are weak. But she stands up for her rights."

JOBS FOR KIDS

"I cannot stand mowing the lawn, and I think the thing I look forward to most as a father is the day when I can look out and see Jack mowing it," said the father of a three-year-old.

There was a time not too long ago when fathers regarded each new child as an extra pair of hands to help with the family business, especially if the business happened to be farming. And you still find big farm families today, even though a new model combine harvester is generally a lot more productive and easier to maintain than your average child. Back in the last century, a father could pick up some extra cash by selling a son for a chimney sweep, and the bustling new industries so abused the huge force of child workers that strict child labor laws had to be written to protect kids.

Further back still, in the Middle Ages, an entirely different attitude toward children prevailed from

the one we're used to. Kids were weaned very late — around age seven — and were then expected to take their places as productive members of the adult community, as apprentices or helpers. Schools for children were completely unknown. The introduction of schools in the seventeenth century and the increasing sophistication of the educational process have resulted finally in a system that prolongs childhood, or at least dependence on family — in our country — through the age of eighteen or even twenty-one.

It would be ridiculous to call for a return to the good old days of the Dark Ages, when a father could get some real work out of his kids. But I think it's worth remembering that kids haven't always been wrapped up for eighteen years in a kind of cocoon of childhood and adolescence — insulated from the world of productive work. Kids are generally capable of taking on greater responsibilities and bigger jobs than we as parents feel we should trust or burden them with. And kids thrive on responsibility; all people do. So there's every possible reason for trying to harness some of the overflowing energy and intelligence of our children and, yes, get some productive work out of them.

I did a quick survey one Saturday of four suburban fathers I was able to collar whose sons and daughters *do* mow the lawn; all four had started their kids as preschoolers on a life of toil — with little household chore assignments.

WHAT JOBS?

There's no butter to churn, no eggs to collect; we can't send a kid down the block to the bakery for a fresh loaf of bread, or downstairs to the corner bar for a bucket of suds — those days are gone forever. In place of a world full of little tasks, many of which could be fobbed off on kids, we have a world of total convenience — conveniences like traffic jams and waiting on line in the supermarket. And you can't get out of the real nuisance tasks, like these, by sticking the kids with them. It takes a fully educated, experienced adult to sit and fume in a traffic jam or stand in a check-out line.

When we do give small kids jobs to do, it often seems more trouble than it's worth. Most fathers I've talked with feel there are very few things a preschooler can do competently, that when a small child has finished with the job, you have to come along behind and finish it up or do it over correctly or clean up the mess the job generated. These are sound observations of how kids work; I'm not going to try to convince you that every four-year-old can do an effective job of sweeping the floor, or even of setting the table. But I would like to convince you that the answer isn't doing all the chores yourself, even if that is more efficient.

Until they are at least four, kids are dying to help out and be given responsible jobs, and real griping and shirking don't usually start till they are in school and find out how older kids act. It may tax your ingenuity to find jobs they can handle, but there will be things each child can do at his own level. Timothy at sixteen months, for instance, did a fantastic job of tearing up the lettuce for the salad. And a couple of months later he took on putting the flatware in the kitchen drawer; he would take the basket full of knives and forks and spoons from the dishwasher and dump it in the middle of the drawer. It wasn't terribly orderly, but it was efficient.

One child at four may love to run the vacuum, while another may still have the same fear of its noise he had at one. And there will be entirely different tasks available in an apartment than in a suburban house. A three-year-old in an apartment house may have the job of advance guard and always run two minutes ahead of the rest of the family to

press the elevator button as they go out. The tasks you assign will have to fit your kids and the circumstances of your lives.

Please consult the kids — who will have marked preferences in jobs and excellent ideas for new ones. One father told me how his son, Kenny, at three, had assigned himself the task of keeping the TV screen sparkling clean; every few days with care and reverence he wiped off the dust from the magic eye with a very soft cloth. Gregory, almost three, expressed a strong desire to wash our VW station wagon — he scoured the front fender and hood with sand and gravel from the driveway because he thought we had let the car get too grimy. "See, Da-Da, I cleaned the car with sand!" What do you do — laugh or get angry? I did both. And also, the next sunny day we took the bucket and hose and had a great time washing the car, and now Gregory knows how it's done.

KEEP IT LIGHT

The jobs you set up for kids should be very light and easy, especially at first. If a child can't make a go of something, it's usually because she's overwhelmed by it, or frustrated by what she thinks is her inability to do it, and almost never because she doesn't want to do it.

Here is a typical scene between father and preschooler; it's a scene I've starred in repeatedly. Dad on a crisp, sunny autumn Saturday afternoon, full of good feeling and enthusiasm, says: "Come on, guy, let's do a job on these leaves. You take your little rake and you can help Daddy rake up all these leaves." But instead of the "Sure, Dad, let's go" that was supposed to follow, the three-year-old throws a long face and a sulk and, "I don' wanna." Shot down again, Dad.

Was it the gung-ho enthusiasm, did you lay it on a little too thick? Did you come on too strong? Not at all; kids love gung-ho enthusiasm. It was probably the way the child understood the proposition; he was being asked to help rake up *all* these leaves. All these leaves! Trees full of leaves! A whole yard full of leaves! And I don't even know how to rake yet. These kinds of misunderstandings happen over and over, no matter how sensitive we are to our kids. We simply aren't equipped always to see the situation from the child's point of view and then act accordingly. But we can try to figure them out in retrospect and the next time around it will be more like this: "Come on, guy, I want to teach you to use your rake the way Daddy uses his. And there is this little place over here by the back stairs that I want you to practice on."

Most jobs can be broken down into steps for a child to master one at a time. Setting the table, for instance, can start at three with just napkins, then napkins and forks, etc. Even picking up the mess in their own rooms — which is the hardest job for kids to come to grips with because it is such a big job — can be broken up into little tasks. But don't expect much success with getting your kids to pick up their own rooms. This is the place where almost every child balks.

GI JOBS

I've found a good source of jobs for kids in the standard operating procedures of the U. S. Army, most of which are designed so they can be accomplished by a four-year-old. From time to time I try out on kids some of the little oddities I remember from my days at Forts Jackson and Bragg. And sure enough, short of cleaning and firing a rifle, a preschooler can do most of the smaller tasks I remember being assigned.

GI Cleaning

Anyone who has ever served in the Army will remember the times when his training sergeant said in his usual personable tone of voice: "You guys get the "#$%–&**$% in there and GI those crappers." "To GI" means to clean something in the traditional GI way. The procedure for cleaning the latrine is to wet the whole room down and cover every available surface with a thick coating of powdered cleanser; coarse brushes are then used to scour mercilessly every object in sight without regard to its need for this abrasive treatment or its ability to stand up under it. Bucket loads of water are sloshed liberally and big mops are used in an effort to rinse away the cleanser. Any reasonable housewife would be appalled to see this ritual performed. But a child of three wouldn't — he'd want to join right in. You have to go barefoot and roll up your pants legs and sleeves to do the job correctly, since the room has to be awash in order to clean it properly.

When there is a bunch of kids around on a warm day at our house and the big old front porch needs cleaning — which is always, since that's where the kids play — out come the buckets and the four mops and the kids GI the living #$%–&**#%$ out of the porch floor. We leave out the scouring powder, but we bring in the garden hose, which adds a little to the hilarity. Children at any age love this job; but a toddler is liable to lose his footing on the slippery deck. So he loses his footing — and everybody gets a

laugh. A three-year-old can do as good a job mopping as most GIs, which isn't such a great job, but if you use enough water, most of the dirt gets spread around evenly. If you haven't got a porch, try a scaled-down bucket brigade treatment on the kitchen floor or in the bathroom; or if Mom won't co-operate here, the garage floor or the patio may have to be GIed from time to time.

Spit Shines

Another GI procedure that really attracts kids is the spit shine. Most preschoolers, especially boys, love to spit — anywhere, anytime. It's the ideal, instant ploy for getting Mommy's goat, and for embarrassing and angering Dad: spit at another kid in company or on the floor during dinner. Sooner or later most parents come down really hard on this one and stamp it out. But sometimes it's almost irrepressible in a four-year-old.

A good military shoeshine gives a spitter an acceptable outlet for this urge. You will have to do most of the work on this, principally because shoe wax is made with petrochemicals and is toxic, so kids shouldn't be left alone to polish shoes. But your naughty four-year-old can supply all the spit for your shine.

The secret of a high-gloss, mirror-surface toe is saliva. It is applied liberally immediately following a thick coating of the shoe with wax; this is then vigorously rubbed in with a soft rag. Additional saliva is added from time to time, and a number of coats of the wax and spittle amalgam may be needed on a dull shoe. Some shoe shiners use saliva freely as they buff the shoes finally to a high polish.

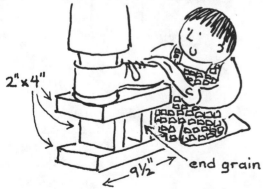

With a young helper, use lots of spit, since he has it right there on the tip of his tongue, ready to oblige. Kids can help with other parts of shoe shining as well. Muddy shoes need to be brushed off —

over newspaper — and then cleaned with saddle soap, which is safe for a child to use. Set your child up for saddle-soaping with a small sponge, a container of lukewarm water, and a lot of newspapers on the floor.

Teach your preschooler to use a rag for buffing. A child can buff her own shoes if you hold them for her; one way is to drape a knee with newspaper and put your fingers inside the shoe to clamp it down on your knee. A good simple shoeshine stand can be glued and nailed together by you and a five-year-old from a few pieces of 2″ x 4″. The hammering will go fast and accurately for your child if you drill pilot holes just a hair smaller than the nails. Use 8d nails, driven from top and bottom.

With a little practice at buffing your shoes, by the time your kid is six, you'll notice that it's a wonder that the rag don't tear, the way he makes it pop — with his hippety, hippety, hippety, hippety, hippety, hippety, hop.

Bed Making

A three-year-old can start making his own bed, and if you spent any time in the service, you'll be the professional bed maker in the family and so the natural teacher of the art. With preschoolers, you have to relax your high military standards; there's no way they can pull the covers so tightly across the bed that a quarter can be bounced on them. But you can teach a three-year-old to pull back the covers from time to time and scrape out the cookie crumbs, Little Golden Books, Hot Wheels cars, and raisins. He can straighten the covers pretty well — particularly if he can get at both sides of the bed. And he can line up his friends Teddy, Dapper Dan, Mushmouth the Raccoon, and the Fonz doll in a fairly orderly row.

At five you may be able to teach the art of making square corners, which for a child can be an accomplishment like learning to tie his shoes. You can't expect a preschooler to make her bed each and every day, but keep after it a little and you may end up with a straightened bed more often than not.

You also can't reasonably expect a boy to make his bed regularly if he's never seen a man do it. I grew up in a household where the beds were always made by women, so it never occurred to me that it might be a task men were good at. It actually came as a surprise to learn in the service in my twenties — after years of near animal disarray at college and as a bachelor — how simple it is to make a bed and how quickly it can be accomplished.

Your kids of both sexes will follow Dad's example in this as in most things, and though the covers will never be tight enough to bounce that quarter on, they'll be plenty tight enough for Dad to bounce some kids on.

Sock Rolling

An army trick that Mom will love when you teach an orderly five-year-old to do it is rolling socks in little balls — and undershirts and underpants into little egg-roll shapes. Anything that will help with the sorting and filing of the clean laundry in a household with small kids is worth trying, and many preschoolers find magic in the way a sock turned halfway inside out can be put on more easily than one tugged on from the top; they are also intrigued by rolling them in little balls. It is also just possible that children who see Dad helping to put away the laundry will be encouraged to help, too.

The step beyond rolling the clothes neatly is arranging them with precision in the drawer, and I balk here. But an orderly kid may be turned on by a job like this — so why not?

PRAISE

Each job should have its share of praise, even if it isn't done perfectly. Because of course the purpose of the exercise is to teach your kids about work and accomplishment in a positive way. You would never go to all the trouble involved just to have some inept help emptying the trash cans.

Your praise will help your child on to the next job and the next accomplishment. So here I am, saying: "That's a really good job you did painting the bottom of the wall," and I realize that quite automatically at the same time with my brush I'm touching up a

place Gregory skipped over, not even a very big skip, but I always like it to be right. His face drops and then he starts on his squealing sillies routine, which is calculated to drive me right up the wall we just painted. I blew it again. By touching up that place on the wall, I told him as plainly as if I'd spoken it: "You did a lousy job, and it has to be fixed." If you must have the job done right, try at least to wait till the kid is out of sight, and then scurry around to finish it up.

If you have started them working young, a day will come when you'll realize with astonishment that they actually are a help. If you have ever grown an apple tree, you know that you plant it and care for it, spraying it regularly to protect it from damage, and you hope year after year that it will bear, and year after year nothing happens, until one summer day, quite miraculously — though you knew it was due all along — there is an apple. If you planted an apple tree when your child was born, when she is six, an experienced worker, and ready to do a good job of picking them, there will surely be apples on the tree for her to pick.

FLEEING

Where do you go when the noise of the household gets you down — do you have a place where you habitually go to hide? Men who had only one child often acted surprised when I asked them this question, as if it were somehow an inappropriate thing to ask; some even got a little huffy: Who would think of hiding from his own kids? they intimated. Men with two kids tended to think it over for a minute and then say: "Oh sure, I guess I usually go down to the garage, where my workbench is" — or out for a walk, or whatever. Men with three or more kids picked right up on this question and answered without a moment's hesitation: "I always come up here to my study; I have it soundproofed," or, "I always grab the dog and take her for a walk." One man told me about his brother, who has seven kids and can always be found in his bedroom playing solitaire.

If you need a quiet moment to do something as selfish as, say, preparing your income tax, try insulating yourself from the family and the rest of the world with stereo earphones, as several fathers told me they do. For getting away entirely, the reference room of your local public library offers a haven where you can do paperwork undisturbed; many libraries are open some evenings till eight or nine — after which the kids have gone to sleep.

MARRIAGE TIME

Every marriage needs an occasional break from family life. That's what grandparents are for — Saturday night off for Mom and Dad to go out to dinner together at a slow-food restaurant or to a grown-up movie, or a whole weekend when you can stay in bed late if you like, do whatever you want with no one grabbing at you with sticky hands, no one crying or complaining or demanding anything. Rita sighs hourly during a weekend when the kids are at Nana and Papa's house: "Oh, I miss having them here so much." But she loves it just the same. And when we all get back together at the end of the weekend, everybody is refreshed and family life is a little less hairy than it was before the break.

If you haven't got handy grandparents, impose on friends or other relatives or cultivate a responsible older baby-sitter you can trust the kids with overnight, but do find ways to change the scene and take time out for yourselves as adults and for your marriage. You won't be depriving the kids or deserting them if you take off a day or so every couple of weeks — they're just as tired of listening to your complaints and directions as you are of listening to their whining.

BIG FAMILIES

Fathers with two or more kids know what a breeze it is to deal with only one. You think back to the good old days when there weren't any complications. What a nice ratio: two parents to one child. When the child wears out one parent, the other may be there to take over. With a second child it's one on one and nobody seems to have any time any more. The third child tips the balance irrevocably: two to three. Some fathers with large families feel that the biggest jump is between two and three kids — that this is the point where the family ends and the gang begins. Other fathers feel that with three you can

still get an occasional chance to deal with each child alone and as an individual, but when the fourth child comes . . .

Here's how one father of four put it: "Now, sometimes I think of it as a pack of dogs. You know how nice dogs can be if you have them separated. You put all of them together and they become a pack. So, especially when I'm tired, I picture them as a pack. I think I recognize all of my children as individuals — I still do if I can keep them alone. But as a group it's hard to keep them all in perspective. The pack of dogs isn't a very good-sounding analogy, but sometimes when you're in a bad mood, that's exactly how it feels."

ALL-TIME CHAMPION FATHER

The world's record for the most children fathered by one man is held by Moulay Ismail, "The Bloodthirsty" (1672–1727), the last sharifan Emperor of Morocco. He is said to have had 548 sons and 340 daughters.

VASECTOMY

When your family grows too large, the most emphatic and permanent thing you can do about it is vasectomy. Usually performed in a doctor's office in half an hour or less and under a local anesthetic, this simple operation severs and blocks the vas deferentia, the minute tubes in the scrotum that carry sperm to be mixed with the fluids that make up the volume of the semen a man ejaculates. By blocking the sperm, a vasectomy is one of the surest methods of birth control known; but only the sperm are blocked, so the operation doesn't tamper with a man's sexuality.

Sex continues as before the operation — after a layover of a week or two. There is no change in performance, except that it's said there is often an *increased* sexual drive for a short time after the vasectomy; erections are unchanged and ejaculations are the same as ever, except that the sperm have been cut off at the pass. The secretions of accessory glands (seminal vesicle, prostate, mucous, and other glands) continue as they always have to produce the lion's share of the semen for ejaculation, and the missing tiny sperm don't make a noticeable change in the volume of semen ejaculated. The production of male hormones is also unaffected by a vasectomy. No bed rest is needed following the operation; warm baths and aspirin usually take care of most postoperative discomfort. The operation produces no noticeable physical changes, only two short scars (½″ to ¾″) at the base of the scrotum. The procedure is not expensive and costs are often covered by medical insurance.

The most serious complications following a vasectomy are psychological, not physical. Before you have the procedure done, you and your wife should be firmly convinced you aren't going to want more children. If you have any hesitation, vasectomy probably isn't for you. And many men do hesitate, feeling they may want to have another child for unforeseeable reasons — should a child die or should they for some reason remarry. If you feel that your financial situation doesn't allow you to have more kids now, but if things work out, you might like to have them later — then vasectomy isn't the answer. During your wife's pregnancy is no time to have a vasectomy; most doctors won't perform one until well after the baby is born. Also, several large religious groups are opposed to vasectomy — as well as to a whole spectrum of other birth control measures.

A vasectomy can be reversed. In a procedure called vasovasostomy, a skilled surgeon working with high magnification can locate the severed ends of the vas deferentia and sew them back together with extremely fine thread. But this is a relatively major operation and there is no assurance that it will succeed, so physicians always advise against vasectomy in the first place, rather than relying on the possibility of reversal later on.

Sperm banking before a vasectomy, however, does provide something like fertility insurance, and may cut down on hesitation before and psychological problems following a vasectomy. With sperm frozen in cold storage, you have a fair chance of having more children through artificial insemination should your world turn upside down in the future and you decide to become a father again. Hundreds of healthy, normal babies have been born as a result of inseminations with sperm that had been frozen and stored.

You will want to be well informed about all aspects of vasectomy before having one performed. Two good sources of information are: Evan McLeod Wylie, *All About Voluntary Sterilization* (New York: Berkley Publishing, 1977); and Gilbert Kasirsky, *Vasectomy, Manhood, and Sex* (New York: Springer Pub., 1972). Both books include nationwide lists of hospitals and clinics where vasectomies are regularly performed.

The first step toward having a vasectomy will probably be talking to your family doctor; he may be able to perform the procedure, or he may recommend a urologist or surgeon. You can also contact your local Planned Parenthood Association for information, or write to the Association for Voluntary Sterilization, Inc., 14 West 40th Street, New York, New York 10018.

At this writing, vasectomy is a man's only truly effective means of birth control. But scientists are hard at work on schemes to suppress the production of sperm. Many substances are known to do this, but most have undesirable side effects; they're addictive or toxic or they increase the incidence of heart attack. The contents of the Pill, actually, would work as a male contraceptive, but men wouldn't accept the consequent reduction of sexual desire and performance. Promising experiments range from a search for antifertility vaccines that could immunize a man against his own sperm to the application of ultrasonic waves directly to the testes to raise testicular temperature, which makes the manufacture of sperm impossible.

DIVORCE

I'd prefer not to end this section on Family with notes on fathers and divorce, but there's no ducking the fact that divorce is what ultimately happens to many, many families. It's said that seven out of ten people in our country will experience divorce, either as children or as adults. There isn't room in the scope of this book to do justice to the topic, and I haven't the background or experience to, but I've included in the Further Reading section at the end of the book, under the heading Single Father, a list of excellent books you may want to look at if divorce becomes your family reality. A family threatened with breakup can use all the help it can get — from books, from professionals, and from friends who have been through it; parents and children need help and should reach out for it.

Divorced fathers have been making headlines in the past decade with their insistence that they be granted custody of their kids by the courts. And the courts are starting to listen to their argument that they can do just as good a job as single parents as mothers can. Organizations of divorced fathers have sprung up across the country to support and advise men who are seeking custody of their children, and also to lobby for change in divorce laws that they feel discriminate against fathers. They have met with some success. Until only recently any mother, no matter how unfit, was usually regarded by the court as the parent of choice — a state of affairs that had existed for about a hundred years, before which children were generally regarded by the courts as the father's property. Today divorce courts have

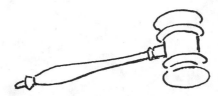

begun to weigh more carefully the claims of both parties and are granting custody to fathers in some cases.

Organizations of divorced fathers are also fighting to enforce the rights of divorced men to see their children, since the mothers often interfere with visitation privileges. The fathers' organizations charge that men face stiff fines and jail sentences for withholding child support or alimony, while their wives aren't prosecuted for cutting them off from their kids. These groups also attempt to get the courts to force live-in boyfriends of ex-wives to leave the homes that divorced men are supporting.

At this time there is no national organization of divorced fathers; the groups are organized locally. If you are interested in contacting one in your area, look in the white pages of the phone book under Fathers, as most of these groups have names like Fathers United for Equal Justice, Fathers United for Equal Rights, etc.; and check under Equal, too, because some have names like Equal Rights for Fathers. You can also write to the "parent" organization in the field: Fathers United for Equal Justice, Inc., 2 Brewer Street, Cambridge, Massachusetts 02138. They maintain a list of similar groups in other states and can refer you to one near you.

Chapter 5

PROVIDING

Providing is a big word for fathers and it's got dollar signs all around it. Since there's no way I can tell you how to supply those dollars, I'm lumping together under the heading of Providing a host of other things that fathers provide for their kids: contributions a father can make to a child's room and play yard; home safety and car safety; health care; insurance; day care and nursery school; and because fathers provide a regular repair service for all the things kids break, a small Fixit section.

PLAY YARD

If you have any room at all outdoors, fill it with equipment your child can use to stretch out those developing muscles and burn up all that energy.

Materials for kids to build with have an important place in a play yard, too — sand, first and foremost, but old tires and bricks, smooth stones, boards and boxes will all contribute to making a play yard an exciting place for a preschooler.

For a toddler, a sandbox, an inflated inner tube to bounce on, and a cheap plastic wading pool for summer are the basic outdoor equipment. A low strap-in swing and a short slide are great additions, and try to provide some low hurdles and objects for a toddler to climb over and around.

A three-year-old can use a swing set, and this is the point to think about setting up a challenging climbing structure. From three on, a child will be able to help you build impromptu playhouses and set up obstacle courses in the play yard, and by stretching your imagination a little, there's no end

to the possibilities for creating a top-notch play environment.

I'm including a number of suggestions below for homemade play equipment, mostly things I've built or set up for my own kids. But if you want to get into fitting out the play yard in earnest, take a look at some wonderful books that include plans for a great variety of father-made equipment; several of the best are listed under the heading Play Equipment in the Further Reading section at the end of this book. And look in the card catalogue of your public library under the headings: Playgrounds, and Playgrounds — Apparatus & Equipment. For a mail-order catalogue advertising some of the classiest and sturdiest outdoor play equipment available, write to Child Life Play Specialties, Inc., 55 Whitney Street, Holliston, Massachusetts 01746.

CLIMBING STRUCTURES

Anything that preschoolers can climb on safely belongs in a play yard, whether it's a huge old fallen tree limb, a defunct rowboat with drainage holes drilled in the bottom, or a bunch of old tires bolted together. A landscape architect, father of two preschool girls, who designs big play areas for parks, put it this way: "Any considerable three-dimensional object is a valid form to put into a child's play area."

A child who spots a sturdy fence will climb on it, and probably the simplest form of jungle gym you can erect in the back yard is a section or two of ordinary post-and-rail fencing. It needn't enclose anything; it just stands there and gets climbed on and over and under.

Designing and building a jungle gym climber is a great project. Below are plans for one I put up in the back yard. I hope, though, that no one will follow this scheme exactly, but only use it for a little inspiration and as a jumping-off place for designing his own unique climbing structure.

Building a climber for your kids will save a little money and produce a structure much sturdier, longer lasting, and probably much more interesting for climbing on than the cheaply manufactured metal tubing jungle gyms sold in big toy stores. Build with wood. Metal piping structures are cold and slippery in winter, and besides, the cost of metal pipe is out of sight. Interesting climbing structures can be made from PVC plumbing pipes, but again the cost of materials is high compared with wood. Cedar 4" x 4"s are the best material for sturdy uprights. Cedar is much softer, easier to work with, and will hold up longer set in the ground than spruce or other fir woods. It is nearly as durable as redwood and a whole lot cheaper. For climbing rungs, 1⅜" closet poles are ideal — "closet pole" is the lumberyard name for dowels over 1" in diameter. Ordinary 2" x 4"s make good horizontal beams

for climbing when bolted to 4″ x 4″ uprights, and 2″ x 4″s can be used for uprights when they are only a couple of feet high.

Used utility poles are very popular for building massive climbing structures in public playgrounds, and can be used in the back yard if you want to erect a truly heavy-duty climber. Local phone and electric companies will sometimes deliver used utility poles to your house free for the asking, but setting them up is a problem because you need heavy equipment for digging them 4′ or more into the ground.

Bolts should always be used to connect parts of anything kids will climb on. Nails will work loose quickly but bolts provide a strong and somewhat flexible joint.

Set a climbing structure up in a place with good drainage so puddles won't form under it when the kids wear out the grass. When the grass disappears, you can add a thick layer of wood chips to soften falls. Sand also makes for soft landings. In a small play area, you can save room by digging a shallow pit under and around a climbing structure and filling it with sand, thus combining sandpile and climber in one space. Big metal toy trucks with sharp edges and other similar toys naturally have to be banned from this kind of sandpile. Never set a climbing structure up on a hard surface like concrete, and

keep it a good six feet away from fences and other obstructions.

You want a climbing structure to be high enough to give kids the thrill of daring, but low enough for safety. For kids three through seven, 5½′ is an excellent height, because an adult, even a short one, standing on the ground can reach a child at the top who needs help. At the top of any climber, I think there should always be a place for kids to sit and ponder the world or eat a peanut butter sandwich — it's like a tree house perch. Onto and around a basic climbing structure like the square "tower" on the one illustrated, you can add any number of exciting features. You can, for instance, bolt on a store-bought metal slide for quick descents, or set up a metal fireman's pole near at hand, or attach a ladder going down at a slant.

I got some expert help with the design of the climber shown here. Daphne, nine, a true monkey on the bars, knew just what kinds of things were needed, and it's thanks to her ingenuity that it has tires to climb through and swing on. Gregory insisted on a bar to hang from and chin on. Timothy was just starting to toddle when it was built, and couldn't use it for climbing, so the framework for a strap-in swing on short chains was included to make him part of the deal.

Building this structure was not a quickie weekend

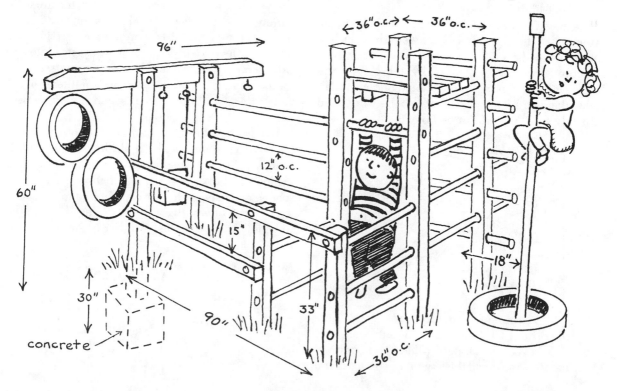

project. It extended over many Saturdays and Sundays. But the effort was great fun both for me and for the various kids who helped with it, and the satisfaction of watching kids swarming all over it is enormous.

Construction Notes

All rough and splintery parts on the wood were removed with a cheese-grater rasp and sanded down. The top edges of the uprights were all chamfered with a rasp to keep them from splintering, as were the ends of the rungs and cross beams.

The 4" x 4" uprights were drilled in advance on a drill press to accept the 1⅜" closet pole rungs. The four uprights of the "tower" section were set directly in the ground in 2' deep holes dug with a post-hole digger. A shovelful of ¾" gravel went in the bottom of each hole to help with drainage and to give the uprights a firm resting place. The two uprights for the toddler swing frame need a better foundation because they are more free standing and take a lot of stress. They were set 2½' down in holes filled with concrete. The bottoms of the uprights were painted liberally with creosote before being set in the ground. Watch out for creosote — it is evil smelly stuff and you don't want to get any on your shoes or clothes, or on other parts of the structure that won't be buried.

The uprights were set loosely in their holes in the ground and the closet pole bars were then pushed through the drilled holes, after which the whole structure was checked carefully for plumb and level, with extra gravel being added under the uprights that were too low. Then the holes were filled in firmly and the dirt tamped down.

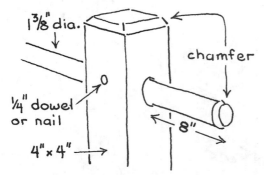

To hold the round bars tightly in place, a ¼" hole was drilled through the upright and into each bar, and a ¼" dowel was tapped in behind a squirt of glue, and then sawed off flush with the surface of the

upright. A galvanized 8d finishing nail driven through the upright and into the crossbar will achieve the same result, but the dowels can be drilled out if the structure has to be disassembled and moved to a new back yard at some future date, while nails would make the structure permanent. Pilot holes should be drilled if nails are used — to avoid splitting the ends of the crossbars.

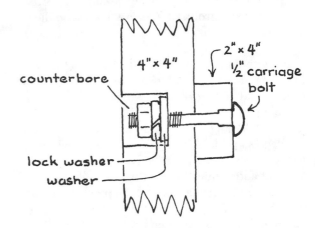

The 2" x 4" cross members are bolted on. At each joint is a single ½" carriage bolt, with the nut end in a counterbore so it will not protrude past the face of the member and catch a child's clothing. Under each nut are a lock washer and a flat washer against the wood. The 2" x 4" crosspieces are included for variety — they give a climbing surface different from the round bars at a different spacing. They also provide a nice high place for a kid to straddle and ride horsy. The tops of the two uprights on the toddler swing frame are notched in the front to accept the 2" x 4" crosspiece, which is held on with countersunk carriage bolts.

The tire on the square tower section hangs on a bar passed through two holes drilled in the tread. It swings a little when kids sit in it, and crawling through and over it is a good challenge for a preschooler. The two other tires are bolted to the frame and to each other. Big washers are used inside the tires, followed with a lock washer before the nut is

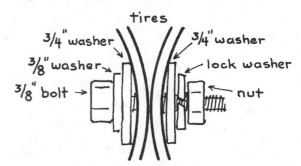

put on. Besides being great for precarious climbing, these tires make good targets for kids to throw balls through. A ¾″ drainage hole is drilled through the bottommost part of the tread of each tire on the structure.

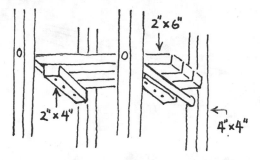

The platform perch at the top of the tower was made by screwing three lengths of 2″ x 6″ to perpendicular cleats made from 2″ x 4″s. It is not bolted to the frame, but rests on the top bars of the tower, with the cleats just inside the bars to keep it centered. It can be taken down and placed in half a dozen different positions on the climber. Positioned on bottom rungs, it becomes a "roof" for a kind of simple playhouse or can be used as a table surface for a picnic meal or working with modeling clay.

The final step was painting all surfaces with several coats of a clear penetrating petroleum-base wood-preserving finish, concentrating particularly on the end grain at the tops of the uprights and ends of the poles and crossbeams. The hardest job in the whole production was keeping kids off the thing for a week and a half until the finish was completely soaked in and thoroughly dry.

Firehouse Pole

Next to a climbing structure or any high place like a back porch, you can set up a firehouse pole for quick exits. Use a 3″ diameter galvanized pipe the length you need, plus 3′ to set in a wide hole in the ground surrounded with concrete. The hole should be at least 18″ square. Your preschooler will enjoy mixing the concrete almost as much as sliding down the pole. Fill the hole with concrete to about 1′ from the level of the ground. Let it set up for a few hours and then fill the rest of the hole with dirt. And no sliding for at least five days while the concrete cures. A pipe cap is needed at the top of the pole to keep kids from sticking their fingers in. Drop an old tire down around the pole to make a bumper pad for soft landings.

Ladders

Ladders can be constructed very quickly, and have many uses in a play yard. You can bolt a ladder to a high back porch to give your kids their own special approach to the back door, or suspend one between two heavy blocks of wood on the ground for crawling across or tricky ladder walking by a five-year-old. A group of ladders can be bolted together with 4″ x 4″ uprights dug into the ground to make a climbing structure with ladder ascents and ladder bridges. For a very simple climber in a tiny play area, bolt the top of a 6′ ladder to a block of wood that in turn is bolted to the side of the house. And if there's no room at all outdoors, look for a place to put up a permanent ladder inside.

2″ x 4″s
1″ dowels
6d galvanized finishing nails

Cut the 2″ x 4″ rails the length you want them and remove all splintery and rough areas on the wood with a cheese-grater rasp and sandpaper. Clamp the two rails together or hold them together provisionally with a couple of nails while you drill 1″ holes for the dowel rungs through both at once. Mark the places to drill by drawing a pencil line down the center of one rail and laying out the centers of the holes along it. For kids three to four, 8″ on centers is a good distance apart for the rungs, but an average-size four-year-old can handle an interval of 12″. A drill press will make the work of drilling fast and accurate.

Cut the dowel rungs 16″ or 18″ long. Separate the rails and tap all the rungs into one rail using a mallet or block of wood. As each rung is tapped in flush with the side of the rail, secure it in place with a 6d galvanized finishing nail through rail and rung. It's a good practice to drill pilot holes for the nails to avoid splitting the ends of the dowels. When all rungs are in place on one side, line them up with the holes in the other rail, tap into place, and secure with nails.

You can paint the rails with bright-colored enamel before assembling or finish with clear polyurethane, but don't use either on the rungs or they'll be slippery. A clear penetrating wood preservative finish can be used on the rungs, and may be used to protect the rails from the weather as well.

Another type of ladder can be made from 4" x 4" or 6" x 6" and 1⅜" closet poles as shown. A single free-standing 5' high ladder column like this makes a good climbing structure for a limited space. You'll need an 8' length to make it, as it should be buried 3' deep in a wide hole with a concrete footing.

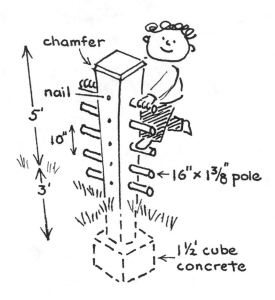

Balancing Beam

An 8' length of 2" x 4" suspended between two heavy blocks of wood (4" x 4" or 6" x 6") will give a three-year-old the heady sensation of tightrope walking. To make balancing trickier for a five-year-old, nail together a few pieces of 2" x 4" or heavier wood to make two blocks like the one illustrated. These will hold the balancing beam with the narrow edge up. The narrow dimension of the 2" x 4" beam should fit snugly in the slot. Turn the blocks upside down, and the beam can be suspended between them broad side up.

Sandbox

The most popular sandpile is always the one the construction workers dump at a worksite. An orderly little sandbox gets much less use. If you have room and aren't at all fastidious about the surrounding lawn, a pickup load of clean sand dumped in a corner of the play yard will make a great hit with your kids.

Boxing in the sandpile will make it a little neater. Select a flat, well-drained spot, preferably with a little shade in the afternoon. Use 2" x 10" construction grade lumber for the sides of the box, and make it as big as you can afford the space and materials for. Between 6' and 8' per side holds a whopping good sandpile. The sides rest directly on the ground, as does the sand — which will mean good drainage. A sandbox doesn't need a bottom.

Lay out the shape of the box with stakes and string, and excavate around the edges so the boards will sit level on the ground. Digging out the inside of the enclosed space, sloping to a depth of about 1½' at the middle will give the box a greater sand capacity — but this step isn't entirely necessary.

The corners of the box can be made with laps or they can be slotted together, as in the illustration.

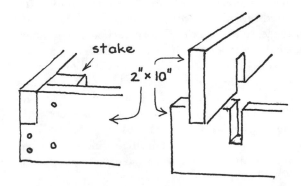

Drive a 2' long stake made from 2" x 4" lumber into the ground at each corner and nail the box to the stakes for stability. If the box is more than 4' on a side, use a stake at the middle of each side — inside the box. Use 10d galvanized common nails to hold the parts together.

Rough spots on the boards should be rasped and sanded to eliminate splintering, and the tops of the stakes can be chamfered for the same purpose. Before assembling the sandbox, paint all surfaces with several coats of a clear penetrating wood preservative and let them soak in and dry thoroughly. Enamel paint — with a good undercoat — may give a snappier look, but probably won't hold up quite as long as the clear wood finish.

A triangular board nailed across one corner is a good addition, not so much as a seat, but as a work surface for playing kids. If the sandbox is big enough, kids won't be sitting demurely on benches around the edge — they'll be out in the middle where the action is.

When cats are a problem in the sandbox, a cover is needed. An old tarpaulin works well, but you'll need ropes fastened through grommets at its corners, which can be used to lash it down securely.

Expensive white sand isn't necessary. It looks a little prettier than brown sand, but kids don't know this or care, and both colors of sand are clean enough for children to play in when sold commercially. A sandbox 6' x 6' takes one cubic yard of sand; an 8' square will accommodate almost two cubic yards.

A huge discarded truck tire makes a fairly good sandbox for a small area. Drill ¾" drainage holes on one side, lay it on the ground, and fill completely with sand.

SWINGS

Hang swings from every stout limb around, or buy a metal A-frame swing set. Don't bother trying to build your own swing framework — it may run higher in material costs for metal pipe or heavy wooden members than the cost of a sturdy store-bought set. Make sure to buy a swing set from a discount house in late fall. These are such big pieces that stores mark them way down just to get rid of them in the off season.

Under swings, you want a soft place for falling kids to land, and good drainage. If a swing set is put in a low spot with poor drainage, when the kids wear out the grass under it, you're stuck with a hard landing surface and miserable puddles under the swings that won't drain off for days after a rain. Wood or bark chips make a relatively soft surface, and won't cling to kids' shoes and get tracked into the house. Don't put sand under swings for soft landings — it invites kids to squat down to dig and play and then get bopped in the head by other kids on the swings. Swings should never be set up on concrete or other hard surfaces, and keep them a full 6' away from fences and other obstructions.

A swing set requires firm anchoring to keep it from rocking back and forth, which can work the bolts loose or even tip it over. Adequate metal anchors that are chained to the legs and pounded into the ground can be bought at the same place you get the swing set. Setting the legs in concrete is cheaper; it also does a slightly better job, is very little more trouble than attaching anchors, and is a treat for the kids, because kids always love to mix up concrete. With a shovel and hoe, a wheelbarrow, a bag of ready-mix concrete, and some kids to do the mixing, the job is done in a jiffy. Cover the exposed surface of the concrete with an absorbent material like leaves or hay to keep it damp for twenty-four to forty-eight hours. And don't hang the swings on the frame for at least five days so the concrete has plenty of time to cure before any stress is put on it. Make sure to use a carpenter's level when setting up a swing framework — the sides should be plumb and the top crossbar level.

Much better than the old wooden board, which cracks little heads that it collides with, are rubber and heavy cloth safety swing seats sold in toy stores. A baby or toddler needs a swing with arms on either side to enclose her, and a strap to hold her in.

Baby Swing

A stable swing for a baby or toddler can be made as a plain box construction with the rope threaded through holes drilled in the sides and passing under the seat as shown. The materials are:

> 4' length of clear 1" x 10" pine
> 6d finishing nails
> 1 belt (cloth OR leather)
> ½" rope

Cut two 11" lengths of 1" x 10" for seat and back, and two 10¼" lengths for the sides. Draw a pencil line across the middle of each side and mark on it the

spots for drilling the ½" rope holes — they should be 2" on centers from the edges of the boards. Cut two narrow slots 8" apart in the bottom edge of the back for the seat belt. All surfaces should be sanded smooth, and the exposed edges of the boards should be sanded round or chamfered. You can decorate the swing by drilling a pattern of ½" or ¾" holes in the back. Assemble the boards with glue and 6d finishing nails. Pilot holes for the nails will save splitting the wood. Finish in a bright color of non-toxic enamel over enamel undercoater.

Any sound cloth or leather belt will do for the seat belt. Thread it through the slots, looping around the back, and test it for size on your child, making new holes with a punch or awl.

A covered porch is a great place for a baby swing, or hang it indoors or out — 5' is a good length for the ropes.

Tire Swing

The standard tire swing is made by looping a rope around a tire and hanging it from a tree. The rope doesn't last long, however, because the bead of the tire (the metal hoop imbedded in the rubber around the hole) cuts into the rope. To eliminate this prob-

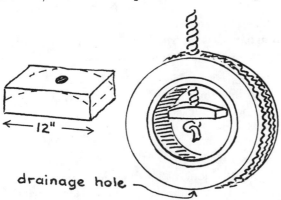

lem, cut a 12" length of 2" x 4" to the contour of the tire as shown in the illustration, and drill a hole for the rope through its center. Another rope hole is drilled in the tread of the tire. The rope passes through the tire and the block and is tied in a big knot under the block, which is then pulled into the tire to support it. Hang a tire swing low for pre-schoolers — a foot or less off the ground — and well out from the trunk of a tree. It's more for climbing and clowning around on than for serious swinging. Look for a tire with a big center hole for this type of swing, and drill a ¾" drainage hole in the bottom of the tread.

Sit-down Tire Swing

You need a saber saw and a fine-tooth blade to cut this excellent swing from a tire. Use the smallest standard tire you can find. Steel-belted radials are no good — they're too hard to cut, and the edges of the steel bands could cut the swing user. Draw the cutting pattern on the tire with chalk. You can leave only the bead rings and a seat about 10" wide, as shown here, or you can leave about a third of the tire intact for a swing with a back. A cushion helps in a tire swing with a back.

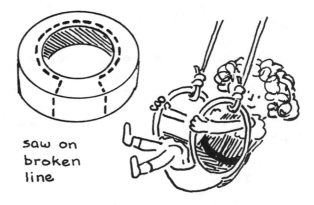

saw on broken line

Tie a rope securely to the top of each bead hoop. If you use chains, loop a short piece of the end of each around the top of the tire bead and bolt it firmly to itself, or join with a repair link. When bolting chain together, use a large flat washer on each side of the assembly and a lock washer directly under the nut.

I've seen swings exactly like this priced at $39.50 in a mail-order catalogue, so you save a bit by making it yourself — a project that won't take much more than an hour.

Hanging Swings

A small indoor or porch swing can be hung from heavy-duty eyebolts screwed into pilot holes in overhead beams. Outdoor swings, however, should have more powerful support at the top.

If you loop a rope or a chain around the limb of a tree, protect the limb with an old piece of garden hose split lengthwise and wrapped around the chain or rope. When a chain is wrapped too tightly around a limb or other support, the first link will act as a pivot, wearing quickly and breaking. Join the chain with a short bolt, flat washers on either side of the assembly, and a lock washer before the nut is put on. A rope can be joined with the whipped joint shown here.

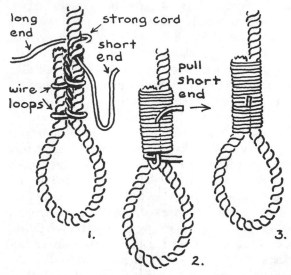

Heavy-duty eyebolts fastened through holes drilled in a strong limb or other horizontal support bar provide a better way to hang a swing. Holes

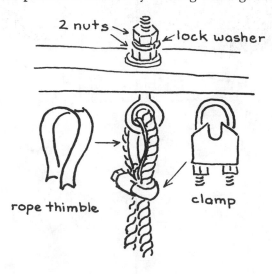

drilled in a limb will do little or no damage to the tree. Use a large flat washer under the nut, and, preferably, the bolt will be long enough to take two nuts for added safety protection. A rope can be attached to an eyebolt using a heavyweight metal rope thimble inside the loop and a steel rope clamp to secure the short end of the loop. A heavyweight S-hook, firmly crimped shut, will join a chain to an eyebolt.

Ropes or Chain? Ropes are cheaper than chain and have a nicer feel, especially in winter, but they wear out much faster and they are affected by the weather — a swing on long ropes will be several inches higher after a rain than it is on a dry day.

For hanging a baby swing, ½" hemp rope is sufficient, but go to ⅝" for a well-supported board swing, and ¾" for a tire. With nylon and polyethylene rope, you can use lighter weights — ½" is enough for a tire or board. Never use clothesline, which simply isn't strong enough for any swing.

There's no need to buy expensive welded link chain. Cheaper woven wire chain is sufficient for

swings used by preschoolers and school-age kids, too — the proper size is known as 3-0 and has seven and a half links per foot. S-hooks can be used for many chain joints, but should never be left open; always crimp both loops firmly shut. Chain repair links and cold-shut chain repair links are also handy for joining chain. An S-hook or repair link should always be heavier than the chain being joined.

Eight feet is about the maximum safe length for swing ropes or chains, and a baby swing should be hung on shorter supports — about 5' long.

Rope Ladders

Rope ladders are a great indoor or outdoor challenge for kids age four and a half and older. The simplest is made by suspending a length of ¾" rope with plain overhand knots tied in it at 12" intervals — or make the interval shorter for a small child. At the bottom end, to give your child a step up, make a whipped loop as in the illustration above. Be sure to make it much too small to act as a noose.

A ladder with ½" rope sides and 1" dowel rungs is

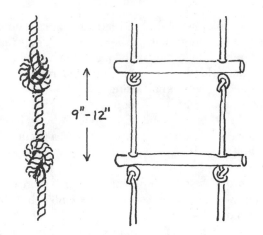

also easy to make. The rungs can be 14" or 16" long with holes drilled for the rope 1½" in from the ends. Space the rungs 12" or less apart with knots tied under them; 5½' is a good length for a vertical rope ladder for a preschooler.

PLAYHOUSES

A playhouse can be as elaborate as you want to make it — or as simple. I go for simple ones knocked together from scrap materials because preschoolers will stay involved in the construction of a structure that goes up quickly, and will learn a lot from the experience of building it with Dad.

A big cardboard box can be converted into a playhouse in minutes. Just cut doors and windows with a sharp knife wherever your child thinks they should go, leaving them hinged on one side so they open and close. Or help a five-year-old cut the doors and windows with a keyhole saw or wallboard saw. Appliance stores often give away huge cardboard boxes for the asking. Cardboard of course won't stand much weather, so a wooden crate or a huge wooden cable reel is a better find. Cut a door and

windows, make sure there are no nail ends jutting through the wood, and add whatever improvements you and your kids can think of — some cloth stapled inside to cover the doorway or as curtains at the windows, a box or an overturned bucket for furniture.

Or start from scratch, making a framework of 2" x 4"s and adding scrap siding or light plywood. Any construction method is great, but the best plan is one you and your kids figure out together.

A playhouse needn't be a conventional house-type structure. One father showed me a wonderful roofed log fortress he'd made with 6' lengths of trees that had been cut to make a larger back-yard clearing behind his house. He and the kids had dug a circular trench about 6' in diameter and set the long logs upright in it. The logs had been reinforced and tied together with pieces of scrap wood nailed to them on the inside, and a piece of plywood had been set on at a slight slant for a roof.

Use any material you have at hand — especially if it's free or very cheap. Tires can be bolted together to make simple structures with lots of nice circular windows for kids to crawl in and out of. Polyethylene sheeting, which can be bought inexpensively in big rolls from any lumberyard, can be used to cover virtually any type of framework. Across is a plan for a polyethylene-covered teepee. Pup tents and other structures can be made from this see-through plastic material tied down to stakes with ropes. To make strong grommet holes for the rope, cut 3" doughnut shapes from the sides of used plastic bottles (milk or bleach), sandwich the polyethylene between two of these and staple them together with about eight staples. Then poke a hole

polyethylene sheet

through the polyethylene in the center of the doughnut and put through the rope.

Impromptu playhouses don't need roofs, and anything that represents walls is fine. A super-simple play structure can be made using three or four closely spaced young trees as a framework and stapling plastic sheeting "walls" around them. If the walls are high enough off the ground, preschoolers can crawl under to get inside; or cut a slit partway up one side for a door.

A playhouse can be quite small, because kids like to go into a tight dark place and giggle. A flashlight will help if it's very dark.

Plastic Teepee

This see-through teepee is great in the fall and spring, when the sun keeps it warmer than the outside air. We even had a couple of family picnics crowded into its cozy warmth in the fall. In summer the inside gets hot and steamy and the grass on the floor grows tall. But open the door flap and in half an hour the draft clears the condensation out — the same wonderful draft that in a real teepee carries the cooking smoke up through the small hole at the peak. The materials you'll need to build it are:

> six 8' saplings OR 8' lengths 1" x 2"
> 10' wide roll 4 mil thick polyethylene
>   sheeting
> galvanized medium-weight wire
> 2 empty bleach bottles
> staples and staple gun

Peg a 3' length of string in the ground in the middle of the flat place where the teepee will go. At six roughly equidistant points around the circle that the end of the string describes, use a crowbar or a pickax to gouge holes in the ground for the thick ends of the saplings or the 1" x 2"s. The teepee poles are pushed into these holes as far as they will go, which will probably be about 6". Gather them at the top, allowing about 1½' to stick up above the juncture, which is bound together with the galvanized wire.

The cover is cut from the polyethylene in the shape of a big semicircle with about 1' extra at the ends for overlapping. Cut it about 4" longer than the distance between the ground and the intersection of the poles so it will reach the ground all around. Wrap the cover on for fit, holding it in place with clamps.

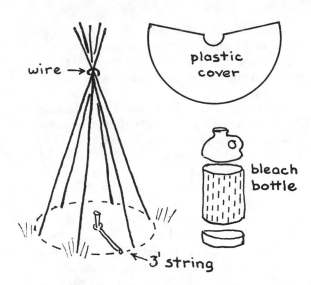

Cut off the bottoms and tops of the well-rinsed empty bleach bottles and cut the sides into ¾" strips — running up and down. These strips are used between the staples and the plastic sheeting to keep the plastic from ripping. Work around the teepee from pole to pole, stapling the cover down. Stretch the material fairly tightly between poles. Use three bleach bottle strips per pole and plenty of staples. At the pole where the material meets, overlap and staple at the top, but leave part unstapled for a flap door.

TIRES

Every play yard needs a collection of defunct tires for kids to build with, roll around, and sit in — children find dozens of uses for them. Make sure, though, to drill drainage holes in tires before leaving them outside, or they quickly become a nuisance, filling with rainwater, which freezes solid and heavy in winter, breeds mosquitoes in summer, and gets all over kids who pick the tires up. Drill three or four ¾" holes per side. A block of wood to hold the sides apart will make the drilling job easier.

If you're sensitive to what the neighbors might think about unsightly old tires in the back yard, make them sightly by painting them bright colors with nontoxic rubber-base paint. Two-tone tires are very snazzy.

Kids will sit and "ride" on a tire buried halfway in the ground, and crawl through the semicircular hole, and jump up and over. Before burying a tire, drill some ¾" holes in the tread part that will be underground, to help with drainage.

Tires can be bolted together in dozens of arrangements for kids to climb on and into. Use ⅜" machine bolts with big flat washers against the rubber on both sides and a lock washer under the nut.

Old tires aren't hard to come by. In every dump and behind nearly every gas station are all you can use, free, and thank you for carting them away. Avoid tires with rips or slashes that a child could catch a hand or finger in.

INNER TUBES

Tire inner tubes are great for kids of every age. At one, an inner tube is a big soft obstacle for a child to climb. It makes a bouncy horse for a one-and-a-half-year-old who straddles it and posts up and down. Some preschoolers like just to sit in a big inner tube, as in a magic circle, and think; some pretend a tube is a car or a boat and sit in it and drive; some roll them around, others use them as sleds in winter, and all kids bounce on them.

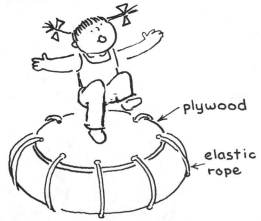

To make an inner tube bouncier, cut a circle of ¼" plywood to fit the top. Drill holes at intervals around the edge, and tie the plywood circle and the tube together with light rope as in the illustration. Elastic rope does an even better job. This trampoline can be used indoors or out, but don't leave it

outside or the weather will quickly destroy the plywood. For a weatherproof trampoline like this you'll have to use ½" or ¾" marine plywood, which is expensive, and paint it with several coats of spar varnish. This assembly makes a nice raft, too.

Most gas stations will give old inner tubes away free for the asking — but if you ask in July or August, when everybody and his brother is asking for inner tubes to float in, you may find the filling station owner demanding a steep price. A dump is another good source. An inner tube you get free will usually have a hole in it. Punctures are easily mended using a small, cheap kit of patching materials that you can get from a hardware or auto supply store.

GARDEN HOSE AND WATER SLIDE

Standard equipment in every play yard are a garden hose for summer and a father to spray water on the kids.

Make a wonderful water slide by laying out a big sheet of plastic on a grassy slope and keeping it thoroughly wet with the hose. When the kids hit this, they go skidding. Any big plastic dropcloth will do; the heavier the gauge, the better. Standard 4 mil thick polyethylene sheeting — the kind used widely in construction — is perfect and can be bought in rolls from any lumberyard or building supply store.

Weight down the top end of your water slide by wrapping the plastic around a heavy board, or use big smooth stones and make sure the kids stay clear of them. Put the slide on soft, grassy ground, because you and the kids will do plenty of hard-hitting belly flops on it. Move it to a new spot on the grass every half hour, or the grass will be cooked by the sun shining through the plastic. You can use a lawn sprinkler to keep the water slide doused down.

An inexpensive molded plastic wading pool is a play yard must for toddlers in the summer, and your kids will keep on using it for years. Kids should be supervised in a wading pool, because a small child can slip and drown in even a couple of inches of water.

RIDING PATH

Most kids could spend the whole day pedaling around on a trike or big wheel if there was anywhere to ride. If there aren't safe sidewalks in your neighborhood, but you have some room around the house, the nicest thing you can do for a preschooler is to lay out a long path of concrete, flat paving stones, or even bricks. A circular path for riding round and round is much better than one with a beginning and end where kids have to turn around to pedal back.

WORK AREA

A little work area makes a great addition to any play area — a flat raised surface for kids to use when they're drawing or painting or making things from play dough. A low table will do the trick, or even some boards laid across blocks.

If there are no paving stones or concrete walkways in the play yard where your child can draw with chalk, she'll love helping to mix and pour a small concrete slab especially for chalking. Keep it close to the side of the house or somewhere else well away from open places where kids run and tumble.

In a corner of the play yard, you can loosen the dirt with a spading fork or shovel to give a five-year-old a spot to do some serious digging. And if there's a sunny corner, try digging it up and helping your child plant his own little garden; see p. 311 for more on gardening and preschoolers. A child may not harvest much produce from his own corner garden — most preschoolers are so investigative and impatient that they dig up the beans the day after they're planted to see if they're growing. But a few plants will take hold and your child will be super proud of them.

MAINTENANCE

Bolts work loose and sometimes rust out and break off under the dual onslaught of kids and weather that play yard equipment is constantly subjected to. As important as setting the equipment up in the first place is keeping it in safe operating order. Every few weeks, make an inspection tour of the play yard, wrench in hand, checking for tightness every bolt at every connecting point on swing frame, climber, slide, etc. Also keep a sharp eye on swing chains and ropes, and replace them when they appear worn. A check like this doesn't take long and is a big deal for the child who helps you by carrying a few extra tools.

Replace rusted bolts, and when metal equipment starts to lose its paint and rust forms at most of the joints, scrape the rust down with a wire brush, rub with emery cloth, and repaint the whole piece of equipment with rust-resisting undercoater and bright-colored enamel — let the kids pick the new color.

Since he turned five, Gregory has delighted in the loud squeaking of his swings, but for two years before that it drove him batty and he begged me nearly every week to lubricate the swing chain connectors. I found that spray graphite does a little better and more lasting job than ordinary household oil.

Check wooden play structures for splintery areas, though your kids are checking for these every day with their hands and will usually point them out. Rasp and sand down rough areas. A wooden structure finished with clear penetrating wood preservative should be given a coat or two of the same finish every three years to help it stand up to the weather. Keep kids away until the finish is thoroughly soaked in and dry.

Once a year, poke around with an awl at the base of wooden uprights set in the ground to check for rotting. If you catch rotting when it is still only superficial — say ½" deep — you may be able to save the upright. Dig around the post to discover the extent of the rotting. Chisel out the weak spot down to sound wood, and paint with several coats of wood preservative.

KIDS' ROOMS

The ideal home setup, of course, has a spacious playroom to contain the major part of the kids' clutter — but how many young families have that kind of room to spare? Any sort of playroom, no matter how small, is a godsend, so consider fixing up part of a basement, or attic, or even dividing a larger room. Most of us, however, are stuck with making the most of a child's bedroom so it can be used for sleep, play, work, and a multitude of other purposes.

No matter how it's decorated, the biggest contribution you can make to a child's room is to provide ample storage space — shelves on every available wall space to store toys and books; boxes and drawers so things can be put away easily and the decks cleared for action. A child who has easy, open access to all her toys and other paraphernalia can use them when she likes, and use them imaginatively. In a cluttered room, though, a child can become confused by the jumble of toys, blocks, and books, and will pick through them, fiddling with each for a short time and then tossing it back in the pile, never settling down to a long, satisfying period of work or play with one thing.

Shelves in a kid's room don't all have to be low down where he can reach the stuff on them. Build them right on up to the ceiling and store things at the top that are seldom used. If they're in view, they may one day catch his eye and his interest, and he can always ask Dad or Mom to get them down. Make sure, though, that high shelves are securely anchored to the studs in the wall, because every child will climb wherever he can get a foothold. You might also build a ladder with dowel rungs (see p. 107) right into the shelf setup to give an approved path for climbing.

A closet, even a fairly small one, can be fitted with more shelves for toys, and the closet floor can be used as a little walk-in play area. Kids, especially boys, don't wear many clothes that go on hangers, and these are short, so they can be hung up high and out of the way.

Put up a row of clothes hooks at child height in the closet or on a wall. No kid will fold clothes neatly and lay them on the end of the bed without overwhelming badgering from parents, but even a two-and-a-half-year-old will get into the habit of hanging up pajamas and clothes if there are hooks handy.

Ideally, hooks should always be a little higher than a child's head, to avoid injuries from running or falling against them.

A toddler can use a sturdy low worktable to advantage, and from three on, it's a must in a child's room. A preschooler loves to work at a "desk" — especially if she knows that's what Daddy does. The worktable will be used for drawing, painting, clay, nail hammering if it's sturdy enough, climbing, jumping, block building, bedroom picnics, and dozens of other uses and abuses. A folding easel makes a nice setup for painting, but isn't altogether necessary — most kids will get more mileage out of a flat table surface for painting, and some much prefer it. Almost as important as a good working surface is a good light to go with it. The best lighting comes over the left shoulder for right-handers, and over the right shoulder for lefties so a shadow isn't thrown across the work by the working hand.

An indoor trapeze with rings and a low swing is a terrific addition to a child's room at four. You can get indoor trapeze sets with fittings that allow them to be hung in a doorway. Rather than blocking a doorway, though, you can install a trapeze from heavy-duty eyebolts screwed into pilot holes in ceiling beams in the middle of a child's room. When not in use, it can be rolled up above everyone's head and hooked in place with open S-hooks.

BUNK BEDS

Built-in bunk beds are a favorite project for handy-man fathers, but after talking to half a dozen men who built them only to have their wives complain bitterly for years afterward about how hard they were to make up, my advice is to use ordinary beds if at all possible, and find another project that will be better appreciated. Mothers crack their heads against the top berth when they're straightening the bottom one, and they find it almost impossible to straighten up the upper bunk — the height and the railings are too much to contend with.

To be fair about this, I have talked to a couple of satisfied bunk builders. One had done a beautiful job of constructing two upper berths above built-in closets and a cozy low play area, and the advantage of the extra storage space had offset the disadvantage of high beds. The other had built an upper over his son's bed that was only used for occasional overnight visitors.

One possibility for extending the space in a child's room without the drawbacks of bunk beds is to build a sturdy play loft over low beds, or, even better, over a storage area. The ladder going up to the loft adds excitement to the room setup, and a metal fireman's pole for quick descents will make the place into a preschooler's dream room. A trundle bed — a small bed that rolls out of the way under a larger bed during the day — is another satisfactory method for winning space in cramped quarters, but mothers complain that the small bed always has to be pulled out for naps and when the child who sleeps in it is sent to his room to think about a misdeed.

If you can't resist the temptation to build bunks and you want an excellent detailed plan for beds set with the upper at right angles to the lower, an arrangement that saves a lot of space, look for a copy of Sunset Books' *Easy-to-Make Furniture* (Menlo Park, California: Lane Publishing, 1977).

CHALKBOARDS

Nail inexpensive ⅛″ hardboard to any low place on a wall, paint it with chalkboard paint, and your two-and-a-half-year-old or older child has the ideal place to draw. The bigger the chalkboard, the better; 4′ x 4′ is an excellent size. The hardboard, smooth side up, can be nailed around the edges to the studs in

the wall with 1½″ wire nails, or use wallboard nails and cover their big heads with lattice or other molding strips to make a trim border. If the hardboard buckles in the middle, tack it down to the studs in a few places with 1½″ wire nails. Both tempered and cheaper untempered hardboard are fine for this purpose.

Chalkboard paint is sold in most well-supplied paint stores. It comes in green and sometimes in a snappy-looking deep blue. Rough up the smooth side of the hardboard a little with medium sandpaper before applying the chalkboard paint.

Any blank surface in the house can be turned into a chalkboard — you can tack it to the front of a toy box or the back of a door. The kitchen is a terrific place for a low chalkboard on a wall or the side of a cabinet — the chalk dust can be easily cleaned up from the kitchen floor.

BULLETIN BOARDS

From one or more 4′ x 8′ panels of homasote, you can make a huge bulletin board for a child's room. Homasote is much less expensive than cork, much easier to put up, and it can be painted to match the walls of the room, or painted a snazzy color for contrast. Cover as big a wall space as there's room for — no matter how big you make it, there won't be room for all of your child's drawings and paintings, family photos, and pictures clipped from magazines of Bert and Ernie and Mickey Mouse. Besides, a big bulletin board can become a kind of learning center where you and your child post pictures of new things he's interested in — photos of animals clipped from magazines for a toddler, or big paper letters when he's learning the alphabet, or a clock face with cardboard hands that turn when he's work-

ing on time. Change the display frequently to keep it fresh and catch your child's interest and imagination.

Homasote can be nailed directly to the studs in a wall using roofing nails. The big nail heads largely disappear when the bulletin board is painted, and then disappear completely under the things pinned to the board. If it's necessary to make a seam between two panels of homasote to fill the space you have, cover it with 1⅜" lattice molding held on with long brads. For a neat job, you can trim around the edges with lattice or any other type of molding strip.

Get a big supply of push pins from a stationery store. They cost more than thumbtacks, but they make it possible for a four-year-old, who would be all thumbs struggling with thumbtacks, to pin things up easily by herself.

Save scrap pieces of homasote left over from putting up a bulletin board for your child to drive tacks and small nails into with a hammer. It is the ideal first nailing material because it doesn't offer as much resistance as wood.

FIBER DRUMS

A father who works in a chemical plant showed me big fiber drums with light metal bottoms and tops that he had brought home from work and converted into wonderful deep storage bins for the kids' room. His two boys had decorated the outsides with bright paintings, and into them went anything big. No small toys or little parts, because the kids are forever dumping out the contents and using the drums as playthings. They love to climb in and crouch down at the bottom — the drums are about two thirds the size of a garbage can. Laid on its side, a drum becomes a cramped play cave, or one child can lie inside while another rolls it back and forth across the room.

If you can't get fiber drums as surplus where you work, look in the Yellow Pages under "Barrels and Drums" for a supplier. They come in a wide variety of sizes for different types of storage, but definitely get one big enough for your child to fit into. If the top is designed to snap on, get rid of the snap fasteners so a child can't be trapped inside. Drums can be covered with contact paper or wallpaper cut into designs, or painted with latex paint or kids' tempera. If the kids are going to decorate the drums, paint them a solid light color first for a handsome effect.

CHILDPROOFING AND SAFETY

Childproofing a home is a double job. You want to arrange the place so your child isn't exposed to hazards, but at the same time you want to set it up so she has every reasonable opportunity to explore and investigate, play in, learn about, and enjoy her home. Putting everything in the house up out of reach or under lock and key and sticking the kid in a playpen will keep her safe, but she'll be bored. The trick is to eliminate the dangers without getting rid of the challenges and the fun. See p. 45 for more thoughts on safety and giving a child maximum access to the interesting things around her.

The task of childproofing isn't a one-time affair that's taken care of when the baby comes home from the hospital. Every six months or so you find that there's a major new childproofing job to be done, because your child can reach new levels and get into new mischief. Most of the basics of childproofing are outlined below according to age, and Car Safety, Poisons, and Fire are treated under separate headings. Other safety measures are discussed throughout this book under appropriate headings, for instance, Tricycles and Two-wheelers (p. 272) and Lawn Mowing (p. 309). And of course every house or apartment building has unique hazards. Some of these you'll spot and correct, and meanwhile your child will use all his ingenuity in discovering and calling your attention to the others.

BABIES

A new baby gets full-time protection. He's never left alone, except in a safe bassinet or crib (see p. 41 for notes on bassinet and crib safety). He's always held in the bath and on the changing table. You take care that nothing he handles presents a threat; common sense, for instance, dictates that a string of beads or a pacifier cord won't go around his neck and possibly choke him. He's never given sharp or small objects, and toys for a baby are always unbreakable, with rounded edges, and much too big to swallow. A baby seat is always on the floor, where it has no chance to fall. And since a baby spends most of his first six months on his back or asleep, he doesn't contrive to get into much trouble.

SIX MONTHS

Somewhere in the middle of her first year, a baby starts to crawl and explore, and every object in reach goes into her mouth for the taste test. The fifth month is a good time to get the house ready for her, and this is the point at which you do the lion's share of babyproofing. Go at it from the baby's level —

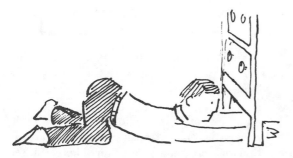

down on the floor. With a little crawling around, you find pennies or straight pins forgotten under the couch or in the little space between the bookcase and the wall — I found broken glass under a radiator and realized we'd never had any reason to look

under the radiators before. You notice that the electric cords from lamps and the TV hang down in nice free loops ready for a baby to tug on. You see sharp corners on low pieces of furniture or maybe a nail or screw protruding from the bottom of a low table. You realize the fireplace screen can be pulled over with a little tug. All these problems can be corrected so your new crawler will be able to roam around freely and check the place out.

Wires and Outlets

Plug all unused outlets with child-resistant blanks — they are cheap and can be bought in any hardware or variety store. The blanks prevent a child from plugging into 110 volts by shoving a bobby pin or the tines of a fork into the interesting socket.

Keep all wiring in every room out of reach, or secure it so a tug won't bring a table lamp crashing down. This usually means some rearranging so

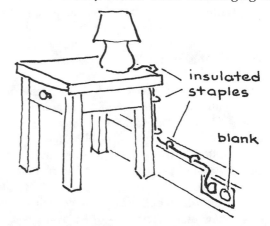

insulated staples

blank

cords and outlets are safely behind heavy pieces of furniture. Exposed wires can be fastened firmly to baseboards and secured along the backs of table legs and other pieces of furniture with insulated staples.

Kitchen

The kitchen is the highest risk room in the home, but a baby spends a lot of her time crawling around its floor, because this is where the action is. It won't be long before she'll be prying open low cabinet doors and pulling out low drawers, so make sure all the things in them are safe for her to handle and play with. Rearrange kitchen storage so that pots and pans and other harmless containers are stored under the sink and in the low cabinets. Canned foods can go under the sink, too. All kitchen cleansers, bleach, wax, etc., go up out of reach on a high shelf. Locking them up in a cabinet at the child's level isn't an adequate safeguard. If you don't know whether or not some product is toxic, put it out of reach anyway.

Give a child his own low drawer in the kitchen to keep toys in and allow him regular access to plastic containers and metal pots and pans, and he will feel he's part of the operation. Even though everything at his level will be safe to handle, you'll still want to restrict his access to some low cabinets, or the pots will always be out in the middle of the floor.

You can stretch big rubber bands between cabinet handles to keep a child out, but they are a nuisance to remove and replace each time you want to throw something in the trash or get a frying pan. Child-guard latches are widely available in hardware and child specialty shops, and they quickly repay in convenience the hour or two it will take you to install them. These catches come in a number of styles, but the basic design is essentially the same: the catch goes inside the cabinet door or drawer and allows it to be opened only an inch; an adult can release it at this point with the touch of a finger, but a child can't get at it.

In order to be effective, child-guard catches have to be installed within an inch of the opening edge of a cabinet door, or the opening center of a pair of doors, and often magnetic catches have already been installed in this position. Unscrew the magnetic catches and move them along an inch or two, fill the old screw holes with plastic wood, and install the child-guard latches, using the old holes if they are in a convenient position — the plastic wood will set up and grip the new screws. While you're installing catches on lower cabinets, you might as well put one on a high drawer where knives and other sharp kitchen utensils may be stored, against the day when your child will be up and climbing.

A crawler won't be able to reach the stove top yet, but start early explaining that it is HOT, and get in the habit of using the back burners first and always turning pot handles to the back of the stove.

Eliminate tablecloths for the duration — a baby will pull on the skirt and bring down the hot soup.

Bathroom

Nonslip stick-on strips go on the floor of the tub when the baby starts to bathe in it, and your child is never left alone in the bathtub — a child can slip and drown in seconds, even in shallow water. Be careful with hot water, too. And keep all medicines, cosmetics, cleaning products, and shoe polish high up in cabinets.

Gates

Install gates at the tops and bottoms of stairways. There's no great advantage in the type of gate that slides open to lock snugly against the sides of a doorframe and saves you from screwing hardware into the woodwork — it has to be put aside whenever it's taken down, which means finding a place to put it, and you end up always tripping over it. Standard wooden folding pantograph-type gates are the best. The few screws that hold the hinges and catch in place won't do the woodwork any harm. When the gate eventually comes down, the screw holes can be filled with plastic wood or a latex putty compound, and touched up with a dab of paint. The filled holes will never be noticed, because they are way below adult eye level. If it's easy to arrange, install the gate at the bottom of the stairs across the third stair. This gives a baby a good climbing place to practice on, but saves her a long fall.

Gates seem very much in the way at first, but after a while opening and closing them every time you go up or downstairs becomes an automatic reflex.

Newer houses often have widely spaced iron railings between levels and beside stairs that are no protection for a crawling baby or an older child. On some the rails are so wide apart that a school-age child can easily squeeze through between them. Heavyweight nonslip vinyl floor matting that comes in long narrow rolls can be woven in and out through the rails to prevent falls. This kind of matting is usually translucent and isn't particularly ugly — you can find it in hardware stores and housewares departments.

Small Dangers

A child can aspirate (inhale) and choke on any small object. Some of the worst things for babies and toddlers are very attractive to them: popcorn, nuts, chewing gum, and uninflated balloons. Toys shouldn't have small parts that can be pried loose.

Plastic Bags

Get into the habit of tying all light plastic bags in knots and throwing them out. With his head in a garbage bag or dry-cleaner's wrap, a child can quickly suffocate.

ONE YEAR

When she's up and clomping around toward the end of the first year or in the beginning of the second, your child will be able to get to the tops of tables where you've been putting things out of reach, and soon she's climbing on everything and going everywhere. Keep an eye on her. Fancy china ashtrays and tippy end tables soon find their way into closets and storage. Now is the time to redouble your efforts to keep the kitchen safe, to put all medicines and household cleaning products, etc., under lock and key, to fence in the yard. Now you're extra careful always to fasten doors that lead to driveways, apartment building hallways, storage areas, swimming or wading pools, stairwells, etc. Check out the windows — some may need guards or latches that allow them to be opened only so far. A hook and eyelet fastener high up on the outside of a bathroom door will help defeat a toddler's urges to dabble in the john and break her neck climbing into the tub.

You can't save a new walker from the thousands of pratfalls and spills he'll take, but you can roughen the soles of his new shoes with coarse sandpaper to give him a little extra traction.

This is the stage at which you learn to protect yourself against the little hazards a child constantly throws in your path. You learn always to look at the stairs before going up or down, because for years to come there will always be a toy on one to trip you. Every night after I lock up, I automatically kick

wide paths through the children's clutter so there will be clear routes to the doors and the basement in case of a fire in the night.

Lock and Key

Now is the time to put all medicines and other toxic items in the bathroom in a locked cabinet, including cleansers, toilet bowl cleaners, cosmetics, and shoe polish. Keep a key handy hanging on a nail or stuck to a magnet in an out-of-the-way place, and keep spare keys in your wallet and Mom's purse. Toothpaste, Band-Aids, and other harmless things can go in an unlocked cabinet over the sink.

All toxic and poisonous kitchen items should be stored high up on a shelf inside a closet. The closet can be locked, but the best arrangement is to cover the dangerous shelf with its own locked sliding or hinged door. That way, the bottom part of the closet can be used for convenient storage of brooms, etc.

In the garage and around a workbench, also provide locked storage for insecticides, pesticides, paints, fertilizers, gasoline, and other toxic substances. See p. 300 for shop safety, and p. 309 for pointers on storing power tools and other equipment for outdoor work.

Fences

Fencing is the most costly item on the childproofer's list. You don't need to spend a fortune and make a play yard look like a maximum-security prison with a 5' chain-link wall around it. The least expensive 3' fencing will contain a toddler, which is all you're trying to achieve, because when she reaches three, she'll find her way over, under, or around almost any barrier you can erect. If looks aren't important, use 2" x 4" mesh galvanized fencing 3' high hung on standard 4' metal fence posts. With a good wire cutter, pliers, and a small sledgehammer to drive the posts, two people can enclose a large play area with this kind of fencing in an afternoon.

TWO

A two-year-old can start to learn about dangers, but don't count on warnings and safety lessons having a lasting effect, because a two-year-old wants to try everything, especially the things he's been told are off limits.

You can tell a child is two if she has a big welt on her forehead — this is the age for falls and smashing into things. Glass doors are a great hazard at two. The bottom panel of a storm door should be fitted with safety glass; if it isn't, replace it with plexiglas or cover it with a grille. Use furniture to block a straight run at a big sliding glass door, and remove interior hinged glass doors for the duration. Large decals on glass will call a child's attention to it, but a giddy runner may still crash into it.

Two is also the age when kids break and run in a parking lot and dash toward the street when your back is turned. Don't turn your back. And get tough with offenders.

Two-year-olds make it their special goal to search out and swallow toxic and poisonous substances. See the article on Poisons below for thoughts on frustrating this effort.

THREE–SIX

A three-year-old starts to learn and accept some restraints. You still want to keep his world hazard-free, but now the emphasis can start to shift from full-time vigilance to teaching him safe ways to act around water, fire, traffic, how to handle tools and kitchen equipment safely, and you even begin to trust him alone for short periods. Set firm limits on where he can ride on a tricycle and start now to teach him the right way to cross the street. The age at which a child can be allowed to cross a street alone will vary from four to nine, depending on the child, but more on the kind of traffic in the street.

At four, five, and six, as she wins your confidence, your child will be allowed to roam farther afield, but always make it clear just how far, and be sure she knows the territory and how to get back. Make it your business to scout out your child's world, including the neighbors' back yards, and satisfy yourself that she isn't exposed every day to attractive hazards like an unfenced pool, a deep hole, or an abandoned refrigerator or washing machine with a door that could trap her inside.

CHILDPROOFING GRANDPARENTS

Grandmother always has cookies and candy for your child, but she may also have drain cleaner under the sink and heart attack pills on the night table in her bedroom. Tactfully help grandparents — or other relatives or friends — take basic childproofing safety measures before your child stays with them.

The grandmothers I know insist on leaving fragile ashtrays and bowls of flowers on low tables and then constantly shooing toddlers away from them and having fits when they get broken or overturned. Tact and persuasion seem to be no match for this syndrome.

CAR SAFETY

Always buckle your kids in. Cars are the number-one brutalizer and killer of little kids — way out ahead of all the diseases, way ahead of child abuse, way ahead of other types of accidents. Every year a thousand children under five are killed on our highways, and 150,000 are seriously injured. In a crash, a child who isn't strapped down in an adequate restraint device becomes a projectile — and a very heavy one. In a nice slow 20 mph collision, a 15-pound baby is hurled forward with the irresistible force of 300 pounds. Kids playing loose in a car are not only in danger themselves — in a collision they can be violently slammed into other passengers and even injure other kids who are properly safeguarded.

On a baby's very first car ride — on his way home from the hospital — he should be strapped securely in a rear-facing infant seat — not held in his mother's arms. A mother's arms may cuddle and comfort a baby, but they don't do a bit of good in an accident.

If the adult is wearing a safety belt, the force of the collision will tear the baby from her arms and hurl him forward. If adult and baby are strapped in together with the same belt, the adult's weight, vastly increased by collision forces, can press the belt deeply into the child's body. And if no belt is used, the child can be crushed between the hurtling body of the holder and the interior of the car.

Strapping your kids in for each and every ride may be a little inconvenient, but it is the only way to give them reasonable protection. There is no way to make it safe for children to ride unrestrained in the front or back of a car, station wagon, van, truck, or towed camper or trailer.

When you buckle your kids in faithfully and habitually, they grow up used to it, and *expect* to ride with a strap. It also helps if they see Dad and Mom always buckling up, too. Of course they try to squirm free, and even a one-year-old will figure out ways to unbuckle a harness or safety belt, but on the whole it becomes a habit — as good a habit as a person can have.

You may have trouble figuring out just what kind of infant or toddler restraint system to buy, because a bewildering variety of these is offered by auto dealers, department stores, and juvenile specialty stores — and some that are offered are inadequate since the federal government has been lax in setting standards. For accurate up-to-date information on the best crash-tested devices, write to Physicians for Automotive Safety, 50 Union Avenue, Irvington, New Jersey 07111; send twenty-five cents and a self-addressed stamped business envelope and ask for a copy of the excellent pamphlet *Don't Risk Your Child's Life*. You can also write for information to Action for Child Transportation Safety, Inc., 400 Central Park West, #15P, New York, New York 10025. *Consumer Reports* magazine is another good source of information about car safety devices.

Infant Seats

Properly designed infant car carriers face the rear of the car seat. The baby, half reclining, is strapped into the bucketlike carrier with a harness, and the carrier is held down firmly on the car seat with a lap belt. The standard make — the General Motors Infant Love Seat — is widely available through G.M., Ford, Chrysler, and American Motors dealers, as well as in department and juvenile specialty stores. Some other infant seats listed as satisfactory by the Physicians for Automotive Safety (see address above) can be converted to serve as front-facing seats when your child is old enough to sit up without support.

Do *not* use a "car bed" — it won't provide adequate protection for your baby.

For a newborn riding in an infant seat, roll up a receiving blanket and put it under her shoulders and head for extra support and comfort.

Toddler Restraints

When a child is old enough to sit up without support, he can switch from the rear-facing infant seat to a forward-facing toddler restraint, and here you have a choice of several different types.

Shields Shields are the favorite device of the safety experts. The child sits directly on the car seat and a big padded tunnel-shaped shield is placed over her. This is then buckled down with a lap belt. No harness is used to hold the child in place. The one problem with a shield is that a squirmy kid can wriggle down through it and out the bottom. If your child isn't terribly squirmy and accepts some direction, a shield is an excellent choice.

Car Seats The most common device is a solidly built seat raised somewhat off the seat of the car; the child is strapped into the seat with a harness and the seat and child are then secured with a lap belt. Many of these devices also have a tether strap attached at the top of the back. When a child rides in the back seat, this strap *must* be connected to an anchor clip bolted into the rear window ledge or the back floor of a hatchback or station wagon. If the child rides in the front seat, the tether strap can be connected to a buckle of a lap belt in the rear seat. But in any position in the car, the back tether strap has to be used to hold the child seat firmly in place, or the seat will lose its protective value entirely.

tether straps

Before buying a child seat, make sure to note if it has a back tether strap and determine whether or not the anchoring clip can be installed conveniently in the rear window ledge or back floor of your car. Parents often buy seats with back straps and neglect to use them, either because they find it's impossible to install the anchor clip or because they put off installing it. If there is any chance this will happen in your case, buy a seat designed to be held down only by a lap belt.

If your child's seat has both upright and reclining positions, lock it into upright and leave it there. The reclining position is not safe, and it's not necessary, because kids go to sleep in almost any position in a car — including bolt upright.

Safety Harnesses   Safety harnesses are less expensive than car seats and provide good protection. To work effectively, though, a harness must be secured with a back tether strap like the one described above under Car Seats.

Hand-Me-Downs   Be extra carefull about taking a hand-me-down car restraint. Until quite recently, children's car seats weren't designed for safety, but only to lift the child up to the level of the windows, and most old seats are just plain dangerous. The worst — which happily are beginning to disappear into junk heaps — were designed to hook over the back of the car seat.

Try to get the manufacturer's directions for using a secondhand child seat. If they haven't been saved, write to the manufacturer for a copy, because correct installation and use are often the keys to whether or not the device will protect your child — as with the back tether straps described above.

Four Years and Up

Kids over four who weigh forty pounds can switch from a "toddler" seat to the regular car seat and lap belt. Put a firm cushion at least 2″ thick under your child so the lap belt will go across his *lap*, rather than riding up on his abdomen, where it could hurt him in case of a collision. And make sure the belt is snug across his lap.

A shoulder harness should only be used if it crosses your child's chest — not her neck. Kids are usually ready for a shoulder strap when they reach 55″ in height. When not in use, a connected shoulder strap should be behind the child, not tucked under an arm. The owner's manual for your car will probably give further information on the use of shoulder straps.

Car Safety Tips

The middle of the back seat is the safest place in a car for a child to ride. But this position loses some of its safety advantages if you're driving without another adult and are always turning around to check on the baby behind you.

If no child seat or other restraint device is available — say in a friend's car or for extra kids in yours — it is safer to use a lap belt than to allow a child to ride loose. Boost the child up on a pillow to try to keep the lap belt across his lap rather than around his abdomen. But always try to use a proper restraint rather than settling for makeshift.

If grandparents are taking your child for a ride or a weekend — or anyone else, for that matter — make sure to transfer her car seat to their car. Demonstrate and explain how the seat should be installed and used, because most grandparents have had no experience at all with child car restraints, and would just as soon the grandchildren rode loose in the front "death" seat, free to climb around the car — exactly as you did when you were growing up. Properly instructed grandparents, however, who understand the importance of the restraints, will be just as careful as you are always to buckle the kids in.

Some foreign-made cars are equipped with roll-up lap belts — called inertia reel belts — which aren't adequate for strapping down child restraint devices. Replace them with standard fixed belts that can be tightened down securely. If the lap belts in your car are too short to go around a safety device, your automobile dealer may be able to provide belt extenders.

Kids get restless on a car trip of any length — whether or not they're strapped in. Setting them "free" of a safety device to play in the car for a while is taking a big chance for a very small gain. Instead, stop often and regularly on long trips so the kids can get out and be free of the whole car for a short while and really have a chance to work off some of that pent-up energy. See p. 182 for thoughts on long car trips with kids.

POISONS

Almost the first thing a baby or a toddler does after picking up a new object is to pop it in his mouth, and there he may be testing it with more sophistication than an experienced French wine taster uses to savor a great vintage. Children have more taste organs in their mouths than adults. With age we lose taste buds from the palate, the sides of the mouth, and the top of the tongue. So a baby is literally better equipped than the wine taster. And, boy, does he ever use that equipment.

All poisonous and toxic substances should be kept out of reach of babies and locked up as soon as a child starts to stand and toddle. The list of common household items that are toxic is almost endless: cleansers, cleaning fluids, wax polishes — including shoe polish — ammonia, bleach, cosmetics, medicines, insecticides, fungicides, pesticides, paint, paint thinners, gasoline, etc., etc., etc. Some are more dangerous than others. Some are killers. Don't bother with fine distinctions — if it isn't food, lock it up.

Locking up is only half the battle, because many childhood poisonings occur when medicines or toxic substances are left out briefly. Buy medicines and poisonous products in containers with child-resistant caps whenever possible, but regard these only as a last line of defense, and not a terribly effective one. And get into the habit of always putting medicines and toxic products away immediately after use. Never put turpentine, paint thinner, or some other notorious poison in a soda bottle, cup, or other container regularly used for food — that only invites a child to take a swig — as does liquor left in a glass from the night before. Don't call medicine "candy" when you're trying to talk a child into taking it — she'll spend all her ingenuity trying to get more of the "candy."

The chance of a child eating nonfood substances is increased by disruptions in the home, so take extra care during stormy periods. And watch out for repeaters — a child who has eaten a toxic substance will often do it again.

Always have on hand a bottle of syrup of ipecac and a can of activated charcoal — both of which you can buy in any drugstore. The ipecac will make a poisoned child vomit, and the charcoal may be needed to counteract residual poison. When a child has swallowed a toxic substance, don't induce vomiting immediately, but call a poison control center or your doctor for expert advice. If the child is unconscious or having fits, vomiting will only aggravate matters, and some poisons will do as much harm coming up as going down — these include strong corrosives like lye, drain cleaner, acid, as well as gasoline, kerosene, and other products containing petroleum distillates such as furniture polish, waxes, and lighter fluid.

Poison Control Centers

Purple-faced Barry, four, had just eaten a mimeograph stencil. His worried father called the Manhattan poison control center immediately and described the situation. "That's all right," came the calm reply. "Mimeo stencils aren't toxic. You could give him a glass of milk to wash it down." Particularly in big cities, where they have considerable experience due to the volume of business, the people who staff poison control centers are real pros and can readily tell you if something your child has eaten will do harm. And if it can, they will tell you what steps to take.

Post the number of your local poison control center prominently on or near every phone, and always call if your child has eaten anything that isn't food. The number will be listed in the emergency numbers section of your phone book — or call Information. If you live in a small community, particularly a rural one, get the number of the center in the largest urban community nearby. Small centers naturally have a small volume of inquiries and therefore may not have the expertise you will find in a large city. This expertise is worth the added expense of a long-distance call.

When you call, be prepared to describe the problem in detail. Have in hand the bottle the pills came from, the container the cleanser was in, or part of a plant identical to the one your child ate.

Poisonous Plants

Babies and toddlers should be watched carefully around plants, and older kids should be taught never to nibble on leaves, twigs, nuts, berries, bulbs, or to suck the juice from flowers, because some of the commonest, most innocent-looking plants contain poisons. Eating Christmas mistletoe berries, for instance, can lead to convulsions and coma, and the needlelike crystals of calcium oxalate in the ordinary house plants philodendron and dieffenbachia, or dumb cane, can swell the tissues surrounding the windpipe, blocking it and killing the child who has eaten the leaves.

All house plants should be hung from ceiling hooks or brackets well out of children's reach. Some, of course, are harmless, but eating the dirt from a house plant container can also be a disaster for a child. Other common house plants to be particularly careful with are: crown of thorns, poinsettia, autumn crocus (sold for forcing), lantana, and Jerusalem cherry, a cousin of the deadly nightshade.

Many hedges and ornamentals planted around houses contain dangerous toxic substances. Rhododendrons and azaleas, boxwood hedges, yew, privet, holly, mountain laurel, wisteria, and English ivy are some of the commonest. Oleander, daphne, and the golden chain tree are killers.

Garden flowers can be dangerous, too. Watch out for lilies of the valley, sweet peas, daffodils, foxgloves, iris, caladium, monkshood, larkspur, and delphinium, among others. Even the pretty little buttercup packs a mean punch. And the bulbs of lilies, daffodils, etc., store up strong doses of poison.

Parts of some food plants are toxic. You eat the stems of rhubarb, for instance, but the big leaves can kill a child, and green potatoes or shoots from a brown potato are toxic.

Poisonous plants abound in the woods, swamps, and fields: baneberry, jack-in-the-pulpit, marsh marigold, bittersweet, water hemlock and poison hemlock, Jimson weed (also known as thorn apple and angel's trumpet), many mushrooms, pokeberry, chokecherry, bloodroot, black nightshade, deadly nightshade, false hellebore, black locust, horse chestnut, and oak trees.

Seeds often contain concentrated doses of a plant's poison. Castor bean seeds, for instance, are killers. Never let a child chew on jewelry made from strung beans or seeds. Even though the jequirity pea (or precatory bean) is lethal, it frequently is found in jewelry, dolls, and other souvenirs of the tropics.

The lists of poisonous plants given here are not comprehensive. They are merely meant to suggest the extent of the dangers to children and point out some of the commonest perils.

Poison Ivy   Teach kids to recognize poison ivy and avoid it. A three-year-old can learn to spot it every time. It's lying in wait for kids all over the place, but most often in areas of partial shade — under bushes at the edge of clearings, and along the edge of woods. It twines under and around other plants and sends tall vines up trees and abandoned buildings.

The stems are hairy, and the leaves grow in groups of three, turning red in spring and fall, deep green in summer. To the untrained eye, many harmless plants look just like poison ivy — Virginia creeper is a dead ringer except that it has more leaves to the cluster, and even innocent three-leaved raspberry plants are look-alikes. It won't hurt your kids to steer clear of all of these until they can make a positive identification.

The sap that contains the chemical irritant can be released by bruising any part of the plant at any time of year. A first brush with poison ivy usually produces only a minor rash, but the more often you come in contact with it, the worse the effect. It is said that washing with strong yellow soap immediately after exposure will prevent or reduce the rash, but I've never found this effective.

The only sure way to protect kids from it is to get rid of it. Check for poison ivy every spring around the edges of the play yard and in other places your kids regularly play, and kill it. You can try uprooting it, wearing gloves and other protective clothing, but parts of the root will usually be missed, and these will send up new shoots. Poison sprays available from garden shops are much more effective. Don't burn uprooted poison ivy plants — the smoke is said to carry the irritant.

Poison sumac gives a similar rash, but it's seldom found near houses, because it prefers to grow in wet places and swamps. It usually has a bushy form and bears greenish flowers and white fruit. Don't confuse it with harmless sumacs like the staghorn sumac, which have red fruit.

Lead Poisoning

Many people think that lead poisoning endangers only kids who live in crumbling tenements where paint is peeling off the walls. But it can strike a child who lives in the grandest old mansion house, and if it isn't caught early, the consequences can be irreversible brain damage and even death. All that's needed are some chips of old leaded paint, which used to be used in all buildings, inside and out. Kids will put anything in their mouths, and some have a nasty condition called pica, which means that they regularly eat nonfood objects. Also, it's said that leaded paint chips taste sweet — like candy.

The biggest hazards are peeling and chipped windowsills, doors, ceilings, and walls — plaster chips contain lead, too — in old houses. Old children's furniture and old toys are often covered with leaded paint. When a lot of sanding and scraping are done prior to painting an old building, inhaling the dust is dangerous for adults as well as kids.

If you live in an old home where walls and woodwork are in good condition, there's no serious immediate danger, but keep an eye open for tooth

marks on the windowsills. When paint and plaster are cracked and falling, act immediately. Scraping off chipped places and painting over them with lead-free paint will help by cleaning up the situation and arresting the chipping, but it won't eliminate the hazard, because lead from the old paint will leach up into the new paint. On badly peeling places, as a temporary measure, scrape or sand off the worst parts and cover the whole thing with contact paper. The only sure ways to get rid of leaded paint are to strip and sand woodwork and paint it anew and to cover old walls with paneling or new wallboard.

You can have paint chips analyzed for lead content by your local health department, but if you even suspect your child has eaten some, have his blood lead level checked by a doctor. Lead poisoning has to be treated early to be cured, and some kids show no symptoms until it's too late. Symptoms that a child *might* show are unusual irritability, poor appetite, stomach pains, persistent constipation, and sluggishness or drowsiness — but don't wait for symptoms to appear.

To protect against the danger of lead poisoning, the federal government has imposed fairly stringent regulations on the paint industry. Since February 1978, all "consumer surface coating products" have been restricted to 0.06 per cent lead by weight of the dried film — a level generally considered safe. Previous regulations imposed in January 1973 set the limit at 0.5 per cent, also an acceptable level, but paints manufactured before that time contained larger quantities of lead. Artists' paints and related materials are exempted from the lead regulations.

FIRE

Install smoke detector alarms above every stairwell, or in the hall of an apartment. Some good local fire and building codes now require this precaution in all homes.

Fire drills are great fun for kids, and should be held at least every year — preferably more often. Map out the house or apartment and try to establish two escape routes from each room. Know exactly what you will do to get to the baby or help the kids, and hold fire drills using a doll while your child is still too young to participate. When the kids are older, a meeting place should be designated outside, well away from the building, and kids should know how to get out fast.

Sleep with bedroom doors closed — they may hold back smoke, flames, and fumes from a stairwell or hall long enough for everyone to get out by another route. When you smell smoke or hear the smoke alarm, don't rush out into the hall. First, feel the door — if it's hot, the hallway may be filled with deadly heated gases.

Explain to children as young as three that they should feel the door before opening it, and tell them to stay low to the floor during a fire, which may save their lives, because smoke and hot gases rise, leaving cooler air near the floor. A five-year-old will definitely be able to understand and remember a lesson like this if he practices crawling during a fire drill.

A window may be the only way to get to a baby or a child. If it won't open, break it with a shoe, chair, or other object, and clear off the jagged edges. A blanket can be thrown over the sill to protect your child from cuts.

Once everyone is out, don't go back in for any reason. Now is the time to call the fire department from a neighbor's phone, or turn in an alarm. Ask your local fire department for decals that can be placed on doors and windows to indicate to firemen where children's rooms are.

Preventing fires in the first place by keeping your home free of fire hazards is, of course, vital. Remember that a child with access to matches or a lighter or the knobs on the stove is a serious fire hazard. At four and five, kids are especially keen on matches. Keep fire extinguishers charged and know how to use them.

In explaining fire to a four- or five-year-old, parents often drive home the point that a fire is safe only if it is in a *closed* container — meaning, of course, a fireplace, stove, etc. Children don't always understand exactly what is meant, and have been known to light fires in closets, thinking they are doing something safe in a *closed* place.

A child of four or five also has difficulty visualizing the destructive power of fire. Simply *telling* him that fire destroys or that it can burn down a house won't make much of an impression. Get him to feel the weight of the logs before they go into a fire, and later show him the scant shovelful of ashes they have been reduced to. Or get him to make a big pile of crumpled newspapers in a fireplace, and point out how quickly it is consumed when you light it.

A child of four or five can learn what to do in case her clothes go up in flames. She'll have a grand time practicing rolling up in a rug to smother the fire, and the fun of practicing may help her remember not to run and fan the flames. Try to teach her that *any* rug or blanket will do, or she may try, when the chips are down, to run for the *specific* rug she practiced with.

HEALTH CARE

In this book I have purposely avoided including nonexpert health care advice and first aid instructions.

For ready reference in an emergency, first aid directions, and to help you understand your pediatrician's advice, every family needs a copy of Dr. Spock's *Baby and Child Care*. Three excellent additions to the family health library that go into more

detail than Dr. Spock on many health care questions are: Jack Shiller, *Childhood Illness* (New York: Stein & Day, 1974); Jack Shiller, *Childhood Injury* (New York: Stein & Day, 1978); and Boston Children's Medical Center, *Child Health Encyclopedia* (New York: Dell, 1978).

Bone up on mouth-to-mouth resuscitation and practice it with your child; learn how to help a choking child; and learn as much as you can about first aid, preferably by taking a Red Cross course.

Keep health care books all together on a convenient shelf and always put them back so you know where they'll be when your child is screaming with pain and you call the doctor and the answering service says he's out. Having to search for a book just adds another layer of anxiety. A worried father makes a lousy diagnostician when he's trying to calm a frenzied mother and meanwhile fighting it out with the index to a health care book. If the problem seems at all urgent, get a doctor on the phone, or head for the emergency room.

PEDIATRICIANS

A good pediatrician can be a kind of third parent in charge of your child's health, so choose carefully. Recommendations from friends and neighbors will usually be your best guide for finding the right doctor. A call to your local medical association or, even better, to the pediatrics department of a nearby hospital with a medical school affiliation or teaching staff can help.

Ordinarily you select a pediatrician a month or so before your first baby arrives, and the pediatrician is on hand at the birth. Call the secretary of a prospective pediatrician and ask if the doctor is board certified. Certification by a national board is some assurance that a doctor is thoroughly trained and well qualified, but isn't absolutely essential — some excellent physicians do not take the board examinations. Also ask the secretary about the doctor's prices if you're interested.

Try to meet with a prospective pediatrician, if only briefly, to determine whether this is someone you'll be able to like and trust, someone who will explain problems clearly, and freely answer all the questions you'll have as worried parents. If your wife intends to nurse the baby, make sure the pediatrician is a warm advocate of breast feeding and so will be helpful and supportive on this score (see p. 36 for more on this question).

If you can fit it into your schedule, take your child for some of her routine "well baby" inoculation visits so you can maintain your relationship with the pediatrician and stay in touch with the progress of your child's health care. Some fathers avoid these visits out of a sense of embarrassment — they feel the doctor will wonder what they're doing taking the child around rather than being at work where they belong. The two pediatricians I mentioned this syndrome to insisted it had never crossed their minds to wonder why a man had time to bring his child for a visit, and both said it was refreshing for them to deal with fathers from time to time.

On a visit to a pediatrician, ask all the questions that are on your mind, especially the questions you feel are dumb — they're usually the best ones. Doctors are invariably rushed — it's their way of life — and even the best explainers try to get away quickly. So block the doorway of the examining room and get off all your questions. Among other things, you're paying handsomely for the answers.

Always ask the doctor to write "Label" on a prescription. Doctors often neglect this notation, and without it, pharmacists will usually type only the dosage and directions on the label. "Label" indicates that the full name of the drug should be typed as well, and it is always best to have this information.

HOSPITALS

If your child is ever hospitalized, insist that you or your wife stay with him. Some hospitals and doctors resist this, but it can be arranged with an extra cot, and it is vitally important not to cut a child off altogether from home and parents on top of a medical problem — he needs your comfort and reassurance in this altogether strange and scary place.

When an operation or other hospital stay is scheduled in advance, try to prepare your child. Some hospitals have helpful preadmissions tours for kids. Books like *Curious George Goes to the Hospital* can also help a preschooler learn about what lies ahead. And your own made-up story about a little girl just her age who went to the hospital can explain about anesthesia, operations, and other mysteries, and reassure her that it *will* hurt, but she'll come through fine.

HURT KIDS

Hug a hurt child in a great big father bear hug. That's the basic first aid measure for anything more serious than a tumble and less serious than a sprain. Just fold him in, and hold on tight. You can't spoil a hurt child by hugging. Little spills, scrapes, bumps, and clashes with other kids can usually be ignored, and most parents stop comforting a toddler after every fall when it becomes clear that she'll go right on about her business after a short cry of protest or indignation. You soon learn to sort the minor incidents from the medium-sized ones that need a hug, and the real injuries that need a call to the doctor or a dash for the emergency room. If you haven't seen what happened, your child's cry — how loud it is and how long it persists — usually gives you a fairly good clue to how badly hurt he is.

For a bad bump, augment hugging with an ice cube. You can put the ice cube on the place that hurts, but it will end up in your child's mouth, where it will do the most good — distracting her from the source of the pain. Similar to ice cube therapy in its effectiveness is candy therapy.

Don't be stingy with Band-Aids. The tiniest scratch on a child over two requires a bandage.

Because adults have told them it is so, children are uniformly convinced that Band-Aids actually make the cut better. They believe in them and believing makes them work.

Serious medical problems are another matter altogether. No father is ever prepared for the long, anxious vigils with a sick or injured child, or for the pain of holding down a screaming baby while the doctor probes or the nurse injects.

INSURANCE

When your baby is born, every insurance agent for three counties around takes note of the announcement in the paper and writes to suggest that you take out a life insurance policy. I asked an experienced insurance underwriter who has a daughter in nursery school if there were any other types of insurance that a prudent father should acquire.

Standard family health care insurance policies — like Blue Cross and Blue Shield — automatically cover new family members, and the premiums aren't increased with each new baby. But do check on the provisions of a major medical policy, as these vary considerably from state to state.

If your car is used to transport groups of kids to nursery school or day care, insurance companies recommend that you increase your liability limit. The basic liability coverage limit in my state, for instance, is $15,000 per person and $30,000 per occurrence. With car pooling and other child passenger situations, insurance companies suggest that you go to at least $100,000 per person and perhaps $300,000 per occurrence.

Homeowner's policies include high standard liability coverage that normally won't need to be increased when neighborhood kids start to congregate around your house and hurt themselves on your child's swing set.

DAY CARE AND NURSERY SCHOOL

As a novice father overhearing conversations between Rita and her women friends about child care programs, I never understood a word. It was pure shoptalk. For both full-time and working mothers, child care is a crucial issue. It involves their children's activities and needs, but it also allows mothers time for *theirs*. So they are quick to pick up on all the ins and outs, the subtleties and nuances of the business.

If you'd like to have a part in deciding what kind of early experiences your child will have outside your home, for a start, you have to get straight the various basic types of child care. The following is offered as a kind of primer or glossary to acquaint you with some of the terms.

There is a major distinction between *home-based care* and *center-based care*. A home-based situation is sometimes called *family day care*, but is more often called *baby-sitting*. You take your child to another person's home, where she cares for him and usually her own and others. This is the most common arrangement for infants and very young kids of working couples. *Infant care centers* exist in some places, but they are unusual in our country — perhaps because they remind us of the state-run communal nurseries in the Soviet Union.

When children reach three, more possibilities open up, all of which can be referred to loosely as *preschool programs*. Most of these are center-based rather than home-run affairs. The main distinction in preschool programs is between *day care* and *nursery school*. A day care center is set up to provide for children from morning to night so that both parents can hold down jobs. Many open their doors at seven-thirty, serve breakfast and lunch, and keep the kids till they are picked up by tired parents at six in the evening. Nursery school programs, on the other hand, have much shorter hours — usually three hours in the morning — and some meet only a few days a week. The nursery school is the usual choice of families with full-time mothers. Day care and nursery school usually start at age three because most kids are toilet trained by this point — an important consideration for the staff — and because most kids at around three can handle and even thrive on a little separation from the nest. "Readiness" for preschool, though, varies greatly from child to child and is an important consideration when you are deciding on a program. Many day care centers offer nursery school as one of several programs, and nursery schools come in a dizzying variety, some of which are discussed below.

Nursery schools sponsor some offshoot programs, for instance, *toddler groups*, where Mom can take a two-year-old several times a week for a couple of hours of play with his peers. And mothers often band together to form *play groups*, which start at around age one. In these, each mothers takes a turn having the small group for a few hours in her house or apartment while the others take a break.

This is by no means an exhaustive survey of the possibilities available in child care, but it should give you enough of the vocabulary to get you into the conversation.

WHY PRESCHOOLS?

A miserable ice storm had pulled all the traffic off onto the shoulder of the road one morning and threatened to turn us back for home. "But I have to get to nursery school," wailed Gregory, four. "I have to be *teached*."

All the preschool kids I know are eager to be "teached," and this really is as good a reason as you can have for sending them to nursery schools and day care centers. There are, of course, a variety of other compelling reasons for early education, the most important of which is that a preschool experience gives a child a chance to learn about and adjust to a group. For at least thirteen years in the future, your child will be a member of a group in school, and it is something he can't learn about at home unless you have half a dozen kids.

It probably will cost money — there are very few public preschool programs available. But if there's any way to squeeze some more out of that tight budget, you may want to weigh some of the real advantages to you against the cost.

A nursery school program, even one that's limited to a few mornings a week, relieves a full-time mother. It may not be as big a relief as she would like, but it's a letup after a three-year, twenty-four-hour-a-day commitment to a single cause. And this breather can only improve morale in your household. A slightly relieved mom means a slightly relieved child. When you pay for preschool, you are paying, among other things, for the possibility of an easier-going household. Now, that's a good buy.

Costs for nursery schools and day care vary widely, even within a single community — so shop around. Check into co-operative nursery schools, too. These cut the costs of operation — and therefore the cost to you — by having the mothers take turns as teachers' assistants. The fathers in a co-op get together for occasional weekend work parties to do much of the routine maintenance of the building and equipment. A co-op though, like any do-it-yourself scheme, isn't primarily a money saver — it's a way to get involved. And parents who get involved in their kids' preschool are liable to be the parents who will stay interested and involved throughout their children's education — another bonus for the whole family.

As you look for the right preschool, cost will naturally be an important factor, but I hope it won't make you settle for a place you feel isn't just right for your child. A place with rigid teachers or loveless or unenthusiastic ones can be just as destructive to your child's morale as a dead-end job could be to yours. Preschool is the very start of a child's career in education, and kids should start off on the right foot.

CHOICES

If you're looking for a preschool program in a small town or rural area, you may have to go some distance just to find one, let alone a good one. But in the city or suburbs, you may be confronted with many programs to choose from, each claiming some great advantage for your child over the others. Some boast fancy equipment, some claim curriculum advantages, some appeal to you on philosophical grounds.

In making your decision between competing claims, I hope you'll brush aside a lot of the nonessentials and get right to the point. Are the teachers good? The best equipment, the most sophisticated curriculum, the soundest philosophical grounding isn't going to make up for a teacher who is a cold fish. Your child's important relationship is with the teacher, not with the teaching equipment.

You probably won't have time to go from pre-

school to preschool to find teachers you feel a real rapport with. But if your wife can narrow down the field, try to get a chance to meet and talk with the most likely candidate. You can tell little or nothing about a preschool teacher unless you see her in

action, so this will mean taking time off from work. Most preschool programs will welcome your sitting in and observing what goes on. I'd be suspicious of one that didn't.

Don't be alarmed if things seem noisy and chaotic. The kids in preschools are only learning about social behavior — they haven't mastered it yet. Visitors to mainland China are always impressed with the orderliness of the kids in preschool programs there. They march in little rows, sit neatly and quietly, and recite and perform on cue. But what these visitors often overlook is that the kids are being specifically trained to grow up as orderly, obedient adults, members of a social and economic system altogether unlike ours. Our kids are being trained to enter an adult world where self-reliance is a ruling virtue, not unthinking obedience to authority.

Recognizing a good teacher isn't easy. You'll have to rely mostly on instinct. But there are a few things to watch for. A good preschool teacher will always approach kids on their level — not just leaning over, but actually bending at the knees to be face to face — and she will look at the kids directly, not off to the side, as she talks to them. A good teacher will be spending the greatest part of her time with the kids themselves — not in straightening up or coping with materials, and not chatting with other adults. A good teacher will appear to be on top of things — coping with the needs and demands of a group of three- or four-year-olds can easily get the better of an inexperienced person. And you'll want to notice how the children respond to the teacher, whether they seem relaxed with her and come to her readily for comfort and help.

One thing to avoid in evaluating a preschool teacher is using the same criteria you might use, say, to evaluate a new employee for your business. You are looking for someone who is great with kids, not necessarily someone who is poised and confident with other adults. One excellent test of a teacher is simply to take your child along when you go to observe. If they hit it off, you may not need to look further.

The ideal teacher here is called "she" because the overwhelming majority of people who work in preschool programs are women. But men make excellent teachers and if there's a man or men on the staff you can assume you're dealing with a healthy situation where your child will see a balanced, two-sided version of the adult world.

Educational Policies

If you have a choice of preschool programs, you'll hear about "open learning" groups, play schools, Montessori schools, schools that emphasize early reading, and a host of other possibilities. There are fairly clear distinctions between the educational policies of the different types of programs. To make a very long story as short as I can, I'll divide them roughly between "teaching" programs and "socially oriented" programs.

Socially Oriented Programs Basic to most American-developed theories of preschool education is the idea that children need to adapt to a group situation and that this social adjustment — rather than the early learning of specific skills — is the major task of the preschool. Play schools and nursery schools wouldn't dream of neglecting the intellectual development of their pupils, but many are committed to the principle that social development has clear priority.

The practical application of this idea is that kids are eased into group membership. They are allowed much autonomy and "free play" — but this is usually balanced with organized group activities and more structured "learning experiences." In this

kind of school, play is regarded as a child's natural avenue for learning, his method for exploring and coming to terms with the world. So an effort is made to provide a stimulating environment for imaginative, creative play — which means interesting toys, good playground equipment, and tools and materials for activities like carpentry and arts and crafts.

At their best, schools of this sort are attempting to produce kids who are ready for the discipline and order they will find in kindergarten and school, but who at the same time retain a strong sense of themselves as individuals. The end product that is envisioned is a kind of American ideal — a self-reliant person confident in social situations, and also bold, imaginative, and independent.

Teaching Programs The "teaching" type of preschool has a different order of priorities. The most widely known of this type, the Montessori schools, are found throughout our country. They are only very loosely affiliated, but all share similar instructional materials and a common historical background. The Montessori method grew out of the pioneering work of the Italian physician-educator Maria Montessori. In the early years of this century she had great success teaching underprivileged children in the slums of Rome in a program that might be compared to our Head Start programs. The Montessori schools of today derive their orderly, structured approach to early education from methods that proved successful in that setting. Naturally, the methods have been adapted somewhat over the years to fit other situations and new communities. But the underlying philosophy of the Montessori-type school is that preschool children thrive on structure and order, and that by systematically presenting them with interesting learning materials, they can be stimulated to develop a spontaneous interest in their work. The Montessori school at its best seeks to achieve the "spontaneous self-discipline of children when happily occupied."

The Montessori schools are enjoying a boom period at present. They have existed in our country since the thirties, but were eclipsed and almost disappeared during what might be called the "permissive" era of American child rearing. During the late forties and fifties, the vanguard of American preschool education was interested in an "unstructured," "free" preschool environment, and the Montessori method was regarded as overstructured and manipulative. Being a European import didn't help the Montessori method much during that period either. American educators are proud that our system encourages individual discovery and problem solving, and are quick to criticize European education for relying too heavily on rote learning. But in recent years, parents have reacted strongly against the permissiveness of the last decades, and structured early learning has become a *cause célèbre*, so the Montessori schools, with their well-defined structure and orderly teaching approach, have re-emerged on the scene.

The Montessori schools are only one example of a "teaching" type preschool. And within the broad groups of "socially oriented" and "teaching" preschool programs, there is wide variety and even intragroup dispute over goals and methods. If you look around, you can find a spectrum that ranges all the way from irresponsible freedom farms to hard-nosed three-R rote factories. Happily for parents and kids alike, most preschools — regardless of philosophy — in actual practice fall somewhere near the middle of this spectrum and strike a happy medium between encouraging social adjustment and giving a child a first taste of structured learning. Happily also, except where a school assumes an extreme stance, the philosophy behind what is going on disappears almost completely in the hubbub of daily activity, and the success or failure of the program comes to depend almost entirely on the quality and strengths of the teachers in it. A lot also depends on the quality of the kids in the school and of their parents.

So when it comes to deciding on a preschool for your child, try to base your decision less on what you read in the school's brochure than on what you see actually going on between the teacher and the kids.

Physical Setup

You'll want to satisfy yourself that a day care center or nursery school is safe for your child and that it's kept clean and in good repair. There should be plenty of room outdoors for running, and interesting equipment for the kids to climb on and build with — a pile of old tires is a good indication. Inside, you should expect enough room so that quiet activities (story reading, puzzles, letter blocks, etc.) are done in one space, while big, noisy play (trucks, hammering, kitchen and house games, etc.) are

reserved for another room or space. A separate place for arts and crafts projects is also a sign of a good nursery school or center.

If you see a bunch of kids sitting in front of a TV, you are in warehouse for children, not a place where they will learn and grow.

A place with lots of spiffy new equipment may impress you. But unless it was built and equipped last week, this could be the last place you would want to send your child. If the toys and jungle gym are in mint condition, you can bet the kids aren't getting a chance to use them. And some over-regimented, profit-minded places do just that — keep the kids from using the equipment so it will stay new-looking to impress prospective customers. No thoughtful parent wants to be a "customer" or a "consumer" of early education. You're not buying a commodity, you're arranging for a very big chunk of your child's life. So look for a place where the equipment is worn, even a little dog-eared, but immaculately clean and kept in order.

FIRST DAY

For a three-year-old the first day away from home is going to be traumatic, no matter how wonderful the center or nursery school, no matter how carefully you prepare your child or how cleverly you handle the situation. About half the children scream their heads off the first day, and the others choke down their feelings, but the feelings are there anyway.

As a father who leaves home every day, you are in an excellent position to help your child understand what she'll be getting into out there, away from the nest. She has seen you leave weekday in and weekday out since she's known you, and she knows that you make it back every evening — maybe a little the worse for wear, but still in one piece and even sometimes ready to have fun with her. You can explain that going to nursery school or day care will be like what Daddy does each day — unless you hate your job, because she will love hers. And you can reassure her that the people she'll meet in the outside world will be very kind and helpful.

It's important for a child to visit the new preschool with a parent before going it alone. This probably won't fit in with your schedule, but your schedule may well allow you to take your child on the morning of the first day. This is a task that Mom traditionally handles — amid tearful farewells. But a three-year-old will be much more used to saying good-by to you than to Mom.

Plan to stay around for fifteen minutes to give your child a chance to get accustomed to the place with a familiar person there for reassurance. It won't

help, though, to stay on longer than this. And when you've said good-by, the best policy is to move out sharply with your jaw set firmly and your heart hardened to what you know your child is going through.

STAYING IN TOUCH

A preschooler's idea of what Dad does all day at work is often hazy at best. I've asked dozens of fathers if *their* idea of what their kids do in preschool is any better than their children's understanding of what they do at work. Many say that the picture is just as dim on their end. "What she does there all day is a mystery," says one father who is always presented with works of art to praise, but can't seem to pry out much information about his daughter's day. "It could be she goes there and draws two pictures and comes home."

For the first weeks or even months, fathers report, they get enthusiastic feedback from their kids — voluntary daily reports. But then the reports slack off in most cases and when Dad asks: "What did you do today?" the answer is "Nothing. . . . Not gonna tell you."

Some fathers find that it helps to be specific. "If I ask Stephie Ann [four] pointed questions about what she did, I can get fairly accurate responses: 'What did you do at play time?' 'Did they read you a story?'" says one father. "'What did you do at work today?' isn't going to turn *me* on. Maybe I'd just say, 'I sat at the desk and answered the phone all day.'"

Other fathers who use this excellent tactic of pointed questioning for prying out information find they can usually get the conversation rolling most easily by going directly to the central issue of a child's day: "What did you have for a snack?" "What did you eat at lunch?" Your child's special friends give you another avenue of approach: "Was Cristin there today? What did you do together?"

The questions here are all going in one direction — from father to child. But: "What did *you* do today, Dad?" Has your child ever asked that? Have you ever told him? It's just possible that a father's job of prying information out of his kids about their day would be a good deal easier if he were in the habit of volunteering information about *his*.

Parents' Meetings

Evening parents' meetings will help you stay in touch with your child's world. Fathers recently have begun to get involved in their children's pre-school education on this level, in some communities, it seems, more than in others. An artist father in Manhattan reports that all the fathers show up for the monthly parent discussion groups at the day care center his two-year-old attends. Where we live in the country, though, a father at a preschool meeting looks like a rooster in the hen house. If you live in a community where fathers don't commonly attend preschool meetings, I can assure you that your smallest effort to make contact will be greeted with respect and appreciation. No one will think you a sap for being at the meeting — least of all the other dad who may show up. You're saving him from being a minority of one. Also, remember that child care institutions are staffed almost exclusively by women, and they're delighted to have a man to deal with occasionally.

Your child's teacher or "care-giver" can tell you a lot about him. She sees an entirely different side of him than you do at home, and she knows much more about him than you might suspect. I don't mean that you need a detailed daily report — neither teacher nor parent has the time for this. But do stay in touch and get to know the teacher — who can be a valuable ally and source of information.

Father-Child Days

A relatively new development on the preschool scene is the special father-child day, and in many places these have proved to be a tremendous hit. The nursery school sets aside a Saturday morning and invites all the fathers to come with their children. Attendance at these events is strikingly high — few fathers miss them. Not, I think, because this is an occasion every man longs to attend, but because the kids really put the pressure on. They regard this as an event of the utmost importance — a chance to show off their fathers to the other kids and a chance to show Dad their world.

Lots of men who have been dragged to these affairs have had a perfectly good time and have given their kids a proud moment and a rich memory. A year after the event, one father told me, his daughter Courtney, four, remembers the father-child day fondly and talks about it all the time, and "Even now, Jessica [seven] asks why they didn't do it when she was in nursery school. She feels slighted."

If your child's preschool doesn't sponsor a father-child day, perhaps you'll introduce the idea at the next parents' meeting. You might want to model yours on the excellent Halloween pumpkin-cutting party I've heard about from several fathers whose kids all go to the same suburban co-operative play school. Fifty fathers showed up; the school supplied the pumpkins and cider; and my sources claim that a great time was had by all. A theme like this will probably draw in a few extra dads. For the kids, though, the pumpkins could matter less — the big deal is that Daddy comes to their place.

PRESCHOOL PRODUCTS

The only regular links many fathers have with their kids' daily activities at preschool are the styrofoam ball with toothpicks in it, the dark blue cupcake, the daily drawing. Kids present these with pride and a need for praise that is so insistent we all recognize it and supply the applause.

Some parents even go overboard in an effort to make their kids feel good about the things they've made, and lay the compliments on thickly. A child doesn't necessarily need rave reviews when all he's done is put a feather in a construction paper band to make a Native American headdress. Overpraised

kids catch on quickly to what's happening, and sometimes react in a way that seems totally perverse — they become disappointed with the things they make. They know on the one hand that they are being conned — it *is* just a feather in a band — and on the other hand that there is no way they can actually live up to the lavish praise they are getting. These are the children who may eventually lay down the paintbrushes and refuse to try new projects.

I certainly don't mean to discourage you from saying that the plaster hand print is wonderful or interesting or whatever you feel about it that is positive and relatively honest. We all need encouragement — all the encouragement we can get. The point is simply that a child will get the most mileage out of the experience of making and presenting a pasted paper collage or a soda straw sculpture if it is treated with *genuine* interest.

By the way, you will have to eat the dark blue cupcake.

An important refinement of the praise-giving session is the trick of saying, "Tell me about it," rather than, "What is it?" Naturally, the first thing that comes to your lips when you're presented with a scribble drawing by a three-year-old or a rock with macaroni pasted to it by a four-year-old is: What is it? But look at it from your child's point of view. She has been waiting for hours for your return to show you her drawing of a lion in a cage or the noodle-studded paperweight she has made for your desk. She *knows* that you will know what it is, just as she does. So "What is it?" is about the last thing she expects to hear — it confuses the situation and it can be insulting. She was expecting "Thanks for the useful paperweight," and all she gets is "What is it?"

You, however, still don't know what it is, so you can't meet her expectations perfectly. But you can try "Tell me about it." And variations like "Tell me the story you were thinking of when you drew it." Sometimes you will learn its identity, and other times you'll discover an interesting truth — it wasn't originally meant as something; it actually was just meant to be a scribble drawing or a rock with noodles.

You can also cheat, pretend you know what it is, and say, "Thanks so much, it looks just great." But kids who get this treatment get wise, and they turn the tables: "What is it, Daddy? You have to guess what it is."

Preschool products can be great jumping-off points for father-child discussions and projects. When the inevitable feather headband comes home, why not find a picture book about Native Americans for the bedtime story, or talk about Indians and the Wild West at dinner, or set up a quick toy teepee with sticks in the yard or pencils inside?

Dad as Art Critic

The role of art critic is one that most fathers find themselves unprepared for. Each evening as you examine the day's productions, you nod and praise and sometimes wonder if there is anything in this scribble worth praising. Or you become so excited when your child draws a first happy face that you shout, "Genius!" and rush out to buy a set of toxic oil paints for a three-year-old.

One useful point: in the long history of art there has never been such a thing as a recognized child prodigy. In music, prodigy is a fairly regular phenomenon, but in the plastic arts it simply doesn't exist. Some children draw, paint, and make sculptures wonderfully, some clearly do better than others, and some kids show a strong early attachment to art work that may — or may not — last a lifetime. But a child's art doesn't progress in an orderly way. A young artist doesn't acquire one skill after another, practicing and perfecting it as he forges on toward technical mastery. This is possible for an extremely gifted child pianist — the progress chart for her skill and art may look like a straight uphill climb. The child pianist, though, is performing adult music with an adult technique on a full-size piano. The child painter, on the other hand, is drawing and painting what a child sees of the world or feels about it, with a child's naïve techniques. As his view of the world changes, so, too, does the look of his pictures. These changes go in a fairly regular, predictable sequence and aren't always — at least to adult eyes — for the better.

Here is a brief rundown of roughly what you can

expect from a child's early artistic development. Each child works, thinks, and progresses individually, so these are only milestones to watch for. Your child may work months or years behind or ahead of these general predictions and still be doing fine.

ONE: Scribbles. You'll notice that the scribbles all go in one general direction at first. A big step for a one-year-old is when the scribbles cross each other in two directions. Next, usually, come circular motions. The child is fascinated by the movement of her hand as she scribbles — the pattern that is being made isn't yet a real concern. If you want to see the pattern clearly, give your child a nontoxic marker, which — unlike a pencil or crayon — makes a clear line with little or no pressure. Supervise marker drawing since the tip of the marker will go into your child's mouth as often as it goes on the paper. Developed scribble drawings, which some kids continue to do through four, often show emotion. There are happy scribbles, angry scribbles, hurt-feelings slashed scribbles, etc.

MID-TWO to THREE: Faces begin to show up in drawings. At first, just a circle with eye dots and a mouth line — but, interestingly, almost from the first face, you can see whether the expression is happy or sad. From earliest infancy, faces are a child's major point of focus and interest, so it's only natural that they are the first things you actually recognize in a child's drawings.

THREE: At some point during this year, the face drawings become a little more sophisticated. The head will sprout first arms and then legs — no body in between. Now a child will like to paint with big brushes and will fill the whole paper boldly — with one color. Later, she will divide up the paper with lines or patches of different colors, making bright abstract paintings that can be very attractive to adults. When the picture is finished, if it reminds your child of something, she'll give it a title: "This red thing here is a turtle in a race." But she didn't start out to draw a turtle — it just appeared.

FOUR: A young artist discovers color mixing. Fascinated with this process, he mixes and mixes until the colors blend to produce a nice uniform diarrhea brown. It's hard not to be a little disappointed by this development if it follows some bright, cheerful "abstracts." But this passes. The colors become clearer and figures start to show up in paintings as well as in drawings. In the drawings, you see bodies asserting themselves between head and limbs. A four-year-old starts to know in advance what he will draw, rather than drawing it first and naming it at the end.

FIVE: If she's had any practice with paints, a child is now well out of the mud-mixing period and is enough in control of the materials to put interesting details into the pictures. The pictures usually represent things we can recognize: houses, trees, people, rocket ships.

FIVE to EIGHT: This period is the heyday of children's art. Kids draw and paint boldly and directly, and they have enough co-ordination to put down pretty much what they want to. At seven or eight comes a big change, when every child begins to be more aware of the world outside his immediate family and school. This new awareness of the adult world makes kids feel compelled to get the drawing "right" in what they take to be an adult way. So the bold, clear pictures disappear, replaced by small, tightly drawn efforts at rendering.

Look closely at your child's picture — it can give you a rare glimpse into her mind. It's not a picture of the mental equipment that we are giving the child — the adult, verbal part of her mind. It's a peek directly at her native child perceptions and feelings, because with markers and paints she has a way to record these that doesn't depend in any way on words or on letters learned from "Sesame Street," or on logical thought. Her pictures can get right down to brass tacks and tell it like it is — to her.

FIXIT

Glue a broken wooden toy back together for a toddler, replace a dead battery, or even plug the radio back in and you're a miracle worker in your child's eyes. I'm kind of proud of the fact that Gregory's first sentence was "Daddy fix." Sometimes he used it as a command, but it really felt great when he'd use his sentence to brag about what his dad could do: "Daddy *fix*."

When your first child is a toddler, you can stay abreast of the things that get broken, but after a few years the pile of fixit jobs at the end of the workbench becomes a mountain.

TOY REPAIR

Fixing up a cracked or broken wooden toy is a breeze — a little white glue and a C-clamp, and the thing is back in operation the next day. If a piece has been smashed beyond repair, you can always cut a new one from wood and add it in.

Plastic and metal toys, however, present more complicated problems. When a thin piece of plastic breaks, joining the edges or ends with cement — even tough epoxy or miracle cement — is seldom the answer, because your child will put the same strain on the joint that broke it in the first place and it will be back on your workbench within a day. Some sort of splint or reinforcement is in order, preferably one made from a piece of similar plastic material. Scraps of plexiglas can be used as well as pieces cut from heavy-duty detergent bottles and defunct plastic containers. On a large plastic toy with a big crack, you may be able to splint or reinforce the break on the inside with a piece of wood held with roundheaded wood screws driven through from the front of the plastic — use washers under the screws. Worn or broken parts of sturdy plastic toys can sometimes be rebuilt with wood putty.

Unfortunately, not all cements suitable for one type of plastic will work with another. The best cement for joining acrylic plastics is acrylic plastics solvent. It is sold in plastics specialty stores and is applied with a syringe-top squeeze bottle. You hold together the pieces to be joined, lift up one edge a fraction, and squeeze some of the thin liquid into the joint. As you hold the pieces tightly together, the liquid melts both surfaces a little and welds them in place. Pieces can also be held in place with masking tape stretched tightly between them for cementing with acrylic plastics solvent. Vinyl plastic menders, epoxy, and other cements and glues will also bond some plastics.

A hot-melt glue gun is invaluable for small fixit jobs. Anything can be bonded with hot glue — wood, plastics, cloth, metal, you name it — and different materials can be bonded to each other.

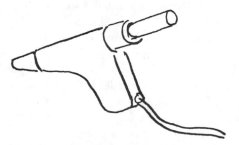

Hot glue won't work on a big or even a medium-size job, because the bead of glue will be cooling and nearly set before you can get the parts together. But gunk a little heated glue on for any small repair, get the parts together fast, and you have a strong, slightly elastic joint. If the edges of the pieces to be joined don't fit together exactly, the hot glue can be glopped on thickly to fill the space. It helps to work with hot glue in a warm place.

You'll find that cotter pins come in very handy for repairing riding toys and other things that are assembled with cap nuts on the ends of metal rods. When the cap nuts pop off, as they inevitably do, they usually can't be replaced unless there's a very well-stocked hardware store in town. Drill a hole through the end of the rod and insert a cotter pin. Drilling is easier if you first make a dent with a center punch to start the drill bit in.

The most valuable fixit tool award goes to the needle-nose pliers. Tiny screwdrivers are a great help, too.

Put aside the assembly instructions for any expensive new toy or piece of equipment, or cut the name and address of the manufacturer off the box so you'll be able to write for a replacement if some critical part breaks.

Refurbishing

Old toys can often be given new life with a little glue in the joints and a fresh coat of paint. Always use paint clearly labeled nontoxic and for use on children's furniture and toys; see p. 284 for more on painting toys. Older toys were often painted with dangerous lead-base paints. If you're restoring one, the best course is to strip all the paint off with paint remover, and start again from a clean surface. Rusted metal toys can be restored if the rust hasn't gone too deep. Scrape with a wire brush, sand with emery cloth, and repaint with nontoxic rust-resisting paint.

Lubrication

A well-placed drop of oil or squirt of spray graphite will often get the working parts of a toy operating again. Vaseline makes an excellent lubricant — it's safe enough to use around babies and will take the squeak out of crib sides, carriage wheels, tricycle wheels, etc. Nontoxic beeswax sticks also come in handy — they're sold in auto supply stores for car door lock lubrication.

Battery-Driven Toys

If replacing the batteries doesn't do the trick, the problem nine times out of ten is with the contact terminals and can be fixed in a jiffy. The contacts are the little pieces of metal that touch the ends of the batteries. Sometimes a battery has worked its way loose, which can be corrected by gently prying up one or both contacts with a screwdriver blade to achieve a tight fit. The more common problem is corrosion on the contacts, which interrupts the electrical circuit. Clean the contacts with a pencil eraser or scrape them lightly with fine sandpaper or the edge of a penknife — a few touches will make them shiny and operative again.

The next step is dismantling the toy to see if a wire leading to the motor has come loose, and resoldering it if it has. Beyond that, it's pure tinkering. Preschoolers delight in examining the innards of toys. If you take the trouble to disassemble one, make sure to show your child the working parts and explain how they function. Keep small parts all together in a dish or bowl, the way a watchmaker does.

Sometimes gear wheels will be completely frozen with rust or other parts of a drive mechanism will be broken irreparably, but the little electric motor will still function. Salvage it. You may be able to set it up to drive a small homemade toy. Or solder on a couple of short pieces of light wire and provide a fresh size D battery that your child can touch on both ends with the wires. A preschooler will love to listen to the hum of the motor and feel the little shaft spin around.

Alkaline batteries have a much longer life than conventional ones and are worth the extra money when used in a child's phonograph, tape recorder, etc., which will be used with some care over a long period. But use cheap, cut-rate batteries in small toys and flashlights, which have a brief life expectancy. Tape flashlights tightly — a child will manage to disassemble a taped flashlight, but it will take her a while. Replace batteries as soon as they wear out, to avoid leaking, and replace all of them at once — if one still has a little life in it, it won't for long.

Inflatables

Few inflatable vinyl toys survive the first week. If the kids' teeth don't do them in, somebody sits on them and busts a seam.

If you can't see the hole or hear or feel the air escaping, inflate the toy and put it in the bath with the kids. Preschoolers love the detective work of following the air bubbles to their source. Dry the toy and mark around the puncture or rip with a dark-colored crayon or pieces of tape so you can locate it for patching when the toy is deflated.

Some inflatables come with peel-off adhesive-backed mending patches. More effective than these, I find, are vinyl sealers sold in hardware stores — sometimes in a tube, sometimes in more liquid form in a bottle. These are variously known as plastic mender or vinyl plastic repair. Before applying a patch or sealer, make sure the area surrounding the puncture is thoroughly dry. For a big rip, try patching with a scrap piece of similar vinyl material held on and sealed around the edges with vinyl sealer.

BOOTS, SHOES, SNEAKERS

The same pair of rubber boots can serve several kids. Big holes and rips can be repaired with an inexpensive, easy-to-use tire and inner tube patch kit, which you can find in any hardware or auto supply store. Small rips and places where the rubber looks old and develops a crackly surface can be coated with a wonderful substance called Magic Rubber, which comes in a tube and is sold in hardware stores. It is black neoprene rubber in liquid form, and it dries in a tough, flexible skin. Several coats build up a really durable patch. A repair made with the material from a tire patch kit will last longer if you coat around it with Magic Rubber to prevent kids from prying at its edges.

Shoes and sneakers shouldn't be handed down from child to child. New shoes adapt themselves to the wearer's foot, but a thoroughly broken-in shoe or sneaker is liable to adapt the wearer's foot to its configuration.

Tears in kids' shoes and sneakers can usually be repaired at home. Patch rips and holes with scrap pieces of canvas applied from inside the shoe if possible. A hot-melt glue gun provides the perfect elastic glue joint for shoe repairs. The vinyl plastic menders discussed above under Inflatables also do a good job of cementing patches in shoes. Kids never wear holes through the soles, because they outgrow the shoes before they have a chance to.

Before winter, it's a good practice to treat all leather shoes with a waterproofer. Shoe stores carry a variety of waterproofing substances.

Recycled Shoes

Here's the perfect vehicle for teaching a five-year-old to tie her shoes. Any old shoe can be adapted with wheels — sneakers, moccasins, loafers. Mom's old platform shoes can be drilled through easily to accept dowel axles.

The wheeled baby shoe illustrated is made by first cutting out a rectangle from the sole to accommodate the 1½″ diameter front wheel. You will need a sharp knife for this as the sole will probably be as tough as shoe leather. Cut the wheels from ½″ wood; see p. 282 for suggestions on making wooden wheels. The front wheel spins around on a fixed axle, so use a 3/16″ dowel through a ¼″ hole. The axle is shoved in between the two layers of the sole

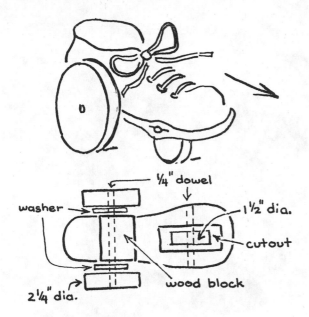

after you separate them with a screwdriver blade to admit it. Glue will hold it in place.

Now carefully pry up the rear of the insole. The ¾" block of wood shown in the illustration is drilled with a 5/16" hole to accept a revolving ¼" axle — drill toward the rear of the block and very close to the surface of the block that meets the sole of the shoe. Two roundheaded wood screws coming down from inside the shoe hold the block on; they screw into the front of the block, away from the axle hole. Add some glue when mounting the block and use washers with the screws if the heads have to hold against soft material inside the shoe. Make sure in

mounting the rear block that the axle will be aligned parallel to the front axle so the shoe will run straight. Use one or more metal washers on each side to keep the rear wheels from touching the sides of the shoe and slowing down the works. Glue the wheels on the ends of the axle and glue down the rear part of the insole. Add long shoelaces if you have a five-year-old who is ready to learn the skill of tying them.

Now, doesn't that beat having those old baby shoes fossilized in bronze?

If you're set on preserving your child's first shoes for posterity, perhaps you'll want to use the handsome contemporary-looking display technique one father showed me. He'd found a plexiglas box the right size in a plastics store. He cut a piece of ½" plywood to fit loosely in the box, and covered it with deep blue velvet, glued on. The baby shoes were screwed down over that, and the plastic box was pushed down over the base — the cloth wrapped around the edges of the plywood makes it fit snugly in the box.

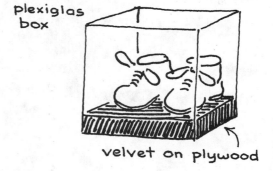

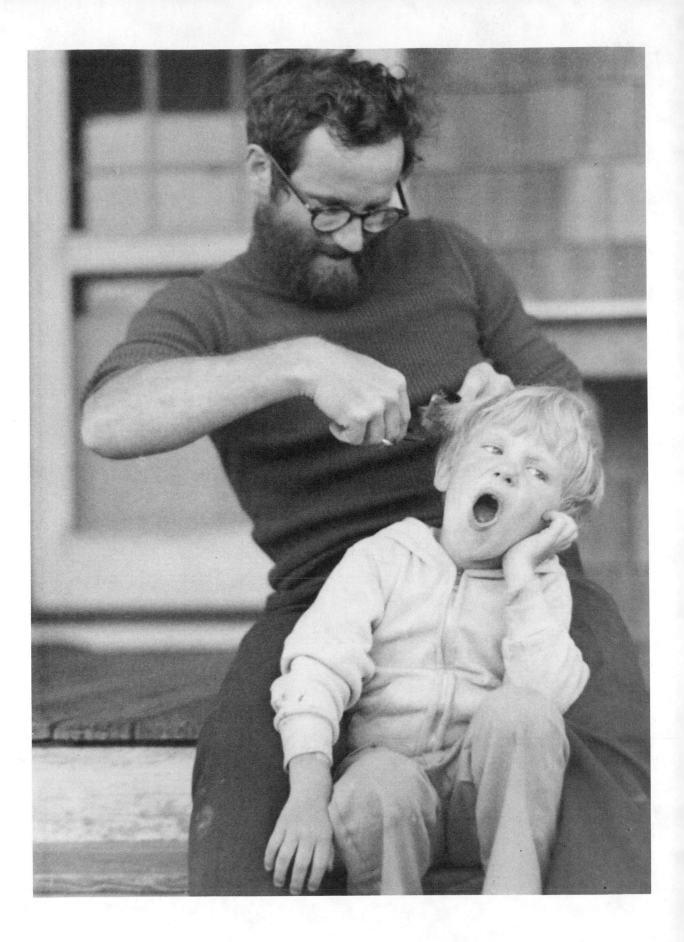

Chapter 6

EVERY DAY

A father's weekday life with his kids is usually crowded into a few brief hours, mornings and evenings. But a lot can be packed into those short time slots — family breakfasts and dinners, father-supervised baths and bedtime rituals. These little daily encounters make up the real bulk of a man's relationship with his kids. Weekends are great for long hours together and special outings, and of course there is always that expectantly awaited vacation when there will be days on end to spend with the family. But fathers whose schedules rob them of day-in, day-out contact with their kids often find that it's not easy to get back in touch with their children when that vacation finally comes.

Men who travel a lot for business and are gone two or three weeks at a time always say that they come back to find their kids have been transformed completely while they were away — they hardly recognize them. Especially during their first six years kids constantly change in dramatic ways — the same child at six months and again at a year is two entirely different people, and it only takes a matter of months for him to metamorphose again . . . and again . . . Even when you're home every evening, sharing your kids' day-to-day lives, these changes keep you pedaling hard to stay abreast. To me, one of the fascinating things about daily living with kids is that it never stays the same for long. Before you have kids, you expect fatherhood to be somehow stable and stodgy, but it is never that — you're too busy changing the conditions of your life to keep pace with the way the kids have grown, and changing your strategies to keep up with the way their behavior has developed.

BEHAVIOR

Every child goes through good times and bad — stages when he's so charming you could hug him every time you look at him and others when you wonder how you can stand to have him in your home.

Many of these stages come at predictable intervals in the lives of most children. In recent years, psychologists and other researchers interested in child development have plotted the sequence of behavior stages in great detail and with some accuracy. There are, of course, many exceptions to the general patterns they point to — because each child is an individual and follows a unique course through life. Some lucky parents even claim that their children don't go through the so-called Terrible Twos.

Knowing in advance what kinds of behavior you can expect from your child at different ages can help you cope when you are suddenly faced with an apparent "behavior problem." It may just be that your child has moved forward into a stage in which *all* kids are "behavior problems." The knowledge that you aren't alone and that your child isn't a special disaster will be a great comfort.

The following is offered as a brief guide to behav-

Birth   Six Months   One Year   Terrible Two

ior in the first six years. It touches only on the major landmarks. For the subtleties, look at some of the books listed in the Further Reading section at the end of this book under the heading Child Development.

INFANT: Babies are generally easy to live with. They eat, sleep, and cry when they need something — and there are no big surprises.

ONE: A one-year old is nearly always a delight — her responses to the world and the people close to her are positive and charged with the excitement she feels at coming alive intellectually, learning new things. But around eighteen months, and sometimes as early as fourteen months, kids discover the idea No, and many are so intrigued with it that their behavior for months afterward is shaped by it. The whole household can be upset by the grumpy negative attitude of a child at this stage and his perverse refusals to co-operate as he practices the new-found power of No.

Many kids, in my experience, miss this stage or only get a mild case of the Nos, but watch out, because few steer clear of the famous Terrible Twos.

TWO: It's most often at around two and a half that kids turn into Terrible Twos. This stage is designed as a test of your patience, resolve, and good will as a parent. A two-year-old is in the process of discovering his identity and individuality. Awed and confused by the scary implications of independence from Mom and Dad, but nevertheless intent on exploring this possibility to the full, he arrives at a tactic that he'll use again as an adolescent. He takes stock of all the things his parents approve of and expect from him, and then exerts his independence by doing quite the opposite. Two is the time for "tantrums." And a Terrible Two issues imperious

orders to his parents while refusing to comply with even your most lovingly expressed requests.

In this atmosphere, parents often grow tense and argue between themselves. I've never seen a study to substantiate it, but I suspect that the separation and divorce rate in families with Terrible Twos is much higher than in the general population.

Many fathers, when their children are two, suddenly discover that their work load has increased dramatically, and begin working evenings and weekends. They are avoiding not only an obnoxious child, but also an exhausted, harried wife who has been beaten down all day by two-year-old behavior. Of course a father who avoids the issue only adds to the problem by withdrawing his support from his wife and his guiding hand from his child. Parents who hang in there *together* can share the harassment and also the joy of seeing their child's behavior suddenly and miraculously take a turn for the better.

THREE: This year is a gift to parents who have been through the Terrible Twos. A three-year-old — in general — is a joy to have around.

FOUR: Because it is a less well known phenomenon that the Terrible Twos, the so-called Out-of-Bounds Fours comes as an unpleasant surprise to many parents. You get another strong foretaste of adolescence in this stage as your child "acts up" outrageously and pushes beyond every limit you try to set — again, apparently, in a crude effort at exerting his independence. And again the situation can be eased by a father who is on hand to help both mother and child.

One limit that almost every four-year-old pushes beyond is the Truth. Parents are usually shocked when they discover their darling telling whoppers

Three   Out-of-Bounds Four   Helpful Five   Six

for the first time. No child, of course, is naturally dishonest, but every child at around four figures out for the first time what a lie is and how it might be useful, and proceeds to use lying as one of dozens of tough tests of his parents' resolve. For more on four-year-olds and the truth, see p. 207.

FIVE: A very good year — another gift to parents. At five, kids are wonderfully co-operative and their general attitude of self-assurance and purposefulness can make everyone in the family feel great. Of course, five-year-olds aren't perfect; they get upset and grumpy and ill-mannered from time to time, but then, don't we all?

SIX: Six-year-olds tend to be a little moody and unreceptive at home. It may seem hard to get your messages through to your child at six, and you may sense a gulf developing between you. Meanwhile, she will be attentive and eager at school as she tunes into a new life away from the nest.

MORNINGS

CLANG go the toy cymbals at six in the morning, a full half hour before the alarm — CLANG, CLANG. "Gregory, cut that out. Right Now! Why are you doing that?"

"My friend Barry told me to do that — when everybody is asleep, he said I should clap these cymbals."

Barry is six months older than Gregory, so he is always providing him with useful new approaches.

Fifteen minutes later I have two little guys straddling my back and bouncing until the sleeping giant heaves off covers and kids.

BACK RUBS

When the kids attack you in bed in the morning, try channeling their energy and turning some of it to

your advantage instead of ending up pummeled and sore. Teach a three- or a four-year-old to give you a back rub — not the massage rubbing kind, but a workover with short, soft karate-type blows from the sides of both hands. At four Gregory learned to do this in about five minutes, and he does such a good job of it that I come away feeling refreshed. Even when he gets silly and starts hitting in earnest, he's not strong enough yet to do any damage.

SHAVING

Every father who shaves soon discovers what a big deal this is for his kids. Kids love ritual things and adult things, and shaving is both. If you use an electric razor, the kids will be turned on by the hum, but I hope you'll also give the old-fashioned method a try and maybe even switch when you discover what this lathery production means to your kids. With a one-year-old, you're playing his favorite game — peek-a-boo — behind the suds. Where did Daddy go? And in jig time your familiar, reassuring face is revealed by the razor. Kids get to squirt the shaving cream out of the can — and sometimes to play with it in the tub. For a three- or a four-year-old you are always Santa Claus in his white beard, and kids this age can join you in a little shaving.

Gregory and I made a very realistic-looking toy razor by pounding a piece of dowel into a tight hole drilled in a little rectangle cut with a sharp knife from the sidewall of a discarded tire. Timothy, at one and a half, insisted on having a razor, too, by pawing at his face and screaming. So we made another, and now every morning when there's time, we all lather up and scrape off the foam.

If you use an electric razor, your child can make his own from any small block of wood and a little

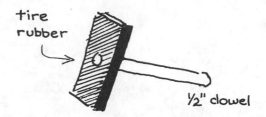

buzzing. Don't bother helping him fit it with a wire for an imitation electric cord, because he'll surely try to plug this into a socket.

Girls get to shave, too — their faces if they're not fussy; legs and underarms if they want to do things properly.

Father's Moustache

Fathers with beards and moustaches report that their face hair gets tugged and tweaked at first, but that babies learn fast and this slows down quickly. In one family, Mom was forever cheering the baby on as she yanked at Daddy's beard: "Pull, Pam, pull!!" But since she reached four months, Pam has neglected the beard; she pulls at Daddy's glasses instead.

Kids whose fathers have beards don't learn much about shaving. I asked a boy of four whose dad sports a full set of whiskers: "What is shaving like? Where does a man do it?" "Shaving," said he knowledgeably, "is like on his forehead and in his hair." But a nonshaver doesn't miss all the fun — beard and moustache trimming can be made into an impressive production for the kids.

A man who has two preschool daughters told me he had shaved off his moustache one day pretty much on whim, while he was alone in the house. Later in the day, Emily, two, arrived home and came running in. "She got within four or five feet of me and *froze*. Looking at me. 'What's the matter, Emily?' No response. She wouldn't talk, period." Emily's dad showed her shaving in pantomime. He hung his finger on his lip for a moustache. All to no avail; she was clearly afraid of him. Amanda, five, took this drastic change pretty much in her stride, but it was days before Emily would accept her clean-shaven dad.

TOOTHBRUSHING

Joining Daddy every morning at the sink for toothbrushing gives a child a source of pride, and it builds a habit that can cut down on the ruinous dental bills that loom in your future as a father.

A child's teeth should be brushed from the time the first one appears — which varies widely among children. If a brush won't fit in the baby's mouth, use a finger, a piece of gauze, and some toothpaste. Brush up and down — in the direction the teeth grow — and brush the gums as well. Make this a daily routine that your child will grow up with and never think to question. Let her grab the brush and do it herself as soon as she likes, but be sure to continue also to brush *for* her until you're satisfied she's doing a thorough job. A mirror mounted at your child's height encourages brushing.

The right kind of early introduction to dentistry can cut down remarkably on a child's anxiety over visits to the dentist. Ask your dentist about a get-acquainted visit for your child sometime between ages two and three. This can often be arranged as part of your regular checkup. Your dentist may let your child stay with you and watch while he performs some routine procedure. Seeing that it doesn't hurt you is sound evidence for your child that there is nothing to worry about. And many dentists will take a few minutes to let a child sit in the big chair and show him how some of the equipment works, because dentists know that a child who has cheerful, positive, early experiences will look forward to going to the dentist and won't scream and bite when the chips are down. Playing dentist games with your child at home before a first visit can help him understand what's going on and enjoy it.

A few more pointers for avoiding big dental bills:

Baby teeth are not immune to decay, and a sugary nightly bottle can rot out a whole mouth full of them, causing big problems for a child — water is the best drink for a toddler's nightly bottle and will help her fall asleep as well as any other fluid. Specially designed nipples and pacifiers are available that aid in the proper formation and development of teeth and mouth. If your local water is not fluoridated, check with your dentist and/or pediatrician, who may want to add a fluoride to your child's diet as a supplement, like vitamins.

DRESSING

If you help your kids get dressed in the morning, as soon as they're able to do anything for themselves, start backing off and let *them* do the job. And even before this, with kids from one and a half on, try to think of yourself as a dressing instructor rather than a valet. Being able to dress themselves is one of the first big steps toward independence for kids, and one they are eager to take — so try to help them move along at a brisk pace. If you're too generous with your help, a child will learn to depend on it, and the whole learning process can bog down.

With patient instruction and good techniques, by the fourth birthday, most kids will be able to put on their clothes alone — after a fashion and with help on fasteners. By five and a half, dressing skills have been refined and kids do a pretty capable job, even accomplishing shoe tying, though there's a good chance the shoe that gets tied will be on the wrong foot. So you aren't out of a job for years, but you switch over from instructor-helper to supervisor sometime after four.

A one-year-old is a great comedy act as he stands on one foot jabbing at the other foot with the toe of the shoe, trying to put it on — kids need systems for putting clothes on, orderly routines that eliminate most of the difficulties they encounter. Learning a simple set of basic dressing positions is a major step in the right direction: standing for shirts; sitting on chair or bed for pants; and sitting on the floor for socks and shoes.

Coats

At two and a half a child can put on her own coat, jacket, or front-opening shirt if you lay it on the floor at her feet; the collar should be closest to her and the coat should lie on its back with the front opened

wide to show the armholes. The child bends over, puts a hand in each armhole, picks the coat up, throwing it back over her head and simultaneously thrusting her arms into its arms — and it's on. The child is proud and you've saved a couple of years of coat holding.

Shirts

Pullover shirts and sweaters have a habit of getting stuck around the face. Teach kids to bunch up the shirt and start with the hole, pulling it wide and prying it on from the *back* of the head; when the hole is over, then the arms can be shoved through. Taking it off, the procedure is reversed: arms out; then grab the bottom of the collar and pull up and back across the face and over the head.

Pants

Around three, putting on pants gave Gregory fits — two feet in one leg, and then when that was straightened out he'd squirm and writhe on the floor, but they wouldn't pull up. So we worked out the Potato Sack Jumping Race Pants Method, which works just the way the name describes it. Gregory would grab the pants at the two sides of the belt and tug and hop and tug and hop until they were up.

Socks

The best socks for kids are heelless tubes that can be pulled on any which way. If your child has socks with heels, turn the tops out and down, so that the sock is halfway inside out, with the heel section clearly protruding. The child pulls this onto his foot

with the heel part naturally down, and then rolls the top section up around his ankle. Gregory believes that this simple expedient is magic.

Shoes

Every child should have a shoehorn at two and a half or whenever she starts making halfway successful attempts at putting on shoes. Kids adore a shoehorn; it's one of the first tools they can learn to use that actually helps them perform a difficult task alone. Put a cord on the shoehorn and hang it up somewhere convenient so it won't disappear into the bottom of the toy chest.

Also teach your kids from the start to pull open the laces so the shoe will be easier to put on; if they don't learn to do this, you'll have to do it for them thousands of times.

Laces

Since you're the parent who most often has shoes to tie, you're the logical teacher of this skill, and often the one the kids seek out. A four-and-a-half-year-old can usually learn the simple overhand knot that begins the bow. Demonstrate it often with big pieces of rope and get your child to practice it on a large scale — say with a length of clothesline. Gregory and I do knot lessons with licorice whips, and when we want to tie something really fancy, we use

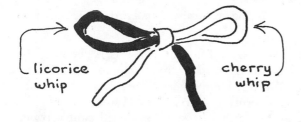

one black licorice whip and one red cherry-flavor whip. At four most kids will practice knot tying by the hour if you give them enough rope.

When the first part of the shoe knot is mastered, move on to the bow; again demonstrate and practice it on a large scale; and break it down into short steps. Actual-size practice, though, is the most important part of working up this complex skill. Your child can practice on a shoe that's not on her foot at the time to make the job easier; or make a shoe car like the one on p. 140 for bow-tying practice.

Give your child a "handle" on bow tying by explaining that the first loop is a horse's head and neck, and that the second loop is a cowpoke's lasso thrown around to catch the horse.

Don't bother to push your child on shoe tying; he is probably pushing himself a little too hard already, because shoe tying is a major mark of status in his world. Younger kids talk with reverence in their voices about a five-year-old who can tie his shoelaces.

Speed Dressing

With a child who is dawdling at dressing herself, you get nowhere at all by complaining that she is dragging her feet and slowing down the rest of the family — that line draws a total blank. Try the positive approach of a speed dressing contest — many kids like an exaggerated hurry-up routine. Some kids, though, will just keep tugging at the same sock for half an hour and refuse to be jollied into a little snap and precision.

TOILET TRAINING

Few fathers play a major part in toilet training — it's an effort that requires being on hand all day, every day. But with a boy you will definitely be the chief demonstrator-instructor; kids learn by observation and imitation, and your son will have to pick up his skills in this department from you.

When you are around and your child — whether son or daughter — is making progress, your approval will cheer her on to further successes. A child learns to use the pot mostly to please her parents, to win their approval, and a father's approval is a keenly sought after prize. Huzzahs and group cheers aren't called for each time your child succeeds on the potty, just honest hearty congratulations.

Many "programs" for toilet training are available to parents, and you and your wife should consider with care before you settle on one. Responsible child care experts pretty well agree on waiting till the end of the second year to start bowel training — the first step. Dr. Spock's section on toilet training is fine; perhaps even a little better is pediatrician T. Berry Brazelton in *Infants and Mothers* (New York: Dell, 1972), whom Dr. Spock quotes on toilet training. I'd avoid books that claim a child can be toilet trained in a single day — too many hopes and pressures will ride on that one day.

A Step Up

When Gregory moved from the little pot to a seat on the big one and started bladder training in earnest, he and I made our first woodworking project together — the little step stool shown here. He was just a few months over two, so I sawed the 2″ x 4″s, but we did the other sawing and hammering, holding the tools together, and we had a grand time of it. Gregory was super proud to be working with Daddy with the tools and even prouder when the thing was together and in use and he realized its significance

to him. It only lifts a child up 4″ — but that's a giant step toward growing up. Incidentally, a girl can use a step up, too. The materials you'll need to make a similar stool are:

15″ length 2″ x 4″
25″ length 1″ x 4″
6d common nails, galvanized

shellac OR varnish OR polyurethane OR contact paper

A few coats of finish are necessary, because this item will get soaked from time to time. I'm too impatient to bother finishing projects with coat after coat of varnish, so Gregory and I simply covered the two top boards of his stool neatly with contact paper, which has stood up through two toilet trainees.

FAMILY DINNER

I've been searching for someone with a sure-fire solution for keeping small children on an even keel during family dinner. A way out of "I don' wanna eat *that*," and "YUCK — awful," as well as "How many times do I have to tell you not to blow bubbles in your milk?" and "No, you may not have dessert until you've finished your dinner." If anyone has the answer, it hasn't, as far as I can make out, been made public yet.

But no matter how disagreeable family dinnertime may get — and it can be outrageous in our house, with two little guys goading each other on to ever sloppier feats of food play — I think it's still worth the effort to sit together as a family and work at getting the kids to co-operate and enjoy family meals. Dinner in many homes is the main everyday family event, and the only alternative — an early meal for the kids — simply wipes out most of the weekday family sharing it's possible to have.

A first baby, except that he spills and slobbers a little, makes a charming dinner companion. And most kids are "good eaters" for the first two years. In fact they're usually omnivorous — Timothy would

grab at the beam from the flashlight and try to cram it into his mouth to eat it. At two, though, kids commonly turn into finicky and fussy eaters. The little guy who has cheerfully stuffed down everything in sight may start to push food away. And this is the point at which conscientious parents begin to feel driven to make the child finish his green beans. Your child hardly touches his food for a couple of days and you begin to suspect he'll starve to death if he doesn't eat those green beans. At two, however, the pediatricians assure us, a child's caloric need isn't as great as it previously was; it's okay if he eats a lot one day and then stores it for days of fasting — it's called chipmunk eating.

Regular appetite returns, but then about a year and a half later, at three and a half, you often have another "problem eater." At this point kids commonly refuse any food that's offered; they want something else instead or the same thing prepared differently. This syndrome apparently has nothing to do with caloric need but is a manifestation of the three-year-old's power hunger, his desire to "run" his parents.

Around four years old is when food bargaining usually starts in earnest — the child eats the dinner to get the dessert. Many parents feel there's something "wrong" with this, that they shouldn't "bribe" the child with goodies. This is, however, a situation that almost all four-year-olds set up, and note that it is created by a child's idea of how things should be; parents don't create it by offering bribes. Kids insist on this game and I have yet to hear of a viable alternative. So relax; if you don't like to think of it as a bribe, call dessert "positive reinforcement" as it is called by child care experts. And bribe your child with it as he expects you to.

When a preschooler acts foolishly at the table and holds off on eating, often you realize she is simply looking for attention. So you have another positive reinforcement commodity to barter with besides dessert. Your child will probably take you up on it if you state it plainly: "If you eat your food, I'll pay attention to you while you do."

Prodding one child to eat green beans over a variety of objections at a variety of ages isn't such an onerous task. But family dinners really get tricky when you have two or more kids. The baby gets attention by dropping food on the floor and turning his bowl over on his head, so naturally the older child copies him to get the same attention. And then the older one, now wound up, does some Bronx cheering, which the baby then immediately copies, and so it goes, back and forth across the family dinner table. Now it becomes a major effort to stay calm and on top of the situation. Whole meals can be spent correcting both kids, banishing the older one, listening to vehement protests — no one's digestion is improved.

Occasionally, though, none of this happens; both kids are alert and they eat without complaints or spills, and wonder of wonders, we are in the midst of a family conversation. Perhaps it's only by contrast to the meals where the kids act up, but there's something extraordinarily refreshing and impressive to me about a successful, peaceful, conversational family meal.

SPECIAL MEALS

One easy way to improve a family dinner scene that keeps collapsing — at least for the short run — is to take a break with a special meal. Just change the scene — in the summer a picnic will do the trick. Kids love eating outside, or in any new place, for

that matter, and the change will usually distract them enough to interrupt their fixed patterns of idiotic dinnertime behavior.

A picnic can be staged almost anywhere — out on the lawn, or in a nearby park. But even in winter you can have picnics for the kids — indoors. Just lay out a picnic tablecloth — preferably oilcloth — on the living room floor, or in any other room. As a special reward for Gregory and Timothy, we occasionally have a picnic upstairs on the floor in their room. Going on location for these special meals is made a lot easier, we've found, by using the huge family tray that Gregory and I manufactured. We can usually crowd everything that is needed for the meal on the tray for one trip each way, so the picnics aren't time-consuming and full of jumping up and running back and forth. All you need to make the tray are:

    18" x 24" piece ¼" plywood
    8' length any light molding
    brads OR small finishing nails
    paint OR contact paper

There's nothing at all to making this tray, so it's a good short project for a father and a five-year-old. Cut the molding to fit around the edges of the tray; you can miter the corners if you want a neat job, or for faster work, cut 16" and 22" lengths and leave a gap at each corner. Glue the moldings on and drive brads or nails through from the bottom of the plywood. Either paint the whole thing or cover the plywood with contact paper before attaching the moldings with nails.

Without moving from the usual dinner table you can change the scene for kids, at least during the winter, when it's dark early, with candlelight — it is just as romantic for a child as it is for an adult. Usually the kids are so interested in the candles they forget to act up. The most special dinner of all in our house is a candle-lit picnic in the kids' room.

Any noticeable change in the meal, in fact, is likely to improve dinner behavior. If you hardly ever cook, your infrequent efforts as a gourmet chef will probably be greeted with your kids' keen interest, and children seldom say Yuck to dinner if Dad cooks it; for more on fathers and cooking, see p. 320. Chinese food with chopsticks or Mexican night with everything rolled up in tortillas can change kids' dinnertime attitudes — or make them worse, if they are turned off by the exotic food.

Imaginative changes in the way food is presented to a child will sometimes make him sit up and take notice. One father told me he had conned a picky two-year-old who refused food by presenting him with "dangerous dinners" just bristling with toothpicks — and this little excitement had converted him back into a good eater.

THANK YOUS

Around one and a half or two, when she's learning labels for everything, your child can say a little grace at dinner that will help her practice the names of all the things on the table. "Thank you [for] these hot dogs; thank you [for] this broccoli," etc. She'll probably leave out the preposition "for," but she'll get the names of the foods right, and she may actually understand something of the sentiment she's expressing. Rita and I will never forget the dinner when Gregory — completely unprompted — added after "Thank you [for] the mustard," "Thank you [for] this mommy; thank you [for] this daddy."

BATHS

Supervising the nightly bath is a favorite of many fathers. It's a relaxing time to spend with young kids. Soaking in the tub, children calm down and can be easygoing and receptive — except, of course, if you even mention washing their hair.

I find that my kids learn things more easily in the tub than anywhere else, so it has always been the place where we practice new songs and nursery rhymes and where I teach them the names of the planets and the names of the great men on the coins from my pockets. It's also a good place for discussing serious matters with preschoolers, since they're open and usually pretty attentive in the tub. Other fathers agree with me that they're apt to understand what you're trying to get across a little more clearly than they might somewhere else. If you're trying to help a preschooler grapple with a problem, I think the relaxed atmosphere of the bath puts him in a good frame of mind for focusing on finding solutions.

There are plenty of good water sports for small children and their fathers at bath time — more of that appears below. If you want to get the kids clean in the midst of all these other extraneous activities, toss a capful of shampoo or some kids' bubble bath into the water at the beginning of the bath and the movement of the children in the tub will clean them up pretty well, except for faces and behind the ears.

TUB FLEET

Gregory was so pleased at three and a half with the ship he hammered together from old scraps of wood that he vowed to build many more — "a million collection of ships." His fleet isn't that big yet, but it's growing.

Illustrated here are some bathtub standards that can be made by father and child as good projects to share in the family workshop. The materials are scrap pieces of wood and dowels. The drawings show spiffy finished models. There's really no need for painted waterlines and portholes and ribbon flags — I've put those in just to make the illustration look presentable. To your child, any homemade boat will look just like the *Queen Elizabeth* on her maiden voyage, even if it's only a few pieces of wood nailed together, and especially if your child did most of the work.

Ordinary white household glue isn't waterproof

enough for boats; it gets gummy when it's wet and the pieces will come unstuck. So stick with nails or supervise the work closely if you use a toxic waterproof glue. Galvanized nails are probably best since they resist rust and don't bend up as easily as aluminum nails do when a child hits them.

If building the boat is your project — not your child's — and you want to make a good clean job of cutting the bow, mark the center line on the wood and then use a curved edge (French curve, large dinner plate or platter, sole of shoe) to draw identical curves on either side. Don't try to saw along these lines; the most professional carpenter will do a

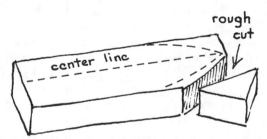

sloppy job. Rough cut the waste away, leaving some wood on the waste side of the lines, and then use a cheese-grater rasp to get down to the lines. A five- or a six-year-old can do some of the work of bow shaping if you help set it up well (see section on kids in the workshop, p. 298, but don't expect hairline accuracy until your child reaches the teens.

A boat that turns out top-heavy and tips can be righted by adding some roundheaded brass screws along the keel line.

Of all wooden toys that are likely to be made by fathers and kids, bathtub boats need a preserving finish most, because the wood takes a beating from

the water and turns dry, grainy, and a little splintery. In an ideal world there would be time to paint little boats with nontoxic enamel and/or with spar varnish, which is used on real boats because it stays slightly pliant and so won't crack up easily. If you are orderly and can hide what you're doing from the kids, maybe you'll manage to paint some bathtub boats. But Gregory and I, hard at work on his million collection of ships, have never yet gotten to that stage on one — the pieces are barely together before it has to be launched in the tub.

Motor Boats

Illustrated here are three methods for achieving the same result: the standard rubber band stern-wheeler. The stern wheel itself is made from two

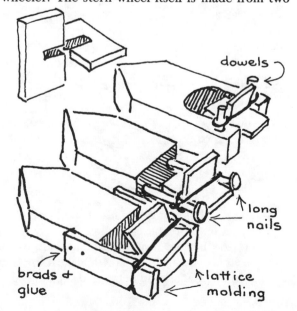

pieces of light wood — lattice molding is perfect — notched and glued together as shown. These little racing boats are good outdoors, too, in a toddler's wading pool, or wherever there's water and room.

Burger Boat

Here's the flagship of the bathtub fleet. To make this sleek-hulled beauty, you will need:

scrap piece of 1″ wood
1½ clean styrofoam hamburger boxes
12″ length ¼″ dowel
white glue and waterproof glue

Drill a ¼″ hole in the scrap piece of wood and punch or drill one in the top of the complete hamburger box. With white glue fix the dowel in the scrap wood. Now push the dowel mast through the hole in the box top from inside. Apply an even bead of white glue all the way around the edge of the box bottom. Glue the wood piece to the floor of the box as you close the lid. Check to be sure that the white glue seals the top and bottom together. The white glue isn't waterproof and will get sticky in the tub, so wait till it's dry and smear a light film of Duco or some other waterproof glue over the joint to seal it — too much waterproof glue will melt the styrofoam. A hot-melt glue gun will do a quick waterproof job of sealing the box together.

Make small holes in two sides of another box lid and push it onto the mast for a sail. If you want to decorate the Burger Boat with a flag, before you start assembly use a coping saw to make a thin slot in the top of the mast and at the end slip a piece of ribbon into the slot and wrap and glue a short part of it around the dowel.

Blowing on the sail makes the Burger Boat move forward at a good clip. Three and a half or older is a good age for this boat.

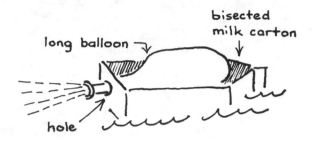

Bath Toys

Instant bathtub toys can be made from many ordinary household containers. Styrofoam meat wrappers make good rafts, and a plastic egg carton rides high in the water. A one-year-old will enjoy putting small things in the egg compartments — Weebles, Fisher-Price people, little plastic blocks.

Plastic bottles and cups float well, and are more useful if you do some minimal doctoring and turn them into funnels and water sprinklers. For a sprinkler, just punch holes in any plastic container, using a nail or a small drill bit; fill it with water and sprinkle the kids.

Kids in the bathtub spend much of their time and ingenuity trying to scuttle and dunk and sink the boats and other bath toys — which looks a little counterproductive to adults. But notice that in a kid's experience more things float in the tub than go under: boats do it, bars of soap do it, even rubber duckies do it. So kids take floating pretty much for granted, but they are very interested in its opposite. Make sure to include some objects that won't just

bob back up every time they go under. Two-liter plastic soda bottles make great submersibles, because adding water makes them go down very slowly.

A couple of yards of clear vinyl tubing from a hardware store make an excellent bath toy. We use a length of tubing to siphon water from the bathroom sink down to the tub. Gregory gets to suck on the tube to start the siphoning. He also loves to use the tube for blowing bubbles up through the bath water.

Anchoring toy boats was one of Gregory's favorite games at age five. He made anchors from anything heavy enough to do the job — an adhesive tape spool or a metal toy car tied by a length of string to the boat.

When too many bath toys start to accumulate and Mom threatens to banish them because there's no more room on the lid of the john, get a plastic string bag from the dime store and use it to collect all the small things; hung up on a hook, it allows the toys to dry out.

BATH FEARS

At three and a half, Gregory was deathly afraid of having his hair washed and rinsed under the hand-held shower in our bathtub. I went ahead and did it anyway, as a test of my own will and determination. And when it was over, Gergory said: "But I *didn't* die when you poured water on me." "What do you mean?" I asked. "Cause the witch died." It turned out that he had seen the *Wizard of Oz* months before on the TV, and had been more than a little impressed by the scene at the end, where the

Wicked Witch of the West is permanently doused with a bucket of water. Of course he'd kept it quietly to himself over the months — the secret knowledge that he, too, would be turned into a puddle in the tub.

One classic bathtub fear that many kids go through very early in their lives — in fact often the first big terror a child can express in words — is the fear of going Slurp down the bathtub drain. She sees all the water go down and comes to the reasoned conclusion that she, too, could go down the same way. The problem of the relative sizes of her body and the drain hole apparently doesn't come into play in her reasoning — big and little aren't too well sorted out in her scheme of things, so it doesn't occur to her that she'd have trouble fitting through. A child who's afraid of going Slurp down the drain can use a crash course in size relationships with clear physical demonstrations that big objects don't fit through tight holes — that her elbow won't fit through a finger ring and that her baby doll can't be stuffed down the drain.

HAIR WASHING

Hair-washing time is when you're afraid the neighbors will be listening and turn you in for child abuse. Even when the name of the shampoo promises there will be no tears, kids cry and carry on when you wash their hair. One father told me he gets good results with positive reinforcement — promises of lollipops and bubble gum. A little trick that will work a few times is getting the child interested in washing a doll's hair; meanwhile you wash hers.

"Tearless" shampoo does help; and you can start

when your child is still only a few months old to get him used to water being poured over his head and face, though conditioning like this can be easily reversed by a shot of real soap in the eye, or just by a child's whim. A washcloth rolled up and held to the child's forehead as you rinse his hair will help to keep water and soap out of the eyes, but a child-size diving mask may solve the problem. A child who washes his own hair — which can start around four and a half — is less likely to cry than one who has to be operated on.

Fathers are usually pretty good about brushing their daughters' hair, because it's novel and fun, but it's easy to neglect brushing a boy's hair, just as it's easy to forget to do your own. Kids comb and brush for themselves before they are even a year old, but the scalp needs the exercise of the extra pressure you can give to the brush.

TOWEL SLINGS

Make sure you give your kids an after-bath ride in a towel sling. I learned this wonderful trick from a father who did it regularly for his son, five, and daughter, three. Since I introduced it into my Wednesday-night bath ritual, the kids have joined their mother in her insistent demands that I supervise the bath more than once a week.

Simply wrap an open towel around your child's back and under her arms, and gather the two ends in front of her in your hand. Pick her up and swing.

The towel can also wrap the other way — across the front and under the arms and gathered behind. Timothy at one and a half wasn't too young for towel swinging. You can probably handle two kids at once, but two hands on the towel give a surer grip. Keep the swinging pretty gentle, though, because you'll lose the whole soothing effect of the bath if you get the kids worked up at this point, which can blow bedtime and mean starting from scratch to calm them down. Save rowdy towel swinging for the beach or for earlier in the day.

BEDTIME

Every kid ends up with a bedtime ritual that has to be repeated, just so, each night — Daddy has to kiss the Teddy bear or she can't go to sleep. A few simple procedures like this, a short prayer, a formula for saying good night — it's all fine because it gives the child a smooth transition from waking to sleeping —

a reliable, comfortable feeling that sets her up for falling asleep. Some kids try to add dozens of steps to the ritual, but don't let it get too involved or you may find it becomes counterproductive; a twenty-step ritual is no longer a quiet, familiar rite of passage that lulls the child — it has become a major production that demands her attention to get through. And it can take up a lot of your time.

Before the ritual comes the bedtime story, and I think this is one of the really wonderful things a father can share with small children on a regular basis. For many fathers who work long hours or who commute long distances, the bedtime story is the *only* thing they can share with the kids every day during the week. Start as early as you like; many kids at six months enjoy looking through books. When they are learning the names of things in the second year, you can have a great time "reading" mail-order catalogues together at bedtime. Gregory's favorite literature for months toward the end of that year was a mailer from a western boot company — he'd look at each page and each and every boot: "Shoe, shoe, shoe, shoe, shoe . . ." Magazines are fun at this point, too, because they have pictures of cars and men and houses, all things that a child is eager to point out and label with his new words. A good bedtime reading and storytelling habit can go on as a family tradition for years into the future. Even after a child learns to read for herself, reading aloud can continue to be a regular close family event — in homes where it's practiced it sometimes wins out in competition with prime-time TV shows.

After a good story and the incantations of the ritual, some kids still have trouble falling asleep. The same deep-voiced father lullabies that work on babies (p. 33) continue to knock out toddlers and preschoolers. And try back rubs — when kids can't get to sleep it's often because they're keyed up and tense, and a slow massage around the back and shoulders with your big comforting hand may do wonders.

"Close your eyes," I say every night to Gregory and Timothy. "Count those sheep. And go to sleepety, beepety, beepety . . ."

"BEEP," they shout, and out they go like lights.

BEDTIME ROUGHHOUSE

Fathers are always getting shot down for playing too roughly with the kids at bedtime. Here is an excerpt from a letter by Teddy Roosevelt to his son Ted in 1901:

> *Recently I have gone in to play with Archie and Quentin after they have gone to bed, and they have grown to expect me, jumping up in their tommies, expecting me to roll them over on the bed and tickle and "grabble" in them. However, it has proved rather too exciting, and an edict has gone forth that hereafter I must play bear with them before supper, and give up the play when they have gone to bed.*

Sound familiar? The "edict" here is the only way to manage the situation. Play bear much earlier than bedtime, or the kids won't be able to settle in. But then, a little very gentle roughhouse can't hurt — like the towel slings suggested above.

STORYTELLING

My father told wonderful stories — tales that no right-thinking parent would dream of scaring his kids with. They were also totally indiscreet, considering the make-up of our household. A housekeeper named Mrs. Hickerson lived with us, and she was a tough old bird — when she was irritated, which was most of the time, she'd drag my brother and me, seven and six, around by the ears. Mrs. Hickerson was the central character in my father's stories — Mrs. Hickerson the Witch. I've forgotten most of her evil doings now, but I can never eat a biscuit without remembering the "tooth-breakers," as we called them, that the real-life Mrs. Hickerson baked each week, because in every story my father told, we insisted on having the part about Mrs. Hickerson the Witch baking her stones in the oven. What wouldn't I give for a tape recording of those tales!

Many of the fathers I've talked with are storytellers, and the yarns they spin for their kids will be stuck in their children's minds just as those stone biscuits are stuck in mine. A lawyer entertains his three kids by the hour on long family car trips and at night before bed with the endless saga of netherworld characters called Giesel Troll and Gray Malcon and Froelicher, a frog; the general format is borrowed wholesale from the Hobbit sagas of J.R.R. Tolkien, but the characters are home-grown.

Their personalities are closely modeled on members of the family, and their continuing adventures simply grow, one on another.

An accounting manager for a large corporation describes the creative process that brought about his preschoolers' bedtime favorite, "The Tale of the Greedy Father": "They accused me of being greedy one night when I ate the last doughnut. So I said, 'Let me tell you a story about the Greedy Father.' I try to include them in the story. You know, I never refer to any of us by our real names, but it's us. The basic story of the Greedy Father — naturally he's the hero — is that he has the children's best interests at heart and the reason he's denying them the sweets and goodies is for their own good. One day they run away from home but they don't have any money to buy food, and they get very cold and hungry, so they come back. The Greedy Father is overjoyed to see them, and sorry they ran away from home, and he promises to give them all that they want to eat. So they sit down to a positive orgy of sweet things, and of course they get stomach-aches, and then they tell the father they realize he was right all along. I have a grouchy candy store operator that I throw in there. He takes the seven cents away from them and gives them one little stick of gum, and throws them out of the store. But they really love it. I gauge the length according to how fast they go to sleep."

A prep school English teacher draws the inspiration for the stories he tells his two kids, six and three, from the peculiar adventure of his aunt, who was chased through the woods by a moose in Maine. The stories are about Maurice Moose and his lovely wife, Maureen, and their children, Mike and Michelle. Maurice Moose no longer worries women

in the woods; he has become thoroughly domesticated, and the plots of the stories concern the family affairs of the Mooses of Maine — the arrival of a new baby, the celebration of Christmas.

Almost all the storytelling fathers I've talked with have made the same important discovery: Whatever the story is about — moose or mice, sharks or sweet teeth — the part that brings it home to the kids is that they see themselves in the characters — always disguised, but the disguise is a thin one so they can't help but know it's *them*. If you will think back to the literature course you took in high school or college, you'll remember this vital point being harped on and drummed into the students: In great literature, the reader will always *identify* with the protagonist. And that also seems to be the key to great storytelling for kids — that the kids will always identify themselves with the main characters in the tale.

Story Material

If you'd like to try some storytelling but hesitate, as several fathers have told me they do, because no original theme or plot comes to mind, just remember that your kids have no interest in your originality. What they like to hear is a story about themselves told by their dad. The plot, character development, and all the other trappings are secondary at best; they can range anywhere from silly and trite to absolutely masterful and the kids will like the story just as well.

If you need a plot and characters, steal them. Borrow them if you have scruples. Take them where you will — from books for kids, or the funny papers, or the cartoons on TV. Shakespeare, the most "original" genius of our language, is famous for having stolen his plots wholesale — lifted from popular books and plays of his day. Maybe all you need is one bold act of literary piracy to set you up as a storyteller.

There's no formula for the perfect bedtime story and kids are so very different and original that a favorite for one family or one child may be a dead bore for another. One thing you have going for you, though, is that not many kids younger than six ever do get bored. In fact, your only reason for making the story interesting is that you'll have to listen to it yourself dozens of times as you retell it on demand.

There are a few useful guidelines for good stories that fathers have known about for centuries. Use animals — little animals for the littlest kids, and bigger ones as they grow. Bunnies and chipmunks for a two-year-old; dogs and cats for a three-year-old; sharks, dolphins, dinosaurs, and whales at four. Children and animals can mix freely in stories. One father tells David, two, about a little boy named Daniel who is riding his tricycle on the sidewalk when he is challenged to a race by a talking turtle; a bunny hops up and joins in, and a blackbird officiates, and it's a very exciting race with a lot of nip and tuck and neck and neck and huffing and puffing and wild cheering at the finish line by the front porch steps.

That's another important part of the story — hamming it up with plenty of razzle-dazzle, if that happens to be your style, or with comic accents if you enjoy that kind of thing. Go ahead and throw yourself into the act; play the fool; you are in the privacy of your own home.

Using animals, actually, is only one part of a much broader and more useful general rule for bedtime stories: fit your tales to your kids' interests of the moment. If they are excited about superheroes, you can give them the adventures of Superfather and the Lost Children; if it's bicycles, you can do the "Tale of the Runaway Two-wheeler"; if it's tea parties, you can swipe your material right out of *Alice in Wonderland*. Or even combine your interests with theirs: "The Dallas Cowboys Meet Jabber Jaw the Shark."

One set of stories you have ready-made, absolutely no imagination required — what you did as a boy. Some kids like this type of story best of all; one father told me his three preschoolers shoot down all his bedtime songs and made-up stories and will listen only to this type of account. Of course if you like to use your imagination, there's no law against embroidering these boyhood reminiscences a little:

"How Your Dad as a Lad of Seven Defeated Bionic Bigfoot at Arm Wrestling."

Even the news of the day will yield an occasional bedtime story. Here is a true-life tall tale that I picked up from the radio news one evening driving home. A dolphin in a West Coast aquarium swallowed a large bolt, which became lodged in his throat. Medical technicians attempted in vain to reach the bolt with specially designed long-armed instruments. When technology failed, someone clever called in a professional basketball player — the longest arm on the West Coast. He simply reached down the dolphin's gullet and yanked the bolt free. I don't think I could count the number of times I've had to tell this one over.

Whatever the source of your stories, no matter how simple or elaborate you make them, do yourself and your kids a big favor and turn on a tape recorder some evening when you are in good form. The tape you make is something your children will treasure in years to come, and you may even get a chuckle out of it too, thirty years hence. See p. 335 for notes on making clear tape recordings.

Morals

Don't hesitate to use stories to drive home points or to teach your preschoolers lessons you want them to learn. No child ever listens to a lecture, but all kids are all ears for a story. They're attentive and they're quick to understand the point.

Also, a story about a child with a similar problem can be an enormous help to a child who is grappling with something difficult.

Con Job Stories

An important variation of the bedtime story is the story that's told entirely by the child — with a little bit of help from Dad. One evening when you know your preschooler has been somewhere special during the day — on a trip to the aquarium or to visit Grandmother — try this little con job. Let's say you have a three-year-old named Mary. Tell her: "One day a three-year-old girl named Martha, who lived in faraway Metuchen, went with her mom and two friends on a visit to the big aquarium there, and she saw . . ." I'm not going to claim that every preschool child will pick up the ball from there and run with it, but several other fathers I've talked with who use this approach agree with me that it yields at least twentyfold what you get with a simple "What did you do today, honey?"

Another story formula that works on roughly the same principle is perfect for kids at around two and a half. Say your child's name is Justin, and his favorite cartoon character is Mickey Mouse. "One day Mickey Mouse visited Justin's house and he asked Justin to show him everything. So Justin showed him his own room first, and in it were . . ." A two-year-old is still learning the names and labels for everything and will enjoy rattling off all the things he knows as he shows them to good friend Mickey.

READING STORIES

How many of the juvenile books you read to your kids do you really enjoy? There are probably a few; it's hard not to fall for Babar and later for Dr. Doolittle. But the majority of the books you'll be called on to read are going to be something less than fascinating to you: *The Daffy Little Duck, Toby Runs Away, The Bingity-Bangity School Bus*. Each child will find her individual tiresome favorites. An insurance underwriter told me that his daughter, four, regularly picks out her own books. "In fact," says he, "there are a couple of books that mysteriously disappeared because I can't stand them."

You get so you read with no enthusiasm, plowing through deadpan. "I feel like the tired priest at early morning Mass who can get through the whole service in eleven minutes flat," a father of two preschool boys said, describing how he read his children's favorites. The odd thing, though, is that almost no amount of contempt you show toward *Toby Runs Away* is likely to dampen your two-year-old's enthusiasm for it. It's part of a ritual that he can find meaning in, no matter how indifferently you read the story.

A quick examination of the plot may give a clue to the source of this fanatical attachment. In this particular book, Toby runs away; he has fun on his romp; but soon it starts to rain and he is lost and a little scared. A friendly mailman takes him home to a glass of milk and Mom. Not much of a story, perhaps, for us, but a crucial tale for a little person whose major concern is setting up independently in the world, who wants to go it alone, but who is still dependent for almost all his needs on Mom and Dad. His every scream and defiant act asserts his independence, but he knows there is no way he'll actually be able to run away for a while. Toby does this for him and his involvement with Toby-hero is the same thing we experience in literature that moves us. *Hamlet* lives through the years because each of us has some of Hamlet in him; each of us has wondered at some time, no matter how fleetingly: "To be or not to be?" And every child at two or two and a half is thinking, though he couldn't formulate it in words: "To be independent or not to be? That is the question."

With a story like *Toby Runs Away* the interpretation is obvious enough. But every child finds other favorites that no amount of adult ingenuity can infuse with interest, on any level. Kids become attracted to things for reasons we can't begin to guess at, and they aren't able to explain when we ask: "Why do you like *The Little Kittens' Christmas* so much?" I figure if they're drawn to it, they must need it. But do I have to read it over and over and over?

Why not tape-record these tiresome favorites when you've read them over for the fortieth time and lost all interest? Give the recording your best shot: plenty of gusto and enthusiasm. And then the next time: Click . . . "Once upon a time there lived four little kittens . . ." But if you do this, please

don't turn on the recording and leave the room. Stay there and turn the pages. I'm sure you've noticed that the real point of bedtime stories is being close and cozy and sharing something. The tape won't save you any time here, but while you're away at work during the day, your child may play your rendition of *The Little Kittens' Christmas* over so often that she, too, will be stone bored with it in a month or two. But will Mom — subjected to this barrage of tape-recorded drivel — applaud your efforts?

STORY SPECIALS

A little variety in the bedtime ritual may keep you from going stale. That wonderful warm feeling of closeness a child gets when Dad is holding her and reading a story isn't restricted to any one particular location. Kids love a change of place, and you may, too. You can change the scene without even moving from your usual story perch on your child's bed. Just get the sheet up like a tent — you are the tent pole — and read the story under there by the glow of a flashlight.

This same sort of conspiratorial setting can be achieved in any room by turning out the lights and reading by candlelight. If it's warm and clear, definitely go outside for a bedtime story — with a flashlight or a candle or that wonderful Coleman lantern you bought years ago for camping but never used after the kids arrived. Out under the stars you may end up forgetting about the story and looking at the universe instead.

Try reading a story in the back seat of the family car. It is a very intimate place, as you will remember from other back seats and other partners. Your child will love to get you alone here in *his* place — and it is very much his place if he regularly rides in the back in a car seat.

All these nighttime settings are perfect for ghosts and monsters and creepy-crawly stories, and I know lots of fathers who love to tell these, and plenty of kids who love to hear them. But preschool kids don't tolerate scary stories well; they are very literal-minded, while at the same time they haven't made a sharp distinction between fantasy and reality, so they can easily take ghosts in a story for the real thing. Kids will usually ask for scary stories when they want them and are ready for them, since they know plenty about ghosts and monsters from their friends and the TV.

Flashlight or candlelight reading doesn't have to be spooky at all. In fact, if it's just cozy and familiar it's liable to help a child to *like* the dark.

Major Productions

Preschoolers love a bedtime story that's made into a major production, and all it actually takes for a major production is a few little frills. Let's take *The Three Bears* for an example. Each member of the family gets a role, and it's straight type casting; Mom may have to double as Goldilocks if you have only one child actor. You can have rehearsals at dinner if you like — this will make mealtime a delight for the kids, though you may not like it much after the thirtieth time.

For a truly major production of *The Three Bears*, after a few rehearsals, record your family dramatization on tape. Work in some sound effects: the joyful chirping of birds as the bears set off on their morning walk in the woods, or maybe a few bars of Beethoven's *Sixth* to give an appropriate pastoral background. Other special effects will include loud slurping as Goldilocks eats the porridge, a clatter of sticks and blocks when the chair collapses under her, and heavy snoring when she gets into baby bear's bed, all of which are eagerly supplied by kids. But only you, Papa Bear, can supply an angry and outraged growl. And make sure that Mama Bear hams it up, too.

Any of the classic kids' stories will give you plenty of material to work with. I like *The Three Pigs* because it gives me a chance to do the time-honored trick of crinkling cellophane next to the microphone for the sound of the fire that cooks the wolf at the end of the story — while Gregory yowls piteously. He gets to do some pretty strenuous huffing and puffing in this one, too.

NIGHTTIME FEARS

One morning when he was just four, Gregory said: "I dreamed about the Three Little Pigs last night, Daddy." "Did the Big Bad Wolf come?" I asked. "Yeah," said Gregory, his face breaking apart, "and he stood by my bed and he thought I was one of the pigs."

Even before he's two, a child wakes in the night screaming and though he can't tell you what's up, you sense that he's been having a nightmare, that he's gripped by fear. And when kids start to have enough command of the language to tell us what they're afraid of, the occasional glimpses we get into their sleeping and waking fantasies are startling. Gregory's dream images sometimes haunt me more than my own do; another morning his nightmare story went this way: "The monster wouldn't stop chasing me and *he wouldn't take off his costume*."

The first nighttime fears you hear much about are the bears-under-the-bed sort — the monsters in the shadows that keep a two- or a three-year-old from going to sleep. These monsters and bears are very real to the kids who fear them. There's no line between fantasy and reality for a child of two or three, so telling her that the monsters don't exist isn't going to do much good. She needs protection from them rather than reassurance that they are only in her mind.

Kids see their fathers as superprotectors. Eric, nearly four, told me: "I rode with my daddy on my daddy's motorcycle. In the woods. But I didn't open my eyes to see cause there was a monster in the woods. And my dad looked out and he killed him." Dads are forever slaying dragons for their kids — it's the simplest and most effective way of dealing with these earliest fears. One father told me how he stood by his son's door nearly every night when he was two, evicting the fearsome Squogs one by one, saying, "All right, you, now get out there and stay out and don't come back." Once in a while, he noted, a monster would give him a really hard time

and he'd have to throw him out bodily — with lots of loud noises.

One practical help you can give a child who's scared of things in the dark — at any age — is to turn the light on. There's no law that says a child has to sleep in a dark room and most kids can go to sleep in any light if they're tired.

A policy to avoid in comforting a child who wakes up with nighttime fears is taking her into your bed. It'll work perfectly, but do it once or twice and you have a habit established that's hard to break. Staying by the child's bed while she goes back to sleep may be a little less convenient in the short run, but over the long haul it's far easier than taking her into yours.

As children grow older, the sources of their nighttime fears become more complex and the fears themselves take on a different character. A child of four or older may be terrified by the face he "sees" in the shadow the night light throws on the wall or the monster he insists is lurking in the hall. But he's also learning that there is a line between fantasy and reality, so he's not as certain that the bugbear truly exists as he would have been a year or so before. Now you can start to help him sort out what the monster is, to understand that the monster is in his head, just as a dream is — it doesn't *really* happen. Simply debunking the monsters won't help much; they still seem genuine in a sense to a child, but a sympathetic explanation will help.

Probably the best help you can give a child who's scared of things — of anything at all, night or day — is help in finding her *own* way to deal with the fear, to confront the monster, to resolve the problem. The monster *is* in your child's mind and your chas-

ing him out of the room isn't going to do the trick any more. Maybe it will work temporarily, but the old mental monster will keep coming back. Your child has to slay this dragon for herself if he's to stay dead.

You may be able to give your child an effective weapon for coping with the monster. Rita gave Gregory a magic blanket that did the trick at four — the same old dog-eared red quilt, but she told him to pretend it was magic and the next morning he reported: "I put my big blanket over my head and over my raisin box and over my teddy, and pretended those monsters weren't there, and know what? — they didn't bother me."

And often kids are able through their own resili-

ence and gutsy determination to cope with their nighttime fears and work out solutions and resolutions with no help at all from Dad and Mom. Gregory, looking absolutely angelic one morning, asked, "Know what I dreamed about, Daddy?"

"No, what?" I asked, thinking maybe sugarplums or Santa Claus.

"Bloodsuckers."

"What?"

"Bloodsuckers. They're about this long . . . no, about *this* long, and they suck your blood and so I grab them and cut them and suck their blood back."

Ah, sweet innocence of youth. But he sure took care of those bloodsuckers.

TV

What do fathers in the TV industry do about their kids and TV? Producer/director/actor/TV dad Michael Landon, for one, doesn't let his kids watch it during the week — except his show. It's not that he's opposed to TV for kids; it's just that he'd rather they learn to read.

TV is such a pervasive force in our children's lives that no father is entirely indifferent to it. One man told me he uses every tactic he can think of to turn his two girls away from its seduction: "We ridicule the TV, just as a matter of course." This man quipped that his proudest moment as a father had come "when Melissa [six] told me she thought the Donny and Marie show was silly." His message had gotten through. Another father defends TV for kids: "As a research scientist, I end up looking at a screen all the time. Our kids are going to be deciphering information from looking at screens, so they might as well get used to it."

The push-button baby-sitter has been a member of the American family for a quarter of a century now, and parents have started to come to terms with it. Our parents were a little befuddled by this new phenomenon — they had no guidelines from their parents, no body of experience to draw on when it came to making decisions like: How much TV should the kids watch? What programs? How late at night? But thoughtful parents have come to understand the need for setting up firm family rules limiting the amount of time kids spend as passive spec-

tators. And we're starting to be able to use the TV to our advantage as parents — not just the selfish advantage of keeping the kids occupied on Sunday morning so we can sleep late, but the real advantage both to children and parents that TV offers for early education. And TV programming — especially noncommercial programming for preschoolers — is growing up and learning how to enrich children's lives.

"Sesame Street" and other similar shows have made decisions about TV relatively easy for parents of preschoolers — these are shows most parents *want* their kids to watch. The hard decisions come in the future. Preschool kids are pretty well insulated from violence on the TV, though some parents worry about the violence of the cartoons — just as some Victorian parents worried that the Punch and Judy shows were too violent. And preschoolers do get occasional glimpses of what "adult" TV is like. One father told me he was driving a group of children when he heard a five-year-old ask his kids in the back seat: "Did you watch 'Starsky and Hutch' last night and see the guy strangling her with the pantyhose?" "Suddenly," he said, "you realize that your children are being brought into contact with something that you don't want them to be brought into contact with — and you have no real control over it."

No, we don't have any influence over what our kids pick up from their playmates, but as parents we are in full control of what they watch on TV and I think we should exercise that authority. It's a matter of personal choice just how many and what kinds of programs kids should watch, and every family will work that out differently. But we can and should give our children a clear and understandable structure in this part of their lives as in all others — well-defined hours, specific shows, and click, it's off when we say it's off. Start this early and try not to knuckle under to griping, screaming, tantrums, or pouting, and you have a head start on the tougher years ahead. The hours and schedule are always subject to reappraisal and change and Specials when Charlie Brown is on at Easter, and the kids' interests are always taken into consideration, but the final decision is a family one, and Mom and Dad reserve the full power of the veto.

I've noticed that fathers in general are more critical of TV and less tolerant of their kids watching it for long hours than full-time mothers are, in general. For mothers, the TV is an ally; it occupies the kids while Mom gets something else done for them, like cooking their dinner, and on a rare occasion when she — God forbid — does something for herself. Mom isn't likely to bad-mouth so good an ally. But for fathers the TV doesn't render such a regular and important service. Some fathers even find a rival in it. Arriving home tired from work, many men are greeted not by the cheerful hugs of their little loved ones, but by the coarse noise of "The Electric Company" and the "glazed look," as one father described it, of their kids glued to the tube.

One father I know, a news weekly journalist, expressed his personal and professional hostility toward the TV by refusing to have the family set repaired when it broke down. He then taught his three daughters to say things like: "Our family is much happier now that we don't have a TV; we even have conversations sometimes." They mouth this propaganda very prettily and very earnestly for company. But where are they each afternoon and every evening they can get away? At the neighbors' house across the back hedge, where the TV works. And I know several people who as adults are TV junkies, all-night movie addicts, because their domineering fathers refused to allow TV in the house. The TV is a powerful adversary for one man to take on singlehanded.

Some parents feel their kids will be "culturally deprived" if they are refused any of the TV shows they want to watch, that their children won't be able to keep up with their peers if they don't see all the same things the other kids see. Unfortunately there is a tiny germ of truth in this argument. TV is undeniably a force in American culture, and preschoolers "deprived" of "Sesame Street" won't have the same familiarity with their ABCs and numbers as kids who have watched it regularly — unless their parents are careful at-home teachers. But why a child should be culturally deprived because he has never seen a woman strangled with pantyhose, I can't imagine. Especially if meanwhile he is instead doing something "culturally enriching" — looking at a book, building with blocks, playing in the sandbox, or going on a hunt with Dad for night crawlers. There are few things a child can do that won't be culturally enriching.

It is children who are warehoused in front of a screen who are being culturally deprived. And so is a child who is allowed to gorge herself as she chooses, morning and night, on the tube. Giving a child a free hand on the TV dials is like giving her carte blanche at the candy store.

But then there are always those wonderful days for a kid at Grandmother's house when she *may* eat all the candy she likes and watch every cartoon on TV. She arrives home hung over, fagged out — but it *was* fun.

LITTLE PEOPLE IN THE TV

Toddlers when they watch TV believe they are seeing tiny people in a box, tiny people who talk and sing and who sometimes are scary. As parents we are often startled to discover this misperception when our kids at three have enough command of the language to tell us what they are seeing. It takes careful explanation to disabuse kids of this notion; they have no particular reason to give up an idea that has been with them since probably before they can remember, the perfectly reasonable and demonstrable notion that their friends Bert and Ernie are there in the room with them each day *in* the TV.

Mom and Dad say, "But they're not *really* there, they are only pictures." Which is not that much different from Mom and Dad saying, "But *we're* not really here; we are only pictures." So what? Real or picture, Bert and Ernie are friends and Mom and Dad give hugs and food.

After much ingenious explanation on your part — you show her photographs and talk about cameras — your child decides to please you and go along with your idea that they are not really there, they are only pictures. But does she really believe it? I love to ask preschool kids what they see on TV because their answers are usually nicely phrased, learned by rote, and their look is almost always sheepish. And often a five-year-old, if you catch him unawares, will say right out: "There are little people in there."

TV POSTURE

Take a look sometime at how your kids are sitting to watch the TV. Nice straight backs, attentive expressions on their faces? Highly unlikely. Chances are they're slumped down in the softest pieces of furniture in the room, spines bent around in the shape of the letter *C*. When our kids get to be teen-agers, we'll gripe at them for not holding themselves upright, just as our parents griped at us for slouching.

The floor is a fine place for kids to sit to watch TV, and backless seats encourage good posture. With a little furniture rearranging, you can probably devise a setup that allows your kids nowhere else to sit in front of the tube but on the floor or a low child seat.

ADVERTISING AND KIDS

One afternoon close to Christmas I walked into the living room, where Gregory, two, was watching a TV commercial. "Daddy, Daddy," he said excitedly, "I *want* that. . . . What is it?"

You notice early in your kids' TV-watching career that they pay a lot more attention to the ads than to anything else. A toddler, busily engaged with some interesting activity like tearing the day's newspaper into small pieces while Dad watches the evening news, will stop what she is doing abruptly and turn her full attention to an ad for hemorrhoid suppositories. This is of course no accident; vast sums of money have been expended and a sparkling array of human talent has been orchestrated to make your toddler's head turn — and yours — at the very mention of these life-supporting necessities in suppository form. As adults, we can chuckle at a pretentious ad and pass it off with a joke: "You know where they can put their suppositories . . ."

But a toddler — without your sense of humor, your background, your language, your knowledge of the world — responds directly to the *appeal* of the message. She doesn't need language to know that she is being told convincingly and insistently that this is something she *needs*. And she is being told this by an obviously authoritative source, the sincerity of which she will for years to come have no reason or grounds for questioning. Daddy and Mommy pay close attention to what they are told by the TV — she has observed this to be so — and she will do likewise.

As your child grows older and can understand the actual message of the ads, he begins to gravitate toward ads that are directed specifically at him — candy, toys, soda, hamburgers, sneakers. Here is a typical scene between a five-year-old and his dad:

Five: "But, Dad, I *need* this kind of sneakers."
Dad: "Why do you need this special kind? They cost more than the others."
Five: "They will make me jump high. They help me run better."
Dad: "But it's *you* that does the running and the jumping, not the sneakers."

Five: "Oh no, it's true, Dad. The sneakers do the jumping. *They told me on TV.*"

You're going to have a hard time convincing this little guy that he is wrong. He has authority on his side of the argument. And much as we may hate to admit it, the TV is an authority that a child will often listen to with more attention and respect than he listens to Dad and Mom.

If the problem were merely that the child and his dad were being conned into buying an expensive pair of sneakers, the issue could be resolved easily enough. Dad says, "No, I don't want to disappoint you, but we have to get the ones that cost less," and the child learns a useful lesson about disappointment. And that would be the end of it.

But I think that we need to recognize that the issue here isn't so simple; the immediate resolution will be the same in any case, but what is happening here is much more far-reaching than a simple con job. The child has learned to accept the word of an oracle that tells him over and over in beguiling and attractive ways that he is inadequate as a human being, that *he* doesn't do the jumping, the sneakers do; that he isn't the one who supplies the fun, the toy does; that he is strong only through the good offices of the cereal he eats. Kids haven't even had language long enough to form realistic images of themselves when they fall prey to this strange attack on their egos. The TV ads will never help them form positive images of themselves as independent, thoughtful people; the ads can lead them to only one conclusion — that they *need* specific products in order to be healthy, happy, strong . . . that the sneakers *do* the jumping.

I don't mean to imply that there is a willful conspiracy on the part of advertisers to turn us all, from infancy, into pathetic boobs whose personalities are defined by the things we consume and who need those things in order to feel we exist at all. But the effect is much the same as if there were such a conspiracy. We all know people who have grown up this way, and I think many parents see this pathetic boob in their own preschoolers. I certainly see it in Gregory when he attacks his radiantly fresh-complexioned mom: "But, Mommy, you *have* to wear make-up. It says so on TV."

Further on down the road comes the day — at around seven or eight — when kids discover that the ads on TV are a sham, that the authority they have trusted since infancy has feet of clay. This is a disillusionment parents can't take lightly. Among

other things, how on earth are Dad and Mom to be trusted by a child who has discovered that the other authority in the family living room is a fraud? How is anyone or anything to be trusted? Child psychologists are constantly confronted in their practice by the turmoil that is created in children's lives by their discovery of the TV's deceit — or is it the world's deceit?

We're certainly in no position to shield our kids from the world's deceit. But I think we owe it to them at least to try to help them sort out the notions they're picking up from the TV. The job isn't an easy one, because the competition is a powerful, successful industry that knows how to sell things to kids. A head-on confrontation of the issue won't work; if you simply debunk a TV ad, your four-year-old will take the side of the advertiser and you'll end up arguing with the child. But you can teach your kids that the ads are there to sell things, that they are very different from the stories and the news.

Why not a little skit in which you try to sell your five-year-old something he regards as shabby and useless by praising it highly? You grab a battered, defunct sneaker and say: "Buy this beautiful sneaker, this sturdy fine sneaker. It will give you happiness and eternal life." "But, Dad," says he, "you don't understand; *that's* not the kind of sneakers I need. I need the red ones." Teaching is slow work. Try the skit the other way around; see if your child can learn about salesmanship by pretending to be a salesman. Come at it from any angle where your child leaves you an opening.

If you present your side of the story convincingly and sincerely, and without going for the throat of your opponent — which will only make your child feel he is personally under attack — you'll get a hearing. You won't be believed at first, but keep after it, and slowly over months the light may dawn in your child's mind and he may discover to his astonishment that Daddy was right, that it is *he* and no object or gimmick, he alone, barefoot and unencumbered, free and proud, who is doing the jumping.

Action

A busy parent-founded group called Action for Children's Television (ACT) has taken on the TV Goliath and has managed through lobbying and grass roots political pressure to win a few battles, though the war is still in progress. ACT concentrates its efforts on the two major parent-TV issues: advertising and violence. It has won concessions from the industry like the elimination of vitamin ads from children's programs and the reduction of weekend commercial time. If you're interested in helping this cause as a member of ACT, you can write for information to: Action for Children's Television, 46 Austin Street, Newtonville, Massachusetts 02160.

TV TOGETHERNESS

Many kids like TV best when they sit in Daddy's lap to watch it. If you're enjoying watching something, it's a good bet your kids will pick up on your enthusiasm and share it — whether it's football or ballet, tennis or a documentary about dolphins.

It's also an excellent idea to watch some of the shows your kids watch. A number of men have told me they look at "Sesame Street" by choice. But even if you aren't turned on by kiddie TV, watching your children's shows from time to time is a kind of courtesy to them, like taking the time to meet their friends. In fact it is exactly like meeting their friends, because each child believes that the characters she sees on TV are just that — her special friends.

Kids turn to Daddy for approval in every aspect of their lives. If Sarah at two and a half knows her dad approves of Big Bird, she has won a little confidence; she knows she has picked a friend well. This is a very small thing in both their lives; but Sarah's eventual confidence as a woman isn't won all at once with a big dramatic gesture; it is built up of many, many such little things.

Chapter 7

SPECIAL EVENTS

In families where Mom is on hand every day, kids naturally come to think of Dad as a special events man — his realm is weekend outings, picnics, trips, vacations, celebrations — all the goodies.

OUTINGS

An ecology-minded father told me how he had taken his two preschool girls on a Sunday outing designed as an object lesson to teach them about the evils of pollution. He drove them on an inspection tour of the hideously polluted East Texas waters near where they lived, pointing out the scummiest horrors. At nursery school a week later, when the teacher asked Mary-Jane what she had done over the vacation, she bubbled with excitement and pride telling how her daddy had taken them to see The Pollution. She loved it. It was beautiful. She told about the snacks they had eaten on the trip and what a wonderful time they had.

I think this tells the whole story of kids and outings. Wherever you take children, they will love to go. About nine tenths of the pleasure is in being with Daddy and going *somewhere*. The kind of place you pick to go to may count for very little.

The simplest, shortest little "outings" will delight toddlers and preschoolers. There's probably no better excursion as far as a two- or a three-year-old is concerned than a walk around the block with Daddy — especially if it's at night in the dark. There's mystery and excitement in the dark, but all the reassuring familiarity of the neighborhood streets and your big hand to hold onto. And these walks in the dark will go on for years.

A preschooler doesn't have to go to Disneyland to find novelties. Nearly everything he sees or does is quite literally novel. If you live in the suburbs or the country, for instance, your three- or four-year-old may never have ridden on a bus. When he was three, Gregory and I hopped a public-service bus one Saturday norning for a ten-minute ride each way between two suburban towns. We shared a piece of coffee cake at a luncheon counter at our destination, sitting on the high stools and discussing the ride on the bus; we walked around town a little, checking things out, and we were back to our starting point within an hour and a half. Short and Sweet. Gregory still talks about that little jaunt, remembering all the details, especially the coffee cake. For him it was an event of major importance — his first ride on a bus.

ELABORATE EXPEDITIONS

Big-deal planned-ahead outings are often a bust. The kids get worn out long before the circus is over or before you're ready to leave the fairgrounds, and you end up with a sobbing child on your shoulders for the long trek to the car in the parking lot.

One family on a trip to Washington, D.C., took their two preschool boys to see the wonderful new Air and Space building of the Smithsonian collections; what an exciting visit for two youngsters — planes, rockets, moon landing modules, the works. But it had been a long hot day and in the huge exhibition spaces the kids quickly grew weary and a little restless. As they left the museum, their father asked cheerfully: "Now, what did you like the most?" Quentin, three, was certain of his answer. "Getting out of there," he shot back.

The last thing I want to do is discourage you from exposing your kids to the world — show them everything you can. But at the same time it makes sense to be realistic about how much your child can take at his age, and to be ready to quit when your child is. Otherwise you can easily wind up at the end of a trying day thinking: "Look at all the trouble we went to just to please the kids, and look at the way they act. . . . Why, the ungrateful little . . ." I catch myself falling into this one sometimes, and I have to back off and take stock of the situation and accept the fact that they're not ungrateful, they're really just worn out.

So go into major outings with your eyes open and your expectations low and your kids will probably

disprove everything I say here and romp through six hours of amusement park rides and ice cream cones with never a whine or a whimper.

FATHER-CHILD JAUNTS

Mom may like father-child outings even better than family excursions; she'll have a break and some time for herself. And you'll have some uninterrupted time with your child. You needn't while away your few weekend hours at a park watching your child on the swings and feeling uncomfortable because you aren't accomplishing any of the hundreds of tasks around the house or apartment that need your attention. Because whatever you do will be an "outing" for your child.

Babies are portable and can go wherever you do. And you can take a preschooler along to a lumberyard or an auto parts store, or down to the garage to talk to the mechanic about the problem with your motor — and your child will have a thrilling adventure. Sure, it's a little more trouble — at the garage you may have to steer her clear of an oil drain-off pan or take a wrench or two away from her as she explores and inspects the place. But many fathers I've talked with find these trips their favorite times with their kids — just doing together the things that need to be done. It gives you a companion while you take care of dull chores, and it gives your child new experiences and tremendous pride in being able to go along to grown-up places and share something of your world.

"Luke is my right-hand man," says one father of his son, three. "I take him everywhere with me. I don't drag him around — passed out and falling asleep. But if I'm going someplace, he's more than welcome to come along. . . . He considers my friends his friends; he hangs out with them; he likes them. I think any little kid likes to do what he sees his father doing."

I've noticed, though, that if I have the kids with me making the rounds of weekend chores and errands, they will be *with* me and relatively easy to manage if they have the sense that they're part of the operation, that we've set out to accomplish things as a kind of team. But when I'm distracted and my attention is taken up entirely by the chores, that's it for the kids — they drift off into back-seat bickering and general irritating silly behavior. It seems to happen every time they get the feeling that I'm only dragging them along out of a sense of duty and to give them an airing. Of course it happens, too, every time they get tired.

If you have time to *enjoy* doing kiddie things, by all means take your children to the swings or the zoo or the fish hatchery. And besides going places that kids traditionally like, try a few that you enjoy. Just be sure you're ready to leave when your child has had it. You obviously can't take a three-year-old to a ball game and expect her to sit through all nine innings. Though you can take the same child to a golf match and expect to spend some of the time watching and some of the time chasing her around the fairways; and both of you will have a great time.

DIVORCE AND OUTINGS

Several separated and divorced fathers I talked with while I was working on this book said things like this: "Oh, you'll have to put in a really meaty section on outings. I'll buy a copy of the book just for that part." Especially for newly divorced fathers, outings can loom as the major practical question as weekend after weekend they and their kids search for novel diversions.

The new bachelor pad is small and bare and doesn't seem like the right kind of place for kids. Or weekend visiting means driving a hundred and fifty miles and staying at a motel, and you figure a motel room's no fun for a child either. "You really want the kids to have a good time when you've got them," a recently divorced father of a five- and a seven-year-old told me. "I know it says in the books that you're not supposed to spoil the kids and compete with their mother — you're not supposed to overdo it and go everywhere and buy them everything. But hell, what would you do? You don't want them to have a lousy time while they're with you."

One of the realities of the weekend visit is that it is *long*; there are hours and hours each day to fill up. This same man pointed out that he'd almost never spent a full day together with his kids before the divorce and special outings had been rarities back then: "There wasn't time to catch up on the stuff that had to be done around the house — clean out the gutters, put up new storm windows, there was always something on the weekend. . . . We never took the kids anywhere."

But a divorce changes all the priorities and fathers end up weekend after weekend with the kids and one or two days to "kill." So it's circuses and amusement parks and afternoon movies and every meal at McDonald's — a hectic round of kiddie pleasures that can be just as tiresome, fatiguing, and finally stultifying for a preschool kid as it is for his well-meaning dad.

The "weekend dad" *does* need to arrange for plenty of outings — there's no way around it. But there can be much, much more for a divorced father and his kids. And as time goes by, most men in this situation shift from "entertainment" and "outings" to more ordinary things, and the kids do visit in the bachelor pad, which has become a little more like home. As the father's life fills itself back out after the divorce, he finds more and more to share with his kids on a solid, personal level.

For a while, though, outings are the almost inevitable central issue, so I hope this section will be meaty enough for a father who needs it.

BE PREPARED

On any excursion that's going to last much more than an hour, whether it's a family trip or a father-child special, some advance preparation is called for. The younger the child, the bigger the bag of stuff that has to be dragged along. With a baby or toddler naturally you need the whole kit: disposable diapers, wipes, bottle(s), food, spoon, bib, paper napkins, extra clothes, a few small toys, pacifier, etc. If you leave behind something the baby depends on, you've had it. And you need a baby carrier of some sort — see p. 29.

As a child grows older, the amount of paraphernalia is reduced, but you still should come prepared for most eventualities, which means: small toys, children's books, wet towelettes, a box of raisins — never forget the raisins; they can be given out one by one. The books will get you through a lot of nuisance situations like squirmy long bus rides, and if your child wears out during an afternoon jaunt, you can always find a bench somewhere to sit down and change the pace by reading a story.

Through age two and a half or even three, a big plastic bib is very useful. Put it on for ice cream or lollipops, or any food for that matter, and you'll win points by returning home with a (relatively) clean kid. The bigger the bib, the better; I like the ones that cover everything but the legs.

You can't cram all this stuff in your pockets when you go out alone with your child. If you're embarrassed to carry it in the same bag your wife uses, get an airlines tote bag. An insulated bag is best of all if you're carrying bottles with formula.

WHAT TO DO

In some larger cities you can find guidebooks written specifically about attractions for children. Big-city newspapers often feature weekend listings of kiddie events and attractions: plays, concerts, puppet shows, etc. — and in smaller places, too, the paper will list special events for kids. The one common problem with all these sources of information is that they are seldom very specific about the age groups for whom the events and attractions are intended. You'll have to rely on your sense of what your child is ready for, and maybe call ahead to make sure you're not way off target.

You should find a copy of a children's guide — if there is one published for your city or area — in the bookshop of any local museum, particularly a children's museum. Here's a partial listing of currently available children's guides:

LOS ANGELES
Lila Weingarten and Thea Granz, *Where to Go and What to Do with the Kids in L.A.* (Price, Stern, 1972), $2.95.
Stephanie Kegan, *Where to Take the Kids in Southern California* (Chronicle Bks., 1977), $3.95.

MINNEAPOLIS-ST. PAUL
Elizabeth S. French, *Exploring the Twin Cities with Children* (Nodin Press, 1975), $3.50.

NEW JERSEY
Michaela M. Mole, ed., *Away We Go! A Guidebook*

of Family Trips to Places of Interest in New Jersey, Nearby Pennsylvania, and New York, 4th ed. (Rutgers Univ. Press, 1976).

NEW YORK

Claire Berman, *Great City for Kids: A Parent's Guide to a Child's New York* (Bobbs, 1969), $3.95.

Sandee Levinson and Michael Levinson, *Where to Go and What to Do with the Kids in New York* (Price, Stern, 1972), $2.95.

Ray Shaw, *New York for Children: An Unusual Guide for Parents, Teachers and Children*, rev. ed. (Dutton Sunrise Bk., 1974), $2.95.

OREGON

Nancy M. McCarthy and Joyce Tuggle, *Now Where? Places in Oregon to Go with Kids* (International Scholarly Bk. Service, 1977), $3.50.

PHILADELPHIA

Richard S. Flood and Lydia S. Hunn, eds., *Philadelphia for Children*, rev. ed. (Hadley Group, 1975), $2.95.

SAN FRANCISCO

Franz T. Hanzel, *Great Family Fun Guide to San Francisco*, rev. ed. (Comstock Editions, 1975).

Mary Lewis and Richard Lewis, *Where to Go and What to Do with the Kids in San Francisco* (Price, Stern, 1972), $2.95.

Elizabeth Pomada, *Places to Go with Children in Northern California* (Chronicle Bks., 1973), $2.95.

WASHINGTON, D.C.

Elizabeth P. Mirel, ed., Green Acres School's *Going Places with Children in Washington*, 8th rev. ed. (Washingtonian Bks., 1976), $3.00.

Ray Shaw, *Washington for Children: An Unusual Guide for Families, Teachers, and Tourists* (Scribner, 1975), $3.95.

CROSS-COUNTRY TRAVEL

Alvin Schwartz, et al., *America's Exciting Cities: A Travel Guide for Parents and Children* (Crowell, 1966), $4.95.

Many of the best outings, however, are simple ones that don't rate a listing in any guidebook. Below are suggestions for places to go, things to do that are sure-fire hits with toddlers and pre-schoolers.

Ducks

The all-time favorite outing for kids from one year old on is duck feeding. Ducks like stale crackers; in fact, they'll eat any stale baked goods they can get. Corn kernels make good duck food, too; ducks will catch them in the air and dive for them.

To find the nearest duck pond, just ask other parents. You may "grow out of" duck feeding pretty quickly, but your child will go on loving it year after year, long after you'd assume he was too old for it.

Small Airports

Small airports get five stars at the top of my personal list of recommended weekend outing places for preschoolers and their fathers. There's one near us that specializes in towing up gliders and on weekends there's a glider being taken up or one circling silently and drifting in for a landing every five or ten minutes, so there's plenty of activity to watch that's interesting both to the kids and to me. And at this field — though I can't vouch for all small airports — nobody minds if we wander around at will and examine all the small planes and gliders. It's also very open and grassy, so the kids can run long distances. We go a couple of times a year on sunny days and stay for maybe forty minutes. And we always take along toy airplanes and a piece of string for a game of toy plane and glider.

Also try hang-glider ports.

Tricycle Tours

As soon as your child can ride a tricycle well, you can take excursions with her where you walk fast or jog slowly and she rides. Kids on trikes and big wheels are always restricted to a driveway or a sidewalk in front of the house; a tricycle tour gives a child the chance she's been longing for to peddle

block after uninterrupted block. If it's steep and hilly where you live, throw the tricycle in the trunk of the car and go to another neighborhood — a flat one. Even if you live in a flat neighborhood, go somewhere else from time to time for a tricycle tour; your child will be delighted by the change of scene. Uncrowded paved plazas in parks and in front of big public buildings like museums make wonderful tricycle tracks.

Tricycle shopping is another favorite for a three-year-old. If you're going to be visiting a number of closely grouped stores, take the trike along and let your child ride between the stores and park by the door of each one you go into. You can do this even before tricycle age if your two-year-old has mastered some early riding toy. Tie a box or basket to the tricycle handle bars so your child will have somewhere to put a little purchase.

Parks

City dwellers with kids soon know all the public parks for miles around — grassy ones for running and well-equipped ones for climbing and sliding, and the zoo. For some variety in your parks, try college campuses. Most have lawns for running and walls, trees, and outdoor sculptures for a little climbing, and there's often something going on — a football rally or a protest march — that will be an exciting event for your child. And at most colleges and universities you're perfectly free to roam about, indoors and out, as your please.

Rides and Excursions

Climb on board any train or trolley, bus or boat — for a preschooler, the ride will be more interesting than the destination.

There's magic in ferries. Waiting on the dock, Eben, five, heard his father say, "Look sharp, the ferry is coming." Thinking of Tinkerbell, he asked, "Is she going to take us one at a time or all together?"

Some other kinds of transportation, like steam railroads, still hold that magic for many fathers. One man told me: "Amber [six] and I have been on every steam excursion railroad in Pennsylvania and New Jersey. My father worked for a railroad, so I grew up around trains. I've got trains in my blood — there's no denying it." You can find out about steam railroad trips in your area through ads in the newspaper and notices posted in railway stations. The trains usually make short runs on the weekends and most of the passengers are in family groups. On some old trains for a dollar extra you can ride in the caboose up in the cupola. If you and the kids like your first excursion railway, it will lead to many more — there's a regular subculture of steam excursion enthusiasts and at each old railway you will learn about many others from handouts and ads.

To interest a child, though, a train doesn't have to be an authentic period piece, or have anything else special about it — going on any mode of transportation makes the outing.

Stores

Almost any store you take kids into will have some special attraction for them, but there are some that you can visit with kids just as you might take them to feed the ducks.

In the evening a pediatrician takes his two preschool boys to the lawn tractor department of their local Sears store, where the salespeople let them

climb on the riding mowers and "drive" them to their hearts' content. The sales force in your local Sears outlet may feel differently — but it's worth a try.

Most kids love a visit with Dad to a hardware store because there are so many things to examine, but they especially like a hardware store if there's something in it for them, and there often is — a key. Hardware stores and locksmiths usually save the key-copying machine's mistakes and will give one of these rejects to your child if you ask.

Pet stores, naturally, are favorites, and bakeries usually give cookies to kids.

Your kids will find their own favorite stores and insist on going back. Gregory loves a clock store near his grandmother's house that has a room full of old pendulum clocks; he stands there in awe, listening to them all tick.

Your favorite store may be a big attraction for your child. One father told me how he and his daughter, four and a half, regularly stop by the Brick Church Pipe Shop, where they both inspect the fine pipes and tobaccos.

Toy Stores   One place I studiously avoid taking the kids is a toy store. There's just too much here and it makes a child's head spin. You're stuck with his agonizing decision between two plastic toys; he can afford only one with the fifty cents you've given him. And he *wants* everything else in the place, but obviously can't have it. Toy store visits are all too often painful for a child and for the adult with him. Grandmothers love to take kids to toy stores. Let them.

If you feel compelled to take your children to toy stores, here are some thoughts. After age four and a half you'll have a better time and so will your child; by this time kids have gotten under control some of that powerful need for instant gratification that drives them through their earliest years. At four and a half a child can examine the things in a toy store, making careful decisions about what he wants for Christmas.

Any child you take into a toy store should be well prepared in advance. Tell exactly how much money can be spent, and narrow down the field of what it may be used for. "Pick out anything you want" is likely to drive a child up the walls; it's too much of a decision. Limit it to a ball or a doll or even to a narrower category, so there won't be too many choices.

Grocery Shopping

I put grocery shopping under outings because for kids it's almost always fun. Here is a father talking about supermarket trips with his daughter, six: "Colleen's main interest is shopping and spending money; she goes batty about shopping — which is fine because I can't stand it. And when we go shopping, Colleen is usually a real shot in the arm because she gets an honest pleasure out of what to me is a real chore. You know, picking out this kind of hash and this kind of dog food — she loves it."

There's a lot to do with kids in a grocery store. With a toddler you can go through the aisles teaching and practicing all the names of the food and enjoying his excitement when he comes across one he knows: "Ap-ple, Ap-ple!" And this same beginning talker can "read" many of the labels — for instance as you cruise through the pet foods section, where friendly cats and dogs appear on every package.

As a child gets older you can play food-spotting games as you circulate through the aisles: "Now, tell me when you see the eggs." "Shout out when you see the doughnuts." By age four, many kids have developed a startlingly accurate mental catalogue of their standard family fare and will remind you to buy things that have been left off the shopping list.

The store is for buying and as soon as a toddler begins to understand this, she quite naturally wants to buy something too, and you have a beggar on your hands, or a demander: "Buy Me That." A sound policy for keeping the peace and teaching her not to beg is to buy her something, but definitely not That. Make it something she likes that's on the regular shopping list and that you need — raisins or cereal or cookies. Your child gets to "buy" something, but it's a family thing, not a personal treat.

Of course there will be a few personal treats, too, along the way. The problem is that every toddler and preschooler desperately longs for a treat every time he sees a store; he gets all hyped up on anticipation, and if no treat is forthcoming he's crushed or he throws a tantrum. It helps if you always let a child know ahead of time — on the way to the store — exactly what to expect. Get all the cards out on the table so there won't be any surprises: "No treats today. We're just doing the shopping." Or, "Today as a special treat you can have a box of animal crackers."

And then there's the gum machine gauntlet that

you have to run entering and leaving. If you capitulate early on and set up a pattern of handing out nickels, there's no turning back. But if you can hold out firmly through age three — which means plenty of complaining and screaming — your child will learn that you aren't a nickel and quarter dispenser, and will be extra pleased when you occasionally *volunteer* a nickel for the gum machine.

City Walks

Walking through city streets or the streets of a town, kids usually have to keep pace with adults. There are specific places to go, goals to be achieved, things to be bought. Kids enjoy this kind of brisk adult activity — until they get tired — but they enjoy a slow city walk in an entirely different way, and more on their own terms. If there's time, I like to slow down to the kids' pace every now and again and let them take the lead. You end up examining with care many things you would ordinarily have stormed right past — maple seedlings growing up in the crack between the paving, or acorns in the gutter. And you go into stores and public buildings you would never have thought to visit. Gregory since he turned three can't pass a church without asking to go in and look at the stained glass — so I have seen the insides of some lovely churches and synagogues that I would never have investigated on my own, and some very dull ones as well.

It's one of the strange burdens of fatherhood that day and night without interruption you're "in charge" of a child's life, responsible for its direction, and I feel somehow lighter when I'm with the kids but for the time being they are leading me.

Picking Fruit

One of the best possible family outings is a visit to an orchard where you can pick your own fruit or a farm where you can pick your own berries — look for advertisements in your local newspaper. Some big orchards grow so many different kinds of fruit that they will supply you with a list of the ripening dates of many varieties of cherries, peaches, and apples so that you can come back week after week throughout the season and pick the ones you favor.

Kids love to pick any fruit, but cherries — in early summer — are probably the biggest treat. The trees are usually low, and with the branches weighted down by fruit, even a two-year-old standing on the ground can easily pick dozens of cherries. Peaches and apples require a little more care in handling, and often a boost up onto Dad's shoulders.

Berries, especially strawberries — which get squished — are a little harder for young kids to cope with than tree fruit, but great fun nonetheless. Watch out for poison ivy, which you sometimes find growing cheek-by-jowl with berry plants.

Your kids' plastic sandbox buckets make good containers for the fruit they'll pick, as do cardboard boxes. Also take along a large container of water for washing the fruit — which has almost always been sprayed with chemicals — so your kids can safely eat some of the fruits of their labor.

Country Rambles

In the country with a preschooler, stop along the road to chat with the cows, and go into a cornfield and walk down the tall, endless rows of towering plants. You can stop the car on a drive and get out to do these things and have other country experiences, but much better is to bicycle slowly along back roads with your child in a kiddie seat behind. If you live in the city or in town, put your bicycle on a rack on your car and switch to pedal power when you get to the country. Pick level terrain and watch out for country drivers on back roads — they're reckless. But on a bike you're going along at an easy pace and you and your child can stop whenever and wherever you like to take a closer look at the things along the roadside. See p. 271 for more on child carriers for bikes.

Always stop by lakes and streams; there's inevitably something about water to intrigue a child, if it's only the chance to throw in some pebbles.

Woods Walks

I've asked dozens of fathers what their favorite activity with their kids is. Walking in the woods goes at the top of the list of favorites — way ahead of playing ball and roughhousing. Several fathers told

me they had vivid memories of walking in the woods with their own fathers, and naturally it was something they wanted to do with their children.

You don't have to be a knowledgeable naturalist, able to give a lecture on flora and fauna, to take your child for a walk in the woods — though it's very useful to be able to identify poison ivy and steer clear (see p. 126). Knowing a little about wildflowers, ferns, and mushrooms may make walks in the woods more interesting for you, and a preschooler always loves to be able to identify a few things; then he can search for and keep spotting his game. Say it's spring and there are jack-in-the-pulpits in the woods; a preschooler who recognizes jack-in-the-pulpits will zero in on them, and before he's through he will have found dozens of jack-in-the-pulpits and be delighted with his ability to recognize them. For a primer course in nature or if you want to learn more about the things you are seeing on your woods excursions with the kids, try the widely available Golden Nature Guides — these little books have a wealth of information for families who walk in the woods.

Make sure to stop by streams and brooks, not only for the kids to play by the water, but also to check the mud along the bank for interesting footprints (see p. 236 for more on animal prints). Kids like to visit "animal neighbors" in the woods. If you spot an animal's hole, the kids will get a big kick out of shouting greetings down into it, though no mammal in his right mind is going to respond. See p. 232 for more on preschoolers and nature.

You really don't need anything planned for a walk in the woods — except to make sure you know the way back out. There will always be things to do that you wouldn't have expected and the kids will easily find them. We're lucky enough to have woods right behind our house, and every time I go back there with Gregory and Timothy they find new adven-

tures — rocks or fallen trees to climb on, sticks to pick up and build with, white bark to peel from a fallen birch limb, salamanders under stones, a toad to hop after . . .

If you don't have woods nearby and have to go to some trouble to get to a state park, call your walk in the woods hiking or backpacking to make it into a big deal. Your child can carry crackers and an apple in a knapsack or on a hobo stick for a snack in the woods. If you intend to do real backpack hiking with the kids, some short, light practice forays are essential anyway. But walking in the woods is a different activity entirely from backpacking. In hiking the object is to cover distances — it's an achiever's activity. Woods walks are for enjoyers — you don't have to get anywhere, just into the woods, and the kids will take it from there and find out what there is to do.

Camping

Camping for families means anything from air-conditioned luxury in a Titan home on wheels to very plain living in the open. Young kids and even babies fit well into pretty much any style of camping except for a bare-essentials survival course.

But ask any kid what camping is and she'll tell you — it's sleeping in a tent. The first trip alone with Dad to spend the night outdoors is an event of major importance for a child. Here are thoughts on how to go about it from a father with lots of experience in camping — he's on the board of directors of a camp in Maine where he was a counselor for six years, and he's introduced three sons to the great outdoors: "I think camping's one of the neatest things you can do, but I really think they've gotta be five or six years old. . . . We didn't go hiking. We brought the car, and I found a campsite where I could bring the car right down by a stream and we'd just move like a hundred yards away from the car. . . But it's amazing, when you're in a tent, you could be a million miles away or up on top of a mountain as far as they're concerned. A lot of the fun is just building the campsite — putting the tent up and then making

a lean-to — Alec [five] is absolutely fascinated by the idea of building a lean-to. . . . I find that one long day and a night is more than enough."

Keeping it simple is always the best way with preschoolers — you aren't going to turn a five- or six-year-old into a true outdoorsman on the first night out. A tent and the sound of crickets provide all that's needed. Make sure to have a good bright light along — a big battery-powered lantern that your child can handle himself is better than a kerosene or white gas fueled lantern.

With any camping trip, whether it's plug-in luxury or roughing it, success depends on your equipment and how familiar you are with it, so if your tent is new, set it up at home and make sure you know how everything else works before you set out for the campsite. If you're new to the outdoors, you can ease into it with your child at her slow pace; perhaps your first night out can be in your own back yard. Your first campfires can be charcoal briquettes in a hibachi — that's plenty authentic enough for a preschooler, and marshmallows can be cooked over the coals of a hibachi, which in the end is the whole purpose of the campfire.

Get a copy of the *Boy Scout Fieldbook* and with its help you can introduce yourself and the kids to some of the refinements of camping — a little at a time. The first trips, though, the important part is setting up the tent — with as much help as possible from your child — and sleeping in the tent. If you haven't got a tent, try to borrow one the first few times so you'll get an idea of whether or not you and your child like the outdoors before investing in one. You'll also be able to gauge better how big a tent you'll want to buy if you've slept out a few times in a borrowed one; this is a big help considering the bewildering variety of camping equipment that's available.

Here's a checklist of absolute essentials for a first overnight camping trip with a preschooler; also throw in any other camping equipment you have, and gear for fishing or a short hike in the woods or flying a kite or whatever else you like to do outdoors with your child.

> tent (best with a sewn-in floor)
> ground cover
> sleeping bags OR bedrolls
> extra blankets
> inflatable mattresses and pillows optional
> large flashlight
> cooking and eating gear
> cans of beans, Vienna sausage, etc.

> marshmallows
> large containers of water
> toilet kit
> towels
> sweaters
> **rainwear, boots**
> 3 extra changes of dry clothes (especially socks and shoes)
> john paper
> shovel (if no toilets will be available)
> kids' books
> familiar stuffed animal or doll

Deciding what foods to take and assembling the cans and boxes and cooking utensils will provide at least half a week's worth of daily excitement before the excursion. Make sure your child has his own knapsack or laundry bag or other kit to carry some things in. And don't forget to take along some things that are familiar to your child — books that can be read in the glow of the flashlight in the tent, and a doll to snuggle up with for easy sleeping.

Five is not only a good age to start camping trips — I'd say it's *the* age. At five most kids are able to handle sleeping in a strange place, and will actually enjoy it — but also a five-year-old is a great cooperator and usually a pleasure to be with, so the success of the venture for both child and father is almost assured.

Beaches

All beaches are wonderful for kids — oceans, lakes, rivers. Just come well prepared with suntan lotion and some provision for protecting a baby from the wind and the sun — like the windbreak described below. I find that the tamer the beach and the more crowded it is, the more fun the kids have. Wild stretches of deserted beach with high crashing surf are for romantic adults. Kids like a place where there are other children to play with and where the waves are small so they can do a lot of wading.

Windbreak For a baby on a windy beach you'll want to put up some kind of protection. A high sand castle will do a good job, but without any digging you can make a very effective windbreak from:

> 3 OR more 4′ lengths ½″ dowel
> beach towels OR any cloth
> big diaper safety pins

Shove the dowels deeply into the sand — you can

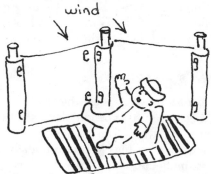

sharpen the ends to make this easier — and pin the ends of the towels or cloth around them to form a simple cloth wall. For more than one section, pin each new one to one that is already in place.

Sand Castles   It's a toss-up which is the more effective destroyer of sand castles, the waves or a small boy. Kids will help a little in building a sand castle, but their real forte is tearing them down. With a big enough shovel you can build faster than the kids can destroy, and get up a ring of fortifications that will act as a kind of combination windbreak and playpen for a one-year-old, or as a climber for a preschooler. Plastic beach shovels are no good. Take along a full-size garden spade for really turning over some sand; or for portability get an army surplus fold-up entrenching tool — the collapsible foxhole shovel. And take an entrenching tool or a good small garden spade for a child of four or older.

If you're fussy about your sand castles and want them to stay intact for the waves to wash away, leave the kids at home.

Sand Crabs   Make sure you dig for sand crabs with a preschooler. You can find them by digging almost anywhere along the water's edge at the beach, but you'll find multitudes of them if you dig where there is some offshore protection like a sand bar. You only

need to go down about the depth of your hand, and just keep turning over sand till you find some. If you hit a good place, a four-year-old will be able to dig plenty for herself. With kids of five or older, sand crab races are good sport. On the shout of Ready, Set, Go, the sand crabs are released; they dig furiously, and the first one under the wet sand wins.

Shell Collection   The bags full of shells that inevitably come home from the beach never seem to find a home. A month later, when the kids are thoroughly bored with them, set them up with hammers to crush the shells into fine pieces. Crushed shells make an excellent addition to any garden soil — they're a fine source of lime. And preschoolers of course delight in doing the smashing and crushing. The shells should be in an old burlap bag or something similar for crushing — confining them in a bag makes the job easier and keeps small pieces from flying into kids' eyes.

Museums

Babies make excellent museum-goers. For the first couple of years you can take your child along to any adult museum with little or no trouble; just strap the baby in a front or back carrier, or push her around in an umbrella stroller. One thing to watch out for: some museums don't allow strollers — though others appreciate and encourage their use and even provide them. So call before you go and ask if you can use one. Afternoon nap hour is a good time for a museum visit with a baby — she'll sleep through the whole thing.

After age two, though, museum visits are less fun and are apt to be disasters. This is the unanimous opinion of many artists and other avid museum-going parents I've talked to. Especially in a crowded painting gallery, an active two-year-old or a preschooler will have a miserable time. Look at it from the child's point of view. First, here's a room full of people and none of them is paying the least attention to him. Second, the things they are looking at are high up, out of range, and are of no particular interest. And third, he's way down where it's stuffy and airless with only knees and crotches to look at — the tall crowd of adults is intimidating. Kids protest vehemently in a place like this; hoisting your child on your shoulders helps for a while, but a half hour of this is really pushing it. So if you want to see a special exhibit you know will be crowded, get a baby-sitter.

Uncrowded museum galleries will be easier to manage, but preschool kids tire quickly in almost any kind of adult museum. There are some exceptions. Most preschoolers will get a big thrill from seeing suits of armor and the mummies in an Egyptian collection. Another major exception is a museum of natural history. A four-year-old dinosaur enthusiast can have no bigger treat than a look at the bones of mighty Diplodocus and the hideous toothy grin of Tyrannosaurus rex. Whale- and shark-loving kids will see the objects of their passion here, too. In fact, there's something in the natural history museum for almost every preschooler. After all, it's just a big indoor stuffed zoo.

Art Galleries

For exposing your kids to painting and sculpture as preschoolers, try taking them to commercial art galleries, which are ordinarily less crowded and less imposing than museum galleries. Theoretically, kids' minds should be open to anything you introduce them to; you'd expect a preschooler, with no background in art criticism, to be uncritical and generally turned on by all new things. But in practice, a child of four or older will say, "Yucky," or "*Ug*-ly," or, "I hate it," to paintings and sculptures, just as he does to the new foods he tastes. We continue to make these same judgments throughout our lives, sometimes because the things we see or taste are new and we don't understand them, and sometimes because they are in fact Yucky.

Some types of art are more immediately appealing to preschoolers than others. Kids particularly like kinetic (moving) sculptures and light sculptures, and they are fascinated by holography (laser-projected three-dimensional pictures).

Bring along an opera glass or a magnifying glass to help stimulate your child's interest in looking carefully at the things being exhibited.

Children's Museums

A children's museum is another five-star outing. Everything is at a child's height; there's not so much that it becomes overwhelming; and the emphasis of the exhibits is on things kids traditionally love — dinosaurs, model airplanes, phosphorescent rocks. Four is a good age for a first visit to a children's museum, but take along a younger brother or sister, who will delight in the feely-touchy exhibit that is standard fare in most children's museums.

Libraries

A trip to the library rates six stars on my five-star outing list. It also goes at the top of the rainy day list.

I don't think eighteen months is too early to start a child on a library habit with an introductory visit to the children's section. From age two and a half, you can make fairly regular visits and borrow big piles of books. The process of borrowing and returning books in itself is a great lesson for a two-year-old. He thinks of all things he uses as MINE, and having to return library books provides him with substantial proof that this view of the world doesn't cut it.

Picking out books is a great game for kids; you can steer your child to books you think will be interesting, but let her do most of the selecting. While you're there, sit down with your child and read a story or two. No one will be disturbed; librarians like to see parents reading quietly to their kids; that's what the place is set up for.

Check the bulletin board; libraries often sponsor special events for kids: films, story-reading hours, seasonal parties.

Theater and Movies

Before your child's first live theater or first real movie, you think how exciting live performers or the big silver screen will be for him, but for a three-year-old, the most impressive feature of a first play or movie may be that it's very dark in there. Many theaters that have special children's presentations are sensitive to the fact that young kids get spooked in the dark, and they don't turn the lights down all the way in the audience, but it's best to prepare your child for a blackout.

A good way to explain the darkness of a theater to a three-year-old is by comparing it to the "special" darkness of a birthday, when we put out all the lights in the room and the only light comes from the candles on the cake to show off the most important part. This is a comparison that a three-year-old can understand quite well.

Eating Out

Eating out with a baby is seldom more complicated than going out on a dinner date. One father remembers the good old days before his first child started to toddle: "We'd pick him up sleeping and go out and have dinner — we used to go to a Chinese restaurant a lot and he'd lie right there in the booth and never wake up. But we can't do that now."

After your baby is sitting up and taking in the world, you can kiss good-by to unhurried, easygoing meals in restaurants — or you can add the price of a baby-sitter to the price of the meal. When your kids are in grade school, you may be able to have sit-down, digestible meals in family restaurants, but for now you're pretty well stuck with fast-food places.

The problem isn't children's manners or even their behavior so much, because most kids do okay in a public place, especially at the start, when there are new things to see. The problem is the sit-down wait for the food to arrive. Kids grow impatient and this gets the meal off to a bad start. Once a child knows that it's possible to have a burger instantly in a junk-food place, she simply won't be satisfied to order and then sit and wait.

There are a few ways around total capitulation to the fast-food industry. In big cities look for restaurants with cafeteria-style service, which eliminates most of the problems you have when eating out with preschoolers. Self-service doesn't have to mean steam-table food — I've eaten Greek shish kebab and Maryland crabs in restaurants where you carried the food to your table on a tray. You can also try occasional sit-down restaurant meals, but definitely go to family-style places where the person who waits on you will understand what you're up against and will know how to help out. Go early, a little before your kids' regular mealtime, or late, having fed them lightly at home. Take along storybooks for the time after the menu, and quiet toys or a pad and crayons. Don't bother with drinks and appetizers — that will only drag things out longer. Inexpensive Chinese restaurants are excellent for family meals because Chinese food is always cooked quickly by stir-frying and is usually served fast.

One well-organized father had an excellent scheme for restaurant meals with his two kids — three and seven. The family keeps a copy of the menu from a nearby family restaurant where they are "regulars." An hour ahead of mealtime, Dad writes out the family order on a note pad and calls it in. They arrive punctually, and no sooner are they seated than the food is served. Now, that's fast food. Of course setting up a similar deal depends on finding a pretty accommodating restaurant. Pizza places are usually happy to put the pie in the oven when you call ahead.

Fast Food   The fast-food industry caters to the preschool set; kids can do no wrong as far as the management is concerned. But some rules are in order. The booth seats are low and it's hard for a preschool child to eat and drink with a straw while sitting down, so we made up a fast-food restaurant rule in doggerel rhyme: "It's allowed in our family to kneel on your heel — but *not* to squirm like a worm." Gregory recites this every time we eat in one of these places, even sometimes as he squirms, but it has helped him along a bit in the direction of self-

control. You can make drinking with a straw much easier for a small child by cutting off a third of the straw with a sharp pocketknife.

Managers of fast-food places will often arrange a behind-the-scenes tour of the kitchen for your kids, or bring a whole group of neighborhood kids. The tour will have to be set up in advance for an "off" hour and probably not on a weekend.

CAR TRAVEL

"My sister lives down in Tuckertown, and it's just a hundred miles away," said one father. "Well, we don't get any farther than Somerville, which is only fifteen miles, and the kids are saying: 'Are we there yet?'"

Another father remembered an easy long car trip with his child all the way from the East Coast to the Rockies — but the child had been five months old and slept most of the time. Now that his family has expanded and his kids are eight, seven, and four, there's no more cross-country driving. They fly out to the Rockies and rent a car there to head for the hills.

Many families extend the sleeping baby stage as long as they can get away with it — by driving only at night. With the kids in pajamas sound asleep in their car seats, you can usually drive straight through for three or four hours, and carry them in, still sleeping, to bed when you arrive.

For longer trips, where the kids will be most or all of the day in the car, you need extra time for making lots of stops along the way, and advance preparations so there will be much more for a preschooler to do than kick the back of the driver's seat.

There's a real "them and us" setup in the way families ride, with parents in the front and kids in the back for safety. The kids sometimes can't even hear what you're saying to them when you're driving, and if you're driving well, your whole concentration is on the road, not on what's going on in the back seat. So it's easy to feel insulated from the kids and to develop a kind of tunnel vision when it comes to long trips. The kids begin to seem like disagreeable passengers who have to be coddled and appeased from time to time by tossing them back some food. I find that it helps if I can think of the destination as only one part of the trip, rather than seeing it as an all-important goal to be reached after hours of dreary hassle. Then I can think of the travel time as a possible source of family good times. And the kids do much better when they're part of the trip from the start, helping with packing and planning and map reading.

The most important thing, though, is always variety — frequent change of pace and scene, which means toys, snacks, stops, games, songs, stories, sleep, and whatever else you can do that works. As soon as your kids start to fall apart, you want to be ready with a change — a new activity, something new to eat. And when they slack off, you want to be alert to their need to be left alone to their own perfectly good devices.

CAR TOYS

Some well-organized families keep a special cache of car trip toys stowed away in a closet, which keeps these things fresh and novel for the kids. One family, for instance, who have a six-year-old and four-year-old twins, keep a box for trips that includes toy binoculars, a magic slate, snap-together plastic building toys — all things that are especially good on the road.

Another good approach to toys for a trip is to get your child to pack her favorites of the moment. A box or a small suitcase or overnight bag to pack toys and books will make a child feel like a real part of the preparations. When Gregory turned four I gave him my old battered attaché case that had moldered in a closet for eight years. With his attaché case, he acts as important as a bank president as he makes major decisions the day before a trip: "Dad, do you think I should take Stretch Monster or my rubber shark?" He crowds quite a stack of Little Golden Books in there, and a pad and crayons, and some little cars.

Before he graduated to the attaché case and real status, we had an old laundry bag that Rita helped him pack with favorite toys. But we kept this in the front seat and handed something back whenever he began to wear thin. Now that he's older, he naturally has control over his own things. But now Timothy's toys are in front in a bag, and he is handed things item by item.

SNACKS

This army of yours, as Napoleon observed, marches on its stomach. When Gregory was younger, I was always intrigued by the elaborate snack preparations Rita made. Every quarter hour or so, out of a bag would come some little box or bottle or container — things like cardboard bouillon cube boxes and plastic Easter eggs. These would be passed back to Gregory, who would play with the boxes long after he ate the few raisins and other small health goodies they contained. There would be dozens of these for a trip, and at the bottom of the bag was always a box of raisins from which all the containers could be replenished. Timothy has been cheated out of this ritual because with two kids there's

hardly time to get everybody into the car, let alone futz around with little boxes. But there is still a big bag full of raisins, healthy cereal, fruit, and pretzels. Not much to drink, though. Kids who drink a lot on a trip always want to stop. If the snacks are metered out with care, many kids will eat their way through an unbroken three-hour drive.

STOPPING

The hardest part of long car trips for me is adding in the extra time for stopovers, picnics, pit stops, scenic overlooks, and rest breaks. I figure how long it will take to get from here to Boston — six, maybe six and a half hours — and then I have to tag on at the very least an hour and a half for stopping and it's up to a full working day's drive and I'm almost ready to call off the trip. But the funny thing is that the parts of the trip I always remember — and usually with pleasure — are the stopovers, the picnics, the pit stops, and the scenic overlooks.

When we stop, the kids are ready to play hard, and so am I. We run or jog or do toe-touching exercises, or child-lifting acrobatics, or piggyback rides, or ring-around-the-rosy. And we always have a ball in the trunk for kicking around, and a Bionic Family Stick (p. 259).

If your kids are asleep, fine, drive right on through till they wake up, but when they're awake try not to let two hours go by without a stop. A stop and a workout can change the scene and the pace enough to quiet antsy children down for the next leg of the journey.

The best places along the highway to take a break are the grassy rest stop pull-offs with picnic tables — the ones without a big restaurant and filling stations and machines full of candy and trinkets that present one more nuisance when the kids start to beg for quarters.

Picnics and Meals

The more food you can carry in the car, the better. Picnics along the way really break up the trip, and even if it's raining, you can always eat in the car.

Restaurant stops aren't quite as refreshing for the kids because they go from the confinement of the car to the confinement of manners. But a restaurant is another scene and the more often you vary the menu of the trip, the more easily things will go. Hit restaurants well ahead of or behind regular meal hours to avoid the slow-down of crowds, using snacks to stave off the children's hunger. Depend more on the food you bring to provide the kids' regular diet and nourishment than on the hot dog they will ask for in a restaurant and then not finish. That way, you can stop at the junk-food places the kids love — and that you can afford — and everyone will still be decently fed.

Unadvertised Specials

Some traveling families have special treat times on long trips — a grab bag of trinkets or a party at lunchtime with some party hats and balloons. Make these *unadvertised* specials so you don't just give the kids one more thing to beg for. And spring them as needed.

Pit Stops

Refueling stops can be great for family trip morale, but only if the kids can get out and see what's up. Unless there's pouring rain, we all climb out and the kids inspect the gas pumps and then we check the tires with a tire gauge that I keep handy in the glove compartment. I'll bet we could get in the *Guiness Book of Records* for the number of times we've checked the tires. Gregory fell in love with the tire gauge when he was just two, and now he has introduced Timothy to it and they both insist each time we stop for gas that we use the "tire checker." We also keep a close watch on the oil level; Gregory wipes the dip stick with great pride, and Timothy gets "second wipe." With some extra time to kill, we also check the blinker lights to make sure they're functioning properly; Rita stays in the car and works the directional lever and we stand in front giving exaggerated hand signals to tell her which way to blink.

If you're the kind of driver who has to press on through and you find yourself pushing way past the point of your kids' endurance, one way to force yourself to take regular breaks is to buy only half a tank of gas or less each time you refuel.

Stand-up Swing

In the trunk, where it's always handy, we keep the simple device shown in the illustration — which we call a stand-up swing. At least three men's room urinals out of four are too high for a preschool boy. But preschoolers, instead of being reasonable and

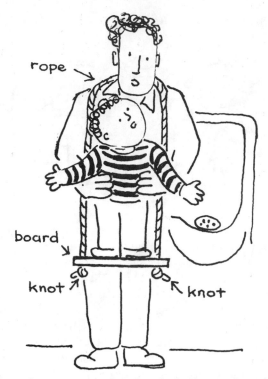

using the pot, insist on using the high urinal — it's a status thing. As all fathers of boys discover, it's awkward to hold a child up in the right position, and it becomes more awkward as he grows — until, of course, he's tall enough to stand on his own.

Gregory and I have had a lot of fun with this swing and now Timothy is learning, too. It may take you all of fifteen minutes to make one like it. You will need:

14" length 1" x 4" pine
3 yards clothesline

Drill holes 1½" from the ends of the board and thread the ends of the clothesline through them, tying them in heavy double knots that can't be pulled back through. Adjust the swing so that it hangs at the right height for you and your boy, which will be a little below your knees for a two-and-a-half-year-old, and leave some extra line so the swing can be lengthened later — just tie the extra ends of the clothesline together under the board.

If you start this with a two-year-old, practice at home to see if he'll be able to manage. With a child this young, you'll still be doing most of the supporting with your hands. As he grows, though, he'll get used to standing on the swing, and a practiced three-year-old should be able to balance pretty well on it while using the urinal.

Kids also like to sit on this swing as on a conventional playground swing and be spun around by a whirling father. If you try this, make sure not to take all the pressure of the rope on the back of your neck. Drape it across your shoulders, and twist it around both forearms, holding it firmly in your hands. Also have your child reach around behind your arms and hold on tightly to them.

Breaks on Long Trips

On a trip of more than a day, if you see something along the way that looks like fun, why not stop? It could be a national park or a construction site, a lake or a small airport — whatever you happen across. This way the trip becomes a series of little unplanned adventures for the kids and they are likely to stay interested in what lies ahead.

Our highway systems are so efficient that it's much harder than it used to be to have "adventures" like this. You get on the big highway and you can just keep on truckin' till you get there. But if you can afford the time, try occasionally taking a secondary road that parallels the big one. Say you have to come down off the highway for gas; check the map and see if there's a smaller road that will run along near the highway, taking you through small towns and countryside, and put you back on the big road after ten miles or so. We do this sometimes and on about half of these side jaunts nothing interesting turns up and it's a waste of time; but the other times we find places to stop where the kids can see new things — we happened on a wonderful river raft race once this way and another time ran smack into a small-town bicentennial celebration.

Or say the whole family hits rock bottom driving on a rainy day. Maybe you can break the spell by stopping in a town for a shopping spree in a dime store, or even take in an afternoon movie.

PACKING THE CAR

It falls to Dad's lot to fit all the equipment in for the safari. Which is simple enough if you're driving something like a reconditioned school bus, but with a standard-size family car and a one-year-old, you find yourself with a mountain of paraphernalia on the sidewalk that looks as if it will never fit in — and often it doesn't.

From late in the first year through about three are the logistical years. With a newborn first baby you often make it hard for yourself by bringing too much stuff along — including a nonportable bassinet. But you soon discover that for much of the first year a baby can travel very light and can indeed sleep in a dresser drawer. It's when the baby moves up to a crib that the mountain of paraphernalia starts to pile up: crib, playpen, stroller, even a full-size baby carriage. And then Grandmother says she has no high chair — why don't you just throw yours in the car and bring it along?

In fact you do need some kind of traveling crib setup until your child is around three and a half and old enough to sleep on a couch or on a floor with a bedroll. A small folding playpen will do double duty as a traveling crib. This and a folding "umbrella" stroller are the two essentials for this age bracket — you won't get that much more use from a full-size carriage. And try to get Grandmother to ask around among her neighbors; someone often has a spare high chair to lend. But make sure there will be a high chair of some sort, and take one along if you must, because this is a corner you will not enjoy having cut — especially if you're visiting older people who expect a little order in your child care style.

Car-top Rack

The "logistical years" are the time to get a car-top rack for big items, which needn't be terribly expensive if you buy the two-bar type from a discount house or a large camping supply place. Make sure you get one with legs that sit firmly in the gutters of the car roof and have thumb-screw fastening clamps that reach under the gutters to hold them fast. Suction cup models are inadequate and may dent the car roof if heavily loaded.

Car-top racks often have holes in the crossbars at regular intervals, through which you can thread lashing ropes, but unless there's a load on the rack, the holes whistle loudly as you drive along at anything over 30 mph. Simply tape the holes shut to stop the whistling; aluminum-color heating duct tape is a good choice for this job.

In tying your load on, you don't need to make a maze with your ropes; just make sure everything is held down securely and can't move in any direction. Here is a diagram of the basic knot — the double hitch — you will need for lashing things fast.

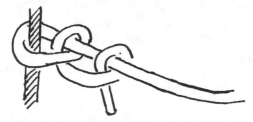

GROUP SINGING

You can get some good mileage out of group singing. The older the group, the more miles the singing will cover. Start at two years with "Old MacDonald" and work up to round-robin numbers like "Drive, drive, drive your car — boldly down the street. Merrily, merrily, merrily . . ."

A good song for the car is the oldie "Ninety-nine Bottles of Beer on the Wall." Gregory and I have converted this one to bottles of pop for preschool consumption. And we cut back to ten bottles for a start. At four many kids will be able to count backward from ten, having learned it from "Sesame Street" and from Countdown and Blast-off, a popular nursery school game.

All the golden oldies you can remember from the fraternity house or summer camp are adaptable in this same way and each new one will squeeze out a few more miles. Make up your own songs, too, using familiar tunes like "Skip to My Lou" and adding words about the trip, your family, friends, your child's nursery school. Preschoolers will pick up on this and add contributions of their own.

Also, try carrying a few quiet musical instruments — not a whistle that will drive you crazy, but something like the rubber band zither (p. 244).

STORIES

Kids like stories just as well on a trip as they do at bedtime. On the road you have ready-made story lines all around. Say you're driving through the country — why not tell a tale about farm animals you see or about children on a farm? Or an eighteen-wheeler passes you hauling bananas — why not tell

the story of the bananas in the truck, where they came from and where they're going? Or just improvise on the story of the trip you're taking. If you're on the way to Grandmother and Grandfather, tell all about them and all the things you did with them when you were young. Or make up a family just like yours riding down the highway to some similar destination, but then let them stumble on fabulous adventures.

With kids of six and older a good family story game can be played where you start a tale and each person adds a new part. As it makes the rounds, you pick it up again and it's going in a new direction you never intended or imagined when you started it out.

TRAVEL TAPES

You can easily bring along the kids' favorite music and stories on tapes that they can play on a cassette tape recorder in the back seat. Gregory and Timothy spend long quiet private times listening to their tapes of *Peter and the Wolf* and Woody Guthrie in the car. Their tapes will always keep them occupied and serene through an hour-and-a-half ride, and once provided us with five straight hours of easy car travel.

SCENERY

Children aren't scenery buffs; they concentrate more on what's going on inside the car. One reason for this is that kids know very little about what they're looking at. You can fill them in simply by talking about the terrain and the things you pass. This is just a matter of extending the old "Look at the pretty moo-cow" routine, and making it more interesting and informative: "Look at all those cows; why do you think they're all in that one corner of the field?" "Look at those fields; what do you think is

growing in them?" "There's a factory. What kinds of things are made in factories?"

Gregory has made the same hour drive to Nana's house hundreds of times since he was born. About halfway there is a mountain with a fairly steep grade on either side. One day when he was three it occurred to me that he never talked about this mountain crossing and that he might not even recognize it as that. And sure enough, when I pointed out that we were going up, up, up the side of the mountain, and then leveling out when we hit the top, and then the nose of the car was pointing down to go down, down, down the other side — it came as a revelation to him and he clearly learned a big lesson about mountains. Since then, whenever we get to the upgrade, he explains that we are going up the side of the mountain, and now we're at the tippy-top, and now we're going down to the bottom. Everything in the world is new to a kid.

NO-LOSE CAR GAMES

License plate games are for grade school kids and older. With preschoolers, you need simpler schemes and things that are easier to spot than small numbers on a moving target. It's also a good idea to start with games that are noncompetitive. Preschool kids are easily hurt and frustrated by competition; a three-year-old loser is a really bad loser — grumpy, surly, altogether unpleasant to be around. So there's no point in setting up a "game" that may produce this kind of a loser on a long car trip. Kids learn their bitter lessons about competition from all sides — from friends and brothers and sisters. We don't have to *teach* them about competition by overmatching wits with them in win-lose games.

The Color Game — which is a staple in cars with preschoolers — is a good illustration of how you can set up a game noncompetitively. Each person in the car picks a color: "I'm red"; "I'm green"; and so forth. As you see something your color you shout it out: "Red stop sign." "Green Plymouth." "Yellow stripe." There are two ways to play this game. Competitively managed, you keep count of how many reds or greens you see, which is usually a little fun for an adult since there is a small element of sport in it. But any adult can trounce any child at this in minutes unless he takes a big handicap like the color purple. And then you have a child loser on your hands. If the game is played noncompetitively, with each player simply shouting out color spottings, preschoolers will play for just as long as they will when a tally is being kept, and everyone in the car will be a winner because no feelings will be hurt.

You've of course noticed how intensely competitive preschool kids are when they get into a win-lose game — they're worse than adults and will always go at it tooth and nail. So it is hard to appreciate the notion that preschoolers don't need the thrill of competition to keep them going, that they will play a game for the sheer pleasure of playing it. It helps me to understand the situation if I think of the noncompetitive game as being like a game of toss or catch. Just back and forth, no teams, nothing at stake, and it can keep going for a long time in an easygoing way. I think that's the level at which it's useful to play games with preschool kids.

You may not get much fun out of spotting fifty-three blue objects along the highway and not even getting credit for them, but you may get fifteen miles out of it — the critical fifteen miles between the point when the kids start breaking down into the "sillies" and the time you get to the next rest pull-over. The Color Game car start as early as your child knows anything about colors — say around age three — and will last long past the time when you are thoroughly bored with it.

Rhyming

Starting at age four and a half, you can keep up a pretty lively rhyming game. Simple setup: "I see something that rhymes with ants." Everyone tries rhymes until someone hits "pants" — which is what I saw. Whoever gets "pants" picks the next rhyme. The object can be inside the car or out on the road and if no one gets it you can give broad hints: "I'm wearing them on my legs."

If this is a little too advanced, just drop back a notch. "What is a word that rhymes with bee?" And your child can earn a little praise by picking see or ski, key or knee.

Observation

There should be a pad and crayons or markers in any well-equipped family car and with these a non-driving parent can make a list of things for a child to look for beside the highway — with simple pictures illustrating the things. The list can have things like a house, a tree, a cow, a cloud, a police car, an American flag, and whatever else you feel like putting on it. Your child can mark a big X across each thing as he spots it. Throw in a few tough ones to drag out the

game, but not too tough, because of course the point is for the child to find them all and get some praise for each find. A three-year-old can play a simple version of this game and you may be able to keep it going through age six or later by making it increasingly difficult and switching the emphasis from pictures to words as your child learns the letters — *C* for cow — and starts to read.

Guess What I Saw

This is the primitive form of Twenty Questions. From age four a child will enjoy being the center of attention in this game and will be able to hold forth answering questions that try to pin down what she saw. The answer system can be "warm" or "hot"; or

"yes" and "no." Was it bigger than a toy box? Did it have four wheels and a light on top?

Directions

With children confined in car seats and belts, Simon Says games are about as much exercise as you can provide between rest stops. The driver is left out of these games and they are of course more fun if there is a group of kids, but one child — of three or older — will enjoy doing them alone. Simon says, Wag your head. Simon says, Wave your hands. Simon Says, Knock your knees. Kids like to touch body parts: shin bones and behind the ears and shoulder blades. Leave out the part of Simon Says where kids are put "out" for making a mistake — it only ends the game prematurely and gives you a sore loser.

A variation is Do This and Add Something. The first player claps his hands; the second claps her hands and pulls on her ear; the third claps his hands, pulls on his ear, and raps on his head . . .

Actor and Mirror

With a couple of preschoolers in the back seat, suggest a game of reflections. One child is the "actor" and the other does the mirror image of the "actor's" movements. Fairly contented children will keep this up for quite a while, but don't introduce it to kids on the verge of silly behavior or you'll get nothing but giggles. Mirror image yawning is the best part of this game.

Counting

At four and five kids like to practice counting, and the basic game is called Count Up to a Million. If you child makes it up to forty-three with you supplying every other number, that's pretty much like a million at four and a half. For this game you don't even need objects to count — just numbers. But kids will also enjoy picking out something to keep track of: campers, panel trucks, yield signs. Show a five-year-old how to tick things off in groups of five on a pad of paper so he can keep an accurate tally.

When overexcitement reaches a crescendo five or ten minutes before you arrive at a familiar destination, set your child to counting twenties. "We'll be there when you've counted to twenty fifteen times." Which may get you almost to the door.

Maps

Always keep track of the progress of a long trip on road maps, marking how far you've gone from time to time as you stop. Use a different color marker or crayon for each leg of the trip so the kids can see how you've progressed.

A good road map game for a six-year-old is Alternate Routes. Give the child a map on a hard surface — a clipboard comes in very handy on long trips — and show him how to mark a route with a crayon. The purpose of the game is to trace along as many alternate routes as possible between two points, preferably the points you're traveling between. The routes can be ridiculously roundabout, but they all have to lead to the right destination.

Quizzes

Make up simple quizzes on any scheme you like. For instance: What animal gives us milk? What animal gives us honey? How do carrots grow, up or down? Which is juicier, an apple or an orange? I find these quizzes are pretty good puzzles for me while driving — they don't demand too much attention, but they keep me thinking hard to come up with more quiz questions at the right level.

Along the same lines is Opposites, which three-year-olds love because they are sorting out the world and getting everything paired up. What's the opposite of hot? Of little? Of sit?

CB RADIO

Gregory, at five, found his own solution to the problem of what to do on a long car trip. He designed and we built together the CB radio pictured here. He

had admired a friend's plastic toy CB and was begging to buy one, when he came up with the idea of making this one instead. Its body is a scrap piece of $^5/_4"$ x 6" lumber. The main switch is a short piece of dowel nailed onto the side: it moves back and forth to bring in other operators and alternately to let Gregory talk to them. The dials are a variety of bottle caps — like plastic ones from milk bottles — and they are held on with galvanized roofing nails. The microphone is a heavy plastic yogurt container top joined by a length of scrap bell wire and a nail. The dial is drawn on with a marker.

It's a homely little number, but Gregory and I had a grand time making it — discussing what to use for dials and how many there should be, and searching for the right jar lid for a microphone, and so on. And best of all, Gregory now sits in the back seat jabbering away in his own unique CB language. I hope there are other kids on wooden CBs in the back seats of other cars picking up his messages. He keeps asking: "Can they *really* hear me on my CB in the other cars?" no matter how often we tell him No.

We have made a similar CB set for Timothy, who broadcasts important messages over it: "Wanna Cookie . . . Wanna Cookie . . ."

STEERING WHEEL

Every kid wants to get his hands on the steering wheel of the family car, and you spend a lot of time trying to frustrate this desire. A big help is simply getting a child his own steering wheel.

One Saturday afternoon Gregory and I drove over to the local junk yard, which happens to be a pretty classy place; it has a printed sign on the door that says: "This is not a junk yard. This is an automobile disassembly and recycling center." They had indeed disassembled a lot of cars and there was a pile of at least a dozen steering wheels — from

---

which Gregory chose one with a small picture of a Mustang in the middle, and in mint condition. What a difficult decision; he seemed to be living through his wildest fantasy — not only a dozen real steering wheels in one place, but a chance to choose one all his own.

Of all the things I've done for Gregory and given him over the years, the steering wheel is far and away the most appreciated; I'm thanked for it over and over. The steering wheel comes with us everywhere in the car, but not as a toy to play with on the way, because it's a heavy object that could become a dangerous projectile in an accident — it rides in the trunk. In the kids' room I drilled a hole in the side of some shelves and fitted in a piece of dowel on which Gregory can mount the steering wheel and "drive" to his heart's content.

INTRA-AUTO PHONE HOOKUP

In our family car we have a front seat-back seat father-child telecommunications hookup — which is just a two-yard-long piece of 1″ clear vinyl hose from a hardware store. Any piece of garden hose or other tubing will do. Talk into one end and your voice carries clear as a bell through to the other end, which is held to the receiver's ear.

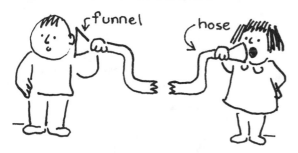

You can fit the ends with small funnels shoved in and taped on; they make excellent microphone/receivers. Actually, though, holding the end of the tube in your fist and talking into it will achieve the same thing.

The problem with using this phone is getting the kids in the back to speak into it softly so they don't smash your eardrums. I play whispering games with my passengers. I speak into the phone so quietly they can't possibly hear my voice over the sound of the motor, except through the tube phone, and I say: "If you can hear my quiet voice, say, 'Wonton soup.'" And a little voice from the back seat chirps, "Wonton soup." Then I say, "Now I am speaking even more softly; if you can hear me still, say, 'Noodle pie'" . . . A preschooler will keep repeating the code words as long as you can keep up the whispered chatter.

The big moment comes when your child is able to reverse the game and give the softly spoken directions himself for Dad to call back the code words. It will take months to achieve this, though, because the intra-auto phone offers too tempting an opportunity to blast Dad out of the driver's seat with a loud screech.

Hose phone hookups can be made around the house, too, or between buildings if you have a long hose and a close neighbor with kids the same age. A defunct garden hose with the hardware cut off is perfect for this purpose; and again funnels can be used for microphone/receivers. Hose phones are superior in every way to the tin can and string phone systems that bedevil kids by working only if the string is pulled absolutely taut. The hose can go around corners, up, down, in any direction, and the voices will still carry through clearly if it isn't crimped.

CELEBRATIONS

BIRTHDAYS

Many fathers told me they duck out of birthday parties, but I think they're missing something, because I always get a kick out of these events and every man I talked to who had gone to his kids' birthday parties had enjoyed himself. Of course it's a drag if you hang around on the fringes with the mothers. The fun is right in the thick of things with the kids. One of the good parts of birthday parties is that you get to meet all of your child's friends; and your child will be super proud to introduce Daddy.

You can be the life of the birthday party if you feel like it. Competitive games like Pin-the-Tail are too

advanced for preschoolers because the competition will produce pathetically disappointed losers — so the party needs entertainment that everyone will enjoy, not just the winner. Why not do your old magic tricks? Or play songs at the piano or on the guitar? Whatever you know how to do — and you don't have to do a professional job, because you'll have an enthusiastic audience and a very proud child whatever the quality of the performance.

Showing cartoon movies will make a big hit with the preschool crowd. You can often borrow or rent films from a well-equipped public library; and check with the library for sources for renting a projector. If you work in an office, ask around — there may be a company projector that you can borrow for the weekend. Home-movie makers have their most receptive audience (outside of the grandparents) at the birthday party. This crowd will even get excited about a showing of your family slides.

My favorite part of birthday parties is giving rides in the back yard. Two sure-fire hits are the wheelbarrow ride (p. 310) and the Daddy-go-round (p. 257). There shouldn't be more kids than you can handle, because you'll keep preschool birthday parties small; a good rule of thumb is one guest per year of age — and there'll always be an extra guest or two that the birthday person insists on inviting. Big parties are unmanageable and no fun. With a small group, each kid can have a turn at everything that happens.

Party Games

Everybody should be a winner in games played at a preschool birthday party, or at the very least, no one should lose. A follow-the-string treasure hunt will end in a prize for every child. This game is good with kids of four and older. A five-year-old will have a lot of fun before the party helping lay out the strings — which can be as long as you like and run anywhere. Tied to the far end of each one will be a trinket, so even if a kid starts reeling in, she'll get what she's after. Use a different color string or yarn for each child if you have them. The object of the game isn't to get to the treasure first — just to get the goody.

Standard party games are easily adapted for no-lose playing. Musical chairs, for instance, is great fun for preschoolers if no one is put out. Just keep taking away chairs and everyone eventually ends up on everyone else's lap on one chair, which is many more laughs than the traditional way, where nearly everyone loses and the lone winner gloats.

Try other noncompetitive games, too, say a musical conga line; or pair the kids up if they're five or older and see if they can hold a balloon between two heads or two chests.

Balloons

For a birthday party you'll want to blow up lots of balloons. But sore-cheeked and winded fathers have discovered that it's no mean task to inflate the cheap little balloons that come in the economy pack from the dime store. A filling station owner, father of three, uses his air compressor for this task, but suggested a stand-up bicycle pump for the less well-equipped dad.

A bicycle pump not only does an excellent job, it has a terrific bonus — it can be operated efficiently by a three-year-old. The cheapie balloons fit a standard bike pump nozzle perfectly, but with bigger, better balloons, you have to hold the neck tightly around the nozzle, or wrap it with a tight little rubber band (the size used for orthodontic braces).

At birthday celebrations at our house, the kids

blow up the balloons themselves on the pump, and this is always one of the big events of the party. Kids as young as one and a half enjoy working the pump handle and with a little help can inflate a balloon. Children who have been to our house and blown up balloons this way always search around for the red bicycle pump when they come back for a visit, so we keep it handy in the kitchen closet with a supply of little balloons.

Failing a bicycle pump, soften the balloons by filling them with water after stretching the necks around the end of the kitchen spigot.

But remember that uninflated and popped balloons make dangerous playthings. Kids love to suck on these and will suck them right on into the windpipe. So always supervise balloon blowing and as soon as a balloon pops, commandeer the remains and throw them away.

PURIM

The jolliest day of the year for Jewish children, Purim is celebrated with dancing, singing, masquerade parties, and Purim plays. All this merrymaking commemorates the escape of the Jews in Persia from destruction at the hands of the villainous prime minister Haman — the story is in the Book of Esther.

Shown here is a plan for making a traditional Haman knocker, a Purim noisemaker that's used in temple services and as a child's toy. When the story of Esther saving the Jews is read, each time the

name of Haman is mentioned, the knockers are clapped back and forth to make enough noise to blot out all mention of his name.

To make one, you'll need:

> scraps 1″ pine stock
> 2¾″ length 1⅛″ lattice molding
> one 1¼″ nail

Cut pieces shown in the illustration. The platform has a rectangle cut out of its center with a coping saw or chisel to accept the 1″ x 2″ handle; they are held together with white glue. The handle is notched to accept the knocker arm — a 2¾″ length of 1⅛″ lattice molding. The knocker arm is glued into a ⅜″ deep mortise chiseled in the bottom of the hammerhead. Drill pilot holes for the nail in the handle, and a larger hole in the knocker arm that will let it swing freely back and forth so the hammerhead will smash into the imaginary head of the evil Haman.

Purim is celebrated on the fourteenth day of Adar, a month in the Hebrew calendar — which means that it falls in February or March. But a child with a Haman knocker can whoop it up any day of the year.

EASTER

Every year at Easter egg dyeing time I show off my favorite trick — blowing eggs with a vacuum cleaner. And every year Rita is annoyed because it wastes eggs — and the kids are delighted.

With an awl or a thin knitting needle you carefully poke a hole in the end of an egg; push it all the way through and make a hole coming out the other end. Wiggle the awl a little as it goes through, because you want to pop the yolk. Now you attach the vacuum cleaner hose to the exhaust side of the cleaner, press one end of the egg to the open end of the hose, and turn on the vacuum cleaner — which blows the egg white and yolk out the other hole and into a waiting bowl.

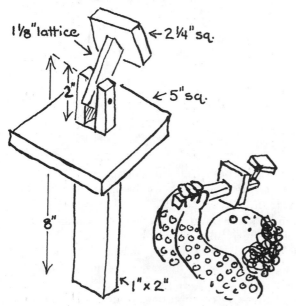

MOTHER'S DAY

Always on the second Sunday in May. This is an occasion for touching sentimental remembrances and thoughtful gestures. Prod the kids into making angelic prerehearsed speeches of thanks to Mom. Have a family party where Dad and the kids cook the meal. And have a Mother's Day cake at the end with candles even though it's nobody's birthday — candles make the party for the kids.

In our family, we treat Mother's Day a little like St. Valentine's Day — with red hearts cut out of construction paper. Tiny Timothy scribbles on paper hearts and puts them in an envelope for presenting. When Gregory was just three, we worked together with a coping saw to cut out a small heart shape from lattice molding; we painted it red and attached a safety pin to the back with tape so Rita could wear it. Kids older than this prefer to make things without a lot of help from Dad, so each year I cut some hearts out of lattice and red plastic jar lids and let Gregory figure out what he wants to do with them. One year he drilled holes in them and strung them as a bracelet, and one year he glued them to a blocky little wooden car we had made some weeks before. He thought that would be a nice present for Mom, because she needed a toy car. And it was an excellent present, because any child-made object will be loved on Mother's Day — especially one that Dad has helped with.

Going to the store with Dad on a special mission to buy a gift for Mom can be a very big deal. I take the kids to a cheap variety store and let them pick something out themselves. Their first ideas are usually pretty wide of the mark — Mommy would like a Fred Flintstone coloring book or a bucket of plastic Slime — but after inspecting everything in the store and some serious discussion, they'll come up with something perfect.

The standard Mother's Day present is flowers for planting; in our part of the country, pansies are the usual choice since it's early spring and these are blooming colorfully in their packs from the nursery. The kinds of flowers that will be best vary from place to place according to the weather. For transplanting flower plants to the garden, choose an overcast or drizzly day, as sunshine will wilt them and set them back. Flower plants usually come twelve or half a dozen growing together in a shallow box. The dirt should be thoroughly wet for transplanting. Remove the whole clump from the box and, working gingerly with your fingers, separate the individual

root clumps of the plants. Preschoolers can help by digging holes for planting with a trowel and spraying in lots of water from the hose. Flower plants should usually be set in the ground just a little deeper than they were growing in the nursery pack.

Three Wishes

For the last two Mother's Days, we've had a Mother's Three Wishes special event at breakfast. Rita is sitting down and being *served* breakfast and she gets to make one wish each for what she would like Gregory, Timothy, and me to change in our dealings with her — kind of a New Year's resolution for the other guy. We try hard to make the wishes come true, though most of them end up after a while the way New Year's resolutions always end up.

FATHER'S DAY

Always on the third Sunday in June. Father's Day is an afterthought to Mother's Day. It was made an official national holiday by act of Congress only in April 1972, whereas Mother's Day, which was celebrated first back in 1908, has been a fixture on the national scene since 1914.

An organization called the National Father's Day Committee has been presenting fatherhood awards to distinguished Americans since 1942, when Douglas MacArthur became the first National Father of the Year. The list of others similarly honored at Father's Day awards dinners in New York includes presidents and statesmen. This organization gives many awards in special categories, too, like Music Father of the Year and Humanitarian Father of the Year. Here, for instance, is a list of Sports Fathers of the Year for the seventies:

1970	Bowie K. Kuhn
1970	Jack Nicklaus

1971   Brooks Robinson
1972   Roger Staubach
1973   Bob Griese
1974   Tom Seaver
1975   Johnny Miller
1975   James "Catfish" Hunter
1976   Luis Tiant
1976   Dave DeBusschere
1977   Roy White
1977   John Newcombe

In 1978 there were eleven National Fathers of the Year, including Thomas P. "Tip" O'Neill, Jr., Dr. Martin Luther King, Sr., and Yul Brynner. And in the last decade, the group has awarded the big National Father of the Year honor to:

1970   Frank Borman
1971   Henry M. Jackson
1972   Spiro T. Agnew
1973   Charles H. Percy
1974   Gerald R. Ford
1975   Edmund S. Muskie
1976   Edward M. Kennedy
1977   Andrew Young

There are also Southeast and West Coast regional Father's Day awards dinners and similar events in Dallas and Chicago, where most of the fatherhood honors go, as on the national level, to politicians and other celebrities.

So no matter how good a job you do raising your kids, there's not much chance you'll be tapped as National Father of the Year.

Father's Hammock

Ask for a good hammock for your Father's Day present — it's one piece of equipment no father should be without. It's great for relaxing, but it's also the perfect way to enjoy babies and little kids — just swinging with them. I can't think of a more peaceful thing to do than to lie in a hammock with a baby asleep on my chest.

HALLOWEEN

A father is an excellent trick-or-treat escort for a preschool kid, and in a city neighborhood where there is any chance of Halloween foul play, Dad should definitely go along. Make it a family affair with both parents or go in a big neighborhood group, parents included, for fun and safety.

Try to keep Halloween tame — just a little bit of scary stuff goes a long way with preschoolers' vivid imaginations. Preschool kids are willing to take spooky goings on quite literally, even when they are explained and the ghost sheets are taken off. Every home with little kids should have a pumpkin lantern, though, glowing in the dark — make sure to eat Halloween supper to the grinning glow of one.

Jack-o'-Lantern

I talked to several fathers who had all had a terrific time at a Halloween father-child pumpkin-cutting party given by the co-operative play school their kids all attended. One of these men told me, though, that there had been many fathers at the party who hadn't known how to cut out a jack-o'-lantern. It's hard to believe that this simple time-honored craft is disappearing, but just in case some reader doesn't know, here's how to:

With a sharp knife cut a roughly circular top plug with the stem in the center; the diameter will be about 5″ for a medium-size pumpkin; angle the knife toward the center as you cut so the top will fit back in securely. With newspaper laid out on the kitchen table, let your kids scoop the seeds and pulp of the pumpkin out into a bowl with a big spoon. A child can then draw a face on the pumpkin with a black marker. Then, using the marker face as a rough guide, cut out eyes, nose, and mouth — triangles are the easiest shape to cut for eyes and teeth in the mouth. Some people like to cut a small hole for the nose and shove in a carrot, parsnip, or turnip. Another nice touch is fastening on green or red pepper quarters with toothpicks for ears. Inside the

pumpkin, in the center of its floor, make a tight shallow hole for a short candle — a melon ball cutter is the perfect tool for making the candle hole. Shove in a short candle, light it, and put the top back on. The top can stay on until it's charred and dried out, at which point it should be removed. On p. 315 are tips for pumpkin growing to help you start your jack-o'-lanterns all the way from scratch.

Walking Warlock

I can't resist playing one slightly scary little game each Halloween. It is said that when witches and warlocks used to assemble, they would light their way through the night to the coven with pumpkin head lanterns, and that the glowing grimacing heads bobbing through the night would scare the wits out of any curious passers-by. I take the pumpkin head from the dinner table and go out on the lawn in the dark, where I walk around with the lantern, lifting and lowering it, and howling a little. From inside the window, the kids see only the glowing face of the pumpkin floating through the blackness. Rita tells them it's only their daddy, but of course they can *see* that it isn't.

THANKSGIVING

One morning shortly before Thanksgiving when he was four, I was driving Gregory to nursery school and talking to him about what Thanksgiving was, how it was a time to give thanks. Gregory said: "Well, God gives us all this good stuff, so maybe we should give God a present."

"What kind of present?" I asked.

"How about a machine for making people?" Gregory suggested.

"How would it work?"

"See, God is always making people. And it's hard. So he wouldn't have to do it the way he does any more. He could throw some junk and some bones into that machine and turn the handle and make people."

HANUKKAH

A great holiday for preschool kids with lots of candle lighting and presents for eight days in a row, Hanukkah is celebrated in December.

Each night of the eight days of the Festival of Lights, one more candle is lit in the menorah, a candelabrum that holds nine candlesticks. The ninth candle is called the shamas, or servant, and is used to light the other eight. A menorah made by father and child will make the lighting of the candles even more wonderful for the child. Menorahs can be made in many shapes and out of any material you can work easily. A good simple plan for a father and child working together with a brace and bit (see p. 303) is to drill nine candle holes in the wide side of a

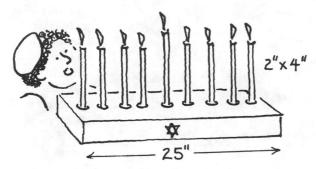

25" length of 2" x 4"; space the holes 2½" on centers. The diameter of the holes, of course, will depend on the kind of candle you plan to use. Let your child decorate the menorah with paints or glue and colored glitter.

The candles of Hanukkah are a symbol of religious freedom. When the Maccabees triumphed over the Syrians in 165 B.C., they rededicated the Temple in Jerusalem with the lighting of lamps. Hanukkah recalls this event and has become a way of celebrating the remarkable survival of the Jewish people and their identity.

CHRISTMAS

Make the most of reading *The Night Before Christmas* — it's the only important epic poem in our culture that has the domesticated dad for narrator and hero.

If you want to play Santa Claus, go ahead, but don't expect to fool your kids — at any age. They'll always spot Daddy under the disguise.

When you do Santa's job, make sure to leave some clues to show that he was there. Some kids find ashen footprints leading from the fireplace to the pile of toys under the tree. Always leave a sandwich and milk out for Santa before the kids go to bed, and a carrot for the reindeer, and make sure the milk glass is drained and that a crust or some big crumbs are left on the plate for evidence.

Tannenbaum

You'll want to buy a Christmas tree that's relatively fresh, so there'll be no hazard of fire from dryness. To test a tree for dryness, grasp it by the trunk and gently bump the bottom against the ground. If many needles fall, it's too dry. Also try to snap a smaller twig; if it snaps easily, the tree is too dry. Sometimes you can get a tree that has been treated with a flame retardant. In any case, always

keep the base of the tree wet by using a water-holding stand.

Until the kids are at least three and a half, tree decorations that are within reach are in jeopardy. One solution is using unbreakable decorations on the lower branches. Or get a small tree and put it up, securely held in place, on a table or shelf out of reach. The kids will climb and grab for the ornaments even if the tree is up high, so don't expect glass balls to last in any situation. Also make sure the tree, whether big or small, is firmly braced and held in place to keep the kids from toppling it. Attach braided picture wire around the trunk and at the other end to good-size screw eyes screwed into the woodwork, and brace in as many directions as you need to for stability. If you put a small tree up on a table, you may be able to fasten the stand securely to the table with a C-clamp.

Batteries Not Included

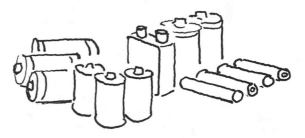

Christmas Day is battery day in most American homes, and every year there are hundreds of thousands of disappointed kids across the nation whose parents and grandparents neglected to heed those all-important words in small type on the package: "Batteries Not Included." I know an enterprising teen-ager who turns a nice profit each Christmas selling batteries at inflated prices door to door in his suburban neighborhood.

Make sure you have a good stock of film on hand, too. Fathers are always being caught with only two shots left on the roll as the kids gleefully open their presents and flash around those perfect radiant smiles.

Partial Adult Assembly

On the box the Christmas toy comes in you always find the words "Partial Adult Assembly Required," a phrase that can mean anything from five minutes with a screwdriver to a whole night's work using every tool you own as well as the "special tool supplied" for fastening the cap nuts. Included with one riding toy I assembled — an ambulance — were acorn nuts, push nuts, pal nuts, hex. nuts, face lock nuts, lock washers, sheet metal screws, roundhead bolts, truss head shoulder bolts, truss head bolts — and that's just fastening devices; you should have seen the parts list.

It makes a lot of sense to do these adult assembly chores a couple of days ahead instead of waiting for Christmas Eve. Some assembly jobs last for hours, and you may want some sleep on the night before Christmas. Also, many toys that require assembly are held together with cap nuts, which means pounding to drive these onto the ends of metal rods, which means wreaking havoc on the quiet of Christmas Eve — Bang, Bang, Bang, and there go those visions of sugarplums. Mothers are not at all keen on Christmas Eve pounding.

There's one little advantage to "Partial Adult Assembly Required." If the toy has an obnoxious noisemaker, you can leave it off or alter it so it doesn't function. One Christmas as I assembled Gregory's heart's desire, a dark blue plastic Batcycle, I though about cutting off the stiff plastic blades that would make a terrible racket as the back wheels revolved against them — but I reasoned that Gregory probably wanted the noisemakers because his friend's Batcycle had them, and I dutifully put them in place unaltered. We suffered for five months with the nerve-racking noise those clickers made as Gregory pedaled his Batcycle around the house; Rita and I were constantly getting angry at him for riding it and making him stop or chasing him outside. One day I thought to ask Gregory: "Do you *like* that noise?" "No, Daddy, I hate it. It hurts my ears." We were both delighted when I cut the plastic clicker blades off with a sharp knife, and he pedaled off swiftly and noiselessly on his usual rounds.

Visions of Sugarplums

For months before Christmas, preschoolers muddle over and talk about what they want for Christmas — it's the number one topic of conversation at nursery school. Listen carefully to what your kids think they want; it's a matter of the gravest seriousness to them and you want to intervene before some impossible desire has become a controlling passion. The earlier you discover that she is expecting a pony, the more time you have for diplomatically letting her down.

Try to limit the list of desired presents to one or two things you know you can supply. If the price isn't right, you can always say that Santa can't bring such fancy things. And when your child decides she wants both a Barbie doll and a Farrah Fawcett, you can point out that Santa brings only one of the same kind of toy and that you have to make up your mind. Kids are pretty willing to accept Santa's rules.

The first Christmas that Gregory really knew what was going on — when he was four — I tried to prepare him for possible disappointments by telling him repeatedly that Santa Claus sometimes doesn't bring *exactly* what a kid wants, and when we talked about why this was, Gregory developed the useful rationale that sometimes the elves run out of plastic, so they can't make enough toys to go around. Nonetheless, I'm sure he would have been crushed if the elves had run out of plastic before they made the toy he wanted.

Chapter 8

TEACHING AND DISCIPLINE

The most concrete and useful thing any parent can know about discipline is simply the original meaning of the word. It means *teaching*. The word *disciple* — a first cousin to discipline — has held on a little more firmly to the root meaning. But so many meanings and connotations have attached themselves to the word discipline — military discipline, the whips and chains "discipline" of the porn world, your own sense of self-discipline, which is one of the hardest things you have to cope with in life — that to many parents discipline can seem like a very heavy piece of equipment to introduce into a relationship with a small child.

Just translate "discipline" and read "teaching" instead. It's an accurate description of what you do with kids: teaching them how adults behave and how they can get themselves to behave in the same ways; teaching them the limits; and teaching them good habits you want them to establish for a lifetime.

We all know that by ancient tradition the father was expected to be The Disciplinarian in the family — the natural and only disciplinarian-punisher. The stern authoritarian father of the past was working at home. If he was a craftsman, his kids were in and out of his shop all day and, as they grew older, became helpers and apprentices. If he was a lawyer, his office was in his house and for his peace of mind and the good of his business he had to keep quiet and order in the place. If he was a farmer, the kids were workers in the family business from a very early age.

Practical necessity seemed to demand that fathers assume a tough authoritarian stance — it's easy to understand how a man with the success of his business at stake might lean a little heavily on the kids if they weren't co-operating.

Since the Industrial Revolution, of course, the whole structure of work has changed and most fathers now work far away from squalling babies and rambunctious preschoolers. The change in working habits brought with it a new style in father discipline — the "wait until your father gets home and hears this" syndrome. Dad became a heavy, an enforcer. And mothers took advantage of this setup to unload some of the inevitable guilt they felt when correcting or punishing the kids. They saved the dirty work for Dad. Kids under this regime were regularly punished long after they'd forgotten about the crime. And fathers were stuck with only a single aspect of the big disciplinary/teaching job — the part that hurts you as much as it hurts the child. If there had been a book called *The Father's Almanac* published in 1895, the section on Discipline would have been a comparison of the merits of birch rods and ash wood paddles. "Wait till your father gets home" is heard less and less in American homes, though it still lingers.

In most homes, we've replaced this syndrome with the humane notion that justice must be swift — particularly for young kids — and correction and punishment are done on the spot by the parent who is present, so the child will understand why he's being corrected and learn something more from the punishment than simply to fear his father and tremble when he returns in the evening.

The parent who is usually on hand when the kids misbehave is a full-time mom. Dad's away at work. So does this make *her* the natural and only teacher/disciplinarian in the family? Does this mean that she inherits all the authority that a home-working father once exercised, and that a modern dad should opt to stay clear of this part of child rearing, to concentrate his energies on playing with the kids and teaching them about baseball?

Emphatically not. But of course we all know families where that is exactly what has happened, where Mom is the boss and the enforcer and Dad is an extremely popular fellow who comes home evenings and weekends to hack around with the kids. Many fathers relish this popularity with their children and are afraid they'll lose it if they deal out punishments or correction. And other fathers just feel uncomfortable in the role of "disciplinarian"; some men tell me they "avoid" disciplining their

kids, others that they "shirk" it, still others that they just don't feel they are effective as disciplinarians.

This is fine in the short run and may even be a good deal for the fathers who manage to avoid what they feel is a distasteful obligation. But it can't be too good for the kids involved, because they lose the most effective natural *teacher* they can have — a father.

The work of a teacher is only partly corrective punishment, and it's a small part at that. Think back over the teachers you had in school and you'll remember that the ones you respected and learned the most from kept order firmly, but weren't tyrants. A good teacher is liked and respected precisely because he or she does manage to stay on top of the situation. There's no formula for achieving this and the results will look to an outside observer very different for different teachers — according to their personalities and style. One may run a tight ship, while another's idea of useful order may be a relaxed atmosphere where students can openly contribute their ideas. But the core result is always the same: enough order is maintained for everybody's activity to prosper — the students are free to learn and the teacher has their attention.

In the family, ideally a father is "teaching" toward pretty much the same end — the kind of order in which everyone's needs are respected and everyone's work can go forward uninterrupted. It's a hard job, because it means teaching civilized ways to little people who start their course of instruction without even having a grasp of language, let alone any idea of how they are meant to behave — such a difficult job that you clearly need more than one teacher. And of course that's one of the reasons we band together in families. Mom is very much a teacher, too — usually the home room teacher.

You and your wife will have regular faculty meet-

ings to figure out how to approach your child's education/discipline, and to agree on common policies so your child won't be confused by entirely different treatment from different quarters. You'll find yourselves discussing things as silly as whether pulling the cat's tail is a major offense at one year, to be dealt with sternly, or the result of an uncontrollable urge that can pretty much be winked at. And you'll find yourselves discussing the same silly problem again and again as your child grows and learns, and pulling the cat's tail does become a willful and gratuitous meanness.

EARLY INSTRUCTION

A baby arrives in your life as a refugee arrives from another country — he needs to learn the language and the customs before he can pick up his life, get a job, earn a living. Both baby and refugee look helpless at first, but if they meet with warmth and understanding and get into a good language course they are on the way to competence in no time.

That language course is the first instruction/discipline a baby gets. You start teaching your child language the day she arrives; it's as natural a thing to do as the phrases you use to do it: "Hi there, kid; it's good to have you with us." You talk to your child and eventually she gets the message and starts to talk back.

Meanwhile, though, this beginner has gotten up off her back and started to crawl around the classroom, sometimes disturbing others and often endangering herself. Here the job of teaching gets a little rougher. You need techniques to deal with these problems — better techniques than constantly telling the child No and swatting hands, which is a dismal bore for both parent and child. Sure, we all have to fall back on these in an emergency. When your kid is running out into the street, you don't stop to think of a clever way to deal with the situation. You rush after him shouting, NO! And when you're irritable and your child is yelling, it's hard to avoid Nos and swats. But the rest of the time, the nonemergency times, the relatively calm times, you can do some constructive teaching/disciplining, and it doesn't demand much more of your energy than perpetual No-ing.

By constructive teaching I don't mean something terribly clever and arcane, something that only an expert in child development would be capable of. I mean things as simple as handing a baby a toy when she's bent on playing with the knobs of the TV, and if that doesn't work, picking her up and moving her to another room. Kids handled this way don't get the idea that No is the most common word in the language — so common that it can be blithely ignored. In fact, the less Nos you manage to use in situations that don't pose a serious threat to your child or your things, the more likely it is that the big NO will be effective — the big NO when you spot your child lunging toward a hot burner on the stove.

Distracting a baby with toys is the first technique you master. A firm command of No may catch a baby's attention and stop him from doing something immediately, but it isn't going to prevent him from trying it again five minutes later, and it's likely to make him cry like hell with frustration, which is the last thing you're looking for. So you offer a baby something else to do, which distracts him and gets him operating in a way you approve of.

But once you get this down, so too does the baby — he's grown some and become a toddler and now he's not so easy to distract — because he's learned your trick. Hand him a rattle while he's having fun scratching the finish off the coffee table with a spoon and you get nowhere. Phooey on your old rattle; you can't fool me; this is much more fun. So you pick him up — probably with some loud protests — and carry him into the next room. By the time he gets there, and can't see the coffee table, he's ready to do something else, hopefully something more constructive.

This works for a while, and then one day you realize that it, too, has been found out. Your child has grown older and wiser and no longer forgets the coffee table the minute he leaves the room that it's in. He remembers it quite well now and back he heads to finish the job. Time for a new tactic, and happily by this point most kids can understand some spoken directions.

Meanwhile, you have managed to reserve No and swats on the hand for the biggies — eye gouging on another child, hanging over a window ledge on the third floor, that kind of thing. And meanwhile, also, you have babyproofed the household so there aren't a million and one hazards that have to be Noed and so that your most prized possessions are safe from harm and don't have to be guarded with constant vigilance. But hopefully you'll leave some of your good things around — so there will be things in your child's life that *are* off limits, and she can start to learn this from the first moment she can understand it. See p. 118 for more on babyproofing.

Meanwhile, also, you will have come up with novel solutions to the particular little problems your household and your child create. A stereo buff father kept moving his Marantz receiver to ever higher shelves as his toddling daughter learned to climb to get at the dials, which she loved to turn just as her daddy did. The stereo equipment was on such a high shelf he had to step up on a straight chair to play a record, when he had a good idea and the next Saturday took his daughter to his favorite audio store. There they bought for a few dollars a defunct Quadraphonic receiver that bristled with knobs and dials, but which had all its output transistors blown out. Dad mounted the Quadraphonic receiver at the toddler's level and the problem was solved.

I haven't wandered off the subject of discipline — buying that broken receiver was an excellent disciplinary measure at that age and for this situation. She wasn't learning to steer clear of the real receiver and she was obviously driven by a powerful urge to get to its dials and imitate Daddy by turning them. A toddler hasn't the self-control yet to overcome that kind of urge. She wasn't born with the "conscience" that we use as adults to overcome our strong urges (when it works), and it will be a while before she learns enough about the world and what is expected of her to be able to build a functional conscience for herself. As an older child — say at three and a half — she will readily accept directions to leave the dials alone. So this father saved his toddling daughter a possible bad fall and himself a lot of useless preaching and Noing by getting her the used receiver. And he also got her a splendid toy.

The point here isn't that a new toy will solve any problem. It's that an original thought by a parent is liable to solve one.

The useful early techniques for distracting babies and moving toddlers from the source of the trouble teach you the value of finding ways around confrontations, and this knack — though the methods will change with the seasons and the years as your kids grow — will put you in a strong position to concentrate on the important part of discipline — teaching your child what you and the world expect of her. Nose-to-nose disputes with kids usually lead nowhere — except to headaches. Just as nose-to-nose confrontations between men lead nowhere — except to six-gun duels if the men are in a western movie and wars if they happen to be politicians or generals.

But teaching your child what the boundaries are, and sticking by those boundaries, even if it means from time to time getting backed into a nose-to-nose confrontation — that may accomplish something.

ACTING UP

Kids act up and misbehave for a thousand different reasons — because they're tired, or angry at you, or trying to get your attention — and with a little detective work you can often figure out the cause of some particular outburst or tantrum. Just as with a baby you can go through the old checklist when he screams — Diaper? Bottle? Burp? — at most ages you know your child's moods and ways and problems well enough to run down a kind of mental catalogue and spot what's up — the daily and momentary influences.

But there are also much broader patterns determining how kids act, generalized "stages" of growth that all children commonly go through. So that as each child grows, she becomes a series of distinctly different people. At one year you have a charmer in the house, a joy to be around. But then the charmer learns No and practices it — in everything she does — and at eighteen months this same lovely child has metamorphosed into a negative grump, just as surely as a playful tadpole turns into a croaking frog.

And your attitudes toward her change, as do the ways you handle her.

If you're lucky and she misses this first predictable personality slump that most kids go through in the latter part of the second year, she probably won't miss the next big Down — the so-called Terrible Twos, which is usually the Terrible mid-Twos. At three she's liable to be a delight again. You breathe easy and it's smooth sailing till you hit the squalls of four. A four-year-old swings back and forth from the best she's capable of to the worst — and she's learned what lying is and experiments with it boldly. A five-year-old is easy to live with — co-operative, purposeful, sure of herself and her place in the world. A six-year-old, all eagerness, attention, and competitive energy at school, may be a bit moody and hard to get through to at home.

Each of these children — even though they are all the same child — needs something different from his parents. And one of the basic things he needs is the understanding that he is going through a stage — that it *will* be over. The negative times at eighteen months, two and a half, and four are like foretastes of adolescence — and we all remember what *that* was like. During these times, kids are trying hard to assert their independence, and just as adolescents always do, they manage to figure out all the things their parents disapprove of, and then proceed to do these with a vengeance.

If it's just a stage, should you try to ignore the misbehavior, wait it out, and be pleased when it goes away? If you do, I think your kids have spent a lot of time and strenuous effort begging for your interest and instruction, without getting the feedback they're after. Just as children's behavior is part of a broad scheme, parents' responses to it are part of a scheme. Kids push the limits, cross the line, and they are asking Dad and Mom to hold the line, show them that it *is* there and why it's there. Again it's the job of teaching/discipline.

The job is made slightly easier if you recognize that your kids are going through stages. You can make some allowances and avoid some head-on collisions because you know what's up, and that it will be over. But this doesn't let parents off the hook. We still have to teach our kids firmly what we expect of them.

Child development researchers have categorized the stages of children's growth and behavior in voluminous detail. Though your child may defy all of their predictions, the patterns they call attention to can often give you an accurate picture of what your child is going through and why. See the Further Reading section under Child Development (p. 340) for reliable sources in this interesting field.

THE POSITIVE SIDE

At least three quarters of the big discipline/teaching job can be concentrated on the positive side of things — with never a No or a Don't. When kids do things you like, you praise them. We praise and applaud new accomplishments like learning to walk, and by the same token we should try to praise new accomplishments like playing peacefully with another child or asking for a cookie instead of demanding it. Since these acts are the norm for adults, we sometimes forget to recognize them as the giant steps in the right direction they are for a child.

By praising behavior you approve of, you make your child want to repeat what he did that won the praise. Oh, there will be plenty of backsliding to the old, disapproved behavior — no lesson is ever learned the first time it's read through. But kids are looking for approval from Dad and Mom — it's as strong a force as any in determining how they act. And if your child knows he can get your approval by *not* kicking the back of the driver's seat, he is likelier to keep his feet down.

It's hard to remember to notice and remark on things like this and it may seem an elaborate courtesy to extend to a small child. But it certainly won't harm anything at the end of a car trip to say, "Thanks, I enjoyed that kickless ride."

It also feels good to be able to tell kids things like this. So often you get stuck in the dreary grind of correcting a child for one thing after another. "Settle down now . . . No, that's not the way . . . If

you'll just come over here and let me help you . . . Darn it, I *told* you it wouldn't work that way . . ." You know the scene if your child is over three. There's no fun in it, and not much instruction either — but we're stuck with it because we're human and we're fathers. For me it's like a jump in a clear cold mountain pool on a raging hot day, to be able to say, after one of these dismal sessions of nagging: "Hey, I'm proud of you for doing it that way . . ." It's the best part of discipline/teaching.

Another positive step is giving kids small rewards for doing things you want them to. Many parents shy away from this tactic because it sounds like bribery. And it is bribery if you use it all the time and your kids learn that they can always set up a "deal." "Sure, I'll be quiet if you buy me a whistle pop." Kids learn quickly to drive a hard bargain, and if you get in the habit of haggling back, you find yourself being fleeced. Of course, steer clear of bribery and bargains. But an occasional treat as a reward for some act you admire isn't a bribe — any more than an Olympic gold metal is a bribe to make a young athlete run fast. It's deserved recognition.

Lollipops and gum can work wonders in shaping good behavior, but rewards don't always come in candy wrappers. Your affection and approval are among the most effective rewards; sometimes the prize will be a smile or a hug or even a wink.

In the jargon of the social scientists, the whole positive approach is known as *positive reinforcement* and it is sometimes spoken of as a *behavior*

modification technique, which makes it sound like a method for manipulating experimental animals. But it's not that way at all. By trying to approach children always from the positive side, you set an optimistic tone for your lives together, and you tell them loud and clear that you respect and appreciate their efforts to learn. That's hardly manipulation. It's good manners, good morale, and good sense.

There's no age limit on the positive approach — it will work with all kids, with your wife, with people you see every day at work . . .

PROPAGANDA

"I propagandize my kids to get them to do what I want," one father told me. "I lay it on really heavy, butter it up thick, repeat it till they know what I'm talking about. I figure the advertisers and the media are getting through to them with their dumb messages, I might as well pump 'em a little with the things I believe in."

Propaganda — advertising if you prefer — works wonderfully on kids and it's easy to adapt for your purposes as a father. A preschooler's thinking is very direct — no subtleties, little room for doubt — and kids are totally open to suggestion. Notice sometime how they salivate when they see a hamburger ad on TV.

Take a simple example. A four-year-old is getting into the habit of saying at dinner: "*Get* me something to drink!" in the most demanding way. Irritating. You can tell him: "No, *don't* talk to me that way!" But if you do, you'll probably end up saying, "No, don't talk to me that way," at every meal, getting more and more irritated, and using harsher measures to stop your child's demands. In the end you succeed only in creating a fixed ritual — nasty demand countered by annoyed parents.

Try in the first place to propagandize this four-year-old with a positive idea of what you expect from him. Telling him No and Don't — besides antagonizing the kid and polarizing the situation — doesn't give him any idea what might be *acceptable* behavior. And though he may seem very grown-up and capable in many ways, he may have no idea at all what would be correct. So tell him: "A good way to say that would be: 'Gosh, I don't have anything to drink. Could you get me something to drink, please.'" This won't sink in right away, particularly

if the child is stuck for the moment on a lot of nasty "Get me's." But keep up the good propaganda. Give him five different sweet and charming speeches to choose from to use for getting a glass of milk. And don't give him any milk until he uses one. The idea will get through. After a week or so he may be making up his own pretty little milk speeches.

Unfortunately, this approach can't be applied across the board to all situations. Among other things, it takes a razor-sharp wit to come up with a positive slant on every situation, and events constantly overtake you. It takes a very cool head to say anything but NO when you find your three-year-old poking the baby in the eye with a Tinkertoy dowel. But after the shouting has died down, you can do a little propagandizing and teaching even on this count.

Baby poking and baby shoving are crimes of passion and they are regular repeat offenses. Propa-

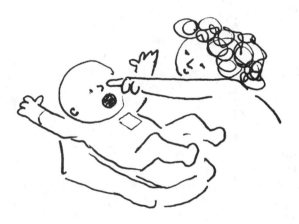

ganda can help, because with patience you can explain and demonstrate to an older child gentle, acceptable ways to behave with the baby, and she will try to do them to please you. Punishment will help, too, in this situation. But with all the good intentions and good techniques you can muster, you probably won't be able to root out the jealousy that explodes when one child lays into another.

Propaganda, though, *will* offer the baby attacker an alternative system that she can try to use, and this system will become part of the "conscience" she is building, and the attacks on the baby will become a little less frequent — especially when the baby grows up a bit and learns to counterattack.

SETTING LIMITS

A major part of the job of discipline/teaching is in figuring out exactly what it is you want to teach. Defining where the limits are. The broad goals are ones most parents agree on, even take for granted. We all want our kids to learn to control their behavior so they'll be able to live in a world with other people. But beyond that come the practical, everyday decisions as to what the limits should be in your own home and for your own very individual kids.

I'm talking about decisions like these: Should the kids be allowed to use the garden hose whenever they like, and if not, when may they use it and under

what conditions? Is actual sitting necessary at the dinner table, or is kneeling on the chair orderly enough — and at what age? Is it okay for a three-year-old to give his dad the Bronx cheer — because it *is* funny — or should this be treated as disrespect and stomped out?

These are hardly earthshaking decisions. A child's eventual success or failure as a competent human isn't riding on any or all of them. Every family will decide them differently, according to the personalities of the decision makers, because they don't involve the direct teaching of recognized, established norms. So why bother to decide them at all? Why not let these little things work themselves out in the course of events?

Why not? Because kids want to know. They want concrete guidelines on the day-to-day affairs of their lives, so they will know how they are expected to behave. They want to know *precisely* what the limits are so they can either stay within them or push just past them to see if you really meant it.

If we don't give our kids clear limits, we stick them with a major dilemma: What *is* the world like? What *does* it expect? A child needs an immediate and reliable source for information this important. And obviously a child can't work with abstractions and generalizations like "good behavior" and "moral conduct." She needs day-by-day answers: "Is it okay to paddle with my hands in the toilet?" "Do I *have* to

eat this yucky stuff?" "Can I stay up till the next commercial?" These are the kinds of questions kids are looking for answers to.

If we can supply the answers and set the limits for them, our kids will take over from there, systematize the material, and shape the big answers for themselves. They will see the pattern emerging as all the little limits point them toward "good behavior" and "moral conduct."

A one-year-old needs limits for his own protection. A two-year-old wants the limits so he can flaunt them and show you he's independent. A three-year-old will use the limits to help build a working "conscience." A four-year-old will systematically test the limits by pushing past them to see if they stick. And most five-year-olds will settle graciously into trying to live within them. But at every stage, from the moment they can understand anything you tell them, your kids will make good use of the limits you set.

Many small matters you can decide arbitrarily, but there are a couple of things to watch out for in setting limits. Whatever the demands we make on our kids, we should be pretty sure they are physically capable of meeting them, and emotionally ready for them, too. By this, I don't mean anything very complex; you don't have to be a Ph.D. in child development to be sensitive to the fact that a five-year-old can be expected to sit still at the dinner table for a little while, but the same thing can't be demanded of a two-year-old. It can probably be forced on a child of any age, but is it worth it in the long run? Kids need clear, firm limits to work within, not unreachable goals or harsh restrictions.

How do you present limits? Certainly you aren't going to carve them on stone like the Ten Commandments and awe your kids with a list of Thou Shalt Nots. The limits will be established as answers to children's questions and as instructions that are repeated day in and day out. And they will change from week to week as your kids change and you get glimpses and insights into what they need.

When you're going into a new situation with a child, though, say a visit to a store she's never been to before or to people she's never met, a detailed set of rules and restrictions clearly laid down beforehand will help a preschooler control her behavior. If she knows beforehand precisely what you think she should do in the situation, she'll have an easier time living up to your expectations.

Kids also need responsible explanations of the

limits. A father of four put it this way: "I think the worst thing in the world is just to lay down a bunch of rules and then walk away. Well, those rules are fine, but if somebody should question the rules later on to the kid, the answer 'My father said it's no good' doesn't hold up. That's all right for a while, but when he starts to realize and to question, he's got to have more of something to grab hold of — not just, 'He said it was wrong,' but *why* he said it's wrong."

Lying

Most parents are shocked when at age four their child starts to lie. She's always been so good, you think, she's never done anything like this before. Before four kids don't know how to lie. At four they do it because it's new and they find that it's sometimes useful and effective. But most of the lies a four-year-old tells are whoppers that you can spot a mile away. When lying starts you naturally come down hard on it and try to stomp it out.

Besides drawing the line and being firm about lies, though, some positive fatherly teaching will go a long way. Without some background explanation and practice a preschooler can't distinguish precisely between lies, jokes, and stories. They all have a common element as far as he's concerned — you tell something that's not true. It's confusing for a four-year-old that people laugh at a joke, listen with interest to a made-up story, but get angry at you when you tell a lie. The difference between these forms lies in the motivation of the speaker, which is a sophisticated notion for a preschooler to grasp. A child eventually figures out the difference by himself, after first adjusting to the situation either by

getting better at lies so they won't be detected and draw your wrath or by deciding not to tell them for the same pragmatic reason. But with your patience and instruction he can learn what a lie is from the start and why people don't like one, and he may choose to concentrate his newfound ability to stretch the truth on telling outrageous tall tales and bad jokes.

"Bad" Language

When a preschooler brings home a "bad" word and tries it out for effect, he expects to get a rise out of you. He also wants you to help him categorize his new four-letter treasure as "bad," because kids like to have things neatly polarized — bad words and good words — so they can say the bad ones when they feel the itch to get in trouble.

$$\#**!\&?\#\%***!!!$$

For helping your child prune her vocabulary of some of the "crap" she hears all around, a useful distinction that she can understand is whether it's a kids' word or an adult word. When she says, "That's a lot of crap. Is that a bad word, Daddy?" you can try something like: "It's not a word for kids; it's a word that grown-ups sometimes use, and, yes, I think it's a bad word. Use a kids' word like *junk* or *crud.*" Give your kid a whole tough alternative vocabulary of approved kids' words: SHOOT! SHUCKS! DRAT! BLAST! RATS! ACID! DARN! ETC.! ETC.! Your kids are still going to surprise and embarrass you with four-letter words at inappropriate times and sometimes delight you by using them at precisely the right moment. But the distinction between kids' words and grown-up words gives a preschooler a clear idea of where those words belong. And preschool kids tend to stick with children's words in most cases. Every child over the age of three knows the adult four-letter word for "poopies," but kids use their own version for years.

Here is an interesting thought on children and bad language from Robert Burton's *Anatomy of Melancholy* (1621): "Diogenes struck the father when the son swore."

CONSISTENCY

Whatever their personal styles of discipline — and these ranged from laissez-faire avoidance to toe-the-line authority — almost all the fathers I talked to stressed the importance of *consistency* in dealing with their kids. Some of them had learned its importance roundabout — by being inconsistent — while others had come to respect it as a method that got results.

One man put it this way: "You have to be consistent. If your kid's doing something you don't like, and just because you're kind of tired or you've got a hangover, or whatever, you let it slide, then the kid doesn't know — he doesn't understand that next time you don't have a hangover or you're not quite so tired . . ."

We all learn as parents that children thrive on order of all sorts. We notice that our children play more contentedly and imaginatively in a room that's straightened up than in one that confounds them with a messy jumble of toys competing for their attention. We find that they are much happier if they have very regular hours for meals, nap, bedtime, and we notice how cantankerous they can be when they're thrown off their schedules. These kinds of order obviously give children an important sense of stability and security. And the *consistency* that so many fathers talk about in terms of discipline is just one more orderly structure that we can give them to make their lives — and ours — a lot easier and often a lot happier.

Consistency means sticking by the limits you've set up, and following through in the same way with the same reward or the same punishment as often as you need to. It means not giving in to screaming and pouting. It means explaining the same thing hundreds of times till it sinks in. It also means a united front from Dad and Mom — the kids will know that there is no easy appeal to a different court, that they will find the same brand of justice wherever they turn, from parents who have discussed and agreed on how the important issues should be handled.

Of course you can be *too* consistent. You always have to watch that you don't slip over into rigidity — because there's such a thin and easily crossed line between helpful consistency and deadly dogmatism. Such a thin line that often it's impossible to know which side you're on. I feel like the dreariest of dogmatists each evening at dinner when I say:

"No, you may only have your dessert if you finish your supper first." And yet I know that Gregory has come to depend on that ritual phrase, that it is nearly as much a piece of his dinner-eating equipment as his knife, his fork, or his spoon.

Another part of consistency is the phrases — most of them instructions and most of them negative — that we find ourselves stuck with and repeating dozens of times a day. "Use a quiet, indoor voice." "Stop opening the refrigerator door." "Be gentle with the baby." These phrases never seem to have the desired effect — or any effect at all. The whole family is bored with them. So should we save ourselves the trouble and not bother? I don't think so. It looks like we're stuck with this one as parents. We're like workers in tedious repetitive jobs on an assembly line, day in and day out turning the same bolt in the same direction with the same wrench. The worker is so wearied by his job that he becomes indifferent to the fact that the cars coming past his wrench are getting built and that his turn of the bolt is a small but nonetheless vital part of the process.

The message does sink in after a while. At least by age twenty-one kids seldom need to be reminded to use an indoor voice or stop opening the fridge. You never notice the exact moment at which you stop saying these things. It's like the disappearance of pain. You hate it while it's there, but you never notice as it leaves — it's just gone and it won't be till much later that you remember.

KIDS' IDEAS

On matters of discipline, parents consult child care experts, they consult their own consciences, they consult between one another. About the only person who isn't consulted is the child who is the object of all this. At the beginning of the course of discipline/teaching, kids are too young to make any contributions — it's a straight lecture course, not a seminar. So when your children are old enough to have something constructive to contribute, you're usually so used to *not* consulting them that it hardly even presents itself as a reasonable thing to do.

I'm not talking about making discipline a democratic family process in which preschoolers have an equal voice — that's a cute idea, but hardly practical. I simply mean asking kids from time to time what they think a proper punishment should be for a specific act. Or asking them in a quiet, fresh moment how they feel when they are punished for particular things. As you know, preschoolers are very open, and they are likely to surprise you with thoughtful answers as well as perspectives on the situation you hadn't considered.

You're apt to discover, for instance, that a four-year-old is carrying around attitudes like this: "Children do bad things, but grown-ups never do." In fact, this particular misconception haunts the mind of nearly every preschooler, and of course it's not at all the point you're going to so much trouble to drive home with discipline/teaching. I discussed this with Gregory, at four, and he said boldly: "You make mistakes, Daddy." But then very apologetically and backpedaling like mad, he added: "But almost never!" Kids seldom voluntarily tell you about attitudes like these; it takes some prying to get them to the surface, where you can help a child deal with them and learn differently.

Confirmed nonspankers are liable to discover, by asking their children, that their kids' ideas about corporal punishment are very different from their own. At nursery school, in the park, wherever they congregate, kids discuss the important issues in their world, and punishment is one of the liveliest topics. They swap stories: "My daddy swacked me." "My mommy whupped me." Unless your kid is in solitary confinement, by age four she'll know plenty about spanking and it will more than likely be what she regards as the norm for the correction and guidance of kids. I'm not saying that you ought to spank because other parents do. But it's worth considering what your kids *expect*, and asking them about it. Many parents who resist spanking, but finally give in under intense provocation, discover — to their great surprise — that the spanking clears the air.

Sometimes for kids it will be the swift, clearcut, and realistic way for the situation to be resolved. Even in some sense a way out for the child.

Solutions

Preschool kids can make a very positive contribution to the discipline/learning scene by finding their own solutions to their own problems — a process that you can encourage and assist at every turn. Say your three-year-old is racing from one room to another. "Stop running!" may not even attract her attention. Try grabbing her and saying: "I can't let you run indoors. Can you find something else to do?" That may get her thinking along new lines, but also prod her with suggestions: "How about listening to a record? How about doing a puzzle? . . ." You're working toward the moment when she'll say: "Hey, *I* have a good idea — I'll . . ."

Or two kids fighting over a toy may need your arbitration. If you can display the diplomacy of a Henry Kissinger, you may be able to lead them to finding their own solution: "Let's take turns. I'm first . . ."

Helping kids find their own solutions isn't an easy task and it won't produce quick results. In the two situations above, the running child would probably have ended up on the couch pouting, and the kids fighting over the toy would probably have had to be separated when they renewed the argument, this time fighting over first turn. It will take months or even years of patient work before you see clear indications that the idea has gotten through to your child, before you discover him one day without any adult help, arbitrating a sticky issue with a neighbor child: "Now, let's find a different way; maybe you can give me half . . ."

For my money, though, this is effort well spent, because your child has learned that problems needn't create dead ends. He's learned that a problem is a road to a solution and he's learned to look for positive steps to take every time a problem emerges.

ACTION

The phrase "Actions speak louder than words" must have been coined by a parent with preschool kids. "How many times do I have to tell you that?" I find myself saying — and I hear my own parents saying the same thing to me. I wasn't listening either. If I was making noise, I was listening to my own noise; if I was running from room to room there wasn't time to stop to understand a direction, even if the direction was Stop. Kids get giddy and wound up and they *don't* listen to what you tell them.

You can shout louder in an effort to be heard, or you can take action — pick up this stone-deaf troublemaker and move him somewhere else. To a corner, to his room, to a "quiet chair." The place

you move him to will vary with his age and his needs at the time. And the amount of time he'll be able to stay put there to consider his misdeed will start off at about fifteen seconds and after years of practice hit a possible outside limit of ten minutes at age five or six — unless he's tired and forgets and falls asleep.

When you want to interrupt what your child is doing, it's action that does the trick, not talk. If the offense is trivial, you'll move her to something new

that's fun. It's the tactic you learn with babies and toddlers, but it continues to work — with changes and refinements — until your kids are too heavy to pick up and move easily. When you move your child from something destructive or especially irritating to you, you also have to do some talking and explain precisely why you're moving her and why you're angry.

A four-year-old who has been mesmerized by his own screaming voice hasn't even registered your three reasonable requests for quiet, and when on your fourth you look and act angry and move him to his quiet chair, he may have no idea at all what is going on. When the tears stop, ask him why you moved him, and you'll find out what he's thinking: "Because you hate me, Daddy. Because you're angry at me." He's dead wrong — you're angry at what he did, not at him. But how is he to know this unless you explain it with care? And you have to explain this distinction over and over in many ways for years before your kids fully understand it. But each time this misunderstanding crops up, you can clear it up with an explanation of what your child did that was wrong, and a big warm father bear hug — when you're satisfied the message has sunk in.

PUBLIC PUNISHMENT

It's rare and noteworthy when you see an angry parent in a public place pick up a misbehaving child and without a word leave the room or the scene, to reprimand the child in private. This habit is to me the most attractive public trait a parent can have — not because it avoids unpleasant and embarrassing scenes, but because it allows the child to save face.

When a kid gets a well-deserved dressing down or swat in front of a crowd of strangers in a store or in the park in front of friends, the pain is doubled, and pointlessly. The important part of the disciplinary message can be gotten across in private — out in the parking lot in the car, or down the street in a quiet place — and without heaping humiliation on top of blame.

I'm always impressed when I see a parent do this, because I know that anger quickly takes over in punishment situations like this, and that it takes a very even temper to remember to pick your child up and get away from the audience.

Fathers in general are much more easily embarrassed by the misbehavior of their kids in public than full-time mothers are. Mothers get used to it, and they have a surer sense that other people — especially other mothers — who witness it will understand and forgive. But for a novice father, a two-year-old's temper tantrum at the Burger King can be a really humiliating experience. Grin and bear it — it happens to everybody.

SPANKING

Though preschool kids, from comparing notes with their friends, are usually perfectly at home with the idea of spanking, it can be a real bugbear for some of their parents. Whether or not, how hard, how often — all the ramifications. If you look in child care manuals that are ten years old — from the now

generally repudiated "permissive" era — you discover that they either duck the issue or imply that you should never spank. More recent authorities are likely to say that it's okay from time to time, but imply that most of the benefit goes to the spanker — who works out his frustration by doing it.

Meanwhile, confident parents make their own decisions about what to do, using common sense considerations like this one from a father of four: "If I had not been spanked as a child, I might wonder if it was going to hurt the child, but I don't believe it's going to hurt." And here's a father of three: "You know, spanking your child for running out in the street isn't child abuse." Still another father, who has two preschool boys, said: "Spanking for me is like the H-bomb of discipline. I sure as hell don't want to use it, but if I gave it up, it would be like unilateral disarmament, and I figure there's no reason to dump the whole arsenal if I can keep it as a deterrent. And it is a deterrent, 'cause you can bet that kids respect spanking."

Parents who hesitate, trying to be "modern" or "permissive" and never spank, and then are provoked into it, are often delighted with the results: they feel better, the child feels better. Instead of hating you as a tyrant, an infrequently spanked child may well respect the fact that you will take a firm stance.

How hard? Here is the father of a four-and-a-half-year-old: "When she knows she's done something really wrong, you can just barely tap her and she'll break out into tears. By the same token, you can be teasing with her and hit her even harder and she'll just laugh."

What age to start? With a baby or a toddler, a tap on the hand gets the results you're looking for. When the tap on the hand doesn't get the attention of a really terrible two or three-year-old, it may be time to switch.

Naturally, spanking in some circumstances can be the worst solution. If it's done in a fury or with no attempt to talk things through, or as the last straw in a squabble that starts and ends in misunderstanding, it can only aggravate matters. But if it comes as a response to a child's forcefully and extravagantly stated demand for limit setting — which is to say he has found some perfect way to drive you up the wall and moving him to a new place and reasoning with him don't help . . . Or if your child has done something that you have every reason to want to discourage — like getting lost in the woods or pushing her little sister downstairs . . .

Many fathers feel that their bark is as good as their bite, that a deep-voiced growl can command as much attention as a swat, and that the growl is a father's most versatile disciplinary tool. For many kids the growl will do the trick, but I think it's only one of many useful disciplinary tools. And ahead of it *and* of spanking, in ascending order of versatility and usefulness, I'd have to put a father's patience, his understanding, and above all, his ability to *Teach* his kids with every tool and technique at his disposal.

A CHILD'S DON'TS

Kids get Don't This and Don't That from morning to night. It's always refreshing to hear a preschooler, with right on her side, turn the tables:

"Don't smoke that cigarette, Daddy."

"Don't lean back in the chair, Dad."

"Don't chew the ice. It's bad for your teeth."

"Don't put your feet on the coffee table."

"You oughta untie your shoes when you take them off."

UNEQUAL JUSTICE

"If I growl at Marc, he is crushed — he just falls back crying. Serious crying, not alligator tears — I mean he is crushed that I had to talk to him that way. Where with Lucas, you can talk to him that way and he'll look at you and smile and keep right on doing it."

No matter how even-handed their father would

like to be in dispensing justice to Marc and Lucas, there's no way he can treat them identically. They are two years apart — two and four — and they are two very distinct personalities. He will have to escalate a little with Lucas and tone things down a bit with Marc.

Before we have children and we see this kind of thing going on, we're quick to say: "*I'll* never treat *my* kids differently that way." You have to be a parent to know what this is all about. Even with a single child, you still don't have that clear understanding of the profound differences between kids' personalities that you get when there are two children in the house and you experience it first hand. In talking to a lot of fathers it was interesting to me to notice that the more kids a man had, the more he seemed to talk about the differences between them, differences that you become acutely aware of because they color your relationships with your kids and make it impossible to treat them identically.

As children, we shove some of our natural jealousy toward our brothers and sisters off on Dad by saying: "He favors Mary," or, "He always coddles little Joe." As parents, we begin to understand what really may have been behind this. Mary and Little Joe had special needs that Dad had to meet. It wasn't necessarily his favoritism. Their personalities shaped his responses to them.

We're dealing here with a fact of life, the wonderful fact of human diversity. Kids have recognizable personalities from the day they are born. Their genes stamp them with pure biological individuality, and their experiences, ages, and stages mark them ever more indelibly as special entities. They can't be treated identically because they simply are not identical — even if they're look-alike twins.

Of course we should *try* to deal evenly and give evenly to our children. Surely we'll figure out a way to give our love equally. But for the rest, we can only try, though we can point out to our kids — often and in ways they can understand — that they *are* special and different, and that each is treated in a special way because he is unlike all others. That's what we are saying when we explain: "It's okay for Timothy to do that, because he's one, but I can't let you do it, because you are a big boy and know better." It's one of the hardest lessons for a child to learn, but when he has finally understood it, it is a basic part of his understanding of how the world really works.

EMANCIPATION PROCLAMATION

Abe Lincoln took many a severe whipping as a boy from his backwoods father. With his own children he adopted a strikingly modern notion of discipline that didn't fit at all with the prevailing view.

He treated them with great kindness and respect and encouraged them with praise. His wife, Mary Todd, remembered and wrote down this little family Emancipation Proclamation that the great man had uttered: "It is my pleasure that my children are free, happy and unrestrained by parental tyranny. Love is the chain whereby to bind a child to its parents."

Some of Lincoln's contemporaries, however, weren't too impressed with the practical results of this regimen. William Herndon, Lincoln's early law partner, wrote many years afterwards of Sunday visits by Abe and his boys to the law offices they shared: "Lincoln would turn Willie and Tad loose in our office, and they soon gutted the room, gutted the shelves of books, rifled the drawers, and riddled boxes, battered the points of my gold pens against the stairs, turned over the inkstands on the papers, scattered letters over the office, and danced over them and the like. I have felt many a time that I wanted to wring the necks of these brats and pitch them out of the windows, but out of respect for Lincoln and knowing that he was abstracted, I shut my mouth, bit my lips, and left for parts unknown."

Chapter 9

LEARNING WITH KIDS

"Daddy, can a woodpecker poke a hole in an elephant's skin?"

"Flies are the one animal we can kill — right? Why can we kill flies?"

"What was this hot dog when it was alive?"

"Where is God?"

"How did dinosaurs brush their teeth?"

The floodgate of questions opens up at about age four, and from there on out you're faced with daily posers. Many are hard to answer, but you seldon hear one that doesn't deserve an answer.

Gregory wants to know about God, motorcycles,

sex, salamanders, death, guns, rockets, quartz crystals, skin color, prehistoric animals, divorce. Nothing he sees or hears about escapes untouched by his curiosity. He's interested in things I haven't given a thought to in years and in others that I've never even noticed, and as he explores new territory, I find myself exploring along with him — grabbing books right and left to fill myself in so I can supply the answers he's looking for, and sorting out my ideas and opinions about the tough issues like Sex, Death, and Religion till they're clear enough in my mind that I can boil them down for preschool consumption. When Gregory and Timothy want to know how things work — why it doesn't rain inside the house, how the picture gets into the TV, where the rocks come from — it's right back to basics. If I can't explain, we find a book from the library that can. We disassemble toys to see what makes them tick, do simple experiments, build primitive machines. I haven't learned so much in years.

SUPPLYING THE ANSWERS

Quick, clear, to-the-point answers will keep a preschool child's questions coming — growing sharper all the time. It's kids who get the feedback of good answers who learn to ask better questions, and it's the astute question askers who learn the most.

Asking a child lots of questions in return also keeps up the flow of her Whys and How Comes.

Kids love to be quizzed so they can shine by answering correctly. Not tough quizzes that put them on the spot, but questions that get them to practice things they've learned recently or know well. Preschoolers don't get turned off or worn out by too many questions the way adults do. They ask so many themselves, they must expect questions in return.

With the questions flying in both directions — from child to father and from father to child — everybody learns.

READINESS

When you notice your child at nine months pulling himself up on every piece of furniture he sees, you know it's time to start walking lessons, and for every other skill or accomplishment you're likely to see indications from your child — clues that tell you he's ready to go.

It's always possible to teach a child something long before she's "ready for it" — but it's hard work. You can practice weekend after weekend with a three-year-old teaching her to catch a ball in her hands instead of with her outstretched arms as she naturally tries to do at this point, and with a lot of fairly dreary effort you may help her work up the skill. On the other hand, you can have a terrific time kicking the ball around with her at three and wait till she's four and a half, when her developing co-ordination will allow her to grab the ball with her hands. You can push arithmetic problems on a four-year-old who is learning the sequence of the numbers, and with a lot of practicing you may help him learn a few sums by rote. But if you help him concentrate on the part he's really interested in — counting — until he has it squarely under his belt, you will start to see an interest in adding and subtracting showing itself naturally at five. That's the time to get out the apples and oranges for some concrete math at the kitchen table. The learning

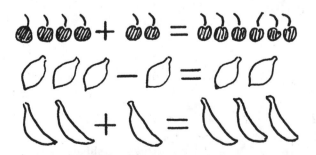

will go like a breeze and you'll soon have to switch from fruit to crayons to do bigger sums in a small space.

Even though it's possible to predict with some accuracy the age at which most kids will be physically and intellectually ready to learn a particular skill, each child advances very much at her own rate. There may be months between the "readiness point" for walking of two kids in the same family, and later on, between the same two kids there may even be years between the points at which they are ready to start reading.

There are always exceptions in every task — the two-year-old who learns to cast with a rod and reel, which is usually a hard job at six; the kid who can tie her shoes at four instead of the usual five and a half; the mechanical whiz who can keep a screwdriver in the slot and twist the screw out at two. Every child develops a precocious specialty or two, and if you spot your kid starting on a new skill and strike while the iron is hot, you may be able to help her work it up into something for the whole family to brag about. Gregory at two and a half would always look closely at the faces on the coins I'd take out of my pocket and show him, and he'd ask who the men were. He was so interested in the faces that, with a little regular coaching, it was no time before he had names for all of them — Abe Lincoln, Thomas Jepferson, Roosevelt Franklin on the dime, and Ike with no hair on the big silver dollar. He gloried in the attention and applause he'd get from adults when he named them, and he really wowed the teller at the bank by identifying Alexander Hamilton on a ten-dollar bill. But it was a relatively easy conquest for him, because all kids at two and a half are learning names — thousands of names for everything and everyone around them.

Problems crop up, though, when it's the child next door or your brother's kid who is being bragged about. Johnny has learned to ride a two-wheeler at three. Your child is five and can't. It's easy enough to conclude that there's something wrong with your child; and your child is sure to decide there's something wrong with him. A five-year-old, however, has time to spare for learning to ride a bike and doesn't need extra pressure from Dad and from himself to succeed. The best help you can give him — besides bike-riding lessons — is to help him try to understand that Johnny is fast; he isn't slow; each kid learns at a different rate. If he can appreciate this, the intense pressure he may feel to keep up won't stop him from trying altogether.

The best judges of a child's readiness for new accomplishments are always her parents. Books, including this one, can only estimate when most kids are ready for this or that. Friends, neighbors, and relatives who push their kids and exaggerate their accomplishments will tempt you to push your kids beyond what they're ready for. But you see your kids every day and know their interests and abilities. If you can stay one small jump ahead of them, trying to keep things at the level they've reached, you'll help them sail through early learning.

LOOKING IT UP

A child acquires a wonderful habit naturally if her parents help her look through books for answers to her questions. A one-year-old who likes kitties will be thrilled with a library book about them. A three-year-old who is into rockets will be blasted off by a kids' book about space exploration. By four and a half a child who is used to looking things up will be able to understand how an index works and how it gives you command over all the answers in the book. The library card catalogue is another ready

source of information that a preschooler can easily appreciate — it's not a mystery that has to wait till college years to be revealed. A four-year-old who wants to know about rain or wolves or racing cars can find illustrated books about them by searching the card catalogue with Dad or Mom.

I always like the fresh perspective Gregory brings to an adult book. Looking through a big history of art text together when he was nearly five, we came across a full-page color illustration of an ancient Greek plate with a picture on it of Herakles wrestling a lion. "Hey, look," says Gregory, "this guy is a superhero, 'cause he's fighting a lion. Do you know who winned the fight?"

From about age four and a half, most kids are happy to join you in looking at illustrated adult books that will interest both of you. Even though many kiddie books are extremely informative and well illustrated, it can be a refreshing change of pace to share with a child a thick adult volume full of photos of whales or railroads or arachnids.

Learning from Kids

It's always a surprise to learn something from a small child, because you're sure you know much more than he does. Or you hope you do. Sometimes I wonder. Gregory, at four and a half, was asking his usual questions about sharks at dinner: "If mouses lived next to the ocean, would sharks eat them? How come a killer whale eats sharks? Sharks eat garbage. Do sharks smell the garbage?"

"No, Gregory," I said, "Sharks can't smell. Fish don't have noses." Rita chimed in: "Sharks don't have noses because they are fish — they breathe through gills instead, which are slits on the sides behind their heads." We were doing as model modern parents should, and answering our child's questions intelligently and to the point.

The next day I was in a public library. My eye happened to catch on the Natural History shelves, and a little voice at the back of my mind asked: "Do sharks smell the garbage?" With a moment's browsing I found a book called *The Sixth Sense of Animals* by Maurice Burton (New York: Taplinger, 1973), and the chapter headings led me to "The World of Odours." The words leaped off the page:

> *A first-class clue to the smelling abilities of the higher animals is in the proportions of the brain. In the front of the brain is a pair of olfactory lobes in which the information from the olfactory membrane is processed. In fishes these are relatively large. In sharks they are enormous, and sharks find their food mainly by smell.*

Reading on, I discovered a whole World of Odours that I had never suspected the existence of. The ink of the octopus, it turns out, isn't used as a smokescreen under which to retreat from danger, as most people believe. The ink disperses too slowly in the water to make an effective screen. Instead, it contains a chemical that interrupts the sense of smell of the moray eel, who preys on the octopus and hunts him largely by smell in the murky depths.

Taking a hint from this passage, Gregory, Timothy, and I have done what we call the Octopus Experiment half a dozen times. With an eyedropper we squirt ink, and sometimes bright food coloring, into a large bowl of water. But the ink always takes a full countdown of ten to start to spread — plenty of time for the moray eel to see and seize the octopus if the ink were only a smokescreen. And then Ding on the kitchen timer and the ink diffuses beautifully through the water, which is the part the kids like.

I think Gregory's question has been answered. "Do sharks smell the garbage?" Incidentally, in case you were wondering, it is true that sharks eat garbage, or trash, to be exact — old rusted pieces of metal and other debris are always turning up in sharks' stomachs.

TOUGH QUESTIONS

How do you explain things to your child that make no sense to you? "Daddy, why are there bad guys?" How do you help a kid come to terms with grim realities? "Dad, how come Jamie's daddy doesn't live in his house?" Tough questions. And there are Sex, Death, God — which always fascinate preschoolers.

Sex

Short answers will do fine. A three-year-old who asks where babies come from isn't looking for a lecture on obstetrics, but he is looking for straightforward, reliable information. The question will come up year after year, and each time your answer can be a little more sophisticated, a little more informative. Comparisons with animal behavior may help you get across your message, but the birds and the bees are poor examples to pick since the ways they do it are so different from the way we do.

In bookstores and libraries you'll find a variety of illustrated books designed to help parents introduce their kids to sex and reproduction. There seems to be one for every taste, even including a few in what to me is very bad taste. One of these, which is extremely popular, is illustrated with cartoon pictures of an ugly comic couple in bed together and makes sex seem a silly affair, while another features close-up photos of nude children exploring each other's bodies. But you can also find clear texts with

attractive illustrations that can help you organize your ideas and give you an orderly way to present the material to your child when you feel her repeated questions and detailed interest make her a good candidate for beginning sex education. An excellent book of this type is Andrew C. Andry and Steven Schepp, *How Babies Are Made* (New York: Time-Life, 1968).

God

Kids start to ask about God at age three. They hear that God made everything and ask: "How did God make the street lights? How did He make my sneakers?" The idea of God is a particularly hard one for preschoolers to understand, because He can't be seen, and children learn best through concrete experiences — seeing and touching. But even with this serious handicap to understanding, it's often surprising and touching how well a preschooler seems to come to grips with the concept of God. "God made Hisself," announced our four-year-old theologian one day from the back seat of the car.

There are also concrete ways a preschooler can get a handle on religion. Children love an exciting story like David and Goliath, where it's good guy against bad guy. And they understand that Jesus was a very good man when it's pointed out that he loved little children. Kids will always understand best stories and ideas that fall within their experience and interests.

Discussing theology with a preschooler forces you to decide exactly what it is you believe so you can put it in terms a child may understand. Gregory one evening was saying that God had made him, and Rita was trying to convince him that Mommy and Daddy had done it. I tried to mediate and explain that we were acting as agents for God, which only confused Gregory and started a little argument with Rita. Disgusted with the uncertainty of opposing notions, Gregory said: "If I throwed God and you both out, I could make myself all by myself — and Timothy too." An interesting Existentialist point of view.

Death

Preschoolers want to know about the difficult part of death — where your soul goes — which is what parents always go to great lengths to explain. But they are even more interested in the tangible part, the easily explained part — the mechanics of death. What do they do with all the bodies? Where do they put them? How? Matter-of-fact practical stuff. Ice, embalming fluid, caskets, backhoes, shovels, fires. There's nothing morbid about this interest. It's just healthy curiosity to know about everything, including how it will all end. A four- or a five-year-old will be fascinated by a short visit to a graveyard and a good explanation of how the graves are dug and what the stones say, because it will show her what does happen to all those dead people.

Explaining why a friend or a relative died and coping with your grief and your child's is another matter altogether. The death and burial of pets usually introduces children to death in a realistic way, but nothing prepares a child — or an adult — for the death of someone close.

Divorce

Perhaps the toughest question kids throw at parents is Divorce. Few children get through the preschool years without learning about it from friends — and sometimes from direct experience. A child who learns that daddies and mommies can break up and move apart will reach the conclusion that it will happen to her dad and mom — and she will be afraid. For a child, the fear of divorce is probably much more compelling and frightening than the fear of anything else, including death. Divorce is something horrible that happens to kids she knows — why should it not happen to her? Her questions can't be dismissed lightly with: It can't happen here. Because they are earnest questions about a serious matter, they deserve attention and thoughtful explanations of what divorce is and how it does affect many kids, but doesn't happen to many, many others.

EXPLAINING

Many fathers don't wait for their kids to ask all the questions, but go ahead and explain things wherever they are, whatever they're doing: how the brake stops the car, why the smoke is coming from the chimney, why you turn the hamburgers over when you cook them, where the water comes from before it gets to the faucets. Their kids are delighted to have this kind of information and ask to have it repeated again and again.

A preschooler wants instruction that is so basic it often doesn't occur to adults to supply it. He's fascinated to learn about mundane things that we take totally for granted: how a hammer functions, why people wear shoes, what windows are for, how pockets work. You don't have to stick only with bedrock basics, though, because he's excited to hear what you have to say about complex subjects, too — electricity or the life cycle of a tree. But he'll listen with the greatest attention when you show him exactly how a hinge works or how a brush distributes paint.

Questions like "Can I cut this rock with a sharp piece of glass?" aren't just silly ramblings. They're efforts to understand the basic properties of things. Tell what will cut a rock, and what things sharp glass will cut — including a kid's fingers. With good, hard information about everyday objects, materials, and simple machines, a child's ingenuity and imagination have the wherewithal to start functioning. It's a preschooler who has worked on basics who runs to get the bicycle pump to blow out a candle, who invents her own novel method for cracking peanut shells by riding over them with the front wheel of her tricycle.

Experiments

Long abstract explanations, of course, get nowhere with a preschool child. You have to keep everything short, and preferably you have some object or picture to talk about — a physical way to demonstrate your point.

Gregory, Timothy, and I like to call demonstrations Experiments. It makes them seem very important. Our experiments are usually super simple. Gregory will ask: "Which is the toughest, wood or metal?" So I'll get him to smack a 2″ x 4″ with a crowbar to find out, and then see if he can dent the crowbar by smacking it with the wood. For a further

experiment, we'll get a tin can and see what a good whack with a 2″ x 4″ will do to *thin* metal.

When Gregory wanted to know at three and a half why it didn't rain inside the house just as it did outside, we did an experiment. We put some toy figurines and toy furniture outside on the grass and turned a square plastic dishpan upside down over them to represent a house, and then we rained on the house with the garden hose, really giving it a storm from right overhead. But the figurines and furniture inside stayed dry, and Gregory learned how a roof functions.

I've included below instructions for some slightly more sophisticated experiments, most of which demonstrate scientific notions, but which primarily are great fun to do with kids. Many involve candles, balloons, food coloring, and other things that traditionally delight children, and these things are the most interesting part of an experiment at first for a preschooler. With repetition, the point of the exercise will sink in, too. And you *will* repeat the experiments — kids never let you get away with doing something only once.

Gas-filled Balloons   For this great rainy-Saturday quickie you will need:

    1 funnel
    2 teaspoons baking soda
    1 small beer, ale, OR soda bottle
    ⅓ cup vinegar
    1 small balloon

Using a funnel, help a four-year-old put the baking soda in the bottle. The vinegar is then poured into a balloon, also using a funnel. You now stretch the neck of the balloon over the mouth of the bottle. Pull the balloon down pretty far and hold onto it,

because the reaction between the vinegar — which your child will pour from the ballon — and the baking soda produces enough carbon dioxide and pressure to blow the balloon right off the top if it's on loosely. The mixture fizzes and bubbles and the balloon expands until it's plump and full.

A variation on this scheme is to put Alka-Seltzer in the bottle and pour water in from the balloon.

Still another method creates a hot-air balloon. Stretch an empty balloon over the mouth of an empty bottle. Now place the bottle in a deep saucepan with warm water surrounding it, and heat slowly on the stove. As the air in the bottle grows warmer, it expands and inflates the balloon. The hot-air balloon is less spectacular for a child than the other two, because the balloon doesn't get very big.

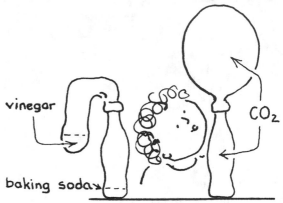

Shiny Pennies   Break the piggy bank and empty your pockets — gather up all the dirty old pennies in the house. This little chemistry experiment will give them all a brand-new luster. A preschooler can mix up in a cup a solution of:

    4 tablespoons salt
    ½ cup vinegar

When all the salt has dissolved, your kids can put in the filthy pennies and stir them around in the cup. The solution works quickly, but let the kids keep stirring this witch's brew for a while. Help dip the sparkling shiny pennies out with a spoon and drain them on paper towels. Gregory and Timothy voted this their absolute favorite among all the dozens of experiments we've performed.

Ice   Try freezing water in some eccentric shapes. Kids love to make a big ice ball by filling a small balloon with water from the tap and popping it into the freezer. For a cold hand, fill a rubber glove with

water — then use clothespins to hold it wrist-upright inside a gallon milk carton with the top cut off.

Freeze a penny in the middle of a cube of ice, or a small toy in the middle of a block of it. First, you freeze about half of the cube or block. Next the penny or toy is placed on this layer and the mold is filled the rest of the way with water and put back in the freezer. A paper milk carton of any size makes a good mold for a block of ice; paper cups and plastic containers will give you a variety of shapes.

Kids get a kick out of putting food coloring in water that will be frozen, and they'll be interested to find that you don't get evenly colored ice — the color mostly goes to the middle. Any ice shape you make will be licked and gnawed on till it disappears. Add a little fruit juice for a touch of flavor, and always give kids a large plastic basin when they play with ice shapes.

Midwinter is the best time for ice experiments — you can do big ones without taking up any room in the freezer. My kids like to make a frozen "lake" in a big plastic basin; they bring it inside and "skate" toy figurines around on its surface.

Cutting Ice   Freeze a large block of ice using a quart milk carton for a mold, or an ice cube tray without the dividers. Arrange it as a bridge between the seats of two straight chairs, or between blocks that will keep it a couple of feet off the ground. Wrap a

piece of wire around it and attach some heavy object at the bottom — a hammer will do. A basin or newspaper underneath will catch most of the dripping. The wire cuts slowly through the block of ice and falls through below. But mysteriously the ice is still perfectly intact. As the wire works its way down, melting a path as it goes, the water flows up into the crack and refreezes, sealing the gap. What will you have to do to cut the block cleanly in half? Another experiment.

Colored Water   This experiment may seem too simple to you, but it will probably be your child's favorite. Help a three-year-old or older child fill small clear bottles with water and then squeeze food coloring into them — the primary colors that are supplied, and mixed colors, too. That's really all there is to it. Kids delight in watching the coloring dye the water and the colors mixing to make new ones, and they like to see a bright light shining through the jars. When your child is through admiring the colors, cap the jars and put them on a sunny windowsill, where he can continue to marvel at the light streaming through them.

Along the same lines is the Whirlpool Experiment. With a wooden spoon or rubber spatula, your child stirs around and around in a deep container full of water until she has a good vortex going. When it's really swirling, she squirts in some food coloring or ink.

Missing Oxygen   When the oxygen is burned up inside the bottle, the water rises dramatically to take its place. You will need:

> 1 candle
> 1 bowl (soup or other)
> food coloring
> 1 glass quart bottle

Drip some wax from the candle in the center of the bowl and make the candle stand in it. Now put

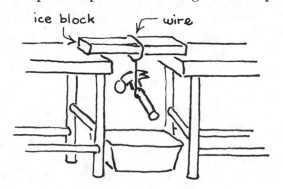

ice block   wire

bottle

food coloring →   water ↓

water in the bowl, but not to the rim — leave room for the bottle. Your child can squeeze a few drops of yellow food coloring into the water. Light the candle. Place the inverted quart bottle over the candle. Soon you will see the flame die and then the water will rise impressively in the bottle to displace about a sixth of its volume, which has been vacated by the oxygen burned by the candle. Now your child squirts in some blue food coloring to turn this into a two-tone experiment — the water in the bottle will stay yellow, while the surrounding water in the bowl will turn green.

From this experiment, a child can learn that fire needs air, with its oxygen, to keep burning — something she doesn't learn by blowing out candles, which seems to demonstrate quite the opposite.

Candle Snuffer Make a candle snuffer with the help of a five-year-old so he can experiment with cutting off the oxygen from the candle flame. Supervise his experiments. The materials are:

> 1 twist-off metal bottle cap (wine OR whiskey OR soda)
> 1 wire coat hanger

Wine and whiskey bottle caps are best because they're deeper than soda bottle caps. Better than all of these, if you can find one, is a *metal* 35-mm film can. Pry the plastic or cork liner out of the cap. Punch a hole for the wire in one side of the bottle cap, where it meets the top. Punch two holes on the opposite side of the cap and about ½" apart from each other. Cut out the long, straight bottom section of wire from the coat hanger. Push it through holes on opposite sides of the bottle cap. With pliers, bend it as shown and pull the short end back through the third hole. Pinch it together inside the cap to make the assembly permanent. Crimp over

coat hanger wire

bottle cap

about ¾" at the other end of the wire so your child can't use it as a sharp poker.

Evaporation At age three, kids want to know how rain and snow work. Gregory and I did an experiment that convinced him that the water really was going up into the sky to be formed into clouds and eventually to fall on us again. On a hot, sunny morning we took an old shallow pan, put some water in the bottom, and set it out in front of the house in a sunny spot. Immediately, Buckram the cat came and drank the water. So we refined the experiment by wrapping a scrap piece of hardware cloth across the top of the pan to exclude animals — only the sunlight could still get at the water. Gregory ran back and forth for two days checking the level of the water at least every half hour, and when it had finally evaporated he was fully persuaded that the work had been done by the sun, because Buckram couldn't get in there to drink it.

Silver Egg Hold an egg in the flame of a candle until it is thoroughly blackened with soot. You may want to hold it with kitchen tongs to avoid singeing your fingers. Preschoolers love to see the egg grow black — among other things, this experiment may be your child's first introduction to the fact that fires make soot.

When the egg is nicely blackened all over, put it in a white cup with water to cover it. Reflections of light will make the sooty egg look very silvery, which delights a four-year-old almost as much as seeing the egg charred.

Shadows One of the first experiments you'll do with your child is making shadows. Cast any strong light on any light-colored wall, and hold a baby up between. She'll wave at her own shadow and yours, but it may be months before she has any idea whom she's waving at.

For a preschooler, shadow pictures like the ones illustrated are especially exciting if you make them outside at night, casting the shadow on the wall of a building with a big flash lantern or the headlights of a car. Indoors, try throwing shadow pictures on the ceiling of a dark room with a candle.

Help a five-year-old make some cardboard cutout figures to manipulate in front of a light for a shadow play. You can trace the outlines of superhero figures from the comics, or make simple paper doll shapes or heads with eyes, nose, and mouth cut out as for a jack-o'-lantern. For a big production, set up the

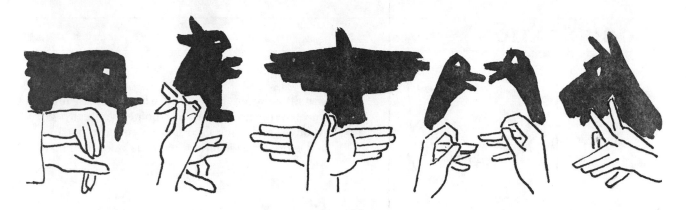

family slide screen and cast shadow pictures or a shadow play on it with the projector's light.

Surface Tension Get a four-year-old to shake ground pepper all over the surface of a large bowl of water, covering it fairly evenly. If your child touches the water at any point with a wet bar of soap, the coating of pepper will crack up dramatically and withdraw, leaving big open spaces in the water. The surface of a body of water has properties that resemble those of an elastic skin under tension. The soap reduces the surface tension at the point it touches, but the surface elsewhere retains its tension and so pulls the pepper away from the area of reduced tension.

For another neat demonstration of surface tension, arrange wooden matchsticks on the surface of a bowl of water in a circle, with one end of each matchstick pointing toward the center — like the rays around a child's drawing of the sun. Now your child touches the center of the surface, in the middle of all the matchsticks, with wet soap, and the sticks all move outward toward the rim of the bowl. To reverse their direction and attract them to the center, dip a lump of sugar into the middle and hold it there. The sugar part of the experiment has nothing to do with surface tension, but it's fun to watch. The sugar absorbs water, which sets up little currents that move the matchsticks toward it.

Floating Egg Have a five-year-old place an egg carefully in a glass of water. It sinks. Try another egg. It sinks, too. How to get it to float? Your child can add 5 tablespoons of salt to the water and stir until it's completely dissolved. The egg floats. Put out another glass with plain water and your child will delight in switching the egg with a big spoon from floating to sinking, and he can switch the glasses around while your eyes are covered and make you guess which one the egg will float in. He can also squirt different colors of food dye into the salt and plain water to add another layer of interest to the experiment.

To achieve the odd effect of an egg floating in the middle of a tall glass of water, fill the glass halfway with salt water and place the egg in. When it's floating there peacefully, very carefully and slowly pour unsalted water down the side of the glass to fill it.

Floating Ball Attach the hose of a vacuum cleaner so it is blowing out. Now place a Ping-Pong ball in the center of the stream of air. It will stay there, suspended in the steady stream. This experiment demonstrates Bernoulli's law, but it also gives a child a great suspended target to strike at with a short stick. An air-filled balloon weighted with paper clips can be suspended above a vacuum-cleaner air stream, too.

ORIENTATION

A baby has to learn to distinguish between her own body and the rest of the world, and as she grows, she has to discover her individuality again and again. When he was nearly two, I heard Timothy proudly chanting a word I'd never heard from him: "Ti . . . Ti . . . Ti . . ." So I asked him what it meant — what was his word? He kept saying it to make me understand, and I asked several more times. Suddenly he stammered loudly: "I AM ME." What a discovery! He'd been chanting his own name to tell the world that he had it figured out.

He can also use a lot of help figuring out exactly who ME is and where he is.

Roots

Before they reach age two, kids focus on how they're related to the people around them. There's Mommy, Daddy, Brother, Friend, Grandmother, etc. A two-year-old wants to know all about his roots and will go over with you the names and relationships of everyone on the family tree as often as you can stand it.

At four, kids love to hear stories about relatives or ancestors. When Gregory wouldn't eat potatoes one night, I told him that my father's father had come to America from a place called Ireland, where all they had to eat was potatoes. He was very impressed with the idea that all they ate was potatoes, that there weren't any hot dogs or granola bars or Bubble Yum. I had to tell the story several times before he understood the part about how the potatoes wouldn't grow one year, which meant there was nothing at all to eat, so they had to get in a boat and come to this great land of plenty, and that's why he

was sitting where he was with a heaping plate full of uneaten potatoes. But the point eventually got through, and since then he's eaten more potatoes and every time we have them he asks for the Potato Story.

Place

You can usually teach a three-year-old enough of her address for her to get herself home with the help of a policeman, and by five and a half a child may be able to recite address and telephone number and even dial 0 in an emergency, if you've worked on it — but don't be too sure your child will remember any of this in a pinch.

A preschooler's address sounds super important if it includes United States of America, planet Earth, Universe. When he wasn't quite three, I started teaching Gregory about his place in the universe. We used grapefruit, oranges, and lemons laid out in a line on the floor for the planets — Earth was an apple and Pluto was a marble all the way at the far end of the room. After a few sessions of this game, Gregory knew the names of most of the planets and a few little facts about them — how Venus and Mars were our neighbors, and Saturn had rings, and Pluto was tiny and far, far away. He learned about orbits by doing a planet Earth imitation: I'd stand in the middle of the room being the sun and he'd run around me, trying also to spin as he went.

To show him how we go from night to day as we circle the sun, I stuck short pieces of toothpicks in a Nerf ball to represent Gregory and Rita and me standing on Earth, and then I orbited it around a light bulb sun in a dark room while Gregory watched fascinated as the toothpicks went from day to night and back to day. "What is the earth like?" I asked Gregory a few weeks later. "It's a thing like a Nerf ball with toothpicks shoved in."

Try this demonstration of our movement in relation to the sun. Early in the morning, trace your child's shadow on the sidewalk with chalk. Do this again at noon, and again in the late afternoon, adding a few more tracings in between if there's time. Mark the spot where your child stands with an X, or trace the outline of her sneakers, so she'll be in the same position each time.

Maps

Show a three-year-old where he lives on a map or globe and he'll find it the next day with ease and pride. He'll also learn to point out a few other landmarks in a child's world — principally the North Pole, where Santa lives. A favorite bedtime story at our house is leafing through an outdated atlas and talking about what happens in the different places: oranges come from Florida; this is Rumania, where the famous Count Dracula lived; Russia is where Peter and the Wolf are from; here is Japan, and you have to fly in an airplane to get there. A three-year-old will give the impression that he understands how the map represents the actual place, but his ideas on this score are still vague.

With a five- or a six-year-old you can begin to draw maps of your house or your neighborhood and explain how they work — that the map is a small picture of a place the way a bird sees it, that it stands

for the place just as a doll or a figurine stands for a person or an animal. You may be surprised how difficult it will be for your child to grasp the concept, but keep drawing maps and eventually it will sink in.

Treasure maps help. With your child, hide a candy treasure in some obvious place — say at the base of a tree. Then draw a simple map of the immediate area with a big X marking the spot, and help her follow the map from building to bush to tree to get to where she knows the treasure is hidden. When you think the idea has started to take hold, try hiding some candy by yourself and providing your child with an X-marked map.

Nationality

By three, most kids can spot and identify a McDonald's sign half a mile away, and they know the difference between the McDonald's sign and one on a Burger King. But ask many of these same kids to identify the flag that flies in front of the post office and they say: "Huh?"

Maybe in our post-Watergate, post-Vietnam world some parents are embarrassed to tell their kids about the flag, afraid they're passing on chauvinism. But flags are made for kids. A preschooler who can spot the American flag and tell about it has a valuable piece of knowledge that he can trot out over and over again, because there are flags everywhere. And the flag will give him a sense of belonging to something important — he is an American and there's a special flag for that. It will be years, of course, before he can understand in any depth what it means to be an American, but recognizing the flag and identifying with it is a first step.

Time

Gregory, age four, asked to borrow a compass: "I need this compass at nursery school to tell when lunch is."

"But a compass tells where you are," I said. "North, south, east, west — not what time it is."

"I know," said Gregory impatiently, "but it also tells lunch."

Telling time by the clock is a complex skill; you can wait till your child is five or six to work on it — when she has counting mastered and understands a little about how numbers function. Before that point, however, kids have a natural sense of time that you learn to use when you have to describe when events will take place. Everything is related to mealtimes. A child's internal clock has three basic positions — breakfast, lunch, and dinner. A two-and-a-half-year-old can usually understand when something will happen if it's expressed as right after breakfast or a little before dinner.

A child's year is similarly built, on two basic dates — her birthday and Christmas. She can learn the seasons in order at four if they are related to these two important milestones. "Your birthday is coming in October," you explain, "and that's in the fall." This treasured bit of information will be gone over a thousand times. "My birthday is coming when the leaves fall off the trees — right, Daddy?" "My birthday is coming in October. That's right after Thursday." "How come my birthday is coming in October?"

MECHANICS

Kids are learning the ABCs of language earlier than ever before. Why not also the ABCs of technology and machinery? A preschooler can understand levers, pulleys, winches, inclined planes, drive belts, gears — because they all make terrific toys.

Lever

Can your four-year-old lift the family couch? Let him grunt and fume a little trying. Then give him a stout lever 3′ or 4′ long — a 1″ dowel will do perfectly. Show your frustrated thirty-eight-pound weakling how to put one end of the lever about a foot back under the edge of the couch and lift up on the other end. Up comes the couch and up come your child's spirits — to the top. "Ta-ra!" he shouts as he attacks the wing chair with his lever. "Super Muscle."

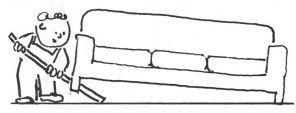

Rollers and Wheels

Find a heavy object with a flat bottom that your five-year-old couldn't possibly budge — a concrete block or a full toy box. Help her pry it up with a crowbar or other lever and get a couple of 1″ dowel rollers under it. It's of course best to have at least three rollers — two under the object being moved at all times and one being replaced from where it's been left behind, to the front. With rollers, your child will find, she might be able to move stones big enough to build a pyramid.

A preschooler is so used to wheels from seeing them everywhere that he takes them for granted, just as adults do. Demonstrating how rollers work should give him a fresh viewpoint on wheels. Talk about wheels and take a look at some on toys, cars, tractors, bikes, etc. — examining what they do — until you're satisfied your child has some understanding of the concept. Put that same concrete block or full toy box on his little red wagon so he can see how efficiently wheels do the same job the rollers did.

Inclined Plane

Gravity is such a tormentor and frustrater of kids, forever smacking them against hard floors when they trip and smashing cups to smithereens when they drop them, that a three-year-old understands what you're talking about when you explain that there's a force called gravity that pulls things down. She can appreciate the notion that an apple will always fall — it will never float as it would in space.

A ramp builder of any age is equipped to put gravity to work. The inclined plane, your child will discover, helps gravity move an object from one place to another. Some of the best ramps are made in the sandpile and on the beach. The marble and track system illustrated here is perfectly suited for a father and kids playing together indoors. The inclines are cove moldings in this shape:

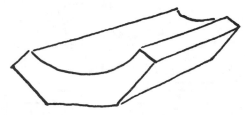

You can get them from a building supply store, or make your own with a router. Four or five 4′ lengths will give you plenty of track. The purpose of the exercise is to set up a complex downward route for a marble (or Ping-Pong or other small ball). Start at table or chair height and build downward using pieces of furniture, boxes, blocks, books — whatever comes to hand — to hold the ramps up. Getting the marble to turn a corner requires some ingenuity, and precisely placed blocks or books for backstopping, and the ramps have to be adjusted to just the right tilt so the marble runs fast, but doesn't overrun the corners. Gregory and his friend Jesse and I like best to set up a series of ramps that bring the marble around and back to the neighborhood of the starting point so we can simply take it from the plastic margarine tub in which it lands and place it back on Go, to chase down after other marbles that

incline made from a 1" x 4" board with sides of 1" x 2" glued and nailed in place makes a heavy-duty ramp. A three-year-old can help build it if you set the work up carefully and drill pilot holes for the nails. This is an excellent sanding project for a preschooler since no one will care if it's sanded with the grain, but it should be splinter-free, and the smoother the track, the better the cars will run. A sanding block will make the work easy and fun.

One end of the track can be propped up on a chair to give it a good pitch. At the floor end, staple or glue a piece of thin cardboard so the cars can run right down to the floor without a sharp drop-off. Show your child that the more steeply inclined the track is, the faster the race will be run. A starting gate can be made from a piece of cardboard or a block of wood cut to fit the width of the track — your child sets cars behind it at the top and then Ready, Set, and the gate is lifted.

are already in motion on the track. We add a few gadgets and gimmicks to this Rube Goldberg setup, too — tunnels made from cardboard tubes, and cardboard gates for the marble to push through, and precipitous drops from one level to the next.

Try other toys on these tracks; Weebles, for instance, wobble down wonderfully. A favorite game in our house is the flying toboggan run. We set a molding ramp up high and steep with a drop-off at the bottom and a container to catch the toboggan and rider. The toboggan is a big spoon placed bowl downward on the incline so the bowl sits level to hold a Fisher-Price figurine for a fast ride. I make up

an extra-length track by tacking a short piece of lath across the bottom of the joint between two sections of molding.

Auto Incline

The little metal cars that clutter up your household don't get the workout they deserve — the Matchbooks and Hot Wheels, etc. Most of them have good fast wheels, but a track is needed. An 8'

Centrifugal Force Spinner

The same little cars you use with the Auto Incline make a very dramatic demonstration of how centrifugal force works. Test this out first with a straight-sided frying pan and a Ping-Pong ball or other small ball. With the frying pan on the floor, holding the handle, you rotate the pan in small circles until you've set the ball circling around its sides. The ball is being pushed outward by centrifugal force and held in on its course by the pan walls. Now you can switch from the circular motion to a straight, short back-and-forth sliding of the pan

— as you might do to keep a pan of little fish from sticking while they fry — and the movement will keep the ball in motion. Perhaps you remember doing this, as I did, when you were a kid. A four-year-old will pick up the knack fairly quickly.

cardboard

It was Gregory's idea to substitute a little metal car for the ball, and even though I said it would never work, it ran splendidly. I'm forever learning that kids have perfectly good ideas. Not only did the car run in a circle as the ball does, it ran on the wall of the pan, climbing it in seeming defiance of gravity — and it climbed so fast it flew out into the room. With a deep pot the car has further to climb and you have enough control to keep it from flying out. The best pots for this have straight sides that make a right angle with the floor, and a long handle helps. Try all the larger pots in the kitchen, and you may also have to try several little metal cars to get the right one — some are top-heavy, turn over, and refuse to go flashing around the pan, humming on their little wheels. The high speeds you achieve on this steep-sided circular track equal the action of any commercially made toy race track I've seen.

Put down a piece of cardboard or some other scrap material to protect the floor when you do this. Rubbing a pot or pan back and forth directly on linoleum or wood is likely to leave a black mark that will be hard to get rid of.

The next step is to pick up the pot with the car spinning in it, and turn it as if you were pouring out soup, all the while keeping up the steady back-and-forth action. Now the car is doing a spectacular loop-the-loop. This, however, is a refinement for Dad that few preschoolers will be able to match.

Pulleys

For a child it is an extraordinary discovery that by pulling down she can make something go up. One pulley of any sort hung from a hook in a ceiling or doorway or tied to a tree limb, will keep a three-

and-a-half- or four-year-old busy for long stretches of time.

Show your child how the pulley works by tying a string to any object and letting her haul it up and down. In a plastic bucket tied to the string, friends like Teddy and Holly Hobby can go for a ride to the ceiling. A pulley and bucket is only good as a toy if you can trust your child not to sit directly under the bucket and let go of the string. It is also not a toy for more than one child unless an adult is there to direct traffic. If two or more kids are left alone with this setup, one will always contrive to have his head under the descending bucket.

Why not a homemade pulley? You and your child can manufacture one in minutes from a spool and a

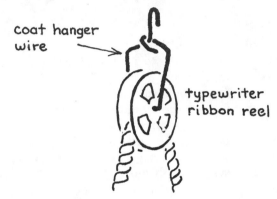

coat hanger wire

typewriter ribbon reel

piece of coat hanger wire. Reels from movie film, typewriter ribbon, etc., will also serve, or an imitation spool can be made by gluing cardboard discs to the ends of a short length of thick dowel and drilling a hole through the center. With pulleys so easy to make, maybe you and your child will work out an elaborate multi-pulley setup with the string going over and down and back and around . . .

Catapult

A ruler or yardstick or any other thin, flexible piece of wood instantly becomes a wonderful mechanical toy when C-clamped to the edge of a table top. The end of the catapult can also be held down by heavy books or your hand.

Use only *soft* objects as projectiles — a piece of foam rubber, a big art gum eraser, or a handkerchief wadded up and held in a ball with string or rubber bands. Preschoolers like to call a catapult a diving board and set a box below it on the floor for the projectile to dive into. The catapult is a grand toy for a four-year-old when you're nearby to supervise, but be sure to dismantle it when he's through.

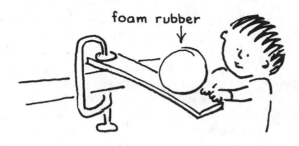

foam rubber

Basic Machine

With a good big set of Tinkertoys, you and your child can put together and test a great range of simple machine possibilities. But Tinkertoy models don't hold up for long with a five-year-old working the crank, so Gregory and I built the sturdy basic machine illustrated here.

Child power on its big crank drives it. Its inner tube rubber drive belt can transfer power from the small diameter of the lower crankshaft to a large wheel on the drive shaft above, building up considerable force (torque), or the drive belt can be stretched from the large wheel on the crankshaft to transfer power to the small diameter of the upper shaft, producing speed. The difference between the two setups and their mechanical capabilities is so dramatic at this size that a preschooler learns a very basic and vital lesson in mechanics simply by playing with the machine.

With the drive system arranged for speed, the machine can send a propeller flying around — or a color wheel or anything else that fancy dictates. It spins several times faster than the child is turning the crank, but with this setup the machine can't do any heavy work — merely touching the propeller will stop it. Arranged in the other sequence, however, the drive shaft creeps around, developing so much torque that even by grasping it tightly in both hands, your child won't be able to stop the drive shaft from turning when you operate the crank. Set up this way, the machine can perform heavy tasks. Gregory likes to attach a strong rope from the drive shaft through a pulley on a tree limb to the handle bars of his tricycle, and while I stand on the frame of the machine to weight it down, he cranks to pull the tricycle up off the ground.

Tying a rope around the crankshaft gives a further way to use the machine — as a simple winch. Gregory ties the far end of the rope to the handle of his wagon, puts stones in the wagon, and pulls it toward the winch. We've also had a lot of fun mounting the machine at the top of the jungle gym in the back yard so the kids could pull up a lunch of peanut butter sandwiches in a dumb-waiter bucket.

This machine isn't a particularly easy toy for a child to operate alone — it's designed for a father and child working together. There are dozens of possibilities for driving things with it — just get your imagination to work, and alter the machine as

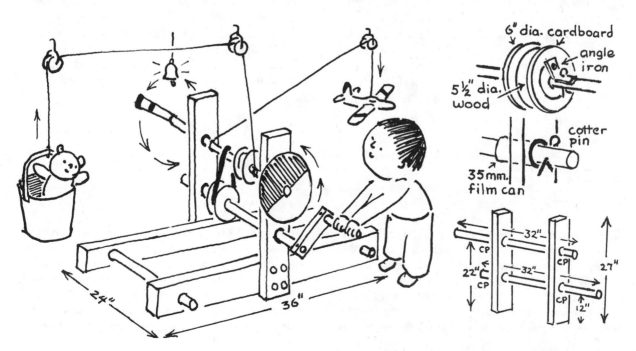

you go, adding new mechanical capabilities when you need them. To make alterations simple, the shafts and drive wheels are held in with cotter pins for quick disassembly and rearrangement.

The materials you'll need are:

> 6′ length 2″ x 4″
> 52″ length 1″ x 4″
> 22″ length 1″ x 2″
> scrap pieces 2″ x 6″ OR $5/4$″ x 6″
> scrap pieces ⅛″ hardboard OR heavy
>   cardboard
> four 3′ lengths 1″ dowel
> six 1½″ cotter pins
> two 1″ angle irons
> 4 plastic 35-mm film cans
> eight ¼″ x 2″ lag bolts with washers
> 4d and 6d finishing nails
> 1 discarded tire inner tube

Clamp the 3′ long 2″ x 4″ sides of the base together, or tack them together temporarily with nails, and drill the holes for the 1″ dowels. Drive a 6d finishing nail through each dowel joint to secure it. A pilot hole drilled for the nail will avoid splitting the end of the dowel.

Clamp the two 1″ x 4″ uprights together and drill 1¼″ holes for the shafts. Use four lag bolts with washers under their heads to fasten each upright to the base. Insert in the holes plastic 35-mm film cans with the bottoms sliced off, to act as smooth bearings for the 1″ dowels. Any amateur photographer can give you plenty of these little containers, or ask for some at a photo store, where there are usually dozens in a throwaway bin under the counter.

To make the drive wheels, draw two 5½″ circles on 2″ x 6″ stock or $5/4$″ x 6″ stock. Drill a 1″ hole in the center of each circle and then cut out the wheel with a jig saw, saber saw, or coping saw. Discs 6″ in diameter with a 1″ hole in the center are made from sturdy cardboard or ⅛″ hardboard and glued to both sides of each wheel — they keep the drive belt from slipping off. An angle iron is attached to each wheel with a roundhead wood screw and held to the drive shaft with a cotter pin. The cotter pin passes through a hole drilled in the shaft and opens out on the angle iron.

The drive belt is made from a discarded tire inner tube, which you can get free from any gas station. With sharp scissors, cut a cross section of the tube ½″ less wide than the drive wheels you've made.

To make the arm of the crank, drill two 1″ holes 6″ apart on centers and 8″ from each end of the 22″ length of 1″ x 2″. Then cut off the ends of the piece 1½″ from the centers of the holes, making it 9″ long overall. This procedure avoids splitting the ends of the 1″ x 2″ with the 1″ bit. Assemble the crank with glue and 4d nails through each dowel joint, drilling pilot holes for the nails.

Cotter pins are inserted in holes drilled through the shafts at the points marked *CP* on the drawing.

Make sure your child helps to assemble the Basic Machine so she'll learn from scratch what it's all about. Many of the assembly operations can be done by a five-year-old, including turning the bolts — preferably with a socket wrench or a vise-grip pliers clamped on their heads.

When the machine is all together, tack a 1′ piece of lath or other thin wood to the face of the top shaft on the end opposite the crank. This propeller will whirl around with the machine set up to produce speed. Hang a bell or a piece of metal pipe where the propeller can hit it as it goes around, and make it ring. And start thinking of other "jobs" you and your child can do with the machine.

ELECTRICITY

To show a preschooler the power of electricity, take a pocket comb and rub it briskly on real woolen cloth — a sweater, coat, or jacket. A comb charged this way with static electricity will attract and pick up light objects — tiny scraps of paper, small pieces cut from cork or styrofoam, wood shavings, sawdust, peanut skins, or the lint from the bottom of your pocket. Kids quickly get the idea and do really vigorous rubbing to charge up the comb. The small objects stay stuck to the comb until they acquire a charge, at which point the two charges repel one another and the little things drop off.

A charged comb will bend a thin stream of water by attracting it off course. Just turn on a tap so there's a fine stream, and get your child to charge up the comb. He should hold it near, but not touching the water. Make sure also to show him that an uncharged comb won't attract the water, and neither will a tablespoon or a salt shaker. It's good science to demonstrate that the effect can only be produced with a charge, but this kind of demonstration is also vital for a preschooler's understanding of what's going on. His few years' experience of the world are so limited, for all he knows, any object held near water will attract it off course.

Try a charged comb on some soap bubbles, too — it makes them dance around when it moves toward them. All of these effects work best on a dry winter day — when the comb will get its strongest charge. Try these next two only on a very dry winter day, when the air crackles with electricity. Charge up a comb and use it to lead a Ping-Pong ball across a smooth surface, like a puppy trotting along behind. Give your child a wide paintbrush to use to stroke a charge of electricity into pieces of light paper — say 4" squares. These can then be placed flat against a wall and they'll stay there, held up by electricity.

Electromagnet

To make an electromagnet you need:

> 1 large nail OR bolt
> 1 size D battery
> 8' length bell wire
> duct tape OR adhesive tape
> tacks

Use the biggest nail you can find; an 8" or 12" spike is best. A 4" or 5" bolt will do well, too. Show your preschooler that the nail or bolt isn't already a magnet — it doesn't attract or pick up the tacks. Strip an inch of insulation from each end of the bell wire and help your child wind it onto the nail as in the illustration. A four-and-a-half-year-old can do an excellent job of wrapping the wire — it should be bound on fairly tightly; it needn't, however, be neatly wrapped, but can overlap and loop back across itself. The longer the wire and the more turns

around the nail, the stronger the magnet will be. Tape one end of the wire to the flat, negative end of the battery. Now when your child touches the other end of the wire to the positive end of the battery, the nail becomes magnetized and will pick up the tacks. An electromagnet only works while the current is on, so the tacks will drop off when the wire is removed from the positive end. To make a more or less permanent electromagnet toy, strap the battery tightly to the wire-wrapped nail with a couple of strips of tape so your child can hold the whole assembly in one hand and use the other hand to activate it.

Lights

Show your preschooler how the electricity stored in a battery will light up a bulb by making a simplified version of the workings of a flashlight. Start with one size D battery, a flashlight bulb, and a narrow strip of aluminum foil. While you hold the end of the bulb and the positive end of the battery

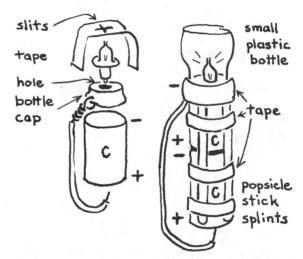

together, your child can hold one end of the foil against the flat, negative end of the battery and touch the side of the bulb's collar with the other end of the foil. It will light up.

With these few materials, you and your child can easily build a primitive flashlight:

> 1 metal screw-off soda bottle cap
> 1 flashlight bulb
> 1 size C battery
> 12" length bell wire
> duct tape OR adhesive tape

Remove the plastic lining from the bottle cap and

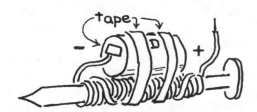

punch a tight hole in the top of it for the flashlight bulb. Punch or drill a small hole for the wire on the side of the bottle cap. Push the bulb in from the top of the cap. Strip 1¼″ insulation from the ends of the wire and put one end through the small hole in the side of the cap, wrapping it securely around itself so it is held tightly to the cap and will maintain contact. Cut a 4″ piece of tape, and in the center of it cut crossed slits that will allow the bulb just to pass through. Pull the tape down around the bulb. Place the bulb assembly so the bottom tip of the bulb is in contact with the flat, negative end of the battery, and secure the ends of the 4″ piece of tape tightly to the sides of the battery. A second strip of tape strapped around at right angles to the first will make the assembly more secure. Now your child can touch the positive end of the battery with the free end of the wire to light the bulb.

A five-year-old can be trusted to be careful with this flashlight and not smash the bulb for at least a day. Or you can protect the bulb with a small plastic bottle fitted over it and taped onto the battery. To make the light brighter, use a splint made from corrugated cardboard or popsicle sticks and tape to add another battery pressed tightly behind the first, or even put three batteries in series — the 12″ bell wire will be long enough for three batteries.

By working on this project, a child sees how electricity is transferred from the battery through the wire and the bulb. And with the principle down, he and you can go on to more elaborate lighting arrangements.

NATURE

At four and a half a child turns over every stone he passes, looking for insects and snakes, and a year later his collections of rocks and the animals from under them may have taken over your household. A child's curiosity about the terrain and the plants and animals around him is boundless, and you can help to stimulate that curiosity and keep it fresh.

Take weekend walks in the woods, the country, a wooded park — but also make a careful survey of the plants, insects, and other creatures in your own back yard or neighborhood. Even in the midst of a big city Nature holds her own in vacant lots and in the cracks between the paving. Unless you're a professional naturalist, you won't know the names of all the things your child collects or have the answers to all her nature questions without consulting a lot of books. Every good public library has a wealth of books both in the children's section and in the adult Natural History section that will help you identify wildflowers, lichens, beetles, or whatever else interests your preschooler. The books in the widely available Golden Nature Guide Series are very useful to have handy at home.

ROCKS

A child's first nature collection is usually a heavy one — rocks, pebbles, stones. They're everywhere and they're easy to gather. They accumulate in pockets and on counters and you're not allowed to throw them out. Your budding geologist will be excited to see pictured in a book the same stones he's found in the back yard or among the pebbles in the driveway. By learning some of their names, he'll be able to zero in on the kind of rocks he wants to concentrate on collecting. Say there's quartz in your neighborhood and he's attracted to the shiny crystals — soon little piles of quartz will start to gather everywhere you look and he'll be a quartz expert.

If there are big rocks or rock outcrops near where you live, your preschooler will discover them and use them for climbing. When she starts gathering stones, show her how to chip a specimen piece from a big rock with a hammer and cold chisel. Attack the rock in cracks and at corners. A good rock specimen will show one well-weathered surface and one freshly cut one. A good rock specimen is also small, which makes it easy to lug home in a shopping bag. A five-year-old will be ready to do some hefty rock chipping with hammer and cold chisel. A special geological hammer with a sharp end is useful for this work, but is certainly not essential for a preschool beginner. Goggles should always be worn for chiseling on rock, as chips may fly.

A ⅝″ cold chisel is a good size for this work. If you want to hold the chisel so your child can get two hands on the hammer handle for extra heft, clamp a vise-grip pliers on the chisel at a right angle to it — which gives you a firm handle that you can hold out of range of your child's blows.

For a child who really gets into rock chiseling, keep a pile of brittle medium-sized rocks indoors for rainy-day chipping.

ANIMALS

Children want to get to know their animal neighbors, but most animals are kid-shy. Even the domestic cat disappears when a toddler approaches — he knows his tail will be pulled. And when a preschooler goes to gather some of the animals that attract him, he has a hard time. A six-year-old is usually still short of the co-ordination it takes to catch a frog, net a butterfly, or even trap a lightning

bug with his hands. Included below are notes on a number of small animals you can introduce to a preschooler that she can easily collect and examine. Worms are a favorite and special father-child worm-hunting techniques are discussed on p. 267 under Fishing.

A child can keep small animals — beetles, slugs, caterpillars, toads, turtles, salamanders, etc. — for a short time in jars and boxes covered with screening and supplied with water and the kind of food the animal is used to, but I think it's always best to get kids to let animals go after a day or so. Then catching

them is a matter of making new friends — saying hello and sending them on their way. This way, a child learns to respect and value the animal's freedom. Also, preschool kids aren't ready for the responsibility of regularly feeding and caring for pets. Even easy-to-care-for domestic pets like dogs and rabbits can wait till a child is seven or eight and can take on a little of the responsibility.

Attracting neighborhood animals to your yard helps kids get to know them. A bird feeder brings dozens of animals flying right up to your window in the winter, where your child can watch them closely. You may also enjoy attracting wild rabbits to a place in your yard where your child can watch them from a window — that is if you haven't got a garden that you're interested in protecting from the ravages of the bunnies. Just put rabbit pellets, which you can get from pet shops and grain stores, in a shallow bowl or pan and place it near a thicket or thick hedge — a rabbit needs cover like this nearby so he won't fall easy prey in the open to cats and dogs, or a fox or hawk. Rabbits may also be attracted to a corn stake feeder like the one illustrated, which

a preschooler can make by driving some 10d or 12d galvanized nails through a piece of board and pushing on ears of corn. Squirrels will go for the corn, too, and you might even attract pheasants or quail if there are any nearby. And of course planting some carrots and lettuce without a fence will bring rabbits from far and near; woodchucks will probably congregate, too.

If there are chipmunks in your neighborhood, but none right around your house, you can try to get a family to move in by making a rough pile of stones, which is a good outdoor project to undertake with a preschooler, who will love hauling the rocks in her own wagon. The preferred home of chipmunks is an old loose stone wall with lots of nooks and crannies to hide in and burrow under, and that's how a rock pile to attract them should be constructed.

Small Creatures

Wood lice, which a child can find in every damp, rotten piece of wood or under any stone, are land-living crustaceans, cousins of the lobster and the shrimp; slugs are mollusks; spiders are arachnids, not insects; and worms are in an order all their own. A preschooler can understand the variety and fascinating individuality of the small creatures if he isn't constantly told that they are all Bugs.

Take a close look with your preschooler at some of the small animals and you'll both want to learn more about how they operate. Gregory and I examined a spider's web one day. Why didn't the spider get caught in her own web? he wanted to know. I didn't know, but the spider book we got from the library explained that the straight, radiating lines of the web and the central hub, where the spider sits waiting for her prey, are made from a dry thread, after which the spiral of sticky thread is added on, secreted by the spider from a different gland. So the spider has straight dry paths to travel on through the web, and doesn't get stuck.

Pitfall Trap Set this wonderful trap for beetles and other small creatures with a child of three or older. Dig a hole just the right size to set in it a tin can or a deep, narrow glass jar. The open top should be flush with the surface of the ground, and over the top it's fun to construct a little roof to keep out rain and slightly larger animals who might snap up your catch. Set small stones around the trap and lay a piece of board on them for the roof. A little piece of meat or fish in the jar will act as bait, but isn't entirely necessary. Various beetles, including the black burying beetle and the familiar ladybird beetle, may stumble into this trap, as will other insects like ants and earwigs, and you may find animals like spiders, centipedes, and wood lice. Once your prey have fallen in, they won't be able to escape up the steep sides of the trap.

Set out your trap in the evening. A damp, overcast night will yield the biggest catch, because many insects and other small creatures need a damp environment to survive — that's why they hide under rocks during the day. In an especially dry spell, or on a cold night in winter, few creatures will be prowling around to be caught. Place a trap near a compost heap or a pile of rotting leaves and the considerable small animal traffic in the area will produce a big catch.

You won't have to remind a four-year-old to check

the Pitfall Trap first thing in the morning — she'll be up and ready for this the way she is up and ready on Christmas morning.

Insect Hunts To gather a variety of insects fast, have your child hold an open umbrella upside down under the low branch of a tree or bush. Then you hit the branch from above sharply with a stick. A light-colored umbrella is best for this job, because you'll be able to see your large catch easily.

A light bulb outdoors near a window will attract hundreds of moths for your child to watch on a summer night.

A beetle-hunting six-year-old will love to have the two halves of a small circular pillbox adhesive-taped to his thumb and index or middle finger, or use any other small box with a lid that fits over the bottom. Outfitted this way, he can sneak up on his prey, and Snap — Got Him. With this setup, your child will also need a container to hold the beetles and other creatures he snaps up.

Daddy Longlegs A four-year-old will be afraid of a daddy longlegs, certain that he is a spider and will bite — until her daddy explains that daddy longlegs is friendly and harmless and it's fun to let him walk around on you. Though he is an arachnid, a cousin of the spiders. Now this child will have a new playmate whenever she spots a daddy longlegs.

Crickets A cricket makes a good pet, but don't let one get loose in the house — indoors they do a lot more than chirp cheerfully on the hearth. They get into food and eat holes in everything made of cloth. A good cage for a cricket can be made from a large bottle — clear plastic is always better for preschoolers than glass. Help your child put some soil, preferably with growing plants, in the bottom of the jar. Add a cabbage leaf or other greens for the cricket to eat, and close him in with a piece of screening held in place with string or a rubber band. From time to time your child can drop a little corn meal saturated with water into the cage to supplement the cricket's leafy diet, and sprinkle or mist-spray in some water to keep the atmosphere moist. You can try keeping more than one cricket in a cage, but they are likely to fight, and crickets fight to the finish.

Slugs   In minutes at any time of year except winter, a child can collect dozens of slugs. They're far and away the easiest land animal to capture. In any garden or yard you see them everywhere following a shower, or if it is early in the day and dewy, or overcast and wet. If it's dry, your child can turn over stones, old boards, anything that will hold a little dampness under it. A child's plastic toys left out in the grass overnight will usually have slugs clinging to the underside the next morning. The slugs hide under things for fear of drying up, which means death. Their soft bodies need moisture — they and their cousins the snails are mollusks, close relatives of the octopus and other aquatic animals like cockles and limpets.

A fastidious preschooler who doesn't want to pick up the slimy slugs can learn to scoop them up between a couple of pieces of cardboard, or with spoons. Your child can collect them in a tin can, but make sure to help him transfer them to a clear glass container of some sort, because the best part of the show is watching through the glass the muscular ripples of the underside of the slug's "foot" — light

and dark bands moving as the slug picks up the parts of the sole in succession to lift them forward. He glides along through a road of slime he produces

from glands under his head, and preschoolers are particularly fond of this yucky performance.

Your child will enjoy spraying water into the slug container with an atomizer to keep the environment comfortable. Slugs will eat almost anything you give them in the way of greens; they also like paper.

Mammals

Many kids become ardent animal trappers at four. They put together a couple of sticks and some tangled string and threaten to catch a bear with it.

Gregory, Timothy, and I have had a lot of fun from a big box trap that we use to catch the woodchucks who constantly attack our garden — the humane kind of trap that doesn't injure the animal, but snares him alive in a cage. We find the woodchucks' burrows in the spring and set the trap at an entrance, loaded with lettuce. Next morning, there's usually a fat, unhappy woodchuck in the cage. The kids get to see him up close and stare at his beady eyes, big teeth, and coarse fur — and then we put the caged woodchuck in the trunk of the car, drive ten miles down the road, and let him go in some woods. We've also caught raccoons who were eating the sweet corn and turning over the garbage cans, and exported them from the neighborhood — the kids loved seeing these masked marauders at close quarters. Use a couple of sardines for bait and you can't miss catching a raccoon.

Smaller "live" traps can be used to catch mice if you live in a neighborhood with less wildlife. Hardware stores often carry ingenious devices like the "Tin Cat" I have that will round up half a dozen mice at a time — they run through a little baffle to get at the smelly cheese bait and then can't get back out. A preschooler delights in baiting a trap like this, and in watching the mice scurry around in it before you let them go, down the road a piece.

A child will want to touch and hold any animal you catch, but the best course is to let him take a good long look, and then let the animal go. If a wild animal of any sort bites — and even a deer mouse may nip — you have to allow for the possibility of the animal being rabid, and the next step is a painful series of shots. So do any handling of the animal yourself, wearing leather gloves — and only if you're experienced in handling animals. Be especially leery if a squirrel stumbles into your trap. Surprisingly, these little charmers are among the most dangerous animals around; the tamest of squirrels may bite, and many squirrels carry rabies.

Always put a trap out in the evening, because most small mammals are nocturnal, but don't set one outdoors on a cold night or the animal you catch may be injured by the cold. And always check a trap in the morning — an animal left too long in a trap can starve.

Better Mousetrap This nutty-looking pitfall trap will actually catch mice. It's also harmless both to the mouse and to the child who helps you set it up. The materials are:

> 1 piece heavy cloth OR paper
> 1 deep steep-sided plastic wastebasket
> 1 plank
> cheese OR peanut butter
> string

Set the Better Mousetrap up indoors or out, wherever you know there will be mice. Outdoors, hang the bait from a limb or branch. Indoors you can C-clamp a piece of 1" x 2" or other stick to a straight chair for a bracket to suspend the bait above the trap. Tie the paper or cloth cover on around the rim of the wastebasket and cut crossed slits for the mouse to fall through. You may need to use boxes or

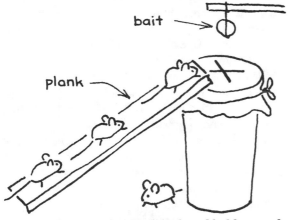

a chair to help prop up the plank and hold it steady. The plank needn't lead upward from the floor — it could be arranged to give a mouse a path downward from a countertop or straight across from a low wall outside. Once he falls in the wastebasket, the mouse can't scramble back up the steep sides.

To use peanut butter, the most effective small mammal bait, let your child smear some on a small piece of bread, and hang the bread over the trap.

Observe the same cautions about handling caught animals outlined above.

It can be a huge disappointment for a preschooler

when a trap she helps to set doesn't catch an animal, so prepare her well beforehand by explaining that even the best laid mousetraps oft times go awry.

Wildlife Sleuthing

A day or so after a snowfall, take your preschooler out on a tracking expedition. You needn't go deep into a virgin forest to find animal tracks — there will be cat and dog footprints anywhere, and in most suburbs you'll find the tracks of rabbits, squirrels, mice, raccoons, and possibly skunks and weasels.

Play sleuth along some human trails, too. Say you discover the sharp heel prints and pointed toes of a woman in fancy boots. Follow them down the sidewalk. Which way did she go at the corner? Your child picks up the trail again on the other side of the street and the boot prints lead right to the door of the beauty parlor.

By following animal tracks, with patience and great good luck, you may discover the evidence left at the scene of some drama — the parallel tracks of a fox and a rabbit, and then scuff marks and blood in the snow. But a preschooler will have more luck and just as much excitement from following the footprints of a neighborhood dog that lead to a fire hydrant. When you've gone some distance tracking in the snow, ask your child if he knows how to find his way back to where you started.

It's a little harder to find animal tracks in the warm parts of the year and in places where it never snows, but look in dusty and muddy places and there will usually be a few.

Pictured are some common prints. A knowledgeable tracker can "read" the pace of the animal by the arrangement of the tracks. When, for instance, a rabbit, squirrel, mouse, or rat runs, his big hind feet land in front of his small front feet. A walking deer often places his hind foot in the print of his front hoof, so you see deer prints that look like double exposures; and deer prints 10' to 20' apart will show you where the animal took a leap. Take a ruler along and help a five- or six-year-old measure the distance between the paw prints of a cat — 5" to 8" indicates walking, while a spacing of about 30" shows that the cat was running. Dog prints vary greatly in size depending on the breed of dog. Cocker spaniels, for instance, leave a 2" print, but an Alaskan husky will make a print 4" long. See if you and your child can decide which prints belong to the Smiths' Fido and which to the Joneses' Rex.

cat dog

deer

front

hind

running
rabbit

raccoon

hind
front

running
gray squirrel

hopping
sparrow

sunflower seeds. These are expensive, though, and the big greedy bluejays may fly in and grab them all before the smaller birds get a crack at them. Some special types of feed attract specific types of birds. Finches, for instance, dote on thistle seeds. Garden specialty stores sometimes carry a wide range of bird feed.

If you do start to feed the birds, make a commitment to keep it up for the whole winter. The birds who are attracted to your feeder come to depend on it as their source of winter food, and suddenly stopping may mean hardship for them. The same birds come back day after day and not only will your child learn the names of the various types if you help her find them in a guide to the birds, she will also get to know them as individuals — the junco with the feathers missing from his tail, and Mr. and Mrs. Goldfinch, who always arrive as a family.

Seed Dispenser   This bird feeder can be made in a short time by a father and a child of three and a half or older. You will need:

> 1 tin can
> 2 pie tins of different sizes
> nylon cord
> 1 flat stick (popsicle)

Remove one end of the can with a can opener. Help your child punch a few triangular holes around the side of the can at the other end using a church key punch-type opener. Punch holes with a nail for

Birds

Set up a bird feeder so your child can see it well through a window from where he sits to eat and soon he'll know by name many of the birds he shares his meals with. Even a two-year-old can identify various types of birds and will proudly say chickadee or tufted titmouse or cardinal when he sees one. He'll discover that the different kinds of birds have different eating habits — that the nuthatch can stand upside down on a hanging perch as he eats, while the sparrows prefer solid ground under them and eat the seeds the other birds drop from a feeder. We keep a large supply of birdseed in a five-gallon lard tin, which is an extra bonus for the kids because they occasionally get to play in the seed — they use it like a small indoor sandbox, running their hands and arms through, which feels sexy, and lifting seed with the bucket on their Tonka crane to dump it into a plastic dishpan. Mixed birdseed from the grocery store will make plenty of feathered friends, but you'll attract more birds if you add extra

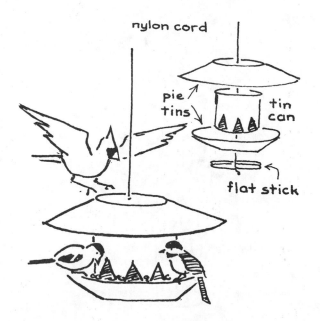

nylon cord

pie
tins

tin
can

flat stick

the string to pass through the centers of the pie tins and the bottom of the can. String the whole thing together as in the illustration, with the flat stick tied on at the bottom to hold the structure together. Hang this near a window from a tree limb or bracket. Pull up the large pie tin on top and fill the can with seeds, which then spill out the holes at a measured rate as the birds eat them from the lower pie tin.

Suet Feeders Birds miss insects in their winter diet and suet (beef fat), peanut butter mixed with an equal amount of corn meal, or kitchen fat (bacon grease) will make up the lack and provide some body heat. You can't just lay a big chunk of suet out on the windowsill, though, or a large bird — a jay or starling — will carry it off whole. Here are a couple of suet holders that a preschooler will enjoy helping to make.

Using a brace and bit (see p. 303), help a four-year-old or older child drill ½" holes in a piece of wood about 3" in diameter and 14" long, with the bark and twigs left on — the bottom end of a discarded Christmas tree is about the right size. The holes should slant down and be about 1" deep. If there are no small twigs on the wood, help your child make some perches for the birds by drilling ¼" holes and inserting glue and 3½" lengths of ¼" dowel. Your child can then push into the holes peanut butter/corn meal, suet, or kitchen fat that

has been melted and mixed with birdseed and allowed to cool. Fasten a screw eye in the top and hang it up by a wire from a tree limb or a bracket extending out over a window.

An even simpler suet feeder is made from the kind of plastic string bag that lemons come in from the supermarket. Your child can fill it with suet and help tie it tightly for hanging. A child can also stuff peanut butter/corn meal into the crevices in a large pine cone. Hang it up and small birds will perch on it to pick the peanut butter from the nooks and crannies.

Every kid expects the birds to start using a feeder immediately, but it may take them a week or longer — even in midwinter — to become regular customers. Your child will find that it's worth the long wait.

Water Animals

Brooks, streams, and ponds teem with life, and though most aquatic animals are too quick for a preschooler to catch, there are some she can easily gather and examine.

By running a kitchen sieve through the waters of a pond or slow stream, a five- or six-year-old can capture quite an assortment of creatures — water boatmen, diving beetles, dragonfly nymphs, back swimmers, giant water bugs, maybe a tadpole or a minnow. The sieve will work better if it's bound to the end of a pole. Take along a large light-colored pan to empty the catch into so your child can see

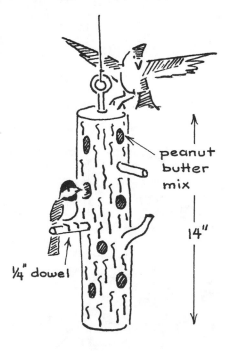

peanut butter mix

¼" dowel

14"

what she's captured. Watch out for the larger water insects — most of them bite.

A night expedition to look at water insects is a real treat for a preschooler. Seal a flashlight and some rocks for weight in a big glass jar. Tie a string around the neck of the jar and sink it in shallow water in a pond, lake, or slow stream where your child can lean over and get a good look — a low bridge or small dock is a great place to do this. The light will attract water insects just as a lamp will attract moths, and many water insects are active at night.

Caddis Fly Larvae Show a four-year-old how to turn over rocks and stones quickly in a brook or on the edge of a stream or pond and look closely to see the little animals scatter. Attached to many of the stones your child will turn over will be what at first may appear to be short twigs — from ½" to 1" long.

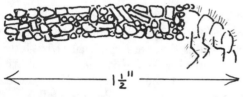

They're easy to pry off the stone, and when your child looks carefully, he'll discover an animal in a tubular house.

Caddis fly larvae live in pools, lakes, rivers of all sizes, running brooks, and wherever they live, they attach bits and pieces of the local building material together to form protective tubes around their soft bodies. In slow or stagnant water, caddis larvae make their cases of lightweight materials — bits of reeds and leaves — but in a swiftly flowing brook, their cases will be constructed from tiny pebbles. The materials are beautifully fitted together and held in place with a silklike substance made by the animal. The larvae start spinning this silk and attaching things to it almost as soon as they hatch from their eggs, and as they grow, they add onto the upper end of the tube, from which the legs and the head with its sharp-edged jaws protrude and carry out the construction. The soft, long abdomen is held firmly in the casing, as your child will discover when he pulls one of the cases apart.

There are insect collectors who specialize in gathering caddis fly cases from all around the world, because of their great variety. A preschooler who is introduced to these creatures will make a huge collection of the local ones. This is an animal that a

four-year-old can gather many of quickly, and there is the added fun of wading and the intrigue of turning over the stones. Knowing about these little cases also gives a child a useful piece of knowledge to show off — because few older kids and in fact very few adults know about these home builders and people are always fascinated when they see them for the first time.

PLANTS

When he blows a dry dandelion, get your child to examine with you the tiny, perfectly designed parachutes that carry the seeds to their destination, and talk about how the dandelion uses the wind and kids to help it colonize lawns. Check out the workings of Nature's helicopter, the maple seed, and explain how it flies along to start new trees in new places. When you take a burr out of a child's clothes, explain that the burr has used her for a vehicle to get to a new place to put down roots. But will this burr get a chance to start a new plant if your child throws it in the wastebasket? No, she says. But what if it travels in the trash to the dump and grows up there?

Look at leaves one day — get a five-year-old to collect a leaf from each plant within reach, and put them in a box or spread them out on paper to compare them for size and shape and color. Most kids won't collect leaves of grass when they do this, even though they may be the most plentiful leaves around; and make sure your child has some evergreen needles in this leaf-comparison collection.

Kids are always told that wood comes from trees, but they seldom understand the connection. You can help a preschooler appreciate how this works by explaining how a sawmill cuts lumber from the trunks of trees, but she'll really get the idea if you split a small rectangular piece out of a log and help her plane it into a small, smooth board. Getting her to drive nails into a log is another good demonstration — for a preschooler this is proof positive that the log is made from the same thing as a 2″ x 4″.

Helping to plant seeds and working with you in a garden will give your child a really close experience of the life cycle of plants (see p. 311 for more on kids and gardens), as will helping with house plants. Below are a few indoor plant "experiments."

Seed Writing Use seeds that sprout quickly and easily — mustard greens and cress are perfect. Put a piece of flannel or other cloth that will hold water in a shallow pan and get a four-year-old to write the initial letter of her name with the seeds on the damp cloth, putting them on thickly. To keep the whole thing moist and hurry germination, stretch plastic wrap across the pan, cover with newspaper to keep it dark, and put the pan in a warm place. The newspaper and plastic come off as soon as the seeds start to sprout, and the pan then goes in a sunny window — preferably on the south side of the house. The letter grows up neatly in little plants.

Seed writing can of course also be done indoors on dirt or outdoors in the garden.

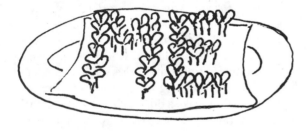

Bean Growing This scheme allows your child and you to see both how the bean sprouts upward and how the root pushes downward. You'll need:

> 1 pint jar
> blotting paper
> tape
> lima bean seeds OR other bean or pea seeds

Line the jar with a cylinder of blotting paper, using tape at the seam to keep the paper pressed open against the walls of the jar. Then place a few seeds between the paper and the glass so they are suspended about halfway up the side of the jar. Lima beans are probably best for this purpose, or use a variety of bean and pea seeds if you have them.

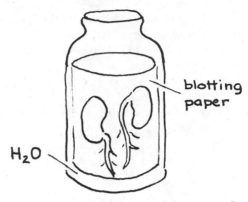

Some water goes in the bottom of the jar, and it is then put in a warm, dark place until the seeds sprout.

If a seed has been placed with the root end uppermost, you'll see that the root will turn and head downward, and the plant will also make a 180-degree turn to head for the sun.

Rising Color This experiment demonstrates how water rises through plants. Stand a stalk of celery in a glass of water that your child has strongly tinted with food coloring — red is a good color. After a while the colored water, rising up through the tiny tubes in the celery, will color the stalk red. Try splitting a stalk of celery halfway up the middle and putting the ends in two glasses with different color dyes for a two-tone experiment. A very strange effect can be achieved by the same process, using a white flower like a carnation. Split its stem and place the two sides in different color dyes. When the colored water rises to the flower, you get a two-tone flower.

Cut the celery stalks to expose a cross section of the tubes that carry the water through the plant.

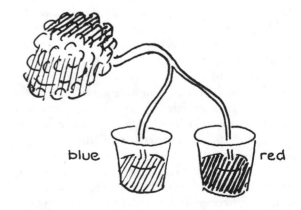

blue   red

MUSIC

One father, home from a grueling day troubleshooting computer information systems, takes out the French horn he's played since the first grade and puffs away while his three preschool girls line up for turns at working the valves. A film maker, who gets home regularly half an hour before the family dinner, grabs the banged-up guitar that's been with him since high school and strums a few chords; it's the beginning of his daily Father's Hour for his two preschool boys. They join in and sing along sometimes, or play near him, and meanwhile Mom has a break from child care to cook dinner — some break . . . but actually it is a relief for any full-time mother at this harried hour.

Music cuts wordlessly across the generations and everybody can join in. It's a language that even babies understand — talk to a baby with a lullaby or clapping hands or tapping spoons, and she'll know what you're telling her. Of course there are generation disputes over music — as early as two years, a child may drive you nearly out of the house by insisting on hearing some inane kiddie record played forty times over, and at four or five your kids will already have pop music idols that you may not love. But year after year the whole family can return to the common ground of the golden oldies. And if you have musical instruments, they will become common family property and your kids will learn to play them as soon as they have enough co-ordination.

Music gets passed along from father to child; there's Woody and Arlo Guthrie, and old Johann Sebastian Bach, who played his fingers to the bone to support his twenty kids. Bach patiently taught all his kids to play instruments, and we still have gay little pieces of music that he wrote especially for the clavier books of young Wilhelm Friedemann and Magdalena Bach. A wonderful household — and many of the brood grew up in this supercharged musical atmosphere to be eminent musicians in their own right.

One father I talked with is a painter whose daily workout on the piano is almost as vital a part of his regimen as his work with brushes and canvas. The pieces he practices are sophisticated and demanding — things like J. S. Bach's *Goldberg Variations*

— but when his toddler, Saskia, is around, they play *her* music. "I'm sharing with her as much as I can," he says. "Since she was nine months old she's been playing with the piano — every day — because I play." She operates with only two or three fingers and she's never banged the piano, which is an 1888 Steinway concert grand. "She wanted to play. Saskia has plenty of things that she can bang with and she knows she can't bang the piano. . . . She has her Mother Goose songs and nursery things that she sings and I'll play them with her. I take her little finger very gently and do 'Three Blind Mice' or 'Ba Ba' — she'll say what she wants to play and I'll play it with her. And she'll sit there in my lap very patiently and as soon as we finish she'll say, 'Ba Ba,' and we'll play it again, and we'll do this again and again and again. When she's by herself she'll get up on the piano stool — she almost split her head open the other day when she fell off. And she'll play quietly for about a minute and a half, but she loses interest unless I'm there and she can get the tune." It takes two — father and child — to get the tune.

But what about a father with a tin ear? No real problem. You can start with the ABCs of music along with your kids. I'm including below suggestions for making a number of simple instruments. If you and your children find you enjoy making and playing some of these, they're only a start. You can go on to inventing your own instant instruments and making them from anything around the house that goes bang or tinkle, and you can also find in your public library many books full of plans for homemade instruments — two of the best are listed in the Further Reading section of this book under the heading Music.

Kazoos

Among instant instruments, the kazoo is king. It's noisier and sassier and easier to put together than any other common toy music maker. The classic home-built kazoo is made of these elements:

    wax paper
    1 toilet paper roll
    1 rubber band

You stretch a piece of the wax paper about 4″ square across one end of the tube like a drumhead, and hold it in place with a rubber band. The paper needn't be taut, just flat. Some kazoo makers like to punch a hole in the tube with a pencil about an inch back from the wax-papered end. The hole lets out the air when a child blows into the instrument instead of humming, and saves the wax paper from being blown off.

The kazoo is played by humming into the open end. Some players go da-da-da or doo-doo-doo, but it comes through as humming and the humming sets the wax paper vibrating and the tube amplifying and the resulting sound makes the heart grow glad.

You can make a kazoo from virtually any tube-shaped object. Length doesn't particularly matter — a long mailing tube will do fine and will look a little like an alpenhorn. Napkin rings are perfect.

For a family kazoo band, you and your kids can assemble enough instruments in minutes. A four-year-old can do most of the assembly work alone. A baby can learn to play the kazoo almost as well as a three-year-old but she will shove her fingers through the wax paper and slobber up the paper roll. For a baby, a commercially made plastic kazoo is probably best.

Percussion Sticks

A little drilling and sawing on the end of a 1″ dowel produces an instrument that makes a loud, crisp clacking note. With a ¼″ bit, drill a pilot hole 1½″ deep in the center of one end of a 5½″ length of 1″ dowel. Follow this with a ½″ boring bit to the same depth. A drill press will do the job easily and accurately, but a perfectly good result can be achieved with a hand electric drill and some care.

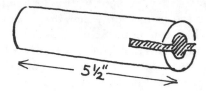

Now, with a backsaw or other narrow saw, cut a kerf across the hole you've drilled, again to the 1½″ depth. Your child strikes the doctored end of the dowel with another 1″ dowel to play it. Percussion sticks that produce other loud notes can be made by varying the diameter of the dowel and the diameter of the hole.

Musical Nails

Hanging nails on threads to make a primitive chime is a musical exercise that's often done with preschool kids, but even though it's known as musical nails, there's not much music in it. The nails you're likely to have handy — 8d, 10d, even 20d nails — hardly yield a tinkle. A 60d nail is 6″ long and it still hasn't much tone. What's needed is big nails.

Most hardware stores carry 12″ spikes, which are commonly used to fasten together railroad ties. Hung by a heavy thread, one of these will give a clear, bell-like tone, and a group of them make excellent chimes. The note can be changed by cutting off a piece of the spike with a hacksaw, which

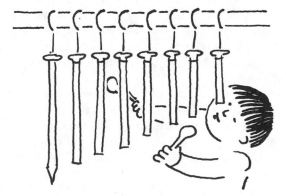

goes quickly. File the cut end smooth. By cutting seven spikes each ¾″ shorter than the last, and leaving one intact, you make a series of notes that approximates a modern whole-tone scale.

Hang the nails 2″ apart from a length of dowel or other stick. Heavy-duty thread is best for hanging them, and not much of it, because long threads will tangle when a child hits the chimes. The dowel holder can be suspended between the backs of two straight chairs so your three-year-old can bang on the nails with a spoon or another 12″ spike. And a father with a little musical know-how will be able to pick out a tune on them.

Ground Bow

The old washtub bass, made with a string, a broom handle, and a tub, is the familiar American version of the universal one-string instrument. All around the world, one-stringers are made in different shapes with the materials at hand. In England, for instance, a tea chest takes the place of the washtub. The Ugandan version is called a ground bow and is made with a flexible stick, a string, and a hole in the ground covered with bark. A slightly Americanized version of the ground bow makes a great short project for a father and kids on a late summer evening. You will need:

> shovels (adult and child sizes)
> heavy string
> 30″ x 30″ piece ⅛″ plywood OR hardboard OR
>   wood paneling
> stones
> 6′ flexible stick

Kids jump at any excuse for digging a hole, and this is an excellent excuse. Make the hole washtub size, or somewhat larger and deeper. The string is passed through a small hole drilled or punched with a nail in the middle of the 30″ x 30″ hole cover; tie a large knot in its end so it can't be pulled back through. The cover is placed over the hole and weighted down with stones. The thick end of the stick is shoved as deeply into the ground as it will go, at about five feet from the center of the hole. Bow the stick deeply and tie the free end of the string securely to it near the top. The bowed stick will pull the string taut.

Then pluck away. The ground bow produces a wonderfully rich deep bass sound that can be varied by flexing the stick. If you have a bow for a stringed instrument, try sawing on the string with it.

In Uganda, this instrument is played by children, and in America a three-year-old or older child will love it; Timothy, at one and a half, also plucked away on it happily. The Pygmies of the Congo make a similar ground bow, but they have a second player, who drums with two sticks on the top of the pit cover — an arrangement that can easily be worked out with American kids.

The ground bow is a double treat for preschoolers. As a bonus they get a fresh pile of dirt and a nice new hole to play in.

Mini Gut Bucket

This juice-can one-stringer is no Johnny One Note. The sound can be altered up and down by

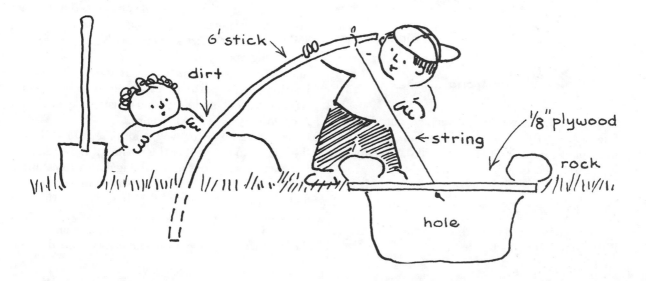

flexing the long neck and by pressing down on the string. The materials are:

    1 No. 10 juice can
    36″ length 1⅜″ lattice molding
    two ⅛″ x 1″ stove bolts with nuts and
        washers
    heavy string

Remove one end of the large juice can with a can opener and crimp down any protruding sharp edges with pliers, or file them off. Drill two corresponding holes in the lattice molding and in the side of the can for the stove bolts. The nuts go inside the can and the washers go between the wood and the heads of the bolts. Drill or punch a small hole for the string in the top of the can toward the side away from the wooden neck. Push the string through from the top and tie a large knot in the end so it can't be pulled back through. Drill a hole for the string near the top of the neck, and thread the free end of the string through it. Now bow the neck and bring the end of the string around it and tie it securely in place. The bowing of the neck will pull the string taut.

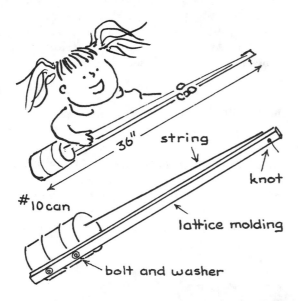

36″ string

knot

#10 can

lattice molding

bolt and washer

Any child over one will strum away on the Mini Gut Bucket. It is best played held under the arm like a banjo, but a younger child will stand it upright like a washtub bass.

Rubber Band Zither

A preschooler can make this instrument with very little help. All that's needed are:

    1 sturdy cardboard box
    rubber bands
    2 pencils

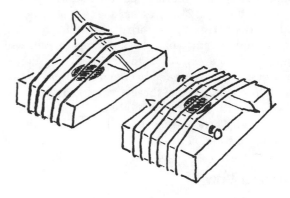

Cut a circular sound hole in the box and show your three-year-old how to stretch the rubber bands around the box. Different-size rubber bands will give a variety of notes. Once the bands are stretched on, your child can push the pencil bridges under them to hold them off the surface of the box. Not much to it. But to a preschooler, this is a very exciting project. It's quick and *he* can do it himself — plus it plays music.

Also illustrated is a rubber band zither with a triangular "comb" that will produce a graduated series of notes from a number of identical rubber bands. The comb can be made from any light piece of wood; cut small notches where the bands cross it, and fix the comb in place with glue.

DANCING

Kids will always dance, even if you don't. But they'll do much more of it if they see dancing around them and know that it's part of everybody's life — not just something special that's done on TV. A baby, as most fathers quickly discover, is the world's best ballroom dance partner. A baby loves to be swept right off his feet, and there's no resistance; you swirl and dip — you're Fred Astaire.

Babies start dancing well before they can walk — they jiggle to the beat of the music. And real dancing can follow the onset of walking with astonishing speed. In our house, Timothy was on his feet only four days when he started the slow, slightly rhythmical turning that is a baby's first dance.

As kids grow, dancing with them takes on more the character of ring-around-the-rosy, the dance favorite from about one and a half through six — the best part is seeing Daddy fall down. Many fathers like to strut with their kids to recordings of Sousa marches and the like. Gregory, Timothy, and I do a kind of stylized chase around the living room furniture and through the other rooms, with everybody stomping, or jogging, or sneaking around, depending on the spirit of the music — and chasing and being chased at the same time.

It's fun to discuss with preschoolers what the music sounds like to them — whether it's big or little, sad or happy. Kids are very perceptive about music in ways you wouldn't expect. Preschoolers like the game of assigning animals to different musical sounds — pretty much the way it's done in *Peter and the Wolf*, so that flute music will be birds chirping and part of the *1812 Overture* may sound, as Gregory put it at four, like dolphins jumping out of the water.

Watching kids dance can be one of the great diversions and treats of parenthood. Every child isn't a Nureyev, but most of them are — they're born to dance. Give them plenty of music and a little applause and they'll perform — spontaneously. Try introducing your child to different kinds of music that aren't the usual fare in your home — which is easily done by turning the knob on the radio. If you listen exclusively to classical music, you may discover that your one-year-old would prefer to clog it to some bluegrass, and if you're a rock fan you may find that your child digs Beethoven. Actually, Beethoven's *Fifth* is a childhood classic; almost every toddler and preschooler will prance around excitedly to its driving beat, giant-stepping with the big, tough parts, and tiptoeing during the hushed intervals. Make sure, too, that your kids hear some ragtime. If that doesn't get them dancing, you can save the money you might have spent on tap and ballet classes.

Bells and Jingles

Tying bells on a dancing toddler — or on any child, for that matter — is always good for some fun. Use the little round bells that are sold at Christmas time and tie them with light string to a belt or a hat.

Metal soda bottle caps make good dance jingles. Pry out the plastic liners and let a preschooler hammer them flat against a hard surface like a sidewalk. Drill or punch holes in their centers and get your child to string them together for jingling

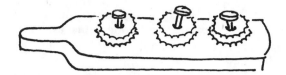

bracelets. Or mount them in pairs on a piece of scrap wood with nails so they will clack together like tambourine jangles when shaken.

RECORDS

A public library collection of children's records is a special blessing for parents — it means that you can constantly change the kiddie music in your home instead of always being stuck in the same old groove that everyone in the house has heard hundreds of times to the point of distraction.

Around three years, most kids can operate a battery-powered record player. Look for the kind that is designed especially for preschoolers, with the tone arm safely ensconced in the lid to discourage kids from tinkering with it. Use alkaline batteries — they cost more than conventional ones, but their long life is well worth the initial outlay. If your child proves to be a true discophile and runs the record player through a set of batteries in a month's time, it will pay to buy an inexpensive AC-DC converter from a stereo store so the record player can be plugged in — save the instructions that come with a record player, because they will tell what kind of converter to use.

A child's battery-powered record player can last for years if its owner is taught from the start exactly how to use and respect it. But there are limits to the durability of these machines. A father of four tells me that his gang can destroy any record player made.

CONCERTS

The best concerts to take kids to are held outdoors — band concerts, bluegrass and folk music festivals, relaxed outdoor chamber music concerts in parks. Events like these are often organized so families can sit picnic-style on the grass and listen to the music, but the kids can get up and run in the park, or the baby can cry and be carried off out of hearing without anyone being particularly disturbed. Take along a bag of toys and books and some food that's not too crunchy, and expect to spend less time listening to the music than chasing the kids around the greensward.

Bluegrass festivals are the ultimate in relaxed, homey music making. We go to these from time to time, not out of any great love for country music, but because they're so much fun for the kids. And because the kids see people getting together in a wonderful, easygoing way for the pleasure of making music. Usually there are as many people with instruments as there are spectators, and impromptu groups are formed in every corner of the lot, often with whole families of musicians — Dad on fiddle, Junior at nine on bass, Sis on guitar, and Mom

playing banjo. The kids dance wherever they like and everyone is glad to have them crowd in close to the musicians to watch how the instruments are played.

TV concerts give you another relaxed way to share music listening with a child. No one in the audience is disturbed if your kid is restless, or if you point out the instruments and teach your child their names, or even if everybody in the family decides to get up and conduct.

If special indoor children's concerts are offered where you live — and you can afford them — you won't find a better one-time Saturday treat for a four-year-old or older child. But wait till he's at least six to buy a season subscription.

PHOTOGRAPHY

At age five most kids can operate a simple camera and can learn some of the fundamentals of photography. Before that, a child loves to snap shots with a plastic toy camera or a couple of blocks of wood knocked together to look a little like a camera. When you get out your camera, your child runs to get hers, and you photograph each other photographing each other photographing each other.

Skin Photography

To demonstrate for a preschooler the fundamental notion of photography — that pictures are made with light — try some summertime "skin photos." Before he goes out in the sun at the beach or in the back yard, help your child draw his initial(s) on his own skin with adhesive tape — or make any other

pattern he likes. Fry the child nicely in the sun, remove the tape, and you have a sharp image made by the sunlight. The best time for this experiment is naturally at the beginning of summer, when kids are still pale all over. Replace the tape several days running and you get a clearer image.

Camera Obscura

This simplified version of the old camera obscura shows a five-year-old how the light from the subject passes through the lens hole of the camera and falls on the film, and it is a neat introduction to the way the image is turned upside down in the process. The materials you need are:

    one piece cardboard (approximately
        18" x 24")
    aluminum foil
    tape
    one candle

With a knife, cut a small hole — say a 2" square — in the middle of the cardboard. Cover the hole with a piece of aluminum foil held in place with tape. With an awl, compass point, or other sharp instrument, punch a hole in the middle of the aluminum foil. The hole should be about $1/16$" in diameter and should be round with clean edges.

At night, place a table near a white wall and put

the candle on the table in a holder. With the room darkened and the candle lighted, line the cardboard up as in the illustration so that the upside-down image of the candle flame is projected on the wall. You may have to move the candle and the cardboard around a bit to get it in focus. When your child blows gently at the candle, the inverted picture of the flame dances on the wall.

Magnifying Glass Photos

Any magnifying glass with two convex surfaces, preferably a large one, will project an upside-down image of a bright scene onto a white surface. Use any white paper — a heavy sheet is best — and stand in a fairly dark room near a window on a sunny day. Hold the paper parallel to the window with the magnifying glass between them. By moving paper and glass back and forth a bit you'll quickly bring into focus on the paper an inverted picture of the outdoors. You can get a sharp image with this technique by standing under a shade tree on a bright day, or by standing in a dark corner of a room at night to project a picture of a brightly lighted part of the same room.

"Living portraits" are great fun to make with a group of kids. In a very dark room aim a bright directional light at a child's face and use the magnifying glass technique to project a live photo of him on the paper. Kids wave excitedly at their upside-down pictures — which wave back.

Box Camera

This quickly made "camera" projects on its translucent inner screen an upside-down image of any bright scene or object it is pointed at, just as an actual camera projects a picture on a piece of film. In one end of a shoe box cut simple eye holes as in the illustration, and in the center of the other end poke a peephole about ⅛″ in diameter using a sharp tool and trying to make a clean edge. The tracing paper screen across the center of the box is held in place with tape. Now you just put the box top on and aim the camera. A dark blanket or coat draped as in the drawing will make the image much brighter.

Real Photos

Instamatic-type 126 cameras seem to have been designed for use by preschoolers — the chances of making a mistake have been eliminated. Loading the film is as easy as operating a jack-in-the-box. Then it's just aim and push the button. The only part a five-year-old may need regular help with is advancing the film between shots, which is a bonus because it allows you to slow down her picture-taking rate and keep her from shooting all the film in a few minutes.

For a first camera, buy the least expensive 126 available; at this writing you can get one for a little under ten dollars. Or, of course, a hand-me-down is even better. These cameras can take pretty much abuse, but any camera is essentially delicate, so teach your child to handle it with care, and keep it in a special place so it doesn't become an everyday toy. A real camera is such an important grown-up piece of equipment, a five-year-old will try very hard to handle it correctly. A loop of heavy string added so the camera can be hung around your child's neck will save it a few falls.

At a camera store — though usually not at a drugstore — you can get black-and-white 126 film. Both the film and the processing are cheaper than color. A preschool-age photographer will take pictures of everything in sight: the neighbors' car, the TV antenna on the roof, a coffee cup on the table.

Since we can't afford the developing and printing to encourage this kind of exploration, Gregory has been appointed Official Family Photographer. When we have guests or a family event like a birthday, out comes the camera. Everybody poses for the official photographer; he gets off a few memorable shots; and the camera is put away until another occasion.

Make sure to teach your child to hold her breath just as she's going to snap the shot, which will help her freeze in position with the camera steady as she squeezes the shutter button.

Use the fastest photo processing facility you can find. A kid whose film is out being developed will beg you every day for the prints.

ARTS AND CRAFTS

Here is a tall tale about a small boy's arts and crafts project and his dad that comes down to us from the first century A.D., told by the writer Thomas:

> *This little child Jesus when he was five years old was playing at the ford of a brook. . . . And having made soft clay, he fashioned there of twelve sparrows. And it was the Sabbath when he . . . made them. And there were also many other little children playing with him.*
>
> *And a certain Jew when he saw what Jesus did, playing upon the Sabbath day, departed straightway and told his father Joseph, "Lo, thy child is at the brook and he hath taken clay and fashioned twelve little birds and hath polluted the Sabbath day." And Joseph came to the place and saw, and cried out to him, "Wherefore doest thou these things on the Sabbath, which is not lawful to do?" But Jesus clapped his hands together and cried out to the sparrows, "Go," and the sparrows took their flight and went away chirping.*

Kids today don't have this same dramatic flair for showing how important their play dough birds are to them, but you can be sure if they could, they'd make them fly for Dad. Making clay birds and pipe cleaner dogs, pasting collages and painting pictures are the daily work of preschoolers, and a vital part of a child's job of learning how he can manipulate things and fit them together to make new things.

It would be a pretty insensitive dad who would storm in like old Joseph in the story and try to stop his child from making clay birds. No one would dream of actively discouraging a child from "ex-

pressing herself." But even though we know it's right for a child to do plenty of this "creative self-expression," it's a rare father who is found similarly expressing himself, and thereby giving his active backing and full stamp of approval to this important part of his child's life.

Many men who would enjoy a little workout with the magic markers or get a kick out of squeezing some clay hold back because they're uncomfortable with crafts work. They feel it requires some special skill or training they never had, that it is outside their realm. "I can hardly draw a straight line," is the rationale. "I haven't got a scrap of talent."

You will notice that any child of three, with no special skill or training and probably no "talent" at all, will have a wonderful time working on a great variety of arts and crafts projects. This child isn't exercising some remarkable creative urge; he is no Leonardo. He's merely having a good time making objects out of materials that he can handle easily and competently.

When a father teaches his kids the fundamentals

of using woodworking tools and wrenches and other things that he's familiar with, he is helping them move forward toward the adult world. But by stopping for a few minutes to work with your children with crayons or finger paints, you pay them the compliment of joining in *their* activities, of using materials that *they* feel comfortable with.

My wife has taught parent-child arts and crafts classes for years, and she knows that it takes a while for the fathers who come to these to loosen up and get into the swing of the thing. She tells of one particularly uncomfortable father who simply stood by fidgeting, watching his four-year-old as she worked on the projects. This went on for several Saturday mornings, until one day he absently picked up a marker and doodled a stick figure while his daughter drew a big face with arms and legs jutting out from it. "This picture I drew is my daddy," she announced, and then added with great pride: "And look, my daddy drew a picture of *me*." The man beamed with pride, too. And after the class he came up to Rita to say: "I think I was afraid she'd see I couldn't do it." After that day, he was the most enthusiastic member of the group.

Below are a few ideas for father-child arts and crafts projects. They are all things that require *no* training. If you want suggestions for going further into arts and crafts with your kids, borrow from your public library a copy of the classic in the field: Victor D'Amico, *Art for the Family* (New York: The Museum of Modern Art, 1954).

Yucky Squeeze Painting

Into Ziplock plastic bags, help your kids squirt shaving cream and pour poster paint, mustard, catsup, food coloring, and/or any other substance they can think of that will make a gooey concoction. Seal the bags and let the kids squeeze them and work the colors together. Squeeze one yourself — it's fun. Try different combinations of colors. Shaving cream with a spot of catsup, for instance, will demonstrate how pink is mixed. Several colors together will at first produce a rich marble effect and then turn to yucky brown.

This is the cleanest messy project possible, but put down plenty of newspapers first for insurance. The bags hold up under some vigorous squeezing, but the seam can always pop. Put smocks or aprons on the kids, too. An excellent painting smock can be made from an old shirt too frayed for you to wear any

longer. Your child can wear it with the sleeves rolled up or cut off, and buttoned up the back.

Shared Self-Portraits

You'll need a big piece of paper for this, because you'll lie down on your back on the paper while your child draws your outline with a big marker. But first you'll trace her outline on another piece of paper so she'll know just what to do. Trace as many details as you can find — fingers, shoelaces, braids. A three-year-old may have some trouble marking your outline, but should get a great kick out of it anyway. The difference in the sizes of the two pieces of paper used for these portraits is fascinating to kids.

You can get brown paper in rolls the right size for this project at a dime store. Or if you are lucky enough to have a real old-fashioned butcher nearby, make an excursion to his shop some Saturday with your child and ask him to sell you some long sheets of butcher paper from his roll. Make sure to get enough to do everybody in the family, too — Mom and the baby and the dog — though you may have to hold some of these down to trace their outlines.

The next step, after the outlines, is for each person to fill in the features and clothes of a self-portrait within the outline. Use whatever markers or paints you have, and just draw or paint the way your child does — as the spirit moves you. This becomes even more of a game if the self-portrait shows you as you would like to be, not necessarily as you are. So that a child might draw on a ten-gallon hat or a superperson cape, and a father might picture himself lying on a beach towel or wearing a matador's suit of lights. Drawing it full size is a lot like dressing up for a costume party.

Each child will fill in the self-portrait according to the stage she's reached in drawing. A six-year-old will be able to add some pretty interesting details, while a three-year-old will probably scribble in the space. The older child will be drawing what she thinks she looks like; the younger one, what he knows he *feels* like, because there are happy scribbles and angry ones, and proud scribbles and so forth.

Finger Paints

Shaving cream is a father's finger paint. Kids love to squirt it on a slick surface — an oilcloth table cover, formica countertop, or cookie sheet — and run their hands through it.

I was raised in a pretty old-fashioned way and never did finger painting as a child, which my wife, with her arts and crafts teaching background, finds shocking. She blames many of my foibles and most of my personal rigidity on this basic lack in my education. Dr. Freud, would you agree with this analysis? At any rate, one afternoon I managed a great psychic breakthrough by joining Gregory at the kitchen table and finger painting with him.

At first I felt inhibited as I dipped finger by finger and doodled. It seemed to be no fun and messy. But then I decided I might as well go the whole route, so I put my palms in the paint and the heels of my hands and heaped on some more paint and started slipping and sliding in it up to my elbows. And right there I felt thirty-eight years of anxieties, aggression, hang-ups, and frustrations slip out through my fingertips into that primordial ooze. I can't promise the same kind of release for everyone, but it's worth a try, seeing as how it's a lot cheaper than sessions with a shrink.

For instant finger paints, squirt shaving cream into separate containers or in separate mounds on a washable surface, and let your child dye it with food coloring. You can also raid the icebox for some natural dyes. Beet and berry juices make fine coloring agents, and spinach water makes a nice pale green that the kids will greet with "Yuck," just as they greet the spinach that was cooked in it.

Paper for finger painting should have a slick surface so the stuff can slide. Use big sheets and don't be stingy — go through a lot of paint and paper.

Finger painting is best done as an outdoor summer project, because the kids can strip down and paint with their toes and knees if they like — and so can you. And at the end, clean-up can be accomplished quickly with the garden hose. If you do finger painting indoors, work on the floor and lay down plenty of newspaper so you can go at it with no holds barred.

The very best place, though, for indoor finger painting is the bathtub. Make up some big batches of colored shaving cream, strip the kids down, and let them decorate the inside of the tub. If you have a shower stall with washable walls, all the better — there'll be more surface to decorate. How deeply you'll want to get into this yourself is a matter of personal choice, but the best part for you will come at the end, anyway, when you turn on the shower to wash the whole crew off, or slosh them with water from a small bucket.

With finger painting, the end product doesn't matter much. The fun is all in the doing. It's like making mud pies — you don't *eat* those at the end, and you don't really have to hang up finger paintings.

Junk Sculpture

Little boys especially are intrigued by the idea of junk sculpture, because they love junk. You can use any kind of junk, which is to say, whatever comes to hand. Take a shovel, for instance, and lay it on the ground. Then help your child find light-colored stones or some bottle caps for eyes and maybe a pencil for a mouth. Is there a mop handy for hair? A four-year-old will quickly pick up on this and start to assemble junk from all over — brooms for arms and legs, silverware for fingers, and your old boots for the feet.

Work at any size you like. On an out-of-the-way beach or any empty lot you and your kids may be able to assemble enough old pieces of wood and containers to put together a mammoth construction. If it looks like something, fine. If it doesn't, just call it modern art. The fun is in putting it together. And maybe get a snapshot to remember it by.

For small-scale junk sculpturing, keep a couple of boxes somewhere — say under your workbench — into which you will throw bottle caps, broken toys, odds and ends of hardware, wine corks, sturdy cardboard food containers, etc. This kind of junk piles up rapidly. Your child can put the pieces of junk together into abstract constructions, using glue and wire, nails and pieces of wood to hold it together. Kids of five and six begin to be interested in making sculptures that look like things — a cow made from a salt box with pieces of dowel shoved through holes for the legs and a block of wood glued on for a head.

If you're at all handy, you'll be able to help your child put the junk together the way she wants it to go. On a project like this it's easy to take over and make a lot of suggestions: "Wouldn't this look better if you put it over here?" Try to stay in the background, though, and act as a resource man who supplies materials and some occasional assistance. Let your child make all the important aesthetic judgments and figure out what she wants to make and how it will go together. If you get the itch to take over and "improve" your child's sculpture, grab some junk and work on one of your own.

Mobiles

Mobiles are just hanging junk sculptures. Help your child drill holes in scrap pieces of light wood, bottle tops, pieces of cardboard, and other junk. With wires through the holes, a child as young as three can hang things up. When a preschooler is using wire, crimp over the ends with pliers to make handling safer.

For a mobile framework to hang things on, you can suspend a coat hanger or an onion sack or a piece of hardware cloth. And for a big production, you can string a wire across a room from ceiling molding to ceiling molding and hang several mobile frames from it. Any light object can be hung on a mobile frame — don't forget colored paper, and the loop chains that kids make with it. The pleasure you get from making mobiles is the same pleasure you get from hanging ornaments on a Christmas tree.

Chapter 10

PLAYING WITH KIDS

When Alcibiades went to visit the great sage Socrates, he found him on a hobby horse, romping with his kids. One day when I went to visit my brother-in-law, who is a pediatrician, I found him on the floor with John, five, and Quentin, three, all building elaborate houses with an enormous set of plastic blocks. "This is Daddy's Lego," John announced. "He got it for his birthday." And often when I look across into the play yard next door I see my neighbor, a strapping six-foot construction worker, playing with his two preschoolers in the massive sandbox he built for them — they have big Tonka construction machinery to push the sand around with.

ROUGHHOUSE

Corporal play beats corporal punishment hands down as a tool for fathers. And fathers always have their best fun with the kids dealing out the rough treatment. All parents know that a cooped-up child is a whiny one or worse, and that regular exercise leads to rosy cheeks, sound sleep, and a cheerful disposition.

I find that a good session of roughhousing one evening usually produces a happier child the next day. Results are quick, but not instant. That is, a heavy workout won't wear down a four-year-old and make her fall asleep instantly. You're much likelier to be the one who's worn out. And too much exercise at the wrong moment — the end of a long napless day — will be downright counterproductive and make a child so giddy that sleep won't come for hours.

Now, while your kids are still small, is the prime time for throwing them around. A preschooler makes a terrific acrobatic partner, but in a few years he'll be too heavy to lift.

Some of the acrobatic routines that parents often do with kids should be avoided. Swinging a child around by the arms puts too much strain on the joints at the elbows and shoulders — weak points in the human anatomy. Always hold kids around the body, under the arms, to swing them — they get just as giddy being swung this way. And then there's the very commonly done flip, where the child walks up your legs, leaning backward while you hold her hands, and then you flip her in a wide somersault, still holding her by the hands. This flip also puts too much strain on the weak shoulder joints. Avoid it. In this section are descriptions and step-by-step illustrations of several somersault routines that give a child just as exciting a flip — but safely.

When you're doing acrobatic stunts, it's always best to be outdoors on soft grass, or on a mat of doubled-up rugs, and well away from furniture — particularly tables and cabinets with hard, sharp corners.

Again

Timothy, at one and a half, decided the name of this routine was Again, because whenever I did it with Gregory and his friends they'd plead: "Again. Again." Of all the many tumbling routines I've done with dozens of little kids, this is far and away the most popular.

The step-by-step illustration shows how it works. Grabbing a child by the waist or under the arms, you lift her up onto your shoulder — either shoulder is fine, but let's use the left shoulder for the explanation. The child will be facing behind you with her abdomen on your shoulder (step 1). Now take her left ankle in your right hand and lower her down your back, meanwhile reaching around behind her with your left hand (step 2). You press her body between your left arm and back, controlling the rate at which she slides downward. Next, you reach down and back with your now free right hand and grab the closest leg (step 3). Your left hand then catches the other leg.

At this point the child can reach out with her hands to the ground and walk away from your back on her hands. Most kids prefer, though, to swing up

through your legs, bringing their arms through as in the illustration (step 4). You then clasp the child's body between your legs, letting her legs fall backward. With your hands, you now reach over her shoulders, hook under both arms (step 5), and pull her to a standing position facing you (step 6). And now you're ready to do it Again.

Both the explanation and the illustration probably seem complex. The actual routine is extremely simple, and easy to perform. Once through and you'll have the hang of it. A toddler is easy to lift each time he wants to do it Again, but bigger kids can ease your burden by taking a run and a leap up as you bend at the knees to catch them on your shoulder.

Low Somersaulting

Here's a good low assisted somersault for a toddler. Kneel down with your right arm held out from your side, and your hand open with the palm up and thumb back. Your child approaches behind your right arm (step 1). Grasp his far side with your right fingers, and with your left hand grab the material at the back of his shirt below the collar (step 2) — no tight collars, please. Now simultaneously lift up with your right arm, turning it forward, and push down and around with the left to guide him slowly through a complete somersault, landing on his feet. The extended right arm acts as a kind of pivot, around which his body turns, so that by step 4 your arms have crossed one another. Perform this gently

1.   2.   3.   4.   5.   6.

clamp legs

grasp cloth

loose
collar

1. 2. 3. 4. 5.

and over a soft landing place, and make sure you're holding on with both hands at all times.

For another low toddler somersault, kneel down and hang your left arm down and a little behind you with the palm of your left hand turned up, creating a step for your child to climb on to get to your shoulder (step 1). With some huffing and puffing and an assist from your right hand reaching over your left shoulder, she scrambles up your back and gets in position with her abdomen on your shoulder and her head forward. Now grab the cloth on the back of her shirt right below the collar with your right hand (step 2) — again no tight collars. Pull forward and down gently with the right hand, meanwhile laying the open palm of your left hand firmly on her lower back to guide her slowly through the somersault to a two-point landing.

Left and right are used here only for convenience in explaining — switch sides if it's more comfortable.

High Somersault

With a child of three and a half or older, you can add some height and excitement to somersaulting. The procedure is identical to the first low somersault described above, but you now sit on the edge of a bed, which makes your job a little easier, and your child climbs up on the bed to approach from behind your extended arm.

Tumbling Team

The tumbling routine illustrated on the next page can start with kids as young as one and a half, though it's a little tricky getting a toddler to go around to the starting point by your upbent legs. With very small children the work is all done by Dad. Older kids, though, learn to throw themselves through the flip, so that your job is more one of guiding and assisting, instead of actually hefting the child.

grasp cloth

loose collar

1. 2. 3. 4.

Do this one only if you're feeling strong, because it will give you a good workout, and once you're down on your back, your child won't let you up till she's had her fill — and a kid's fill of tumbling takes a lot longer than a father's.

You need an open, clear place to do this, without furniture near to crack heads, and a doubled-up rug for your child to land on. The child approaches from behind one of your jackknifed legs. With a toddler, you'll sit up to grasp him (step 1), and then roll back as you lift him gently through the tumble. You grasp a toddler around the body — not by the arms —

holding your hands with the thumbs stretched forward and the fingers down so the thumbs go toward the child's back. You may find this handhold a little awkward at first, so squeeze tightly to assure a firm grasp. Your leg does a lot of the work (steps 2 and 3), gently lifting and throwing the child up and over. Between your leg and your hands, you guide the child through a full somersault to the point where you want him to land — on his feet. The landing point will be behind your head and a little to the side — the same side as the leg you use for lifting.

An older child will learn to take a short run and a little leap up onto your knee, so you can stay on your back, catching her with your arms outstretched and throwing her through the somersault. With a two-year-old or older child, you'll find that a better grip is achieved by grasping her firmly by the shoulders.

As she goes up and over, your thumbs will automatically push into her underarms. Again, your leg does much of the work of lifting and tossing.

Gregory named this routine Glunk for his own obscure reasons when he was two and he believed that there were two types of Glunk, one called Spaghetti Glunk, which was when he landed to the right of my head, and another called Noodle Glunk, when he landed to the left. It took him till he was well past his fifth birthday to differentiate well between left and right, but he never had trouble telling Noodle Glunk from Spaghetti Glunk at two.

Upside Down

You can do this little routine with any child old enough to stand. You and your child stand facing one another; he places both hands on your thighs just above your knees, then bends a little with head down between your legs. You bend over from the waist and grab him by both thighs, holding your hands so the thumbs point down. Now slowly and gently pull out and up so the child is upended, and ends up facing the same way you're facing. Don't jerk the legs up quickly or you'll put a strain on the child's back and neck — just bring them up at a nice even pace. The child's hands pressed against your legs also act to reduce any strain on his back.

Once he's hanging upside down, you'll probably transfer your hold, one hand at a time, to his ankles. When he's had enough hanging upside down, he can walk away on his hands through your spread legs.

Colossus

Many toddlers figure this one out for themselves. They push on your legs until they're spread apart in the stance of the great Colossus at Rhodes, and then chase round and round one leg or set up a figure-eight chase around both of them.

Tickling

Many fathers find that they can tickle away a child's silly behavior. Some kids, however, don't respond by calming down after the tickle fest, but only get more and more slaphappy — in any case, it's worth a try.

It's a rare kid who doesn't love to be tickled, but many reach a point — watch for it at age four — when they begin genuinely not to like it. Your child will always let you know that he likes it by squealing: "Don't do that, don't do that." But let up for a second and he wriggles toward you for more and usually says, "Why did you stop?" This is a technique that little girls refine and carry with them into womanhood, and for that reason, I think that little girls deserve a few extra tickles.

Daddy-Go-Round

Kids who ride on the Daddy-go-round give it a five-star rating by always begging for more, and I give it five stars, too, because it never fails to make me happy and giddy with laughing. You need two kids of about equal weight to balance you out, and they should be at least four years old, so you're sure they'll be able to hold on tight.

Stoop down, bending at the knees, with your arms held straight and a little out from your sides and with your hands palms upward. The kids straddle your hands, facing you. Each hand works as a seat — cup it to grab the child's butt securely. The child wraps his arms around yours and clings.

Now you simply lift and spin — around and around — until you're too dizzy to go on. It's a short ride because you get dizzy fast, but it's always hilarious. Lifting and twirling two at once may sound like hard work, but it's surprisingly light — the motion and centrifugal force must cut down a little on the weight of the kids.

Proper Piggyback Mounting

It's easy enough to pick up a one-year-old and set her on your shoulders. But I think every three-year-old should be taught the proper way to mount his dad. You can see piggyback mounting done in correct form at any circus; the performers never struggle or toss around awkwardly as one climbs onto the other's shoulders. The technique is simple.

1.   2.   3.

You kneel on one knee, with the other leg bridged out to the side. Your child steps up on the bridged leg with her foot (step 1) — left foot for a left bridged leg or right foot for a right-side bridge. She then throws her other leg up and around your far shoulder (step 2) and pulls herself up behind it. This makes getting on almost as special as the ride.

Leap Mounting

A four-and-a-half-year-old can do a more exciting kind of piggyback mounting — a Zorro leap that's straight out of old-time Hollywood. Your child starts from a fairly high place like a bed. You stand a little distance away with your back to him — and keep your knees and back bent a little. He jumps on your back in the low piggyback carry position with arms around your neck and legs around your sides — not on your shoulders, which would really jolt your neck. You can reach back to catch his legs and feet to help him hold on as he lands. A child who learns to do this loses interest in the actual piggyback ride for a while. He wants to spend the time hurtling onto Daddy's back, and from ever greater distances.

If your child isn't much of a jumper and is at all hesitant about trying this, encourage him to do it first from very close up, with the gap between you and him so small that he can keep a hand on your shoulder the whole time. As he gets into it, he'll ask you to move farther and farther off.

This Zorro-style mounting may sound like something you would rather not have happening to your back. I've been surprised to find myself still very much in one piece and with no back strain at all after a full hour of this with a dozen eager preschoolers. The shock of the landing isn't great and you can absorb most of it by keeping your back and knees bent to give a little with each landing.

Double Piggyback Ride

If there's anything more fun for kids than a ride on Dad's shoulders, it's a double piggyback ride — one kid on each shoulder. Sure, it's a little heavier, but it's double the pleasure. It's also the only simple way to avoid sibling squabbles between two kids who both want to ride on Daddy at the same time. Two kids of the same size make this double ride a little easier on you, since they balance you out — like carrying suitcases of equal weight. But you can manage two who are several years apart. Many fathers I've talked to do it all the time.

Shoulder Stand

The next step up from piggyback for a young acrobat is standing on your shoulders, and a slightly abridged version of this circus stunt isn't at all beyond the ability of a four-and-a-half-year-old. As you probably remember from having done this in the water, in order to stand on your shoulders, your child will first have to kneel on them. Now take her wrists firmly in your hands and have her put one foot up on a shoulder. She will press down with her straightened arms and you will push up against them as she lifts the other foot into position and herself into an almost stand. Don't go beyond this point to a free stand. Hand-held assisted standing is totally satisfying and exhilaratingly high for a preschooler, and it's safe. Your child is well supported in this position and it's difficult for her to fall from it — she'll just sit back down on your shoulders if she slips.

Bouncing Swing

This fantastic bouncy giggle inducer was developed by a group of experts in the roughhouse field — some four- and five-year-olds I was playing with at the local nursery school. We figured out together how to make it from:

> 1 old tire inner tube
> 14" length 1" x 4" pine
> staples OR tacks

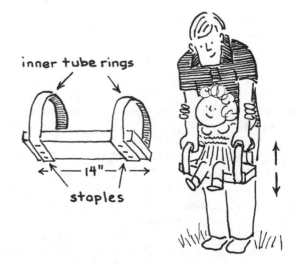

A big thick inner tube is best. You can get defunct inner tubes free for the asking at most gas stations, or take them from any dump. With scissors cut two 2½″ wide sections from the inner tube. These wide rubber bands are then stapled or held with heavy tacks to the underside of the board as in the illustration. That's all there is to making it. If you have a thin inner tube, you may want to double the bands for added strength.

Grasp the tops of the rubber circles and hold the seat down so your child can get on. She should hook her arms around behind yours and hold onto your arms with her hands. And then it's Bounce, Bounce, Bounce . . . Do your bouncing over soft grass or a doubled-up rug. The rubber bands are strong and durable, but naturally they won't last forever. It's so easy to cut more and attach them that I put fresh bands on regularly.

Wear gloves when you operate the bouncing swing. I left the nursery school the day this swing was invented with big blisters from bouncing fifteen kids who would not quit.

Tug-of-War

Preschool kids are notoriously poor at co-operating and sharing, but give them a chance to show a father up at tug-of-war and they'll pull together like a practiced team. A group of four four-year-olds will be able to pull you a short distance if you don't tug too hard, but a bigger group may beat you fairly and drag you clear across the yard.

Kids love the feeling of power they get from moving such a mountain as a father. They get the same thrill from pulling your weight on a toboggan or sled — which should take only two five-year-olds on hard, level snow. On the grass in the summer, pulling Dad on a toboggan is a great challenge, and it's a great triumph when several kids pulling on the rope and a couple pushing from behind get the burden going.

Bionic Family Stick

You can at least double the possibilities for tussling and roughhousing and exercising with your kids with this very simple piece of equipment — a 2½′ length of 1″ dowel. Dowels are available at all lumberyards and most hardware stores. Some of the stick's dozens of uses are outlined below.

The stick is a swing. You hold it near both ends.

Your preschooler sits on it and hooks his arms around behind yours, holding your arms tightly with his hands. You lift him up and spin around till you're dizzy.

The stick is a chinning bar. As you lift it higher, like a weight lifter pressing bar bells, your four-year-old — holding onto the middle of the bar — tries to pull up to a chinning position.

The stick is a hurdle. Grasping one end, press the far end of it up under the low bottom of an upholstered chair or some other low piece of furniture. Your three-year-old will jump over it again and again as you sit or kneel there holding it horizontal. If she misses, the hurdle collapses, which is an essential feature in the design of good hurdles.

The stick is a very jouncy horse. Rest one end on the seat of an upholstered chair and hold onto the other end — you will be standing for this. Your child straddles the stick-horse and you provide the action by pumping up and down. Your arm is the neck of the bronco, and most young cowpokes will have to cling tightly to it to keep from being thrown.

The stick is an oar. You and your child can do a great row, row, row your boat sitting facing each other on the floor with knees bent, both holding the stick-oar. Try it standing, too, and get your child to lean way back when he rows.

You and your child will find many other uses for the stick. One of the beauties of an object this simple is that it sets a child's imagination on fire. Kids will think of many ways to use even a very complex piece of equipment, but real leaps of imagination come when a child confronts something like this that doesn't give him any clues to how it should be used.

In our house, this exercise dowel is always referred to as the Bionic Family Stick, a name arrived at after much discussion, and one that I think suits it perfectly.

Run-through Delight

The same 2½′ dowel that functions as a Bionic Family Stick — fitted with a couple of dish towels — becomes a Run-through Delight for toddlers and preschoolers. Even a crawler will go back and forth under this with glee.

Wrap about 2″ of the short side of each dish towel around the dowel and fasten it with safety pins. The result will look like a pair of dowdy curtains on a curtain rod. Just hold this by one end with the towels hanging free and near the floor, and your kids will run back and forth through it screaming with laughter. To make this a permanent item, the parts of the dish towels that wrap around the dowel can be

sewn instead of held with safety pins. The dowel slips out at the end of a run-through session to resume its identity as the Bionic Family Stick. On a long trip, I throw the Bionic Stick and the dish towel curtains in the car, and use them to exercise and wear the kids out when we stop at rest pull-offs along the highway.

Suspended between the seats of two straight chairs, the Run-through Delight becomes a low, crouch-behind puppet theater. It also makes a perfect matador's cape, with sword along the top to stiffen it. Who in your family is the bull — father or child? Here we are always switching roles and even el toro shouts, Ole!

Dad's Daily Exercises

Whether you do the daily dozen, the Canadian Air Force program, or hatha-yoga, make sure to perform your exercises where your child can get into the act. A baby or toddler will try to imitate every move you make. Help her by counting cadence or chanting the steps of the exercise.

Jogging, of course, is the big exercise craze of the moment, and it's possible to include preschoolers in jogging if you take it very easy and trot short distances with them. This is fun for everybody, but it won't get you into shape. Real jogging, on the other hand, cuts a lot of time out of your day that you might be able to share with the kids. Switching from jogging to the old daily dozen, with the kids included, could give you a rewarding family activity to replace the loneliness of the long-distance runner. Or how about switching to bike riding — also excellent exercise — with a child seat mounted behind?

Basic Father Exercise

The deep knee bend is a father's basic exercise. It gives a man with small kids the wherewithal to get close to his children — right down on their level. Leaning over doesn't have the same effect — it means that you are coming from somewhere else.

You know how happy your child is when you lift him up to the level of your face. It's not all in the exhilaration of being lifted; a lot of the pleasure is simply in being on your level. Nearly the same result can be achieved with a deep squat to your child's level.

A regimen of deep knee bends is a simple physical way to work on closing the generation gap between you and your kids. There's not much room for confusion and misunderstanding between people who can look each other in the eye while they're talking. And if you get in shape to bob down to your child's level regularly, you'll start to see the world from her vantage point, which can't help but give you a better appreciation of where she's coming from.

BALL GAMES

In soccer-playing countries, kids are part of the national sport right off the bat. A toddler in Italy or Venezuela or Greece can kick a big ball around and he's already in the swing of things. But American toddlers and preschoolers are presented with a whole array of throwing and catching sports — football, baseball, basketball — years before they'll be good at throwing and catching. Only when they've reached five do most kids develop the co-ordination needed to catch a small ball with their hands, the way adults do — before that it's all awkward grabbing with extended arms. So kids are stuck for a while with seeing this fascinating sports world all around them and just not being able to get into it in a practical way.

One father, a former defensive end for the New York Jets, said: "The kids today really get exposed quick. With the TV and listening to the parents and all . . . I've got a little nephew right now and he knows how to get down in a three-point stance and he can say, 'Hut one, hut two, hut three,' and he can't say Mommy and Daddy too well yet. But he's getting his football together. I think sports is always good and the younger you can get them active in that, the better — it seems that's an area to let a kid *grow* a little. Where they may be shy and bashful as relates to other things, in the sports field, it just brings people right on out, and can do a lot for the kids."

And we definitely can get kids into our national sports as early as they can shout "Hut one" — by playing with them at these sports *at their level*. So

that in football, for instance, you concentrate on the three-point stance and handing the ball off rather than on throwing and catching it.

But kids beg for games of catch, and every father naturally wants to oblige. Which is great — except that occasionally this turns into a very serious business between a preschooler and his dad as both become determined that the child will learn to do something that may be as much as a year or two out of his reach. When this happens, Dad will be disappointed that his child isn't able to perform, and the child will be disappointed in himself and ashamed that he can't live up to what his dad expects — and all along it has nothing to do with his ability or lack of it; it's just his age and the unrealistic expectations that father and child have both built up.

Each child develops at her own rate and there *are* some early throwers and catchers, even early baseball hitters, but these athletic prodigies will show themselves without any special prodding or pushing. All they will need is a game of catch to show their stuff, or a plastic bat and some slow straight pitching from Dad.

A good policy on ball games is to expect little and be pleased with your child's successes.

CATCH

You sit on the floor with your legs spread and roll a 4″ ball to a baby or toddler in the same position, and the ball goes back and forth like a wordless conversation. As the years go by, the rolling game turns into slow bounce and catch with a big ball and eventually to easy catch with smaller balls, and when kids are in school the ball is thrown harder and harder, but always it's the same easygoing back and forth between father and child. It gets crisper, but it's always the same good conversation.

A toddler can catch a 7″ ball pretty well — if you throw it right. Your child holds her arms straight out in front of her and you lob the ball right on top of them from very close in. She'll usually bend her arms to grasp the ball when it lands on them. And she'll run after every missed ball when your toss isn't accurate enough.

At three and four, catching is still done with the arms straight out in front — a procedure that's very different from the way older kids and adults catch a ball, with the elbows cocked at the sides and the hands doing most of the job. Three-year-old catch is a matter of embracing the ball with outstretched arms — pulling it in. When a three-year-old goes at it too hard, the ball spurts up or down out of his big hug. Those extended arms can create another problem for kids of three and four, because they get so excited waiting for the ball that they end up batting at it with the stiffened arms instead of pulling it in.

Get a child who is having trouble catching to sit on a high stool and hold out his arms as usual. Explain that he can pull the ball in instead of batting at it. Sitting on the stool changes the pace and the scene, so he's able to change technique, too. Being seated also gives him a lap — and between his lap and his arms closing around the ball it's hard for him to miss a slow fair throw. Bouncing the ball up to him from a hard floor makes his job of catching even a little easier.

Big-embrace catching goes on until at five most kids start to use their hands on the ball. We take this kind of catching for granted because it's what we naturally do as adults, but for a preschooler it's a giant step forward from coarse grabbing to a complex co-ordination of eyes, arms, hands, and fingers. Smaller balls can enter the game of catch at this point. And telling a child to keep her eye on the ball is relevant here where it doesn't make much difference with a younger child. Watching the ball is all-important now, and a child with eye trouble will fall behind in ball catching at five or six.

Throwing ability seems always a little better than catching ability to me, but basically it follows the same pattern. Younger kids push the ball away from themselves with arms and hands, while older kids learn to hold the ball in one hand and throw it.

KICK BALL

Though toddlers and preschoolers are slow to develop catching skills, they never have trouble kicking a ball around. If he's given the chance to play it, kick ball, or soccer, is almost always a preschooler's favorite ball game — because he's good at it. It gives him satisfactions that a clumsy game of catch can't provide. A three- or four-year-old can kick a ball pretty much in the direction he wants it to go, and there's plenty of fast action chasing after it. You don't need goals and teams and rules with preschoolers. Well, one basic rule — no hands on the ball. But otherwise the game is all in the running and the kicking, and the ball gets kicked *to* another player or past her — whichever way it happens is fine.

A 7″ ball should be standard equipment in every home with kids, from the time the first baby can crawl around. It will get pushed and rolled for a while, and then it will start to get its kicks. Even a one-year-old will chase the ball around laughing and booting it.

BASEBALL

The wider the bat and the bigger the ball, the more likely it is that a preschooler will connect with a pitch. A fat plastic bat will improve a kid's batting average, and use a soft rubber ball — softballs are too heavy for small children. The pitch has to be perfect and slow, and the kid's luck has to be running. Batting is a complex skill for older kids, but preschoolers will insist on trying, so give them every advantage.

A five- or six-year-old may enjoy swatting at a stable target for practice. With a shot of shaving cream from a spray can, make a mark on a small tree or post at the height of a perfect pitch for your child. When she connects with the "ball," the evidence will be on the bat. You can make the mark permanent with a dab of paint so your child can practice alone anytime.

A solid rubber ball suspended by a string makes a good target for batting practice, too. Drill or poke a hole through the ball with a large screwdriver. Use sturdy cord and make a knot in it about 10″ from the end. Then push the end of the cord through the hole in the ball with a screwdriver and make another large knot beneath the ball so it's sandwiched tightly

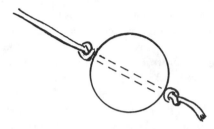

between the knots. The cord can be hung from a tree limb or a clothesline or a bracket extending out from the corner of a building. A hanging ball should be taken down when no adult is around, to avoid the chance of a child getting dangerously tangled in the cord.

The hard rubber or plastic cones used to mark highway construction are perfect for five-year-old batting practice. The batter just perches the ball on the top of the cone and takes a swat at it.

Batting isn't the whole game, and you can get a child to concentrate on a part of the sport that he can handle at his present level of co-ordination — base running. Put out markers for bases — sections of the Sunday paper are good except on a windy day — and explain how the players run, slide, and steal bases. Your child can tear along the baseline and slide dramatically as you "field" the ball and throw it to Mom on second.

KIDDIE FOOTBALL

You don't have to wait for the Little League years to get kids together for sports. There must be other dads in your neighborhood spending Saturday and Sunday with their preschoolers, and with a little organization you should be able to arrange a very silly and enjoyable football game. Don't leave the neighborhood moms out of the fun either, but be

prepared to lose the little girls from your team. Preschool girls — at least the ones I know — segregate themselves by sex in the most alarming and idiotic way. They say things like "The boys are the strongest; the girls are the sweetest" and insist on being cheerleaders at the football game. So teach them a cheer: "Football, Football, RAH, RAH, RAH!" This is no time for consciousness raising.

Six players are enough for a game and eleven are too many. The best kind of ball for the three-to-five set is made of dense rubber foam; cheaper inflated plastic footballs work fine, but a dog can destroy one of these with a single chomp.

The super-simple rules of kiddie football should be explained carefully at the start. Kids get to run with the ball but only dads get tackled — and piled up on, and mauled. Make a big deal of the huddle and use lots of football jargon, but don't bother trying to get everybody together at a line of scrimmage. And don't set up opposing teams that might actually win or lose. Preschoolers aren't ready for a win-lose situation. Well, everyone at every age is ready for a win situation — but losing is a different story, and when you're four, it's murder. I've talked with a number of fathers who have tried, as I once did, to organize groups of preschool kids into small teams for impromptu games of touch. They and I all learned quickly that it's not worth the effort. Teamwork isn't a regular part of early childhood. A group of preschoolers is a group of individuals, each with a personal mission. Each kid wants the ball and wants to run for a touchdown — that's the part of the game that counts.

In every huddle, besides stage-whispering what secret play is coming up, assign the next ball carrier — everybody gets a turn, and in order. After the huddle, a father takes the ball and hands off to the carrier, who runs to the other end of the yard with the other kids following. Touching doesn't put a guy out in this game. Every runner scores, and there's cheering each time. Yell, "Tackle," from time to time as a cue to the kids to gang up on one of the fathers.

After a couple of sessions you may want to introduce some refinements like centering the ball and kicking off. A couple of adults can demonstrate and you'll probably have an attentive audience, but don't expect all the kids to pick up on these fine points or care.

Working alone with a child who's particularly interested in football, concentrate on basics. Teach the three-point stance, how to bark out orders, how to take the ball with both hands and abdomen when it's handed off. Do a lot of handing off, which a child can manage, and only a little passing, which is difficult. Rushing and blocking are fun, too. A father makes a first-class practice dummy. Or stuff a duffle bag with old clothes and get your five- or six-year-old to draw an ugly, evil face on a piece of cloth, which you'll tack to the duffle bag with needle and thread. An angry kid can work out a lot of aggression on a blocking dummy.

I've read in magazines that in some parts of the country preschool-age kids are organized into realistic kiddie league teams with real pads, helmets, and uniforms, real pressure to win, and real injuries. It would be difficult to think of a more farfetched, thoughtless, perverse, or downright cruel thing to do to children.

BASKETBALL

Dribbling is out of the question for most preschoolers, though your child will love watching you do it. And she'll try again and again. Remind her from time to time that it's something she's not yet ready for, an accomplishment that will come much later — after she has learned to tie her shoes, and after she is able to blow a bubble with gum.

A four-year-old may manage to sink a few shots with a light ball — if he's only got a few inches to go to push the ball in. Set a toy basket up just at the height of your child's extended arms. And tell him how the really tall pros just reach up and drop the ball through. After all, why should a four-year-old have a bigger handicap than Wilt the Stilt?

Wastebasket shooting is another good basketball preliminary. A five-year-old may do fairly well at the distance of a yard. Avoid a game where you and your child take alternate shots at the basket — you'll overmatch her easily, which can dishearten and turn her off to the game. Instead, feed your child the balls and let her make all the shots.

FISHING

Preschool kids are lured to fishing just as powerfully as a bluegill is lured to a wriggling worm. Every kid wants to go fishing with Dad. And every dad — especially if he's an angler — plans for the day when he'll take his kids fishing.

You can have a terrific time fishing with a child of any age, but it's important to tailor the fishing trip to your child's abilities. Many fathers have told me of fishing trips "ruined" by preschoolers who became bored and restless after twenty minutes or half an hour. All preschool kids are likely to be bored and restless after a half hour of *anything*. Fishing has a

magical appeal, but not magical enough to extend a child's natural attention span. So if you expect to do a lot of fishing and one of the purposes of the trip is for you actually to catch fish, make sure you have another adult (Mom) along to help out when restlessness sets in.

Or plan ahead for the restlessness and go fishing in a spot where there are other attractions besides fish. Stick with the simplest kind of fishing — still fishing from the bank or shore. Take a child out to troll from a rowboat, for instance, and you've created a multitude of problems. You have to be constantly alert to whether he's climbing overboard, and then when he gets bored there's nothing else to do, nowhere to go, and he starts scuffing his feet on the floor of the boat, which scares all the fish away. If you're beside a small brook, on the other hand, when a five-year-old grows restless, you can help him set his pole up on a big forked stick, and he can go downstream a little to wade or turn over stones to find insects, and come back to fishing when he's ready.

Before age four, children don't need actual fishing equipment. Most pre-fours will be joyfully content with a stick and a string tied to the end, and will play for long periods (up to half an hour) dropping the string in the water, or "catching" underwater weeds by pulling them up on the end of the stick.

If you fish regularly, the whole family can go fishing together from the time your child is born, and she'll grow up around your fishing gear, learning by watching what Daddy does. In families like this, the kids starts in early to use sophisticated equipment. I've seen a three-year-old cast from a dock with a rod and spin-casting reel, and I've heard tell of a four-year-old who landed a twelve-pound blue from his family's cabin cruiser. But these, like all fish stories, are special cases. For most kids, six is the age when they acquire the co-ordination to start spin-casting. And four is a good age to set most kids up with some real tackle, actually trying to catch fish.

FIRST FISHING TRIP

If you're a seasoned fisherman, you'll know what tricks and secrets you want to pass along to your child, and you'll have a tackle box full of lures and flies and hooks that will be a treasure chest in her eyes and will be her school of fishing. As she asks about each fascinating rubber crayfish or shining spoon, your explanations of how they're used will help her learn how fish are caught.

If you know nothing of fishing, you have a lot to learn before you can pass it along to your kids. Instead of muddling through how-to books, find a fishing friend to help you introduce your child to the refined and complex art of angling — someone with a treasure chest tackle box that your child can wonder at and explore. Fishermen usually jump at a chance to initiate kids into the mysteries of their art.

Whether you're a veteran fisherman or not, though, there are a couple of fundamental principles to get across to a four-year-old if he's to understand and enjoy fishing. The first is simply how

fishing works — how the fish is attracted to the worm, but when he goes to eat it, he gets the hook instead. Draw diagrams to illustrate how the hook catches in the fish's lip, or demonstrate with a hook and a light plastic bottle to represent the fish, or with a real fish. Kids are fascinated by the idea of tricking the fish and will go over this valuable new piece of knowledge for months.

The second important thing a kid needs to know about fishing is that you don't always catch a fish — that the fun is in trying and you can come back another day and keep trying. You change your bait or your tackle, or you go to a new spot, but you always keep at it until you catch that elusive fish. A preschooler can easily be disappointed and turned off if she believes, as kids naturally do at four and five, that all she has to do is toss in the hook and bait and the fish will catch themselves.

Of course, there are some spots where all a kid needs to do *is* toss in a hook and the fish will catch themselves. There's a pond not far from where we live where dozens of pumpkinseed sunnies come dashing to the edge if you toss in a crumb of bread or even a pebble; they'll bite at anything on or off a hook, and the kids can catch as many as they like. They're all too small to fry, though, so they get tossed back in after a few minutes in a pail of water, where the kids can examine them close up. Ask around among neighbors who fish and especially among grade school kids who fish — someone may know a spot just like this where you can take your child for a successful first go at angling.

A reel like the one described on the opposite page makes an excellent rig for a four-year-old if you fish from a dock or the side of a bridge. For fishing from the side of a brook or pond, a pole of any sort will do — a straight sapling, or a ½" x 4′ dowel, or a length of bamboo. Tie on a line or fix it more securely through a hole drilled in the end of the pole — 6 lb. test monofilament is strong enough for any fish your child will catch, or use nylon string sold for hand lines for your child's ease of handling. Your child will want to use as big a hook as he can get — the kind that looks like a bent harpoon. Let him use one of these monsters from time to time, because it's fun, but if there are pan fish around and you want him to have the thrill of hooking one, make him settle for a small enough hook, because a big hook will never catch a small fish. Light sinker weights are essential, but a bobber isn't. Except that a pre-schooler loves a bobber. Anything that floats can act

as a bobber; you can press any plastic bottle into service or one of your child's floating bathtub toys. Or you can buy a real honest-to-goodness red and white plastic bobber from the fishing supply store. The trip to the tackle shop — with its fantastical displays of fluorescent plastic worms and minnow-shaped lures bristling with barbed hooks, plugs and jigs and spinners — is just as important a part of a fishing expedition for a child as sitting by the stream waiting for the suckers to nibble.

A preschooler will feel very important if she has a small box to carry her gear in, just as Dad carries his. And you'll need a bucket for the catch and a can for the bait. The best bait is always worms, because kids like to hunt worms just as much as they like to catch fish. The illustration shows how the worm is hooked so it will wriggle dramatically to attract the fish.

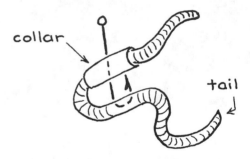

Show your child how to tell the front from the rear of the worm by putting it on the ground and watching which way it crawls.

Make sure to take along many snacks, or a picnic meal, and come supplied with a storybook and a toy or two so your child will have several alternatives to sitting and holding the fishing pole. Taking along a friend of your child's may help, too. Two kids fishing together stimulate each other's interest and keep each other going longer than one child alone will usually last. Getting up before sunrise for a fishing trip makes it a major adventure, and it's the best time to catch fish, anyway.

A preschooler's fishing enjoyment will be greatly improved if you pass along some useful angling lore. Kids love the game of trying to think as the fish would, trying to second-guess and outmaneuver him by figuring out where he'll be and what kind of food he'll be looking for. They like the detective work of finding a shadowy place along the edge of a stream where fish may be hiding between the rocks, or looking for a place where the water runs fast or whirls around, washing beetles and larvae and other food to the waiting trout. And they like to tiptoe along the edge, trying to whisper so as not to startle the fish.

Kids also love, on a hot day, to fall into the stream. Hang their clothes on a bush to dry in the sun and let them wade around for a while if it's shallow enough. The clothes will be dry in no time, but don't bother to put them back on till you're ready to leave, or your kids will only jump back in.

If no fish get caught, on the way home you and your child can figure out new tactics for attracting the fish on the next expedition.

Fish Reel

Here's a fish-shaped reel that's just right for a four-year-old. You can make it from a scrap piece of 1" x 4" about 7" long. With a saber saw, bandsaw, or coping saw, cut out a fish shape like the one illustrated, taking care not to crack the wood at the corners. Smooth with sandpaper. Drill a small hole from the top of the back fin through to the notch for the line; the end of the line is passed through this hole and knotted as in the illustration. Another

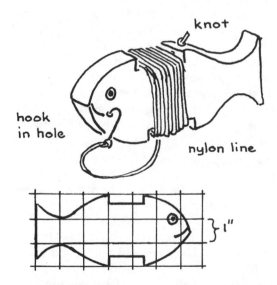

small hole drilled at the mouth of the fish will hold the hook out of harm's way when the line is wound up. Enamel paint over enamel primer will make the fish look spiffy, and will protect it against water. Use a nylon string hand line with this reel — rather than fishing monofilament. Reel fishing is best done from the edge of a dock or the side of a small bridge.

CASTING

A six-year-old is ready to learn to cast. A child should learn on a thumb-trigger operated spin-casting reel rather than the more difficult bail-type spinning reel. You can outfit a kid with rod and reel — at this writing — for less than ten dollars.

Before your child goes fishing with a new reel, get her to practice with it on the lawn, using a practice weight instead of a hook. When a child starts to cast, she wants to heave the thing, to use it with the same force she'd use on a baseball bat or a golf club, so if you set up a close target, she'll always overthrow it. Besides trying to convince her that she's using a sensitive piece of equipment that takes only a flick to send out the line and baited hook, make her sit down in a chair to cast, as she'd have to do in a boat. This will restrict her movement, forcing her to take advantage of the flick of the rod.

For early fishing expeditions with a spin-casting reel, choose a dock on a lake or by the ocean, where overcasting won't make any difference. Avoid small streams and overhanging branches. Sophisticated operations like dry fly casting in a trout stream are still years in the future.

A BUCKET OF WORMS

The best part of fishing for a four-year-old is catching the worms, because there's an excellent chance he'll get some.

Night Crawler Expedition

A hunt in the dark with Dad for night crawlers is a preschooler's idea of heaven. You'll need:

    1 flashlight
    red cellophane OR a translucent red plastic
        food container lid

1 covered plastic container
damp earth and/or leaf mold

You'll also need some worm lore. Only if he knows the ways of the wily worm will your child be able to trick him and catch him whole. Earthworms spend the day underground since they can't survive in sunlight. All night, particularly after a rain, they are out on the surface, dragging rotting leaves to their tunnels, where they cycle them through their digestive systems and produce the rich "castings" that greatly improve the topsoil. When the sun comes up in the morning, the eyeless worms don't see the light as we do, but scattered over their bodies are receptors that allow them to distinguish between light and dark. These receptors tell the worm to get back in its hole — the early bird is on the way. In fact, it's usually the late worm that gets caught by the early bird.

If you sneak up on night-feeding worms and shine the white light of a flashlight on them, they spring back into their tunnels almost before you can see them, since they sense that daylight and danger have come. So you cover the lens of the flashlight with a piece of red cellophane or translucent red plastic, holding it on with a rubber band or tape. The worms can't sense the red light as well as they can the white. But you still have to walk stealthily and move softly as a mouse and reach quickly to grab a night crawler before it retreats into its tunnel. A young hunter will want to yank hard and pull the worm out, and will probably pull it apart, getting only the top half, since the worm usually has a tight grip on the walls of the tunnel with its lower half, using its powerful muscles and holding on with the tiny stiff bristles that it also uses as an aid for crawling. Your child may already know how tightly the worm clings to the walls of his tunnel from watching a tug-of-war between a robin and a worm. The robin is patient and doesn't tug too hard, and eventually the worm weakens and relaxes his grip.

You can help to release the underground grip by pressing down on the soil around the worm with one hand while pulling the worm with the other. Don't grip the worm by the head; grasp it close to the hole. Kids get a lot of partial worms before they learn to do this, but no great harm is done. The worm will live, and if you keep it for a while it may even grow a new tail. But contrary to popular belief, the missing tail will not go off on its own as a new worm. By working as a team with Dad pressing the ground and

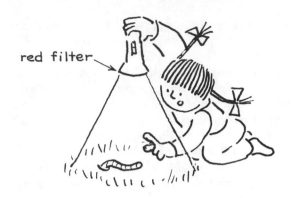

red filter

child pulling on the worm, you may even get a few out intact.

Keep the worms you gather in a plastic container, which should be half filled with damp (not soggy) soil or leaf mold so they will feel at home. Some small holes punched in the lid will let in enough air. They will survive this way for a few days in a cool place. If your child wants to feed them, they are very fond of damp oatmeal, pablum, coffee grounds, and chopped beet greens or carrot tops.

The best place to hunt for night crawlers is on a closely cropped lawn under shade trees and the best time is after a rain. You can create optimum conditions by scalping your lawn with the mower and watering it heavily the afternoon before your night crawler expedition. Any child will help with the watering. If you don't have a lawn, wait till after a rain and go to the lawn of a nearby safe park or college that is kept carefully manicured — there will probably be other shadowy figures there already wandering through the night with red flashlights.

Sawing Worms

This daytime method for gathering worms depends on an entirely different ruse. The worms are tricked into thinking they are being chased by their arch predator, the mole, which drives them in panic to the surface, where you and your child gather them.

If you are very light on your feet, you can sneak up on a molehill as it advances, with the mole at work underneath, and as the crust of the earth is heaved up you will see the worms scrambling to escape to the surface in headlong flight like the people of Pompeii as the volcano erupted — if you will excuse my making a mountain of a molehill. Moles are very sensitive to vibrations in the earth, so this is a rare sight indeed — the progress of the molehill stops immediately if the mole detects a footfall. Earthworms, likewise, react to any disturbance of the earth, which is their built-in defense against the moles. It's a defense system they sorely need since moles feed primarily on worms and will eat as many as three hundred of them in a day.

To convince the worms in your neighborhood that they are about to fall prey to the predatory mole, use:

> 18" pointed stake
> 1 board
> hammer OR mallet
> plastic container with soil

Your child can drive the stake into the dirt — about two thirds of its length. Then rub the board back and forth across the top of the stake, leaning heavily on it as you "saw" — the purpose is to make the stake vibrate. If there are any worms nearby, they should be driven to the surface. You can achieve pretty much the same result by wiggling a stick in loose garden soil, but there's more drama in stake and board "sawing."

Baiting Worms

Like a night crawler hunt, baiting a trap for earthworms has the appeal of a nighttime prowl for your preschooler. You will need:

> burlap
> coffee grounds OR oatmeal
> flashlight with a red shield
> plastic container with soil

In the late afternoon, wet the burlap, wring it out, and spread it on the ground where you suspect there are worms. Sprinkle it with damp coffee grounds or damp oatmeal, both of which are great treats for worms. After dark, the earthworms, coming to the surface to feed, will work their way

through the loose weave of the burlap to get to the bait on top.

A couple of hours after dark, you and your child sneak up with the utmost stealth. Grasp two sides of the burlap and pull it up with a decisive jerk. A few worms may be on top, and more will be trapped in the mesh. First, gather the worms that fall to the ground, and then the ones on the top surface of the burlap. A red-shielded flashlight will be a help on this hunt, as it was for catching night crawlers. The best job for a four-year-old is holding the light, but she should get to scoop up some worms, too.

Digging Worms

Should none of the schemes described above yield worms, you have no recourse but to dig. This will not be a come-down for a preschooler, whose enthusiasm for worm catching is boundless. From age four on, kids are good at digging. Six-year-olds often report having dug through to China. You don't need that deep an excavation to get a worm. Four to six inches of soil turned over with a small spade is plenty. It's best to sort through the soil with fingers, to avoid chopping up the worms with the spade.

Spring and fall are the best times of year; in a dry midsummer it's sometimes impossible to dig up a worm, and if it's cold the worms will have retreated deep into the ground. Good places to find an abundant harvest of earthworms are: shady spots, particularly the base of a maple tree; wherever you find damp soil, rotted plants, or thick clumps of weeds; a compost heap or pile of rotting leaves.

If you dig in several places and *still* can't find any worms, it may be because you live in a relatively new housing development, where the bulldozers pushed aside all the topsoil before the houses were built, and the evicted earthworms haven't yet recolonized the place. Or you may need the advice of an expert. Stop the first kid you see over the age of eight carrying a fishing rod, and ask him where to dig.

CRABBING

Crabbing with traps has all the same glamor and allure that fishing holds for kids, but none of the drawbacks. There's plenty going on to keep a three-year-old occupied and entertained, and a four-year-old can do the important part of the job herself — throwing out the trap and hauling it up onto the pier minutes later full of lively creatures. Success is almost assured, and preschoolers go nearly wild with delight as they haul in trapload after trapload of crabs. No long waits as there are in fishing, no going home without a nibble.

Taking your child crabbing requires absolutely no experience on your part. The people in the bait and tackle store where you buy the trap and line will tell you where to go to use it. You want to do your crabbing from a pier, dock, or causeway of some sort, not from a boat, which is difficult with kids. Several different designs of trap may be available. All work equally well, so the cheapest is your best bet. One trap will be enough for a start; if your kids get hooked on crabbing, you can always add more.

For bait, you can bring chicken parts from home, which are a great favorite of crabs. Legs are easiest to tie into the trap and last the longest, and three legs should be enough. A chunk of bait fish bought from the bait store will work equally well. You tie the bait securely into the middle of the assembled trap, and your child can throw the trap — on the end of its line — into the water. When it hits the bottom, the trap opens and hungry crabs swarm over the chicken or fish. After three or four minutes, your child tugs sharply on the line, which pulls the sides of the trap closed around the crabs, and then the trap is hauled in.

From this point on, you take over the work. Kids have a marvelous time examining the crabs, but don't let your child handle them or get close enough to be bitten. A bite from a crab is really mean. Handle live crabs with kitchen tongs, always approaching them from behind. It's a good policy to wear heavy gloves, and two pair of tongs will make your job easier. If a crab grabs someone's finger, he's not going to let you pry his claw loose. Cut the claw off or break it off, which will loosen its grip.

Keep your crabs in a bucket with some damp seaweed. Don't put water in the bucket.

It adds to the excitement of the crabbing venture to go early in the morning, as the sun is coming up, which is an excellent time for catching crabs — especially if the tide is coming in. An incoming tide means that the crabs will be moving in with it toward the pier or dock. Ask for information on the times of the daily tides at the bait and tackle shop. Also make sure to ask about local rules and restrictions governing crabbing. You'll want to know the legal size limit so you can throw back the small ones.

Here is a list of equipment you'll need on a crab-trapping expedition:

> trap(s) and line
> bait (chicken legs OR fish)
> string
> kitchen tongs
> work gloves
> sharp knife
> pliers
> bucket(s)

CYCLING

Among the fathers I've talked with, bicycling goes at the top of the list of favorite father-child sports. One man was pedaling his second daughter, two, around on the child seat he had ridden in behind *his* father years before.

Kids can ride with you from age one through six — if they don't get too heavy. Forty pounds is about the maximum for a rear-mounted seat. Too much weight slows travel down, unbalances the bike, and can also damage the axle threads, since the rear carrier is mounted directly on the rear axle. Child carriers mounted on the handlebars are only good through about thirty pounds, when the extra weight makes steering too difficult.

Two fathers I talked with had seats mounted both front and back. One man had twins and the other had kids two years apart, with the lighter one naturally riding in front. Both of these two-child pedalers report that the extra weight isn't too much to manage. On the contrary, one was doing ten-mile jaunts on hills and the other was riding ten to fifteen miles at a time on fairly level roads.

If you're new to bicycling or the added weight of your child makes the bike feel top-heavy and awkward, you may want to practice for a while with some other, less precious cargo strapped in the seat until you get the feel of the thing. When your child is riding with you, the rule is: Easy does it. Sudden or jerky movements should be avoided, because the

child's weight unbalances the bike. And take corners slowly and wide with the bike almost upright. Early Sunday morning, when there's not too much traffic, is the best time. Avoid hills if you can, and ride in low gears even on a straightaway.

If you're up against hills and you have a three-speed bike, you can get the gear range lowered by having a bicycle shop install a larger rear sprocket in the back wheel. With more teeth on the sprocket, all the gears shift downward. This makes the bike easier to pedal, but you lose most of the speed of your high gear, since it's now down around where your middle gear was before. Some English bikes can be modified without sacrificing high gear by the installation of a two- or three-socket derailleur system, but this is more expensive than switching to a bigger rear sprocket.

You'll need an extra shot of air in the tire under the child you're carrying.

A front-mounted carrier allows you to see and talk to your child, which is a big advantage, but you should probably use a rear-mounted type if you have only one child. With it, the bike is more stable, and it can be used for many more months than can a handlebar model. Avoid baby seats designed to clip onto the frame of the bike — they can't be mounted securely and in this position the child interferes with steering and pedaling.

Many parents like the brightly colored molded-plastic rear child seats, but somewhat more useful than these are fold-up child seats, which can be knocked down and used for carrying objects other than a child. Any child carrier should have sides, foot rests, and — most important — effective shields for keeping the child's feet out of the spokes. A safety belt is also essential, and use a full baby harness for a child under three.

On a bike, you and your child can see much more of the world than you do from a car — because you're a little higher up and because you can take it in more slowly. And since you're not whizzing by at 55 mph, you can always stop and check out something you see that's interesting, whether it's a brook or a wildflower or a new store on the highway. Where we live there are hills wherever you turn, so we limit bike excursions to a short run down the only fairly level road and take along a sandwich for a picnic at the end where it gets too steep. But in the summer, when we go to the shore, the first thing I do is rent a bike with a child carrier, and we get our money's worth out of the rental fee just roving around and checking out everything for miles around.

TRICYCLES

A two-year-old is ready for a tricycle as soon as her feet will reach the pedals. Low-slung plastic trikes are much safer than the conventional metal-tube style because they're hard to turn over, and because the big spokeless plastic wheel in front eliminates the danger of your child's catching a foot in revolving spokes.

Try to teach your kids not to go down steep hills on a tricycle, because the momentum they gather makes it almost impossible to stop. The trouble is, however, that riding fast down a steep hill is exactly the point of the tricycle as far as most kids are concerned. Riding double is another hazard you can try warning against — it greatly increases the instability of a tricycle.

If you're buying a trike, make sure to check for pedals and handgrips with rough surfaces — not smooth, slippery plastic ones. Check a tricycle regularly for loose handlebars and seat, broken or missing parts; keep everything tight with an adjustable wrench and squirt a little household oil into the wheel bearings from time to time.

Kids never have a sidewalk long enough, so they really love a tricycle tour where Dad walks and they ride for block after block; for more on tricycle touring, see p. 173.

Preschoolers learn to maneuver tricycles with extraordinary skill and accuracy — it's one realm where kids operate with true precision. Set up an obstacle course for an accomplished tricyclist so he can really show his stuff; the obstacles can be cardboard boxes or trashbaskets or anything else light that will turn over if it's hit.

TWO-WHEELERS

A child can keep riding a tricycle until his knees start jamming up under the handlebars, which will usually be when he's six or later, but if he's big and strong and has a good sense of balance, he may go to a two-wheeler as early as four. Most kids make the big switch from three wheels to two somewhere in between those ages. All kids I know *want* to make the switch as soon as they can.

A first two-wheeler is usually a 16″ bike — the measurement is the diameter of the wheel. Try to get a hand-me-down for this one, because you can only squeeze a few years out of it before your child has grown enough to be ready for a 20″ bike at six or seven.

There's one big problem with a first two-wheeler — there has to be somewhere safe to ride it, particularly in the early stages when the rider is still concentrating entirely on keeping upright and not on where she's going. She needs a clear path and definitely won't be ready to steer wide of cars or pedestrians. So you need a quiet sidewalk or a little-used park and flat terrain where possible. A good guideline is: the busier the neighborhood, the later a child should start on a two-wheeler. Because if she's going to have to contend with traffic — even pedestrian traffic — she better be fast at learning.

Another index of when your child is ready for a two-wheeler is how well he does on a tricycle. A strong candidate is a kid who can turn on a dime, can consistently miss a moving target like his toddling sister by a half inch at full speed, and who can pedal around backward effortlessly in circles. The backpedaling is important for being able to set the coaster brakes on a bike.

Choosing a Bike

If you're buying a first bike new, you'll have many choices to make. First will be the choice between a very cheaply made toy-quality "sidewalk bike" and a better quality, but much more expensive, child's bike that may last through a couple of kids. The cheaply manufactured 16″ bikes are made with nonstandard parts and usually can't be repaired, so they can become instant junk, but with a little care one should hold up through a single owner. The cheap sidewalk bikes are sold in big toy stores and discount houses, but go to a bicycle shop if you want high quality.

Be sure a first bike is equipped with back-pedal coaster brakes — some of the cheaper ones are made even without that essential. Also check for pedals with rubber treads since some bikes come with slippery plastic ones. A boy's first bike should

be "convertible," which means that it will have a top bar that can be removed until he's learned to mount with ease and then can be put back in place so the other kids will stop teasing him.

On a first bike and all future bikes, avoid "banana" seats; kids will always ride double on a banana seat, and that causes many accidents. Other "high-riser" features like tall handlebars are also wrong for a first bike. High-risers are show-off 20″ bikes that are highly maneuverable, and grade school kids use them for jumps and "wheelies." Many people consider them unstable, however, and difficult to steer, so if your child waits to start bicycling at six on a 20″ bike, don't let him start out on a high-riser. Also, many 20″ bikes are equipped with hand brakes, because the 20″ bike is used for years until the switch to a full-size bike around eleven or later. But a six-year-old should definitely have back-pedal coaster brakes — he won't yet have the strong grip that's needed to stop a bike with hand brakes.

A learning bike shouldn't be cluttered up with a lot of accessories that will distract the rider. Kids will insist on a bell, which is okay — but be sure your child understands that ringing the bell won't magically clear a path for her; she has to stop for others. Cover the bike with reflectors and reflective tape; you want your child to be as visible on it as you can make her.

A child should fit his first bike well — you don't want to buy it a couple of sizes too big with room to grow. Perched up on a bike that's too large, a child can feel insecure — and he'll be right, because he will be insecure. The experience may scare him and

set back the time when he'll learn to ride. One size guideline is that the length of the child's leg (measured on the inseam) should be 2″ or 3″ longer than the wheel diameter. Even better, of course, is to have the child try out the bike in the store. Your child should be able to mount and dismount easily when the seat is all the way down, and a boy should be able to straddle the frame comfortably with his feet on the ground.

Riding Lessons

Many children's bikes come equipped with training wheels. If you want your child to learn to ride on *two* wheels, remove them. Training wheels sit up an inch or so from the ground, so in theory a child can balance the bike between them, but in practice she soon learns to lean a little to one side to take advantage of the stability of an extra wheel. So she actually continues to ride a *tri*cycle, and she also develops a false sense of security and completely misses the central issue in bike riding — balance.

Before your first practical lesson, show your child — and yourself — how the balance of a bicycle works, by rolling a large coin across a smooth floor. The coin stays upright, balanced on its edge, as long as its forward momentum keeps it rolling. When it slows down it plops over on its side.

You need a place for bike lessons where there's plenty of room and no traffic; try a school parking lot on the weekend. The smaller the bike you use, the easier it will be for your child to learn. Ideally, his feet, or at least the balls of his feet, should touch the ground when he sits on the seat. Because the best way for him to master the simple balancing feat of bike riding is for him to scoot the bike along by pushing on the ground with both feet at once — rather than having you run along holding the bike erect. This way he can get the feel of balancing, and as he starts to coast short distances, he'll almost automatically bring his feet up onto the pedals. With his feet in position, as the coasts grow longer, he can begin to pedal. It will be wobbly at first and there may be some spills, but practice will get him there.

Most kids, however, will want the security and reassurance of having Dad run along holding onto the bike. This isn't going to help teach balance, but if it makes your child feel better about what she's doing — fine. Try to stay behind the rider, with your hand cupped around the back of the seat. And let go from time to time so she really will be balancing.

Most kids don't learn on the first try, but they catch on after a while if they aren't rushed. Short daily workouts — say ten to fifteen minutes each day — will do the job much more efficiently than long, overserious sessions of practice.

KITES

Every father wants to introduce his kids to the powerful, magical pull of the kite on the string. It's a kind of Hollywood dream vision of what a dad does with his kids. The dream vision can be made a reality with a preschool child, but it may take a lot of care and patience — and you'll need the perfect day with the perfect wind. It's also best to be prepared for the dream to be smashed early on. Gregory nearly wiped out our kite-flying ambitions one summer day by leaning on the frame of a box kite that he thought looked strong enough to support his forty pounds. He felt wretched about what he'd done, and I can't say I was too happy about it either. But with some extra sticks and string and glue and time out for extensive repairs, we were finally able to get our venture off the ground.

Think of a kite as *your* toy, which your child can help out with — a little. A flimsy construction of sticks and paper is just too vulnerable to expose it completely to the helpful ministrations of a four- or five-year-old. You'll be doing all the work of launching, flying, and reeling the kite back in. A preschooler can lend a hand on the string when the kite is aloft, but only to get the feel of it — you won't want her taking over.

With all these drawbacks as a father-child project, why bother? I'd asked myself this question dozens of times the day Gregory smashed my kite, but then there we were on the beach with the mended kite soaring in the high wind and a little boy tugging against the string with me, and then running dizzily to chase the dancing shadow of the kite back and forth across the sand, and his excitement running as high as the kite — and I knew why I'd bothered.

If you're new to kites, save yourself the trouble of making the first one from scratch. You can buy beautiful, easily flown kites inexpensively for a start. Get the delta-wing type, which aren't rigidly constructed, so it's harder for a helpful preschooler

to put one out of commission. These are made roughly in the shape of the Greek letter delta (Δ), with a long edge at the back and two shorter edges meeting in front, and are often decorated to look like birds in flight; the string is attached to a smaller triangle of material sewn to the underside of the main wing.

The very light, cheap twine labeled kite string, which is usually about 8 lb. breaking strength, will do okay in a light breeze, but a strong gust will snap it. Spend a little more and get 30 lb. breaking strength kite line or use fisherman's monofilament — also 30 lb. If you have fishing gear, put the kite line on your spinning reel and play the kite like an airborne trout. You won't need the whole length of the rod — just the first section, with the line playing through a guide at the end.

You'll need a good breeze and a very open place — a sparsely populated beach or a treeless hilltop or open country. My favorite place is a frozen lake in winter. *Never* fly a kite near power lines, and also stay well away from roads and highways and airports.

Messages

Message sending is the Big Event of kite flying for a preschooler. When the kite is flying high, place small pieces of paper, cut or torn as in the illustration, around the string and tape the slit together.

They will skitter rapidly up the string, carried right on up to the kite by the wind. Kids love this trick and will send up as many messages as you can supply, so make up a few dozen of them in advance, rather than having to tear them with one hand and your teeth while holding onto the kite string reel with the other hand. Try different sizes and types of paper, and twist the corners of some to make the messages spin as they go up. Kids also like to write actual messages on the pieces of paper. A four-year-old will write a few letters or her name if she knows how, and a five-year-old will write "Hi, Kite" if you spell it out.

Releasing a parachute from an airborne kite is fun, too. Use an ice trigger to do this on a hot day. To make the trigger release, put the ends of two short pieces of string into one section of an ice-cube tray, add water, and freeze. One string is tied to the kite string directly under the kite, and the other is tied to the top center of a simple kid's parachute made by tying strings to the corners of a handkerchief and tying a small weight like a clothespin to the strings. When the kite is up, the sun will melt the ice, sending the parachute floating down. Store the ice trigger in a thermos jug till you're ready to use it.

Streamer Kites

Colorful crepe paper streamers make "kites" that preschoolers can handle easily and have a fabulous time flying in a windy place. Kids as young as one and a half will delight in waving the streamers around and watching them flutter in a strong breeze. Tie one end of a streamer to a short stick and it becomes even more fun to manipulate. A five-year-old with two long streamers on sticks will put on a lively performance.

A windy beach is a perfect place for streamer flying, but keep the kids clear of the water. The dye from wet crepe paper makes a miserable mess.

SNOW PLAY

Winter is cabin fever time in households with young kids — they're cooped up and ready to burst. It's the time to step up the roughhouse play and get everybody outside as often as you can manage it — and that's the hardest part, because the temptation is always to stay in. It takes forever to organize any kind of winter outing. There are scarves and snowsuits and sweaters and hats and boots, and the kids never co-operate with putting them on. You feel like sitting on them when they kick and struggle as

you try to pry on the rubber boots. And as soon as all the clothes are on, somebody inevitably has to use the john.

But it's not more trouble than it's worth — the consequence of leaving kids inside all winter in front of the TV is disaster.

Building with Snow

Wet snow, while it's still fresh, is one of nature's finest and fastest building materials. Kids at every age will love the snowman you build, and a four-year-old will be able to help roll the big balls. Make some snow children, too, especially if the snow is old and compacted and you can't roll together very big balls.

Many fathers like to build snow forts — big snow boulders arranged in a tight circle. Add smaller snow boulders here and there and kick foothold steps in the larger ones so that preschoolers can scramble up to the top of the barricades. To make a firm step in a big snowball, push your boot into the snow and work it around, pressing until you feel it's solid. Variations on the snow fort are the snow wall and the roofless snow house — or add a panel of light plywood or cardboard for a roof.

Another favorite father-built snow structure is the "igloo." No need to build this up with blocks of ice in the traditional manner. Just take advantage of any major pile of snow — a mountain left by snow-clearing equipment if it's safely out of the way of traffic, or the pile you make clearing the driveway. Take a spade or shovel and hollow out a shallow place just big enough for your child to crawl in and sit down. It needn't be big or deep — the thrill is that it's a special little place to get into. And making it deep or wide will weaken the igloo, possibly giving it a chance to cave in on your child. It's a good practice to break up or fill in an igloo like this at the end of the day.

Try some small-scale snow building, too. Preschoolers love making snow dollhouses, and a ramp for doll sleds is another good project. A doll sled can be improvised from cardboard, or use the flat bottom cut from a plastic milk jug. A child who has a toy bulldozer or crane will have a fabulous time moving snow with them.

Snow Gym

Gregory, Timothy, and I roll huge snow boulders, but instead of using them for Frosty the Snowman, who can do little but stand there and melt, we arrange them and a board or an old ladder into a winter jungle gym. You can't build very high, but the 3½′ of a really solid snowball is high enough for preschoolers. Lay the board or ladder across between the tops of widely spaced snow boulders, making sure it is firmly set into them. Add some small snowballs for steps up, and kick some more steps in the sides of the big snowballs, as for the snow fort described earlier. Using smaller snow boulders and packing extra snow around them, you can also make up a short snow slide leading down from one of the big snowballs. With a structure like this, it's winter carnival time for kids. Make sure to dismantle a snow jungle gym as soon as it starts to melt.

snow boulders

Snow Writing

With a letter learner, a good winter game is writing in the snow — which can be done by shuffling feet or dragging a shovel. Big letters, small letters — all kinds of writing can be done, just as you do on the sand at the beach.

If you have a squirt bottle — the kind that catsup is served in at lunch counters, or even an empty dish detergent dispenser — fill it with water and food coloring and let your child write and make designs with it in the snow. In Russia, where they are more accustomed to living with snow than we are, it is said that fathers traditionally teach their sons to pee their initials in the snow.

Sleds

A child doesn't need a sled with runners and steering bar till she's in school. For a beginning sled at three years you can improvise with a heavy sheet of cardboard or a large metal or plastic tray. At sporting goods stores you can buy fast-running plastic mat "toboggans." The child sits on one of these with her knees up and pulls the front of the mat up in a curve as in the illustration. If you improvise with a sheet of cardboard, cut handholds at one end so your child can ride as on one of these speedy

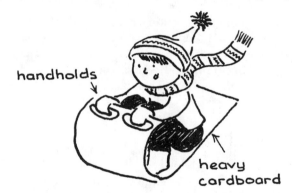

handholds

heavy cardboard

toboggans. The store-bought variety is so zippy it will slide pretty quickly down a steep bank of wet grass, so a child gets to take advantage of even the lightest snowfall.

Start kids easily on very slow slopes. All preschoolers don't take to sledding like ducks to water. Some need a little gentle prodding and with others you'll just have to drop the issue and wait till next winter.

Old tire inner tubes make excellent sleds; you may want to try one of these yourself, or see if your five- or six-year-old can handle one.

Eating Snow

Ask preschoolers what they like about snow, and eight out of ten will say: "Eating it." Keep an ear open for air quality reports when it snows, because your child may be eating a lot more than snow. And bring a shovelful of snow inside and toss it in the bathtub. Your child will get a kick out of watching it melt, and when the water has run off you may be able to see what else he'd be eating along with the snow. I did this in Manhattan once, years ago when I lived there — with fresh pure white snow — and it left a heavy film of black soot in the tub.

If the snow is clean, though, what could taste better to a kid? It will be even tastier if you dress it up a little. Give your child a paper cup to pack the snow in and cover the snow cone with sprinkles — or pour on some syrup, or squirt the top with a couple of drops of food coloring.

Snow cones taste best of all in the middle of summer. If there's some room in the freezer, get your kids to pack snow loosely into clean milk cartons to save for a 90-degree day.

A Closer Look

Take your child outside while it's snowing, carrying a sheet of black paper and a magnifying glass. The snowflakes show up clearly on the black paper, and looking through the glass your child will discover that though every one has six sides, each has its own extraordinary, distinctive pattern.

Skating

In Holland, where *everybody* skates, toddlers start out holding onto child-size chairs on the ice, pushing them along as they go. It's the same principle as using a "walker" to learn to walk.

An agile kid can stand on double-bladed skates at three and a half. If you decide to go in for skating

with a preschooler, be prepared for outings where more time is spent bundling up and putting the skates on, and then taking the skates back off, etc., than is spent on the actual event. But there's a great thrill for a child in standing up on skates, so don't skip it just because of the trouble involved.

Skiing

Big resorts are ready and willing to accommodate preschool kids with baby-sitting and early-learning downhill ski classes, but a number of skiing fathers have told me that for a real family winter sport you should try cross-country skiing. For starters, it costs a lot less than downhill skiing in terms of equipment. And if you live in a place where it snows, you don't have to travel hundreds of miles to the mountains and pay steep prices to ride the ski tow. You can go cross-country skiing over any open terrain, even a golf course if there's no countryside nearby. Kids can start early — four is a good age — and they can keep up with the rest of the family fairly well, because moving on the skis is a little like skating, only easier.

TOYS

Toys are a great common denominator for father and child. There's no age difference between a twenty-five-year-old man and a toddler when both are pushing little cars around on the rug and going: "Brrrrrrrrrrrm, brrrrrrrrrm," and crashing head on.

No language needed, no child psychology, just rev it up and go to it.

In the small poll I've taken, Lego blocks go at the top of the list of fathers' favorite toys. Racing cars on fancy tracks seem to have taken over from model

railroads as the action toy that fathers most often take over from their kids, though there's still a strong contingent of model railroading dads.

Many fathers I talked with had toys of their own — trains or race car setups too advanced for preschoolers, where Dad was the owner/operator and the kids helped play with *his* toy. So many, in fact, that I didn't feel foolish asking for a big motorized Tinkertoy set for my birthday. I set up the electric motor and the drive belt system for the working models. Gregory, meanwhile, adds pieces all over the structure. And Timothy the toddler, refusing to be left out, tries to dismantle anything Gregory and I build. But he has also figured out a constructive way to play with the Tinkertoys — he dumps them all out of the box and then puts them back in one by one. So the three of us share the set, each using it on his own level. But all of us, in fact, use it on the same levels — the level of the floor and the level of fun.

All kids' toys, however, don't appeal to all fathers. As one man put it: "There's not much you can do with Weebles." And it's a rare father who enthuses about Barbie dolls. Simple baby toys — nesting boxes and plastic pop-together beads — also tend to get short shrift from fathers. Toys are such a vital link to children's lives and minds, though, that I think it's worth at least investigating each of the things they play with to see if there isn't some pleasure or activity to share with them through sharing the toy.

Let me try to sell you on the humble Weeble — the little tippy egg-shaped fellow you will surely know if you have a child older than two. The Weeble

is the direct descendant of a traditional Japanese toy called the Daruma, an egg-shaped figure painted to look a little like a Buddhist monk. Like the Weeble, the Daruma has a weight in the big end that brings him upright, no matter how often he is tipped over. It is named after the monk who introduced Buddhism to China and Japan; this holy man sat for nine years in immobile contemplation and it is said that during those years his legs completely withered away. The toy Darumas are likewise legless, but because they are uncapsizable they remind believers of the endurance and the indomitable will of their namesake. This curious tidbit that I came across by chance in a book on the history of toys has given me a new respect for the Weeble, and I have tried playing with him, and sure enough, you can't knock him over — there is no way to keep this good man down. Gregory and Timothy and I have run wobbly Weeble races down a slanted board, and we made a Weeble boat for the bathtub out of a plastic egg carton, and when one of the kids falls and hurts himself, we sometimes talk about how the Weeble will always come up smiling. Which I figure is plenty of use to get out of an object that is only two inches tall.

And take the stock-in-trade baby toys — say the plastic doughnuts that fit over a stake. A one-year-old will play happily enough with these by herself and eventually figure out how they fit — she doesn't need adult instruction to master this. But if you sit on the floor with her and the plastic doughnuts, she will include you in a learning adventure that is very exciting for her, and the two of you can hand the doughnuts back and forth and work at fitting them over the stick. Doing this, you discover that it's fascinating to see her work by trial and error to get the rings on — it's like watching her think. You can't see the process of an adult's thought because it's all done with words and usually behind a poker face, but a child without language thinks with things, and you can see all her blunders and her steps in the right direction and share her triumphant smile when she finally succeeds.

Maybe there is a way to get interested in Barbie dolls, too, though I don't know a single father who has found it. Fathers are often accused of favoring their sons over their daughters, of spending more time with them, demanding more of them, and so forth. Confronted with Holly Hobbie and Charlie's Angels dolls with wigs that curl, does a man have any other choice? Actually I think he does. This is just one aspect of what little girls do in play. It's very clubby and it purposely excludes Dad, along with all men and boys. But preschool girls also enjoy doing almost all the things their brothers enjoy: hammering nails, building with blocks, pushing cars around. The difference that I've found in playing with dozens of preschoolers at our local child care center is that the girls like to be *asked* to do these things, whereas the boys simply gravitate to them. Gretchen won't come up and grab a saw from my hand and start hacking away at the workbench with it, as Hank will. But if I invite her — "Gretchen, how about taking a turn with the saw now?" — she'll come running, all smiles, to saw. And she'll get just as much from the experience as Hank does. So I'm certain that little girls don't have a harem mentality, that they don't really want to shut themselves up for all time with their dolls and miniature kitchens as it sometimes appears. But they may need a little prodding to join Dad in something they'll both enjoy.

BUYING TOYS

Always choose toys that are sturdy, or else Smash, Bam, and it's money down the drain. Age guidelines printed on packaged toys can be generally ignored — except as safety advice. Your idea of what your child is ready for and interested in will be much more accurate than the manufacturer's. The lower limit on age guidelines, though, will tell you at what point the manufacturer thinks the toy is safe for use by kids. On toys with small parts — particularly ones that can be sucked into the windpipe — the lower age limit is normally set pretty high, and with good reason. Until your child is three and you're sure she's not interested in swallowing small objects, stick with things that have big parts. Toys with many little pieces that have to be picked up are a nuisance anyway.

Be super careful with toys for a baby — no button eyes on stuffed dolls, for instance, which could be bitten off and swallowed; everything big, sturdy, unbreakable. No sharp or rough edges or splinters. And plastic toys should be made of tough, resilient plastic rather than the thin, rigid, brittle kind that's liable to crack up with a little use, producing jagged edges and small shards that can be eaten or stuck into ears and nostrils.

All toy packages claim their contents are educational, and they're right. Every object a child handles or even looks at is educational, whether it's a toy calculator that gives back the answers, or a pebble he picks up, or his father's adjustable wrench — because a child learns something new every time he turns around. The kitchen pots and pans are always among a toddler's favorite toys because she learns so many things from playing with them — what they sound like when hit, how they fit into each other, how other things fit into them, etc. An extremely simple toy like a ball or a set of building blocks has a great range of uses, and with it a child can explore many possibilities, so that educationally it will be richer than an elaborate, strictly "educational" toy that may be designed to teach a child one task, and which in fact could be rather limiting.

Don't be conned by highfalutin phrases in the advertising on toy packages like "teaches small motor co-ordination." Picking up a spoon to eat teaches your child small motor co-ordination, as does drawing with a crayon and every other daily act that involves the use of the hands. Your child will learn plenty from any toys he plays with, so the important criteria in choosing them are whether he's ready for them and whether you think he'll have fun with them. It also helps if it's something you'll enjoy playing with, too. You won't pick a winner every time — kids turn up their noses at some toys and ignore others, for reasons of their own, but often the ignored Christmas present reappears months later and becomes the favorite of the day.

TOY WEAPONS

Many parents cringe at the idea of letting their kids play with guns and other toy instruments of war and violence. No kid, however, shares this nice sentiment.

Notice, for instance, what happens in Iceland, a truly pacifist society, where national law prohibits guns of any sort and even the sport of boxing is banned. Icelandic kids have toy guns. They learn about guns by watching imported American TV shows, and their parents give in to their insistent pressure to have them.

Refuse to give a two-year-old the gun he longs for, and he'll turn around and make his own from a stick.

A water pistol, harmless and always fun, provides a compromise ground.

A historical note: Violent toys are anything but new. Archaeologists discovered that in the classical world, Greek tourists at the site of the ruins of Troy could buy toy replicas of the Trojan horse, complete with soldiers inside, to take home to their kids. And during the French Revolution, a miniature guillotine that decapitated dolls was the hottest-selling item in toy stores.

BOXES – THE BEST TOYS

At the end of Christmas day you often find the kids playing with the cardboard boxes the toys came in, and ignoring the shiny new presents. Boxes of every shape and description make wonderful toys.

A big packing box — the kind a kitchen appliance comes in — can be converted into a playhouse in minutes by cutting windows and a door that opens. You can usually have these boxes for the asking at appliance stores.

cardboard paddle

A medium-size box that a child can sit in becomes a car to drive, a boat, an airplane. All that's needed is a little imagination on her part or on yours. You can alter the box to look more like the imagined airplane by adding cardboard wings, or supply some kind of wheel for your child to steer the box/car with. A sit-in box also makes a wonderful indoor sled — push or pull it around on a carpeted floor to give your child a grand ride.

Using colored paper and markers, you can convert a cardboard box into a play stove, or a bunch of boxes into a whole play kitchen, with deep sink and refrigerator included. Attach a couple of sticks behind a box to look like rabbit ears, add black paper to cover the inside, and you have made a play TV set,

in which preschoolers can manipulate their favorite dolls and figurines for actors.

Boxes are easily converted into simple dollhouses; for more on this see p. 290. At Christmas when he was four, Gregory and I made a good Santa Claus toy by setting a paper towel roll through the top of a gift box to represent a chimney in a house. We tied a piece of string to a red Fisher-Price figurine, which represented Santa, and for months afterward, Gregory would sit there twenty minutes at a stretch lowering St. Nick down the chimney and pulling him back out.

A game that Gregory and I enjoy together is converting a box into a fanciful house. He thinks of oddball shapes like hearts and trapezoids and my job is to cut windows and doors in these shapes, leaving hinges of cardboard so they open and close. Then he takes balls of different sizes and tries to roll and push them in through the doors and windows from outside, while my hand on the inside plays the role of the hand of the giant who lives in the house and tries to shove the balls back through the openings to keep them from invading.

No box should be thrown out until a child has had a crack at it.

HOMEMADE TOYS

Any object you make for your child will delight and entertain her. Two scrap pieces of wood that you join with a discarded hinge and screws may be the favorite plaything of a one-year-old. All you need to become a toymaker are hand tools and a table or bench to work at — no special experience required. Always try to include your child in working on a homemade toy, because there's just as much fun in making it with Dad as there is in playing with it —

and far more instruction. A preschooler usually won't enjoy the time-consuming step-by-step process of cutting out and fitting parts, but she will love to be in on the assembly once all the parts are ready to go, and may even be some help with glue and nails and screws. See the section starting on p. 298 for much more on kids in a workshop.

Design your own toys using materials you have at hand or get designs for traditional toys — several good books of toy designs are listed in the Further Reading section at the back of this book. The design of any wooden toy you see in a store or catalogue or at a friend's house is free for the copying — just jot down the construction details while you're looking at it. Below I include some general tips for designing and building homemade toys, as well as plans for some classic oldies that have delighted generations of kids and for some father-and-child-designed originals.

Toy-making Tips

Wheels Put wheels on any block of wood or box or can and you've made a good toy. Or just make a pair of 2″ diameter wooden wheels, join them with a short dowel axle, and give them to a beginning crawler — he'll take them everywhere, rolling them along with the axle grasped in his hand.

The simplest way to make wooden wheels is to cut them out with a hole saw driven by an electric drill. The hole cutout is the wheel, and the saw's centering bit drills a ¼″ hole directly in the center for a dowel axle. Heavy-duty rigidly built hole saws will do the best job but they are expensive. Unless you have a really well-equipped shop, the cheapest hole saw will be the one for you; these come with a nest of interchangeable circular blades and cut hole/wheels up to a diameter of 2⅜″. On ¾″ wood and thicker,

saw only about halfway through. Then turn the work over and come at it from the other side — the pilot hole will line the saw up correctly. This procedure avoids having the saw break through the far side of the work, splintering the edge of the wheel. If your wheels are a little rough around the rims, shove a 3½″ length of ¼″ dowel tightly into the axle hole, chuck the other end of the dowel into an electric drill, and spin the edge of the wheel on sandpaper — a sanding block held in a vise, or sandpaper stapled to the workbench.

Wheels can also be cut out quickly with a coping saw — or with a band saw or jig saw if you have access to a well-equipped workshop. And this will be your only method for wheels over the maximum size of a hole saw. When you cut wheels out this way, make sure to draw them with a compass instead of tracing a circular object, so you will have an accurate mark for the center axle hole.

Small wooden wheels can be made by sawing cross sections of dowels, broom handles, or closet poles (the lumberyard name for dowels over 1″). You'll get straight sections by using a miter box or a table saw, or by wrapping a piece of masking tape around the dowel as a guideline for your hand saw. The problem with these small discs is finding the center. If you don't have a professional center finder, set the points of a compass for the radius of the dowel and draw a circle on a small piece of paper. Place the disc on the circle, aligning them exactly. Now hold the paper and the disc together tightly between finger and thumb and turn them over. Push the compass point through the hole it made in the paper to mark the center on the wooden disc.

You can find plenty of readymade wheels around your home. Jar and bottle caps can be converted to wheels by finding the center, drilling or punching a hole, and mounting with a nail. Spools from thread,

film, typewriter ribbons, etc., make fine wheels. And save the wheels from broken toys.

A dump is a good source for larger wheels to use on a homemade riding toy. You'll probably find a surplus of usable wheels on discarded baby carriages, strollers, tricycles, etc. Otherwise, cut larger wheels from plywood, fill the edges with wood putty, and sand them well. Replacement wheels for baby strollers are sold fairly inexpensively at big toy and baby supply outlets, and these are a good size for small riding toys. Furniture casters can be mounted under a riding toy; they will roll best if only the front two casters swivel around, and the rear two are fixed straight ahead. And if you want to go big time in wheeled toys, try writing to the All-American Soap Box Derby Headquarters, Suite 521, The Ohio Building, 1755 Main Street, Akron, Ohio 44308 — they will send you literature about official wheel and axle kits for building soap box competition racing cars.

Mounting Wheels To mount wooden wheels on a small toy, the best system is a hole drilled through the body of the toy that the axle revolves in, with the wheels glued onto its ends. You may want to add metal washers between the body of the toy and the wheels to keep the two from rubbing together and slowing down the action.

A fixed axle on which the wheel revolves is another good solution, especially for wide toys where an axle hole can't be drilled easily through the body. In its simplest version the fixed axle is a nail driven through the center hole of a wheel and into the body of a toy. Ancient Egyptian toys like the wooden

horse shown here used fixed axles with a crosspiece to hold the wheel on. An ⅛" dowel can be pegged through a fixed dowel of larger diameter to copy this time-honored setup. The cutaway diagram shows a variation on the same theme — a small wooden disc with a hole drilled in its center is glued onto the end of the short axle; the other end of the axle is glued into a hole in the body of the toy, and a metal washer is used as a spacer between wheel and body. Cross sections of large dowels can be used for the wooden discs.

The easiest way to mount larger wheels on riding toys is with fixed axles made from long lag bolts screwed into the body of the toy or into a crosspiece, or axle tree. If the lag bolt is screwed into the end

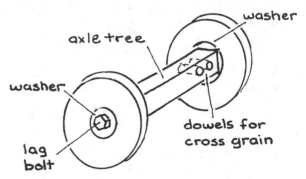

grain of an axle tree it may work loose quickly under rough treatment, since end grain doesn't hold a screw tightly. So first drill one or two 1" holes across the path of the lag bolt axle and insert glue and 1" dowels to give the bolt some cross grain to hold into. Drill a pilot hole for the lag bolt, and use metal washers on both sides of the wheel.

Coffee jar lids and the like make good-looking prepainted wheels for small toys when mounted as in the illustration below. A piece of scrap wood with a hole drilled in its center is glued onto the end of a revolving dowel axle. The jar lid is then centered on the piece of scrap wood and fastened to it with two small roundheaded wood screws; drill or punch holes through the lid for the screws before mounting.

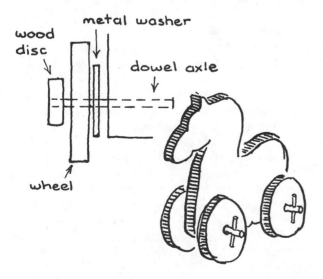

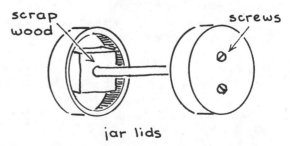

jar lids

Riders Fisher-Price figurines and other common preschool toy figures can go for a ride in any wooden car, truck, boat, etc., that has $^{13}/_{16}"$ holes drilled in it. The holes should be approximately $^3/_8"$ deep.

Mechanisms If you want to design and build homemade toys with some action features — pull or push toys with clowns or animals that bob up and down or ferris wheels or merry-go-rounds that work by cranks — one of the mechanisms pictured here may be the necessary drive system. To give a friction-wheel drive setup plenty of friction stretch a wide rubber band around the edge of the drive wheel.

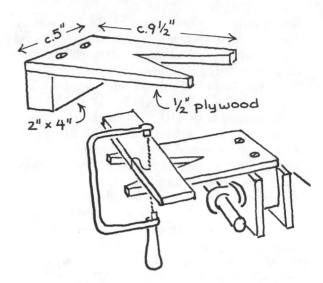

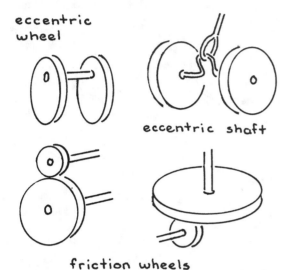

can be made in minutes from a scrap piece of plywood screwed to a scrap piece of 2" x 4", which is then held in a vise. Or just make the top piece with the V cutout and C-clamp it to a table top, which does fine for small work, though the C-clamp will get in the way on bigger pieces.

The teeth of a coping saw should point downward toward the handle when it is used with a jig like this, which is opposite to the way the teeth point on other saws. The cutting is all done on the down stroke with the blade perpendicular to the piece being cut and the handle below the work. To cut out a hole or a shape in the middle of a piece of wood, drill a ¼" hole near the edge to be cut; disassemble the coping saw; put the blade through the ¼" hole and then fasten it to the frame. Coping saw blades are available in a variety of widths — narrow for tight turns and wide for straight cutting.

I like to recycle old mechanisms for new toys. Gregory and I used the spinning base of a discarded lazy-Susan spice rack to make a simple merry-go-round. We just fastened on some figurines from the toy chest and added colorful ribbons on dowel poles as flags to make it look snazzy, and the kids spin it around and around. An orange juice squeezer with a crank-turned mechanism that did a terrible job of squeezing oranges does a marvelous job turning a tower we made with little airplanes spinning around it on strings. And there are always the wind-up motors, flywheel mechanisms, etc., from broken toys. Collect these in a box near your workbench and use them to create new toys.

Coping Saw The coping saw is an invaluable tool for cutting out small parts for homemade toys. It works quickly and accurately if used with a coping saw jig like the one illustrated. This little saw table

Paints and Finishes All homemade toys should be sanded free of splinters, and sharp edges should be eliminated. It's always nice to apply bright paint or a clear finish to a wooden toy, but this is the step I never get to. Gregory and Timothy help me put homemade toys together, and they have to play with them before the glue is even dry — let alone waiting till they've been painted.

If you have time to finish toys, varnish, shellac, and polyurethane all give adequate clear finishes on wood. And for a super-safe chewable finish try Behlen's Salad Bowl Finish, which can be ordered from H. Behlen & Bro., Amsterdam, New York 12010 — product No. B603-00015. The dry film contains only substances approved for use in contact with food by the U. S. Food and Drug Commission.

For colored finishes, use nontoxic enamel paints, making sure that the label clearly states that they are for use on children's furniture and toys. Use enamel undercoater to produce a fine shiny finish, or paint directly on the wood for a mat finish. Small quantities of enamel paint will stay fresh and skin free between jobs if you hammer the can tops on firmly and store the cans upside down.

Your child can paint a wooden toy with her own nontoxic tempera or poster paints and the colors can be preserved and made more vibrant with one or more coats of varnish or polyurethane.

Bits of ribbon and colored paper can be glued on to give colorful touches with less trouble than paint. Contact paper is also excellent for quick decorating.

Plans

Dowel Forest This is a piece of equipment a one-year-old will use every day. Anything small with a hole in it or through it will fit on this forest of perches: Fisher-Price figurines, plastic doughnuts, plastic pop-together beads, plastic bottle caps with holes drilled in their centers, 35-mm film cans. Just take a look through your child's things and yours and you'll find many small objects that will fit on the sticks. Timothy, at a little over one, would sit with me by the half hour playing games on this appara-

tus. He'd move a piece to a new perch and then I'd move one — it was like noncompetitive chess. His favorite game was a kind of miniature peek-a-boo. He'd set a finger puppet or a figurine on one of the sticks and I'd cover it with a little box. "Where did

she go?" I'd ask, and, wreathed in smiles, he'd uncover the figurine.

The only materials you need are:

> 9″ length 1″ x 6″ pine
> 36″ length ¼″ dowel
> white glue

The base plate should be sanded smooth and the edges rounded with sandpaper to avoid splinters, or the edges can be chamfered with a plane or rasp for a good-looking job. Draw a grid of lines in light pencil to get the placement of the dowels, which are set 2″ apart on centers in all directions. Drill the ¼″ holes as straight as you can, with a piece of scrap wood under the work so the drill won't break through the wood roughly. Put some white glue in each hole and tap in the dowels with a mallet or heavy piece of wood. Dowels are easily cut with a coping saw; sand their top ends. Making this toy shouldn't take you two hours.

The dowel forest doesn't lose its usefulness when your child grows older. It becomes a base for building Tinkertoys, which fit on the dowels. A two- or three-year-old can loop rubber bands around the dowels and plunk on them, or run brightly colored yarn in and out and around them to make an abstract piece of weaving or a "spider's web." Your child will continue to find new ways to use it.

It's a good idea to have a small parts bag or box to go with this toy since the little pieces and figurines get scattered and disappear quickly under chairs and beds.

Busy Board A friend of mine built a wonderful toy for his toddler by attaching to a board all the spare pieces of hardware that were cluttering up his workbench. From the second half of their first year onward, all kids love to flip switches, turn knobs, pull handles, push buttons. To make a busy board, all you need are a smoothly sanded piece of wood, a collection of hardware odds and ends, a screwdriver, and a little ingenuity. Use pieces of sewing elastic to add some extra action.

Click Machine A one-year-old enjoys pulling the blocks of this toy apart and snapping them together. You will need:

> 4 wooden ABC blocks (1¼″ cubes)
> light round sewing elastic

Drill holes for the elastic as indicated in the dia-

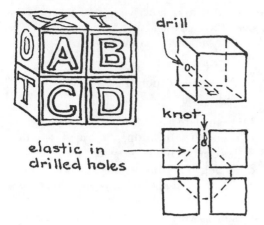

elastic in drilled holes

drill

knot

gram. You will be drilling from the center of one face of each cube diagonally to the center of an adjoining face. Thread the elastic through the holes; pull the elastic as tight as you can and join with a square knot.

The total time for making this shouldn't exceed forty minutes and there is no need for painting or finishing since the ABC blocks make it bright and snappy. These little cubes are cheap and they're indispensable toys for a child of about eighteen months. Kids this age start to build up — straight up, block on block, to dizzying, rickety heights of nine and ten blocks while you watch in awe. So buy ABC blocks in quantity and use them to brighten up toys that you make.

ABC Snake   This toy is made on roughly the same principle as the last one. The ABC snake bites its own tail as in the illustration to make an orderly circle, but a child will twist and bend it into many shapes, wear it like a yoke around her neck, and click the pieces together. You will need:

> 2' length 1⅜" closet pole
> 6 wooden ABC blocks (1¼" cubes)
> round sewing elastic

Closet pole is the lumberyard name for dowels over 1". Using a miter box set at 60 degrees, cut the closet pole into six sections as in the illustration. To help make these cuts easy and accurate, first draw diameters across the two ends of the length of closet pole, as parallel as you can make them. Then join the ends of the diameters to make center lines on two opposite sides of the pole. Now make a 60-degree cut at one end with one center line on top. Rotate the other center line to the top; measure 1¼" along the new center line; start your saw on that

mark, and you produce one of the slices shown. Just keep turning the opposite center line up, measuring 1¼" along it, and making a new cut.

When you have six sections, put each one vertically in a vise and drill as accurately through the center as you can. Also drill holes through the six ABC blocks from the center of one face of each cube to the center of the opposite face. Before drilling the blocks, you may want to lay them out with the other sections and tinker with them to get their letters to spell your child's name or some other word.

Use three strands of elastic, double-knotting them together at one end and threading them through the blocks and pole sections. Pull them as tight as you can and double-knot as close as possible to the last block.

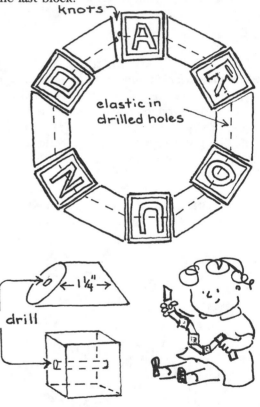

knots

elastic in drilled holes

drill

1¼"

Clang Machine   A two-year-old should have the strength to compress the spring on this toy enough to send the block zinging up the pole to go clang inside the tin can, and will do it again and again and again. Gregory and I invented this one and built it in less than an hour, and it's been a big hit with every child who's played with it. Kids who regularly visit our house go searching for it as soon as they get here. Blake, four, asked, "Where is that Clang Machine?" and that's how it got its name. The materials are:

> 1 block of wood, approx. 4″ x 4″ x 4″
> 36″ length ⅜″ dowel
> 1 wooden ABC block OR 1½″ wooden bead
> 1 compression spring, approx. 3½″ long
> 1 metal washer with ½″ hole
> 1 tin can (soup OR beans)
> 1 roundheaded wood screw with washer

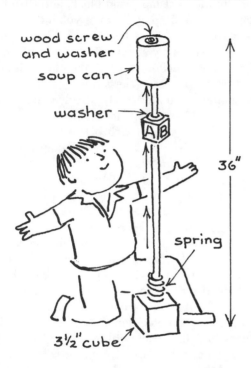

The base illustrated is a cube of 4″ x 4″ lumber but any heavy piece of wood will do. Two scrap pieces of 2″ x 4″ could be glued together to make a similar block.

The dowel is glued into a ⅜″ hole drilled for it in the center of the base. A ½″ hole is drilled through the ABC block from one face to the opposite face. Instead of the block, you can also use an 1½″ wooden bead from an arts and crafts supply store. You can buy the spring at any hardware store. Spring, block or bead, and ½″ washer are slipped onto the dowel in that order. Remove one end of the tin can with a can opener and crimp down any rough edges with pliers or file them off. Drill or punch a hole for the screw in the middle of the end of the can, and drill a pilot hole for the screw in the end of the dowel. Invert the can over the end of the dowel and screw it in place with a washer between the can and the head of the screw.

Self-propelled Spool This self-propelled vehicle is an object of fascination for a child of three or older as it rolls swiftly and silently across the floor, and it's something he needs only a little help from you to make. You'll need:

> 1 large spool
> 1 heavy rubber band
> short lengths of dowel
> 1 metal washer

An ordinary thread spool will make a small version of this, but the plastic 3″ wire spool that Gregory and I used really moves along. If you don't have a big spool, you can improvise one by gluing discs of light wood, hardboard, or heavy cardboard to the ends of a scrap piece of wood (which doesn't have to be round for this purpose), and drilling a ⅜″ hole through the center. The dimensions aren't important — the bigger, the better.

The rubber band passes through the hole in the center of the spool. On one end, loop it around a short piece of dowel and fasten the dowel to the face of the spool with a couple of pieces of tape. On the other side, slip a metal washer over the rubber band, and then slip a longer piece of dowel through the rubber band as in the illustration. Use the longer dowel to wind the rubber band tightly and then set it on the floor. The long end of the stick presses against the floor and the rubber band unwinds against it, causing the spool to turn and roll forward. If one rubber band doesn't supply enough power, use two or more together.

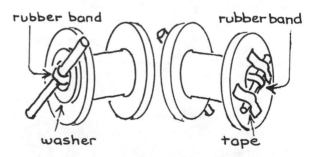

A small spool hasn't much weight and, therefore, little traction. If yours spins around without going anywhere, use a sharp knife to cut lots of V-shaped notches around the rims of the spool, which should make it dig in better on the next try. And run it on a surface that isn't slippery.

Clacker Blocks   You probably remember this golden oldie from your own childhood. The thin blocks appear to be climbing down a ladder, clacking loudly all the way, an illusion that is created as the blocks turn over, one after another, in their double cloth hinges. Made in the traditional way, it takes a child of at least eight to operate Clacker Blocks, but the popsicle stick handles added to this version make it easy for a five-year-old. You will need:

> 30″ length 2″ lattice molding
> 1 popsicle stick
> 2 packets ½″ rayon seam binding tape
>   (9′ per packet)
> white glue
> waxed paper
> tape

Cut seven blocks, each 4″ long, from the lattice molding. Any other wood approximately ¼″ thick may be used and the blocks can be as wide as 3″. Sand the edges of all the blocks. Using clamps, glue the popsicle stick — or any similar light, flat 4½″ stick — across the center of one of the blocks as in the illustration.

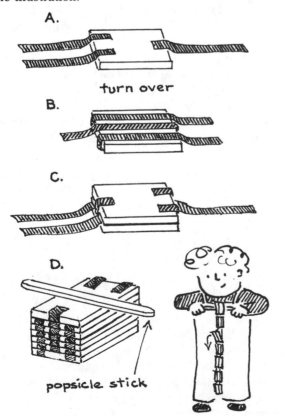

A.

turn over

B.

C.

D.

popsicle stick

Cut eighteen pieces of tape, each about 6″ long. Glue about ½″ of the ends of three pieces of tape to each block, except the one with the handles, as shown at A. When the glue is dry, turn all the blocks over. Now fold the tapes on one block (block No. 1) up and over the face of it as shown at B. Lay another block (block No. 2) on this one as shown at C, and fold the short ends of the tape from block No. 1 up and over, gluing them in place on No. 2. Put a 2″ x 4″ piece of waxed paper over this to keep the glue from sticking to the next tapes and block, and then fold the tapes on No. 2 up and over as you did with the tapes on No. 1. Add block No. 3 and follow the same procedure you followed with No. 2. Add block by block this way, finishing up with the block with the popsicle stick handles — the handles go on top. The tapes should be pulled fairly snugly around the edges of the blocks, but not tightly, so that the blocks will have a small margin of freedom to turn in their hinges. The blocks should make a neat stack when all the tapes are glued in place. Allow the glue to dry thoroughly and remove all the pieces of waxed paper.

Work the clacker blocks a few times yourself so you'll be able to teach the procedure to your child. Hold the popsicle stick handles in the fingers of both hands with all the blocks hanging down in a row. Now turn the handles so the top edge of the block they're glued to turns downward until the face of the block touches the face of the next block in line. If this doesn't set the blocks in motion, turn the handles back the other way until the other face of the top block touches the other face of the second block down, and this will start things going. Keep turning the top block back and forth and the blocks will "move down the ladder" in rapid succession, clacking as they go. Learning to turn the top block back and forth is a little tricky for a five-year-old, but he'll be very proud when he gets the hang of it.

Top   The launching system shown here gives this simple top a really long spin. The materials for top and launcher are:

> scrap piece 1″ x 4″ pine
> 4½″ length ¼″ dowel
> 6″ length 1⅛″ square molding
> 10″ length 1⅛″ lattice molding
> one 26″ shoestring
> short brads

With a coping saw or band saw cut an even 3¼″

diameter disc from the scrap piece of 1″ x 4″, and drill a ¼″ hole precisely through its center. Sharpen one end of the 4½″ length of dowel in a pencil sharpener. Push the dowel through the hole in the disc, gluing them together with the bottom of the disc 1″ from the sharpened tip of the dowel.

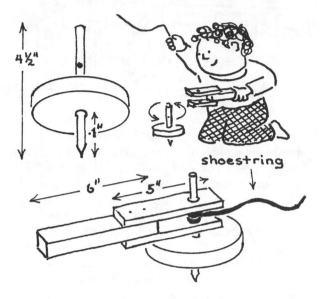

Cut the lattice molding into two 5″ lengths; clamp these together and drill a ⁵⁄₁₆″ hole through both, 1½″ on center from one end. With glue and brads attach 2″ of the other end of each of these lattice pieces to the 1⅛″ square handle as in the illustration. Line them up with care so one hole will be directly above the other.

Place the top in the frame and make a mark on the dowel halfway between the two lattice arms of the frame. Drill an ⅛″ hole through the dowel at this mark to accept the shoestring.

With the top in the frame, insert one end of the shoestring in the hole and turn the top to wind the string around the dowel. Holding the launcher handle so the top is a few inches above a smooth floor, pull strongly on the string with the other hand, which will set the top spinning. A four-year-old may be a little awkward with a top like this, but a five-year-old should be able to operate it well.

Paper Copter Shown here is the pattern for the best paper helicopter that can be made. This is a drop-launched model, so put your child up on your shoulders to set it spinning. In our house the kids take turns sitting on my shoulders to drop the cop-

ter, and the one on the ground hands it back up for more launchings.

Use construction paper, or a slightly heavier-weight paper for best results; ordinary typing paper does a fair job, too. If you hold the paper, a five-year-old who is handy with scissors can do all the cutting on the solid lines. Dimensions and shape don't have to be exact — just a close approximation. The rotor blades are folded in opposite directions along the dotted lines. Weight the bottom end with two medium-size paper clips or one giant paper clip. For a slightly heavier model that a child can launch by tossing it in the air, tape a penny to the end with the tape wrapped around to the other side.

Parachute Drop A preschooler will toss up a parachute made from Daddy's handkerchief hundreds of times, with mixed results, but with this simple contraption — a pulley rigged up on a tree branch — she'll be able to launch it from a truly impressive height, and it will open and float down every time. You need:

    1 small pulley
    1 handkerchief
    1 small toy figurine OR toy car
    string

Tie the pulley to a long piece of string and throw it up and over a good high horizontal tree branch. When it comes back down, put a long piece of string through the pulley, with one end tied tightly to the middle of a parachute made from a man's handkerchief or any other piece of light cloth or plastic. The parachute is made by trying a short string to each corner of the handkerchief and attaching all four

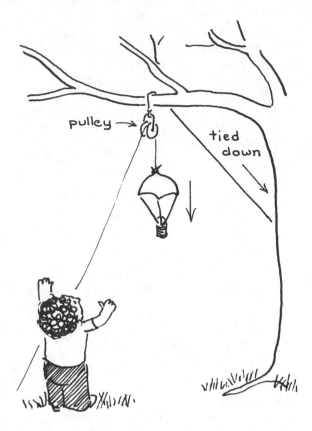

strings to a small weight. A little toy figurine makes a good parachutist, or use a very small toy car — kids like the idea that cars can be dropped by parachute, too, the way the army does.

Now, keeping all your long strings separated so they won't tangle, pull the pulley up to the tree branch. When it's touching and feels fairly secure, tie your end of the string to something stable — a lower limb, a bush, or whatever else is handy. And now the parachute drop is ready to operate. Your child pulls on the end of the other string until the parachute reaches the pulley, and then he lets go, and down it floats. Four is a great age for parachute dropping.

Dollhouses   No-frills dollhouses are the best kind for preschoolers. At eight and nine, girls develop a fascination with tiny details, but until then they don't need elegant dollhouses with scale-model accuracy. Preschoolers — both boys and girls — like a simple structure in which it's easy to manipulate little dolls and figurines. An open "house" similar to the one in the illustration is easily built using 1″ x 6″ boards for the walls, and gluing and nailing them from below to a ¼″ plywood base. Intersecting walls

can be notched together for strength. Dimensions, number of rooms, placement of doors and windows are all up to you and your kids. The scale of a dollhouse like this will be approximately ½″ = 1′, which is right for use with Fisher-Price figurines, Weebles, and other common preschool toys. The standard scale for the fussy fancy dollhouses favored by older kids is 1″ = 1′.

A sturdy cardboard box with a few partitions and some doors and windows cut out becomes a surprisingly durable dollhouse.

Paint or wallpaper the walls; add swinging doors or exterior walls and a roof that comes off; improve this real estate in any other way you like. Or just leave it raw wood or brown cardboard. It will get plenty of use whether it's plain or gussied up.

The cheapest store-bought doll furniture is fine, or make your own from scraps of wood and cardboard, keeping designs simple, as in the illustration. No need to stick slavishly to the ½″ = 1′ scale, because preschoolers aren't bothered in the least by scale incongruities. Assembling a dollhouse and furniture makes a good shop project for father and child.

Figurines   Making dollhouse figurines is a great short project for Dad and a five-year-old. Using a saw in a miter box and possibly a little help, your

child can cut short lengths from dowels — any diameter from ½″ on up. And with a marker she can draw faces on them. Wine corks and small blocky scraps of wood can be turned into little people, too, by adding features. Kids will play with these as is, or you can help your child stick on some scraps of colored ribbon, cloth, or paper for clothes, using white glue.

Dolls Using scrap blocks of wood and dowels, glue, markers, and maybe some paint, you can make dolls along the same lines as the figurines described above, but a little more elaborate. And your child can again help with the assembly, draw the faces, and glue on scraps of ribbon and cloth for clothes.

Father-made wooden dolls are an American tradition — Hopi Indian men still assemble blocky kachina dolls from parts they carve from cottonwood roots. The kachina dolls are carried in ritual dances, where they represent deified ancestral spirits, but at the end of the ceremonies, the kachina dancers give the dolls to kids to use for play.

If you want the arms of a wooden doll to move, drill a hole through the body from one side to the other just under the shoulders, and holes near the tops of the arms, and use a piece of round sewing elastic through the holes and knotted on both ends to hold the assembly together — stretch the elastic tight.

←knot in elastic

Preschool kids love to talk to dolls and puppets. Sometimes they will open up and tell a doll much more than they will tell a parent. If you're looking for information about something your child did or a little insight into his feelings about some issue or problem, you can usually forget about direct inter-

rogation — it hardly ever gets results. But get behind a doll or a puppet and ask all the questions you like, using *its* voice, and you'll start to get some answers.

Airplane Airplane building makes a perfect first woodworking project for a father and a two-year-old. The result won't look like much to you, but it will be a Very Big Deal for the novice carpenter who works on it. You will need:

> one thin piece wood (wing)
> one thicker piece wood (fuselage)

Lattice molding makes a good wing, and 1⅛″ square molding is an excellent shape for a fuselage — or use any other scrap pieces you have handy. The pieces can be cut to any lengths your child likes. She can help you saw them if the saw is held in a miter box. Help your airplane builder assemble the parts with white glue and a C-clamp, or drill some pilot holes for nails and help her knock them in.

Acrobat The father who makes this acrobat is likely to monopolize it to watch with fascination as it somersaults and flips and kicks around. You will need:

> 4′ length 1⅛″ lattice molding
> scrap piece ½″ wood
> ⅛″ dowel
> ¾″ brads
> light string

The pieces can all be cut out with a coping saw. The body/head piece is cut from the ½″ scrap and all the other pieces are cut from the lattice molding. In

the tops of the legs, the "hands," and from side to side across the narrow hips, drill holes for the light string. The arms get ⅛" holes at the shoulders, and the body has a ⁵/₃₂" hole drilled across it from side to side at chest high level.

The legs are attached with a piece of string that passes through them and the narrow hips and is knotted on each side to hold the assembly together. An ⅛" dowel passes through the chest and is glued into the shoulder holes of the arms.

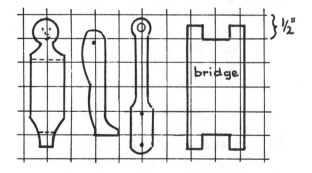

Drill two holes at the top end of each frame upright for the string, and notch the frame to accept the notched bridge, as shown in the diagram. Bridge and uprights are held together with two ¾" brads; no glue is used — to allow the joint to flex.

To join figure and frame, lay the acrobat on a table with his arms above his head, and place the frame so

the top of it surrounds his hands and the bottom is pointing in the opposite direction from his feet. Now make a simple loop of string through the two sides of the frame and the acrobat's "hands." That is, thread the string through the bottom hole in the left upright; through the holes at the finger ends of the two hands; through the bottom hole in the right upright; through the top hole of the right upright; through the wrist holes in the hands; through the top hole in the left upright, and then tie in a double knot. This loop should be fairly loose. You may have to test the action and adjust the loop a little to get the acrobat swinging nicely.

The toy is operated by squeezing together the two bottom legs of the frame, which you will be able to do with one hand, but your five-year-old will need to use two hands. The frame should be held upright at all times so the acrobat can fall back to the hanging starting point, which crosses the strings; then squeezing the legs of the frame together uncrosses the strings and sets him in motion.

Decorate the acrobat by gluing pieces of ribbon or colored paper front and back on the body so he looks like he's wearing a gym suit. Draw a face with a marker on a piece of paper or light cardboard and glue it to the head.

Tumbling Ladder   At two and a half a child should have the co-ordination to set the tumbling block on the top rung of the ladder, and all kids love to watch it work its way down rung after rung. Making this toy requires some woodworking skill and a lot of accuracy. The materials are:

> 9 popsicle sticks OR coffee stirrers (⅜" wide)
> 10' length ½" half-round molding
> 7" length 1" x 4"
> 2 blocks, ¾" x 1⅝" x 3⅜"
> ½" brads

You can buy the coffee stirrers in quantity from an arts and crafts store or save and recycle them. Cut them 3½" long. The ladder is made by sandwiching the sticks between two pieces of half-round molding on each side. Lay two 30" lengths of half-round on a working surface with the flat sides up; mark accurately the placement of the rungs. There should be exactly 2⅞" from the top of each rung to the top of the next rung. Glue the rungs on, preferably with hot-melt glue — but white glue or a fast-setting glue like Duco will do. When the glue is dry, use wood

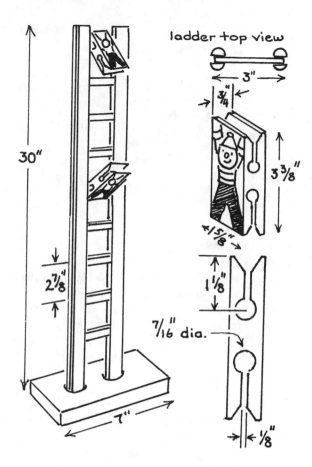

ladder top view

glue to add the other 30″ pieces of half-round, tapping in a ½″ brad at each juncture. Drilling tiny pilot holes for the brads will avoid any splitting of the wood. For a neat job, set the brads below the surface and fill the holes with wood putty.

Drill ⅝″ holes in the 1″ x 4″ base piece for the ends of the ladder. If the ladder ends are a little big for the holes, pare them down with a knife or sandpaper. Glue them in.

The tumbling block is made as shown in the diagram, and will last longer if you have hardwood to make it from. Drill the holes first — preferably on a drill press for accuracy. Now use a band saw or coping saw and carefully cut out the slots and then the slopes in toward the slots from the edges. The slots should be just 1/16″ wider than the thickness of the coffee stirrer rungs, and the diameter of the holes should be just 1/16″ greater than the width of the rungs, so that the block will slide onto the top rung, turn over when the hole is around the rung, straighten itself out as the slot runs past the rung, and then catch on the next rung, riding straight

down on the other slot, turning when the rung is engaged in the hole, and so forth.

You only need one tumbling block, but it's more fun to have two that can chase each other down the ladder. To make the blocks look like tumbling clowns, draw or paint clowns on paper about the weight of an index card and glue them to the blocks.

Homemade Construction Sets

Construction sets are the toys that fathers most often share with their kids. Below are suggestions for a variety of homemade building systems.

Dowels and Connectors Dowels of any diameter and any length can be joined with blocks of wood or other materials drilled with holes to accept them. It's the same principle as Tinkertoys, but with long sections of ½″ dowels and connectors made from 1″ lumber or even chunks of 2″ x 4″, a child can put together substantial frameworks quickly. With this system, it's easy, for instance, to build a crawl-inside playhouse that you can help your child cover with newspaper or light cloth held in place with staples.

Holes drilled in all sides of the connector blocks and at angles will give you and your child a variety of ways to join your dowels. If your child has trouble fitting the dowels into the wooden connectors you've drilled, use a coping saw to cut relief slots across the ends of the dowels.

Connectors don't have to be wooden. I save all the cylindrical cardboard boxes that Parmesan cheese comes in — we seem to use tons of it in our house — and I drill ¼″ holes at regular intervals around these so Gregory and Timothy can build with them and ¼″ dowels. The cans get stacked in towers with the dowels making horizontal walls between them — great for fortress building — and we use them in many other combinations as well.

Actual Tinkertoys offer a wonderful variety of building possibilities — and they're cheap. You can extend the range of a Tinkertoy set by adding some extra elements. A 2′ x 2′ scrap piece of ¼″ pegboard makes a terrific base to build on since the dowels fit the pegboard holes nicely. With a base like this, a preschooler can make a village of framework houses and run little cars around between them. Scrap pieces of ⅛″ pegboard extend Tinkertoy house-building possibilities even further by making excellent roofs and in-between floors. The kids and I like to grab objects at random when we build, so the plastic pop-together beads from the toy chest end up perched on top of dowels like Russian onion domes, and we have marbles and little balls rolling around in mazes created with upright dowels in the pegboard and rolling on ramps improvised from cardboard punched with holes to accept the dowels.

Any wooden toy can have ¼″ holes drilled in it to accept Tinkertoy dowels. Gregory and I have performed this operation on a couple of his wooden cars, which can now be built onward and upward.

Straws and Paper Clips   Bend the two loops of a paper clip apart; pull the free wire in each loop out a little; and you have the perfect connector for two drinking straws. Just shove each end into a straw. The joint can be bent to any angle. A child of five or older can build intricate framework structures with this system. As many as three paper clip connectors can be pushed into any joint. Plastic soda straws hold up best.

Coffee Stirrers and Cardboard   A four-year-old will build cages and castles and jails for the bad guys using panels of cardboard slotted around the edges to accept coffee stirrers or popsicle sticks. Cut the panels in a variety of shapes and sizes from corrugated or (better) heavy plain cardboard. The slots can be made with a knife or a thin saw at intervals of 1″ along the edges of the panels. Cutting the sides of the panels to an even number of inches will make measuring for the slots easy, and will leave a firm square of material at each corner.

You can buy coffee stirrers in quantity at an arts and crafts store, or use wider tongue depressors, which are available at most drugstores. Get a good supply of these flat sticks — kids discover a multitude of uses for them, for instance, stacking them with overlapping corners as in log cabin building.

Natural Construction   In five minutes on a walk in the woods, your four-year-old can assemble enough fallen sticks to build a fine log cabin. Help her stack the sticks with the edges overlapping and she'll get the hang of it quickly. No need to notch the ends — the structure will stay together if it's just piled up. Straight sticks laid side by side make a good roof for a cabin like this. Doors and windows are tricky, though.

Sticks shoved into loose dirt make good fortresses and toy teepees, gathered at the top with string. And a hole dug in the ground with sticks laid over the top makes a doll dugout. Use plastic and cardboard and any other materials you have handy to extend the range of natural constructions.

Homemade Blocks   Don't bother to make wooden blocks yourself unless you like sanding, and unless you have a table saw and a good power sander — preferably a stationary one — to work with.

Hardwood blocks will take the most abuse, but it's hard even to find hardwood, let alone pay for it. Use good quality clear pine or spruce instead. Cheap construction-grade fir will waste your time with endless sanding, and wastes a lot of material when you throw out all the super-rough parts, and the parts with checking (cracks), knotholes, and even oozing sap.

Make the dimensions of your blocks even multiples of the actual thickness dimension of the wood, so they will fit together evenly. For example, with so-called 1″ lumber, which actually measures ¾″, all other dimensions should be 1½″, 3″, 4½″, etc. If you start with 2″ x 4″ lumber, which actually measures $1^9/_{16}$″ x $3^9/_{16}$″, first rip the wider side down to 3⅛″, which is exactly twice the narrower dimension. Then you can cut blocks to length on even multiples of 3⅛″ — i.e., 6¼″, 12½″, etc.

Also make some blocks shaped like this:

Cylindrical blocks can be cut from closet poles (the lumberyard name for dowels over 1″), at lengths that will fit evenly with the rectangular blocks.

For kids up through three, lighter, smaller blocks cut from 1″ lumber tend to be best. When a child reaches four, though, a big set of heavy wood blocks is the best of all possible toys.

Blocks can be left as raw sanded wood, but a clear finish will keep them fresh-looking for a while.

Milk Carton Blocks

Durable light blocks that are great for a baby or a toddler can be made from empty milk cartons. Rinse thoroughly and cut off the sloping tops evenly with a sharp knife. Now shove two milk cartons together, one inside the other, and tape the joint. Use cartons of various sizes and cut them to different heights. Cubes with all sides the same dimensions as the bottom of the carton make for even building.

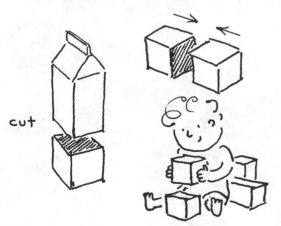

To make a good line for cutting, mark the same height at each corner and join these marks with masking tape. These blocks can be made very snazzy-looking by covering them with contact paper.

Any sturdy small box makes a good building block. Taping it shut will give it a longer life. Cylindrical cardboard food containers — salt, bread crumbs, oatmeal, etc. — can also be added to a set of blocks. And kids' books can be built into block structures for roofs and bridges.

Toothpick Combinations

Use round toothpicks as the structural members for small-scale construction. They can be shoved into marshmallows — both miniature and full-size — or into Juicy Fruit candies, or a combination of these goodies. For connectors that your kids won't gobble as they build, use chunks and pieces of raw potato.

You can also soak beans of any sort for a few hours until they are soft enough to accept the toothpicks. Beans, though, are a little slippery and hard for younger kids to hold, and they sometimes split up when toothpicks are pushed into them. Beans and toothpicks are good for a child of six or older, where the candy and potato connectors can be used at four.

Chapter 11

WORKING WITH KIDS

"They're always helping me," says one father about his two daughters, four and seven, and his son, two. "If we're not building something together, they're with me working on the car or on one of the tractors. You don't get much done. But it's hard to say, 'You have to stay inside with your mother; I *have* to do this outside.' . . . They're good gofers — if they can remember from the time you tell them what it was they were supposed to get. I enjoy having them around. They like to *feel* helpful, too. Even if they're not really, if they think that they're being a help and really adding to the project that's going on, that's satisfying to them. When Russell [two] climbs up inside the hood of the car — that's where I draw the line."

Every kid feels important helping Dad. A two-year-old beams with pride as he carries a few sticks to put on the woodpile, and a five-year-old brags at kindergarten about how she got to help Dad wash the car. Working with Dad is often a bigger deal for a child than playing with him, because it means using adult tools and learning all about adult things.

Some jobs you share are just plain fun. Mixing concrete or mortar in a wheelbarrow, for instance, is the ultimate mud pie. Painting the lower part of a wall, mopping a floor, moving stones, kneading bread, collecting sticks are all favorites, and what child will refuse a chance to spray with the garden hose?

Of course there are places where kids can't be included — like work up on a ladder, or electrical wiring, or cutting with a chain saw. But for the most part there's room for preschool kids in virtually every handyman task. Sometimes it takes a little ingenuity to find a way to fit children in and keep them occupied safely while you get something accomplished. And the job will always take a little longer and require more cleanup at the end when the kids are helping. But for me, at least, the kids are an enormous help on any job. I'm a reluctant handyman, and their eagerness to help and excitement and fascination with the work can turn a dreary chore into pure pleasure.

You don't really notice it, but by small degrees, kids actually begin to be a practical help. Here's a father talking about his three-year-old assistant: "He's getting to the age now where he can help me a lot. If I'm holding something up and I need a screwdriver or I'm working over here and I have to hold this and I need something, he can get it for me. The other day I was working on the car and I asked him to go get a wrench for me — and he came back with it. He walked all the way to the house for it. I said, 'Wow, great, fantastic.' He actually did it." Kids who start their apprenticeship at two and three know the ropes so well by five that they're making a real contribution.

HANDYMAN'S HELPER

A two-year-old is proud to stand by holding tools for you — he can hand you the screwdriver each time you need it. And he can help you turn the screw. A three-year-old can start to fetch tools if they're near at hand and she's learned their names, and by four you have a handy gofer.

On any handyman job you do with a preschooler, it's a good policy to keep tools sorted into two boxes — one well out of reach with chisels, knives, etc., and another near at hand with hammer, wrenches, and other tools that your child can have free access to and examine and play with without doing any harm. Daddy's tools are numbered among a child's favorite toys. Every kid wants to get her hands on Dad's retracting tape measure and his hammer. One father told me that his kids had taken over his under-car creeper as their favorite riding toy and he has trouble getting it back when he wants to change the oil.

There are almost always small tasks your child can accomplish on any job. If nothing easy presents

itself, create a task. Say you're nailing something your four-year-old could damage by missing the nail. Set him up with a hammer and some nails started in a piece of 2″ x 4″ on the floor, and he can pound away, just as Daddy does. Working alongside you this way will make him feel he's part of the enterprise — as much a part as if he were accomplishing half the work.

For more on sharing jobs with kids, see p. 94.

WORKSHOP

"My dad has a hammer, and he teached me to use it," boasts Jordan, four, with immense pride. And fathers, too, swell with pride when they talk about introducing their kids to tools. There's tremendous satisfaction on both sides when father and child go down to the basement and knock together a couple of scraps of wood to make a boat for the tub. No matter how rough or homely the product, both love the experience of working together.

To start your child out with tools, you don't need to be an accomplished handyman with a well-appointed shop. Any sturdy low table will do for a work surface. You'll need plenty of scrap materials to operate on, a few basic hand tools, nails, wire, glue, paint, and you're on your way.

A two-year-old can help you operate a few tools. At three, kids can start their first independent

hammering of nails into soft material and saw pieces of cardboard. Around four and a half they begin to be able to operate some hand tools effectively.

A child who gets early practice with Dad in the workshop will begin at four and five to come up with idea after idea for projects she wants to build: "Hey, Dad, let's make a TV set out of wood." "Let's make a wood hair drier." "Let's build a Super Woman car." With some scrap blocks of wood, some bottle caps for dials and wheels, and a little bit of your help, she'll be able to make them all.

PERFECTIONISTS

"The frustrating thing for me as a perfectionist in the shop," said one father, "was for me to want him to be precise, to drill the hole . . . do it the *right* way."

This was a constant refrain from fathers I talked with, and some had just given up on trying to teach their preschool kids to use tools. The kids couldn't concentrate long enough, wouldn't sand with the grain, got bored or upset when the birdhouse-building project hit a little snag.

But the father I quoted above had stuck with it, and, "What I found is they learn somehow, by golly."

Teaching dozens of children at the local nursery school to work with tools, I've learned by repeated bitter experience how easily kids play havoc with an organized approach. Every time I set up a project and try to lead the kids step by step through it toward a product I have in mind, the whole thing is a bust. They get to a part that entertains them and go no further, or they get distracted and wander off. But every time I manage to get over my natural adult drive to organize and set everything up in advance, and simply get the kids together with some materials and tools and we drill some holes and cut some pieces of wood, the kids get excited about what's happening. They'll say, for instance, "Hey, that looks like a scarecrow," so we'll add a piece of wood for the head to make it look more like one, and maybe C-clamp on a couple of long 1″ x 3″s for legs, and slap on some paint. We have a wonderful time and end up with a 6′ scrap wood scarecrow — or maybe we'll make a crooked house or a rickety stand for acrobats with a rubber Batman poised precariously on the top. The ideas come from the kids and the work is on a level they can enjoy. It's slapdash carpentry for quick — and impermanent — results.

So for a start in the workshop, you can forget about making a simple box as a first lesson in woodworking. Making a simple box with a preschooler isn't simple at all — it requires care and precision and it will bring you both to frustration.

Begin by showing your child how each tool works and help him practice with it on scrap materials. A child wants to hammer nails to feel the power of the hammer and to act like Dad. Joining two boards comes later.

A preschooler may not stick long with a single operation in the workshop, and may even be ready to quit and go out to the sandbox after fifteen minutes — but this doesn't mean that she didn't have

the time of her life while she was hammering with you.

You can definitely forget about precision and doing it the "right" way. A three- or four-year-old who manages to knock a nail in *any* way or who hacks off a ragged piece of cardboard with a coping saw has achieved a big triumph.

Another regular workshop problem fathers have is a compulsion to Help. If a child is working too slowly — which is the way all kids work — or is having a little trouble, there's always the temptation to take the tool away, show how it's done, get on with it. . . . "That's very difficult for me," said one father. "When I get something started I want to get it finished as quickly as possible so I can go on to something else. And that's where I have to back off and let *them* do a certain amount. . . . One of the things that fathers have to have — and it's something you aren't born with, something that develops, and that develops very slowly — is patience. And it takes a lot of work."

TOOLS

Toy tools are junk for anything but imaginative play. They are about as useful to a child for making things as toy food might be for nourishing him. Kids need the real McCoy, tools just like Dad's. Share with your kids the hand tools you have and treat yourself (and the kids) to a few new ones. Fancy tool chests sold for children sometimes contain real and even well-made tools, but usually they don't, and the selection of tools often boggles the mind. Wood chisels for a kid? There's not much a child can accomplish with a chisel except cutting himself. Below I discuss in detail the tools that I and my young friends at the local nursery school have submitted to exhaustive practical tests and have found to work best for preschoolers.

Getting kids started with tools isn't a time-consuming business. One father put it this way: "It's like their questions about sex. They never want to know any more than this much [with a *little* gesture]. If you try to bore them with a long explanation, you're just going to turn them off completely. They're going to stop asking questions. It doesn't take much time to show a kid about a tool. It's not going to take a half hour, it never comes to that."

Most kids want more than anything to go it alone with a tool as quickly as possible, so stack the cards heavily in favor of their success. The material should be soft and easily worked, and it should always be clamped down firmly or held in a vise at a proper height for your child to work on it effectively. The position a child assumes to work with a tool and the technique she uses may not meet "correct" adult standards. Kids choke up on the head of a hammer and have to get up on the workbench to help operate a brace and bit — real aberrations if you insist on doing things by the book. But the "right" way, while it may be great for an adult, may be no good at all for a person who is 39″ tall. Sometimes the crazy-looking stance a child takes naturally will be the right one for her weight and size — though you can of course often help her find a better one. A child who operates a tool in an unconventional way will have no trouble learning good form when she's old enough to manage it. The three-year-old who chokes up on the head of the hammer because it's heavy will be holding it by the end of the handle four years later.

Tools for Two

There are a few exceptions to the rule that a child will always do best operating a tool alone, and these are tools like the plane and the brace and bit that are simply too cumbersome for a preschooler to use by himself, but which he can use very effectively with a father's help. You can introduce these to your child as Tools for Two — tools that need both a kid and a grownup to make them work. If that is clearly understood from the start, your child is less likely to whine, "Lemme do it myself," and the two of you can have a wonderful time together manufacturing wood shavings with a plane or drilling big holes with a brace and bit.

The Tool for Two notion can also help you get around the problem of overwhelming a child with your help on other tools. Instead of giving your child a new saw or some other new tool to use alone, and then, when she can't get it to go, having to intervene and help her operate it — which means she loses face — you can introduce it from the start as a Tool for Two. The two of you can work with it together for a while until she gets the hang of it, and then she graduates to using it on her own. So instead of losing face, she has done the reverse — she has pride in her accomplishment and can go on confidently to another step and another tool.

Shop Safety

An excellent basic workshop safety rule for kids is: Always use two hands. The safest place for both of a preschooler's hands is on the handle of the tool he's using. A free hand is an odds-on favorite to tangle with the descending head of the hammer or the teeth of the saw. You always encourage a small child to use two hands on a glass of milk or a bowl of cereal he's carrying. Why not also on a hammer and saw? Two hands on the handle isn't the "right" way for many tools, but the second hand can provide a preschooler with the extra power he may need — and with a measure of safety.

Once a child is able to operate a tool, he can be left somewhat to his own devices. But I always like to be close at hand, working on a project of my own — far enough away so that Gregory feels independent, but close enough to lend a hand if he needs it, and close enough to make certain he's working safely.

With preschoolers in a shop, you naturally take extra safety precautions. All power tools should be shut off, with their cords disconnected and the wall plugs capped with child-resistant blanks. Make a regular habit of removing the bit from a power drill or router and the blade from a saber saw. Securely tightening a C-clamp on the blade of a hand circular saw or a table saw adds a measure of protection against a child's investigations — or remove the blade. Around power tools, though, and particularly around stationary ones, close supervision is the best safeguard. Sharp and otherwise potentially dangerous tools are naturally kept far out of reach, and glues, paints, solvents, etc., should be stored in a locked cabinet.

All the safe tools in the shop, on the other hand, should be kept low down, where a child of four or older can grab them at will to explore and investigate with them. And nails, bolts, and scrap materials should also be stored where your child can get at them.

Workbench

You can use a chair to boost your child up to your workbench, or you may even try knocking together a simple platform for the same purpose — but you'll soon discover how much the chair or platform is in your way. A low, child-height workbench is the only solution, but it needn't be a beautiful finished job with butcherblock top and drawers and tool holders. The simplest kind of bench will do. In fact, one of the best — because it can grow higher as your child grows — is a piece of ¾″ plywood mounted on two sawhorses made with sawhorse brackets. The 2″ x 4″ legs can be replaced after a few years with longer ones. To attach the plywood top, fasten four 2″ x 2″ cleats to the bottom surface of the plywood with glue and screws so they fit snugly in pairs around the horizontal pieces of the sawhorses. The cleats are then fastened to the sawhorse horizontals with screws.

Another fast and easy bench is made by cutting down the legs on a relatively sturdy old table. Attach a plywood top if it needs a new work surface, and reinforce it if it wobbles. You can save building a real, good-looking workbench from scratch until

your child is ten or older and can take an active part in the project.

The height of the workbench is a function of the size of the kid who is going to use it. Waist height is just about perfect, but add 3″ to grow on. There's no optimum amount of bench surface, but it makes sense to have the top narrow enough to allow your child to reach all the way to the back; and make it as long as you can accommodate, to allow projects to spread out. One nice bonus of a good-size child workbench is that you can borrow it for big projects where you need extra room.

Lighting is an important consideration in placing a workbench. Ideally, it should be near a window with the daylight falling from the back left for a right-handed child and from the right for a southpaw, keeping the shadow of her hand off the work. A window in front of or directly behind the working child isn't a very good arrangement. The first one backlights the work, and the second throws her shadow on what she's doing. Usually, though, you won't have the luxury of a window for natural lighting; but use these same principles in setting up an overhead light to keep the work free of interfering shadows.

With pegboard or a row of nails at your child's height, you can set up and enforce a rule that tools have to be hung up out of the way when they aren't in use. You'll have to abide by this rule, too — if you want it to stick.

Clamps and Vise

Some system for clamping work down tightly to the bench is needed. No preschooler can hold the material in one hand and operate a tool with the other. A child can get by without a vise for a while, but C-clamps are essential. With one large C-clamp a child will have the means to hold work steady for sawing, hammering, and a number of other operations. With a lot of C-clamps, you and your child can fasten together all kinds of impromptu play structures and fanciful objects. For kids, a lot of the fun in this kind of building comes with undoing the clamps and having the structure fall apart.

An inexpensive "light-duty" woodworking vise is perfect for a preschooler; these are usually mounted with a screw clamp so the vise can be moved to different edges of the workbench as needed.

Hammer and Nails

A hammer is usually the first tool a kid learns about. Its purpose is straightforward and easy to understand — bang, bang, bang. Which is simple enough to do with a mallet and the pegs in a pounding toy, but the going gets rougher when you introduce a nail and it has to be started. A kid can get pretty frustrated trying to hold a nail in one hand and hit it with the hammer. The problem can be completely avoided by having your child stick a little ball of clay or play dough on the spot where the nail is to be driven. The nail is then stuck into the clay, which holds it upright while the child starts hammering with two hands on the handle. After a couple of whacks, the clay is removed and the nail is driven home.

Also try starter holes. Drill some holes a hair smaller than the diameter of the nails in a 2″ piece of wood, and present it to a three-year-old with nails and hammer. With a child who wants to go it alone (all kids over three), teach her to operate an eggbeater drill, which is discussed below, to make the holes herself. The perfect nail for kids is the 1¼″ galvanized roofing nail. It has a big head and it doesn't bend up.

By nailing into a soft material like homasote, a child has an easier job of starting the nails alone. With homasote, lighter box nails are good. You can make an excellent nailing toy for a four-year-old using a piece of homasote as a background onto which he can nail small pieces of scrap wood, plastic bottle caps, and other odds and ends to make random patterns. Drill or punch holes in the scrap pieces, and they will hold the small nails upright for starting.

A patient five- or six-year-old can clamp a spring-loaded clothespin to a short nail at right angles at the pointed end. The clothespin will act as a stand for the nail and the child can use two hands on the hammer to start it — or hold onto the clothespin with one hand to steady it.

Holding the nails yourself for a child to start is clearly unwise if you value your fingers. If you insist on doing this, use pliers to hold them; a vise-grip pliers does a fine job.

The best hammer for a child of four or older is a twelve-ounce claw hammer. An eight-ounce hammer is good for a younger child, but it won't drive anything heavier than a tack, and a full-size sixteen-ounce adult hammer is too heavy for a preschooler. When they first start to hammer, most kids choke up on the head and pound with it as if it were a stone. The head is heavy and it's easier to manage this way. But gradually they learn — just as the cave men learned aeons ago — that the handle gives them some mechanical advantage. Don't push a three-year-old to hold back on the handle, because you aren't likely to succeed. But do explain from time to time the advantage of the handle and encourage holding it further down and with two hands. Also try to get your child to smack-tap at the nail rather than hauling back and slugging wide of the mark. A big leap in the co-ordination needed for hitting nails usually comes around four and a half or five.

Pounding nails not only makes a kid feel important, it can be a great way to work out aggressions. Which of course isn't reserved for kids; plenty of fathers use handyman jobs to hammer away at the boss's head or the injustices of the world. An angry kid or a sullen one can work a lot of it off by hammering. A big soft piece of wood, preferably just a little rotten to allow for easy nailing, is a great thing to keep in the cellar or yard as a ready target for therapeutic nailing. Preschoolers delight in smashing beer or soda cans with a hammer, and if you have a short-handled light sledgehammer, let your four-year-old batter a piece of 2″ x 4″ with it.

Pulling nails out with the claw end of a hammer can be just as satisfying for many kids as knocking them in.

Goggles make all hammering safer, and kids love to wear them.

homasote

Tack Hammer

A terrific tool for preschoolers is a tack hammer — sometimes called an upholsterer's hammer — with a magnetized head. It completely eliminates the problem of starting the nail. A tack is picked up by its head with the magnetized end of the hammer and the child hauls back and Slam! he drives it all the way into a piece of homasote with one blow. Kids stand there driving dozens of tacks and feeling exactly like the little tailor in the story who killed seven at a blow. Magnetized tack hammers are usually inexpensive, and are widely available in hardware stores.

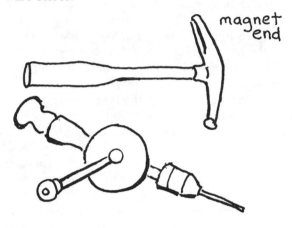

magnet end

Eggbeater Drill

The best drill for kids is the "eggbeater" type. With a minimum of instruction and practice a four-year-old can successfully drill — unaided — holes up to ¼". These crank-and-gear-driven drills use both small twist drill bits — the kind used with an electric drill — and straight-flute bits, with which some come equipped. Limit a child's ready supply of bits to those over ⅛" — fine bits get broken. With an eggbeater drill, a preschooler is pretty much on her own. At first you may have to help hold it straight and exert a little downward pressure, keeping your hand above your child's on the top knob. Teach your child always to hold the drill by that top knob; a hand held too far down the shaft means fingers pinched in the gears.

The eggbeater drill gives a child the means for making starter holes for nails and holes for fitting things together with dowels and wire, but, more important, it gives him a device for just drilling a lot of little holes — which is what he'll enjoy most at first.

Brace and Bit

The brace and bit is often missing from the home workshop, so reliant have we become on electric drills. But I wouldn't give an electric drill to a kid much younger than twelve, and there are a lot of good years of big hole drilling between four and twelve. A good brace is an expensive piece of equipment to acquire; if you haven't got one, try the kids' grandfathers and you may come up with a sound old brace that's hung idly on a basement wall for years.

Introduce the brace and bit as a Tool for Two — it takes a three-year-old and an adult working together to operate it. There is really no way that a preschooler is going to manage this big machine by himself, and this is clear to all but the most die-hard "Lemme do it myself" types; and even they get the point quickly when they try to go it alone.

With a piece of 1" soft wood clamped to the edge of the bench, you hold the top handle and push down. Your child *kneels on the bench*, where she can get a good purchase on the handle. This, of

course, isn't the "right" way for an adult, but it's by far the best way for a kid. Your child cranks the brace around while you hold it steady. There's a heady thrill for kids in seeing the big bit bore through the wood. I drill a lot of holes with my friends at the local nursery school, and they always line up to drill more. Each time the bit comes through the bottom there's cheering, and we write the names of the children next to the holes they've drilled, so that we have a record of which is Keith's hole and which is Lisa's — these labels on identical ½" holes are an interesting source of pride for the drillers.

If your child's arms are a little short for the radius of the turn and the going gets tough, show him how the ratchet action of the brace works. With a little back and forthing on the ratchet system he should be able to get going again. Use only bits up to ½″ — bigger ones are too hard for a child to turn. The brace will also make small holes using twist drill bits.

Eventually you should show your child how to avoid splintering the wood as the bit comes through the bottom. But the first few times around, it complicates matters too much to clamp a piece of scrap wood under the work or to turn the work over and drill from the other side after the point of the bit breaks through. Your child will notice the splintering — kids are excellent noticers — and will ask about it; and then you can show her the tricks of the trade. But first things first, and the first thing is to drill some good big holes. Kids graduate quickly from 1″ wood to 2″ x 4″s.

A suet bird feeder is a great hole-drilling project for a five-year-old and a father (see p. 238).

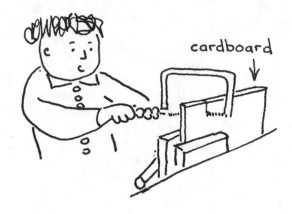

cardboard

Plane

A plane can be the first woodworking tool you introduce to your child — around age two — and I think a father and child can get no closer than when they are working a plane together. You have to envelop a kid in your arms to help him with it. He's standing and you're kneeling and the narrow board to be planed is clamped securely in a low place — I clamp onto a low railing on the back porch. As you and your child work the plane back and forth on the edge of the board, both holding onto the tool, and the shavings start to curl out, you will hear the excitement of a kid who will forever afterward be hooked on using tools. "Those are shavings," says Dad. "Shavings! Oboy! I *love* shavings!" He will hoard the shavings in a paper bag for weeks and you'll be called on over and over to make more.

Coping Saw

The short crosscut saw that comes as standard equipment with sets of tools for children is a difficult tool for a preschooler to operate — it sticks and binds and the relatively large teeth are no help at all. There are several other saws that give a child a much better chance at success. A coping saw, for my money, is the best. It's light and easy for a novice

sawyer to handle and the tiny teeth and narrow blade cut fast and offer a minimum of resistance.

To give her the true sensation of sawing right from the start, introduce your three-year-old to the coping saw as a Tool for Two. Clamp a narrow piece of light material in a vise — heavy cardboard is best, with laths, lattice molding, dry twigs and branches, and bamboo running close behind. Your child holds the saw handle with two hands and you hold onto the frame from the opposite side, and it's back and forth, snicker-snack, and you're through. Kids are usually amazed at how quickly and efficiently this operation goes. If you lend a hand for a while, giving the little extra pressure, heft, and control your child may need, she should be able to go it alone after a very short time. The Tool for Two approach can be dropped quickly if you have a stubbornly independent four- or five-year-old — he will work things out for himself in no time, particularly if the material is corrugated cardboard. If one thickness of cardboard isn't enough of a challenge or it bends too much, fold together double or triple thicknesses.

Use the widest coping saw blades you can buy. The thin blades designed for cutting tight curves break easily and meander widely when a child is operating the saw. Coping saw blades are traditionally mounted with the teeth pointing toward the handle, which is opposite to the direction the teeth point on most other saws. Where a crosscut saw does all its cutting on the pushing stroke, the coping saw cuts on the pull. This distinction will make little difference to a beginner, who will push down on both back and forth strokes, but as your kids progress, you'll want to show them how they can save some effort and saw more smoothly by exerting pressure only on the cutting stroke and coasting in the opposite direction. If your child is slow to set up a good back-and-forth rhythm in sawing, you can add a little encouragement by chanting, "Pull, Pull, Pull," or "Push, Push, Push," depending on the type of saw. Two kids can sometimes operate a coping saw as a team effort, with one holding the handle and the other on the opposite side of the work holding the frame.

A coping saw table like the one pictured on p. 284 is a useful aid for adults and older kids, but preschoolers will be more successful sawing down through thin material clamped upright in a vise. No child cuts a straight line with a coping saw, which tends to look "wrong" to adults. But for a child, the issue isn't making it straight, it's sawing a piece off. In this matter, there are plenty of years in the future to straighten a child out.

Miter Box

A sawing setup that allows preschoolers early success — and straight lines — is the miter box and back saw. The work to be cut can be clamped firmly to the miter box, and the child then works the saw back and forth with two hands on the handle. The miter box holds and guides the saw in the cutting plane, eliminating the possibility of the child's meandering off course and reducing the saw's tendency to stick and bind.

A simple wooden miter box will help if no other is available, but without spending a lot of money you can have a very serviceable metal miter box that will hold the saw firmly above the work. A back saw, which has a square end and a rigid metal strip along its back to keep it straight, is the correct saw to use with a miter box. Some miter boxes can be used with an ordinary crosscut saw, but for a preschooler, the back saw is always best since it is commonly made with more teeth to the inch than a crosscut saw, and the more teeth a saw has to the inch, the less resistance it offers to the operator. To cut down on the resistance of the saw a little more, put a couple of drops of household oil on each side. And of course it should always be kept sharp and free of rust — a dull, rusty saw is a chore for a man to push and will easily defeat a kid.

A miter box should be screwed or clamped solidly to the workbench, and the material to be cut — laths and lattice moldings are good for starters here — should be clamped in place so your child is sawing through the thin dimension. You can lend a hand and a little heft at first if your child doesn't just grab the handle and start sawing down through the wood

right away — which is what will usually happen as early as age three.

Most kids pull back too far on the saw, yanking it out of the miter box, which breaks the sawing rhythm and means stopping to put it back in. This little problem is taken care of easily enough. Drill a hole about ½" from the square end of the back saw, through which you can fasten a machine screw and nut or a cotter pin to act as a stop.

Crosscut Saw

If you have a short crosscut saw, by all means let your child try it. I'm prejudiced against these because I've seen too many kids frustrated by their inability to keep them running straight and by the saw's binding and sticking in the wood. But I also know that a crosscut saw gives a kid a feeling of independence and importance since it is often his idea of a *real* saw because he has seen it illustrated in books — "S is for Saw" — and because he has seen Daddy use a larger version of it. A confident four-year-old will fight it out with this saw and may win. As with all other woodworking, make sure the material to be cut is firmly clamped down. A good material to start on is 1" x 2" and cutting on cardboard may go even faster.

Keyhole Saws

Keyhole saws with fine teeth are fun and relatively easy for preschoolers to cut with, and there are straight-handled keyhole-type saws made for cutting wallboard that have big teeth and allow a child to slice rapidly through cardboard, say in cutting a window into a big cardboard box to make a playhouse or for gouging eye holes in a head-size cardboard box to create an instant mask. All straight pointy-bladed saws of this kind are objects of considerable interest to a preschooler who knows about the sawfish, a relative of the sharks and rays who has a keyhole saw blade with teeth on both sides projecting from his head, which he uses to slash the smaller fish he feeds on. Supervise the use of this kind of saw closely, or your four-year-old sawfish may try a little experimental slashing of her own.

Wrenches

Turning a big bolt with a heavy wrench gives a small mechanic a really satisfying sense of power. "Wow!" said Mary Jane, five, turning a long ½" lag bolt into a 2" x 4" with a vise-grip pliers. "I feel like the Bionic Woman." This thrill is easy to arrange for a child if you have a wrench that won't slip off. With a socket wrench or a vise-grip pliers clamped on, a very small child can turn a very large bolt.

Drill pilot holes in the wood for lag bolts — your child can help with this part if you have a brace and bit or an eggbeater drill. The pilot holes should be the full diameter of the bolt, excluding the screw threads. And get your child to soap up the screw threads before starting to turn the bolt. In doing handyman chores around the house, keep an eye open for other opportunities for your child to fasten things with wrenches. And if you are a builder and design the things you make, consider whether you can fasten your projects together with lag bolts to give your child the thrill of really helping to assemble a big job.

Large nuts and bolts make good playthings for a supervised two-year-old or an older child who can be trusted not to swallow things. A number of attractive toys are manufactured with outsize plastic nuts and bolts, which have some big advantages over the real thing in that they're too big for swallowing and they don't rust.

Sanding

A number of handy fathers have told me that they can't get their kids to help usefully on sanding projects, that they sand across the grain, marring the work. I wouldn't trust a preschooler to sand with the grain either. Kids are a little too inventive and exploratory to be kept in a rut. But there are sanding jobs where there's no grain, and I've seen preschool kids having a marvelous time with sandpaper over long periods of time.

A good way to introduce a three-year-old to sanding is to hand her a very rough piece of wood — say a piece of lath — and talk about how rough it is as she touches it. Clamp the piece down and give her a sanding block — not just a piece of sandpaper. The block can be one of the wonderful heavy rubber ones sold in hardware stores or a short piece of 2" x 4" with sandpaper wrapped on and stapled down. With coarse sandpaper, a child can rub a scruffy piece of wood pretty smooth in a short time. "Wow," she'll say, "I'm really getting this smooth. It's smooth like glass, Daddy."

If your child gets excited about sandpaper, why not make some? Kids love smearing white glue on brown paper from a grocery bag and pouring on sand from the sandbox. Do this inside a box or pan to contain the extra sand that doesn't stick.

Still, can you get any useful labor out of kids with sandpaper if they're always rubbing against the grain? How about that patch you've been meaning to make on the car where it's rusted through at the bottom of the fender? There's a lot of no-grain sanding to be done on the filler material and it's right at a child's height. Or say you and your child make some homely wooden toys — these need to be smoothed to keep splinters out of little hands, and nobody is going to complain about scratch marks across the grain. If you're making or refinishing a fine piece of furniture where appearance is important, but your child wants to help out, surely it would be a help to have the drawer bottoms sanded smooth.

A good method for finishing plywood is to cover it thinly with DAP spackling compound, which you level off while it's still wet with a straight-edged board, scraping right to the top of the highest part of the grain. When this filler material is dry, you simply sand with fine sandpaper, and paint, which achieves a much smoother surface than you would get by sanding the plywood surface carefully in the first place. Here again is a no-grain sanding job.

Fasteners

"How shall we put these things together?" you ask a three-year-old, and no matter whether the things are a pair of steel I beams or two pieces of a broken plastic toy truck, it's ten to one the answer will be tape or glue. These are the fasteners in a child's everyday experience. And when he starts nailing, he'll reach for the 20d nails to fasten two pieces of hardboard together. But a few years of practical experience helping Dad with handyman tasks and putting things together at the workbench will get him on the road to understanding that each material has different properties and each requires a particular type of fastener. The more methods your child masters for joining things, the more elaborate and interesting the things he builds can be.

Wire is a preschooler's easiest and most versatile means for fastening things. Anything that has a hole in it or that your child can punch or drill a hole in can be wired to something else — wood scraps, plastic bottle tops, small plastic bottles, big beads, odds and ends of hardware, marking pen caps, seashells, pieces of cardboard and colored paper, really anything that comes to hand. A four- or five-year-old who has access to a lot of small scrap materials will wire them all together into elaborate and often good-looking mobiles and abstract structures. Wire allows a child to join things quickly and imaginatively without having to go through the many learning steps that would get him to the point where he could, say, build a simple, well-constructed wooden box. That box will come, but much later, and it will be better constructed because your child has dealt with easy materials and fastening techniques and learned their ways as a preschooler.

Long pieces of wire, though, present a potential hazard for kids: a poke in the eye. You can make wires much safer by simply crimping over the ends into tight loops with pliers before giving them to kids to work with.

Tape and glue will be mainstays in a workshop where kids are building. Masking tape is cheap, so you can afford to let your child use the long strips of it that are her heart's desire. White glue is the best kind for kids, particularly an easily washable type

called School Glue. When a preschooler glues two pieces of wood together to make an airplane, it's only seconds before he's ready to fly it or test whether the pieces stick. Hold the glued pieces so your child can get a C-clamp on them, and then put the assembly up high or out of the way and go on quickly to something else. The airplane will be rediscovered the next day, which will be an exciting event.

Measuring

Every kid wants to play with Dad's retracting measuring tape. While she's playing with it, teach her to use it. A five-year-old can learn to read off the number of inches to measure dolls or toy cars or anything else short. A retracting cloth sewing tape is a great tool for a five-year-old — it's just like Dad's only it can't whip around and hurt other kids.

Standard shop tapes unfortunately aren't yet numbered with metric measures, and kids going into school now will be learning the metric system. Keep a metric ruler handy to show your child how it works, too.

Kids love to be measured with a tape, even two-year-olds, who haven't the faintest idea what's going on. Measure your child regularly, not just from toe to head, but between the tips of the outstretched hands as well. And measure noses, smiles, hair length, etc.

Gregory is a measuring enthusiast, so we converted a small toy fire engine into a Measuring Wagon by fixing plastic rulers (one with inches and one metric) to hang where the side ladders were, and adding a pull-out cloth tape on top that doubles as a fire hose.

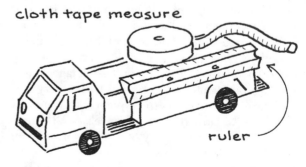

cloth tape measure

ruler

Paint

For some kids, painting is a crucial part of any building project. Others couldn't care less. If yours is a painter, keep a supply of kids' tempera or poster paints and medium-size brushes near the workbench, and let him slap paint on anything he fastens together. To preserve the colors and make them brighter, you can add a coat or two of varnish or polyurethane when the poster paints are dry.

MATERIALS

Jason, four, was given a super fancy toy store tool kit by a generous grandfather, but he couldn't make a thing because he had no scraps of wood to work with — so he got bored waiting for materials and gave the dining room table a thorough going-over with hammer, pliers, and screwdriver. Meanwhile, Martha, five, next door, had gathered up all the odds and ends of wood that the workmen left lying around as they added the new room for her grandmother, who was coming to live with them. And with her wood scraps, no tools, and a squeeze jar of white glue, she built a dozen little houses and a bridge and something that she calls an electric fishing pole.

The more different materials a child has at hand in the workshop, the more widely his imagination can roam when he starts to put things together. Keep all bits and pieces of lumber left over from your handyman activities in a box. If you don't generate many scraps, try nearby construction sites; and some lumberyards and cabinetmakers give away small cutoff pieces free. Also try handyman friends and friends in the construction trades, and you may come up with a gold mine of wood scraps.

There are also some cheap materials that you can buy in any lumberyard that are perfectly suited to woodworking with kids. Rough, thin laths are great for sawing practice and sanding, and gluing together little constructions. Lattice moldings, a refined, smooth version of laths, are more expensive, but nicer to work with. Short end pieces of fancy moldings are often sold very cheaply by lumberyards; these are nearly useless to carpenters, but may be invaluable to kids. Buy lots of dowels — all diameters — they are a mainstay of a good workshop for kids.

Around the house or apartment and at your office or workplace you'll find lots of everyday expendable objects that can be recycled at the kids' workbench.

Keep a box into which you throw jar and bottle lids, small plastic containers, spools, useless hardware, wine bottle corks, etc., etc., etc. A hobby or sport will generate even more good surplus materials. A golfer, for instance, will have lots of extra golf tees. Even if you don't play golf, incidentally, it's worth stopping in a sporting goods store and buying a few dozen tees — they are very cheap and make wonderful pegs for kids to push into the holes they drill at the workbench. Golf tees come in a mixture of bright colors and preschoolers use them to represent little people and to decorate wooden constructions. Get your child to blunt the sharp points of the tees with rough sandpaper.

Gregory and I have a grand time in the aisles of a big hardware store discussing what we might make from the various little gadgets, and we buy whatever we think we can afford, which is usually something like a fifteen-cent plumber's strap hanger, and take it home to convert it into a toy — in this case, a wooden car that looks like this:

An arts and crafts store will have few things of real interest; they usually carry only "craftsy" projects prepackaged and with all the imagination taken out. But an arts and crafts store is the best source for a big box of wooden coffee stirrers, which are great in the shop. Tongue depressors can be bought in quantity from most drugstores.

This list could go on for pages, suggesting items from every store in town as well as all of nature's good building materials — twigs and branches, rocks and seashells. But it could never be complete because there is no material that can be definitively excluded from a father-child workshop unless it's toxic or otherwise dangerous.

OUTDOOR JOBS

The best jobs to share with the kids are always the outdoor ones, where there's room to stretch and holler and make a mess, and the kids can wander off when they get bored and wander back when they're ready to go at it again.

Sweeping the walk, planting bushes, setting up a new swing set, stacking firewood — kids can be included in whatever needs to be done, just as long as it's safe.

OUTDOOR SAFETY

The garage or shed where you keep yard care equipment has to be childproofed just as the inside of your house does. Kids are fascinated by Daddy's things and will explore. Pesticides, weed killers, swimming pool chemicals, grease removers, solvents and cleaning solutions, gasoline — all these and other highly toxic substances are likely to be stored in the garage or shed. Keep them under lock and key; read the label of anything that comes in a can, bottle, or box, and if you're not sure about it, lock it up, too. Don't rely on "childproof" caps — these are only a last line of defense — and don't expect that putting something out of reach will keep a child from getting to it.

When you use outdoor poisons, children should be in the house. A child can be killed by merely licking the top of a can of some insecticides. If you use weed killer or insect spray on your lawn, read the directions carefully and don't allow your kids on the grass until the danger time is over. Also be super careful about the storage of convenient power tools like a cordless electric hedge trimmer — now, there's one a kid could really go to town with. Electric power tools, even ones with cords, should be made inaccessible. And keep children well clear of the area where you are using any power-driven yard tool: edgers, trimmers, etc.

You aren't going to let your child come near a chain saw while you're operating it, or near something so obviously hazardous as a shredder-bagger. If you're working with a chain saw, or felling a tree in any other way, and have kids along, it's always best to have another adult (Mom) with you to make sure everyone is far away from any danger. A tree can always fall the wrong way or bring down large branches from nearby trees with lethal force.

Lawn Mowing

In the summer there's hardly time on the weekend to keep up with the grass and also spend a while with the kids, so many fathers combine the two projects and take their kids for nice long trips on the riding mower, or in a cart trailing along behind. I know this is fun for everybody, so I feel badly pointing out here that these rides just aren't safe. A child should never be anywhere near the rotary blade of a mower. Sure, a child is *over* the blade if you are holding her on the seat, and that seems innocent enough since it's a slow ride. The danger lies in the child's squirming loose — say she wants to get down before the blade has stopped spinning. Or you may become distracted by something unexpected happening; for instance, another kid runs up, attracted by seeing your child on the mower, and you don't see him till he's right up near the blade — you swerve to steer clear of him and have to hold onto your child, too . . .

Kids jouncing along in a cart behind have a jolly old time, but driving the riding mower, you're in no position to see what's going on or do anything about it. Carts can overturn, kids can bounce out.

If you insist on giving your kids a ride on the mower, you can do it fairly safely by removing the blade, or on some models the whole mower attachment can be left off. But why not settle for perfectly safe wheelbarrow rides — which are just as much fun for the kids and will give you a good workout to boot?

Whether you use a walk-behind or riding mower, little kids should be nowhere near while you cut the grass. The best place for them is either in the house, or fenced in on the other side of the house. Even with good protective guards around the mower blade, you don't want a child's feet anywhere near it, and you want to prevent the possibility of a kid running up unexpectedly. Also, mower blades can shoot rocks and other small missiles at speeds of 350 feet per second in random directions. There's always a brittle plastic toy somewhere in the grass that can be smashed to smithereens by a mower blade and shot out in small pieces like shrapnel, or a Matchbox car, or small rocks and pebbles that your kids tossed on the lawn. Keep an eye open for this kind of debris, and especially in the spring before you mow the first time, get your kids to help police the lawn for stuff that may have accumulated over the winter.

Teach your kids to make hand signals from a distance if they need to attract your attention over the noise of the machine — otherwise, they'll run right up to you and shout.

Kids are always interested in a mower, and you can include them in repairing and adjusting it — with the spark plug wire disconnected. If your preschooler has figured out how the mower works, it's much safer if it has a windup start instead of a pull type, or for a battery-start model, an ignition key lock.

GRASS CLIPPINGS

Try not to do the lawn-mowing cleanup job perfectly. Make sure to leave some grass clippings lying around for grass-throwing free-for-alls with the kids.

WHEELBARROW RIDES

One kid in a wheelbarrow will have a great ride, but with two it's like pushing around the proverbial barrel of monkeys. Have them face each other, or sit side by side, or if you have a big wheelbarrow,

crowd in a third. Just be careful to keep the wheelbarrow stable as the kids climb in and out. Hold it firmly by the handles and let them climb up on a box or porch steps to get in. Wheelbarrow rides are great exercise for Dad, but we live in such a hilly place that as the kids have grown heavier, I've established a policy of downhill rides only — kids have to walk back up.

DIGGING

To help you work around the yard, kids need decent tools, just as they need real tools — not toy ones — in the workshop. The shovels, hoes, and rakes sold in toy stores are painted pretty colors, but they don't do a job. They're made with light dowel handles and flexible metal parts, and many just crumple up under a child's first serious efforts to dig.

From a garden supply store, or a hardware store with a good garden tools section you can get your four-year-old a solidly built spade-bladed small shovel with a straight handle that should last for years and will also come in handy around your yard when narrow holes need to be dug. Take the good shovel along to the shore if you go for a vacation —

it'll turn over a lot more sand than a plastic beach shovel can.

GARDEN HOSE

The favorite outdoor job of toddlers and preschoolers is watering plants. You'll do yourself a favor by spending a little extra money on a top-quality adjustable hose nozzle that can be set on a fairly fine spray with the setting locked in place. This will save your saying several thousand times over: "Spray gently; we don't want to hurt the plant." And it will save the lives of many small plants. No child will stick with the gentle spray if she can adjust it to a hard stream.

Kids thrive on messy play, though parents tend to channel them away from it. In summer, when you can hose them down before they come in the house, why not let the kids use the hose in the sandbox? Or even better, loosen the dirt in a corner of the garden for a four-year-old or older child and he can dig holes and pile up mountains and run water in them to create lakes, canyons, rivers, and mud pies.

WINTER WORK

Before they're four, kids can't help you much with shoveling the walk, but they sure like to watch you do it, and at three they'll try hard to lend a hand. By four, definitely provide a sturdy small-scale snow shovel, and assign your child a little place to work on that she'll be able to clear by herself. A preschooler can also move a lot of snow off the family car with a broom.

If you use a snow thrower, keep children inside and away from it.

VEGETABLE GARDEN

Many fathers I've talked with are vegetable gardeners. One had six kids — only one of them still a preschooler — organized into an efficient work force, and their efforts in a model quarter-acre garden are a real contribution to the family budget. Another man had six scrawny tomato plants growing in the only sunny patch near his house — an 8′ square between his garage and the garage next door. Every morning, his wife told me, he and his

daughter Rebecca go out before he leaves for work, and inspect the progress of the tomato vines: "They stand there deciding which flower will give the biggest tomato. But do you think they'd do something as simple as take those poor plants a bucket of water from time to time?"

At whatever level you do vegetable gardening with a child, it will be an education for him just to see that food comes from somewhere besides the supermarket. Pulling a big carrot from the ground is one of the great thrills a toddler or a preschooler can have — it's like Little Jack Horner; when he pulls out the plum he says: "What a good boy am I!"

And when a child pulls up a fat 8″ carrot he thinks the same thing; he's done something really impressive: "What a good boy am I!" Rita and I grow twice as many carrots as we can use and a surplus of beets, too, just so there'll be plenty for our kids and their friends to pull — and we leave a wide corridor next to the carrots and beets so a toddler can operate on them without doing any harm to other plants nearby.

I'm not sure which is capable of doing more damage in a vegetable garden — a woodchuck or a toddler. A toddler pulls out a plant you prize and presents it to you, roots hanging down, with an ear-to-ear smile of pride and then lumbers through the garden kicking and crushing every little seedling within range. You can tell her a million times: "Step here in the path, not there on the plants," but it will do no good — she just keeps stomping along, hitting the plants and missing the spaces in between. At three, she's still at this — perhaps, if you've worked on it, stepping only on every other plant.

So it was remarkable to see Gregory at four and a

half coolly making his way up the paths between the rows of young plants in our garden, and stepping over, not on, the plants as he went from path to path. What a giant step he'd made in co-ordination in the last year. Before, his feet were almost leading him, and now he was able to tell his feet just where to go.

If you have a vegetable garden, kids age one to three belong in it, but only for special occasions like bean planting and radish pulling. The safest place for a toddler in a garden is on your shoulders. Just put him down where the action is — right by the carrots if that's what is going on — and stay close. But after four you may even be able to get a little useful work out of your child in the garden if you explain the job carefully and don't expect too much. Also you want to choose jobs that are possible. For instance, pea picking is beyond many preschoolers — pea pickers need staying power, and it's possible to pull up the whole shallow-rooted vine by tugging at a pod. But pea planting, because the seeds are big, isn't hard for a three-year-old, and most kids, including a one-and-a-half-year-old, will enjoy helping to shell the peas.

Closely supervise seed planting to make sure no seeds go into your child's mouth — some are treated with chemicals that may be toxic. Watch kids around chemical fertilizers and sprays, too.

Stick mostly with things kids enjoy, like watering with a hose, and try others that they can do easily, like pulling small weeds from around big plants — for instance, weeding around full-grown broccolis or corn stalks, where there's no chance of mistaking the plant for a weed. But do try harder tasks, too — several fathers told me their kids at five pick peas perfectly.

If you're going to start a garden for the first time,

try growing some or all of the vegetables that are discussed in detail below — they are things that give fathers and kids great satisfaction, and most are sure successes. Vegetable growing is time-consuming and fairly hard work, and on top of that, it's honestly not all that easy to include kids — but they learn and do become helpers, and I think it's worth all the effort just to see a child's excitement when he realizes that the plants are growing just as he is: "Wow, they got bigger!" When he was three, Gregory and I were watering some seedling cauliflower plants and he asked: "Daddy, how come we don't water people to make them grow?"

Radishes

Every year for three years now, Gregory and I have grown one "cash" crop — radishes. As soon as they're big enough, he pulls them all up with loud exclamations of Wow! on almost every pull. He washes them with a hard spray from the garden hose and we tie them in little bunches of six or eight with string, and load them into the toy wheelbarrow. The wheelbarrow goes into the car, and off we go to Marshall's farm stand down the road, where Mr. Marshall is always pleased to buy our year's production of six or seven bundles of radishes all for a quarter. Agribusiness it's not — but it's got Gregory started on a career in free enterprise.

The first year, he was three, and though I explained the whole procedure carefully beforehand, there was considerable puzzlement mixed with his delight when Mr. Marshall handed him his hard-earned quarter. It was his first sale and he simply didn't understand how selling worked. After much more explaining and two stops back to Marshall's stand to determine whether the radishes had been

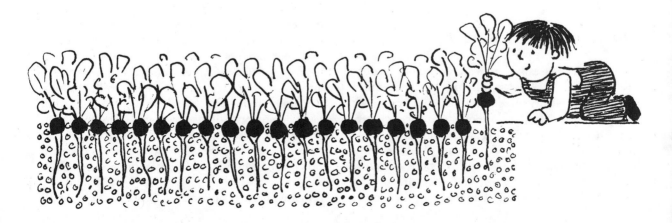

resold, he had it down: "We paid Mr. Marshall the radishes and he paid me the quarter; and then he sold the radishes to some ladies." It was his introduction to economics, and I hope I got it in there early enough that he'll be able to build on it and parlay it into the million dollars his dad will never make. Already he shows signs of going in that direction. At four he was happy enough with a quarter for the lot of radishes, and promptly spent it on candy sticks for himself and Timothy. At five, though, he said: "But, Dad, are you sure we can't get *two* quarters from Mr. Marshall for these radishes?"

Any small neighborhood grocery store would probably be delighted to buy radishes from your child if you want to use this scheme. And you don't need any gardening experience to grow radishes; they are the world's quickest maturing and most easily grown vegetable.

For a cash crop of radishes you'll need a row about 15' long. Two packets of seed should be plenty. The standard variety is called Scarlet Globe and is the easiest to grow. The striking-looking red and white Sparklers are another good variety for the home garden. White Icicle radishes look like small white carrots, and there are long black Spanish radishes, a winter variety, and a whole raft of other unusual types that come from the Orient.

Radishes are a cool-weather crop, and should be planted as early in the spring as you can turn over the ground — which will be shortly after the last snow or as soon as the ground thaws and dries a little. The only secret to getting good radishes is growing them early enough that they don't run into hot weather, which will make them go to seed before full-size roots are formed. The soil needn't be too rich, but it should be turned over and well broken up. Make a ¼" furrow with a stick, and let your child sow the seeds in it. She'll sow them much too thickly, but radish seeds are cheap. Cover the seeds with loose dirt and press it down by walking along the row. Seedlings will probably be up within a week, and even though you've planted very early, they won't be harmed by frosts. When they are 1½" to 2" high, go down the row, ruthlessly pulling out enough seedlings so that the ones you leave will have room to thrive and develop good-sized roots. If they're crowded, you'll get nothing but runts. Garden beginners are usually squeamish about pulling out a lot of little helpless plants, but if you don't, all the plants will end up little and helpless. Leave 1" or

more between plants, which is room enough for fat radishes to grow cheek by cheek.

Don't leave radishes in the ground for more than a few days past the time you decide they're fully grown, or they'll become woody and wormy. Show your child how to grab the stem near the ground to pull — not the greens at the top, which is what he'll naturally try to do, with the result that the greens will come off in his hands and the radish will stay in the ground.

Root maggots may mess up the appearance of some of your radishes. A stiff brush will help to clean them up. Wood ashes from the fireplace, scattered next to the row of radishes, will help to repel the flies that lay the eggs that hatch out the maggots. And strewing wood ashes with a shovel is another favorite job of kids, though a messy one. Try to keep everyone upwind.

Carrots

Super-long carrots that are super easy for kids to pull out can be grown in a narrow trench filled with sand. The sand allows the carrots to grow straight down, giving them a perfect form, where in heavy or pebbly soil, carrots grow crookedly and send out side shoots that make pulling them hard.

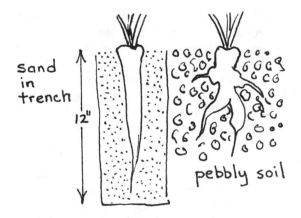

Dig a trench about 1' deep. Your child can help mix the sand in a wheelbarrow with some well-rotted and sifted compost or with a little complete garden fertilizer. Filling the trench with the sand is your child's job, as is sprinkling carrot seed fairly thickly in the ¼" deep furrow you will make down the center of the sand row. Cover the seed with ¼" of sand and water well. Regular watering will speed germination; seedlings often take two weeks or more to emerge. Carrots can be planted as early in spring as the ground can be worked, and in most places as late as midsummer. In the Deep South, carrots can be grown in winter, but summers are too hot for them.

When the tops are 2″ tall, thin them to stand a little less than 1″ apart. Thin again when these carrots are big enough to eat (the thickness of a child's finger), allowing almost 3″ between the ones you leave so they can develop full-size roots.

Any variety of carrot will grow straight and true in a sand-filled trench, but each variety has its distinctive shape, and some, like Danvers half long and Oxheart, are relatively short and squat. Look for seeds for Imperator carrots, which have a long, slim, elegant profile. Long hybrid varieties sold through seed catalogues will give even better results.

Carrots should be pulled holding all stems close to the ground, rather than by yanking on the greens.

Tomatoes

If you're a tomato enthusiast, try a variety that kids adore — Sweet 100s, a relatively new hybrid type that produces bright red cocktail-size fruit so sweet they taste like candy. Hundreds of these remarkably sweet tomatoes grow, mostly in clusters like grapes, on big spreading vines that need support — stakes or a wire-mesh tomato frame. One or two plants of this variety will yield all the little tomatoes your family can eat and your kids can gobble as they pick them from the vines — if they haven't been sprayed.

Seeds for Sweet 100s are available from most of the large mail-order seed houses. Plants for this unusual variety probably won't be available from a local garden store, so you'll have to start your own in paper cups on a sunny windowsill or under lights. Planting the seeds indoors and following their progress is an education in horticulture for a preschooler.

There's not much a child can do to help with growing tomatoes. Setting out the plants is too delicate and precise a task, and a three-year-old picking big tomatoes is apt to drop every other one — squish — into the basket. As a test of my patience and ingenuity and Gregory's ability to follow directions, I've gotten him to help me pick tomatoes every year

since he was two and a half. By chanting: "Gently. Gently. Put the tomatoes down gently . . ." as we worked, I managed to protect all but a couple of dozen fruit the first years, and now Gregory has taken up the chant of "Gently, Gently," as he picks tomatoes, and he does a fair job of it.

Bean Teepee

You'll need at least one bean pole in your garden so you and your child can sit next to the spiraling vine and read the story of Jack and the magic beanstalk. But with four poles, and not much more space, you can grow a living beanstalk teepee and sit inside it at the end of the summer, completely surrounded by vines and beans, to read the story of Jack.

The classic favorite variety of pole beans is called Kentucky Wonder — and these grow just the way Jack's did. Make sure to plant bean teepees on the north edge of the garden so their big shadows won't fall across other plants. To make the framework of the teepee, you'll need:

> four 8′ saplings with small branches left on
>   OR four 8′ lengths 1″ x 2″
> light galvanized wire

Saplings are best, if you can get them, because the side branches give the bean vines and their runners plenty of places to grow out along, allowing the vines to reach across from pole to pole to weave an almost impenetrable fabric of vines and leaves to cover the teepee. Four 8′ lengths of 1″ x 2″ will do almost as well, because the runners are usually strong enough to reach across from pole to pole without support.

Push the thick ends of the poles into the dirt 6″ deep at the corners of a 3′ square, and bind them together teepee-fashion with the wire so that about 1½′ of the poles stick up above the juncture. A three-year-old can plant the beans around the poles. But don't plant beans till late spring, when the weather is settled and the ground is warm. Just dig a furrow in a circle around each pole about 1½″ deep and get your child to drop in eight or ten seeds and cover them with dirt. Press the dirt down firmly with your shoe. A clove of garlic planted by each pole may help deter insect pests. Don't let your child miss the sight of the bean plants shoving the open seeds out of the ground and opening their first leaves, which should happen in about a week. When the plants are up several inches and growing strong, select the three or four most vigorous vines around each pole and pull out all the others.

Now all you have to do is keep down the weeds, but don't cultivate deeply around beans or you'll injure their shallow roots. In fact, it's always better to mulch around beans than to cultivate. You also have to remember to work near the vines and pick the beans only when the foliage is thoroughly dry, since brushing against wet bean vines will spread fungus diseases.

You may find the luxurious foliage of your bean vines full of holes toward the end of summer — the work of the Mexican bean beetle, which is the shape of the familiar ladybug beetle, but tan with eight black spots on each wing. You'll also find the yellow larvae of these beetles, which do most of the damage, eating the leaves bare except for the veins and the upper epidermis. You can try dusting with Rotenone, an organic pest control, but it doesn't always stop these voracious eaters. And you can use chemical warfare if you like, but I'd rather put up with holes in the foliage than have pesticides on the beans.

Pole bean vines bear long string beans over a number of weeks at the end of summer, and will usually keep producing till they're killed by the first frost of autumn. Pick the beans young, small, and tender to use green, or let them mature on the vine and shell them for cooking. A four- or five-year-old will be able to pick some beans from the bottoms of

the vines. The beans at the very top of the teepee will be well out of your reach. To pick them you will need a very stable stepladder or, preferably, a child on your shoulders.

Pumpkins

No family garden is complete without pumpkins for Halloween.

Pumpkin vines sprawl and spread and take up a remarkable amount of space, so put them around the edge of the garden, where they can climb up and over the fence and won't get in the way of other plants. If the vines start invading territory where you don't want them, use sticks shoved into the ground to head them off and fence them out of the area you want to protect. Since pumpkins grow well in partial shade, some gardeners plant them between rows of corn. The vines keep down the weeds that would otherwise grow among the corn. This companion cropping technique is a little better in theory than in practice, though, since it's nearly impossible to avoid crushing pumpkin vines and young pumpkins with your feet as you wade through to pick the corn. Any little-used spot — say alongside a garage or at the partially shady edge of a lawn — is perfect for pumpkins, just so it has *some* sunshine and fairly rich soil.

A cold night will destroy a seedling pumpkin plant, so the seeds shouldn't be sown until late in spring, when the soil is warm and the weather is thoroughly settled. Pumpkins need a long growing season — about three and a half months. In places where the summers are short, the only way to give pumpkins time to mature is to start the plants indoors on a sunny windowsill or under lights two or three weeks before the time you expect to be able to set them out. Cut the bottoms from half-gallon and gallon milk cartons about 3½" high; punch holes in the bottom corners so the containers can be placed in pans for watering from below. Get your child to fill the containers with rich garden dirt and push two or three pumpkin seeds about 1" deep into the dirt in each container. Keep the soil moist at all times. You can cover the containers with plastic wrap and a couple of sheets of newspaper and put them in a warm place — say on or above a radiator — to hasten germination. But check daily and make sure to move the plants to a sunny windowsill as soon as they emerge. When they are a few inches high, choose the strongest plant in each container to keep, and pull out and discard the others. A few days before you plan to plant them, set them outdoors in a partially sunny, protected place to "harden off." When planting, tear off the milk carton containers, being careful to keep the block of dirt intact. Set each one in a hole just a little bigger than the block of dirt and fill in firmly around the edges with earth.

Plant pumpkins — either as seeds or plants — in "hills" spaced about 8' apart in every direction. The hill is just a spot where a group of plants grows. Since pumpkins are heavy feeders, you'll get your best results by digging compost, well-rotted manure, and/or complete garden fertilizer into the ground where each hill will be. Set out two plants per hill or get your child to plant six seeds per hill, 1" deep. Two hills should produce plenty of jack-o'-lanterns for the average family, but the more the merrier. If you've planted seeds, the plants will appear in a week to ten days. When they are a few inches long, select the hardiest two plants per hill and pull up the others.

Many varieties of pumpkin seed are available, from types that produce little 6" fruit to varieties where the pumpkins commonly measure 2' across.

Also available are new bush-type pumpkins that take up less room than conventional vines.

When the vines are sprawling and the big yellow flowers appear, show your child that some flowers — the female ones — are growing on top of bulbous green ovaries that will one day be pumpkins, while others — the male flowers — grow on straight stems. With a small soft paintbrush, you and your five-year-old can play honeybee by removing some pollen from a male flower and brushing it into a female one.

The vines require little care and no cultivation since they keep down the weeds themselves, but they will benefit from watering during a dry spell. As the pumpkins grow in size, some gardeners put boards, plastic, or paper under them to keep them from rotting on the ground or turning white on the down side, but this precaution isn't usually necessary.

For scratching a name or initials in a prize pumpkin, wait till it is almost fully grown, but still green, and cut your legend in, not too deeply, with the point of a sharp knife.

A light frost won't harm pumpkins, but harvest them or protect them well before a heavy frost or they'll turn soft and useless. Cut pumpkins with a long stem, and always use a knife instead of trying to wrench the stem from the vine. Pumpkins brought indoors will quickly turn soft and rot. Store them in a cool place protected from frost — a garage or a covered porch. Pumpkins that are still green when harvested will turn orange slowly; setting them in a sunny spot during the day will hasten this process.

Mammoth Pumpkins For a gigantic pumpkin in the 100-pound-plus class, dig a big hole and put in at least a bushel of well-rotted compost or manure, and mix in a few handfuls of garden fertilizer for good measure. Cover the compost with a layer of topsoil and plant five seeds of a large pumpkin variety like Big Max. When the plants are up a few inches, choose the biggest, healthiest one, and get your child to pull out and discard the others. When that plant has grown and developed three or four pumpkins a little bigger than tennis balls, select the biggest and remove the others, cutting them off with a knife. Then locate the fuzzy growing tip of the vine and let your child break or pinch it off. This will stop the forward growth of the plant. All the energy of the plant and all the nourishment from the compost or manure will now be concentrated in that one

prize pumpkin. If any new blossoms or runners develop, pinch them off.

The big pumpkin will flatten out on one side if it is left always in the same position, so gently turn it from time to time, taking care not to twist or injure the stem. The spectacular pumpkin you produce won't be worth a darn for cooking and eating — but that's not exactly why you and your child wanted to grow it in the first place.

Gourds Gourds are grown very much as pumpkins are. Plant mixed varieties so there'll be a number of different types to dry and hang up and to make rattles out of.

Gourds are very prolific. Half a dozen plants will produce an abundance for an enterprising five- or six-year-old to sell to the neighbors from an improvised sidewalk stand.

Sunflowers

Sunflowers grow up to 8′ and cast shadows, so plant them on the northern edge of the garden, where the shade will fall away from other plants. A preschooler can drop the big seeds every inch or so in a furrow you prepare in the late spring after all danger of frost. Plant thickly, because birds will probably get a lot of the seeds before they have a chance to become plants.

To get the seeds, blackbirds pull up the tiny sunflower plants just as they emerge. Foil the birds by first helping your child plant a row of inverted Dixie cups with their bottoms cut out; space them about 1′ apart. Your child then drops a few sunflower seeds in each cup, and follows them with a light scoop of dirt. By the time the plants emerge through the tops of the cup protectors, they are big enough to hold their own against the birds. This same scheme can be used for planting sweet corn when it is under attack from starlings.

When the sunflowers are a few inches tall, help your child plant a few pole bean seeds near the base of several of them. As the sunflower stalk grows, the bean vines twine themselves around it, climbing up it and using it for support.

MAPLE SUGAR

If you've never seen the sap dripping from a maple tree late in winter, your excitement will probably run as high as your child's if you follow this simple plan for making a little honest-to-goodness, straight-from-the-tree, down-home maple syrup. This is a project that preschool kids adore and can help with. And it has the bonus of fitting neatly into a father's schedule since the sap is gathered late in the day, when you get home from work, and can be boiled down during dinnertime.

The true sugar maple is the hardwood "yellow" or "rock" maple, and you can identify it easily because its leaves turn yellow in the fall. Any other maple tree will do — red, silver, white, or black — but the sugar content of the sap is apt to be low and the final product may be a bit dark for a connoisseur — the highest grade of maple syrup is the lightest in color.

Maple trees are plentiful in a vast part of this country and Canada; in the North from Newfoundland west through Ontario, down into Iowa and Missouri; and in the Appalachian highlands they grow as far south as the Carolinas. If there isn't a maple tree in your yard to tap, maybe a close neighbor has one you can use. You can assure him that no harm will come to the tree if it's over 1′ in diameter. Stands of maple trees that have been tapped for a hundred years and more are usually in better shape than similar stands that haven't been touched.

The method described here isn't going to set you up in commercial production. In fact, you could win the award for persistence by manufacturing a whole quart of syrup.

The sap of a maple tree will run any time, fall or winter, that there is a thaw, but the time to gather the sap is late in winter when there is a pretty consistent run of cold nights and warming days, with daytime temperatures in the forties (Fahrenheit). Depending on where you live, this will probably be sometime in February or March. Professional sugar makers keep a sharp eye on many signs to determine when the sap will start to run. Among other things, they watch the squirrels, who will nip the bark of small twigs and lick the sweet juice when it has started to flow; and as the squirrels leave these twigs, chickadees move in to sip. The sugar maker knows that the best syrup is made from the "first-run" sap, so he wants to get his taps and buckets on the trees at the critical moment. For your purposes, there is a lot more latitude. But don't put it off till the trees bud in March or April, or the sap will have turned cloudy or stopped running for the year.

If you live in a syrup-producing state, you may be able to buy in a country hardware store the tin-plated spouts used by the pros. I prefer to use Nature's own spouts, which you and your kids can manufacture in minutes from branches of sumac, elder, birch, or balsam. Just cut 3½" lengths of branches about ¾" in diameter. These woods all have a soft pith at the core of the branches which can be shoved out with a stiff wire — say an unbent coat hanger — producing a neat tube.

Drill tap holes for the spouts low on the tree(s) and preferably use a brace and bit so your child can do the drilling, cranking the brace around while you hold it steady and press. Old-timers say, "The lower you tap, the more the sap." A good height is 2', and don't go higher than 4'. The tap hole should be drilled about 1½" deep, slanting slightly upward; use a bit of the same diameter as your spouts. The spout should fit tightly in the hole, and can be tapped in with a mallet or block of wood. When it gets wet with the sap, it will swell and fit even more tightly. If the sap is running, it will start to drip out of the spout almost immediately, which is an exciting moment. It's clear and thin as water, and sometimes city folks are disappointed because they expect it to run thick and golden brown.

Professional sugar makers tap directly under a sound limb or above a stout root to get the most sap. Tapping on the sunny, warmer south side of the tree will draw off the earliest sap, and a south-side tap runs well, but a tap on any side of the tree will work. If you tap several years running, don't drill into an old hole or very near one, because the tree converts a narrow vertical strip of sapwood around the old tap hole into heartwood, greatly reducing its sap-yielding capacity. You can tap a tree if it is 12" in diameter; at 20" it can support two taps, and a 30" tree can support as many as four.

For containers to collect the sap, cut or bore holes the diameter of the spouts in the shoulders of plastic gallon milk jugs, directly opposite the handles. The illustration shows how they are hung by a heavy string from a nail (preferably galvanized) driven in 1' or more directly above the spout. Leave the screw-top lid on the jug to keep out rain and snow.

The sap will only drip, never truly "run" — but it can drip three hundred or more times in an hour. The amount of sap you get in a day will vary greatly depending on the temperature, but be sure to check the bottles every evening. Here's a list of the materials you will need to tap a maple tree:

¾" diameter branch of sumac OR elder OR
    birch OR balsam
gallon plastic milk jugs
galvanized nails
heavy string

Tapping the maple tree is worth the effort if only to give your kids a chance to drink a glass of the cold, slightly sweet, and refreshing sap. But the next step will give you real maple syrup.

Boiling Down

In Vermont, sugar makers tap hundreds of trees at a time and use buckets that hold up to sixteen quarts of sap when full. For this scaled-down operation, though, I like to have only about three gallons at a time to boil down, so three to five taps with gallon jugs are plenty. Sap can spoil quickly since heat will make it ferment; so store what you gather in the refrigerator, but not for more than a couple of days, because stored sap makes dark syrup.

Help your kids pour the sap into the biggest pot in the house for boiling down. Here again, you can't compete with the professional setup, which uses huge shallow "evaporating pans" boiling over roaring wood fires in specially constructed sheds — but the kitchen stove will do the job. Old-timers say that you have to boil off 97 per cent of the water in the sap to get syrup, which is a bit of an exaggeration, but isn't far off. So you will do a lot of boiling. Our seven-quart pot usually yields a cup of syrup. This process makes billows of steam, so try to set up a window fan for an exhaust system.

Hours of boiling will go by before you notice any thickening of the sap. Your kids may even have gone to bed by this point, but I let ours stay up for the finale. When it is down to a few cupfuls, start taking it up with a spoon and letting it cool to see what consistency you have. If you have a candy thermometer, you'll have no problem determining when it's ready. Syrup of the right consistency boils at exactly 7 degrees above the boiling point of water. At sea level, water boils at 212 degrees (Fahrenheit), and syrup at 219 degrees. For every 550 feet of altitude above sea level, the boiling point goes *down* 1 degree, so you will have to adjust the temperature down if you live up in the hills.

Without a candy thermometer, you'll have to trust to your intuition and judgment and mostly to luck, as I do, to hit the point when it is neither too thick nor too thin. The old-time test was whether the liquid "aproned" off the edge of a wooden spoon or paddle, rather than dripping, but it takes experience to make this determination. You should watch for a change in the way the liquid boils; it will suddenly begin to boil "explosively" with lots of fine bubbling when the critical point is reached. And remember, the syrup is much thinner hot than it will be cooled. My final product is usually a little too thick or too thin, so we make several batches and boil them all together for a short time later on to get an even consistency. You can strain the syrup through a piece of wool, felt, or flannel if there are many impurities in it. Keep the finished syrup in the refrigerator.

Much of my enthusiasm for maple sugaring comes from having lived for a year in western Massachusetts, where our neighbor had his four kids — who ranged in age from preschool through high school — organized into an efficient maple-sugaring team. They tapped dozens of trees including the ones by our house — with real buckets and taps — and the kids operated the wonderful steamy boiling shed, which produced enough syrup to sell — after they gave a generous amount to the neighbors whose trees they'd tapped. This was the cheerfullest, hardest-working, most co-operative bunch of kids I've ever known, so I connect maple sugaring with happy, successful families and good fathering.

Sugar on Snow

When you've finally got some syrup boiled down, there are much better things to do with it than sop it up with spongy pancakes. When it's first made, let some cool enough to taste it, and have it with sour pickles.

Best of all is when there's still snow on the ground. Take boiling maple syrup and spoon it onto clean snow packed into a pan. It will turn waxy almost immediately. You then twist it up with a fork or a popsicle stick and the kids will eat it all. You may not even get any.

You can also make this extraordinary treat for the kids with store-bought maple syrup. It will be exactly the same confection, but it won't taste quite as good as homemade.

COOKING

Many fathers I've talked with enjoy cooking because it gives them something to do together with their kids that their kids are actually pretty good at. Bread kneading is a big favorite for some fathers and kids on weekend afternoons, everybody poking deep into the dough. Cookie making is another regular for dads; the kids love to measure and mix the ingredients — and lick the spoons.

Children start very young helping out with cooking. A one-and-a-half-year-old will be delighted to lend a hand with mixing, and by four and a half many kids are performing sophisticated operations like cracking raw eggs and depositing them in a bowl with no spills and only a little bit of shell. Preschoolers have often had considerable practice in the culinary arts from baking dozens of cupcakes and brownies at nursery school and helping Mom on quite a regular basis. In fact, of all the "adult" things a preschooler does, cooking is the area where a four- or five-year-old is most likely to excel — from sheer weight of experience.

GIRLS AND KITCHENS

Fathers of girlish girls tell me that they like to cook with their daughters because it's an activity where their interests and abilities can intersect. One such father said: "There's no way you are going to get me to brush the hair of Nan's Bionic Woman doll. I'm no sexist, but I do have *some* pride. . . . But one thing we do together all the time is make waffles in the morning. She does the mixing and I do the grill."

I think this is an important point, because girls and their fathers *do* tend to lose contact during the years from four on, when the child's play is often super-feminized and Dad is huffily excluded along with all other males. The kitchen is a good place to get it back together.

DAD AS CHEF

In talking to a lot of fathers about their contributions to the running of the household, I've been surprised to discover how very many cook one or more meals. It's usually breakfast, but many guys are dashing home from work to put on the burgers and beans for dinner — every night. Especially in families where Mom has a job, too. In fact, taking over some of the cooking chores seems to be the major way that American men have adapted to the just demands of their wives that they pitch in with the household drudgery. A smart move, too, because of course cooking doesn't have to be drudgery. If you're in a good mood and you throw in a pinch of oregano or a dash of Tabasco sauce, cooking becomes an art form, and a pleasure.

Jesse, six, slams his way into the kitchen: "What're we having for breakfast?"

"Eggs," says his mom.

"Who's cooking 'em — you or Dad?"

"I am," says his mom.

"Oh well, I guess I'll have some cereal."

Trouble for Dad. A lot of men find themselves begging their kids to compliment Mom's cooking, too, to keep peace in the house, but kids can be infuriatingly loyal. No hamburger is eaten at our table without Gregory explaining at length that the hamburgers his dad makes taste much better than the ones his mom cooks. Here is President Teddy Roosevelt in 1903 writing about a meal he cooked on a night's camping trip with two of his sons and three of their friends: "As usual, they displayed a touching and firm conviction that my cooking is unequalled. It was of a simple character, consisting of frying beefsteak first and then potatoes in bacon fat, over the camp fire; but they certainly ate in a way that showed their words were not uttered in a spirit of empty compliment."

The point I'm trying to make here is not that fathers are necessarily *good* cooks and certainly not that they are better cooks than mothers — but that kids are, for reasons of their own, great respecters of Dad's cooking, just as they are great respecters of everything else Dad does and touches. If you're a novice in the kitchen, you can burn the burgers, make omelets like tire rubber, even cook the potatoes in bacon fat if you feel like it, and you come up smelling like a rose. And by the time your kids are old enough to be discriminating, you may have improved and worked out some culinary specialties.

KITCHEN GADGETS

A preschooler is the perfect kitchen gadget drive system. Attach a child to any crank and she'll turn it. A three-year-old won't stick with it long, but she'll love the experience and after a couple of years she'll be cranking out some very productive work with kitchen gadgets.

For the price of one electric-powered food processing unit, you can buy dozens of wonderful kitchen toys that squeeze, purée, slice, shred, grate, freeze ice cream, etc. Just make sure there's no way for your child's hand to get near a blade or caught in the works. A toddler gets a sense of magical power from using an egg slicer, the kind that closes down on a hard-boiled egg, cutting it into thin rounds with parallel wires, and the round slices dress up a child's sandwiches and dinner. Look for French-made Mouli food mills — the leaders in the field. Many kitchen gadgets can't be operated successfully by a preschooler alone, but have to be worked by a parent and child together — which is the most fun of all.

BREAKFAST

If you aren't a cook and you'd like to give it a try, start with Sunday breakfast, the traditional father-cooked meal. You have the leisure to foul things up and start over again, and most breakfast foods are easy to prepare. Follow the directions on the Bisquick box, enlisting your child's help with mixing the batter, and you will produce flawless waffles and pancakes. Cook bacon on a very low setting, or fry corned beef hash slowly, turning it occasionally with a spatula — it's hard to mess these up.

Once you have Sunday breakfast perfected, you can branch out into weekday mornings. I used to think I was making a big contribution by cooking every Sunday — I'm an omelet man. But Rita pointed out that Sunday breakfast is only one meal out of twenty-one, and not a terribly important one at that. So I retaliated by cooking my omelets seven mornings a week. I got that down so I could do it all in ten minutes, but the kids insisted on variety, so now I do short-order cooking; I'll cook whatever anybody orders — just as long as it's an omelet or French toast.

French Toast

Kids in Paris don't get French toast for breakfast — they get French bread or croissants. In France, French toast is called *pain perdu*, or "lost bread," and it is eaten only by country folk. American kids, though, are all great consumers of this recycled bread, and it is the simplest thing a father can prepare. You will need:

> 4 slices of bread — preferably stale
> 1 egg
> ¼ cup milk
> 2 tsp. butter OR margarine

Break the egg into a wide shallow bowl and beat it together with the milk vigorously with a fork. Melt the butter in a large frying pan or, preferably, a square electric frying pan, on a medium heat (340 degrees). Dip the slices of bread — one per child — into the egg and milk, covering both sides. Egg breaking and beating and bread dipping can all be done by a three-year-old with your help and by a five-year-old without it. Place the bread in the pan, cutting it to fit two or three slices in at once so the kids won't holler that one got his first. Fry until they are a mottled golden brown on both sides, turning with a spatula.

Cutting the French toast for serving is the important part, though. The great French chefs have always said that the *presentation* of the food is critical — it must please the eye before it pleases the palate. I started out by making Bat Toast — also known as Butterfly Toast — thus:

And because it was an instant hit, I moved on to Bunny Toast:

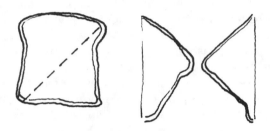

From there to Elephant Toast:

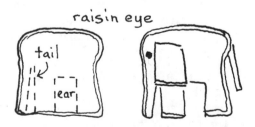

Now I accept all orders. Just name the animal and I'll give it a try. Watch out for fish and sharks — they're hard. If you don't feel up to animals, you can always do gingerbread men and stars and such — even with cookie cutters. And here is a simple Face

Toast for a baby, because babies love faces. The nose is the cut-out mouth turned sideways.

The classic topping for French toast is maple syrup. Applesauce flavored with cinnamon is good for a change of pace. Some kids like French toast sprinkled with a mixture of sugar and powdered cinnamon, and dotted with little globs of jelly.

Crispy-crunchy French Toast

Prepare as above, but after dipping the bread in the egg and milk, also dip it in

1 cup crushed cornflakes

Waffled French Toast

Heat and butter a waffle iron. Let your child mix in a wide, shallow bowl:

1 beaten egg
½ cup milk
2 tbsp. melted butter

Your child can dip six slices of bread in this mixture, coating both sides. Cook in the waffle iron as you would an ordinary waffle. Top with syrup or — for a big treat — a scoop of ice cream of frozen yogurt.

Orange Julio

1 cup orange juice
1 heaping tbsp. instant powdered milk
1 egg (optional)
½ tsp. vegetable oil
1 tsp. honey
5 ice cubes

A preschooler can help you measure all the ingredients into a blender cup. Break the ice cubes up a little by holding each in one hand and smacking it with the back of a large spoon. Blend everything together for about one minute on high speed. Recipe makes two servings.

Banana Zap

> 1 banana OR ½ cup applesauce
> 1 cup milk
> ½ tsp. vanilla extract
> 1 egg
> 2 tsp. sugar

All the ingredients go into the blender. Blend on high speed for about one minute. Substitute applesauce for the banana and this is called an Apple Zap. Recipe makes two servings.

Egg McMarvelous

This is a dish in search of a recipe. Cook eggs any slightly fancy way you like, call them Egg McMarvelous, and a four-year-old will go for them. Create your own specialty around the eggs you cook best. If you're a scrambler, for instance, try drawing a face on top of a mound of eggs with raisins or broken pieces of bacon. All fancy touches are appreciated by kids, and a good name for a dish may mean the difference between total acceptance and your child yucking at it. When he was three, Gregory staunchly refused to eat any kind of stew, but two of his favorite dinner meals were called chicken and vegetables in thick sauce, and Irish lamb with potatoes and carrots in rich gravy.

LUNCH

Dad is the sandwich king in every family. Even Dagwood — the old, outmoded image of the American father as a bumbling oaf inept in every department on the homefront — was respected for his sandwiches. You can always make peanut butter and jelly, or peanut butter and honey, or peanut butter and banana (the healthiest sandwich around), but here are a few others that no child will refuse.

Cream Cheese and Olive

> 1 8 oz. pkg. cream cheese
> 2 tbsp. milk
> ⅓ cup chopped olives with pimentos

For easy blending and best results, start with cream cheese at room temperature, which means remembering to take it out of the refrigerator at breakfast time. Blend the cheese and milk together with a fork in a medium-size mixing bowl until the cheese is soft and a little squishy. Preschoolers like to squish around with the fork after you have softened the cheese initially. Add the chopped olives and let your child stir them in until well mixed. Chopped salad olives are cheaper than stuffed ones and taste the same. Spread on buttered white bread for kids and add a little mayonnaise and a piece of lettuce on your own sandwich.

Cream cheese with jelly, made the same way as peanut butter and jelly, is another childhood favorite. Cream cheese and pickles is an excellent variant

— smear the cheese on a piece of bread, cover with sweet pickle slices, and cover that with another slice of bread. Dark breads, especially pumpernickel, are good with all of the above cream cheese combinations.

Stretch Sandwich

> mozzarella cheese
> white bread
> butter OR margarine

Eating this sandwich made of pully pizza cheese is like stretching hot bubble gum, and kids have a fabulous time. Butter the bread slices well on one side. Cut slices of mozzarella about ⅜" thick and place them between the unbuttered sides of the bread. Cook in a closed sandwich grill, or fry in a skillet, browning both sides, pressing down with a spatula, and waiting till the cheese is completely melted. The silly putty of sandwiches.

BolognaLT

> bologna
> American cheese
> tomato
> lettuce
> mayonnaise
> bread (your choice)

Bologna is regularly debunked these days as a non-nutritious vehicle for carcinogenic red dye and nitrates. But it's the only luncheon meat most young families can afford, and kids love it. Frying bologna is supposed to reduce the evil effects of the dye, and frying also makes it almost palatable for adults. The secret of frying bologna slices so they don't hump up in the middle, thus being burned on the edges and uncooked everywhere else, is to make four slits thus:

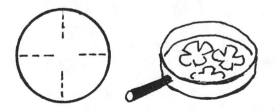

The slits open up when the bologna is fried, and the bologna lies flat in a shape much like the German iron cross. Fry in a little margarine on a medium heat. Turn, and add small pieces of American cheese to the already cooked side. These melt as the down side fries. A couple of slices of this bologna-cheese on toast with mayonnaise, lettuce, and tomato slices rivals a conventional BLT at a bargain price.

Health Soda Pop

> apple juice
> club soda

One part apple juice to three parts soda water, mixed in a glass with ice, makes a drink as attractive to kids as cola or Kool-Aid. But it's cheaper, far healthier, and it may not rot the teeth quite as fast.

DINNER

Most of the recipes below require an outdoor fire, because that's where Dad and the kids have the best time cooking together. The fire can be in a hibachi or any other convenient grill or fireplace. The best one will be low to the ground so kids can easily hold marshmallows over the coals.

Keep a water pistol handy when you are barbecuing steaks, burgers, or sausage, which drip a lot of fat and make flames flare up. The flames can be controlled by squirting with the water pistol, and a five-year-old can usually be trusted with this interesting task. Don't let her get trigger happy or the coals will be doused. At the end of cooking, kids like to help put out the fire. Let them squirt it into oblivion with water pistols. When doused charcoal briquettes dry out, they can be used again.

Around a fire, more effort should go into keeping an eye on the kids than into keeping an eye on the burgers.

Hobo Stove

A griddle-top stove that you can cook pancakes or fry burgers on can be made from a No. 10 juice can or a big shortening tin. Cut and bend back a door as shown in the illustration, and help your child use a hammer and large nail to punch a dozen holes toward the top on the opposite side for a draft. Build a small fire for this stove, use Sterno, or take some coals from the hibachi to fuel it. Heat and then

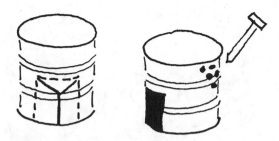

grease the top; wipe off and then grease again before frying.

Stick Cuisine

Holding food on a stick over an open fire is a preschooler's favorite culinary method. Use green sticks cut for the purpose wherever possible. The best length for spear-type marshmallow sticks is 30″

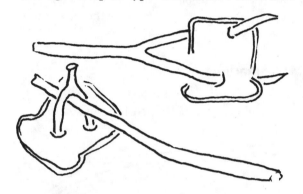

to 36″. The illustration shows a couple of fancy toasting sticks that a five-year-old can use to cook charcoaled French toast. Most of the recipes below involve stick cooking techniques.

Burger on a Stick

long green sticks about 1″ in diameter
1 lb. chopped beef
½ cup finely crushed cornflakes
1 egg
¼ cup ice water
½ cup chopped onion
salt and pepper
8 hot dog rolls

Peel the thick end of each stick. A five-year-old can mix together the ingredients and help shape them on the peeled ends of the sticks. The beef mixture should be squeezed evenly into long drumstick shapes — not made into balls. There should be no breaks or air spaces. Your child can lay these on the grill and use the sticks to turn them from time to time. Twist the sticks to remove them from the burgers as they are laid into the buns.

Budget Kebabs

Use store-bought metal or wood skewers or make your own about 16″ long from straight, thin green sticks, stripping off all twigs, peeling the bark, and sharpening the ends.

hot dogs — 1½″ slices
cherry tomatoes
green peppers, cubed
small onions OR onion chunks

Hold the skewers and supervise as your child pushes on the various ingredients. Pieces of bacon

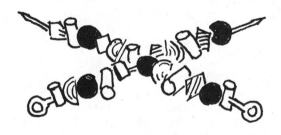

make a nice addition to this dish, but jack up the price. The hot-dog slices can be marinated for thirty minutes in vinegar-and-oil French dressing for a Continental touch. And of course you can use cubes of real meat for a proper kebab — marinate tough cheaper cuts of meat for several hours before spearing on skewers. But preschoolers will like this hot dog version better than authentic lamb. Cook over hot coals, helping the kids turn the skewers.

Aluminum Foil Meal

To prepare this packet of food cooked right in the coals, help your child seal a variety of ingredients into a 12″ double-thickness square of heavy-duty aluminum foil. A quarter pound of hamburger meat will be the basis of the meal, but you and your child can add other ingredients pretty much according to your whim and what's available in the refrigerator. For a conventional stew-type meal, add a slice of potato, a few slices of carrot, some sliced onion and celery, and a little catsup. After sealing tightly, with edges turned so steam can't escape, cook directly on hot coals for about 20 minutes, turning once.

Experiment with other ingredients. Kids have a great time dabbing in a little mustard or adding pickles or duck sauce — whatever comes to hand. Chopped hot dogs can form the basis of the meal, with sauerkraut added, or beans. Use your imagination to come up with other foil-wrapped main courses.

Canned Vegetables

At the edge of the grill, cook canned vegetables right in their cans. Let your child rip off the label, and help him use a can opener to cut nine tenths of the way around the top — leave it attached by a tag to use it as a lid while cooking. Beans can be prepared this way to go with franks cooked on the grill, or you can heat up canned beets, carrots, sauerkraut, etc.

Spinach

If you want your kids to like spinach and grow strong eating it, don't cook it — grow it. Few kids can resist fresh spinach, picked while it is young and used as a salad with garlicky vinegar-and-oil dressing (one part vinegar to two parts oil). Fresh young spinach is sweeter and richer tasting than lettuce.

Some-mores

The campfire classic.

> marshmallows
> chocolate bar
> graham crackers

While your four-year-old is toasting the marshmallow to a nice black char, place three or four

squares of a chocolate bar on a graham cracker. The hot marshmallow goes on top of the chocolate, and this is topped with another graham cracker, making a sweet sandwich.

Try a few variations on the some-more theme. Apple slices can take the place of the graham crackers, or you can substitute chocolate-covered graham crackers for chocolate squares and crackers. Healthy peanut butter can replace the chocolate in the some-more.

Marshmarvels

Split the thick end of a long green stick so the marshmallow can be clamped in it for toasting.

> marshmallows
> chocolate bar OR chocolate chips

Make a deep cut across the middle of the marshmallow and stuff with chocolate. Clamp this in the split stick for toasting.

Hot Banana

> firm banana
> miniature marshmallows
> chocolate bar OR chocolate chips

The miniature marshmallows, or pieces of larger marshmallows, and the chocolate bits are stuffed into a V-shaped trough cut the length of a firm peeled banana. This is well wrapped in a double thickness of heavy-duty aluminum foil and placed right on a bed of medium coals. Cook for about 10 minutes.

Banana Split

Building a banana split with Dad is an exciting event for a preschooler. A five-year-old can cut the peeled banana lengthwise with a table knife. Heap on whatever ice cream and trimmings are available. No need to stick with the traditional three scoops and special toppings. One scoop is plenty, and pancake syrup will do if there's nothing else sweet in the ice box. Jimmies dress up a banana split creation. Banana splits are even welcome in a health food-oriented household. There's nothing healthier than a banana; add scoops of frozen yogurt; top with nuts, raisins, or fresh fruit.

Peter Paul Rubens' portrait of his young son Nicholas.

Chapter 12

KEEPING A RECORD

Years ago, it was only the unusually gifted father who could keep a good pictorial record of his kids' progress, and this section is illustrated with pictures of their children made by some of those gifted dads: Rubens, Rembrandt, and Cezanne. Today, cameras give every father a way to rival Rubens in this department. With a tape recorder, you can go him one better, and keep a record of your child's mind — the things he thinks and says, and the way he says them.

For the excellent advice on still and home movie photography of children that appears below, I enlisted the help of prize-winning documentary photographer Phil Courter, president of Courter Films, Inc., who is forever shooting pictures of his own kids, Blake, five, and Josh, three.

STILL PHOTOGRAPHY

Keep your camera handy, loaded, and ready — when that great picture is happening, you haven't got time to mess around with paraphernalia. If the camera needs film or new batteries for the flash, the perfect moment will be long gone before you have a chance to record it.

Shoot a lot of film when that moment comes and the lighting is right — you may waste some, but you'll get the picture you were after.

BABIES

Soft lighting is the key to getting good photos of a baby. A harshly lit picture of a baby with hard shadows across her face makes her look dreadful. Crowding in for a close-up and blasting away head-on with a flash will create those hard shadows and high contrasts every time, and sometimes it will wipe out the baby's features in a glare of reflected light.

Natural light gives the non-professional the best conditions for photographing a baby. You'll get many of your best baby pictures on a bright cloudy day outdoors, when the colors glow in the soft, diffused light. Photographing indoors near a large window also gives you an ideal setup, but avoid a window situation where splotches of direct sunlight fall across your little subject. Let Mom hold the baby near the window, and you squeeze in close to the other end of the window or the wall to take the picture — so that you are more or less between the subject and the light source. The best rooms for available light photography have light, reflective walls and ceilings. Dark, heavy drapes and dark carpets will absorb a lot of the natural light and reduce the quality of your shots. Turning on lamps in the room will add luminosity to a natural light shot.

If you have to use a flash on a baby, bounce it off the ceiling to diffuse it and to avoid "retina burns," the little bright red spots in the eyes that often show up in direct-flash snapshots. A flash attachment that swivels can be used to bounce the flash off a light wall, and one that unclips from the camera can be pointed toward the ceiling for the most effective kind of bounce lighting. Computing the shutter setting for bounced flash is easy. The shutter speed setting for flash photos is always standard, but the aperture opening (f-stop) varies according to the distance of the flash from the subject. There's often a table printed right on the flash attachment that tells you what f-stop to use at what distance. For bounce flashing, just figure the *total* distance from flash to subject — that is, add together the distance from the flash to the ceiling or wall "diffuser" and

Sketches by Rembrandt of his infant son taking a bottle, 1635.

the distance from the diffuser to the subject; read the f-stop setting from the table; and add an extra half stop to compensate for absorption and light loss.

If your flash attachment is built into your camera, bouncing is of course impossible. Try draping a white handkerchief over the flash to diffuse its glare. Allow one extra stop of exposure (f-stop) for each layer of handkerchief you use. On a simple camera with a Light-Dark setting button, this will mean turning the knob well into the Light position. A bounced or diffused flash can also be used to augment weak natural lighting.

The best time to photograph a baby is when he's bright-eyed and bushy-tailed after a nap, or when he's asleep. A baby is the most unself-conscious subject you'll ever have for your camera. In fact, an infant literally has no self-consciousness — he doesn't yet know who he is. Toddlers usually continue to act naturally for a camera, but when a kid becomes thoroughly familiar with the idea of ME — watch out.

KIDS

As soon as they start to crawl around, kids present new problems for the photographer — their constant movement in and out of focus makes shooting difficult. And by the time they reach three or four, they become outlandishly self-conscious around cameras, giggling and setting their faces in horrible grimace-smiles the minute they see one.

The first rule for making good photos of kids is: Get down on their level. Stoop, kneel, lie down, crawl around on your belly. Shooting down at kids from above will give the pictures a peculiar, distant point of view, and you'll get more of the tops of their heads than of the faces you want to see.

Rule number two is: Use props. Father-photographers can be divided into two camps — posers and candid snappers. Posers quickly learn how difficult it is to get any kid to stay still (actually it's impossible), and candid photographers quickly discover how many good shots are ruined when kids move, or turn their heads just at the critical point. Props are the answer for both posers and candid snappers. A prop can be the wagon your child is pulling, a toy he's playing with, even a flower or a blade of grass he's examining — anything that occupies his attention and interest and keeps him relatively stationary. The best props are the ones a child discovers himself. When you see him busily playing with the dog or building with blocks or clumping around in your shoes, whip out the camera and click away.

If you're an inveterate poser, try presenting your child with props when you're ready to take some pictures. Give a child a big new cardboard box and he'll climb in and out and over it in dozens of postures while you get off a series of interesting shots before he becomes preoccupied with the camera and starts sticking out his tongue. Riding toys, dolls, picture books, kitchen pots and pans, hammer and nails, hats, etc., all make excellent props. A toy camera is fun for a prop — father and child aim at each other and shoot.

A jungle gym is a big, but effective prop — a child climbing on one moves relatively slowly and usually in a single plane, so focusing and shooting are easy. While your toddler still uses a high chair, take plenty of pictures of her eating spaghetti and turning the bowl of bright red beets over on her head — you'll never again have such a stationary or cooperative child subject. A child in the bathtub busily playing with a boat is another great stationary target. And sleeping kids of any age make absolutely serene subjects. Artist fathers who draw pictures of their kids often end up sitting next to the TV set during "Sesame Street" to sketch them — the children's heads are constantly turning, even in this

situation, but at least their bodies stay put for a few minutes at a stretch. Regard the TV as a prop; crouch next to it and get photos of quietly occupied kids.

The family car is one of the best props you can use. Kids climbing on the bumpers make interesting subjects, but more important, the car will date the picture in the future. Nothing adds more interest to a photo of your father as a boy than the shiny new Model T he's standing next to, and my favorite snapshot of my brother and me as kids shows us playing on the running board of the big family Packard. A car in a snapshot looks commonplace the year it's taken, but twenty-five or fifty years hence it is a fascinating antique. Also be sure to snap pictures of the kids with your house or apartment building in the background so they'll be able to see years later the place where they grew up.

"Say, 'Cheese'" never does the trick with young kids — and it makes a four-year-old contort her face into an absolutely grotesque mask. Singing a song *sometimes* helps in a posed situation. But the child has to be in a mellow mood and it has to be the right song, or you get silly singing on top of silly faces. Gregory and Timothy made up their own photo session song — they both croon, "Hummmm, Ba-by, Hummmmm, Ba-by," happily, and wrestle and play with toys as I snap away.

Proper lighting, as for baby pictures, is again critical, and again you'll get good photos outdoors on a bright overcast day and indoors in a bright room near the windows. Full sunlight on a child's face should be avoided — it will make your child uncomfortable and cause her to squint. Below under Quality Shots is a description of how strong sunlight can be used to advantage to make radiant backlighted photos. Always bounce or diffuse that flash, just as described above for baby photography.

Fast film with a high ASA rating (200 or more) overcomes many of the difficulties of child photography. It allows you to use fast shutter speeds and small aperture settings (f-stops) to minimize problems of focus and still have adequate exposure. The fast shutter speed arrests the action, and of course kids are always in motion. But if you use a fast shutter speed with *slow* film, you'll need a wide aperture setting (f-stop), which will reduce the depth of field and make it hard to get the subject in focus. Slow film used with a small aperture will give you the depth of field you need for focusing, but this will have to be coupled with a slow shutter speed, which risks blurring the picture when the kids move. So fast film is the answer.

It's a hard and fast law of child photography that the further away from the child the camera is, the more naturally she'll smile and act. Get in tight for a close-up, invade her space, and you invite silly behavior, especially if she's three or older. A medium telephoto lens (100 mm for a 35-mm camera) is a great help for a father-photographer. With it, you can move well back from the child you're photographing and still get close-up shots.

Try using your camera from time to time as a reinforcer of good behavior. Just as you might dole out cookies or candy as rewards for some conduct you especially approve of, you can grab the camera and photograph your child in the praiseworthy act. An instant camera that develops its own photos is particularly good for this job, because the evidence of merit is right there in a matter of minutes. A long wait for the film to be processed takes a lot of the edge off of this trick, though the simple act of pointing the camera and snapping the picture does act as a big pat on the back. Overuse of this technique, however, may give you a kid who poses at being good — for the camera.

Quality Shots

Use strong sunlight *behind* your child for that one-in-a-million, perfect, magazine-quality photograph. Every weekend cameraman has been told always to keep the sun at his back, shining directly on the subject; the little sheet of instructions that comes packaged with film always tells you to do this. But professional photographers seldom use straight, hard outdoor light. The sun directly on the subject will usually render an adequate snapshot, but it throws harsh shadows across the face and flattens out the picture, making the figures seem to stick to the background.

Properly handled backlighting or sidelighting, on the other hand, can set your child's face off from the background with a radiant halo of highlights around her hair and shoulders, and will create a beautiful mood for the picture. Achieving this kind of effect isn't hard if you work with a light meter. All you have to do is expose for the shadow side so you won't lose all the detail in the picture. When your child is standing with the sun to her back or side, get in close to her and take a light reading on the shaded side you will be photographing, using either a built-in light meter or a reflected light meter (the common type of inexpensive light meter). If you have an incident light meter, point it away from the sun and toward the camera.

Avoid showing a lot of the sky in a backlighted photo, and definitely avoid showing the sun. Shooting from a distance with a telephoto lens will automatically crop out most of the sky, where a normal lens or a wide-angle one will tend to include more sky than you want.

Working for the first time with backlighting, you may blow a few shots, but keep after it, and shoot plenty of film this way, because soon you'll be capturing a rare and elusive quality in your photos, and the people who see them will rave.

Time-lapse Photo

For keeping a record of your child's development, nothing I know of tops the time-lapse photo scheme I was shown by a personnel director who is a spare-time camera buff. Every two or three months, he sets each of his two girls up in front of a white wall wearing a light blue dress, and takes a shot with his camera on a tripod. The girls are still preschoolers, but the piles of photos are starting to mount up, and flipping through them gives a very clear picture of how they have grown since their dad started this project. Imagine carrying this on through a whole lifetime — the child could take over making the photos at some point in the teen-age years, using the kind of automatically timed shutter release that allows you to run around and get in your own picture. And then on your sixty-fifth birthday, you sit down and riffle through the great stacks of snapshots, growing younger as you go . . .

If you want to try this scheme, just remember to organize the situation so that the setting and the lighting will be as consistent as possible. Shooting indoors at night with a flash, and always with the same film and from the same distance will keep the pictures pretty uniform. Do your shooting in a bright, light room, and bounce the flash, as described under baby photography above. Of course your kids will be constantly growing out of their clothes. Taking the pictures at three-month intervals, you may with luck get two in the same outfit, but probably never three. So pick some standard color and type of clothing — like the blue dresses. Dungarees are perfect. You can set a one-year-old of either sex up for a time-lapse photo in jeans and a light-colored shirt and be certain the outfit will be standard equipment for your child at least as long as you'll be snapping the photos.

The time-lapse photo scheme can also be done as slides, and run fairly quickly through a projector to give a movielike effect.

Firsts

My favorite photos of my kids are ones that record their expressions and reactions to important "firsts" in their lives — first day of life, first time sitting up, first steps, first ice cream, first time in the ocean waves, first birthday candle . . .

It's fun, too, to have a bracketed pair of pictures, showing first and last time, as, for instance, first and last rides on the tricycle — there's a lot of time in between and a big size change in relation to the tricycle. First and last days of nursery school make a good pair, and first and last days with a Teddy bear or doll that starts out huge and new as a birth present and ends up years later threadbare, pathetic, but still loved — sometimes there's no last day with these because they have to be kept around forever.

Drawing by Cézanne of his son.

SLIDES OR PRINTS

Many an avid slide photographer converts unhappily to prints after he becomes a father. It's a matter of meeting the demand, and the demand is from Grandmother — and often from Mom, too — for prints. Slides can't be carried in wallets and collected in albums, framed on dressers, and pulled out to show visitors. Switching to prints tends to make you a better photographer fast, because you can't afford to blow any shots at the steep price, or — more often — it makes you stingy with your film.

In another camp are fathers who continue to shoot slides, but who are organized enough to pick out the best ones from time to time and take them to the photo store to have prints made from them. There's a slight loss of quality in this conversion — mainly because the medium is different and the light no longer shines *through* the picture to give the brilliance you get in a slide. The individual

prints are expensive, but you don't have many made, and only the very best shots — which in the long run can be less costly than snapshot prints, where even the poor shots are printed up, at your expense.

Of course there is only one truly acceptable solution: two cameras — one for slides, one for prints.

Displaying Slides

The main objection of mothers to slides is that they can't look at them whenever they like — that there's too much gear involved, what with viewers and little boxes and screens and carrousels. You cut through all these objections and convert almost any mother into a slide enthusiast by putting your slides in *slide protector pages*. These are inexpensive 9" x 11" plastic pages that fit in standard three-ring binders; each page has twenty little windows, each of which holds a slide, and when you hold the page up to the light, you see all twenty pictures. There's no magnification, but most mothers don't mind. In fact, they're delighted to be able to see so many shots of the kids at once. So before you give up on slides, try some of these display pages — they're available at all photo stores. Some are made entirely of clear plastic, but the best kind have a frosted backing that diffuses the light so you see the slides without also seeing the light source through them.

As far as kids are concerned, projected slides (and movies) are always the best way to see themselves. Nothing is more fun than sitting in the dark and seeing a bright, bigger-than-life-size image of ME.

Grandparents can be converted into slide enthusiasts — but won't stop wanting prints as well — if you put on a show for them. Take along the projector and screen and a couple of loaded carrousels to a family dinner or holiday gathering at Grandmother's house and you'll be the hit of the party. Or break out the slides when grandparents visit you. Make the show as long as you like — no one will be bored, and it will be hugely appreciated.

Print Display

Keep prints in albums on a low shelf where the kids can get at them. They'll look through the pictures again and again. One father told me that the first thing his two preschool boys do when they get home from a vacation is to pull out the photo albums — he keeps one for each child.

When you've taken a really satisfying picture of your child, have it blown up as large as you like — which isn't a terribly costly proposition — and frame it or have it inexpensively shrink-wrapped in plastic to hang on the wall of your office or workplace.

MOVIES

All the problems of still photography with kids are compounded when you go to shoot movies. You want lots of action in a film, but kids provide so much of it that they are constantly moving in and out of focus.

Where with still photos it's always best to be back away from the kids, shooting with a telephoto lens, the opposite holds true with movies. A movie telephoto lens or a zoom lens set for telephoto work magnifies all the possible flaws in home movies. It makes the shaky quality of hand holding much more obvious than wide-angle shooting will, and the slightest movement of the child toward or away from the camera will throw him out of focus on telephoto, because of the reduced depth of field. Try always to work in close and low, at your child's level, with a wide-angle lens, or keep a zoom lens set at its widest (or shortest) focal length. This will give you a good depth of field, which minimizes focusing problems.

The zoom lens is a neat gadget, but constantly zooming in and out with it can botch up a good movie by making it appear jumpy. Try to keep it at its widest setting, and only zoom for very special situations.

Every time you stop the camera, move to a new shooting position. Stopping and starting the camera again in the same position a few moments later will produce an awkward "jump cut" — the scene is identical to the previous one, but the kids appear to have been transported mysteriously into new positions. Stopping the camera and moving to a new shooting position, on the other hand, makes a clear and obvious break in the sequence and adds variety to the movie. Zooming, incidentally, doesn't put you in a new position or add desirable variety — you have to walk around to a new place.

Try always to film movies outdoors — preferably on a bright overcast day. Even the fancy new indoor films produce inferior footage compared to movies shot out of doors. If you do film inside, make sure to do your shooting in the lightest, brightest room you have, opening draperies as wide as they'll go or taking them down if they're dark-colored.

It's fun to try to direct kids through little skits, especially older ones who may be able to follow some of your directions. But just as in still photography your best subject will usually be a child who is absorbed in an activity or busily occupied with a "prop," rather than one who has his mind on the camera and the cameraman.

Shoot lots of footage when you're making movies — it won't all turn out well.

TAPE RECORDINGS

Many fathers I've talked to have taped their kids talking and doing songs and nursery rhymes. One had a recording of Jessica at three singing and chattering unself-consciously about butterflies and airplanes. Jessica, now thirteen, cringes when this tape is played, but I doubt she'll cringe when she hears it twenty years from now.

You can start from the minute your child is born to record his voice — if tape recorders are allowed in the delivery room. I have a lusty cry from Timothy made at my leisure on his third day. And that's followed on the tape with laughs and cries over the next months — tickle sessions, dinner eating, splashing and laughing in the bath, jumping in the Jolly Jumper, and some piteous wailing when he had chicken pox at ten months. When he was mastering stair climbing, I followed along next to him on the ascent with the tape recorder, and interjected a little narrative between the sounds of his thumping hands and knees and his heavy panting and puffing as he got toward the top. At the top of the stairs, he gurgles in pure triumph and claps his hands.

TAPING TECHNIQUES

To get high-quality sound, keep the microphone close to your child — no more than a foot away. There's nothing magical about a multidirectional mike — either hand-held or built into the tape recorder. Every time you double the distance of *any* mike from the person speaking, you get only a fourth of the sound you had before. A distant mike picks up background noise as well as the sound of

the speaker's voice bouncing off walls and ceiling, and these reverberations make for mushy sound.

With your child close to the mike, you can turn the recording volume down low, which will give you a clear recording of her voice and pick up almost no extraneous noise. Happily, most toddlers and preschoolers like to talk right into the microphone — they crowd up on it the way people get in close and shout in the ear of someone who's hard of hearing.

Carpeted bedrooms and living rooms are the best places to make tape recordings, because carpets and drapes muffle and absorb echoing and other irrelevant noise. The hard surfaces in kitchen and bathroom, on the other hand, bounce every little sound around and magnify it, reducing the quality of the recording. Naturally, you should avoid making tapes under noisy conditions — i.e., with a vacuum cleaner in the next room, or a dishwasher churning away.

A hand-held mike will usually give somewhat better results than one built into a tape recorder, and it is easier to hold near a child who is moving around. Most cassette tape recorders have a plug to accommodate a hand-held mike. The best kind to get, if you can afford fine equipment, is the semidirectional "cardioid" type — cardioid means "heart-shaped," and this mike picks up sound in a heart-shaped pattern in front of it, while ignoring noise behind it.

Playing back the tape is an important part of any recording session with a child — kids love to hear themselves on instant replay, and this feature encourages them to do more talking. A child as young as two can learn which buttons to push down for playback — with a little help.

Co-operative Stage

Most kids are very open and easygoing around a tape recorder until they are nearly four. You can just push the Record buttons and talk with younger kids about anything they know or are in the midst of learning. At one and a half, for example, you can show your child a picture book and ask: "What does the picture show?" "Kitty-cow." "What does the kitty say?" "Meoooow." "What is this on Daddy's foot?" "Shoe, shoe, shoe, shoe . . ." After several minutes of this you have a succinct catalogue of what she was able to say at this point, and you also have a record of the bright side of her personality — the part you'll be glad to preserve. As the months go by, she'll have plenty more to say into the microphone, and this same easygoing conversational approach will be the simplest way to get her thoughts and opinions on tape.

You can tape a child of eighteen months while he's sitting in a high chair, with the tape recorder right on the tray — but move the high chair from the kitchen to a carpeted room for better sound quality. After age two, you'll find it easier to follow your child around the room carrying the tape recorder, stooping, and holding it or a mike near her mouth.

Silly Stage

From four years old on, you get very little spontaneous talking on a tape. Kids freeze up or they act silly — just as they set their faces in grimace-smiles for the camera at this age. During this stage, try taping only when your child is refreshed from a nap or early in the morning when the day is off to a good start, and stick pretty much with things he knows well: nursery rhymes, songs, counting, alphabet. Otherwise you will have a nice recording of your son saying: "Dumb, dumb, dummies, dum-dum, poopies — eeeeeeeeeek — yucky dum-dums," with maybe some spitting and Bronx cheer noises for good measure. Girls whine and say: "I don' wanna do *thaaat.*"

If you want "candid" conversation on tape after the silly stage sets in, you'll have to go to hidden microphones. You can set the tape recorder and/or mike on a table right behind the back of a couch, turn it on, and then lead your child to the couch from the front side so he won't see what's going on. A picture book or a toy or other "prop" to talk about can get the conversation rolling and will help to keep him in place on the couch. You can also hide a small cassette recorder by hanging it around your neck with a string, under an open-weave sweater, which will put it in a good position near your child's mouth if you're sitting close together on a couch. Avoid moving around with a setup like this or the mike will pick up the rustling sounds of the sweater rubbing against it.

Another expedient you can try if you want the rational conversation of a four- or five-year-old on tape, is ice cream. It soothes Gregory enough so that we can talk calmly at a table with a tape recorder for a few minutes about his world and his ideas. I have an excellent ice cream tape at five years on which he lists eight different species of dinosaur and explains how the hook catches the fish when he goes for the worm.

Kids mellow and become a little more co-operative at five, and taping sessions should go uphill from there on out.

When you were very young it was my delight to play with you all, and I think with a sigh that such days can never return.

Charles Darwin as an older man,
writing to one of his children

FURTHER READING

FATHER

FATHERHOOD

Biller, Henry, and Meredith, Dennis. *Father Power*. Garden City: Anchor Books, 1975. $3.50. Loads of well-meant advice for Dad from a psychologist who has led research into father-child interaction, and a science writer co-author.

Dodson, Fitzhugh. *How to Father*. New York: Signet, 1974. $2.50. Similar to *How to Parent* by the same advice-giving psychologist author.

Green, Maureen. *Fathering*. New York: McGraw-Hill, 1977. $3.50. A journalist's insightful survey of the state of fatherhood in our changing society. Not a how-to prescription.

Lamb, Michael E., ed. *The Role of the Father in Child Development*. New York: Wiley-Interscience, 1976. $18.50. Scientific perspectives on fatherhood by twenty leading researchers in anthropology, psychology, psychobiology, etc. Not for the general reader.

Levine, James A. *Who Will Raise the Children?* New York: Bantam, 1977. $1.95. Informative examination of the changing role of the father in our society — discusses single-parent adoptions by men, shared child care, househusbands, fathers' improving position in custody disputes, etc.

Lynn, David B. *The Father: His Role in Child Development*. Monterey, Calif.: Brooks/Cole Publishing Co., 1974. $6.95. A thorough survey of recent social-scientific investigations of fatherhood. Not for the general reader.

Reynolds, William. *The American Father*. New York: Paddington Press, 1978. $8.95. A psychologist/attorney/father of seven questions many current assumptions about fatherhood.

Schwartz, Alvin. *To Be a Father*. New York: Crown Publishers, 1967. Out of print; available in public libraries. Letters by famous fathers to their children as well as stories, essays, poems, and proverbs about fatherhood.

Shedd, Charlie W. *Smart Dads I Know*. New York: Avon Books, 1978. $1.75. Advice from a Presbyterian minister who writes a nationally syndicated column "Strictly for Dads."

SINGLE FATHER

Atkin, Edith, and Rubin, Estelle. *Part-Time Father*. New York: Signet, 1976. $1.75. Sound advice for separated and divorced fathers.

Despert, J. Louise. *Children of Divorce*. Garden City: Dolphin Books, 1962. $2.50.

Gardner, Richard A. *The Parents Book About Divorce*. New York: Bantam, 1979. $2.95. Excellent guide, especially if used in conjunction with *The Boys and Girls Book About Divorce* (New York: Bantam, 1971) by the same author.

Dolphin Books, 1962. $2.50.

Gatley, Richard H., and Koulack, David. *Single Father's Handbook*. Garden City: Anchor, 1979.

McFadden, Michael. *Bachelor Fatherhood*. New York:

Ace Books, 1975. $1.75. One of few books available on the subject, this free-lance writer's cheerful description of his own easy adjustment to single parenthood may have limited application to the lives of others.

Victor, Ira, and Winkler, Win Ann. *Fathers and Custody*. New York: Hawthorn, 1977. $8.95. The changing custody scene in the courts.

STEPFATHER

Rice, F. Philip. *Stepparenting*. Westport: Condor Pub. Co., 1979. $2.50. Helpful guide.

VASECTOMY

Kasirsky, Gilbert. *Vasectomy, Manhood, and Sex*. New York: Springer Pub., 1972. $4.95. Short and clear, this book answers your questions.

Wylie, Evan McLeod. *All About Voluntary Sterilization*. New York: Berkley Pub., 1977. $1.75. Fully explains vasectomy and lists hospitals and clinics where it's available.

CHILD

CHILDBIRTH

Bradley, Robert A. *Husband-Coached Childbirth*. New York: Harper and Row, 1965. $8.95. The best guide to pregnancy and birth for fathers.

Burton, Jerome, and Rosen, Milt. *The Fatherhood Formula*. Canoga Park, Calif.: Major Books, 1976. $1.50. For the prospective father.

Bing, Elisabeth. *Six Practical Lessons for an Easier Childbirth*. rev. ed. New York: Bantam, 1969. $2.25. A practical guide to the Lamaze Method by its most important American proponent. Dad is included in text and photos, and his part in natural childbirth is well explained.

Donovan, Bonnie. *The Cesarean Birth Experience*. Boston: Beacon Press, 1978. $4.95. A comprehensive, reassuring introduction to a method of childbirth that is being used today with increasing frequency.

Ingelman-Sundberg, Axel, and Wirsén, Claes, with pictures by Lennart Nilsson. *A Child Is Born*. New York: Delacorte, 1966. $9.95. Top-notch photos of fetal development.

Leboyer, Frederick. *Birth Without Violence*. New York: Alfred A. Knopf, 1975. $8.95. A fascinating, poetical look at new possibilities in childbirth.

Montagu, Ashley. *Life Before Birth*. New York: Signet, 1964. $1.95. Prenatal development.

Schaefer, George. *Expectant Father*. New York: Barnes & Noble Books, 1964. $2.95. Primer by an obstetrician.

CHILD CARE

Brazelton, T. Berry. *Toddlers and Parents*. New York: Delacorte, 1974. $5.95. Sensible advice from a renowned pediatrician. Other readable works by Dr. Brazelton are *Doctor and Child* (New York: Dell, 1978), $4.95, and *Infants and Mothers* (New York: Dell, 1972), $6.95.

Pomeranz, Virginia E., with Schultz, Dodi. *The First Five Years: A Relaxed Approach to Child Care*. New York: Dell, 1976. $1.75. Another sound book by a pediatrician.

Princeton Center for Infancy, Frank Caplan, ed. *Parents' Yellow Pages*. Garden City: Anchor Books, 1975. $7.95. About as interesting to read as the phone book Yellow Pages, but crammed with addresses and information, some of it useful.

Prudden, Bonnie. *How to Keep Your Child Fit from Birth to Six*. New York: Harper and Row, 1964. $11.95. Descriptions of exercises to do with your children, many of them designed for fathers.

Spock, Benjamin. *Baby and Child Care*. rev. ed. New York: Pocket Books, 1976. $2.50. The classic.

———. *Raising Children in a Difficult Time: A Philosophy of Parental Leadership and High Ideals*. New York: Pocket Books, 1976. $1.95. Thoughts from the grand old man of child care.

U. S. Department of Health, Education, and Welfare. *Infant Care*. For sale by the Superintendent of Documents, U. S. Government Printing Office, Washington, D.C. 20402; Stock No. 1791-0178; $1.00. The perfect primer for Dad — short and clear, and it touches all the bases. This best-selling government publication is frequently revised and updated.

CHILD DEVELOPMENT

Beadle, Muriel. *A Child's Mind*. Garden City: Anchor Books, 1971. $3.50. A readable popular survey of recent research into the early mental development of children.

Fraiberg, Selma H. *The Magic Years*. New York, Scribner, 1959. $4.95. This wonderful classic offers you a rare glimpse of how children actually think and what makes them tick.

Gesell, Arnold; Ilg, Frances L.; and Ames, Louise Bates. *Infant and Child in the Culture of Today*. rev. ed. New York: Harper and Row, 1974. $12.95. The famed pioneering study in child development, recently updated. Year-by-year descriptions of how children can be expected to behave.

Pines, Maya. *Revolution in Learning: The Years from Birth to Six*. New York: Harper and Row, 1967. $10.00. A journalist's account of research in child development.

Stone, L. Joseph, and Church, Joseph. *Childhood and Adolescence: A Psychology of the Growing Person*. 3d ed., rev. New York: Random House, 1973. *The basic textbook on infant and child development and behavior. Readable, thoroughly informative, and handsomely illustrated.*

White, Burton L. *The First Three Years of Life*. New York: Avon, 1975. $4.95. Practical advice for parents based on researches into early learning by a disciple of Piaget.

HEALTH AND SAFETY

Fontana, Vincent J. *A Parents' Guide to Child Safety*. New York: Thomas Y. Crowell Co., 1973. Out of print, but available in public libraries. Exhaustive study of the subject.

Harmon, Murl. *A New Vaccine for Child Safety*. Jenkintown, Pa.: Safety Now Co., 1976. $7.50. No danger to your child escapes this author's scrutiny.

Boston Children's Medical Center. *Child Health Encyclopedia*. New York: Dell, 1978. $7.95. An excellent new addition to the home medical bookshelf from the staff of world-famous Harvard-affiliated Boston Children's.

Shiller, Jack. *Childhood Illness: A Common Sense Approach*. New York: Stein & Day, 1974. $2.45. A pediatrician who goes into more detail than Dr. Spock.

————. *Childhood Injury: A Common Sense Approach*. New York: Stein & Day, 1978. $8.95.

Spock, Benjamin. *Baby and Child Care*. rev. ed. New York: Pocket Books, 1976. $2.50. Cornerstone of the family medical bookshelf.

MUSIC

Hunter, Ilene, and Judson, Marilyn. *Simple Folk Instruments to Make and to Play*. New York: Simon & Schuster, 1977. $8.95. A banjo made from a plastic milk jug and dozens of other good musical projects for father and child.

Roberts, Ronald. *Musical Instruments Made to be Played*. 3d rev. ed. Leicester, England: The Dryad Press, 1968. Refined homemade instruments.

NATURE

Boy Scouts of America. *Boy Scout Fieldbook*. new ed. New York: Workman Publishing Co., 1978. $4.95. Now available in bookstores, the *Fieldbook* will give you a refresher course in campcraft and help you pass along some nature lore to your kids.

Chinery, Michael. *Enjoying Nature with Your Family*. New York: Crown Publishers, 1977. $12.95. Lavishly illustrated and packed with fascinating nature-science projects for parents and kids of all ages, some of them suitable for preschoolers. Worth every penny of the steep price as your family will use it for years to come.

Golden Nature Guides. New York: Golden Press, $1.95. Handy inexpensive reference books to help your kids identify the wildflowers, rocks, beetles, caterpillars, toads, etc., they collect.

PLAY EQUIPMENT

Dal Fabbro, Mario. *How to Make Children's Furniture and Play Equipment*. 2d ed. New York: McGraw-Hill, 1975. $9.95. Good plans for indoor climbers, cribs, bunk beds, etc.

Friedberg, M. Paul. *Handcrafted Playgrounds: Designs You Can Build Yourself*. New York: Vintage Books, 1975. $5.95. Clear diagrams, imaginative designs.

Hawkins, Reginald. *Easy-to-Make Outdoor Play Equipment*. New York: Macmillan, 1957. Out of print — look for this one in the public library.

Hogan, Paul. *Playgrounds for Free*. Cambridge, Mass.: MIT Press, 1974. $9.95. Terrific ideas and plans for building play structures out of defunct tires, cable reels, and other "trash."

Sunset Editors. *Children's Rooms and Play Yards*. 2d ed. Menlo Park, Calif.: Lane Books, 1970. $2.95. Lots of ideas and a few plans for bunk beds, playhouses, tree houses, climbers, etc.

TOYS

Caney, Steven. *Steven Caney's Toy Book*. New York: Workman Pub., 1972. $3.95. Great fun for father and kids. Plans for action toys so simple to make that kids get the thrill of doing most of the work.

————. *Steven Caney's Play Book*. New York: Workman Publishing Co., 1975. $4.95. More neat projects from a man who really understands what's fun for kids.

Hayward, Charles H. *Making Toys in Wood*. New York: Stirling Publishing Co., 1974. $4.95. Some woodworking skill required to follow these fairly sophisticated plans.

Schnacke, Dick. *American Folk Toys: How to Make Them*. New York: Penguin Books, 1974. $3.95. Designs for traditional action toys that any father can put together — mostly made from scrap pieces of wood.

Schutz, Walter E. *Wooden Toys and Games You Can Make Yourself*. New York: Macmillan, 1975. $4.95. Good workshop projects for Dad.

WORKSHOP

Arnold, Arnold. *The Complete Book of Arts and Crafts*. New York: Plume Books, 1977. $4.95. Excellent advice for introducing kids to woodworking and other workshop crafts. Encyclopedic with clear diagrams, this should be a basic reference book in every home where kids are learning to use their hands constructively.

D'Amico, Victor; Wilson, Frances; and Maser, Moreen. *Art for the Family*. New York: The Museum of Modern Art, 1954. Out of print, but available in most public libraries. The classic on art education for preschoolers, this lively book tells how parents and kids can make art together.

INDEX